THEY WENT AWAY
TO WAR

THEY WENT AWAY
TO WAR

Brian Edward Holley

Book Guild Publishing
Sussex, England

First published in Great Britain in 2005 by
The Book Guild Ltd
25 High Street
Lewes, East Sussex
BN7 2LU

Typesetting in Times by
Keyboard Services, Luton, Bedfordshire

Printed in Great Britain by
Antony Rowe Ltd, Chippenham, Wiltshire

A catalogue record for this book is available from the
British Library

ISBN 1 85776 942 2

CONTENTS

Appendix 609

Bibliography – Additional material (documents at the PRO
and magazines and other named publications of the period are
given in the text) – Publishers

Battle Maps

ACKNOWLEDGEMENTS

I am most grateful to the following people and organisations for allowing me to use material for this book: Mrs Pamela Holt for background information concerning her father, Cecil Henry Westlake, and for access and permission to include excerpts from his POW notebook. Mrs Myra Ellacott, for background information about Horace Westlake and other members of the Westlake family, and for the photograph of Horace. Miss Joyce Watts for the use of the photograph of Alfred Watts. Mr Peter Coe for permission to include a description of the 200th anniversary ceremony and service for the Rifle Brigade which he attended, and for the loan of *The Rifle Brigade Chronicles of 1914*. Mr William F. Dungey, for excerpts from his father's diary of captivity quoted in *The Great War Magazine* (September 2003 issue) published by The Great Northern Publishing Company Limited.

I should like to thank the staff of the Photographic Archives Department of the Imperial War Museum for their help in copying and furnishing me with photographs from the museum's collection, and particularly Yvonne Oliver for her help with the licensing regulations and permission to use the photographs from the IWM archives. The negative numbers of these photographs appear with the images as requested by the IWM. All other photographs are from my own collection.

I have tried very hard, and with varying degrees of success, to locate publishing houses to obtain permission to quote from books and other publications in my collection. Unfortunately, as many of my books were published between 1914 and 1964, some publishers' names seem to have disappeared, and others have been absorbed into other companies or even some between several companies or groups. The number of replies I received was tiny. However, I am indebted to the following publishers I located successfully and who did reply: The Naval & Military Press Ltd, The Random House Group, The Great Northern Publishing Company Limited (as above), The Book Guild Limited and Spellmount Limited.

I apologise to any persons or companies whose material I have used without permission. I can only say again I have tried hard, and that the source of any material used has always been given in the text and in the bibliography.

B.E. Holley

PART ONE

We run through the world to perform our bloody tragedies as often as our enemies permit us… We, poor fools, who have but a moment to live, render that brief space as mutually distressing as we can, and find pleasure in the destruction of every masterpiece which time and labour have produced, leaving behind us nothing but so many hateful memories of the havoc, desolation and misery which we have occasioned.

'Frederick the Great', King Frederick II, King of Prussia, writing to Francesco Algarotti in 1760.

Raison d'être

What I have written began as an aide memoire in a tentative exercise collecting and recording family history, and there it was, just a page or two concerning four of my relatives who, like so many others of the time, rushed to join the army when war was declared on 4th August 1914. Gradually – I suppose because I have always had an interest in the period – this section of the exercise extended and enlarged to become an exploration of the years of war, particularly on the Western Front, while following the fortunes of 'my' soldiers and regiments.

Explanation concerning certain inclusions and exclusions

Whether particularly germane or not, I have included items that intrigued me, or caught my imagination, or aroused my compassion, or I found amusing, or caused me to reconsider previously held

1

views of people or events of those years. For the same reasons I have included statements, opinions, comments, anecdotes, reminiscences, excerpts from articles, and observations from many sources covering the pre-war, war, and immediate post-war years, and I hope these inclusions will help to prevent what can become, all too easily, a chronological but pedestrian procession of troop movements, battles and statistics.

Where I am aware of significantly differing opinions or views concerning an event, circumstances, person or persons of the war years, I have tried to include these – or at the very least acknowledge them. Too often, in my experience, an author will deliver a rather sweeping judgement and/or an apparently definitive statement on a controversial, or potentially controversial, subject but offers no reasons, explanation, authority, or sources to support the stance taken – or alternatively indicates no awareness or willingness to consider an alternative view as being potentially of merit.

On the military side I have not set out to write war-time regimental histories, and although I have concentrated mainly on battalions of four specific regiments, their experiences were generally common to all the troops serving in the same areas at the time, and often other regiments' names could be substituted. Other regiments frequently weave in and out of the narrative anyway. Neither have I attempted to describe in detail, or analyse in depth, the campaigns on the Western Front, and I have left much of the latter stages of 1918 undetailed, as the last of my soldier relatives left the scene during the German spring offensive of March and April. There are many books that take the reader through those final months of the summer and autumn of 1918 when the war, once again, became one of movement after the years of stagnation in the trenches.

Some publications appear to have been written on the assumption that the reader has a good understanding of military formations, equipment, terminology, and abbreviations – e.g. 'Blank had been BGGS SD&T GHQ'.* Alternatively they are written on the assumption that readers have no interest in these matters because little or no explanations or definitions are given; or if given they are perfunctory and tucked away. I have assumed that many people are not knowledgeable, but would like some explanations, provided they are not too detailed or technical.

*Brigadier General General Service, Staff Duties and Training, General Headquarters.

2

It may be idiosyncratic, but personally I *really* dislike having my reading interrupted by being directed to the bottom of the page, or the end of the chapter, or sometimes even to the end of the book, for references, explanations or notes relating to the passage I am reading. In the process of searching I frequently lose the thread, especially if the search for the referral has finally led me to the back of the book to something on the lines of '*Ibid p.146*'. Therefore, I have tried to insert all my references and sources of quotations and explanatory or additional notes as near as I can to the point where they occur in my text. Additionally, at the end of this book, I have listed some 200 books and publications from my own collection that I have found helpful in my researches, and from which most of my references and quotations have been taken.

Finally, I hope this deliberately somewhat unstructured narrative with its amalgamation of general and military background, autobiographical, biographical and anecdotal information, personal recollections, and a very little statistical information – and with no pretensions to be authoritative, learned, or didactic – will prove interesting and informative, and present the reader with some material that, as I was researching, I often wished had been available in a single volume concerned with the period.

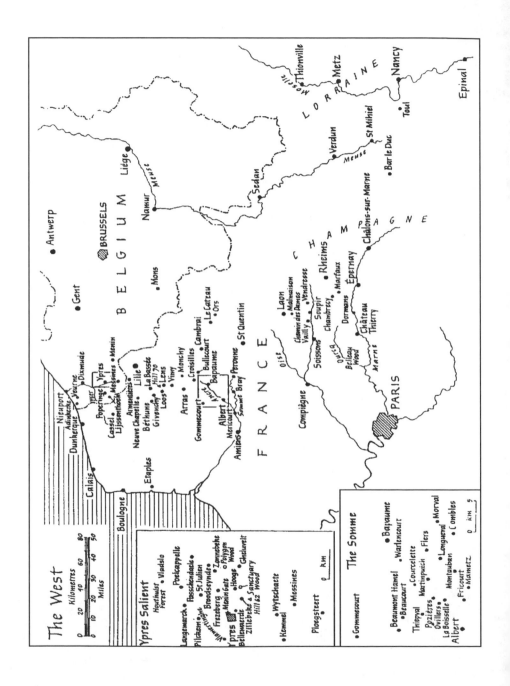

The West

Kilometres
0 20 40 60 80
0 10 20 30 40 50
Miles

Ypres Salient

Langemarck · · Vladslo
Houthulst Forest · Poelcappelle
Pilckem · Passchendaele
· St Julien
Boesinghe · Broodseynde
Frezzberg · Zonnebeke
Ypres · Menin Gate · · Polygon Wood
Bellewaerde · Hooge · Gheluvelt
Zillebeke · Sanctuary
· Hill 62 Wood
· Wytschaete
· Kemmel
· Messines

Ploegsteert

0 km

The Somme

· Gommecourt
· Bapaume
Beaumont Hamel · · Warlencourt
· Beaucourt
· Courcelette
Thiepval · Martinpuich · Flers
Pozières · · Longueval · Morval
Ovillers · Montauban · Combles
La Boisselle · · Fricourt
Albert · · Mametz

0 km 5

Boulogne
Calais
Dunkerque
Nieuport
Adinkerke
Veurne
Dixmude
Etaples
Poperinge · Ypres
Cassel · Messines · Menin
Ijssemthoek · Ypser
Armentières
Neuve Chapelle · Lille
Béthune · La Bassée
Givenchy · Hill 70
Loos · Lens
Arras · Monchy
· Vimy
· Croisilles
Gommecourt · · Cambrai
· Bullecourt
Méricourt · · Bapaume
Albert · · Péronne
Amiens · Somme Bray
· · St Quentin
· Le Cateau
· Ors

Antwerp
Gent
BELGIUM
· Mons
Liège
Namur
Meuse
BRUSSELS
Sedan
Verdun · · St Mihiel
Bar le Duc
Thionville
Metz
Moselle
LORRAINE
Nancy
Toul
Epinal

FRANCE
Compiègne
Oise
Soissons
Vailly
Ouca
Laon
Malmaison
Chemin des Dames
Vendresse
Chambrécy
Marfaux
Rheims
CHAMPAGNE
Épernay
Châlons-sur-Marne
Dormans
Château Thierry
Belleau Wood
Marne
PARIS

4

PART TWO

'Daddy, what did YOU do in the Great War?' Caption from an early war-time recruiting poster depicting two children, a little boy and a little girl, with their father who is seated in his armchair. The little girl, who is sitting on her father's lap, is innocently asking the question, while the boy is beside him on the floor playing with toy soldiers. The father, who from his expression had obviously not enlisted in the armed forces, is unable to frame an acceptable reply. This poster led to the ironic catch-phrase among the troops in the line – particularly when conditions were vile or when engaged in particularly unpleasant tasks: 'What did you do in the war daddy?'

Those who served

Like mine, I am sure that almost every family in the land will have had one or more relatives who served in 'The Great War', and very probably at least for a while on the Western Front in France and/or Belgium. And again, like mine, they will have one or more soldier relatives who, in the words of Rupert Brooke, lie in *'some corner of a foreign field'*.

Perhaps someone who hitherto has not given much or any thought to those times or those relatives who lived and possibly died in them, will be stimulated to attempt to trace and follow the path of a soldier forebear or forebears as I have done with mine, and in so doing catch an echo of their marching feet, the rumble and flashes of the never-ending artillery fire along the front, and the stark illumination at night from the magnesium flares hissing up

5

over 'No Man's Land' where working parties and patrols 'freeze' until the light dies. And most important, think about them a little.

My soldier relatives

Two of my soldiers are brothers; another is one of four brothers serving in the armed forces – unfortunately so far I have not traced the war records of the other three. I know two of them, who were regulars in the Royal Marines, served mainly as DEMS (Defensively Equipped Merchant Ships) gunners, and both were torpedoed on more than one occasion, and one of them was serving in the Falklands in 1918 when the war ended. The third brother was a soldier who was gassed on the Western Front while serving, I think, with the Royal Fusiliers. He was in Canada and in the Canadian Army when his brother was killed in Flanders in 1915, and he then returned to England to join the British Army. The fourth soldier is my father.

Of these four relatives, three served on the Western Front, but the fourth through the luck of the draw, despite joining up in 1914 and being drafted overseas like the others, never served in France or Belgium, or any major theatre of war. Two were killed in action. They both died in 1915, but at different times and places and in different circumstances. One lies in La Brique CWGC Military Cemetery No. 2, close to the British front line in the latter part of 1914 and the spring of 1915 – just on the north-east of the town of Ypres in the dreaded 'Salient' in Belgium. The other has no known grave because like so many no trace of his body was ever discovered. The only record of him is his name inscribed on a memorial panel at 'Dud Corner' Cemetery which stands almost on the site of the Lens Road Redoubt, a German Strong Point in the Pas de Calais in France.

Of the two 1914 volunteers who survived the war, one was taken prisoner when his unit was outflanked and over-run in the 'Emperor's Battle' (*Kaiserschlacht*) in the spring of 1918, and the other, in the parlance of the time, had a 'cushy' war, as he and his comrades enjoyed a virtually pre-war overseas tour of duty in India. Most of the deaths in this battalion were from pneumonia, enteric fever and malaria and not from shot or shell. They did not experience action until 1918–1919 during the third Afghan War, and then it was under

6

the burning sun amid the brown baked hills and arid terrain of the 'Northwest Frontier' (the border area of India and Afghanistan) far from the mud and horrors of the Western Front. And so, most unusually, nearly all these 1914 volunteers survived to arrive home together in the winter of 1919 – and the Old Comrades Association continued to meet until the late 1980s.

The first of these two surviving soldiers died in 1949, and the other 1991.

Their regiments

My particular concerns are with: The 3rd Battalion, The Rifle Brigade; The 8th 'Service' Battalion, The Devonshire Regiment; The 1/5th Battalion, Duke of Cornwall's Light Infantry; and The 1/1st Battalion, The Kent Cyclist Battalion.

In each of these battalions of the four regiments served one of the soldiers related to me (either directly related or through marriage). Their ages ranged from 16 years to 26 years when they queued to join the army like so many others in that first heady rush to the colours in 1914, and of course none of them had any idea of where his enlistment would lead him, or what fate would befall him or his future comrades.

To an extent I have also followed the other three regular battalions of the Rifle Brigade, the two regular battalions of the Devonshires, and the two regular battalions of the DCLI. The Kent Cyclist Battalion (1/1st Kents), however, as an independent territorial battalion, had no regular and service battalions. (A second-line battalion, the 2/1st Kents, was formed in 1914* and took over the home coastal patrol duties from the 1/1st Kents, and soon afterwards a third-line battalion, 3/1st Kents, was formed, but neither features here.)

*Cyril Bristow in his history of the Kent Cyclist Battalion, says the 2/1st Kent Cyclist Battalion was formed in 1915, but my soldier relative was attested into 2/1st Battalion on 5th November 1914, and then when old enough to go overseas transferred to the 1/1st Kents.

The battalions of my regiments were typical of their time in 1914, and they fared neither better nor worse than others around them, but they are important to me because they form links in the chain

7

of my family heritage and history. And although they are typical, each battalion was different from the others in 1914. One was a regular army infantry battalion, one was a first line territorial infantry battalion later re-designated as a pioneer battalion. One was a 'K1 New Army' infantry battalion, and one an original independent territorial cyclist battalion – formed in 1908, and later in the war re-formed with other cyclist battalions to become an infantry brigade.

PART THREE

Now, God be thanked Who has matched us with His hour,

Rupert Brooke. Died 21st April 1915, on his way
to the Dardanelles campaign.

Visiting the battlefields of the Western Front

School groups

While the reality and personal memories of those tragic years slip
quietly into history there is a resurgence of interest in 'The Great
War', and in addition it now forms part of the history curriculum
in secondary schools. Indeed I understand that the majority of
visitors to the battlefields today are escorted groups of school
children, but for them, as the Holts say in an introduction to one
of their excellent battlefield guides: 'a visit is not regarded as an
event within the living consciousness, but as just another school
topic'. I am sure anyone who has walked round the battlefields, or
visited the Imperial War Museum or similar institutions, and has
seen parties of generally uncomprehending and invariably bored
young children and adolescents, local and foreign, milling around,
some clutching 'project paper' questionnaires, or, as I have, picked
up library books about the period covered with scribble and drawings,
will appreciate the sadness – and perhaps the inevitability of it.

About a year after writing the previous paragraph, I received the
then latest copy of the St Dunstan's newsletter, and noticed a
short article in it which read: 'Pupils at Queen Elizabeth Grammar
School in Lincolnshire are raising money for St Dunstan's through
the sales of their own CD of WWI songs readings and poetry.'

The article goes on to say that when the history teacher and a parent organised the first trip three years ago to the WWI cemeteries in France, little did they realise the enormous impact it would have on the pupils, and since then the trips, concerts and fundraising events have got bigger and better. That is certainly good news, and I believe I have an inkling of the identity of the parent concerned; however I stand by my own experiences without in any way detracting from the pupils, the parent, and school staff in Lincolnshire.*

*An ex-teacher in a letter to *Saga* magazine (January 2004) commenting on a proposal to use lottery money to take school children visit the D-day landing areas said: 'When I was a secondary teacher on an educational tour of northern France we stopped at a First World War cemetery and a large majority expressed their complete lack of interest by remaining on the coach.'

Getting to the battlefields

It is very easy to visit the Western Front battlefield areas today, and one can tour either unaccompanied with the help of one or more of the published guide books, or as part of an escorted group through one of the specialist firms.

On the subject of visiting, *The Times*, 9th January 2002, carried a little item of news saying that British war graves in Europe are to be promoted by Eurotunnel as key destinations. The company is intending to launch a scheme in association with the Commonwealth War Graves Commission to attract thousands more visitors to the war cemeteries, museums and battlefields in France and Belgium. A spokesman for Eurotunnel said: 'More and more people are travelling to the battlefields and we are constantly being asked for advice on where to go and how to get there.' (Of course there is also a resurgence of interest in the Second World War, now also becoming 'history', and no doubt 'battlefields' refers to these areas as well.)

There are the towns and locations, as well as the graves and memorials, in the areas of those hauntingly familiar names: Mons, Le Cateau, Armentières, Ypres, Aubers Ridge, Neuve Chapelle, Festubert, Loos, The Somme areas – The Ancre, Arras, Happy Valley, Death Valley, Delville Wood, Mametz, Thiepval, Beaumont Hamel and Guillemont for example – and Vimy Ridge, Cambrai and Passchendaele – to name but a few.

Many motorists take their cars across or under the Channel en route to Continental holiday resorts every year, and as they pass through the Pas de Calais, Picardy or Somme regions of France, some may become aware of the meticulously maintained Commonwealth War Graves Commission (CWGC) cemeteries and memorials. Some very large, some so small it is easy to overlook them.

War memorials vary in style and size; the one at Thiepval, designed by Sir Edwin Lutyens, is in complete contrast to the cold, white, twin pylon monument to the dead Canadians at Vimy Ridge. To me, by its dominant position in the landscape, together with its size, shape and colouring, this vast arch at Thiepval is one of the most oppressive and damning of the war monuments, with its walls listing relentlessly the engraved names, regiment by regiment, rank by rank of those 72,085 British and South African soldiers who were, up to March 1918, and are still, 'Missing' on the Somme sector of the Western Front. Over 90% of the names are of those who died between July and November 1916.

One of the most poignant memorials, and apparently one of the most visited, is The Newfoundland Memorial Park at Beaumont Hamel, with its statue of the caribou, described by some as the defiant caribou and by others as the sorrowing caribou calling for its young who will not return. The caribou was the badge of the regiment and the large statue stands on a raised mound of clay and granite in the park containing trees brought over from Newfoundland. There are 814 names engraved on a panel listing those Newfound-landers who have no known grave.

Ypres and the Salient

In Belgium there is arguably, for Britons and the other Commonwealth nations at any rate, the largest memorial of all, the rebuilt and restored famous (or at the time infamous) ancient and picturesque city of Ypres ('Wipers' to the troops) with its equally famous rebuilt Menin Gate – an entrance to and from the city leading to the then dreaded Menin Road.

Apropos the Menin Road, Philip Warner (*Passchendaele*) quotes from the diary of an officer who arrived as a newcomer to the Salient to join the 7th Battalion of the 60th Rifles:*

11

In August [before he joined them] the battalion had been on the Menin Road, the worst sector of the battle front at Ypres, and a nightmare through the whole army. I could see that the people's nerves were all wrong still: they shivered when the Menin Road was mentioned and talked of it with a horror I could not understand. I wondered vaguely what it was like.

*The regiment today is now a component of The Royal Greenjackets Regiment, as is the Rifle Brigade.

Following the rebuilding and restoration after the war, Ypres today is once again a handsome city, and if it is at all possible a visitor should attend the brief but moving 'Last Post' ceremony that has taken place at the Menin Gate at 8 pm every night of the year since 1929 – with the exception of the period between 1940 and 1943. The ceremony began again in 1944 following the liberation of the town by Polish troops. Other renowned neighbouring Ypres locations such as Hell Fire Corner, Shrapnel Corner and Salvation Corner are close by and easily found.

Sadly, as the increasingly tourist aspect of the city grows, the famous nightly ceremony at the Menin Gate is becoming spoilt by people applauding at the conclusion, and one of the Britons involved in the 'war industry' for a decade told *The Times* correspondent in an article dated 31st October 2003: 'It is tourism, not remembrance now. All that is missing is the jugglers and fire-eaters. This town is living off war.'

Another, who has been involved in research of the battlefields since 1967, was also dismayed:

'It's gone 100 per cent for tourism. There's museums popped up all over the place, but they are collections of battlefield rubbish just in it for the money. It's an industry with a lot of cowboys.' It is an accusation that Mr Slosse of the Ypres Tourist Office is particularly sensitive about. 'It's a daily concern for us. We definitely don't want to be a theme park. Everything we do is done out of respect for the dead – it must always be about remembering,' he said.

The Times, in the same article, commenting on the increase in visitors to Ypres, said that the number of visitors to Saint Georges in Ypres, the Anglican memorial church, has climbed from 80,000 two years ago to 140,000 last year, and the town's main museum, which received 60,000 visitors a year before it was refurbished five years ago, now has 200,000 visitors a year, of which nearly half are British. The article also goes on to comment that the big increase in the number of tour operators, and the coachloads of school children and tourists that now pour into the town, have brought added prosperity to the ancient city, but this influence of professional marketing has also changed its character. It is becoming more and more just a tourist attraction and not a place of memories, history and pilgrimage.

Despite the increasing tourist atmosphere, Siegfried Sassoon was wrong when he wrote his famous bitter poem on the rebuilding of the Menin Gate after the war, *On Passing the New Menin Gate*, with its contemptuous opening lines asking the question:

> Who will remember passing through this Gate
> The unheroic dead who fed the guns?

One has only to attend the evening ceremony to be aware that apart from just tourists there are people there who *do* remember those who served and died, and are deeply moved, and a glance through any one of the visitors' books at the gate will confirm this. There is an annual remembrance ceremony at the Menin Gate on Armistice Day, and the last time I was there, on 11th November 2001, the famous lines of Lawrence Binyon's *For the Fallen* were read by a veteran who, I was told, was 104 years old.

There are some 55,000 names inscribed on the Menin Gate.* These are the names of those killed in the Salient between August 1914 and August 1917 and who have no known grave. Space on this memorial ran out, and the rest of the names of those who have no known grave – a further 35,000 men – who died between August 1917 and the end of October 1918 in the Salient, are recorded on the memorial walls of the Tyne Cot Cemetery a few miles away. These are in addition to those 11,000 bodies lying in the graves at Tyne Cot.

*Those on the Menin Gate include 40,244 British, 6,983 Canadians, 6,198 Australians, 546 South Africans, 421 Indians, and 6 West Indians.

Typical of the mordant humour of the troops on their way out through the Menin Gate on to the hated Menin Road to go 'up to the line': 'Last one out, shut the gate.'

Today, by day, the city of Ypres takes on the aspect of a prosperous bustling town of cafés, shops, municipal and commercial offices, public buildings and churches, and with the streets full of local residents and tourists on foot and in cars. By night, particularly in the late autumn, if one wanders along the hard, uneven, small cobble stones around the silent and softly lit streets behind the tourist spots, it is very easy to feel transported back in time to those war years – to imagine an occasional glimpse of a dim light coming from a shielded candle behind the gratings of the cellars, the sound of muffled voices, the rumble of iron-shod wheels, and the clink and jingle of harnesses from waggons and carts picking their way in the dark amid the rubble and the silhouetted skeletal outlines of the ruins above, lit by flashes from distant guns and the burst of star shells and Very lights.*

*Very light – a rocket fired by a brass pistol to illuminate No Man's Land at night. Invented by Samual W. Very.

Ypres, or Ieper as it is now known, was devastated and almost completely flattened by shell-fire as the war progressed. The devastation of the city by artillery equals that of many of the World War Two concentrated aerial bombings of German cities. Reported by Peter Liddle in *The Soldier's War 1914–1918*, an unnamed diarist records:

> We were not allowed to enter Ypres until dark as it was being heavily shelled. Half the town seemed to be on fire and the glare from the flames playing on the many towers and spires produced a most weird effect made more wonderful as we circled round the town on the far side of the moat and the above shades and shadows were reproduced in the water.

Wilfrid Ewart, (see below) wrote in May 1916:

> I went round Ypres the other day – the Germans were shelling all the time I was there – and saw all the sights of the town, and some strange things ... The whole place is razed to the ground, not a house standing except the prison, but some of the neglected, overgrown gardens are very pretty.

14

Norman Ellison, the broadcaster and naturalist, is reported in *Remembrances of Hell* edited by Davis Lewis, as writing home on 4th October 1916 saying of Ypres:

I am way down underground in a wooden walled alcove ... up above are the ruins and debris of a once fine city, Ypres, now so badly battered and bashed about that it is scarcely recognisable. I have many happy memories of it in the early days of the war, but now it is a nightmare.

Arthur Behrend, writing in *As From Kemmel Hill* says of his time in Ypres in 1917:

Intensely moving though I found it to stand on the Ramparts beside our dug-out entrance in the comparatively calm of a summer evening and watch some fresh Division march – usually in silence – through the Menin Gate on its way to the line, it was more moving still to see its remnants marching back by the same road a week or ten days later.

The Salient

The Front Line area bulging around Ypres was *the* dreaded salient. The German positions dominated the high ground, such as it was, and from these positions could see the entire city and surrounding areas behind, and were able to pour in artillery fire from three sides. 'The Salient' was loathed by all the Allied troops who served there, at whatever time or in any year, even in the quiet times.

Wilfrid Ewart, who served in the Salient in May 1916 with the 2nd Battalion the Scots Guards,* described how the ghost town of Ypres and the surrounding area comes to life as night falls to provide a least a little shelter from the overlooking and all-seeing enemy eyes, and constant shelling by their artillery:

The evening comes, and an hour before dusk the men parade for the trenches in the grass-grown farmyard. By small parties, a platoon at a time, they march away, some to follow cross-country tracks towards the canal, others going by the direct road. It is a calm and lovely aftermath, the sun setting in a golden haze, blue mists creeping up all around; the heat of the day is succeeded by a delightful freshness. Nevertheless clouds of dust rise from the road, for, as dusk falls, the great evening tide of traffic sets towards the trenches. Ration-parties; relieving-parties; all moving in file; motor-lorries, ambulances, motor cyclists, officers on horseback, orderlies on bicycles, quartermasters and quartermaster-sergeants driving mess-carts – all form part of a steady stream that flows through the first battered village... Now the nervous work begins, for often at this hour of the relief the road is sprayed with shrapnel... Presently we pass the stark shell of a ruined house, guardian of a rusty railway-line overgrown with vegetation, and then come to the engineers dump, where all traffic ceases. A congestion of troops in single file is waiting to cross the bridges. One seems to hesitate here on the threshold of fate.

*1916 was generally regarded as a quiet time by Salient standards – except for the period June 2nd to June 13th when the German army mounted a number of attacks at Mount Sorrel – Sanctuary Wood.

When his battalion receives word that the Division is to proceed south to the Somme battle in July, and the first train leaves the railway sidings at Ypres near the old Poperinghe road, he relates:

Cheer upon cheer goes up to the blue sky. It is the men's farewell to Yperz, [Wipers] as they call it. 'To the south!' They know that they are going into action – perhaps in a few days, perhaps in a few weeks – but this matters not a cuss: there is nothing but singing, laughter, and shouting today. For with every mile that hated Salient, the treacherous Canal-bank, the death-stricken city are left farther and farther behind.

By road and rail to-day the relieving corps is moving up to Ypres... For many leagues as far, say, as Wormhoudt – the railway line runs beside the road, and this road carries unending columns of perspiring, khaki-clad troops, unending lines of horse-transport and motor-lorries, unending columns of artillery moving north. And they are fresh from the Somme, these dusty, heat stricken warriors – at least thousands are left behind, and so many thousands are fresh from England – where they have been decimated. They are coming up here – for a rest! God help 'em.

16

Aubrey Smith, author of *Four Years on the Western Front*, said that when the remnants of his battalion were pulled out of the line on May 20th 1915, following the second Battle of Ypres, he and his surviving comrades in the London Rifle Brigade were so delighted to be leaving the dreaded Salient that as they approached the (comparatively) untouched little town of Poperinghe:

> It was a beautiful spring morning and as we passed under the trees overhanging that fateful Poperinghe Road, leaving the war behind us, it seemed impossible that such a blighted stricken piece of country could lie so near at hand.
> What regiment in the British army has not marched up that Poperinghe Road a corporate body of men, and returned weeks, maybe days later as though it had passed through a furnace? How many that went up never returned at all?

The war diary of 3rd Battalion, The Rifle Brigade, reports for June/July 1915:

> The next two months we spent in trenches at LA BRIQUE going out occasionally in billets in the woods at 'A.30' [map reference] between VLARTINGHE and POPERINGHE. No one who has ever been to Ypres wants to go there again and the Battalion had its fair share of this unpleasant spot. After a month or so at La Brique we should all have been glad of a change to any other part of the line. Such names as Forward Cottage, Cross Roads Farm, Hill Top Farm will ever remind us of something unpleasant.

A private in the 1st Queen's Westminster Rifles, Pte. P.H. Jones, in a letter dated 6th August 1915, wrote:

> I have seen Ypres; in fact I am lying there now. We hold the place for moral effect only (our troops would be better off behind the canal), for an ideal. In holding it men have died for a dream.

Ernest Parker, *Into Battle 1914–1918*, writes of his experience on arrival in Ypres as a fledgling member of 'Kitchener's army':

17

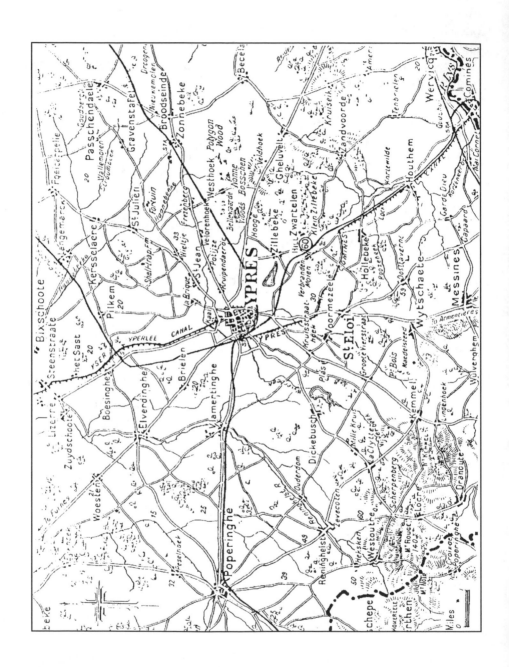

18

At the close of that first day in Ypres we paraded for the nightly working-party in no man's land. With picks and shovels on our shoulders we passed through the Menin Gate and marched down the road as far as West Lane communication trench. Here we got under cover, filing along until we came to the front line. On our way we were continually halting, now waiting until the rear got in touch; now to allow troops to pass us on their way back from the front line. Once or twice the words 'Way for stretcher bearers' rang out, and we held our breath while stalwart fellows carried past blanketed forms aloft on their stretchers. How soon would it be our turn?

In addition to Ypres, other 'Salient' features of the Flanders campaigns can be seen, such as: Hill 60, Ploegsteert, (Plug Street), Messines and Passchendaele, Poperinghe ('Pop'), Tyne Cot and the CWGC cemeteries, memorials and sites that commemorate them.

PART FOUR

They shall grow not old, as we that are left grow old.

Lawrence Binyon. The opening line of *For the Fallen*.
Published in *The Times*, 21st September 1914.

The dead

Prior to 1917 the identity tags worn by the soldiers were of leather or cardboard and many of these rotted in the ground or were otherwise lost when bodies were left lying where they fell. This accounts for many of the 'known unto God' graves. In addition many of the bodies of those killed and left lying in No Man's Land were destroyed or ploughed into the ground by shell-fire as new attacks or bombardments were launched over old ground, and so have no grave. Gerald Burgoyne records in late 1914 in *The Burgoyne Diaries*:

> There on the Southern side of Middlestede Farm, are lying corpses of some hundred or more French and Germans from last September. In front of H1 [a map reference] there are the bodies of some thirty or more Gordons, [Gordon Highlanders] and to my left many more victims or heroes of the mis-directed charge last Monday ... I found the fields strewn with huge unexploded 5 inch shells, fired by the Germans some weeks ago. A dead man just reported to me lying close by. Went out and found he was No. 8863, B. West, Suffolk Regiment ... Horrid job lifting his head to get at his identity disc. I buried him at dusk, and said the Lord's Prayer over him ... three bullets came so close to us'.

A little later in the war no one would have risked his life in similar circumstances. Troops, of necessity, had become – at least on the surface – callous and hardened to the sight of rotting bodies everywhere, sometimes even built into the walls of the trenches. Burgoyne endorses this aspect of trench life with regard to the dead later in March 1915, when describing how his company took over a trench in Flanders from the Royal Scots who had captured it from the Germans in December 1914:

It [the trench] is as bad now as it was then, a mere ditch alongside a weak hedge against which are a few sandbags piled up here and there where they haven't slipped into the bottom of the ditch. It is ankle deep in mud. In some places I sank in half way up my leg. Two or three times I found my feet slipping on rounded substances I at first thought were logs, but they were the dead bodies of the gallant capturers of the trench which still lie there in the bottom unburied but sunk in the mud, and I was slipping and sliding on their limbs, their faces possibly.

There are several corpses still lying about the rear parapet. I can only think the Regiment which has occupied this trench for the last three months has been very slack in not burying these bodies, although when they were first killed it was impossible as the enemy had rifles set on each corpse and men attempting to move them were wounded.

Gerald Burgoyne served with the 2nd Battalion, Royal Irish Rifles, part of 7th Brigade, 3rd Division, during the winter of 1914 and the spring of 1915 in Flanders until he was wounded and sent home. He kept a diary during that time. His daughter Claudia found the papers in a trunk when her mother died, and she had them published. Burgoyne was killed in 1936 in Ethiopia when the convoy of mules he was escorting for the Red Cross was bombed by the Italian Air force.

William Linton Andrews says how difficult it was for civilians and soldiers to understand each other in the matter of burying the dead. He tells of a comrade who had been killed on the German wire:

I wrote to his people giving them a guarded account of his

death, and telling them what a good soldier he was. The father wrote back and said it was very suspicious that I had not mentioned the funeral: surely his son received the tribute of Christian burial, and he would like to know which of his comrades had attended. I explained that the boy had been killed close to the German trenches, and the Germans were sure to take in his body for burial. The father wrote back a letter angrily condemning me for not bringing back his son's remains.

To us at the front, accustomed in a day's journey in the crater area to see the unburied remains of hundreds of men, it seemed amazing that people at home should imagine we could risk the lives of three or four men to bring a body across No Man's Land. There are times when I doubt whether any who were not there will realize the conditions on the Somme and in the Salient.

William Linton Andrews was a journalist who, at the time of his enlistment in August 1914, was news editor of the *Dundee Advertiser*. He wrote a book of his war experiences – *Haunting Years* – and he served in France and Belgium continuously until the early part of 1918 with his territorial battalion The 1/4th, Black Watch. (In 1916 they were combined with the 5th battalion to become The 4/5th Battalion Black Watch.)

But in contrast with these examples of the changing attitude and the hardening indifference to the dead lying around as the war progressed, strangely enough a soldier writing to his parents in mid-October 1918 says:*

On Tuesday we had a long tiring march towards the line to take up our position for the following morning's attack, and at one time we halted for an hour or two in an old trench just across the Schelde Canal. Here we found the body of a dead German – quite a boy he was – and our officer, with our approval, gave orders to bury him. The funeral, such as it was, was just such as we might have given to one of our own men. The padre read the funeral service over him, while the men stood around with bare heads. It was a small matter in itself, but I think it showed a chivalrous spirit. Everyone concerned was profoundly affected by this burial of an unknown boy by his 'enemies' in an alien land … The dead man's identity disks were preserved, and will be, if possible, sent to his relatives in Germany.

*Recorded by Malcolm Brown in *The Imperial War Museum Book of 1918 Year of Victory*.

This seems quite an unusual sentiment and action at this late stage of the war.

During the November 10th Sunday Remembrance service in 2002, there was a touching little ceremony where young pupils from a primary school, somewhere in the West Country, laid posies on the graves of a number of Australian troops who died of influenza in 1918, and who are buried in the local churchyard. The posies are sprays of poppies, rosemary and laurel, and are laid every ANZAC day and Armistice Day. One of the children explained that the rosemary was for remembrance, laurels for valour and poppies for peace. It would be pleasant to think that any surviving family members in Australia would know of this sincere little tribute still being made so many years after the event.

The 'unknown' dead

It has been claimed that on the Somme alone there are 53,409 soldiers buried in unknown soldiers' graves. In Flanders, in addition to those 55,000 inscribed on the Menin Gate at Ypres and the other 35,000 at Tyne Cot, there are the many soldiers who lie as 'known unto God' in the surrounding cemeteries.

The known dead – The young and the old

From my own observation of those who lie in 'some foreign field' there are graves of those whose ages range from 15 years to 67. I understand the youngest recorded is a 14-year-old, Private John Condon, Royal Irish Regiment, who was killed at Second Ypres in May 1915. I have read that no birth certificate exists to confirm it, but if his birthday was, as is believed, in June 1901, then he was still 13 years of age when he was killed. He lies in Poelcapelle British Military cemetery. Another 14-year-old was also claimed but research eventually showed him to be 18 when he died – Private A. Carroll, 22nd Battalion Canadian Infantry.

One 13-year-old who luckily survived was – according to a BBC documentary broadcast in November 1988 – George Maher who was born on 20th May 1903. He said he had always been a big lad and was five feet eight and a half inches tall at the age of 13 and had earned the nickname 'Hefty'. When he told the recruiting sergeant he was 18 he was believed and no proof of age was asked of him. As a result he found himself enrolled in 2nd Kings Own Royal Lancaster Regiment, and in February 1917 he was in France with a draft of newly trained soldiers from all regiments – see below.*

*On the subject of very young servicemen, there is an almost incredible account – but I understand it to be completely authenticated – of a 15-year-old boy, Tom Dobney, who, in the Second World War, flew bombing missions as a sergeant pilot. His true age was only discovered, according to a Mr Stanley Blenkinsop, who after the war became a colleague of Tom Dobney as a fellow journalist on the *Daily Express*, because a photograph of the pilot appeared in the press and was spotted by his father who on recognising him telephoned the Air Ministry to ask why his son was in pilot's uniform when he was only fifteen. (The father was divorced from the boy's mother and knew nothing of his son's enlistment.) The boy was discharged from the RAF, but was allowed to re-enlist when 17, and in 1948 took part in the Berlin Airlift. He died in 2001.

The 67-year-old* was Lt. Henry Webber who was born on 3rd June 1849. In May 1916 he was appointed to 7th Battalion, South Lancs. Regiment, following his repeated requests to the War Office to serve in the army, and joined them in France where he was made transport officer. While he was talking to his commanding officer after taking rations up to the front in Mametz Wood on 21st July 1916 during the Battle of the Somme he was killed by shell-fire. Ironically three of his sons serving in the army survived.

*Every reference I have come across describes him as 68, so perhaps I'm just not very good at sums.

In this same cemetery on the Somme, Dartmoor Cemetery, a father and son are side by side in adjoining graves; Sergeant George Lee, and Corporal Robert Frederick Lee, of 156th Brigade RFA, both killed on 5th September 1916. And, some miles to the north, two brothers lie together in the Ploegsteert area, Riflemen L. Crossley and W. Crossley.

The battlefield cemeteries contain graves of men whose head stones show they performed officially recorded acts of great bravery, and who were awarded the Victoria Cross for their heroism. In addition, and although there is no indication on the headstones, there are 322 graves of soldiers who were executed.*

John Peaty writing an article in *Look To Your Front* by the British Commission for Military History, says:

> Contrary to popular belief, very few were executed for cowardice in the face of the enemy: there were a mere eighteen executions for that offence. The great majority were executed for desertion while on active service ... a man was declared a deserter after an absence of twenty-one days.

Burgoyne writes in his diary on 5th March, 1915:

> I've another man for a firing party. He has just been told off for a FGCM,* and he should be sentenced to death. I told him he had better spend his few remaining hours in prayer and touching him on the chest, I told him, that's where the bullets would hit him. Brutal, I know, but I've no sympathy with a cur. He is always evading coming into the trenches and I hear, ever since he came out here with the Battalion last August, he has scrimshanked all he could to get out of the firing line. I expect and certainly hope he will get shot. Several men have been executed for less, lately.

*Field General Court Martial.

There were also other crimes that warranted the death sentence. Peter Liddle, the author of *Testimony of War 1914–1918*, quotes a case of one conscientious objector, who was given the death sentence on the grounds that he had refused to obey basic military orders after he had been drafted into a unit called the 'Non-Combatant's Corps'. If the circumstances were as claimed then the penalty the court martial awarded 'to suffer death by being shot' seems particularly harsh. The man, Howard Marten, stated in his defence:

I am charged before this court with refusing to drill at the FP Barracks Boulogne. In the first place I wish to state that I do not in my own conscience feel guilty of any offence towards God or man but whether my refusal to obey a certain request which I felt to be incompatible with my inmost belief constitutes a crime I am humanly speaking, in the hands of this court.

The sentence was eventually commuted to ten years' penal servitude, but soon afterwards the Government introduced a special scheme offering conscientious objectors non-military work under less close confinement. Marten accepted these conditions and worked in the prison quarry.

Gordon Corrigan in his book *Mud Blood and Poppycock* cites the cases of two men who were executed for the crime of being asleep on sentry duty. Both were together as a pair of sentries who should have been keeping alert standing on the fire-step in a trench in Mesopotamia. He says these two men, Privates Burton and Downing of the 6th South Lancs, were the only men to be executed for this offence. There were, in all theatres of war, 393 men convicted of the crime, but none was executed until these two men in February 1917. All the other convictions were quashed, commuted or reduced to terms of imprisonment or field punishment.

Another offence was mutiny, for which 56 men were given the death sentence, but only four of these sentences were carried out. Considering there were well over four and a half million British and Imperial soldiers – not all of course on the Western Front – those executed for crimes carrying the death penalty still form an incredibly tiny proportion.*

*According to Antony Beevor, author of *Stalingrad*, the Russians in the Second World War executed around 13,500 of their own soldiers at Stalingrad alone.

The majority who lie below their headstones in the silence and gentle soughing of the breeze are those who were labelled neither cowards nor heroes. There are airmen from the RFC/RAF, and rather surprisingly perhaps there are also sailors and marines. These are from the Royal Naval Division (see below). In the main though the dead are soldiers. Officers and men from all regiments and of all ranks, who were once grieved over by their families, but now lie mainly forgotten and without visit except for the unceasing care of the Commission's gardeners.

Visiting a war cemetery or memorial is a very moving experience, and there are many fascinating and poignant details to be learned about those who lie in these silent plots of land – 'The Silent Cities'. In most cemeteries there is a bronze box at or near the entrance containing the cemetery register with a plan, description of the origins of the burial, and an alphabetical list of the burials. A visit recorded in the visitors' book provided by the CWGC in the box is always appreciated.

The Ministry of Defence (MoD) and the War Graves Commission take great trouble to ensure that the bodies of those buried in the graves are who they purport to be, and if they are unknown, they say so. One battlefield guide told me how incensed he was to hear a schoolteacher telling a group of pupils that 'of course there could be anyone buried in these graves'.

On the matter of schoolteachers who act as escorts to pupils touring the battlefields, yet who apparently lack a basic knowledge of the subject, Gordon Corrigan quotes from a bulletin of The Western Front Association – *Bulletin No. 56, February 2000*, which refers to another schoolteacher leading a group of pupils visiting the Western Front battlefield cemeteries. The teacher, Corrigan says, posed the question: 'Why are there so few officers' graves?' The answer sought by the teacher apparently was that officers took no part in the attack, being safely behind the lines enjoying a good breakfast while their men went to their deaths. If this was accurately reported then such a depth of ignorance makes one despair of what has been and is being fed to the present generation of pupils, and one can imagine what misinformation they in turn will regurgitate to a following generation.

Discovering bodies today

Even today bodies are still being found. *The Times* of 20th June 2001 reported, with photographs, a new discovery by French archaeologists of the bodies of twenty British soldiers lying in a mass grave, their arms apparently linked. The report said the bodies were those from the 10th Battalion, Lincolnshire Regiment ('The Grimsby Chums'). These troops were engaged in the attack around Arras in April 1917. A further four bodies had also been unearthed from nearby – one stated to be a Grimsby Chum, another from the Royal Naval Division, and two unidentified.

However, a BBC programme on 22nd January 2002 revealed that the MoD refused to accept the above findings of the French archaeological team as reported in the newspapers until the details could be established and confirmed. The programme also illustrated the thoroughness exhibited by the authorities who do their utmost to ensure that those buried in the War Graves Commission Cemeteries *are* the bodies of who they are thought to be.

Following this widely reported discovery of bodies, the MoD engaged the services of a forensic archaeologist, Professor Margaret Cox of Bournemouth University, to visit and investigate the site to try to establish the accuracy of the French archaeologists' claims. At the same time the MoD studied their archives and contacted possible relatives of the disinterred soldiers, or people who on reading of the discovery believed the bodies could be those of their relatives, to see if more details could be forthcoming to aid the investigation.

Finally, on the completion of its investigations, the MoD decided that, on the basis of the evidence – an ID tag, a cap badge and medical records – together with Professor Cox's examination of all the skeletons, 'the balance of probability' was that one of the four bodies of the soldiers from the smaller grave was that of 29-year-old Private Archibald McMillan. He was a member of the 15th Battalion, Royal Scots (Lothian Regiment), who had previously and erroneously been entered on a memorial panel of soldiers who had no known grave as Private A. McMillian. Another soldier from this grave was identified under the same heading as a Corporal William Glen also of 15th Battalion, Royal Scots. There was no mention of anyone from the Naval Division or of any other identities being established.

As far as the larger grave of twenty bodies was concerned, the MoD team decided that the only evidence supplied – one helmet, three Lincolnshire Regiment cap badges and a gas mask – was insufficient to guarantee that all the bodies were those of the 10th Lincolns. Nor was it possible to identify any of the men. The strong probability was that the men *were* the Grimsby Chums, but there could also be Royal Scots with them, as the two regiments were attacking side by side and had become mixed together in the battle on 9th April, as the two units advanced. Army records revealed that 21 Lincolns and 26 Royal Scots remained unaccounted for following the battle.

All the soldiers, apart from the two named, were to be reburied in the nearest available military cemetery and their headstones recorded only as 'Unknown soldiers of the Great War known unto God'. (Professor Cox did not accept that the bodies' arms were linked as suggested by the finding team.)

Once the identity of a dead soldier *has* been established, if the family is still in existence and members wish to attend, they are invited to the burial or re-burial ceremony. Two close members of the family can be taken at the expense of the MoD, and all other members are welcome to the ceremony but must make their own travel arrangements and pay their own costs.

On 1st November 2001 *The Times* reported another discovery, the finding of a body of a British soldier in a field near Ploegsteert Wood when the field was being ploughed up. The soldier was identified as Private H. Wilkinson, 2nd Battalion, Lancashire Fusilers, who was killed on the night of 10th November 1914 during the first Ypres battle. He now lies in Prowes Point Cemetery. The article in *The Times* on 31st October 2003 also mentions burials:

> Beneath a leaden sky, a group of Britons crowded into a remote Flanders cemetery yesterday to mark the burial of six unknown soldiers. Just a few years ago such a ceremony would have attracted little attention. Yesterday there were about 100 people present, an indication of the growing popularity of war grave tourism... The priest officiating at yesterday's funeral, Father Ray Jones, said of the ceremony's new found popularity: 'In the three years I have been here, it's really rocketed'.

The article also said, possibly with some exaggeration, that 'the funerals of unknown soldiers take place every few months, as bodies are dug up by builders and farmers.'

PART FIVE

We are the dead. Short days ago
We lived, felt dawn, saw sunset glow,
Loved and were loved, and now we lie
In Flanders fields.

From *In Flanders Fields* composed in 1915 by Lt. Col.
John McCrae. He died in France on 28th January 1918.

The burial of the dead and the Imperial War Graves Commission

The responsible authority for the care of the dead was called
originally 'The Commission of Graves Registration and Enquiries',
and came about through efforts of the British Red Cross Society
in general, and Sir Fabian Ware in particular. As a result of these
efforts the Commission was formed under Ware's command and
took over the work he had started on his own initiative in recording
and maintaining soldiers' graves.

In May 1917 the Imperial War Graves Commission (IWGC) was
established, replacing the Graves Registration Commission, and was
itself in turn re-named in 1960 as the Commonwealth War Graves
Commission (CWGC).

Although there was understandably some opposition at first to
the idea of establishing permanent British cemeteries on the
battlefields, particularly from relatives who wanted to bring the
bodies home, the 'no repatriation policy' was upheld. It was adjudged
that those officers and men who fought and died together would
lie together in their last resting-place, more often than not as though
drawn up on parade, and the Belgian and French Governments
granted free gifts of land for the cemeteries.

31

The French however became concerned by the number of memorials that the IWGC was proposing to erect, and so the number and scale of the Commission's war memorials in France was reduced from twelve to four. Extra land was obtained from the Belgians at Ploegsteert ('Plug Street') to record the names of some of the missing in France. The cost of building and maintaining the cemeteries would be borne by the British and Commonwealth Governments, and the Commission appointed distinguished architects to design the cemeteries and memorials.

The traveller in France or Belgium, if at all possible, should try to visit at least one of the battlefield cemeteries, and take a moment or two while looking at the headstones to think of those lying there, who never came home.

Types of cemeteries

There are three main types of military cemeteries. First, there are the original war-time cemeteries which were made on or just behind the battlefield while the war was still in progress. Many of these were begun by particular regiments, brigades, or divisions, and only a few of these exist – an example is the one on the Bluff in Flanders for the 1st Battalion, Duke of Cornwall's Light Infantry. Then there are the behind-the-lines cemeteries – usually war-time created cemeteries on the sites of former Advanced Dressing stations, Casualty Clearing Stations and Field Hospitals. Many soldiers died of their wounds and were buried in cemeteries like these (see Alfred Watts below). Finally there were the post-war concentration cemeteries. These were burial grounds containing graves moved from small or smaller cemeteries – Tyne Cot, for example.

The cemeteries both large and small, with the exception of the very smallest, are characterised by the distinctive 'Cross of Sacrifice'. The cross varies in size according to the number of graves within the cemetery – the larger the cross the more burials. The Crusader's sword on the cross was originally made of bronze, but it is now plastic.

Below and behind the Cross of Sacrifice lie the ranked graves of the dead soldiers each with a standard simple white headstone 2 feet 6 inches high by 1 foot 3 inches broad. These uniform headstones, originally of Portland stone, but now being replaced with Italian limestone, bear wherever possible the name, age, rank, number and regiment, and the regimental badge and religious emblem (cross, star or crescent as appropriate) of the dead soldier. There is a space at the bottom for a short inscription which could be chosen and sometimes paid for by the family at the rate of $3\frac{1}{2}$d (threepence halfpenny) per word. The Commission at first made this a compulsory charge, but later because some families could not afford it the charge became a voluntary one.

Small traditional British plants and shrubs are arranged and grown on each grave, and headstones of a slightly different shape dotted here and there in the cemeteries denote the graves of German soldiers.

For those who cannot be identified the headstone is inscribed 'A soldier of the Great War known unto God'. The inscription was either originated by, or selected by, Rudyard Kipling, who was a member of the Commission and who lost his son on the Western Front and searched in vain for his grave. According to Martin Stephen, in *The Price of Pity*, Kipling never really got over his son's death, and it did not help, Stephen adds, that numbers of people wrote to him gloating over the death as the just reward for a man who had pushed the cause of militarism so vociferously before the war.

Far away, in Gallipoli, stands an unusual war memorial placed by the Turkish Government at 'Anzac Cove' in 1934. It is unusual because it is dedicated not only to the Turkish dead, but to their enemies, the Australian, New Zealand and all British forces generally who lie there. It reads:

Those heroes that shed their blood
and lost their lives.
You are now lying in a friendly country.
Therefore, rest in peace
There is no difference between the Johnies
and the Mehmets to us where they lie side by side
here in this country of ours.
You, the Mothers,
Who sent your sons from far away countries
Wipe away your tears.
Your sons are lying in our bosom
and are in peace

After having lost their lives on this land they have
become our sons as well.

Alan Moorehead in his book *Gallipoli* published in 1956, makes
no mention of this memorial. He says only:

> For nearly forty years the cemeteries have been tended with
> great devotion by a Major Millington, an old Australian soldier.
> He has a curious existence, for at Chanak on the Narrows,
> where he has his house, he is in a Turkish military area and
> may not move more than a thousand paces in any direction
> without escort. However, the young Turkish conscripts
> accompany him willingly enough as he goes over the peninsula
> month by month and year by year to supervise his staff of
> local stonemasons and gardeners. The Turks find this
> preoccupation with the dead somewhat strange, since their own
> soldiers who died at Gallipoli were buried in anonymous
> communal graves, and until recently almost their only memorial
> was a legend picked out in large white letters on a hillside
> above Chanak. It reads 'March, 1915' a reminder to all passing
> ships that was the day when the Allied Fleet was defeated.
> However the Turkish gardeners work well; no wall around the
> French and British cemeteries is allowed to crumble, no weed
> is anywhere allowed to grow, and now in the nineteen-fifties
> the gardens are more beautiful than ever. Yet hardly anyone
> ever visits them. Except for occasional organised tours not
> more than half a dozen visitors arrive from one year's end to
> the other, Often for months at a time nothing of any consequence
> happens, lizards scuttle about the tombstones in the sun-shine
> and time goes by in an endless dream.

Compared with today the battlefield graveyards on the Western
Front looked very different to Wilfrid Ewart, who visited the Somme
battlefield area in October 1919, with his sister Angela, looking
for a particular grave. He writes:

> And now before us the battlefield stretched afar like some
> wild, undulating moorland; it was only when we looked critically
> through spy-glasses that we perceived the whole area to be
> one of complete destruction; that it was too a vast cemetery...

Nor could the way be easily pursued, for shell-holes of every size treacherously overgrown with weeds and vegetation, not to speak of wires, staves, and the naturally rough nature of the ground, everywhere beset our footsteps. It was impossible to go far without a fall. Hardly less common than shell-holes were the graves of the soldiers – a greying wooden cross leaning at an angle marked usually by the name on a metal label, sometimes nothing at all, and sometimes by the inscription *To an Unknown Soldier* in indelible pencil. At each we paused. Wreckage of the fighting of 1916 not less than that of 1918 lay on every hand. Here was a steel helmet, German or English, dented, comical-looking, once set upon a man's head, now a piece of empty steel; there a shred of uniform, musty-coloured, sodden, and often hardly recognisable ... again, it might be a completely rusted rifle or a gas mask strangely discoloured and forbidding. Fragments of letters we found, photographs of women, and stray names of men who had long since gone to dust. Year-old tragedies lurked on either hand: in this livid green, stagnant pool where a soldier's clothing and equipment, his respirator and rifle, lay adjacent to an oozing, battered grave; in that shell-hole where a blood-stained overcoat and steel helmet suggest what may have happened there... Heaps of salvage litter the way [to the village of Flers] – heaps of iron wiring stakes or pickets, piles of trench mortar bombs and shells, piles of leather equipment, broken trucks from a light railway, many rifles, dug-out frames, and boxes of ammunition – it merges hourly in the green-brown world around and is already grass-grown.

Sir Douglas Haig, in paragraph 16 of his Dispatch dated 19th May 1916, indicates that prior to the battles of the Somme, the War Graves Commission had already established a programme and carried out a surprising amount of work:

16. The Commission of Graves Registration and Enquiries has, since it first undertook this work eighteen months ago, registered and marked over 50,000 graves. Without its labours many would have remained unidentified. It has answered several thousand enquiries from relatives and supplied them with photographs. Flowers and shrubs have been planted in most

of the cemeteries which are sufficiently far removed from the firing line, and all cemeteries which it is possible to work in during the daytime are now being looked after by non-commissioned officers and men of this unit.

PART SIX

The tragic aspect of war is not that it is a conflict between right and wrong, but that it is a contest in which the mass of the combatants on both sides suppose themselves to be champions of the right.

Spencer Wilkinson, Chichele Professor of Military History, Oxford, 2nd December 1914.

The Great War years

The years of conflict from 1914 to 1918 have in one way or another affected all our lives and shaped our nation's future. Winston Churchill, writing in 1930 at the conclusion of his epic insider's review of the period in the third volume of *The World Crisis 1911–1918*, and as yet unaware of the part he had to play in act two of the drama on which the curtain would rise nine years later, said:

> It will certainly not fall to this generation to pronounce the final verdict upon the Great War. The German people are worthy of better explanations than the shallow tale that they were undermined by enemy propaganda.
> ...The German armies upheld her tottering confederates, intervened in every theatre with success, stood everywhere on conquered territory, and inflicted on their enemies more than twice the bloodshed they suffered themselves.
> ...Small states were trampled down in the struggle; a mighty Empire was battered into unrecognisable fragments; and nearly twenty million men perished or shed their blood before the

sword was wrested from that terrible hand. Surely, Germans, for history it is enough!

Now, 75 years after Churchill's comments, it is unlikely that anyone will either have the temerity to pronounce the final verdict upon the Great War, or try to recreate the cadences of Churchill's majestic oratorical phrasing.

Differing views on British propaganda

The 'shallow tale' referred to by Churchill was a German post-war claim that Germany had never been defeated on the battlefield, but had succumbed to a disintegration of its morale, fed by skilful British propaganda – the famous German 'stab in the back' legend. Hitler said that Germany had failed to recognise propaganda as a weapon of the first order, whereas the British had employed it with great skill and ingenious deliberation. One of his first acts on coming to power was to establish a Ministry of Propaganda.

Hitler's tribute to skilful British propaganda does not appear to have found an echo in some British diplomatic circles of the day. In 1916, Le Roy Lewis, at the British Embassy in Paris, wrote to the Prime Minister, Lloyd George, with some asperity concerning the Foreign Office propaganda departments, and for good measure the British Secret Service – which contained some future famous names in literature:

> Our press propaganda, which is apparently run by Lord Newton at the Foreign Office, is worked on peculiar lines. I met here a Mr Masefield,* who is also I believe a novelist, and who informed me that he had been instructed to write up the subject of American help given to the French nation. It is not clear to me how this helps British Interests, but perhaps the Foreign Office may have some recondite reason for this strange effort.

*John Masefield (1876–1967). English poet and novelist who became Poet Laureate in 1930.

The exasperated diplomat continues:

> I saw yesterday a young man called Captain Compton

Mackenzie,* who has been employed for the last year in the Secret Service in Athens. This young man is, I am told, a novelist of some repute, and certainly his stories lose nothing in the telling of them, but his conversation was in my opinion most unwise. If we have Secret Service agents it is just as well to employ discreet people. We have in Spain a certain Captain Mason,* also a distinguished novelist, but whose conduct I am informed by the Secretary of our Spanish Embassy gave rise to a spirited protest on the part of the King of Spain. If we must employ Secret Service agents – and I very much doubt their utility – I should suggest that the profession of novelists might be avoided, and that less brilliant and more discreet persons should be chosen.

*Sir Edward Montague Compton Mackenzie (1883–1972), English novelist and writer who served in the Dardanelles campaign and in 1917 became director of the Aegean Intelligence Service in Syria. A.E.W. Mason (1865–1948), actor (not to be confused with James Mason), novelist, and MP.

At about the same time (in 1916) Maurice Hankey, at the Cabinet Office, passed on a letter he had received from Lord Esher in Paris, to the War Minister:

Something really must be done to improve our official communiqués, which for some time have been the laughing stock of the French and Americans here. The one in which we record with great pomp the killing of two Germans is typical of the stupidity of somebody. You have no idea how unpleasant it has been living among the French through the great Verdun battle. The comments of French and Americans are in reality very unfair to our troops in the field who have through the long winter and spring been fighting every day and losing heavily.

Not a conception of this has been gathered by any Frenchman alive, other than those engaged as liaison officers with our troops. Yet I believe we have all sorts of people engaged on what is called propaganda both in France and in neutral countries.

Cannot you instil a little commonsense into those who direct all this machinery? Two very simple things are wanted here: one is that the British communiqués should be more carefully written, and sent direct to Paris instead of through London which will enable twenty-four hours at least to be saved in the publication of news. The second is that someone who is not a perfect fool should be specially designated to reside here to get in touch with the French press.

I hope you will explain all this to Mr Lloyd George, whose Celtic alertness of mind will grip the importance of it at once.

Support from the Empire

When war was declared the nations of the Empire immediately rallied to the support of the mother country and, in addition to the overseas British regular army troops being hastily summoned home, Imperial troops were also almost immediately on the move to the various theatres of war.

Edward Salmon, writing in *The British Dominions Year Book 1916*, is perhaps somewhat extravagant in his expressions by today's literary and political mores and tastes:

> The God of Battles is the greatest of alchemists and from the dross of party in every land where the Union Jack floated, issued as by magic the finest gold of patriotism. Germany has been guilty of many deadly crimes; the blight of her Kultur menaced civilisation, but we Britons of the Seven Seas at least owe it to her inordinate ambition and her ruthless methods, that we no longer have even a shadow of a doubt as to the desire and determination of the British Dominions and British Dependencies to remain one with the Island Mother.

Having said that, if Salmon is correct in his assertion that a writer in *Der Tag* in April 1915 produced the following, then he was on the right track for the times:

> We [Germany] expected that India would rise when the first shot was fired in Europe, but thousands of Indians came to fight with the British against us. We thought the British Empire would be torn to pieces, but the Colonies appear to be united closer than ever with the Mother Country. We expected a triumphant rebellion in South Africa; it was nothing but a

failure. We thought there would be trouble in Ireland, but instead she sent her best soldiers against us. We anticipated that the 'peace at any price' party would be dominant in England, but it melted away in the ardour to fight Germany. We regarded England as degenerate, yet she seems to be our principal enemy.

Jay Winter and Blaine Baggett in *The Great War and the Shaping of the 20th Century* capture a poignant little story of a family at war that in many respects could be repeated throughout Europe (Albert John Dell below for example). The difference here is that this family, the Goodyear family, lived in Newfoundland, far from the conflict, and yet provided five sons to the army and one daughter to the nursing corps.

Kate, the daughter, nursed wounded soldiers and on one occasion courageously faced and endured the wrath of the hospital matron – not an action to be taken lightly in those days – because, as there was no room other than the corridor, she had placed a soldier in a private ward. He was suffering great pain and could not rest or sleep following his operation for the amputation of a leg. On being reprimanded for putting him in a private room she said to the matron:

> I have brothers ... I have brothers overseas. I don't know where or how they are, and can't do much to help them. But I'll do what I can wherever I am, and I'd like to think that someone would do the same for them. So let me tell you. As long as I am in this hospital, as long as there is an empty bed, no soldier will ever spend a night in a hallway. I Will Not Have It. I shall move them to private rooms if I have to carry them up the stairs myself.

Matron capitulated. All five brothers were casualties. Three were killed, two wounded; one badly.

Newfoundland

Newfoundland at that time was not part of Canada, but existed as a separate British colony of some 250,000 souls, who declared war

41

on Germany with Britain in 1914. The first Newfoundland contingent of about 500 troops sailed to Britain in a small vessel the SS *Florizel* on October 4th 1914, and disembarked at Plymouth on 20th October.

This Newfoundland contingent was enlarged to a regiment, and on 20th September 1915 landed at Kangaroo Beach at Gallipoli, where they joined the 88th Brigade of the British 29th Division, and remained with them until 1918 when they became part of the 28th Brigade of the 9th Division.

The 'Royal Newfoundland Regiment' as it became, in addition to Gallipoli saw service in Egypt and on the Western Front. It was here, on the Western Front, in recognition of its conduct in 1917 in the defence of Masnières, that the regiment was granted the title 'Royal' – a rare if not unique distinction during the war.*

*See below, '29th Division the Battle of the Somme, 1916 and Battle of Cambrai, 1917'.

In addition, some 2,000 Newfoundlanders served in the Royal Navy through the Newfoundland Naval Reserve, and 500 others were formed into a forestry battalion and served in Scotland where they were very popular with the local population.

Caught by the moving family vignette of the Goodyears, I attempted, through *Pilgrimage* by W. David Parsons, to trace the dates and burial places of those three sons killed. Although I found a total of four burials of known Goodyear fatalities in the Royal Newfoundland Regiment, there are also 128 'unknown' bodies in various French and Belgian burial grounds, and I cannot claim success.

According to Winter and Baggett, Raymond Goodyear was killed by shrapnel near Ypres in October 1916. This must have been early in October because, as I understand, the regiment left the Salient on 8th October to return to the Somme area. His brother Stanley was also killed in Belgium when transporting munitions to his unit the following year not very far away at Langemarck* (known to the Newfoundlanders as 'Broenbeek') and where the regiment, as an element in the 29th Division, was engaged in 'The Battle of Langemarck' – part of Third Ypres or Passchendaele.

*Langemarck became the site of a very large German military cemetery and memorial. With its eerie sculpture of four large faceless figures, together with its massed multiple graves and horizontal headstones, it is very different in character from any British one.

42

The cemetery contains over 44,000 burials including a mass grave of 25,000 German soldiers. On one of my visits, which happened to be an Armistice Day, I was surprised to see how many British visitors had left poppies on the graves.

The third Goodyear son to die was their elder brother Hedley. He had enlisted into the Canadian 102nd Battalion while attending the University of Toronto, and he was killed by a sniper on the Somme in August 1918.

To the best of my knowledge I have met and known only one Newfoundlander for any period of time; this was in the 1950s in the Canadian Arctic. Although we never met in person, only over the radio, in our daily contacts he came over as a fine young man and was, I am sure, a worthy descendant of those brave men and women from that earlier war-torn generation who responded so generously to the call in 1914.

Canada, and Princess Patricia's Canadian Light Infantry

The first of the many Canadian contingents to arrive on the war scene was the then unknown but now famous Princess Patricia's Canadian Light Infantry. A most unusual regiment, it was raised initially by an individual private subscription by a Mr Hamilton Gault when war was declared. Its composition was almost entirely of ex-British regular soldiers – and Marines and Royal Navy personnel – veterans of the Boer War in many instances.

Hamilton Gault, a former officer of the 2nd Canadian Mounted Rifles, had served in South Africa during the Boer War when he was nineteen years of age. Now, in 1914, as a wealthy man and a captain in the militia, he proposed to raise a cavalry regiment and he took this idea to the Minister of Militia, Colonel Sam Hughes. Hughes found the idea attractive, but suggested that infantry would be more urgently needed than cavalry, and Gault readily accepted the change.

The proposal was agreed by the Canadian Government and on 8th August 1914 the British Government wired approval also. As a result 'Princess Pat's' was born. The regiment was named after Princess Patricia of Connaught, the daughter of the Duke of Connaught (who was then Governor General of Canada), as she had agreed to become the Colonel-in Chief of the Regiment.

Only seventeen days after the first call for recruits had been made, on Friday 28th August, the regiment embarked to sail for England aboard the liner *Megantic*. Here occurred the first real delay as the Admiralty decided that the ship would have to wait for a naval escort, and to be joined by the first of the main Canadian Army contingent preparing for departure following Canada's offer of 20,000 men.

Again, as with my personal experience of Newfoundlanders, so far as I recall I have known only one (ex) member of the 'Princess Pat's'. This also in the mid-1950s in Canada. On this occasion we met in person when we were both waiting at a base camp at Frobisher, on Baffin Island, for further transport north and west to the Melville Peninsula to a construction site on the arctic DEW line.*

*The acronym for the 'Defence Early Warning' chain of interlocking radar stations stretching from Alaska to Greenland, and then under construction for the American Air Force. At the time the locations were regarded as highly secret.

I don't remember how, but in the course of conversation with this ex-soldier the subject of the Korean War came up, and I mentioned that a friend of mine had served there as a subaltern with the Northumberland Fusiliers, and his experience in Korea had given him nightmares for some time to come. The Canadian mentioned he had been there with the Princess Pat's and asked if I had heard of them. I said indeed I had, and fortunately I was able to assure him, in all honesty, that I had heard nothing but admiration. Just as well perhaps as he was quite a tough-looking customer – in a relaxed and friendly fashion. Apparently I wasn't the only 'old country' man who had discussed his regiment with him. On an earlier occasion, when he was still in uniform and at a railway station waiting for a train, a stranger, after regarding him curiously for a while, spoke to him concerning his regiment. This, it transpired, was Stewart Grainger, a well-known English film actor of the time.

Canada, although having a governor-general appointed by the British crown, retained the right to veto legislation considered harmful to British Empire interests. However the Dominion made no individual declaration of war, but automatically followed Britain. At the time of the declaration of war Canada had only a small regular army although there was a militia in which volunteers served for three years. In the course of the war some 260 numbered CEF (Canadian Expeditionary Force) battalions were mustered. More than 595,000 men were enlisted in Canada; 418,000 served overseas in the CEF, and in addition, among those who served outside the CEF, 13,000 served in the British aviation services, many with distinction. Most famous among these was the pilot 'Billy' Bishop VC.

Australia

In 1914 with 96 per cent of its population from British stock, it is not surprising perhaps that apart from a minority of those of Irish descent there was overwhelming support in Australia for Britain and the war. Led by Andrew Fisher, Joseph Cook and W.M. Hughes, all of whom served as Prime Minister and were very supportive of Britain, the armed services of Australia made a magnificent contribution to the Allied cause. Some 332,000 troops served overseas, of whom more than 212,000 were wounded and 60,000 killed. All the troops were volunteers as the country refused to implement conscription.

New Zealand

Only 25 per cent of the New Zealand population was British born – more than 72 per cent were born in New Zealand and in total there were only some one million and ninety thousand people on the two islands. From this small population more than 124,000 served in the armed forces, 92,000 of whom were volunteers. The first troops of The New Zealand Expeditionary Force left the country in August 1914, for Samoa, and those destined for the Dardanelles two months later.

Throughout the war the NZEF in Europe was commanded by General Godley. They served with the Australians in the ANZAC (Australian and New Zealand Army Corps) in the initial operations in Egypt and Gallipoli, and were re-organised as the New Zealand Division in February 1916, but still fought alongside the Australians in Europe. Less flamboyant than the Australians, they were regarded equally highly as fighting troops; steadfast and brave.

In 1999 while on a 'pilgimage' to Flanders I had the privilege to meet a New Zealand lady who, like me, was visiting the grave of an uncle who had been killed in the area. She was as indomitable as I am sure was her uncle, Gunner Horace Falconer Cobb, who was killed on 11th October serving with the New Zealand Field Artillery on the left of the Australians in the appalling conditions at Passchendaele around Gravenstafel in 1917.

India

Four days after war was declared, two infantry divisions and a cavalry brigade of the Indian Army were ordered to mobilise, and Indian soldiers, still in their tropical uniforms, began to arrive in France in September. They were thrown into the first desperate Battle of Ypres in October, and within a month had won their first Victoria Cross.

The Indian troops suffered terribly from the bitter cold and wet conditions of that Flanders winter, and commanded by Sir James Willcocks The Indian Corps continued to be engaged in local actions in the area around Neuve Chapelle. It was here also that they were heavily engaged in the actual battle of Neuve Chapelle in March 1915, and another Victoria Cross was awarded.*

*To Rifleman Gobar Sing Negi who unfortunately never lived to receive it.

South Africa

Although South African forces were heavily committed to the campaigns in East Africa, some 30,000 were deployed in Europe and in addition an estimated 10,000 South Africans served in the British forces with more than 3,000 in the RAF by late 1918.

The South African Brigade replaced the original 28th Brigade as part of the 9th (Scottish) Division. As such the South Africans were heavily involved on the Somme in July 1916 at Delville Wood where they started in the attack with a complement of 121 officers and 3,032 other ranks. By the end of a week they were reduced to 29 officers and 751 other ranks. In April 1918, in *Die Kaiserschlacht* at the battle of the Lys, they again suffered heavy losses and had to be withdrawn from the 9th Division to refit.

Almost all, if not all, the countries of the Empire sent men to fight the enemy in various parts of the globe, and I have only made reference to the ones with the largest contingents serving in Europe as they form part of my story.

PART SEVEN

Many of the regiments were excellent, but the system was wretched... No one knew anything of the management of an army.

Duke of Wellington recalling his first taste of active service in Europe in 1794. (Charles Messenger, *For Love of Regiment. Vol. 1.*)

Military background – Army reforms

One of the first recorded serious attempts to reform training and tactics was put forward by a Colonel David Dundas, and in 1788 he published *Principles of Military Movement.* Four years later these reforms were adopted for the infantry as a whole. He had his critics. His concept was based on 18th-century warfare, and as the British were to discover to their cost, the French meanwhile had moved on with *their* approach to warfare.

In 1869 Lt. Colonel Sir Garnet Wolsley, later Field Marshal Lord Wolsley of Cairo (he of the expression 'all Sir Garnet' i.e. everything right and proper) published his *Soldier's Pocket Book*. Whether he actually published several books, the first in 1869, and another in 1872, or whether the book was reprinted with a slightly different title I am not clear, as there are references to both *The Soldier's Pocket Book for Field Service* and *The Soldier's Pocket Book, Field Manoeuvres*. Also quoted is just *The Soldier's Pocket Book* which ran to several editions, the fifth in 1886.

In effect, it seems his work reproduced the philosophy of Colonels Coote-Manningham and The Hon. William Stewart when they propounded the formation of The Rifle Brigade in 1800. Wolseley maintained that the gulf between officers and men was both artificial and too wide. He said there was but little sympathy shown to the men and more was required from the officers than assuming all their soldiers needed was drill and discipline.

Wolseley was unpopular in some quarters, as were his views, especially among the most conservative officers, even in the Rifle Brigade when a member of that regiment, and a hero of the Crimea, Captain Henry Clifford VC wrote:

> You must not look upon the soldier as a responsible agent, for he is not able to take care of himself, he must be fed, clothed, looked after like a child and given just enough to make him efficient as part of the great machine for War. Give him one farthing more than he really wants, and he gives way to his brutal propensities and immediately gets drunk.

In 1855 in the Crimea, Wolseley was a captain, and his colonel, Col. Campbell of 95th Foot, described Wolseley as one of his bravest officers. Michael Glover, in his book *Rorke's Drift*, seems to hold a more contemptuous view of Wolseley, describing him as 'malicious, overbearing, conceited and intemperate in speech'. He does however concede that he was a field commander of ability.

One man of influence and farsightedness who did study Wolseley's book and take heed of it was Gladstone's recently appointed Secretary for War, Sir Edward Cardwell, who was Secretary for War 1869–1874. Cardwell was a Liberal and a pacifist, but he saw the need for Britain to have a good modern army.*

*Glover is also less than complimentary about the ideas and reforms of Cardwell. At best he tends to damn the ideas with faint praise, but also implies that the reforms actually made things worse.

As the senior officers in Victorian times were inclined to be conservative and with entrenched views, the resulting hostility towards reform and 'radicalism' in the armed services makes it a wonder that the reformers made any progress at all. In addition, the cumbersome and complex organisation existing at the time of the Crimea War for example makes it difficult to conceive how the army ever got out to the Crimea, let alone with any equipment and supplies and in a position to fight a battle.

In those days, according to Christopher Hibbert, in his *The*

Destruction of Lord Raglan, the Commander-in Chief at the Horse Guards was a sort of Chief of the Imperial General Staff, but he did not command the forces overseas. His power was derived from the Crown, not from Parliament. The Master General of the Ordnance was in charge of equipment, fortifications and barracks, and he also exercised some power over the Royal Artillery and Royal Engineers, particularly in respect of pay and discipline. A board of general officers took charge of clothing. And the Commissariat, a civilian authority and a department of the Treasury, took charge of supplies and supposedly of transport, but in fact had little effective means of moving its supplies.

The Medical Department was largely independent of any other departments, except that of the Secretary-at-War which financed it, and the Purveyors Department, which, as a kind of subsidiary of the Commissariat, supplied it with some but not all its requirements. The Secretary-at-War looked after the pay and finances of the army (except the artillery and engineers) and its arrangements with civilian contractors. He was not responsible for the size and cost of the army, this came under the Secretary of State for the Colonies.

From the foregoing it is not difficult to imagine the muddle, the delays, the duplication, the departmental jealousies and the general bureaucratic nightmare of the system.

Many commanding officers resented and often chose to ignore any instructions or rules that came from 'Horse Guards' (Whitehall). Anyone in those days paying a huge sum of money – up to £40,000 or more – to 'purchase' a regiment did not feel obliged to accept interference with his way of running it, even if he had but the most rudimentary idea of soldiering!

Determined to right the wrongs then in force, Cardwell worked hard to push through military reforms; work that was continued and expanded first by his successor Hugh Childers, and then by Lord Richard Haldane, who held the appointment from 1905 until 1912.

Field Marshal Lord Carver, in *Britain's Army in the 20th Century*, writes that as a result of a general feeling that the army was badly run, and that money could be saved if it was better organised at the top, the Hartington Commission made a report in 1889. One of its recommendations was to abolish the post of Commander-in-Chief, and to establish an Army Board of which the senior member would be a chief of staff. It proved not possible – or not politic –

to remove the Duke of Cambridge, the incumbent, and the post of CIC continued and later was given to Lord Wolseley.

Wolseley had told his staff to prepare a scheme for the mobilisation of two Army Corps and a Cavalry Division and the necessary lines of communication troops for war outside Great Britain. And this was pretty much what Sir John French took with him to France in 1914 as Commander of the British Expeditionary Force.

The army designed primarily for home defence and overseas garrisons

However, the Secretary for State for War, Edward Stanhope, in a memorandum to the Cabinet in December, made it clear that the thinking of the day was that home defence was still the main consideration, but if a force had to be sent abroad to Europe:

> ... it will be distinctly understood that the probability of employment of an Army Corps in the field in any European war is sufficiently improbable to make it the primary duty of the military authorities to organise our forces efficiently for the defence of the country.

The Royal Navy was still seen as being the prime defender of the realm and the Army plans and provisions should be with the aim of meeting various named requirements – among them:

(a) The effective support of the civil power in all parts of the United Kingdom.
(b) To find the number of men for India, which has been fixed by arrangement with the Government of India.
(c) To find garrisons for all our fortresses and coaling stations, at home and abroad, according to a scale now laid down, and so maintain these garrisons at all times at the strength required for a peace or war footing.

There was absolutely no thought of putting a large army in the field in Europe or of establishing a large army on continental lines.

One military innovation in Victorian times, and one designed to foster the feeling of belonging to a regiment, was the introduction of Old Comrades Associations, and following the Boer War (1899–1902), the number of these grew and thereafter continued to flourish. These associations enabled former soldiers, as members of their associations, to maintain contact with their regiments and each other, and to help old and ex-comrades who had fallen on hard times.

Officers' Service and promotion

Cardwell's tasks included a reform to overhaul the officer corps. In his day, as I have said, a wealthy man could purchase a commission in the infantry or cavalry without any prior military training or experience, or indeed any aptitude or feeling for army life. There was no requirement to sit an examination or undergo aptitude tests for selection and qualification. Further, he could purchase promotion to a higher rank in the same way, up to the rank of Colonel. This seems incredible now, but equally astonishing perhaps is that despite this iniquitous system a number of distinguished soldiers did come to the fore.

Cardwell eventually got his way, and in 1871 the purchase of commissions was abolished. Unfortunately this caused a continued blocking of good men for promotion as it was decided in 1876, after deliberation by a Royal Commission, that promotion should be by 'seniority tempered by rejection'. In practice it would seem that seniority ruled.

David R. Woodward, editor of *The Military Correspondence of Field Marshal Sir William Robertson*, says that as late as 1913 only two per cent of regular officers commissioned that year had advanced through the ranks. And between the 1870s and 1880s only an average of from four to five men a year were promoted from the ranks.

In 1908, among other reforms and innovations, Haldane was responsible for the formation of the Officers Training Corps (OTC). This consisted of two divisions, Senior and Junior. The Senior Division was at universities, the Junior Division at public schools and the Inns of Court. In 1914 there were 23 contingents in the Senior Division, and 166 in the Junior Division. Between August 1914 and March 1915 temporary commissions were granted to 20,577 former members of the OTC.

Officers' private incomes

Prior to the war, generally speaking, one still needed private means to live in the manner in which a commissioned officer was expected to live, particularly in the more fashionable regiments. Robert Graves mentions that in his regiment a candidate for a regular commission had not only to distinguish himself in the passing-out examination at the Royal Military College, Sandhurst, and be strongly recommended by two officers of the regiment, but also to possess a guaranteed independent income that would enable him to play polo and hunt and keep up the social reputation of the regiment.

Roger Perkins (see also below), in his study *Military and Naval Silver* gives a fascinating insight into the expenses that a newly joined subaltern was subjected to in a regiment of the line just prior to the Second World War. He quotes as his source a Second Lieutenant Erskine-Tulloch of The 2nd Battalion, The Northamptonshire Regiment, who said newly appointed officers were expected to present the mess with an item of silver on joining and:

> We paid five pounds, spread over as many months, as a joining subscription to the mess. We also paid a monthly subscription equivalent to one day's pay, plus a maintenance charge of about the same amount. There were regular subscriptions to the Band Fund (Major and Captains only), to the Corps of Drums (Subalterns only), to the Regimental Sports Fund, and also to the Silver Fund. There were also small charges for items such as newspapers and magazines, the rental charges for the Mess telephone... In all, I suppose one's basic monthly Mess bill (without drinks) was about eight or nine pounds. There was not a great deal left out of a Second Lieutenant's net monthly pay of fifteen pounds by the time he had given his soldier servant eleven shillings 'extra duty pay', and paid for his laundry. That came to about three shillings a week, and was done by the wife of one of the soldiers or NCOs. We also had the use of a Government horse, for which we were charged a nominal ten shillings monthly forage money.*

*For the benefit of those not familiar with the currency then, twenty shillings equalled one pound.

54

Temporary officers and gentlemen

Some men seeking a temporary commission at the outbreak of the war in 1914 appear to have gained one simply on the grounds of having a socially acceptable background, and knowing someone at the War Office who would give them the necessary introductions. An alternative to the War Office approach was to know the right person in a regimental training battalion. Armed with a letter of recommendation, and followed by a quick interview, they were accepted for training – as in the case of Robert Graves below.

Another method came to the attention of Wilfred Owen in 1915, when he was in London as a visitor from France and saw an announcement on the noticeboard of his hotel saying: 'any gentleman returning from abroad can obtain a commission by joining the Artists' Rifles, subject to age and fitness'.

By January 1915, as there were by now a number of potential officers with basic military training serving in the ranks, it was decided that NCOs and men who were recommended by their commanding officers would be given a short course of four weeks. Those candidates who then were considered suitable would be commissioned and sent to Young Officer Companies, which were attached to Reserve Brigades, for further training while waiting to be posted to their units.

Many private soldiers and NCOs from the Territorial units serving in France and Flanders in mid 1915 were applying for commissions in Kitchener's 'New Army' battalions. As a result, and worried by the loss of experienced men, some battalion commanders in the BEF were forbidding their men to go for interviews in Britain unless they had a written request from the colonel of the intended regiment asking for them to attend. Sandhurst and Woolwich continued to train candidates for regular commissions with shortened courses of four and six months, later extended to eight months and a year.

In February 1916, a new system for training officers was introduced with the formation of officer cadet units. In future, temporary commissions would be granted only to those who had passed through the ranks of a cadet unit unless they had previous service as an officer. The course lasted for four months.

Sir Frank Fox, writing as *G.S.O.*, has this comment on the war-time officers *vis-à-vis* the regular officer pre-war:

The recruits of the old Regular Army before the war came into an organisation which was officered, from brigade generals down to junior subalterns, by specialists. Officers were drawn mostly from a class with a tradition of rule, and were given very close training. Those who came in as officers from circles which had not that tradition were in a minority, and during their course of training learned to conform to the pattern set. Very much of the success of the British Army has been due to the qualities of courage, coolness, and *noblesse oblige* of the officers. The recruits to the New Armies did not have the advantage of coming to an organisation fully officered by men with this tradition of command and technical knowledge of their work. They had to rely for officers on material which was slightly poorer on the average... Recruited officers from the bulk of the community: in many cases very good; sometimes just passing muster; in a few cases distinctly poor. The necessity of a weeding-out was soon recognised.

He describes the ideal officer as being one who should:

Besides being a gentleman and a skilled tactician, [be] a good horse-master, a good house-keeper, and a clever mechanician able to train men to repair a telephone, a saddle, a cooking-pot or a wagon.

Starting at the top, the ranks of the 'Commissioned' officers (those who hold the Sovereign's Commission) were: Field Marshal, General, Lieutenant General, Major General, Brigadier-General (today just 'Brigadier'), Colonel, Lieutenant Colonel, Major, Captain, Lieutenant, Second Lieutenant.

Officer daily rates of pay in 1914

Rates are quoted in shillings. There were twenty shillings to the pound, and twelve pennies to the shilling – written in abbreviated form 's' for shillings and 'd' for pence: Col./Lt. Col. = 23s.0d (£1.3s.0d); Major = 13s.7d; Captain = 12s.6d to 14s.6d; Lieutenant = 8s.6d.

Soldiers in the regular army

During the latter years of the nineteenth century more employment became available, and as a result the required twenty-one years of service in the army became increasingly unpopular, and recruits harder to come by. A number of army reforms introduced trial variations in the length of service for soldiers in an effort to attract more recruits, and at the outbreak of war in 1914, the regular soldiers in the infantry served for a minimum of twelve years.*

*This twelve-year period of service was divided into seven years active service ('seven years with the colours') and five years with the reserves. The exceptions were the Foot Guards who served three and nine, The Horse and Field Artillery who served for six and six; and the Household Cavalry and Garrison Artillery who served for eight and four.

Changes in army uniforms

Field Marshal Lord Carver writes that at the same time as the attempts to improve recruiting by changing the length of service with the colours, Lord Roberts proposed a change in uniform. This was accepted, and from then on soldiers wore the same uniform in peace and in war – khaki, not scarlet, green or blue – and the helmet was replaced by a round peakless cap. The cap proved unpopular and was replaced in 1904 by the peaked cap which survives to this day, although largely replaced in the Second World War by the beret.*

*The beret was originally adopted by the Royal Tank Corps from Roedean girls' school. And I wonder how many paratroopers, SAS, marine commandos etc., today realise that when they are at last able to don their coveted berets, they come to them by courtesy of a famous girls' public school!

The ranks of non-commissioned officers (NCOs) in the infantry

These are: Regimental Sergeant Major,* Company Sergeant Major,* Staff Sergeant, Sergeant, Corporal, Lance Corporal.

*Since 1881 Sergeant Majors in the infantry have been referred to as 'Warrant' Officers, as they hold a 'Warrant' as opposed to a 'Commission' from the Sovereign. There are two classes of Warrant Officers, WO1s and WO2s. Regimental Sergeant Majors (RSMs) are WO1s, and the rank is denoted by the Royal Arms worn on the lower sleeve. Until the reforms introduced by Cardwell, the RSM wore four stripes, and it was not until 1915 that classes of warrant officers were introduced. The WO2s, of which the best known is the Company Sergeant Major (CSM), has the rank denoted by a crown worn on the lower sleeve. Prior to 1915 the senior non-commissioned officer in an infantry company continued to be the Colour Sergeant, a rank introduced in 1813.

Private soldiers

At the very bottom of the army ranks in the infantry is the Private Soldier. Originally he was called 'Private Man' because he only had responsibility for himself – and to do what everyone else told him.

Unlike the rather kindly condescending way in which '*G.S.O.*' refers to the temporary officers and gentlemen recruited during the war, he speaks almost with awe of the volunteers who joined as 'other ranks' at the outbreak of the war:

> The material of the New Armies was such that no recruiting sergeant in 1913 could have hoped to secure. In a fairly typical batch of recruits which I had to take over one day were engine-fitters, brassfinishers, coal miners, agricultural labourers, gamekeepers, two foremen, one compositor, one valet, one pugilist (a champion), one stud groom, one cycle mechanic, one clerk. The wages of these men before they joined was high and only two out of thirty-eight had been of the 'usually unemployed' class... I have seen batches of recruits for the old army before they joined, and they looked usually rather forelorn [*sic*] – men accustomed to be unemployed, men at a loose end, disappointed men, with just a sprinkling of eager men taking to the soldier's life for the love of it. Only after three months of the wholesome life, the wholesome food, the kindly discipline of the Army, would they fairly compare in physique, manhood, and intelligence with the recruits of the New Armies.

Other ranks daily rates of pay in 1914

Sgt. Major = 5s.0d; CSM = 4s.0d; Sgt. = 2s.4d; Corporal = 1s.8d; Private = 1s.0d.

PART EIGHT

The British Army is a loose affiliation of regiments which choose to serve together, as and when the need arises.

Quoted by Roger Perkins in *Military and Naval Silver.*

Regimental changes

One of Cardwell's reforms in the 1880s was to combine two of the numbered regiments into a 'linked' battalion system of county regiments. For example the 48th Foot and 58th Foot merged to form the Northamptonshire Regiment, and the 52nd Foot and 43rd Foot merged to become the Oxfordshire and Buckinghamshire Light Infantry. This new system aroused considerable opposition at first, but gradually it came to be accepted and the previously numbered regiments became either the 1st or the 2nd battalions of the new county or city regiments. Henceforth nearly all infantry regiments were composed of two battalions – among the exceptions were the regiments of Foot Guards who each had three, and the Rifle Brigade and The King's Royal Rifle Corps who each had four.

Although by 1914 the 'new' system of regimental names instead of numbers was completely accepted, the memory of the old system still lived on. Brigadier General J.L. James Lockhead Jack, DSO (1880–1962) records in his diary (edited by John Terraine) that during the retreat from Mons and the stand at Le Cateau, when he had been promoted to staff captain of the 19th Brigade, he had received instructions from HQ 5th Division that he should try to round up some infantry to hold their ground for a little longer and cover the retreat. (There were no reserves left at 5th Division, and his General could give no detailed orders.)

Jack said that, feeling rather daunted and cautiously scouting around, he came upon two companies of the Argyll and Sutherland Regiment (previously the 91st and 93rd Foot) marching quietly back in open order with Colonel Moulton-Barrett at their head. The colonel answered Jack's invitation to oppose the enemy a little longer by at once calling out: '93rd A-B-O-U-T *TURN*', the movement executed on the spot with almost parade ground exactitude. His Highlanders were then led forward to a suitable crest nearby to await the enemy.

The general purpose of the alteration in the titles of the regiments was to try to recruit enough men from within the counties to enlist in 'their' regiments, but this did not always happen because most of the men who enlisted were unemployed, and the amount of unemployment varied across the country. Frank Richards, in *Old Soldier Sahib* says that when he went to India, just after the end of the Boer War, his battalion of The Royal Welch Fusiliers, numbering a thousand odd, was composed of some seven hundred Cockneys and Midlanders in equal number, and not three hundred proper Welshmen. The Welsh grew fewer, and the Midlanders more numerous, until in 1914 the Battalion was sometimes jokingly known as the Birmingham Fusiliers.

Regimental pride

There can be no doubt that belonging to, and being proud of, one's unit is a fundamental necessity in the life of a soldier. This is particularly true of the professional regular British army that has always been small compared with the giant conscript armies of the continent.

Roger Perkins quotes comments in an after-dinner speech made by the Colonel of the Regiment of The Argyll and Sutherland Highlanders in 1947, Lt. General Sir Gordon MacMillan of MacMillan, who said of the war-time battalions:

All those chaps have got what we are blessed with in this regiment, that most priceless regimental spirit. That is the thing we have got to cherish because it is the one thing that makes the soldier fight that little bit longer and a little bit harder than the chap on the other side.

The regular British army was swamped in both world wars by civilian volunteer and conscript replacements and additions, and it was considered vital that the newcomers should feel part of a tradition, be instilled with a pride in their own regiments and know at least a little of the regimental history. It was for this reason that when Kitchener recruited for his 'new armies' in 1914 no new regiments were formed. Instead the number of battalions in the existing regiments was increased.

All regiments like to consider themselves individual if not unique, and this is demonstrated by their regimental histories, their uniforms, their regimental customs, their marching music, nicknames and sometimes by their mascots. Perhaps most of all by their Colours and Battle Honours and cap badges.

Some nicknames bestowed on regiments by others are deliberately less than complimentary, and it is not a good idea for soldiers of other regiments to refer to them by these names unless looking for trouble. These are a few examples of the less scurrilous: The Grenadiers, 'The Grinning Dears'. Many cavalry regiments, 'The Donkey Wallopers'. The Green Jackets, 'The Armoured Farmers', The Queens (2nd Foot), 'The Mutton Lancers'. Some were taken from the initials of the units such as The Royal Army Medical Corps (RAMC), 'Rob All My Comrades', The Army Service Corps (ASC), 'Ally Sloper's Cavalry'. There are many others.

Siegfried Sassoon, writing of the spring of 1916, says that while attending the Fourth Army School at Flixécourt and eyeing the assembled audience of about 300 officers and NCOs:

I improved my knowledge of regimental badges, which seemed somehow to affect the personality of the wearer. A lion, a lamb, a dragon or an antelope, a crown, a harp, a tiger or a sphinx, these devices differentiated men in more ways than one. But the regimental names were probably the potent factor... There was food for thought also in the fact of sitting between a Connaught Ranger and a Seaforth Highlander, though both were likely to have been born in Middlesex.

Peter Coe, an old friend of mine who served with the Rifle Brigade, wrote to me to say he had attended the 200th anniversary of the regiment's foundation. After a service at Winchester cathedral which was full to overflowing and contained a moving ceremony and prayers for the fallen, there was a lunch for 750 guests, and then:

> We formed into battalions for the March Past. In our ranks was one General, a Brigadier, a few Colonels, right the way down to lesser ranks. One grandfather marched with his grandson [the latter served with the Greenjackets]. As many of our number were in their late eighties, it was imagined that we would march at the Old Soldiers pace. But when, on the command *'Stand to your front! Rifle Brigade Quick March!'* the band struck up at full Regimental pace, 140 [to the minute] as opposed to the Redcoats 90, a roar went up from the crowd who then proceeded to clap in time to the drum beat. We were given the *Eyes Right!* when we passed the senior surviving General of the Regiment. It was a very emotional moment. We all managed to stay the course. Perhaps our dressing was a little ragged, but a few refresher hours on the square would soon have put that right.

Views on other units

Disparaging other units, of all kinds, was and no doubt still is a regular pastime in all the armed services. Some years ago I had working with me an ex regular CSM (Company Sergeant Major) of the Irish Guards whose response to any enquiry of mine about any other regiment he had encountered was invariably a dismissive 'we never thought much of them'. His one exception was: 'Old Jerry; now he was generally all right, and when you took him prisoner and shouted at him a bit he'd work very well.' He was referring to the Second World War, but I have no doubt the sentiments would have been echoed by his counterpart earlier in the century.

Incidentally, my ex-Irish Guards colleague once said reflectively to me when we were discussing the Second World War and his own regiment:

> I remember one man in particular, Guardsman Blank. He was an 'orrible little man – lazy, scruffy and useless generally. I decided to smarten him up a bit. Every night I picked him to go out on patrol, and one night he said to me, 'Are you trying

to get me killed?' And I said to him, 'Yes Blank. You have
the choice, smarten up, or go out on patrol every night until
you get killed.' He died at Anzio. But he'd smartened up no
end.

'Of course', my colleague had remarked wryly, when talking about
recruitment pre-war and the intakes of mainly unemployed, poor,
and poorly educated recruits, 'in the Brigade [of Guards] then I
was regarded as a monument of learning and culture.' (He was
also a brave and decorated man, I learned from someone else who
knew him well.) He was also somewhat less than complimentary
about the renowned Brigade of Guards Warrant Officer, RSM Brittain
– not in terms of valour, but as an individual with his increasing
portliness and physical unfitness towards the end of his long service
in the Brigade. He also spoke rather contemptuously of Field Marshal
Montgomery: 'Walking around with two cap badges on his beret.
It doesn't do you know.'

Robert Graves said that when he was an instructor at the Harfleur
'Bull Ring' the chief subjects of conversation were the reliability
of various divisions in battle. It seemed to be agreed, he said, that
one third of the troops forming the BEF were dependable on all
occasions; about a third were variable divisions that contained one
or two weak battalions but could usually be trusted. The remainder
was more or less untrustworthy, being put in places of comparative
safety.

The recognised top-notch divisions were (and again this is entirely
according to Graves) the Second, Seventh, Twenty-ninth, Guards
and First Canadian. The most dependable British troops, the mess
agreed dispassionately, he continued, were the midland county
regiments, industrial Yorkshire and Lancashire troops, and Londoners.
The Catholic Irish and Highland Scots took unnecessary risks in
trenches and had unnecessary casualties, and although in battle they
usually reached their objectives they too often lost them in counter-
attacks; without officers they became useless. English southern
county regiments varied from good to very bad. All overseas troops
seemed to be good. The latest 'new army' divisions and second
line territorial divisions ranked low because of inefficient officers
and warrant officers.

However, according to Sassoon, Graves was given to making
sweeping statements of his own opinions and declaring them as

63

generally accepted principles. Writing of Graves as 'David Cromlech' in *Memoirs of an Infantry Officer*, Sassoon describes him as: 'Big and impulsive with a sallow, crooked and whimsical face [Graves had a broken nose from boxing] – He was deplorably untidy, and known as a "queer bird" by fellow officers, and an expert at putting people's backs up unintentionally... Far too fond of butting in with his opinion before he is asked for it.'

Tony Ashworth, in *Trench Warfare 1914–1918*, while actually speaking on the subject of raiding sorties, makes interesting comments on divisions and the mixture of battalions they contained, and the problems this sometimes occasioned. He says:

> The problem of divisions with élite and non-élite formations was that high command might order élite battalions to carry out not only their own part in battle and trench war but also that of lesser units, which either had defaulted or could not be trusted. This placed a disproportionate strain upon élite units.

He continues by describing an episode during the Somme where a battalion left the battlefield in disarray, whereupon three other battalions of the same division were ordered to re-take the abandoned position; this was accomplished at the cost of many casualties.

Roger Perkins (see above) retails an amusing little anecdote, which may or may not be apocryphal, but at any rate highlights the aspect of regimental pride and superiority. He writes:

> Some years ago a distinguished elder statesman was being interviewed and the talk turned to his life as a young man. In 1944 he had won the MC for a courageous act during the attempt to reach the besieged airborne forces at Arnhem. Unaware that he was posing an unwise question, the interviewer enquired: 'Did you enjoy your time in the army?' His guest visibly stiffened. 'The army? I was not in the army, I was with the Grenadier Guards.'

Could that have been Lord Carrington?

PART NINE

Thank Gawd, we've got a Navy.

'An expression used by army other ranks whenever the
incompetence of military authority became more
manifest than usual' (Brophy & Partridge).

The provision of the Armed Services

As described above, for her armed forces Britain relied upon the
very large Royal Navy to protect her coasts, sea routes and overseas
possessions, and a small but highly trained professional (regular)
army ready to fight in any unrest or local wars that might occur
overseas to threaten those territories. In addition to the British
troops stationed overseas there were the locally raised troops. For
home defence, in addition to units of the regular army, there was
the Special Reserve (previously called the Militia) and also the
Territorial Army.

The navy in 1914

Most of the military resources went to the Royal Navy, and financially
this became a crippling burden as Britain maintained a 'two to one
policy' whereby she sought always to have the naval strength of
twice any possible opponent or competitive industrial nation, and
Germany was rebuilding her fleet fast.

Admiral John Arbuthnot Fisher, First Baron of Kilverstone
(1841–1920) was one of the most influential naval figures of the
age, and an architect of the 20th century British navy. Unconventional

in some ways – even considered eccentric by some people, and regarded as not an easy man to work with – he was largely responsible for the state of readiness and proficiency of the Royal Navy at the outbreak of war that enabled the British Expeditionary Force to have unhindered crossings to France.

However he was not without his critics, and when later during the war both he and Winston Churchill complained about their successors (Admiral Jellicoe, and ex Prime Minister Arthur Balflour) the then Secretary to the Admiralty wrote a counter blast to the Committee for Imperial Defence in 1916 saying:

It must be easy for a man of Lord Fisher's ability to say 'If my advice had been taken how much better off we should be!' unfortunately the converse process is easier still! Why, during the critical years, did Lord Fisher pay so little attention to the subject of mines? Why did he wait until the outbreak of hostilities to discover the value of Zeppelins for maritime scouting? Why was there not as much energy put into the task of increasing submarine efficiency?

These [and there were a lot more objections in similar vein] are considerations which might, I think, have made him more tolerant in criticising other people's performances, more cautious in praising his own.

Fisher had retired in 1910, but was recalled on 28th October 1914 following the resignation of Admiral Prince Louis of Battenberg (the family changed its name to Mountbatten in an attempt to disassociate itself from its German background, as did the Royal Family by changing their name to 'Windsor', see below).

Fisher, and Winston Churchill, who was then First Lord of the Admiralty, got on well at first despite being members of different political parties, but later fell out over the Dardanelles expedition in 1915. Fisher resigned over this as did Churchill, but whereas Churchill continued to be active in the war – including command in the field, and then becoming Minister of Munitions in 1917 and War Minister in 1918 – it was really the end of Fisher's public life.

A 'pro-Fisher' biography of Fisher by Admiral Sir Reginald Bacon *Life of Lord Fisher* provoked Churchill to record in a 'more in sorrow than in anger' vein, the following comments:

They will be read with the interest inseparable from Fisher's strange, dynamic personality. But it is a pity that Admiral Bacon should have discharged his mission in a spirit and method so calculated to revive the animosities, and quarrels which hung around the old sailor's neck.

The British army at the outbreak of war in 1914

The British army of 1914 was a small, regular professional force, backed by the reservists and part-time 'territorials', quite different from the army of mid 1916 onwards when there was virtually nothing left in France or Belgium of Britain's professional 'red little, dead little, army'.

Although in 1916 there were still remnants of the 1914/1915 regulars, reservists and the first line territorial units and other volunteers ('K'1s) who were hastily sent to join the regulars, the ranks of the BEF, from 1916 onwards, became composed increasingly of second and third-line territorial battalions, together with more 'New Army' battalions (see below, 'Kitchener's Army'), and finally the conscripted men, to fill the depleted ranks.

The regular army

The small British army, quite unlike the armies of France and Germany, was a highly trained entirely volunteer professional regular force without any conscripts. It had been described by General von Moltke as 'that perfect thing apart'. It was a perfection in miniature, had never been envisaged or designed to fight in a mass warfare, and it would be overwhelmed by these demands. Haldane in his first speech on the Army Estimates – as quoted by Lord Carver – said:

We live on an island, and our coasts are completely defended by the fleet. Our Army is wanted for purposes abroad and overseas. It is necessarily a professional army; we could not get such an Army by conscription. It must be of high quality; but because of the limited nature of its functions – to strike at a distance – it ought to be of strictly limited dimensions...

We want therefore an Army which is very mobile and capable of rapid transport. For fighting which has to be of a distance and cannot be against large masses of men it ought to be on a strictly limited scale and perfect in quality than in expanded quantity... If the Army is something which is not wanted for Home defence, then its size is something which is capable of being calculated.

The total strength of the British Army in August 1914 was 247,432 regular troops, of which nearly 128,000 were overseas and 120,000 earmarked for the BEF (British Expeditionary Force). There were in addition 224,223 reservists of all classes, and 268,777 members of the Territorial Service. (Again figures vary from source to source, but not by any significant numbers.)

The Militia and its change to the Special Reserve

The Militia was a trained local part-time force formed for home defence in times of rebellion or invasion. The Militia Act of 1775 re-established one or more regiments for each county, raised from volunteers – or conscripts chosen by ballot from each parish. Until 1871, the raising and training of local militias was the responsibility of the Lord Lieutenant of the county, who also appointed officers. In peacetime the Militia assembled for drill and manoeuvres as specified by their local administration. After 1872 they came under the ultimate authority of the Home Secretary. In wartime, after being mobilised (or embodied by royal proclamation), they came under the orders of the CIC (Commander in Chief) and were liable for service anywhere in the British Isles, although not overseas.

In 1908 the Militia was renamed and became the 'Special Reserve', with one or more battalions formed on each regular line regiment. Its role was now more directly linked to providing the regular army with immediate trained reserves in time of war. Cavalry volunteers became the Yeomanry and part of the new Territorial Army (see below). Recruits to the Special Reserve did six months' training as regular troops. Thereafter they were recalled to the colours for one month's annual camp where the routine generally consisted of drill, cross country marching in full fighting kit, gymnastics, parades, sports and games and shooting on the range.

The Territorial Army

Yet another of the results of army reforms and restructuring occurred in 1908 when the old Volunteer Force was dissolved and the Territorial Army created by the Territorial and Reserve Act, dated 22nd August 1907. Lord Haldane had envisaged the Territorial Army as a natural system of enlarging the regular army should the need arise. The Territorial Army came into being on 1st April 1908, and it could be called upon to serve anywhere in the United Kingdom. This Territorial Force was a separate self-contained volunteer army administered by the County Territorial and Auxiliary Forces Associations, and prior to the outbreak of war in 1914 new entrants enrolled for four years, and attended a 14 to 18 day training camp annually and regular local drills.

Initially fourteen Divisions of Territorial Infantry and fourteen Brigades of Yeomanry (Cavalry) were formed, complete with supporting arms and services. A formidable force of Territorial Artillery was gradually created as well. It had no statutory requirement to serve overseas, however, unless units volunteered to the Lords-Lieutenant of their Counties under a 'General Service' obligation (Imperial Service Section of the Provisions for Other Forms of Service).

The Royal Flying Corps

The following article published in late 1914 or early 1915 was written by C.G. Grey, editor of *The Aeroplane*:

> The Royal Flying Corps only came into being a matter of three years ago, the moving spirit in its formation being Lieut.-Colonel David Henderson, DSO. The Royal Flying Corps consists of the Department of Military Aeronautics at the War Office, which controls all personnel and materiel; the central Flying School on Salisbury Plain, where pilots from ordinary flying schools are trained to become military aviators; the Aeronautical Inspection department at Farnborough, – which is responsible for the aeroplanes being fit for use; and the Military Wing, or the fighting section of the Corps... The Military wing is divided into Squadrons each of 24 aeroplanes

and has 24 pilots, under the command of a Major, and each squadron has 6 flights of 4 machines each, under a Captain, the flying officers in each Flight being Captains or Lieutenants according to their Army rank before joining. Also as a rule a trained aerial observer is attached to each pilot, which observer may be an R.F.C. officer or not. Each squadron is a self-contained unit, with its own motor-transport column, motor repair wagons, aeroplane carrying wagons and so forth.

Given the era when it was published – four months after war was declared – one can forgive the author for perhaps a little national hubris, and his 'gentlemen only' stance, for he continues:

In practice the British pilots have proved to be the best in the world, as might be expected by anyone knowing the composition and training of the R.F.C. The pilots all belong to that class of sportsmen and gentlemen which seems the peculiar product of the British Race, and is no doubt produced by generations of horse-riding sporting ancesters. Though the aeroplane, as piece of mechanism is akin to the motor-car, its behaviour in that unstable element the air makes it more like a horse, and so the qualities of a horseman are desirable in an aviator. Possibly for this reason an extraordinary number of fine fliers have come from Australia, where so many fine horsemen have been produced. Be that as it may, the British officer-aviator is noted for his skill as a flier combined with common sense, and military aptitude, the whole, in conjunction with splendid organisation and equipment forming a small but wonderfully efficient flying corps, as the Germans have found to their cost. After four months of war it is firmly established that no German aviator will venture to put up a fight in the air with a British aviator unless he finds his retreat cut off.

I feel his enthusiasm and national pride was rather running away with him. My own understanding is that Britain was quite a way behind with the development of an aerial force compared with some other European countries at the time – despite the vision and hard work put in by both Lt. Col. (later Brigadier-General) David Henderson, the father of the Royal Flying Corps, and his deputy (then Major) Hugh Trenchard – the service in 1914 was a collection

70

of heterogeneous and already becoming outdated aeroplanes, and with no really suitable British engine manufacturers. France and Germany both had much larger aerial forces, and better production of aircraft and engines.

When Trenchard was put in charge of accelerating aircraft production, he continued to order the slow, outmoded, unsuitable machines, whose engines mainly came from France. Britain had to queue for them behind the French aeroplane makers, and as a result put up with poorer and or reconditioned engines. The reason for Trenchard's actions may have been that because the urgent demand was for more aircraft it was quicker to order those already being made than to ask for newer untried and untested designs – if they existed. It was a great pity that Britain had turned down the Dutchman Anthony Fokker when he tried to interest the British powers-that-be in his aircraft designs. The Germans had no such short-sighted reaction, but accepted his offer and placed manufacturing premises at his disposal.

The British army saw the prime function of aircraft as eyes for the ground troops; to perform as it were a light cavalry role above the ground – air reconnaissance to scout ahead of the troops – hence the terms 'scouts' and 'scout pilots' applied to the RFC machines and pilots. In machines where a two-man crew was carried the non-pilot member was called the 'observer' and he wore a half wing emblem on the left breast of his tunic in place of the pilot's pair of wings.

The Royal Navy Air Service

At first it was part of the same administration as the RFC but under a Naval Wing instead of the Military Wing, and it placed quite an emphasis on the construction of airships – again for observational patrol duties like the army for its aircraft. The RNAS also seemed to have more direct control over ordering the types of machines it wanted, and when the service sent its own squadrons to fly on the Western Front later, most, if not all, authorities seem to agree that the RNAS had better aircraft, and were more effective than the RFC who for a long time were hampered by their poorer aircraft and slow delivery of new or improved models (see 1917 below).

Parachutes

Although the observers in static observation balloons were given parachutes to enable them to escape if necessary when under attack from hostile aircraft and when their ground crews could not winch them down to safety in time, neither of the two British air services issued parachutes to their airmen. The decision to forbid parachutes to pilots and observers for the whole of the war was not only heartless but wasteful in terms of lives. Many aeroplanes under attack burst into flames when hit by bullets and the unfortunate occupants, if not killed or rendered unconscious or unable to move, had the terrible choice of jumping to their deaths or being burned to death as the flaming machines plunged to the earth out of control.

PART TEN

The National Service League on the other hand took up the immense and necessarily unpopular task of urging the whole nation to accept a burden from which our insular position and our later history had accustomed us to consider ourselves immune, namely, that of national training for national defence.

George F. Shee, Secretary of the National Service League, writing an article on the winding up of the League in 1921. (The League was formed in 1902, but was never successful in its aims pre-war.)

The numerical increase in the British army as from the outbreak of war

Before the war, barracks in the United Kingdom provided quarters for 175,000 men, but as over one million volunteers had enlisted by the end of 1914 the existing accommodation was utterly inadequate. Tented camps were erected, but towards the end of October when the beautiful sunny hot summer gave way to exceptionally heavy rain and gales, the makeshift camps became quagmires of mud, and the tents blew down.

Gradually but increasingly over the next fifteen months as word spread about their conditions and frustrations – the lack of proper training and weapons, the long delay in being kitted out with proper uniforms, and with the growing general awareness of the stalemate conditions in France and Flanders – the flow of volunteers dried. Despite this, by February 1916, more than two and a half million men had volunteered for war service in the army.

73

Conscription was introduced under the Military Service Act of January 1916, with the age range of 18–41. This was extended as the war dragged on, until by April 1918 the upper age was 51 and medical requirement standards lowered considerably. Ian F.W. Beckett, in his guide to sources in the UK National Archives *The First World War* says on the subject of conscription:

> The same legislation [Military Service No 2 Act April 1918] provided for the conscription of men up to the age of 56 if the need arose, and for the extension of conscription to Ireland. Ultimately, the former was deemed unnecessary and the latter politically impossible.
>
> In any case, conscription was applied selectively. The steady evolution of a war economy and of a manpower policy steadily pushed the army to the bottom of the list of priorities. Indeed in January 1918 the production of timber, iron ore, food, merchant shipping, aeroplanes and tanks all took priority over the army.

By the armistice in 1918 there had been over two and a quarter million men conscripted in addition to the volunteers. This had the effect of bringing a huge increase in the number of women employed in full-time occupations previously considered only for men.

Opinions on the value of a territorial force

Lord Kitchener rejected the territorial force utterly and completely. The reason apparently stemmed from the time when, at the age of twenty, he fought as a volunteer with the French army in the Franco Prussian War of 1870, and gained a poor opinion of the performance of the French territorial troops (French Civil Guard). It would seem he ignored the fact that the British Territorial Army, although not particularly well trained in the art of warfare, consisted of fit and keen young men, and entirely different in outlook and character to the elderly French reservists who unfortunately held the equivalent title *Territoriaux*.

It has been said that Kitchener was also unimpressed by the Citizen Imperial Volunteers and Yeomanry in South Africa, and the performance of the amateur armies in the American Civil War. He had quite different ideas for the army *he* envisaged, and obtained, when he became Secretary of State for War in 1914 (see below).

Other regular soldiers, of all ranks, were also not enamoured by the idea of these 'Saturday soldiers'. Robert Graves, writing of 1915 and holding 'merely' (his word) a commission in the Special Reserve (see above), was very dismissive of the territorial battalions of his regiment, the Royal Welch Fusiliers. He said the four territorial battalions were referred to contemptuously as 'dog shooters' by the regular officers in the regiment and they never accepted them – unlike the 'new army' battalions.*

*Graves was a 19-year-old subaltern at the time and my impression is that his statement on the territorial battalions of his regiment making a poor showing is based on hearsay sessions with other junior officers, and not from personal observation. To the best of my knowledge, apart from 1/4th TF who were made into Pioneers, none of the remaining TF units of his regiment served on the Western Front and so I cannot see that he had any personal experience of their fighting qualities.

Conversely, I have noticed many recorded instances of the high regard that inexperienced Territorial Army troops, who were sent to the Front in 1914 and 1915, felt for the regular soldiers and their battalions when they were placed alongside them, and how well they got on with them.

As an example, Aubrey Smith (see above and below), says that when his 1st Battalion of the London Rifle Brigade reached the firing line in November 1914, they were attached to the 11th Brigade of the 4th Division who at that time were holding the line from just south of Messines to the north of Armentières. For instruction purposes the LRBs were attached to the 1st Battalion The Rifle Brigade and the 1st Somersets and sent to the trenches with them:

> ...thus affording these regulars some measure of relief in their vigil; and no body of men ever had larger hearts and more reassuring words than these troops. They confessed afterwards that on hearing that Territorials were to join them, they never thought they could 'stick it', and were astonished to find the LRBs put up with the discomforts so cheerily. These regulars insisted upon cooking all the meals, relieved our fellows of all possible fatigues and generally set out to be as obliging as they could. We knew them and they knew us by name: we shared out our parcels and newspapers and generally rubbed along exceedingly pleasantly.

75

This part of the line was very undermanned and the line held very thinly. The Germans were not dislodged from this area – Ploegsteert Wood – until 19th December (see 1/Rifle Brigade's part in the attack on 'The Birdcage' below), so it must have been with very heavy hearts that the regulars learned their reinforcements were to be completely inexperienced and untried 'Saturday soldiers' and it was really kind of them to treat the LRBs so well and with such understanding.

A professional soldier, and of somewhat higher rank than Graves, Field Marshal Viscount French of Ypres, surprisingly perhaps, takes a contrary view of the territorial force to those of Graves, Lord Kitchener, and some other regular soldiers. Writing in his book *1914* he says this of the territorials:

> I have spoken elsewhere of what I have always regarded as our great initial administrative mistake in the war, namely, the raising of an entirely new Army, when the machinery for expanding the Territorial Force – especially established by Lord Haldane for the purpose – I mean the Territorial County Associations – was already at hand and would have proved by far the most efficient and economical method of raising the troops required... After Lord Kitchener had made his call upon the country for the New Armies the Territorials found themselves neglected and put in the shade... But the time for the employment of troops other than the Regulars of the old Army arrived with drastic and unexpected speed. The wastage of war proved to be so enormous that the fighting line had to be reinforced almost before the new Armies were in existence. It was then that the country in her need turned to the despised Territorials. It seems to me we have never realised what it was these men were asked to do.

Following the outbreak of war in 1914, ninety per cent of the Territorial force volunteered to serve overseas. Some men held back at first until they could discover how their families would be affected financially; fortunately a number of commercial and industrial organisations, and smaller firms, caught up in the general euphoria, and sharing the general belief that it would all be over by Christmas, arranged for their employees to continue to receive their full wages or salaries when their men volunteered for overseas service.

The original intention for the territorial units volunteering for overseas duties was to use them as 'lines of communication' troops. Their duties as such troops would be guarding docks and railway stations and bridges, unloading trains, escorting and guarding prisoners of war, traffic control duties and so on, thus freeing the regular troops for battle. However, they were put in the line of battle very quickly as the need arose, and the need very soon arose. By Christmas 1914 there were no fewer than 23 territorial battalions in France.

There was, as I have said, but little training for the newly joined recruits to the territorials in 1914. Aubrey Smith MM and Bar, author (aka *A Rifleman*, see above) says that when in September 1914 he and his friends joined their territorial battalion, 1/5th (City of London) Battalion, London Rifle Brigade* – they, like many other units, had no rifles or clothing. 'Drill', he said, 'was conducted by NCOs who were either recruits with a smattering of drill, or those who possessed an aptitude for bawling loudly.

*This territorial unit, The London Rifle Brigade, is not to be confused with the regular army 'The Rifle Brigade' alongside which the 1/5th London Rifle Brigade served, see above and below.

Another member of the London Rifle Brigade of 1914 was the author Henry Williamson (see below).

Shortage of rifles

Michael Gavaghan in his book *Loos 1915* states that at the outbreak of the war there were some 1,241,000 rifles in the possession of troops or in stock. Within two months over 100,000 had been issued as replacements for those lost or damaged. Of the 400,000 required by territorial forces only 240,000 had reached them by mid-December 1914. Of the 600,000 required by Kitchener's 'new army' troops, only 400,000 could be supplied and of those 200,000 were 'training rifles' which were useless at the front.

The territorials, poorly trained or not, show their metal early

The critics of the territorials were generally to be proved wrong.

As early as October 1914, one battalion, 1/14th (County of London) Battalion ('The London Scottish'), who had volunteered for overseas duty and had been sent to France to act as line of communication troops, were flung in to the battle of 'First Ypres' at Messines because there were no other troops available in this last desperate attempt to hold the line to prevent the German breakthrough to the coast.

Not only were these men of the London Scottish completely inexperienced – many of them had been in the army for only a few weeks following the declaration of war – but in addition, as they were rushed into the line, they were armed with the wrong ammunition for their rifles. They found themselves in the front line in the disorientating furore and confusion of the battle, and facing an overwhelming force of attacking enemy. They were fearful, dazed by the noise, and desperately trying to load and fire their rifles, when they discovered, to their horror, their ammunition jamming in the breech. They had been issued with the Mark 1, Long Lee Enfield rifle, that in theory had been modified to take the Mark VIII ammunition, but in reality the rounds jammed in the magazine and as a consequence their rifles could be used only as single-loaders.

Despite this, placed alongside and steadied by the regulars of 6th Dragoon Guards, they held the line, beating off attack after attack. For their performance in this action they received nothing but praise from the regulars, including a telegram of congratulations from Sir John French.

Although not actually present, Henry Williamson provides a graphic description of this action of the London Scottish (whom incidentally he calls the 'London Highlanders'), in his book *How Dear is Life*. To me, his writing of this episode is one of the most powerful and vivid accounts of what it must have been like for these raw troops suddenly being flung into battle with little warning or preparation.

There was one future Hollywood film star there at Messines with the London Scottish, Ronald Colman. And Peter Liddle in his *Testimony of War 1914–1918* quotes another well-known figure, this time from the world of dance and musical entertainment, Victor Silvester, the future world champion ballroom dancer, band leader and broadcaster (famous for his 'Come Dancing' TV programmes). Silvester was at the time a very much under-age member of the

London Scottish, and later, when his real age was discovered, he was transferred to a Friends' Ambulance Unit in Italy where he was wounded and decorated for rescuing wounded under fire. He also served with Argyll and Sutherland Highlanders. Liddle writes that Silvester recalled two particularly harrowing experiences. One was being in a firing squad shooting a deserter, and the other seeing one member of his section lose control in the face of a German attack, with the result that the officer in command shot the man to prevent a spread of panic.

The regular soldier, Frank Richards (see below) says of another territorial battalion, the 1/5th Bn. Scottish Rifles (TF), in November/December 1914:

> Old regular soldiers never held a very high opinion of the Territorials, but as time went on we got to like the 5th Scottish Rifles very much. They were the best Territorial battalion I ever saw, and after they had been a few months with us we never worried if they were on the left or right of us in the line or in attacks.

In passing, the 5th Scottish Rifles was the unit in which the future Lord John Reith (1889–1971), but then simply Mr John Reith, served. He had joined the battalion in 1911, and went to France with them in 1914. Reith became famous in future years as the autocratic and controversial head of the BBC (British Broadcasting Company, later Corporation) from 1927 to 1938, and his account* reveals that even during those early days in France as a junior officer he could be quite an awkward, prickly, unforgiving, rather priggish and sanctimonious customer. At the same time he appears to have been resolute, brave, even at times foolhardy, and conscientious in his duties. In stature he was very big and with an intimidating manner. (He wrote on one occasion: 'It always tires me to stand looking down and listening to little men' – he is referring here to a conversation with the Company Commander of No 1 Company.)

*Wearing Spurs, Hutchinson, 1966.

Reith also remembers that on the march en route to Bailleul, after their arrival in France, his battalion (5th Scottish Rifles) came upon the remnants of the London Scottish, about 350 of them after their exploits at Messines. 'They were unshaven, weirdly clad and caked in mud. There was an awe about this meeting,' said Reith. 'They had already made their name glorious. What would we do?'

PART ELEVEN

You must ask Mummie what a Field Marshal is – I am not sure I know! But he wears a cocked hat and feathers.

General Sir Hubert Gough, then Commander I Corps, writing to his 7 year old niece in 1915 after the battle of Loos.

The structure of the British military hierarchy in 1914

The Army Council

The Army Council had been formed by letters patent on 10th August 1904, for the direction of the army. Headed by the Secretary of State for War, the military members were: Chief of the General Staff, Adjutant General, Quartermaster General, and Master General of the Ordnance. The civilian members were: The Parliamentary Under-Secretary of State for War, Financial Secretary of the War Office, and the Secretary of the Council.

The Secretary of State for War was the army's link with the Cabinet, and on 3rd August 1914 the Prime Minister, Herbert Asquith, appointed Field Marshal Lord Kitchener to the post. Kitchener attended the War Council meeting on 5th August in his new capacity.

Kitchener however was not Asquith's first choice. He would have preferred to reinstate Haldane to the post because the creation of the General Staff, the Territorial Army, and the current organisation of the army, had been due to him. But Haldane's part German education and pro German tendencies precluded his selection at this time. Following the death of Kitchener (see below), Lloyd

George, who had been Munitions Minister, replaced Kitchener as Secretary for War.

The War Council

The War Council was formed on 25th November 1914 because of the unwieldy size of the cabinet. It was formed of members of the Committee of Imperial Defence and its task was to control the conduct of the war. Over the years the composition of its members changed. Originally the military members of the War Council included Field Marshal Sir John French, Commander-in-Chief designate of the British Expeditionary Force, the two BEF Corps Commanders (Sir Douglas Haig and Sir James Grierson), the BEF Chief of Staff, Sir Archibald Murray, and the Deputy Chief of Staff, Sir Henry Wilson.

The civilian members of the Council (which included Asquith, Bonar Law, Lloyd George and Winston Churchill), while they did not always see eye to eye with each other, tended not to trust the army members, 'The Boneheads' or 'Brass Hats'. In their turn, while none of the soldiers necessarily thought highly of each other's capabilities or personalities, they were generally united in their distrust of civilian interference. They referred to the civilian members contemptuously as 'The Frocks' (the formal attire of the civilians included frock coats).

Part of the reason for this bad feeling between the military and civilian members was that scars of the 'Curragh incident' of March 1914* had far from healed, and this would affect the relationship between the army staff and the governing Liberal Party during the early days of the war. There were five civilian members and eleven general officers, with Kitchener poised between them representing no one quite knew what, as he had taken no personal share in the planning for war on the Continent.

*The Curragh incident occurred when the officers of the Curragh camp in Ireland declared they would resign rather than be used to coerce the Ulster Unionists into accepting Irish Home Rule.

An explanation of British army formations in 1914

Commands

In 1914 the United Kingdom was divided into seven areas called Commands and each was allotted regular, special reserve and territorial units. The infantry was formed in six divisions and the cavalry into one. Each formation had its own divisional artillery, engineers, communications and medical support.

Army

An army was a unit similar to an army corps but on a larger scale and a higher level. Its front could be 25 miles in length and was composed of several army corps and led by a full general. By early 1916 there were four British armies on the Western Front, and later a reserve army became the fifth. Each had an establishment of four corps containing three divisions.

Army corps

With a staff of some 24 officers, and commanded by a lieutenant-general,* an army corps was a formation in the chain of command coming between an army and a division. Although it had some permanent fighting units of its own, especially heavy artillery, its function was strategic and administrative with duties to position and direct its three divisions along its frontal sector – of up to about 12 miles.

Incidentally, an army corps should not be confused with units that contain the word 'corps', as in ASC (Army Service Corps), RAMC (Royal Army Medical Corps), RFC (Royal Flying Corps) and so on.

The principal difference between an army – or an army corps – and a division was that armies and/or army corps were headquarters units forming part of the chain of command and they did not hold units on a permanent basis except for specialists.

Infantry division

Commanded by a major-general,* an infantry division was like a small self-contained army. It consisted of three infantry brigades and artillery; an ammunition column; two field companies and one signal company of royal engineers; an ASC (Army Service Corps) divisional train (see below); three field ambulance units and a pioneer battalion (also see below).

A divisional total strength in 1914 was about 600 officers and some 18,000 NCOs and men, and this held until re-organisation in 1918.*

*When the infantry divisions were reduced in size to three infantry brigades of three battalions, in place of three brigades of four battalions, but with more machine guns allocated to compensate for the reduced rifle power. General Jack for one regarded this alteration as most unsound because, he said, in the event of severe casualties, or otherwise trying operations, the two leading assaulting battalions could not both be relieved at the same time, as is desirable – perhaps vital. A further immediate attack would therefore be carried out with one relatively inefficient battalion (because of casualties and battle fatigue) and one fresh one. An ill-balanced arrangement.

Tony Ashworth, in *Trench Warfare 1914–1918*, says of an infantry division of the time:

A division comprised about 20,000 men, organised into 3 infantry brigades – 12 battalions, [until 1918, as above], 4 artillery brigades, machine-gun and trench-mortar units, engineer units and supply transport, medical and signal services. The division was a self-contained and self-supporting unit which held a front line approximately 4,000 to 6,000 yards long ... the division was the largest tactical unit of the war and its main function was to train and direct men in large-scale battles and trench warfare. Further the division was the largest unit to maintain a permanent establishment (larger units such as Corps and Army did not) and might keep its original infantry and artillery units throughout the war... The number of divisions on the Western Front increased from four in August 1914 to sixty four in November 1918.

Divisions were either regular, New Army or Territorial... Of the 57 divisions which served for 3 months or more on the Western Front 12 were regular, 27 New Army and 18 territorial. In some cases, however, these titles were misleading; some regular divisions contained New Army battalions and conversely, but territorial divisions remained entire throughout the war.

Divisions *were* moved between armies at times, but they *usually* retained the same brigades and the brigades in turn their same battalions, but not always.*

*For example, the 3rd Battalion, the Rifle Brigade, was transferred for a little while from 17th Brigade to the 16th Brigade on 24th October 1914, but returned to 17th Brigade on 15th December 1914. In August 1915 the 17th Brigade was transferred to 24th Division from 6th Division.

The Royal Naval Division

This was an unusual division. It was officially formed on 3rd September 1914 from Royal Naval and Royal Marine Brigades consisting of surplus naval reservists supplemented by surplus Kitchener 'New Army' recruits. There were eight battalions named after famous admirals, and Kitchener was very pleased to have these units added to his forces. Winston Churchill, as First Lord of the Admiralty, did all he could to help the formation of this unit.

The Royal Navy Division of infantry was determined not to lose its naval identity and insisted on retaining its own ranks and customs. The White Ensign flew over their land-based camps and to mark the passage of time a ship's bell was rung. 'Permission to go ashore' was requested when a member wished to leave the camp. There were no sergeants or corporals – there were petty officers and leading seamen instead. Field kitchens were called 'galleys'. Permission to grow beards could be and was given. 'Port' and 'starboard' instead of left and right were used. All in all it took some getting used to by the army staff at HQ.

Wherever there was a battle the Royal Naval Division was generally to be found – Antwerp, Gallipoli, and the Western Front. Its losses were so high it had to undergo a major re-organisation, and on 19th July 1916 it became the 63rd (Royal Naval) Division.

The writer, poet, and Independent Member of Parliament, A.P. Herbert,* and the poet Rupert Brooke, both served as infantry with the RND. Herbert survived Gallipoli *and* the Western Front where he was wounded at Arras in 1917, but Brooke died of illness on his way to Gallipoli in 1915.

*A Lost Leader is an example of Herbert's lighter poems – and yet one that carries the undertones of the worry that must have beset many a leader or guide on the march – I have always been much taken with the first verse – much more so than his poem concerning Major General C.D. Shute that brings predictable guffaws and shrieks of laughter (although I am sure it was good for morale, even if not appreciated by the Major General if it came to his ears):

> The men are marching like the best;
> The wagons wind across the lea;
> At ten to two we have a rest,
> We have a rest at ten to three;
> I ride ahead upon my gee
> And try to look serene and gay;
> The whole battalion follows me,
> And I believe I've lost the way.

The divisions with which I am particularly concerned are the following: 4th Division (1st Rifles). 5th Division (1st Devons and 1st DCLI). 6th Division (3rd Rifles). 7th Division (part of which was formed by 8th Devons from 1915 onwards). 8th Division (2nd Devons and 2nd Rifles). 27th Division (2nd DCLI and 4th Rifles). 61st Division (1/5th DCLI). And from 9th August 1915, the 24th Division when the 3rd Rifles were transferred from 6th Division.

Infantry brigade

Normally commanded by a brigadier-general,* and until the reorganisation in 1918 described above, usually formed by four battalions plus artillery, signals, field ambulances, engineers etc.

*The rank of brigadier-general was abolished soon after the war. It was replaced briefly by 'colonel-commandant', and then by just 'brigadier'. I think this was because it was felt there were too many generals for the reduced post-war army. An early war-time book called War Facts & Figures describes the brigadier-general as: 'A temporary or local rank given to Colonels to qualify them to command Brigades or equivalent.'

The brigades I follow are: 11th Brigade (1st Rifles). 14th Brigade (1st Devons and 1st DCLI). 16th and 17th Brigades (3rd Rifles). 20th Brigade (8th Devons). 23rd Brigade (2nd Devons). 25th Brigade (2nd Rifles). 80th Brigade (4th Rifles). 95th Brigade (1st Devons, and 1st DCLI from 12th January 1916).

Infantry regiments

These had been composed, in the main, of two regular battalions; one generally serving at home, and one abroad, very often in India, but during the reforms of the army between 1870–1912 one of the reorganisations was to add a third battalion to the regiments. This was a reserve and training unit that could also have a territorial or special reserve contingent. The exceptions as stated above were the Foot Guards, The Rifle Brigade and the King's Royal Rifle Corps.

Infantry battalions

Commanded by a lieutenant colonel, an infantry battalion consisted of a headquarters company and four rifle companies, and varied from between 800 and 1000 of all ranks. The nominal strength was 30 officers and 977 men per battalion, with 6 officers and 221 men per company. The establishment for a headquarters company – which included a machine gun section – was 6 officers and 93 men.

At the start of the war, territorial battalions were still organised on the 1909 regulations where a battalion consisted of 8 companies of about 120 in four sections, unlike the regulars who had recently been changed to the four companies systems above. Tony Ashworth has this to say of the battalion:

> The battalion figured largely in the lives of most infantrymen, since it was large enough to minister for their basic needs, yet not so large as to seem impersonal; on the contrary, all officers, and most NCOs and private soldiers of a battalion knew each other by sight at least. The battalion was an administrative and fighting unit which not only organised its members in and for battle, but fed, paid and clothed them, arranged their leave and saw to their religious, recreational and medical needs... A battalion [was] organised into sub-groups which comprised: 4 companies, 16 platoons and 64 sections.

Cyclist battalions

Early in the century a new breed of infantry had been introduced named 'cyclist battalions'. Most were linked to county regiments and were numbered as battalions with the word 'Cyclist' in brackets. Several cyclist battalions, however, were formed and served independently.

Pioneer battalions

These were created in December 1914, and an unusual feature of these battalions was that they were attached directly to divisions and not brigades, and often one can only trace them through their parent division – or if one is lucky through a Regimental History.

'New army' battalions

No new infantry regiments were introduced during the war but additional battalions titled 'Service Battalions' were added to the existing regiments, and these newly formed battalions were encouraged to feel they really were a part of their regular 'parent' regiment – with all that the name and traditions entailed. It proved a very wise move as time and again the new Service Battalions fought as gallantly as their regular namesakes, maintaining the traditions and the honour of 'The Regiment'.

It is interesting to note, however, that Lieut.-General Sir Arthur Codrington, Military Secretary to Kitchener, and an advocate of keeping to the existing regiments and not forming new ones, said that he was in Kitchener's room at the War Office when Kitchener was asked what he wanted to call the 'new army' battalions. Kitchener replied that he didn't care what they were called as long as he got the men. So Codrington got his way and the new battalions were raised as additional battalions of the existing regiments of the line and not, as might easily have been, new formations that would be without histories or traditions.

Lord Kitchener, when war was declared, immediately began a recruitment campaign, and so effective was it that his call for 100,000 volunteers was swamped by the response, and by the end of 1914 over one million men had responded. The administration just could not cope with this influx, and an unforeseen result of the massive response was the hardship suffered by many wives and families who received no allotments until all the paperwork had been sorted out.

Like the men who rushed to join the territorial units in August 1914, these hastily mustered 'new army' formations were poorly trained and lacked basic equipment. They spent frustrating months in makeshift camps in poor, and sometimes appalling conditions, and usually dressed in civilian clothes or cheap blue make-shift 'uniforms'. Despite these conditions morale remained high among those territorial and Kitchener's 'new army' battalions already enlisted. For a revealing glimpse of those early heady light-hearted days of 1914, Donald Hankey writes in *A Student in Arms*:

'The New Army', 'Kitchener's Army', we go by many names. The older sergeants – men who have served in regular battalions – sometimes call us 'Kitchener's Mob', and swear to take us to war would be another 'Massacre of the Innocents'. At other times they affirm that we are a credit to our instructors (themselves); but such affirmations have become rarer since beer went up three-pence a pint.

We are a mixed lot – a triumph of democracy, like the Tubes. Some of us have fifty years to our credit, and only own to thirty; others are sixteen and claim to be eighteen. Some of us enlisted for glory and some for fun, and a few for fear of starvation. Some of us began by being stout, and have lost weight; others were seedy, and are filling out. Some of us grumble, and go sick to escape parades; but for the most part we are aggressively cheerful, and were never fitter in our lives. Some miss their glass of claret, others their fish and chips; but we all sleep on the floor, and have only one suit, which is rapidly becoming very disreputable, you can never tell t'other from which.

We sing as we march. Such songs we sing! All about coons and girls, parodies of hymns, parodies about Kaiser Bill, and sheer unadulterated nonsense. We shall sing *'Where's yer girl? Aint yer got none?'* as we march into battle.

Battle! Battle, murder and sudden death! Maiming, slaughter, blood, extremities of fear and discomfort and pain! How incredibly remote all that seems! We don't believe it really. It is just a great game we are learning. It is part of the game to make little short rushes in extended order, to lie on our bellies and keep our heads down, snap our rifles and fix our bayonets. Just a game, that's all, and then home to tea.

....Anyhow, we are Kitchener's Army, and we are quite
sure it will be all right. Just send us to Flanders and see if it
ain't. We're Kitchener's Army, and we don't care if it snows
ink!

Designation of the different types of infantry battalions

The regular army battalions were generally written as either 1st
Loamshires, 2nd Loamshires, etc., or 1/Loamshires, 2/Loamshires.

The territorial battalions who, having volunteered for overseas
service, began to set up second line formations were given fractional
numbers, and when a territorial battalion went overseas on active
service its place was taken by its territorial reserve battalion, and
so on. For example, the 1/5th Battalion of the Duke of Cornwall's
Light Infantry – the territorial battalion going to France – would
be replaced at home with its reserve battalion now called 2/5th
DCLI. From March 1915, third reserve battalions were formed
designated 3/5th etc. In April 1916 the 3/ prefix was discontinued
and instead battalions became known as 'Reserve' battalions.

The 'new army' battalions (see above) were given a number in
the regimental sequence with the title 'Service' to distinguish them
from the regular and territorial battalions, e.g. 8th 'Service' Battalion,
The Devonshire Regiment. The first 100,000 volunteers of the 'new
army' were formed into battalions and referred to as K1 units, and
later, as more volunteers were formed into battalions, these became
K2, K3 and later K4 (2nd Reserve).*

*Further reserve battalions were formed and the naming and numbering system becomes
more complex, but as I am not following any of these units I have not given details.

Altogether eighty K1 service battalions were raised, eighty K2, and
ninety K3. In total there were 557 service battalions, including the
various locally raised Reserves.

Battalion transport

The transport section of an infantry battalion was in the charge of
a transport officer, usually a subaltern, i.e. a 1st lieutenant or 2nd
lieutenant. Among those in the section were drivers, officers' grooms,
brakesmen, and the men with nine pack animals that carried
ammunition. Very important members were the transport-sergeant,

his corporal and a farrier-corporal and such specialists as the shoeing smith, saddler, carpenter and cook. The vehicles were the GS (General Service) waggon, the mess waggon, the company cookers, the water cart, the cart special to the quartermaster's stores known as 'the Maltese cart' and limbers carrying machine guns and ammunition.

Company

The company was the main unit of a battalion. Depending on prevailing circumstances, the size of a company varied, but 230 is a rough guide, and commanded by a captain, or at times, subalterns, depending on casualties. The senior NCO of each company was a company sergeant major. A company was divided into four platoons.

Platoon

As with a company, platoons varied in size, but 60 would be a good average and commanded by a lieutenant or 2nd lieutenant (again according to prevailing circumstances). A platoon consisted of four sections plus a headquarters unit of a subaltern, a platoon sergeant, a runner and combined batman/second runner. By the end of the war a platoon included a Lewis gun section of a two-man gun team and supporting riflemen, and one section trained as bomb throwers.

Section

A section of a platoon was of up to fourteen men led by an NCO usually a corporal.

Variations in size of units

It is difficult to state categorically the numerical composition of any type of units as they varied according to conditions at any one time – e.g. casualties, sickness, men on leave or attending courses, replacement drafts or lack of them.

When a battalion went in to action in the First World War, it became usual to leave behind a cadre of officers and men to ensure some personnel would remain for reforming if the battalion was badly mauled in an attack. This cadre was referred to as a 'Battle Surplus' or 'First Reinforcement' or 'Minimum Reserve'. To give an example, Army Orders in 1916 during the battle of the Somme instructed that the second-in-command, 2 captains, 5 subalterns, the regimental sergeant-major, 2 company sergeants-major, and 10 others per company were to be left at the transport lines as a reserve in case of too serious casualties.*

*See below, War Diary 8th Devonshires on the opening day of the battle of Loos, and Liddell Hart on the opening day of the battle of the Somme.

Replacements

When the system of returning wounded men to their original regiments and battalions broke down, 'Base Details' were sent up the line to those formations most in need of reinforcements at that moment. So a formation on occasions could contain men from a mixture of regiments, whatever its title was nominally. This was a pity because men lost the feeling of being with, and belonging to, their own units and comrades.

Aubrey Smith bemoans this aspect of replacements saying, after the diversionary battle of Gommecourt in July 1916 – where the London Rifle Brigade had suffered heavy casualties:

> A motley collection of drafts from all regiments was ready to make the division up to strength immediately. What annoyed us was the persistency with which the authorities regarded all our units as 'London Regiment', sending say sixteen LRB's to the QWR's* and at the same time sixteen QWR men to our battalion. With a little more thought a good deal of esprit de corps could have been retained.

*Queen's Westminster Rifles, 1/16th County of London Battalion.

Robert Graves says after arrival in France from his training battalion (and this was early in the war), on receiving the order to go up the line he was disgusted to find he was being sent to a regiment other than his own. When he arrived he found all except two of the officers in his company came from other regiments.

At times the ordinary soldier may have been temporarily unsure to which particular army of the BEF he belonged as his battalion was moved around, but he would always think of himself as belonging to his division and brigade, and of course to his regiment.

PART TWELVE

I read a good deal in the seclusion of my tent. One book of interest is 'Rome' by Zola; another 'Ordeal by Battle' by Oliver, [Macmillan, 1915] in which the author quotes the nonsense publicly delivered by two eminent politicians who declared that 'one volunteer is worth six (the other said three) pressed men'. Is it seriously suggested that one British soldier, a volunteer, is equal in battle to six, or even three conscript soldiers of the magnificent German Army? Pure rubbish!

Entry from the diary of Brigadier General J.L. Jack
dated 8th August 1915.

The other armies on the Western Front

The Belgian army

The guarantee of neutrality provided little incentive to Belgium to develop its armed forces, although the king, Albert the First, who had spent most of his life in the army, was keen to do so. He had put pressure on the government to make service compulsory. In 1912 a decree demanded that one member of each household should serve for a period of fifteen months with the colours (field artillery was 21 months and the horse artillery 24 months). However, married men, or those who supported families, served only 4 months. The system did not work very well and at the outbreak of war only about 117,000 reservists were available, and many units were under strength.

The Belgian forces comprised: the regular army, the Gendarmerie, and the Garde Civic. Following reforms and reorganisation in 1913,

95

the army encompassed six infantry divisions and one cavalry division. Each division was to comprise three brigades, each of two three-battalion regiments, and three field batteries integrated at brigade level.

The French army

There had been a great contrast between the work of mobilisation in France and Germany on the declaration of war between them in 1870. The French minister of war had asserted that the forces were ready to the last gaiter button, but events soon showed that this ideal was far from realisation. The munitions of war were in every respect inadequate; the existing railways were not equal to the strain of conveying 300,000 troops to the seat of war; regiments were not organised upon geographical principles – Alsatians had to travel to the south of France to join their colours, southerners were obliged to make their way to Brittany. The result was extraordinary confusion, whereas for the German armies, according to Moltke, everything had been foreseen and provided with scientific accuracy. He said, with satisfaction, that the fourteen days of German mobilisation were some of the most quiet of his life.

The concept of universal military service had been established in France after the French defeat in the Franco-Prussian War of 1870. The law, as it stood in 1913, demanded that all fit men between the ages of twenty and forty-five would serve in the army for three years with the colours and eleven in the reserve, and the remainder with the Territorial Army.

Voluntary service was also permitted from the age of eighteen years, and those men whose compulsory service had expired could re-engage for up to fifteen years. Such *rengagés* received a bounty, improved pay and pension, and in addition such men provided a cadre of experienced soldiers to form a high proportion of the NCOs.

At the outbreak of war in 1914, the standing army comprised some 823,000 men and included 46,000 colonial troops. In the first two weeks of August, 2,887,000 were mobilised.

The German army

The German army, like the rest of the continental armies, relied upon conscription, and the peacetime strength of the German army in 1914 was some 840,000 of all ranks. Efficiently organised, Germany was able to field a large professional army within a few days of war being declared.

Briefly, their system was as follows. In peacetime every German male, from his seventeenth to his forty-fifth birthday, was liable for military service. At seventeen he became automatically liable to serve with the *Landsturm* (Home Guard). From the age of twenty he was eligible for service with the Standing Army and commenced this with a period of service of two years for the infantry – three in the cavalry or horse artillery. This was followed by four or five years with the reserve forces when he was transferred initially to the *1st Ban Landwehr* (Reserves), and then at about the age of thirty-two to the *2nd Ban Landwehr* for the next six. Finally, at the age of thirty-nine he was passed to the *2nd Ban Landsturm* on whose books he remained until the end of his forty-fifth year.

In addition there was a supplementary reserve, the *Ersatz Reserve*, composed of men who for one reason or another were not called in the annual call-up. Men in this category were available for twelve years in the *Ersatz Reserve* and during this time were liable to call-up for three annual periods of training. After the twelve-year period they passed into the *2nd Ban Landsturm*. On mobilisation in 1914 the *Ersatz Reserve* amounted to about 1,000,000 men aged between twenty and thirty-two, and formed a high proportion of the reserve divisions.

There were two other categories in addition to the *Ersatz Reserve* which formed the basis of the German army. One was the *Resanten Liste* – men whose service was put back for one or more years and mainly because of domestic or business circumstances. The second was the *Einjahrige Freiwilligen* – one year volunteers who were men of good education and who undertook to clothe, equip and feed themselves during their period of service. Most aspired to become officers in the Reserve by taking further annual training for two years, and passing a military examination.

Sir John French's view of the German cavalry

Sir John had been invited by the Kaiser to visit Germany in 1911 to observe the cavalry manoeuvres being held near Berlin. Of this occcasion French wrote:

It was an experience I shall never forget, and it impressed me enormously with the efficiency and power of the German cavalry... I have never seen a more magnificent military spectacle than they presented on that brilliant August morning, numbering some 15,000 horseman with a large force of horse artillery, jäger and machine guns ... [Over luncheon] His Majesty asked me what I thought of what I had seen in the morning, and told me that the German cavalry was the most perfect in the world; but, he added, 'it is not only the Cavalry; the Artillery, the Infantry, all the arms of the Service are equally efficient. The sword of Germany is sharp; and if you oppose Germany you will find how sharp it is.'

The army of The United States of America, in France

Following America's entry into the war in 1917, there were plans for the deployment of an ever-increasing number of American divisions in France, but the war ended before even half of the programme could be completed. Even so, by the time of the armistice, there were seven regular, seventeen National Guard, and sixteen national army divisions on the continent. An American colonel, Colonel Stanton, made the famous statement on the arrival of the AEF: '*La Fayette, nous voici!*' Inexperienced, but full of enthusiasm, they were welcomed wholeheartedly by their now almost exhausted allies who by this time were scraping the barrel for men.

PART THIRTEEN

*Victorian Society possessed three main characteristics –
its youthfulness, the speed with which the population
was growing, and its increasing industrialisation and
urbanisation. Between 1841 and 1901 the inhabitants of
England and Wales grew from 15.9 million to 32.5 million,
and by 1901 four-fifths of the population lived in urban
areas. The Population Census for 1871 said: 'Middles-
borough in Yorkshire had a population of 383 inhabitants
in 1831 and now has 39,563'.*

Pamela Horn, *The Victorian Town Child.*

The new century: The times leading to the beautiful summer of 1914

The twentieth century had begun by continuing and accelerating
the great progress in the worlds of invention, engineering, industry
and commerce that had been the hallmark of Victorian times. The
phenomenal urban growth produced dreadful overcrowding and
poverty in parts of most towns, child labour was rife, and so was
child mortality. By the end of the century many children and adults
were still undernourished, and children's education suffered badly
from the constant 'moonlight flits' as families vanished overnight
from lodgings they could no longer afford, and started again
elsewhere.

Poor physique of many working-class youngsters in the aftermath
of the Boer War apparently led the medical officer of health for
Manchester to go on record saying: 'To get good soldiers you must
rear good children, you must see that children are adequately fed.'*

When they were first seen in Britain – following the collapse of the Dardanelles campaign – the height and physique of many Australian troops was commented upon very favourably when compared with many British youngsters brought up in poor urban areas. I remember my mother saying what tall, fine looking boys the Australian soldiers were (there were always a number of them coming to the house when they were on leave, and her older sister, Alice, was engaged to most of them I gather, but fortunately the suitors did not arrive on leave at the same time!)

Times were changing. In 1901, Guglielmo Marconi had pioneered wireless telegraphy by sending morse code signals right across the Atlantic Ocean – from Poldhu in Cornwall to Newfoundland – proving that wireless signals were not affected by the curvature of the Earth. Following this event ships and coastal stations were being fitted with wireless transmitters and receivers and so increasingly vessels at sea were no longer cut off from land and other vessels.* This meant too of course that navy ships could communicate with the Admiralty and other vessels of the fleet over longer distances and were no longer tied by visual contacts. Winston Churchill puts it rather more poetically in *The World Crisis 1911–1918*: 'So now the admiralty wireless whispers through the ether to the tall masts of ships'.

*'Wireless telegraphy' at sea became famous from its use in the White Star liner *Titanic* when her dramatic call 'CQD' and the more recently generally accepted 'SOS' signals alerted the world to her plight. On her maiden voyage on 14th April 1912, she had struck an iceberg while travelling at high speed and was sinking as she transmitted her distress calls.

Aeroplanes had taken to the skies following the Wright brothers' famous successful first flight in Kitty Hawk, North Carolina, in 1903,* and more recently Bleriot had flown across the Channel in 1910. The armed forces of the world were beginning to assemble aerial units.

*Although not the least bit relevant to events, I can't resist including the following. There was a hilarious piece of misreporting in *The Times*, that must be one of its best. Dated Tuesday 9th July 2003, here it is exactly as reported:

> Two British pensioners, Denis Wood and Jack Berkin, both 68, have completed a four-day crossing of the Atlantic in a homemade aircraft based on a prototype of the Wright Brothers' machine that made the first powered flight. They landed at Blackpool Airport after a 4,500 mile journey from Dayton, Ohio.

On reading this incredible story I had so hoped there would be an accompanying photograph showing two elderly, but intrepid, aviators arriving at Blackpool after this epic journey – and having flown in a completely open fuselage, box-kite flying machine piloted from the prone position. The men, I hoped, would be wearing goggles under peaked cloth caps turned back to front, and possibly Plus Fours, and Norfolk Jackets, and despite lying on their stomachs for four days at the controls, able to give a cheery wave to the cameras as they landed.

Surely this should have been the journalistic scoop of all time? After all, the Wright Brothers managed on their first flight only about 30 seconds or less in the air a few feet off the ground, and covering less distance than the wing-span of a jumbo jet, but it would seem our brave pensioners flew for four days, crossing the Atlantic Ocean, and covering a distance of 4,500 miles in their prototype replica, and apparently without the need to refuel during the flight. Sadly I could find no photograph and no further coverage or reference to the event. Such a pity!

Actually, some months later, I discovered that the two men *did* fly across from America, but the aircraft they had assembled was a modern kit aircraft, and of course it looked nothing like the Wright Brothers' original machine; in fact the only connection with Orville and Wilbur was that this self-assembly machine was based on a design principle of the Wright Bothers – having a single rear-mounted propeller and front flaps.

From the beginning of the century there had been a steady increase in the numbers of motor vehicles on the roads. And for some years they had been accepted in their own right and no longer considered as 'horseless carriages' to be preceded by a man carrying a red flag as a warning of approach to other road users. Much of the road transportation of goods however was still by horse-drawn conveyances in 1914, especially for local journeys. To offset this, powerful steam engines pulled trucks and carriages along the network of railway lines that covered most of the country. Telephones, the electric telegraph, typewriters, gas and electric lighting were quite normal, if not always widespread.

London had an underground railway system, and Great Britain still supplied much of the world with manufactured goods. Like the Royal Navy, the British Merchant Fleet too was the largest in the world. The country imported vast quantities of raw materials and in return exported vast quantities of manufactured goods and equipment. And of course there was the Empire 'on which the sun never set'.

Sail had lost the battle to steam, but the masts and yards of oceangoing and coastal sailing vessels could still be seen as these ships were loading and unloading in the docks, or beating their way out to sea. Large numbers of the distinctive shallow draft sailing barges too still plied their trade in the Thames estuary.

Below the surface of this prosperity the picture was not quite so

101

rosy. 1913 had been bedevilled by strikes and other countries were overtaking Britain in industrial output. Germany, with booming industries, was expanding in every way and at the same time complaining of encirclement, and demanding 'a place in the sun' – the desire for an increase in colonial possessions. The antipathy between the Kaiser and his uncle King Edward the Seventh, and continuing with his cousin King George the Fifth, had not helped diplomatic relations between the two countries, and neither had the Kaiser's vast programme of warship building which was seen in Britain as a deliberate and direct threat to Britain's long established naval supremacy.

Despite so much of Europe being ruled by the extended family of the late Queen Victoria, there were, in the manner of many families, quarrels or ill feeling among the members, and there is no doubt that these feelings helped to precipitate the onset of war. Even so, as late as 1913, at the wedding of the only daughter of the German Emperor William II – a grandson of Victoria – King George V of England and Nicholas II of Russia attended, and both these monarchs had German wives as well as the common relationship through the late Queen. The wedding banquet was a great success and omens and political realities seemed far away. But they did not go away.

In addition, France, still smarting from her defeat in the Franco-Prussian war, and anxious to regain lost territories, was more than willing to take on the Germans again.

The Entente Cordiale

In 1904, the British and French concluded an agreement which came to be known as the Entente Cordiale as it seemed clear that, unlike the past, Britain's enemy was more likely to be Germany than France in any future war. In 1906 Haldane authorised the newly created general staff to meet with their French opposite numbers on the understanding their discussions were not politically binding.

In 1910, Sir Henry Wilson asked General Foch what would be the smallest British military force that would be of any practical assistance to the French. Foch replied immediately: 'A single British soldier – and we will see to it that he is killed.'*

By 1911, the Anglo-French plan for the BEF to take its place on the continent to the left of the French should there be a war, had been completed. A tremendous amount of detailed planning under constant pressure from Sir Henry Wilson had been carried out to provide, among other things, arrangements for the rail transportation for men and horses, and to overcome the problems of the differences between British and French railway tracks and rolling stock.

As far as the Royal Navy was concerned, the understood, if not formally stated, 'agreement' between France and Britain was that if the French fleet concerned itself with looking after French and British interests in the Mediterranean, the British fleet would safeguard France's northern shores from being bombarded and battered and left undefended if a war should break out with Germany.*

*See below, Sir Edward Grey's speech to the House of Commons 3rd August 1914.

The Royal Navy had planned its cover for protecting the Channel and Channel ports for the transportation of the army across the Channel, and plans for the mobilisation of army and navy reserves were all in place. In the event, both the mobilisation and embarkation went like clockwork.

Summer 1914

The unanimous opinion is that the summer of 1914 was beautiful and extremely hot. A summer that had begun early, and continued late, with the sunshine seeming endless as crowds flocked to the seaside, or strolled in the warm air through the public parks and gardens where bands entertained. Barrel organs churned out cheerful melodies in suburban streets, and children played hopscotch, or with tops, hoops and skipping ropes. Urchins gleefully called out: 'Whip behind governor!' to the drivers of horse-drawn carts as other children hung on the back of the carts for a free ride and a 'dare'. The children of those families lucky enough to be by the sea worked seriously digging and building sandcastles with buckets and spades before the encroaching tide destroyed them.

Until the feeling that war was inevitable – because Britain *must* stand by her declaration to protect Belgium's neutrality, and fight any aggressor who challenged it – there had been a mood of optimism that year. Prospects were looking good, and although income tax had reached an unprecedented one shilling and four pence in the pound (about seven and a half pence in the pound in today's currency) there was something to cheer everyone. Social change was on its way, nothing by today's standards perhaps, but nevertheless there were schemes for Labour Exchanges, state-funded old age pensions and insurance schemes, and there were people trying to persuade Parliament to give women the right to vote at elections as the suffragette movement gained in momentum up to the outbreak of the war.*

*Lady St Helier, in an article published in *Woman's Sphere* in the early days of the war, writes with restrained well-bred, if not explicitly expressed, horror of the suffragettes, and relief at the changes taking place:

> To those of us who only a few years ago watched with deep anxiety and apprehension the direction in which ambitions and desires of such a large number of English women were diverging, the change of the last year is thankfully welcomed. The unrest, the discontent, has passed and in its place has arisen a spirit of steadfastness and devotion characteristic of the highest standards of women's ambitions. Those who have watched and contrasted the processions of women deputations to the Government then and now, must, even amid the shadow and sorrows of to-day, have felt thankful that in the supremest moment in the history of their country the women of England are displaying the qualities and virtues on which the foundations of our national life have grown and flourished.

The London Season was nearing its end, but still gentlemen in evening dress accompanied by ladies in silk and satin gowns and glittering jewels emerged from stately motor cars outside mansions and hotels in Mayfair. Crowds flocked to the opera and ballet, and attendance flourished at theatres, music halls and the new 'picture palaces' or bioscopes with their silent flickering films and piano accompaniment. Dance halls were finding a new craze as the waltz and one-step were being ousted in popularity by the recently imported fox trot or saunter – to become so ably demonstrated by Vernon and Irene Castle.

PART FOURTEEN

...my two companions were French officers belonging to the General Staff. We each sat at a table in this stifling corner of the Ministère de la Guerre exactly as we had sat the day before, and the day before that. But there was now an enormous difference: today was August 2nd, 1914, France was mobilising for war, and I, who belonged to the Army of another country that had not declared itself, had ceased to be a comrade and had suddenly become an object of suspicion.

Edward Spears, *Liaison 1914*.

War. 4th August 1914: 'A scrap of paper'

Out of the clear blue August skies came war. James Cameron describes it thus in his *1914*:

Bank Holiday Monday had filled London with a sort of fantasy; the city was alive with restless people, gay and tormented, relaxed, tense, bewildered, thoughtful, carefree, obsessed; in the multitudes that moves back and forth along Whitehall was everything from enthusiasm to despair.

Sir Edward Grey addresses the Commons

Cameron went on to say that outside the House of Commons the crowds grew thicker as the time grew near, and the Chamber inside was dressed for high drama. Sir Edward Grey rose, his eyes red-rimmed in a lined empty face, and during a speech lasting for almost an hour he said:

We have consistently worked with a single mind to preserve peace. We have little difficulty in proving it, though little time was allowed... Austria showed a disposition to force things rapidly to an issue at great risk to peace. And the result is – the policy of peace has failed... Yesterday we let France know that we should not allow her coasts to be attacked. This is not a declaration of war. If Germany agrees not to use her fleet – should we give our pledge to neutrality? It is far too narrow an engagement for us. If we run away our respect is gone.

Although not quoted by Cameron, Sir Edward Grey also said in that speech to the House:

I now come to what we think the situation requires of us. For many years we have had a long-standing friendship with France ... the warm and cordial feeling resulting from the fact that these two nations, who have had perpetual differences in the past, had cleared these differences away... The French fleet is now in the Mediterranean, and the northern and western coasts of France are absolutely undefended. The French fleet being concentrated in the Mediterranean, the situation is very different from what it used to be, because the friendship which has grown up between the two countries has given them a sense of security that there was nothing to be feared from us.
   My own feeling is that if a foreign fleet, engaged in a war which France had not sought, and in which she had not been the aggressor, came down the English Channel and bombarded and battered the undefended coasts of France, we could not stand aside and see this going on practically within sight of our eyes, with our arms folded, looking on dispassionately, doing nothing. I believe that would be the feeling of this country.

Grey then poses the question that if we did nothing, the French were forced to withdraw their ships from the Mediterranean, and Britain's interests and trade routes in the Mediterranean came under threat from warring nations in that area, we would not be in a position to guard our shores and the approaches to them, and, at the same time, maintain a large force in the Mediterranean. What then will be the position in the Mediterranean? He emphasised how vital it was to this country to keep open her trade routes. He continued:

In that emergency and in these compelling circumstances, yesterday afternoon I gave to the French Ambassador the following statement: 'I am authorised to give an assurance that if the German fleet comes into the Channel or through the North sea to undertake hostile operations against the French coasts or shipping, the British fleet will give all the protection in its power. This assurance is, of course, subject to the policy of His Majesty's Government receiving the support of Parliament.'

In *his* report of the scene in the House that fateful and momentous 3rd August 1914, James Cameron added:

The lonely challenge came from the Labour Leader. Ramsey MacDonald stood up very straight [and saying to the Foreign Secretary and Prime Minister who had spoken before him]:
    'Your speech will echo in history, but you are wrong. Honour? No such crime is ever committed without an appeal to honour. It was so in the Crimean war, it was so in the South African War; it is so today.'

Later that evening Sir Edward Grey spoke again to the House of Commons saying:

I want to give the House some information which I have received, and which was not in my possession when I made my statement this afternoon. It is information I have received from the Belgian Legation in London, and it is to the following effect: Germany sent yesterday evening at seven o'clock a note proposing to Belgium friendly neutrality, covering free passage on Belgian territory, and promising maintenance of independence of the kingdom and possession at the conclusion of peace, and threatening, in case of refusal, to treat Belgium as an enemy.

107

A time limit of twelve hours was fixed for the reply. The Belgians have answered that an attack on their neutrality would be a flagrant violation of the rights of nations, and that to accept the German proposal would be to sacifice the honour of a nation. Conscious of its duty, Belgium is finally resolved to repel aggression by all possible means.

The Imperial Chancellor's address to the Reichstag

In a speech in the Reichstag on 4th August the Imperial Chancellor, Herr von Bethmann-Hollweg, put Germany's position in terms of brutal frankness:

Gentlemen, we are now in a state of necessity, and necessity knows no law. Our troops have occupied Luxemburg, and perhaps are already on Belgian soil. Gentlemen, that is contrary to the dictates of international law. It is true that the French Government has declared at Brussels that France is willing to respect the neutrality of Belgium as long as her opponent respects it. We knew, however, that France stood ready for the invasion. France could wait, but we could not wait. A French movement upon our flank upon the lower Rhine might be disastrous. So we were compelled to override the just protest of the Luxemburg and Belgian Governments. The wrong – I speak openly – that we are committing we will endeavour to make good as soon as our military goal has been reached. Anybody who is threatened, as we are threatened, and is fighting for his highest possessions can have only one thought – how he is to hack his way through.

James Cameron comments: 'That evening in Berlin thirty thousand Germans gathered around the Bismark Monument to hear Dr Dohring, the Court Preacher, recite the Lord's Prayer, while far away the first of the *Uhlans** cantered into Flanders.

*Scouting cavalry

So, despite the flurry of activity between diplomats and officials, and between embassies and chancelleries, the urgent meetings and telephone calls to prevent the conflict had finally resulted in deadlock. German mobilisation was too far advanced to halt, or at least so claimed von Moltke, and, as the chimes of Big Ben tolled midnight and German troops continued to enter Belgium, Britain's ultimatum to Germany expired. Britain was at war with Germany.

On the previous evening in London the weary Foreign Secretary, Sir Edward Grey, sadly looking into the dusk from his window in Whitehall made his now famous despairing observation to a companion:

The lamps are going out all over Europe, we shall not see them lit again in our lifetime.

In Berlin, after the declaration of war, the British Ambassador, Sir Edward Goshen, paid a farewell visit to the German Chancellor, Herr Theobald von Bethmann-Hollweg, whom he found despondent and despairing. 'Just for a word,' the German Chancellor said to the Ambassador, 'Britain is going to make war on a kindred nation that only asks for friendship. Just a word: "neutrality"! Just for a scrap of paper!'

The Treaties of 1831 and 1839

The scrap of paper referred to contemptuously by the German Chancellor was the Treaty of 1831 signed by the following plenipotentiaries: Palmerston (Britain); Sylvain Van De Weyer (Belgium); Senft (Austria); H. Sebastiani (France); Bülow (Prussia); Pozzo Di Borzo (Russia). The vital articles of the treaty were numbers II and VII:

Article II: Her Majesty the Queen of the United Kingdom of Great Britain and Ireland, His Majesty the Emperor of Austria, King of Hungary and Bohemia, His Majesty the King of the French, His Majesty the King of Prussia, and His Majesty the Emperor of All Russias, declare that the Articles mentioned in the preceding Article are considered as having the same force and validity as if they were textually inserted in the present act, and that they are thus placed under the guarantee of their said Majesties.

109

Article VII: Belgium, within the limits specified in Articles I., II., and IV., shall form an independent and perpetual neutral State. It shall be bound to observe such neutrality towards all other States.*

*This treaty was confirmed by the same six powers in the Treaty of 1839.

Later that fateful Tuesday 4th August 1914, King George V received the American Ambassador. 'My God, Mr Page,' said the King, 'what else *could* we do?'

War! It was true that the former Prussian Chancellor, Otto von Bismarck, some years earlier predicted that 'Some damn thing in the Balkans would ignite the next war', but what had they to do with Britain?* Nobody really could remember Britain being involved in a European war – if you discounted the Crimea, and that was a long way away, and not really European, and also in the previous century. The last conflict, the Boer War, had also been a distant war – like all the other British wars of the Victorian era – and for most of the people at home it had been mainly the subject of newspaper articles expressing opposing opinions. *Goodbye Dolly Gray* was a tuneful memory and the war generally forgotten by the public, although not by the military.

*A fascinating study covering the Balkans in the late 19th century and 20th century up to and including the Great War is *Royal Sunset, The Dynasties of Europe and the Great War* by Gordon Brook-Shepherd.

Mobilisation

In Britain, reservists flocked to the railway stations to report to their depots, mingling with holiday crowds, and officers were instructed to get their swords sharpened. At the Oval cricket ground Surrey was playing Kent in Jack Hobbs' benefit match. The day ended with Surrey 472 for 5, and the score card reading 'Hobbs, bowled Ironmonger, 226'. The next day the army commandeered the cricket ground and the match was transferred to Lords.

So Britain went to war.*

*The actual dates of the opening of the war are as follows: Austria declared war against Serbia on 28th July. Germany declared war against Russia on 1st August. A state of war arose automatically between France and Germany on 1st August. Belgium was invaded

110

without formal declaration of war by Germany on 3rd August. Britain declared war against Germany on 4th August. On 6th August Serbia declared war against Germany, and Montenegro declared war against Austria. On 11th August, Montenegro declared war against Germany; on the 12th France and Britain declared war against Austria, and on 23rd August, Japan declared war against Germany, this being followed by the Austrian declaration of war against Japan on 26th August.

Rumours

If, as it is generally accepted, the first casualty of war is 'truth', then one of the first manifestation of this casualty is 'rumour', and however ridiculous the content, or unlikely the sources, rumours are frequently accepted and given credence, and spread as fact, at least for a while.*

*As a personal example of a war-time rumour I can remember that a few days after that fateful Sunday, 3rd September 1939 (when, as a 10-year-old evacuated with my school from London to Bognor Regis, and while standing on the beach, I had heard, through loudspeakers from Butlin's Holiday Camp, the amplified voice of Neville Chamberlain announcing we were now at war with Germany) the father of the family with whom I was billeted came home with the news that an RAF pilot from nearby Tangmere aerodrome had just brought word from France that Hitler had been killed. On receiving this news the many children in his family leaped up and began dancing around singing:

> Poor old Hitler is dead
> He died last night in bed
> He cut his throat
> With a ten bob note
> Poor old Hitler's dead!

Even at that young age, I felt there was something unlikely about this story, and also if it were true, I could not rejoice in someone's death.

In August 1914, the Russians, who were now our allies, had been reported as sending troops to the west and, it was said, Russian soldiers had been seen in trains in Scotland heading south for embarkation to France, and they still had snow on their boots.

The Germans, now our enemies, were known 'as a fact' to have bicycled into Belgium disguised as nuns, and were busy bayoneting babies in the streets.*

*A further example of rumours and stories of German invaders disguised as nuns that ran rife in both world wars is recorded by the Countess of Ranfurly writing in her diary on 23rd May 1940 in Palestine, where she was living. She had just received a letter from her husband's aunt, Lady Constance Milnes Gaskell, who had been dining in London

111

with the ADC, and a Lady-in-Waiting to Queen Wilhelmina of Holland. The Lady-in-Waiting had just arrived in Britain following her escape, and on the subject of the German invasion of Holland stated: 'Women [Fifth Columnists] were dropped dressed as nuns. Many of the parachutist men who were wounded proved to be boys of only fourteen and sixteen.' The Countess admits that later it was discovered of course there was no truth in the story – highly placed as it was – but she says at the time everyone believed it.

In 1914 Ian Hay relates, unquestioningly it would seem, a story he heard soon after his regiment's arrival in France:

> But the grim realities of war are coming home to us. Outside this farm stands a tall tree. Not many months ago a party of Uhlans arrived here, bringing with them a wounded British prisoner. They crucified him to that self-same tree, and stood round him till he died. He was a long time dying. Some of us had not heard of Uhlans before. These have now noted the name, for future reference – and action.

One must not forget either 'The Angel(s) of Mons', when newspapers, both local and national, reported accounts of the sighting of a host of white-clad horsemen led by a towering angel-figure appearing to guard the exhausted troops of the small British Expeditionary Force as they fell back before the mass of an advancing, and potentially encircling, German army.

Thousands of harmless Germans, people who had lived and worked in Britain for years, were rounded up and put into internment camps. German-owned shops were looted by mobs and the owners assaulted as the word was put around that these unfortunate people were spies.

But, in truth, 'gallant little Belgium' *had* been invaded, we had given our word to defend her neutrality, and the wicked had to be punished. (As described above, both Britain and Germany had guaranteed Belgian neutrality on more than one occasion – in 1831, 1839, and yet again in 1871.) And it must be added that German troops did pillage Belgian homes as they advanced into the country and met with civilian opposition, and a number of civilians were shot.

Ludwig Renn, in *War*, asks, with seeming naïvety, as his unit of the German army advances into Belgium in 1914 and meets a not very friendly welcome from the natives: 'A little house stood on the right. A man leaned in the doorway, his cap down over his eyes, and stared at us. The man hated us. Why must people hate when they make war against one another?'

Edith Cavell

Among the civilians executed was the English nurse Edith Cavell, who at the time was matron of a nurse training establishment, the Berkendael Institute. She had been a resident in Brussels since 1907, and following charges that she had aided 200 Allied troops to escape to the Netherlands, she was arrested. On 11th October 1915 she was executed. This event was naturally seen as being of great propaganda value for the Allies to illustrate the brutality of the Germans. Her last words were reported as: 'Patriotism is not enough: I must have no hatred or bitterness towards anyone.'

Germany reports Belgian atrocities

John Terraine quotes a German seaman writing on 5th August 1914: 'Terrible reports of atrocities against German citizens arrived from Belgium. Our nation is not at all prepared for war, I thought as I read this.'

Terraine also quotes a Captain Walter Bloem of the 12th Brandenburg Grenadiers reporting on his way to the frontier at the same time:

We bought the morning papers at a wayside station and read, amazed, of the experiences of those of our troops already across the Belgium frontier – of priests, armed, at the head of marauding bands of Belgian civilians, committing every kind of atrocity, and putting the deeds of 1870 in the shade; of treacherous ambushes of patrols, and sentries found later with eyes pierced and tongues cut off, of poisoned wells and other horrors.

Spy mania

There seems to have been an obsession too with spies and spying, particularly in the early days of the war, and one wonders how many poor ignorant and innocent peasants in France and Belgium were accused and executed for the alleged offence. Reports abounded of people 'behaving suspiciously'; of people in villages signalling to the enemy by flashing lights at night across to the enemy lines (for what purpose? the intention of bringing a bombardment down upon themselves? Far more likely they were searching in the wreckage of their abandoned homes for possessions).

During the Battle of the Aisne, General Jack was not immune to the prevalent spy mania, recording in his diary in the early days of the war in 1914:

> One afternoon as I was riding near the Fère-en-Tardenois to Soisons road a large open car came flashing along it from the south, the occupants all muffled up in spite of the sunshine. Their appearance and procedure were so like those of an enemy's agents that I would have tried to stop the car had that been possible.

It is an intriguing thought of German agents adopting a special agent's 'appearance and procedures' when travelling on enemy roads! Anyway he solemnly reported the 'incident' thereby increasing the number of barricades on the roads, and guards were exhorted to be even more vigilant.

Refugees arrive in Britain

Almost 200,000 Belgian refugees arrived in Britain in 1914, and by middle of 1915 the number had risen to over 265,000 – and they presented a problem. Technically they were the responsibility of the Metropolitan Asylums Board, but as the war lengthened there had to be some way of integrating them into the economy, but it was not clear how.

Most of the refugees who came to Britain arrived at Folkestone, Tilbury and Hull – and ports in between – in every kind of vessel. Some arrived with money and supplies, others were destitute. In the week that followed the fall of Ostend over 26,000 arrived at Folkestone. On 10th September 1914, Mr Herbert Samuel, on behalf of the government, offered the Belgians the hospitality of the nation, and the Local Government Board was given the responsibility of dealing with the problem. This was an almost impossible task, particularly as the places that were able to offer the most accommodation – such as seaside towns – had little in the way of industry or training establishments. Children as usual were able to adapt most easily and able to attend schools and quickly learn English. There were many difficulties for older people.

A Belgian woman who eventually arrived in France said in an interview: 'We were ruined. The people who could stay at home grew rich with the soldiers. The people who had fled were always "refugees". It was a funny name. There is nothing you can do, you are ruined and they still talk about refugees.'

PART FIFTEEN

We shall never sheathe the sword which we have not lightly drawn until Belgium receives in full measure all and more than all that she has sacrificed, until France is adequately secured against the menace of aggression, until the rights of the smaller nationalities of Europe are placed upon an unassailable foundation, and until the military domination of Prussia is wholly and finally destroyed.

Henry Herbert Asquith, Prime Minister. Speech, Guildhall, 9th November 1914.

The British Expeditionary Force (BEF) August 1914

The British army that embarked for France initially in August 1914 consisted of one cavalry and four infantry divisions (1st, 2nd, 3rd and 5th). It had been planned for six infantry divisions, but Kitchener demurred. The ration strength was approximately 110,000, made up of 66,000 rifles, 7,600 sabres and 400 guns. A little later two more infantry divisions were added to join the other four, the 4th and 6th.

The instructions to the commander of the BEF

Sir John French's orders that he received from Lord Kitchener before leaving for France and arriving at 5 pm on 14th August 1914, were as follows:

Owing to the infringement of the neutrality of Belgium by

117

Germany, and in furtherance of the Entente which exists between this country and France, His Majesty's Government has decided at the request of the French Government to send an Expeditionary Force to France and to entrust the command of the troops to yourself.

The special motive of the force under your control is to support and cooperate with the French Army against our common enemies. The peculiar task laid upon you is to assist the French Government in preventing or repelling the invasion by Germany of French and Belgian territory and eventually to restore the neutrality of Belgium, on behalf of which, as guaranteed by treaty, Belgium has appealed to the French and to ourselves.

These are the reasons which have induced His Majesty's Government to declare war, and these reasons constitute the primary objective you have before you.

The place of your assembly, according to present arrangements, is Amiens, and during the assembly of your troops you will have every opportunity for discussing with the Commander-in-Chief of the French Army, the military position in general and the special part which your force is able and adapted to play. *It must be recognised from the outset that the numerical strength of the British Force and its contingent reinforcement is strictly limited, and with this consideration kept steadily in view it will be obvious that the greatest care must be exercised towards a minimum of losses and wastage.* [my italics]

Kitchener, in his instructions, continues to put Sir John in a very difficult position *vis-à-vis* the French and it underlies Kitchener's distrust and dislike of the whole operation – and possibly too his distrust of Sir John's leadership and reputation as a 'thrusting' cavalry man, and his lack of training for overall command.

Therefore while every effort must be made to coincide most sympathetically with the plans and wishes of our Ally, the gravest consideration will devolve upon you as to participation in forward movements where large bodies of French troops are not engaged and where your Force may be unduly exposed to attack. Should a contingency of this sort be contemplated, I look to you to inform me fully and give me time to communicate to you any decision to which His Majesty's Government may come in the matter. In this connection I wish you distinctly to understand that your command is an entirely independent one, and that you will in no case come in any sense under the orders of any Allied General.

In minor operations you should be careful that your subordinates understand that risk of serious losses should only be taken where such risk is authoritatively considered to be commensurate with the the object in view ... officers may well be reminded that in this, their first experience of European warfare, a greater measure of caution must be employed than under former conditions of hostilities against an untrained adversary.

The final warning:

You will kindly keep up constant communication with the War Office, and you will be good enough to inform me as to all movements of the enemy reported to you as well as to those of the French Army.

The final, somewhat mendacious, paragraph:

I am sure you fully realise that you can rely with the utmost confidence on the wholehearted and unswerving support of the government, of myself, and of your compatriots, in carrying out the high duty which the King has entrusted to you* and in maintaining the great tradition of His Majesty's Army.

(Signed) Kitchener, Secretary of State

*Sir John was dismissed from his command and recalled home in December 1915 (see below) and his job given to Sir Douglas Haig who held the post for the rest of the war.

The BEF to be positioned where? Antwerp? Amiens? Maubeuge?

The only real hitch to occur was when almost at the last minute a dispute arose concerning the actual placing of the BEF alongside its allies. Would it after all be in France, or Belgium? If, as previously agreed, in France, then where? Sir John French suddenly resurrected Antwerp in Belgium, although this had been ruled out earlier.*

*Originally the majority of the General Staff were in favour of a completely independent British force placed to hold Antwerp and the adjoining coast. Admiral Sir John Fisher, who had recently overhauled the Royal Navy, believed strongly, and perhaps not unnaturally, that British action should be predominantly naval. He doubted the military capacity of the French, and expected the Germans to beat them on land. He saw no purpose in ferrying the British army to France to be included in that defeat. In fact, he said, the plan to fight in France was 'suicidal idiocy'. Eccentric though he was apparently generally regarded, seen in hindsight, there is much food for thought in his words.

Kitchener, as stated, wanted only the four divisions of infantry and the one of cavalry to go, and not six, and for them to be staged at Amiens and not Maubeuge. He was eventually overruled and the destination reverted to the previously agreed decision for Maubeuge, just south of the border between Belgium and France.

Kitchener, however, was to be proved right because, as he asserted, the Germans would sweep through the far side of the river Meuse in great force, and if the BEF concentrated at Maubeuge it would be swamped by the invaders before it was ready for battle and forced to retreat. (See also Lord Esher and General Grierson below.)

Churchill was even more prescient on what would happen. Churchill, unlike Kitchener, *was* in favour of the BEF, even though its size was small. 'Such a force,' he wrote in *The World Crisis 1911–1918*, 'is a material factor of significance. Its value to the French would be out of all proportion to its numerical strength' – the same opinion as that expressed by Foch to Sir Henry Wilson above.

On 13th August 1911, three years before the war, Churchill sent a memorandum to the Committee of Imperial Defence following discussions with the General Staff. In this, although he was impressed by the army presentation, he said he believed the Army chiefs were far too sanguine about the power and effectiveness of the French army in the early days of a war.

If the French advanced at the beginning of the war they would, he was convinced, be in serious trouble of losing their advantage of internal communications, and by moving towards the advancing German reinforcements annul any numerical advantage they might for the moment possess. He said the French had no option but to remain on the defensive, both upon their own fortress line, and behind the Belgian frontier. He added that the Germans must be

120

credited with the wisdom of choosing the best possible day and could not be forced into decisive action against their will, except by some reckless and unjustifiable movement on the part of the French.

The French actions and the effect on the BEF

The French, immediately on the outbreak of the war and as the German army advanced through Belgium, threw their armies forward on the attack in accordance with their strategy of PLAN XVII. The plan was stated: '*Whatever the circumstances, it is the C in C's intention to advance, all forces united, to the attack of the German armies.*' This they did again and again and sustained great losses.

French tactics were concerned with the problems of the effective use of mass armies of conscripts – propelling vast numbers of relatively untrained troops forwards quickly and effectively. The French army had a theory of *élan*, the winning psychological effect of massed bayonet charges supported by cavalry and the famous mobile field artillery gun – the quick firing *Soixante Quinze* (75 mm). This policy and attitude of the French high command in 1914 is exemplified by Foch's famous statement at the Battle of the Marne: 'My centre is giving way, my right is in retreat; situation excellent: I shall attack.'

Of the consequences of the French plans and actions Churchill had written:

> A prudent survey of the chances from a British point of view ought to contemplate that, when the German advance decisively begins, it will be backed by sufficient preponderance of force, and developed on a sufficiently wide front to compel the French armies to retreat ... the balance of probability is that by *the twentieth day the French armies will have been driven from the line of the Meuse and will be falling back on Paris*. [My italics]

This was written three years before the war began, and that is what happened almost to the day.

PART SIXTEEN

You are leaving home to fight for the safety and honour of my Empire. Belgium, whose country we are pledged to defend, has been attacked, and France is about to be invaded by the same powerful foe. I have implicit confidence in you, my soldiers. Duty is your watchword, and I know your duty will be nobly done. I shall follow your every movement with deepest interest and mark with eager satisfaction your daily progress; indeed your welfare will never be absent from my thoughts. I pray God will bless you and guard you, and bring you back victorious.

GEORGE R.I.

King George V, message to the BEF on 9th August 1914.

Mobilisation and embarkation of the BEF, August 1914

As the German army marched into Belgium to begin its bid to capture the Channel ports and sweep down through France, the British army mobilised and prepared to embark to take up its position on the left of the French army. Mr Winston Churchill,* then First Lord of the Admiralty, had already some days previously set the Grand Fleet in motion to its war base at Scapa Flow.

*It was not until many years later, after the Second World War, that he became Sir Winston Churchill.

On the afternoon of the 6th August, the Prime Minister was given the all clear for the dispatch of the BEF as the Admiralty had said it could guarantee the safety of the crossing of the Channel, but not the North Sea – which put Antwerp as a landing point out of favour.

Sir Ernest Shackleton records in his book *South*, that on hearing of the mobilisation order as he was about to depart on his ill-fated expedition to the south polar regions, he called all hands on board the *Endurance* and told them he proposed to send a telegram to the Admiralty offering his ships, stores, and if they agreed, all their services, at the disposal of the admiralty. Everyone immediately agreed and the telegram was sent. Within an hour, he said, he received a laconic reply from the Admiralty saying: 'Proceed'.

The BEF assembled at Newhaven, Dover, Southampton, Portsmouth, Bristol (Avonmouth), and Liverpool, with Southampton the main embarkation point for personnel. Embarkation began on 9th August, and on the busiest day eighty trains were run into Southampton docks, and an average of thirteen ships sailed daily. During five days 1,800 special trains were run.

The BEF arrives

GHQ crossed to France on 14th August, and by 20th August the BEF was fully assembled in the Maubeuge area near the Belgium border, and on the left flank of the French as instructed. The French were annoyed by the delay as they felt the BEF should already be in position.*

*Most of the BEF landed at Rouen, Le Havre and Boulogne between 12th and 17th August. It was only by the prompt action and efforts of the British Navy that the troops and materials were able to cross the channel unopposed by the German navy. Hospital ships were also able to cross as required. The French seemed to take this for granted, and with no appreciation, or understanding, of what was entailed in transporting an army overseas.

According to an obituary in the *Daily Telegraph* the first British officer to land on French soil – and incidentally, the first to be mentioned in despatches – was a platoon commander with the 2nd Battalion, Argyll and Sutherland Highlanders. This young officer, after being wounded and awarded the MC, and later a Bar to his MC, and mentioned in despatches again, served as a junior staff officer under Major-General J.F.C. Fuller (of whom more below). The young officer became Brigadier Ian MacAlister, the 13th Laird of Achnacone, Argyllshire, and he died, aged 91, in March 1987.

The small British Expeditionary Force, as it moved up to Mons from its base at Maubeuge to take its place alongside on the left of the French Fifth Army, was unknowingly right in the path of the huge and advancing German First Army of General Von Kluck.

Thus the Battle of Mons began, and once it was realised that the BEF, particularly II Corps, could be outflanked by a whole German army as the 5th French Army on its right was forced back, the battle became 'The retreat from Mons'. This retreat continued through to Le Cateau back to the Marne and the Aisne, and the desperate defence of Paris.

The BEF reservists

A fact perhaps not always remembered, is that the BEF contained a large number of reservists as well as those on its active strength, indeed it has been said that fifty per cent of the total strength at Mons was made up of reservists. For them, some of whom only a few days earlier had been settled in civilian occupations, it must have come very hard to find themselves back in the army and marching mile after mile along the hard cobblestones and dusty roads of France.

General Jack (see above and below), at that time a captain in the 1st Cameronians, says, on the subject of mobilisation, that only one or two of their some 600 reservists failed to report on time. He was concerned, however, that the presence in the ranks of such a large number of reservists – although they were needed to make the battalion up to its War Establishment – was unsatisfactory, because these reservists needed 'tuning up' and conditioning for marching, before being ready for battle.

The BEF reservists were tired and thirsty as they marched mile after mile in blinding hot sunshine; their feet were sore and blistered in their newly issued, but not yet broken in army boots, and with the shoulder straps of their unaccustomed heavy equipment chafing and cutting into them, they sweated in the heat and dust. Each man's kit, consisting of a loaded pack, webbing equipment, an entrenching tool, ammunition, rifle and bayonet, weighed about 80 lb or 36 kg.

As the BEF soldiered on to their destination they chanted and sang irreverent and frequently obscene songs. Under no circumstances, and quite unlike the Germans, did these evoke patriotism, honour or glory. An improbable and inconsequential ditty called *Tipperary* had an almost immortal success which puzzled everybody, including its composer, Jack Judge.*

*Originally Florrie Forde sang the song in a 1913 pantomime without causing comment anywhere. In 1914 a serious-minded clergyman in London thought the melody good but, for the benefit of the soldiers, suggested an amendment in the words from:

> Goodbye Piccadilly,
> Farewell Leicester Square

to:

> Good-bye self indulgence;
> Farewell soft armchair.

To which the troops replied with the inevitable coda: '*Have a banana!*'

Call to the colours

While the BEF was marching its way through France, posters were appearing all over Britain on walls, hoardings, and on the backs of the London General Omnibus Company's red 'double-decker' buses. The posters bore the brooding face of Lord Kitchener* with the caption below reading: 'Your Country Needs You!' And it continued: 'In this crisis your country calls on all unmarried men to rally round the Flag and enlist in the ranks of her Army'.

*Margot Asquith, the second wife of Herbert Asquith, wrote in her book *Portrait of an Imperialist*: 'If Kitchener was not a great man, he was, at least, a great poster.'

Although both Germany and France had huge conscript armies, for Britain there was no hint of compulsory service, despite the earlier efforts of the National Defence League. Kitchener wanted to recruit one hundred thousand men in the first instance in 1914, and he got them quickly and easily (see above). Long queues formed outside recruiting offices, and on the stage Phyllis Dare sang many a young man into the trenches with:

> Oh we don't want to lose you
> But we think you ought to go
> For your King and Country
> Both need you so.

YOUNG WOMEN OF LONDON

=================================

Is your "Best Boy' wearing Khaki? If not don't **YOU THINK** he should be?

If he does not think that you and your country are worth fighting for – do you think he is **WORTHY** of you?

Don't pity the girl who is alone – her young man is probably a soldier – fighting for her and her country – and for **YOU.**

If your young man neglects his duty to his King and Country, the time may come when he will **NEGLECT YOU.**

Think it over – than ask him to

JOIN THE ARMY TO-DAY

==================================

Wording of an early poster issued by the Parliamentary Recruitment Committee in 1914.

My four relatives enlist

This seems an appropriate point to introduce my four young men, in August 1914, as they like the thousands of others queue outside their recruiting offices in the sunshine to enlist in their future regiments. I'll introduce them in the order they enter and then depart my story.

Alfred Watts (17.4.1888–11.6.1915)

Aged 26 years, at Mitcham in Surrey, Alfred enlisted into a regular battalion of the Rifle Brigade. Whether this was a deliberate choice on his part, or whether he was simply allocated to the Rifle Brigade at the recruiting office, I do not know. He was to become Rifleman Alfred Watts, Number Z/2411,* 3rd Battalion, The Rifle Brigade.

*A question, to which I can find no answer, is the significance of the letter Z before his number, Z/2411. I have only encountered this on the headstones of a few graves of Rifle Brigade men, certainly not on all, and not, as far as I can remember, on other regiments. The Royal Green Jackets Museum at Winchester could not enlighten me when I asked. I am indebted to Tom Morgan of the internet website *Hellfire Corner* who wrote to me to say that *Soldiers Died in the Great War* lists 793 soldiers with numbers beginning with Z/. They were all members of the Rifle Brigade.

He was the son of Alfred and Elizabeth Watts, and in 1914 the family lived at 49 Pitcairn Road, Mitcham, Surrey. Mitcham, by then no longer famous for its lavender fields, was now just another suburb and bordered by the boroughs of Tooting, Streatham and Merton.*

*Having said that, even in my time, as a very young child I can remember a small local dairy farm within a few minutes' walk. I used to accompany my mother there to buy milk when we lived in nearby Arnold Road, close to my grandparents.

Alfred, the father, had been married before and had two sons by his first wife. She had died in 1886, and Alfred, the soldier son, was the first child born to Elizabeth and Alfred. He was followed by three more boys, and then twin girls (one of whom died in childbirth), and finally another girl, my mother Nellie, the baby of the family, who was born in 1901.

They were a sociable family, and the house overflowed with relations, friends and general 'waifs and strays' coming around all the time. Alfred, the father, who worked in the printing trade, was also a gambler, and when he had a good win on the horses they all lived very well, at least for a while.

I'm not sure what Alfred, the son, did for a living before he volunteered in August 1914.* I believe he worked in the 'West End' of London, in a firm that imported goods from France and Belgium. He was very generous and spoilt his two young sisters with gifts from these countries, and they adored him.

*I wish now I had asked more about my family when I had the chance, and, unfortunately, much was thrown away or lost when older members died. But, as is natural when one is younger, one's thoughts look forward rather than backwards and I very rarely, if ever, thought or asked about family members or times before I was born.

Horace Robert Westlake (1895–1915)

Aged 19 in 1914, Horace was the elder of two Cornish brothers whose home was in Launceston. Their father, William Westlake, was a farmer and twice married. His first wife – Horace and Cecil's mother – Florence died in 1899, and her widower married his first cousin Miss Anna Maria Westlake in 1900.

William had, or developed, a heart condition and this caused him to give up his farm. He died in 1911 leaving his second wife to bring up the children – the two boys and their sister Gwendoline.

Horace, up to the time of his enlistment, had followed in his father's footsteps, and was working on a farm in Falmouth, 'Penrose Farm'. His occupation when he enlisted was given as a 'horse driver'.

In that hot August of 1914, Horace enlisted in Falmouth, and on being attested and signed up for 'the duration' in one of the 'K1' battalions, he became one of Kitchener's 'first hundred thousand.

Again, I don't know if the choice of regiment was his (Launceston being a border town of Devon and Cornwall), or whether the lists were open for The Devonshires at his local recruitment office and he joined them before the lists closed. Either way he was now, or about to be, a member of 8th (Service) Battalion of the Devonshire Regiment, and he would become Lance Corporal, No. 14662, H.R. Westlake, and the second of the three young men to arrive on the Western Front.

Cecil Henry Westlake (10.5.1897–17.1.1949)

The younger brother of Horace; Cecil, as he was generally known, was to marry my father's sister, Lilian Holley. Before he joined up he was working in Launceston in an ironmongers. His sister Gwendoline also worked there in the ironmongery trade. Aged 17 he enlisted at Launceston in Cornwall into the Territorial Battalion of his county regiment – The Duke of Cornwall's Light Infantry, and he would become Sergeant, No. 240201, C.H. Westlake, of 1/5th The Duke of Cornwall's Light Infantry, mentioned in despatches, and holder of the Belgian Croix de Guerre.

His death at about the time of his daughter's 21st birthday was, I know, a dreadful shock to her. They were very close, but like many others who served in the war, she said he never spoke of his wartime experiences. The family lived in Bristol, and I saw them but seldom as my family lived in London. I do remember that when I was about six or seven years old Cecil drove a Triumph Gloria, and this impressed me as most of the people I knew who were fortunate enough to own a motor car drove Austin 7s, and Morris or Ford 8s and 10s. (One exception was an ex-army friend of my father who owned a Lagonda, which was unbelievably grand, but he ended up in a mental hospital. Whether there was a connection here I don't know!)

The Cecil of my memory was a man of stocky build, physically strong, self-confident and with a brisk manner. I think he regarded me as a bit of a weed, and admonished me, on the rare occasions we met, to pull my shoulders back and stand up straight. Once a sergeant...!

I am sure that his time as a prisoner of war, when his unit was overrun in 1918, must have undermined his health (see extracts from his notebook below). Pamela, his daughter, said that while a prisoner he contracted beriberi (a degenerative disease caused by lack of vitamin B), and he was very ill on his return to England. By the spring of 1918, when he was taken prisoner, Germany was desperately short of food, and many ordinary civilians were close to starving.* Prisoners of war came very low on the list for rations. (And, as in the Second World War, the most unfortunate soldiers to be prisoners of the Germans were Russians.)

*According to A.C. Bell, *The Blockade of Germany, 1914–1918*, at the beginning of 1918 German civilian adults had a diet of only 1,000 calories a day, less than half that generally regarded as necessary for the maintenance of health and efficiency.

Joseph Edward Holley (29.10.1897–23.11.1991)

Aged 16 years, and at Canterbury in Kent when war was declared, the regimental unit Joseph applied to and joined was an independent territorial battalion, The Kent Cyclist Battalion, and he became Private Edward Joseph Holley (he was actually Joseph Edward Holley) Regimental No. 265490.*

*Although 'Ted' Holley was accepted, he was told he could not actually join the regiment until his birthday in October; and that he did.

He was my father. When he was born his parents and his sister Lilian (who, as I have said, later married Cecil Westlake), were living in Reedworth Street in Lambeth, a turning off Kennington Road, not far from the Oval Cricket Ground. Neither of his parents were Londoners. His mother was from Cornwall, and his father from Berkshire.

As a young man my father's father had gone to South Africa, either with or following his older brother Robert, and while there he joined the Kimberley Diamond Light Horse. He also (and I am not sure whether this was before or after South Africa), became a regular soldier, enlisting in the cavalry, the 7th Hussars, at the Hounslow Depot. He saw service in India where the regiment spent a lot of time, and as I have mentioned elsewhere, he served in the same troop with the man who was to become the Commander in Chief of the BEF, Field Marshal Sir Douglas Haig who, at the time being the adjutant, signed his discharge papers.

When my father left school he got a job as an office boy in the City of London in Paternoster Square, just by St Paul's Cathedral. He was a physically active lad, a keen Boy Scout, swimmer and cyclist. He used to cycle to work in the City each morning, cycle back home at lunch time, and cycle back to work after lunch and then cycle home in the evening after work. (He worked from 8.30 am to 6 pm, the usual office hours in those days.)

In the circumstances it was not surprising, I suppose, that while on a cycling holiday in Kent in August 1914 he applied to enlist in the army and into the Cyclist Battalion.

PART SEVENTEEN

Officers and soldiers do not belong to their regiment, they are members of it. They do not serve in their unit, they serve with it. The intimacy of the relationship is reflected in numerous other subtleties of language.

Roger Perkins writing in *Military and Naval Silver*.

Regimental backgrounds

To explain the existence and composition of my four regiments I have included very brief regimental histories, and also given a brief background to the army as it was in 1914, following the reforms of Cardwell, Childers and Haldane.

The Devonshire Regiment

'The Bloody Eleventh' – so named after the severe fighting in Salamanca in July 1812 where the regiment's casualties were more than 300 out of a strength of 400 – is the most senior of the line regiments in this little cameo.

The 1st Battalion, formed in June 1685, raised by Henry, Duke of Beaufort, in Bristol was, like so many others of the era, first known by the name of its colonel, and in this case the regiment was known as the Duke of Beaufort's Musketeers. In 1751 and until 1782 it was listed as 11th Regiment of Foot. Between 1782 and 1881 the name became 11th (North Devon) Regiment of Foot, and finally The Devonshire Regiment.

From its formation the First Battalion served and fought all round the world including the Peninsular War, the South African Wars, the First World War, the Second World War, then Malaya, and Kenya (during the Mau Mau Emergency).

The 2nd Battalion was formed in 1756 and became the 64th Regiment of Foot in 1758. It merged with 1st Battalion in 1816. The battalion was re-formed in 1857 and, like 1st Battalion, served world-wide taking part in the Second Afghan War of 1878–80 and the South African Wars.

The 2nd Battalion served on the Western Front in the First World War, and in the Second World War, it served in Sicily and Italy, and landed in Normandy on D Day. After fighting throughout north-west Europe to Germany, it was disbanded in 1948.

In 1958 the regiment was amalgamated into the Devonshire and Dorsetshire Regiment.

A great-uncle of mine, Robert Holley, writing an account of a walking holiday in the West Country in March 1878 that he and friend undertook says:

> ...and sought the village under the guidance of a youngster whom I fortunately fell in with. Surely never were such sturdy, ruddy boys, seen as those I have had the good fortune to meet and see around this moorland. What possibly splendid recruits for the 11th Devon Regiment some of them in time will make.

Duke of Cornwall's Light infantry

Formed from an amalgamation of the 32nd and 46th Regiments of Foot under Cardwell's reforms, it lies 32nd in the list of seniority of infantry regiments.

The 1st Battalion (32nd Regiment of Foot) came into existence in 1702 as one of several regiments of marines for service in the War of the Spanish Succession, and was known under the name of its colonel. It was disbanded in 1707 after being involved in several battles, but re-formed in 1713. In 1751 the name was changed to 32nd Regiment of Foot, and between 1782–1858, the title was 32nd (Cornwall) Regiment of Foot. During this period the regiment fought in a number of engagements including the Peninsular campaigns and Waterloo.

During the Indian Mutiny, at the siege of Lucknow, the regiment sustained over 370 killed, and 200 wounded, and it was here that it won four Victoria Crosses and was awarded the title of 'Light Infantry' as a mark of recognition for its gallantry. Finally, until the amalgamation in 1881, it was known as 32nd (Cornwall) Light Infantry.

The 2nd Battalion (46th Regiment of Foot) from 1741 to 1751 was known by the name of the colonel – 'Colonel John Price's Regiment' – and it served overseas in the West Indies, Canada and America. In 1751 it became the 46th Regiment of Foot, and this was followed by another change, in 1782, to the 46th (South Devonshire) Regiment of Foot. The regiment fought in the Crimean War, and in 1881 it joined 32nd to become The Duke of Cornwall's Light Infantry. The 32nd became 1st Battalion, and 46th the 2nd Battalion.

The 2nd Battalion was absorbed into the 1st Battalion in 1950, and in 1959 there followed an amalgamation with 1st Battalion The Somerset Light Infantry, and the Cornwalls became 1st Battalion, The Somerset and Cornwall Light Infantry.

The 3rd Battalion was the reserve battalion, and the 4th and 5th Battalions were the territorial battalions.

The Rifle Brigade

Titles: 1800–1803 'The Rifle Corps'. 1803–1816, '95th or Rifle Regiment'. 1816–1862 'The Rifle Brigade'. 1862–1881 'The Prince Consort's Own (Rifle Brigade)'. 1881–1920 'Rifle Brigade (The Prince Consort's Own)'. 1920–1958 'The Rifle Brigade (Prince Consort's Own)'.

Founded in 1800, as an 'Experimental Corps of Riflemen', it was the dream child of two officers, Colonel Coote Manningham, and Lt. Col. The Hon. William Stewart. These two officers proposed to the Duke of York that they form a force of troops that could carry out reconnaissance in terrain difficult for cavalry to function in, particularly close and broken country. The force could also cover withdrawal operations and skirmishing. Assent having been given, they set about recruiting men from existing regiments, selecting them on the basis of intelligence and marksmanship.

These troops, by the standards of the time, were revolutionary. The foundation stone was envisaged as mutual respect between superior and subordinate at all levels, and each member was to be trained to be able to act on his own initiative. Further, great importance was to be placed upon keeping the same officers and men together in each company.

The emphasis was on comradeship, but additionally all ranks

were encouraged to 'better themselves', and to this end a library and regimental school were established. The emphasis was also on fitness and health with the encouragement of games, swimming, sports and dancing. Regimental medals for good conduct, long service, and bravery, were also instituted, and above all, musketry and marksmanship skills were pre-eminent.

In 1803, it was placed among the numbered regiments of the line, and became the 95th or 'Rifle Regiment' until in 1816 it was restyled, by order of Wellington himself, in honour of its performance, 'The Rifle Brigade'.

A recruitment poster issued in 1808 is shown opposite. The layout, punctuation, and use of capitals and the varying type print characteristics are the pamphlet's original, not mine, but who could resist such an appeal? Not many budding soldiers it would seem as the recruiting campaign was apparently very successful and by May 1809 the strength of the 1st battalion was 1,536, and the 2nd battalion 1,579, so a third battalion was formed.

Perhaps, as the following anecdote indicates, the reality of life in the regiment was a little different from that expounded in the poster. I refer to an episode during the Indian Mutiny, when, on 13th June 1858, at Nawabgunge, the 3rd Battalion of the Rifle Brigade, exhausted from having endured days of forced marches in blinding sun and intense heat, and with little or no food, were rushed into action:

As they were becoming overwhelmed by a larger enemy force Quartermaster Harvey galloped over to Hodson's Horse to beg for help. In vain did the officers of Hodson's Horse order their men to advance on the enemy. Seeing there was no help forthcoming Harvey then galloped over to Sir William Russell commanding 7th Hussars* and explained that the Riflemen must be overpowered unless aid came. 'We'll soon clear them', said Russell, and the Hussars accompanied by the officers of Hodson's Horse charged cutting up the regiment with green banners as they fled. During this action, Pioneer Samuel Shaw, 3rd. Bn. Rifle Brigade won the VC.

*For me, there is an interesting family connection between the 3rd Battalion of the Rifle Brigade, which one of my four soldier relatives joined in August 1914, and the cavalry regiment 7th Hussars, in which, as I have mentioned above, Haig and my paternal grandfather, Edward Holley (brother of Robert quoted above), both served, at the same time.

RIFLE CORPS!
COUNTRYMEN!

LOOK, BEFORE YOU LEAP:

Half the Regiments in the Service are trying to persuade you to enlist;

But there is ONE MORE to COME YET!!!

The 95th; or Rifle REGIMENT,
COMMANDED BY THE HONOURABLE
Major-General Coote Manningham,
The only Regiment of RIFLEMEN in the Service:

THINK, then, and CHOOSE, Whether you will enter into a
Battalion Regiment, Or prefer being a RIFLEMAN,

The First of all Services in the British Army

In this distinguished service, you will carry a Rifle no heavier than a Fowling Piece.
You will knock down Your Enemy at Five Hundred Yards, instead of missing him at
Fifty. Your clothing is GREEN; and needs no Cleaning but a Brush. Those Men who
have been in a Rifle Company, can best tell you the comfort of a GREEN JACKET.

NO WHITE BELTS! NO PIPE CLAY!

On Service, your Post is always the POST OF HONOUR, and your Quarters the best
in the Army For you have the first of every thing; and at Home you are sure of
Respect – because a BRITISH RIFLEMAN always makes himself Respectable.

The RIFLE SERGEANTS are to be found any where, and have orders to
Treat their Friends gallantly every where.
If you enlist, and afterwards you wish you had been a RIFLEMAN, do not
say were not asked, for you can BLAME NOBODY BUT YOURSELF.

GOD SAVE the KING! And his rifle Regiment!

HULL, January 11th, 1808.

137

Unfortunately, the original concept of the officer/men relationship in the Rifle Brigade seemed to deteriorate in the later Victorian years, and became more like that in the rest of the army.

In 1966, following another period of army re-organisation, the Rifle Brigade really ceased to exist as it became part of the Green Jackets, a regiment formed by an amalgamation of the Ox and Bucks Light Infantry (1st Bn. Green Jackets), The King's Royal Rifle Corps (2nd Bn. Green Jackets), and The Rifle Brigade (3rd Bn. Green Jackets).

The Kent Cyclist Battalion (TF)

The Kent Cyclist Battalion, formed in 1908, was one of ten original territorial cyclists battalions in the country. Their main role, in the event of war, was to patrol the coastline. In line with existing territorial formations the battalion was composed of eight companies, and it was one of fifteen units of the Territorial Force administered by the Kent County Association, headed by the Lord Lieutenant of the County.

The battalion was drawn mainly from members of the numerous detachments of the volunteer battalions in Kent – including a substantial contingent from the old 'Cyclist Section', founded in 1888, of The East Kent Regiment, 'The Buffs'.*

*Apropos of the well-known expression 'Steady the Buffs', I regret to say that until my father told me that it was not so, I had wrongly assumed that this was originally a command for 'The Buffs' to stand firm in the line of battle. But, as probably almost everyone else is aware, it referred to the precedence and seniority of the regiments of foot: 'Steady the Buffs. Halt the Queen's. Let the Royals go by'.

'The Royals' (The Royal Scots, the First of Foot), are the senior infantry regiment in the British army, and, because of their seniority, also referred to as Pontius Pilate's Bodyguard. 'The Queen's' – or Royal West Surreys, were the second, and 'The Buffs', The East Kents, the third in seniority.

For the first few months of its existence the Kent cyclist battalion was designated as the 6th (Cyclist) Battalion, Royal West Kent Regiment, but it was felt this inhibited recruitment in East Kent, and so the battalion was quickly re-designated 'The Kent Cyclist Battalion' and on 1st March 1909, it was recognised by the Army Council as a separate unit independent of both the West and East Kent Regiments.

Recruitment poster of early 1914 (pre-war).

KENT CYCLIST BATTALION	'G' COMPANY RAMSGATE and DISTRICT.

RECRUITS WANTED.

HEIGHT: 5ft. 2in. **AGE 17:** 17 to 35 years on enlistment

TERMS OF ENLISTMENT: 4 years. When a man leaves the District or County arrangements can be made to transfer to another unit, or (where necessary) for discharge. No penalties are enforced on any man who tries to be a good soldier, but has, by force of circumstances, to leave.

ANNUAL CAMP: 15 days, with pay according to rank.

WEEK-END CAMPS AND TOURS:- Held at certain periods of the year, for which pay and allowances are granted.

UNIFORM: Two complete suits are issued to a recruit – a Walking Out Dress (blue), and a service Dress (Khaki).

PAY: Pay and allowances when in Camp and Special Training for all N.C.O.'s and Men, as per Regular Army (Infantry) Scale, according to rank.

SPECIAL ALLOWANCES: A grant is made of £1 10s. 6d. per annum for the use of cycle, providing the Man attends the full period of Annual Training. 8/- per diem is allowed for the use of a motor cycle.

WORK OF A CYCLIST: Coast Defence Work, Sketching, Road Reporting, Scouting, Dispatch Carrying, Signalling, Machine Gun Work, Rifle Shooting, Infantry Drill, etc. (The work is always interesting).

'The Kent Cyclist Gazette, published quarterly, chronicles the doings of the Battalion.

===

'The Kent cyclist Battalion was raised when the Territorial Force came into being in 1908. The Establishment is 520 all ranks and every man is mounted on cycle or motor. There are Companies at Bromley, Maidstone, Chatham, Folkestone, Tonbridge, Tunbridge Wells, Canterbury, Ashford, and Ramsgate. The Battalion is classed in the Army List as 'ARMY TROOPS,' and a high standard of discipline and efficiency is expected of all ranks.

'Army Manoeuvres, 1913. – The training of the Battalion for 1913, was carried out with the Regular Army on Manoeuvres, and gained excellent reports for its work from Officers of high rank.

'Extract from 'Daily Telegraph,' September 20th, 1913, from 'Our Special Correspondent' on Manoeuvres:

'Colonel Gordon, Chief Staff Officer to the 2nd Division, told me that the Detachment of Cyclist Territorials from Kent have done excellent work during the past few days. They have carried out the somewhat difficult tasks allotted to them with great efficiency, and have proved themselves worthy of the honour of being brigaded with regulars'.

'Young men of Ramsgate and District who are cyclists should consider it an honour to join the Battalion that can earn for itself such words of praise for work done when brigaded with Regular troops.

===

'Applications may be made through any N.C.O. or Man of the Company, or at this Drill Hall, Willson's Road Ramsgate, from the Colour-Sergeant Instructor. The fullest information will willingly be given.

GOD SAVE THE KING.

The Kent Cyclist Battalion was disbanded in September 1922, and the regimental colours are housed, together with the colours of the Queen's Own Royal West Kent Regiment, in All Saints Church, Maidstone. The Colours of the Old Comrades Association were laid up in Canterbury Cathedral in 1979.

7th Queen's Own Hussars

As this narrative started out as a result of family notes and, as I have said, Douglas Haig as well as my grandfather, Edward Holley, served in 7th Hussars at the same time, this a good enough excuse to bring in a little about their regiment.

The regiment dates back to 1685 as The Queen Consort's Regiment of Dragoons. Later, at the time of the accession of George II, The 3rd and 7th Dragoons were renamed 'The Queen's Own Regiment of Dragoons.'*

*I understand that a dragoon was originally intended to be a mounted infantryman and had to be prepared to fight on foot. Dragoons were armed with both musket and sword and rode horses 15 to 15.2 hands in height.

In July 1751, under a warrant from George II, the regiment became the 7th Queen's Own Dragoons, and in 1783 the regiment was converted to light cavalry. A further change of title and dress to 'Hussars' occurred in 1807.*

*Hussar was originally the name of the Hungarian cavalry raised by King Mathias the First in 1458. The name apparently derived from the Hungarian word for 20, as every twentieth household was required to furnish a man for the corps. The term was later used for light cavalry used largely for reconnaissance, or where speed was of the essence. The title was adopted in the early years of the 19th century by a number of British army light dragoons.

PART EIGHTEEN

...I have served alongside a large number of regiments – Guards and Line, Regular and Territorial – over thirty years. They each had their individual character, but all had one characteristic in common. This is the enduring doggedness of the British Infantryman, especially in the face of adversity, and this runs as another thread throughout this History.

Charles Messenger in the introduction to the first volume
of his *History of British Infantry.*

The divisions and regiments at the outbreak of the war

The peace-time distribution of units in August 1914 directly affected their fortunes in the early days of the Great War.

4th Division

Commanded by Major General Snow, until September when he was invalided home and replaced by Major-Gen. Sir Henry Rawlinson (who was then promoted in October, to command the 4th Army Corps) the division consisted of three brigades: 10th Brigade, 11th Brigade and 12th Brigade.

11th Brigade

The 11th Brigade, commanded by Brigadier General A.G. Hunter-Weston (see below – 'Somme'), consisted of four battalions: 1st Battalion Somerset Light Infantry, 1st Battalion East Lancashire

Regiment, 1st Battalion The Hampshire Regiment, and 1st Battalion The Rifle Brigade. Also in the 11th Brigade were units of divisional cavalry, royal engineers, royal artillery, RAMC field ambulances, and lines of communication and army troops – and among the latter were the 1st Battalion, Devonshire Regiment, later transferred to the 8th Brigade, and then to the 14th Brigade (see below, 5th Division).

1st Battalion, The Rifle Brigade

One of the twelve infantry units of the 4th Division, the 1st Rifles were in barracks at Colchester, and destined for a spell of overseas service in the coming September. Instead, the battalion found itself encamped on the playing fields of Harrow school on 18th August, and then, embarking aboard the SS *Cestrian* and arriving at Le Havre in the early hours of 23rd August, finally marched to the No. 3 Rest Camp. The strength of the battalion on arrival was 24 officers, 1 WO, 49 sergeants, 43 corporals, 16 buglers and 848 riflemen; a total of 981.

5th Division

This division, commanded by Major-General Sir Charles Fergusson (invalided on 22nd October and replaced by Major-General Morland) consisted of 13th Infantry Brigade, 14th Infantry Brigade, 15th Infantry Brigade, and 19th Infantry Brigade. There were, in addition, units of divisional cavalry, royal engineers, royal artillery, RAMC field ambulances, and Royal Flying Corps.

5th Division, 14th Brigade

As part of 14th Brigade, the 1st Battalion, The Duke of Cornwall's Light Infantry was stationed in Curragh, Ireland. The battalion moved to Dublin by train, and embarked aboard SS *Lanfranc*. They disembarked at Le Havre on 15th August 1914. The 1st Devonshires, after being split up on their arrival in August (see below), and then attached to Third Division, joined the 14th Brigade on 29th September.

142

6th Division

Commanded by Major-General J.L. Keir, the division comprised the 16th Infantry Brigade, 17th Infantry Brigade, and 18th Infantry Brigade, plus units of divisional cavalry, royal engineers, royal artillery, and RAMC field ambulances.

17th Infantry Brigade

3rd Battalion, The Rifle Brigade, as part of the 17th Brigade, were stationed in Cork, in Ireland. They sailed aboard SS *Patriotic*, and disembarked on 18th August 1914 at Holyhead. Next, they travelled to Cambridge where they arrived the following day and stayed in camp until moving to Newmarket on 31st August.

Travelling to Southampton on 7th September, they embarked aboard SS *Lake Michigan* on the 8th, but they did not disembark (at St Nazaire) until 12th September. The delay was caused by inadequate docking facilities and this was unfortunate, as the troops were urgently needed for the Battle of the Aisne. They entrained quickly for Coulommiers, arriving early on 14th, and marched nine miles to St Ouen, and billeted.

On arrival in France the battalion strength was 26 officers, 1 WO, 49 sergeants, 43 corporals, 16 buglers and 867 riflemen.

8th Division

The division, commanded by Major-General F.J. Davies, reached France on 6th November, and the concentration of the division was completed by 12th November.

This regular division was composed of the 23rd Brigade, 24th Brigade and 25th Brigade, plus units of the Royal Artillery. It also had non-regular units: three squadrons of the Northamptonshire Yeomanry, The Wessex TF Field Ambulance Unit, and a TF signals company.

Although composed of regular infantry battalions, there was a difference between the 8th and the other, and earlier arrived, regular divisions in France. The infantry battalions of the 8th Division had been gathered together hastily at the outbreak of war from different overseas garrisons. This meant that unlike the units in the other regular divisions, the brigades and battalions – and of course the

143

TF and yeomanry troops – had never worked together before. They were strangers to one another.

Despite its unfailing gallantry (the division suffered nearly 64,000 casualties and won 12 VCs), the 8th Division was signally unfortunate in its lack of success in the major offensives in which it took part (see also below).

8th Division, 23rd Brigade

The 2nd Battalion The Devonshire Regiment was in Cairo in August 1914, and on 13th September embarked aboard the SS *Osmanieh* and arrived in England on 1st October. At 2.30 am on 5th November, in torrential rain and through a sea of mud, the battalion moved out of the camp at Hursley Park near Winchester, to Southampton, in order to join the 23rd Brigade of the 8th Division, and embarked aboard SS *Bellerophon*.

On arrival in France the battalion strength was 29 officers and 983 other ranks. They spent two days in a rest camp, but before the division had completed its concentration, the battalion, together with the 2nd West Yorkshires, was ordered to proceed to Neuve Eglise and report to the Cavalry Corps.

25th Brigade

The 2nd Battalion, The Rifle Brigade was encamped at Kuldana, in the Murree Hills in India, at the closing of a seventeen-year period of foreign service. This service had included both the Sudan and the South Africa campaigns, and the battalion was due to return to England on 29th October. Instead, leaving Kuldana, the battalion arrived at Bombay to embark aboard the SS *Somali*, and sailed for England on 20th September 1914. They landed at Liverpool on 22nd October, where they entrained for Winchester, and arrived there on 23rd to camp at Hursley Park, to join the 25th Brigade.

On 5th November they took ship again aboard the SS *Victorian* and arrived at Le Havre on 7th November, and marched to No. 1 Rest Camp. On 14th they went into the trenches as brigade reserve at La Flinque, 1 mile south of Laventie.

The battalion's strength on arrival in France was 28 officers, 1 WO, 51 sergeants, 40 corporals, 16 buglers, and 881 riflemen.

27th Division

This division, like the 8th, also arrived on the scene in France in November, and two of its three brigades (80th, 81st, and 82nd Brigades) contained 'my' battalions.

82nd Brigade

2nd Battalion, Duke of Cornwall's Light Infantry. At the outbreak of war the battalion was in Hong Kong, and engaged in rounding up German residents who were then interned. The battalion arrived in England, at Devonport, in early November 1914, with a strength recorded as 21 officers and 881 other ranks. It then formed up as part of the 82nd Brigade, and arrived at Le Havre on 21st December 1914. The battalion entrained for Arques, and from there marched to Wardrecques, and billeted in two factories.

80th Brigade

4th Battalion, The Rifle Brigade, having completed ten years of its tour of foreign service, was at Dagshai, near the northern frontier of India, when war was declared. They sailed from Bombay in mid October, and arrived at Devonport about 18th November. By 23rd December 1914, they became part of the 80th Brigade.

The battalion strength was 27 officers, 1 WO, 50 sergeants, 42 corporals, 16 buglers and 822 riflemen. On arrival in France, on 27th December, they were billeted near St Omar, and began work on a reserve trench system around Blaringhem and Steenbecque.

An unusual unit in the 80th Brigade – which, in addition to the 4th Rifles, included 2nd King's Shropshire Light Infantry, 3rd and 4th King's Royal Rifle Corps – was one of the first, if not *the* first Canadian battalion to arrive in Europe, the 1st Battalion of Princess Patricia's Canadian Light Infantry. Not only was this Canadian battalion early on the scene, but it was, as I have said above, a unique formation.

61st (South Midland) Division

This was a second line territorial division, and my interest in it is because its pioneer battalion was 1/5th Bn. Duke of Cornwall's Light Infantry (TF).

On 4th August 1914 the battalion was at Bodmin, and then moved to Falmouth where it became part of the Devon and Cornwall Brigade, Wessex Division. After moving to Salisbury Plain at the end of August the volunteers for foreign service were posted to the 1/4th Battalion. As the 1/5th Battalion was now under strength it was replaced in the Wessex Division by 1/6th Devons.

In April 1916, having become a pioneer battalion, the 1/5th DCLI landed in France at Le Havre on 22nd May 1916. As a pioneer battalion, the 1/5th, apart from one occasion, never belonged to a brigade in France, but directly to a division (see definition of 'Pioneers').

Notes on my battalions

The Duke of Cornwall's Light Infantry

Although The Duke of Cornwall's Light Infantry was the first of the regiments to arrive in France in 1914, the 1/5th Battalion was actually was the last of my three units to reach the Western Front, and the last of the four to go overseas.

The Rifle Brigade

At the outbreak of war in 1914 the four regular battalions* of the Rifle Brigade were, in accordance with the routine of the Cardwell System, equally distributed between the United Kingdom and Foreign Stations.

As part of the 80th Brigade the 4th Rifles would be sent to Salonika in 1915 (see below, and Robertson's comments on this theatre of war) and they ended the war at Rabrovo with the rest of their Brigade – except for the Canadians, who had been transferred, but this was still in the future.

*The Rifle Brigade's 'Special Reserve Battalions', the Fifth and Sixth, were cadre formations for the supply of reinforcements in time of war. In 1914 both were in their stations on the Isle of Sheppey in the Thames Estuary where, for the next four years, they trained recruits and found drafts to fill the ranks of the four Regular and eight Service Battalions of the Regiment.

The Devonshire Regiment

The 1st Battalion landed at Le Havre on 22nd August 1914 from the SS *Reindeer* and was the second of my regiments to arrive in France. They marched at 4.30 am to No. 1 Rest Camp, and here the battalion was divided, and placed on line communication work, with each company going to a different location. The battalion strength arriving in France was 29 officers and 983 other ranks.

The Companies did not link up again until 11th September 1914. On 14th September they were pushed forward to reinforce the 8th Brigade of General Hubert Hamilton's 3rd Division. When they were relieved on 26th September they had suffered over 100 casualties, and on 29th September, they were transferred to 14th Brigade, 5th Division, to replace the 2nd Suffolks who had been almost annihilated at Le Cateau.

8th (Service) Battalion

This is the Devonshire's battalion I am following in most detail. It was formed on 7th August 1914 as a 'K1' battalion, with the nucleus provided by the officers and NCOs detached from the 1st Battalion, together with Captain Holland, and Lieut. Kekewich, who at the time were then at the depôt. (Kekewich would be killed at Loos – see below.)

As there was no regular major available, an officer was brought in from outside to command the 8th Battalion. He was Lieut. Colonel Grant, of the West African Regiment. He was gazetted on 19th August, and his second in command was Major Carden, DSO, a retired officer of the Devonshire Regiment. There was a shortage of subalterns, but at last they appeared; six came from Oxford University, three from Cambridge University, three from the Artists Rifles (see Wilfred Owen for further comments on this unit), the rest straight from public schools.

A number of recruits came in quickly, including old soldiers who had served their time with the reserve and had now volunteered to rejoin their regiment. After a short stay at Exeter the 8th Battalion left its native city for Aldershot, and in the middle of September it was moved to Rushmore Camp, at Aldershot, as part of 14th Division. In November 1914 it moved to Barossa Barracks at Aldershot, and then in December to billets in villages south of Farnham.

The Kent Cyclist Battalion

The battalion paraded regularly for instruction and drill and attended camp for a fortnight in the summer of each year. It was in camp at Broadstairs when war was declared on 4th August 1914, and it immediately mobilised and began its planned role by patrolling the coast of Kent.

Battalion headquarters were established at Canterbury, and stations were set up at rough intervals of six miles around the coast of Kent, from the mouth of the Thames, to Jury's Gap on the marshes near Rye, on the border with Sussex.

PART NINETEEN

Over the last half century these Generals have come to be regarded by the public at large as a group of aristrocratic, incompetent, callous cavalry officers, who spent the war in châteaux well behind the lines and sped millions of brave young men 'up the line to death', causing a loss from which the British nation has never fully recovered.

Robin Neillands, *The Great War Generals on the Western Front.*

The main British army commanders involved with the Western Front during 1914–1918

Field Marshal Horatio Herbert Kitchener (1850–1916)

First Earl Kitchener of Khartoum. Known as 'K of K', or 'The Hero of Khartoum', Kitchener was immensely popular with the public, but less so in government and military circles. Commissioned into the Royal Engineers, he had served as an intelligence officer behind the Dervish Lines in 1884. Later he achieved success in the Sudan campaigns of 1898–9, but he did not do so well as Commander in Chief in the later stages of the Boer War. Now, in 1914, he regarded the purpose of the BEF with misgivings, and its Commander in Chief with less than admiration.

On Christmas Day in 1914, a visitor found Kitchener as usual in his large room at the War Office. The room was hot, and the air sluggish, as two large fires blazed, one at each end of the room. When a visitor arrived and commented on the appalling state of the atmosphere, Kitchener said, with a shiver: 'Very likely, but I have not spent a Christmas in England for forty years.' He was a stranger to England.

As I have said above, like Admiral Fisher, Kitchener did not believe the BEF's six divisions (in the region of 100,000 troops) would be likely to have much effect in the impending clash between France and Germany; each of whom was able to field up to seventy divisions when mobilisation was completed, and reserves brought in (Churchill puts the German figure much higher than this).

Kitchener believed the regular army, with its professional officers, and especially NCOs, to be too precious and indispensable as a nucleus for training the larger force he had in mind. He thought it criminal folly to throw the army away in immediate battle under what he expected to be unfavourable circumstances. His was almost a lone voice in saying the war would not be a short sharp bloody engagement, but would go on for years, and Britain needed to develop a massive army, together with the resources to look after it. This would require an immense national effort, he said.

Professor Barbara W. Tuckman (*The Guns of August*) says of Kitchener:

> Standing at a distance he was able to view the war as a whole, in terms of the relations of the powers and to realize the immense effort of national military expansion that would be required for the long contest to begin.

Like most senior officers, and the nation in general, he was against conscription. In addition he disliked the concept of the Territorial Army, and had little time for it. He believed in the need for a massive force of civilian volunteers to come forward for training and service to form a 'New Army'. 'We must be prepared,' he said, 'to put armies of millions in the field and maintain them for several years.'

In principle he generally, but with reservations, recognised the need for concentration of the military force on the Western Front. He loyally supported the tactical policies of French and Haig, but his reputation suffered from the Dardanelles campaign. He offered to resign in 1916, but this was refused. The government wished to remove him from the scene however, and was pleased to send him to head a mission to Russia to meet the Tsar, to show support for the Russians, and to discuss the progress of the war generally.

On Saturday 4th June, after having had lunch with the King to discuss his impending trip to Russia, Kitchener and a party of eleven took the train for Thurso and Scapa Flow where they were to embark for Archangel. The following day, after lunching with Sir John Jellicoe aboard the flagship *Iron Duke*, he went across to the cruiser *Hampshire* which was to take him and his party to Archangel. The weather was atrocious, and with a worsening north-easterly gale Jellicoe suggested delaying the departure until the weather abated, but Kitchener, who prided himself on being an excellent sailor, declined the offer, and at 5 pm the *Hampshire* sailed with an escort of two destroyers. By 7 pm the weather had become so bad that the captain of the *Hampshire* detached the destroyer escort and proceeded alone.

Exactly one week earlier, the commander of the German submarine *U75*, Lt. Commander Kurt Beitzen, on his way to the battle of Jutland, had laid a few mines as he passed Marwick Head in the Orkneys. At 7.40 in the evening of 5th June, forty minutes after the departure of the escorting destroyers, the *Hampshire* struck one of the mines, heeled over to starboard, and sank within fifteen minutes. Neither Lord Kitchener, nor any member of his party, was seen alive again. Twelve survivors made it ashore on a raft, and seventy-five bodies were washed ashore, one of them a member of Kitchener's staff, Lt. Col. Fitzgerald.

Peter Liddle in his *Testimony of War 1914–1918* shows photographs of the written pages of a diary kept by a young girl who worked in her father's photographic shop in Kirkwell, in the Orkney Isles. She writes a moving account of those sad days in 1916 when the news of Jutland broke locally, and she reflects the esteem in which Kitchener was held in the public's eye and expresses the popular sentiments regarding him:

Saturday June 3rd [1916]. Rumours were afloat that a naval engagement was going on on Wednesday 31st May, but I could not believe it true. Last night Jim and I worked until 11 pm putting new glass in a large picture for one of our fleet men on the *Bellerophon* when Maggie came in and told us a battle had really taken place [Jutland] and 10 of our ships were sunk. After that I could do no more work for thinking of all our men who had pictures in to be framed and who poor souls might never come back. Such a lot of fleet men [The Grand Fleet based Scapa Flow] come in with pictures to be framed. I kept hoping all night the sad news might prove untrue so

151

this morning one of the men of the *Royal Oak*, one of the ships in action, came in with some pictures to get framed and told me it was too true. They can't tell very much so he said 'It's all very sad and that's all I can tell you'. We had heard the *Marlborough* was sunk but he said she would come back all right in a little while. Poor chap he was so hurt because he could not get word to his friends of his safety. All day on Saturday the Territorials were burying the dead in Longhope – so we were told. What a gloom was cast over the town, and how depressed we all were to think of our noble ships and brave sailors and officers going down that summer night on the North Sea or off the coast of Jutland.

Wednesday night: Just as I was preparing for bed last night word came by wireless that a cruiser was blown up off Mawick Head. A wild storm was raging so I could not sleep for thinking of the poor souls struggling in the water, and such a wild coast that no help could reach them in such a storm. This morning we heard it was the *Hampshire* and later we heard that it was Lord Kitchener and all his staff were on board. I kept hoping such a calamity would prove to be untrue.

Thursday. Alas it is too true and every soul on board perished except 10. Willie was up at [writing unclear] today looking for the bodies who might be washed ashore. This seems to be a black week in the history of the Empire.

Sunday. 11th There's a memorial service in the cathedral tonight for Lord Kitchener. His loss is the greatest calamity the nation has got since the war began. The weather keeps cold, not like June.

Lord Beaverbrook writing of Kitchener says:

The people did not reason about Kitchener, they just trusted, and that mere trust was a priceless asset in days when life was being torn up by the roots and the firmest mind might well fall into doubt or fear. Men simply said: 'Kitchener is there; it is all right.'

...It was the personality of Lord Kitchener which gave him the immense prestige which compelled the government to employ him at any cost. All this immense reputation was partly substance and partly of that longer shadow which concrete objects cast in the rays of the setting sun. Lord Kitchener was a great and obscure figure. He had always been successful in everything he had undertaken in distant lands... [He] was the best-advertised man in the Empire, because he refused to advertise; he had found a royal road by which the Press was compelled to talk about him, if only in sheer annoyance at his silence. And something of the mystery and fatalism of the East was added to the hard practicality of his mind.

He was a shy man, frightened of the politicians, and ill at ease with nearly all of them. He had the soldier's professional and professed distrust of the class – and only Grey and Asquith surmounted the prejudice... He added to the soldier's inability to explain that curse of nervousness which prevents a man from speaking at the moment when he should and must speak if he is to prevail in council.

Lloyd George once said to me [of Kitchener] he was like a great revolving lighthouse. Sometimes the beam of his mind used to shoot out, showing one Europe and the assembled armies in a vast and illimitable perspective, till one felt that one was looking along it into the heart of reality – and then the shutter would turn and for weeks there would be nothing but a blank darkness.

On February 9th 1916 Kitchener paid his last visit to Haig's headquarters, and Brig. General Charteris describes the meeting and the two men as follows:

To Haig the essential method of arriving at a decision was complete knowledge and study of all the factors, and then a considered and most firmly held judgement. A decision arrived at by a conscious mental process of this nature is not easily disturbed by any man; in Haig the strongly developed self-confidence emphasised the tendency. He would willingly consider any new factor and amend, if necessary, his judgement to meet it; but unless there was a new factor he was not ready to re-open consideration of a problem on which he had arrived at a conclusion. Mere 'opinions' weighed little with him. He required logical reasoning.

In temperament and characteristic they [Kitchener and Haig] were totally distinct. To Haig's reasoned arguments Kitchener had nothing to offer except unconscious mental processes, arriving with amazing frequency at correct conclusions. With Haig it was logic, with Kitchener instinct or genius... Haig had mastered every detail of military affairs; Kitchener had surprisingly little knowledge of detail.

Kitchener had wide interests outside military matters – art, science politics, literature claimed their share of his mind; Haig's whole mind and life were concentrated on the army and on the war... Both soldiers had inflexible wills, both had great self-confidence; each vied with the other in supreme devotion to duty. Neither made many intimate friends – yet both had the power of gaining loyal service and devoted attachment from those who worked closest to them.

Kitchener was given a funeral ceremony with full military honours and amid much public grief, but it would seem there was less grief in political and military circles.

Field Marshal Viscount French of Ypres (1852–1925)

French was one of the few 1914 commanders to have come out of the Boer War with an enhanced reputation. There he was remembered for his dash and vigour, and perhaps this was unfortunate when he was appointed Commander of the BEF, as it might well have been part of the reason for the restrictions and difficulties Kitchener imposed upon him regarding the use of the British Expeditionary Force in France in 1914.

Kitchener apparently did not trust French's judgement, and he wished to keep the small regular British Army as intact as possible, and feared to see the force wasted by French's potential impetuosity. Kitchener's written restrictions and caveats in turn could have accentuated the way French acted – at times alternating between excessive caution and overconfidence.

French, an Ulsterman, was sixty-two years of age in 1914. Unusually he had begun his service career in the Royal Navy, but suffering from sea-sickness he switched to the army and was gazetted into the 8th Hussars. He was not a rich man, but enjoyed society life, and this led him into debt. On one occasion Sir Douglas Haig bailed him out by loaning him £2,000 – a large sum in those days.

He was the archetypal cavalry general and one who, in the early days of 1914 at any rate, still really believed that the cavalry had a powerful part to play in modern warfare. He was very much against the cavalry being used as mounted infantry, an idea that had gained many adherents, including Smith Dorrien and which the Boers had put to such good effect in South Africa.

In his own account of the first year of the war, *1914* (published in 1919), wherever possible he extols the exploits of the cavalry and denigrates the II Corps Commander's actions. For example, when talking about Smith Dorrien's II Corps he writes:

> The superb gallantry of the troops, and the skilful leading by Divisional and Brigade and Battalion Commanders,* helped very materially by the support given by Allenby [at that time Commander of the Cavalry Division], and Sordet [The French cavalry leader whose men were loaned to help, see below] saved the II Corps, which otherwise would have been pinned to their ground and surrounded. The cavalry might have made good their retreat but three out of the five Divisons with the 7th Brigade must have been lost.

*No mention of the Corps Commander, Smith Dorrien, the only one not to get a word of praise, whose actions, it is generally accepted, saved the day.

It is ironic that while always stressing the value of the cavalry in 1914, later, whether he realises it or not, he has to support the use of mounted infantry tactics by the cavalry, as when he describes an action between German and British cavalry. He writes:

> A Squadron of 18th Hussars, under Major Leveson, took up a position by this line of trees, *dismounting* [my italics] in the corn storks, and was immediately charged by a German squadron [cavalry] in perfect order, in line at close order. The 18th Hussars met the charge with well-directed fire at close range, and the German squadron was almost annihilated. A few passed through the firing line and were shot by the horse holders. A second charge was attempted shortly afterwards, but did not approach closer than 400 yards.

155

Accounts of French say that he was an excitable man, and given to outbursts of temper. Unlike Kitchener, who was tall, broad shouldered and inscrutable behind his solemn blazing eyes and 'walrus' moustache, French was short, stocky, florid, and usually looked on the point of apoplexy – particularly when wearing his cavalryman's stock in place of a tie. It is said he swung between extremes of pessimism and optimism during his leadership, and he bore grudges. In 1914 he certainly did not like his immediate French neighbour, General Lanrezac, commander of the French Fifth Army and with whom he needed to work closely, and this dislike was reciprocated. It was doubly unfortunate that neither spoke the other's language.

In the same way as had his French counterpart General Joffre, Sir John French had been named head of the staff without staff experience, or study at staff college. He was pitched into a position for which he was not equipped, although in the field he had shown himself to be a man of courage and resource.

French had important social contacts, and was allied to the Liberal governing party. At 62 he was two years Kitchener's junior, although he looked older. It was said that he had the mercurial temperament associated with Irishmen and cavalry officers. His dislike of Smith Dorrien, the II Corps Commander, was intense and long standing, as I mentioned, and he is generally accepted to have traduced Smith Dorrien when he demanded his recall in 1915.

Winston Churchill, who had got to know French well over the years, had a high regard for him, and says in *Great Contemporaries*:

> French was a natural soldier. Although he had not the intellectual capacity of Haig, nor perhaps his underlying endurance, he had a deeper military insight. He was not equal to Haig in precision of detail; but he had more imagination, and he would never have run the British Army into the same long drawn-out slaughters.

Churchill of course was not a pronounced 'pro-Westerner' like Haig and Robertson, he was generally in favour of what became known as the 'indirect approach' hence the Dardenelles, Salonika, Egypt etc., campaigns – much detested by the 'Westerners' (see below). French himself says that as trench fighting developed (by the end of 1914):

I began dimly to apprehend what the future might have in store for us ... it required the further and more bitter lessons of my failure in the north in the last days of October to bring home to my mind a principle in warfare of today which I have held ever since, namely that *given forces fairly equally matched, you can bend, but you cannot break your enemy's trench line.* [My italics]

To catch a glimpse of the then Commander in Chief of the BEF, by an observant and trained eye, W.L. Andrews (mentioned elsewhere), recalls an occasion in 1915, when his unit, 1/4th Black Watch, was visited and addressed by Sir John following their introduction to battle at Neuve Chapelle:

We were keen to see the commander upon whose shoulders so historic a burden rested. Having seen many celebrities in my reporting days [he was a news editor on the morning paper *Dundee Advertiser* before joining up in August 1914], I did not expect much; famous men are usually disappointing. French no doubt was a great soldier, but we could not expect him to show it in a speech. All the same, he made an excellent impression. He was as we expected, a heavy, bowed, squat-shouldered man of the cavalry type, but we were not prepared for his exceedingly incisive way of rattling off a speech, a few phrases at a time.

Field Marshal Sir Douglas Haig, 1st Earl Haig of Bemersyde (1861–1928)

Haig was another cavalryman – commissioned into 7th Hussars* and 17th Lancers – and the most written about British military figure of those times. He has been castigated by a number of authors – particularly Australian and Canadian sources, and writers using these sources as the basis of their main criticisms.

*As I mentioned in Part Seventeen, as matter of family history, my paternal grandfather served as a private soldier in the 7th Hussars at the same time as Haig who, as adjutant, signed my grandfather's discharge papers. And should I be reproved for using the rank 'private' instead of 'trooper' the lowest rank in this cavalry regiment then – and this was in the latter part of the nineteenth century – was still called a 'private'. It was not until the early 1920s that the rank generally became a 'trooper' in all the cavalry regiments.

Haig was the son of a wealthy Edinburgh distiller, and, according to Charteris, the death of his father in 1878 left no great blank in Douglas Haig's life. His mother was a far greater influence. Sadly she died while he was still in his teens, and his older sister, Henrietta, then played a large part in moulding his character. Throughout the whole of Haig's life there existed between them a strong bond of affection and comradeship.

After prep school he was destined for Rugby but he didn't achieve the necessary entry standard, and eventually he was sent to Clifton. In 1880 he entered Brasenose College, Oxford, where he appears to have distinguished himself at polo but little else, and his academic studies held no interest for him.

His sister Henrietta steered him in the direction of the army as a career, although he would seem to have been lukewarm about the idea. Once at Sandhurst he found his vocation quickly, and when he left he was first in order of merit, and with the Anson Memorial Sword, as Senior Under Officer, and with a high athletic record.

He left Sandhurst as he entered, without any close friendship for any of his contemporaries, but while there he began a pattern, which he followed when he commanded the BEF, of rigidly apportioning his time to a fixed timetable, including his leisure hours.

There is a common criticism of Haig that he sat and failed the entrance examination to the Staff College. The conclusion to be inferred from this is that he was 'not very bright', especially taken in conjunction with his failure to pass the entrance examination to Rugby, and leaving university without taking a degree. Charteris, in his biography of Haig, says that Haig sat the examination to the Staff College, but was failed in the medical examination. Apparently Haig, like one in ten of the male population, suffered from a degree of colour blindness – but there is no mention of academic failure.

In 1896, thanks to the good offices of the Duke of Cambridge, Sir Evelyn Wood and General Fraser – and following the introduction of a new cavalry drill manual which he had written in conjunction with Sir John French – Haig was nominated for, and accepted into, the Staff College, despite his failure in the medical earlier.

He is reported to have shown little interest in women, but when the time came, and after a very brief courtship, he married well, and as a result gained entry to Court circles; and this did his career no harm. He had served as an advisor to Haldane, and was designated to take command of the 1st Corps of the BEF under Sir John French's overall command. A degree of animosity existed between French and Haig, and this increased as the war progressed, although they had apparently got on well together in South Africa during the Boer War.

Haig, it is also said, was critical of Sir John French's leadership; he distrusted his military knowledge and flinched from his uncertain temper, and didn't care much for his personal character. They tended to avoid each other. Haig, who was 53 when the war began, did not have the gift of self-expression in public, but he confided a lot in his diaries, and although I have not been able to read them, other than quoted extracts, his diary comments apparently do not always match his more public statements.

When Robertson became CIGS (Chief Imperial General Staff) he and Haig, although not close, had much the same ideas on the conduct of the war in as much as they both believed the outcome could only be determined on the Western Front. They were both against the 'easterners' and any 'side shows'.

Haig was always impeccably dressed, dour, noticeably taciturn, and much given to long and heavy silences that were sometimes interpreted as rudeness. He was steady, careful, resolute and reluctant to change his mind and, it is generally agreed, with a not very flexible mind.

When Haig became CIC after Sir John French in 1915 he carried an incredibly heavy burden of responsibility right through to the end of the war, and his armies were of a size undreamed of by British commanders in previous years.* But the burden, however heavy, was one he certainly did not wish to relinquish.

*As an example; Wellington commanded an army at Waterloo of some 67,000 men in a battlefield covering 5 miles. Haig, in 1918, commanded over 1,000,000 men, and at times his battlefield covered 128 miles.

According to Charteris, Haig was not a man able to gain devotion or personal affection of the men and armies he commanded, but he did not seek such things; he was too reserved and had no fund of small talk. He rarely spoke to the men, Charteris continued, except to put a purely official question – about their food, or their billets. Seldom, if ever, did he try to strike a more personal note. Charteris relates:

On one occasion indeed, on the urgent representations of his staff, he did make an attempt, and asked a somewhat elderly man in the ranks: 'And where did you start the war?' The reply, 'Nowhere sir; I didn't start the war', effectively checked any repetition of the effort.

At the conclusion of hostilities, Churchill says of Haig:

In 1919 Haig walked ashore at Dover after the total defeat of the German army and disappeared into private life. He was 58 years of age, and he was given no work. As he left the gangway and set foot on the pier at Dover he was transformed from supreme responsibility to a retired country gentleman. He felt it badly even if he did not show it publicly. When censorship was lifted and criticisms of his campaigns ran rife Haig said nothing. He neither spoke nor wrote in his own defence in the years that followed the war.

The author Denis Winter says of the comments above by Churchill:

These phrases have an elegant ring and were in line with the majority opinion at the time, but, as Churchill must have known, they bore no relation to the facts.

The picture of Haig painted by Churchill was not quite that depicted by Brig. Gen. Charteris either, who wrote in his biography of Haig:

It was not until July 1919, that he [Haig] finally gave up his command abroad, and retired to take over the duties of Commander-in-Chief of the Army in Britain. In his office at the Horse Guards he sat at the table which 100 years before had been used by the great Duke of Wellington... Innumerable decorations were conferred on him. Foreign countries vied with each other in doing him honour. France, America, Italy, Belgium, Portugal, Japan, Serbia, Roumania, China, each gave him their highest orders. He was created Earl Haig, Viscount Dawick and Baron Haig of Bemersyde. The Sovereign conferred on him the Order of Merit – the highest order in his gift. His own countrymen in the House of Commons voted him £100,000.

In the post war years he had played a prominent part in the formation of the British Legion.

Haig died on Sunday 30th January 1928. He retired for the night at 10.30 pm and his brother John heard low moans coming from the bedroom. John Haig rushed in and found Haig sitting on his bed gasping for breath. He died a few minutes later.

Lieutenant General Sir James Grierson

A brief appearance, as Grierson who was the designated commander of the BEF II Corps unfortunately died before he could take up his command. This is one of those intriguing 'what if?' scenarios – what if he hadn't died, but had taken over from Sir John French in 1915? Grierson was regarded as one of the cleverest and most capable commanders in the British Army. He was, unlike most of his contemporaries, a linguist speaking fluent German and French. He had a deep knowledge of the German army, and he astonished French officers by his fluent French, and his knowledge of French military history.*

*Lord Esher in 1913 led a committee that had undertaken an overhaul of the military establishment following the shock of the Boer War. This in turn had created a Committee of Imperial Defence to govern policy pertaining to war. Grierson was appointed the Director of Military Operations, and as a result of an exercise based on the assumption that if war broke out on the continent, the Germans would sweep through Belgium in a wide flanking movement north and west of the Meuse, he and his assistant General Robertson came to the conclusion that there was little chance of stopping the Germans unless the British arrived on the scene quickly and in strength.

Grierson, according to contemporary sources, was a man of vision and humour, and 'a good trencherman'. Well read, and much liked throughout the British army, Sir John French regarded his loss as a calamity to the BEF. He wanted Kitchener to replace Grierson with Plumer; instead he got his bête noire, Smith-Dorrien.

Lieutenant General Sir Horace Lockwood Smith-Dorrien (1858–1930)

Unlike French and Haig, Smith-Dorrien was not a cavalryman. One of 15 children and the son of a soldier, he was originally destined for the Rifle Brigade (95th Rifles), but after leaving Sandhurst he was commissioned into what was to become the 2nd Battalion, The Sherwood Foresters, and later commanded them.

He was a tall, hot-tempered man, with a lantern jaw, and a kindly, although not outgoing, personality. He cared for the welfare of his men and was widely regarded as a good soldier. He showed great personal courage in the Zulu Wars when the British and African troops were overwhelmed at the Battle of the Isandhlwana.

In 1914, absorbing the major part of the German attack at Mons, he was left to his own devices for a week until Sir John French ordered a withdrawal. Smith-Dorrien, on his own initiative, halted the withdrawal to turn and face the attack at Le Cateau. French praised him highly for this but later retracted this praise, and animosity between the two men increased, especially after Smith-Dorrien was made commander of the Second Army (as the expanded II Corps became).

In the actions in Flanders around the Ypres salient he pleaded with French to allow him to withdraw to more defensible positions in order to reduce casualties. French refused because by now holding Ypres had become a point of honour for Britain, and following the first German gas attacks in April 1915, Smith-Dorrien was forced to order more costly attacks. Sir John French relieved him of his command in early May 1915, putting out the story that Smith-Dorrien was unwell and had to go home, and he never really held an active command again.

It has been said that when he was sent home the British Army lost one of its best leaders. Plumer replaced him as Commander of the Second Army.

General Herbert Charles Onslow Plumer, 1st Viscount Plumer of Messines (1857–1932)

An infantry soldier, Plumer was 58 when he arrived in France. Of Yorkshire stock, although born in London, he was educated at Eton and Sandhurst, and in 1876 he was commissioned into the 65th Foot – 1st Battalion, The York and Lancaster Regiment as it became.

He fought against the Dervishes in 1884, and took the Staff Course from 1885–87. During the South African War he commanded Rhodesian, New Zealand, Canadian and South African Troops and, apparently, earned their liking as well as their respect.

He arrived in France in 1915 as a corps commander, to command

162

V Corps in Smith-Dorrien's Second Army (as the Second Corps had then become, and with Haig in command of the First Army – previously the First Corps). Plumer, it is said, disliked the way French got rid of Smith-Dorrien, even though it gave him command of an army. He had a good reputation before arriving in France, and while serving on the Western Front he was considered to be highly competent and a popular general. In fact, although one or two of the First World War commanders came out of the Boer War with enhanced reputations, Plumer was possibly the one British general to come out of the First World War with an enhanced reputation.

The unfortunate aspect of Plumer was that he really did look like the later 'Col. Blimp' figure created by David Low. He was a shy man, slightly built, but by now somewhat stout. He wore an amiable expression, although his delicate features were hidden behind a huge 'walrus' moustache. He was a disciplinarian, but he also had a sense of humour. He believed in trusting his men, and led from the front. He was referred to as 'Daddy' or 'Old Plum and Apple' by his troops. His watchwords were: 'Trust, Training and Thoroughness'.

Leon Wolff in his *Flanders Fields* describes Plumer as follows:

Sir Hubert Plumer's hair had turned white during his two thankless years as warden of the Salient. A heavy responsibility had been his, with no chance for glory, for there was hardly a point within the loop of ground held by his Second Army which German guns could not enfilade or fire into from behind, a state of affairs hardly calculated to improve the nerves of this commander or his troops. None the less he had made of the Salient a nut so hard to crack that the enemy had not not tried to do so since 1915. An ideal officer to hold any position in bulldog fashion, Plumer was a prim little old man with a pink face, fierce white moustache, blue eyes, a little pot belly mounted on tiny legs. As he walked he panted and puffed.

Arthur Behrend recalls in *As From Kemmel Hill*:

Only the other day a friend, glancing through what I have written, mentioned that he had attended some course at Second Army headquarters, and at the end Plumer addressed them and said, 'When I send a staff officer up the line and he comes

163

back and tells me what he found wrong, I stop him and say I want to know what you found right.'

Most of Plumer's war was spent in Flanders. For a time, in late 1917, he was appointed CIC British Forces in Italy, but was recalled to Belgium to take a major role in the conduct of the Battle for Messines, for which he had been planning since 1916.*

*Messines was the first battle on the Western Front since 1914 where the defending (German) troops suffered more losses than the attacking (British) troops, a difference of some 8,000.

Even such a considerate commander as Plumer can get out of touch with the front line conditions. General Jack (see above and below), records an instance in his diary in October 1918, during the fighting around Ypres, when Jack, who was now a Brigade Commander, received a visit from Plumer:

> [Plumer] asked heartily, 'well Jack, how are your men?' He seemed astonished to be told that they were pretty tired, but would be fit to attack again with a few days' rest. After all, when he put the question, the Brigade had been out of the line for little over 24 hours, following eight days of more or less severe fighting, outposts, marching, hard work in bad weather, without shelter, without sufficient rest, and sometime short of food. Plum is most human, but it is the old story: those who live right away from the troops engaged cannot possibly understand the strain and weariness affecting fighting troops at the front... The Brigade is returning to the front tonight.

As far as I am aware, Plumer left no personal papers, or books or articles concerning the war, but I think I am right in saying that he was generally accepted as a very good commander, as well as an honourable man.

General Sir Henry Rawlinson (1864–1925)

An old Etonian, Rawlinson was another who, unlike Haig and French but like Plumer and Smith-Dorrien, was an infantry officer, and not a cavalry officer. He was commissioned into the King's

Royal Rifle Corps (60th Rifles), and after 8 years, in 1892, he transferred to the Coldstream Guards.

He gained considerable experience in India, Burma, Egypt and the Sudan, and later in South Africa during the Boer War. He sat for, and passed into, the Staff College, and it was here he formed a lasting friendship with Sir Henry Wilson.

Rawlinson established a fine reputation in South Africa as a fighting commander, and returned home with quite contrary views to those of Sir John French on the future use of cavalry. Rawlinson was convinced that the day of the lance and sabre cavalry was finished, and that infantry was the only way to solve a battle. The cavalry, he said, must be trained to fight on foot as weapons increased in range and firepower. These sentiments did not endear him to Sir John, who became one of his most bitter enemies.

Rawlinson was sent to France in 1914 to take command of the 4th Division but arrived just too late to take part in the Battle of the Aisne. After a bid to rescue the Belgian army trapped at Antwerp, his force was absorbed into the main BEF, and named IV Corps, in time for the First Battle of Ypres.

His career had its ups and downs in France. He fell out frequently with French who was quick to find fault with his actions, and who of course disliked him anyway for his views on the cavalry. Rawlinson was a man not afraid to speak his mind to his superiors, such as Haig and Kitchener, and he maintained a strong streak of independence. French blamed him for not throwing in his reserves at Neuve Chapelle at the vital moment, and Rawlinson in turn blamed Davies (see below). Rawlinson said that his experiences at Neuve Chapelle convinced him of the 'bite and hold' tactic rather than the major breakthrough propounded by Haig (see Gen. Hubert Gough below).

Rawlinson also had brushes with Haig, but Haig appreciated his abilities, and gave him command of the 4th Army, and the main role in the Battle of the Somme in 1916. They disagreed with each other over the tactics for this battle, but finally Haig, as CIC, prevailed. Rawlinson stayed in command of the 4th Army through to the armistice in 1918.

General Sir Edmund Allenby (1861–1936)

Appointed to command the cavalry division of the BEF in 1914,

'Bull Allenby' (so called because of his physical appearance and his violent temper) is regarded as a general who did not appear to do particularly well on the Western Front. As Commander of the Third Army from 1915 to 1917, he was accused by his critics of being profligate with casualties. He disagreed with Haig, and disliked him, and Haig, who reciprocated his dislike, wanted him removed.

Fortunately for Allenby he had the support of Lloyd George, by then Prime Minister, who despatched Allenby to Egypt as Commander in Chief. Here, freed from headquarters, and operating an independent command for the first time, he was a revelation. The open warfare of Palestine suited his cavalry background, and he was very successful in his operations. He was highly regarded, both by his troops, and the local Arab population, where the Arab version of his name, 'al-Nabi' the prophet, was taken as fulfilment of the prophesy to free the Arabs from Ottoman control.

General Julian Hedworth George Byng, Viscount Byng of Vimy (1862–1935)

Byng was a man of interesting antecedents – his grandfather led the Guards Brigade at Waterloo, and earlier, in 1775, another relative, Admiral Byng, was shot by the French. Byng, like Haig and French, was also a cavalryman. His regiment was the 10th Hussars, and following distinguished service in command of the South African Light Horse in the Boer War, he was given command of a cavalry division in the orginal BEF in 1914.

In 1915 he took over the Cavalry Corps, and later in that same year he was sent to the Dardanelles. Here, he conducted the only success of that ill-fated expedition, the withdrawal. In May 1916 he was back on the Western Front and given command of the Canadian Corps, and in 1917 he assumed command of the Third Army, taking over from 'Bull' Allenby.

His big reverse was at Cambrai, and probably his big success was Vimy Ridge in 1917. As far as I am aware, Byng has not been faulted for his leadership of the Third Army during the major retreat in the spring of 1918.

Despite a biography, nobody seems to have much else of consequence to say about Byng as an army commander. All I have found really are the comments that 'his personable ways won him many friends' (which sounds as illustrative as 'a useful term's work'

166

on a school report) and 'one of the better generals of the war', Byng was awarded a peerage and a gift of £30,000. After the war he became Governor General of Canada, and two years before he died he was created a Field Marshal.

Another 'worm's eye' view of the great, this time from George Coppard, who, writing of Byng in his book *With a Machine Gun to Cambrai* says:

> Suddenly I ran into a party of staff officers accompanying Sir Julian Byng, GOC the Third Army, on a tour of inspection. I wondered if I were seeing things. When about to pass by me, the General noticing my bandaged head, stopped and said, 'are you wounded?' I replied, 'No sir', 'Boils'? queried the general. 'Yes sir', I said hoping that he, in an expansive mood, would wave a hand and say 'send this boy down to the reserve for a couple of days' rest'. I had no such luck. 'Beastly things. I've had them myself', he said, and with that the General and his entourage moved on.

Lieutenant General Sir Henry Horne (1861–1929)

If Byng is difficult to pin down, then artilleryman Horne, as one writer puts it, 'is the unknown general of the Western Front'. He was commissioned into the Royal Artillery in 1880, and in the First World War he served in France where his rise was steady. Between August and December 1914, he was commander of the Corps of Artillery in Haig's I Corps – designated as 'Brigadier General Royal Artillery', or 'BGRA'.

He was promoted to became a divisional commander – 2nd Division, in 1915 – and further promoted to Lieut. General, and given XV Corps in 1916. He commanded the XV corps in the Battle of the Somme, where I have read some passing criticism of his actions – or lack of them – and in 1917 he was given command of an army, the First Army. And it is here in his career that I found a comment: 'He handled his army with skill and was respected, if not greatly loved, by all who served with him.'

It would seem Horne kept no diary, wrote no autobiography and had no biographer. And his wife, according to one source, destroyed all his letters. One letter to his wife must have been preserved by someone however, for Malcolm Brown quotes it in his book of

1918. The letter was written on 11th November 1918, and the date made him think back to the beginning of the war as he writes:

> I think we may well regard Nov. 11 1918 as a red letter day, and it was on Nov. 11 1914 that the 1 Corps, in which I had the appointment of Brigadier General Royal Artillery, defeated the great attack of the Prussian Guard – an attack which was planned to break down the British resistance and to open the road to Calais! Now the mighty German nation is completely humbled and the great German Army, which regarded itself as the most powerful fighting machine in the world, is in retreat to its own frontiers, broken and defeated!

General Sir Hubert Gough (1870–1963)

Martin Middlebrook, author of *The Kaiser's Battle*, says of Gough that he was a controversial figure before the war because of his role in the 'Curragh Incident', and says his action in this (his support of the Ulster Protestants, saying he would resign his commission rather than use troops against them) made for him the first of several groups of enemies.

Gough came from a famous army family; his uncle, his father and his brother had each won the Victoria Cross. In April 1915 he became a Divisional Commander, and in July 1915 he was promoted a Corps Commander. By the spring of 1916 he was commanding an army. He was 45 years old, by far the youngest of the senior generals in France; seven years younger than Rawlinson, and ten years younger than Haig.

'Thruster' Gough commanded a cavalry brigade in August 1914 and it is said that it was he who gave the first order to the BEF to open fire in August 1914. Promoted over the heads of others in 1916 to command the reserve corps for the Battle of the Somme, this force now became the 5th Army. He came to prominence later when Haig was searching for a man who shared his vision for a decisive breakthrough, and picked on Gough.

It seems generally accepted that Haig made a serious mistake putting Gough in charge of the 1917 Third Ypres or 'Battle of Passchendaele' campaign. Gough knew nothing of the conditions in the Salient, and no concept of what the fighting there would be like. There could not have been a worse place for a dashing cavalry commander to take charge. Gough himself seems to have agreed. He says in his autobiography *Soldiering on*:

> It was a mistake not to entrust the operation to Plumer, who had been on that front for more than two years, instead of bringing me over on to a bit of ground with which I had practically no acquaintance.

The reason behind this 1917 appointment, it has been said, was that Haig, desperate to breakout from the stalemate of trench warfare, saw that the only way to break through to the open country was by means of a concentrated and, if necessary, prolonged infantry attack to create a gap and then fling the cavalry through it. Tanks were mechanically unreliable, too slow and difficult to manoeuvre quickly, and once the initial surprise and fear they had generated among enemy troops had been overcome, they were often unable to cope with the churned up, deeply cratered and waterlogged ground, and so cavalry was still seen as the only way to exploit a move quickly into open country.*

*As a passing aside on cavalry, although I am saddened when I think of the fate of so many cavalry horses, and transport horses and mules, and I am delighted that horses will never again, at least I hope, be used in battle; for those detractors of the use of cavalry in that war, and the contempt expressed for the commanders who advocated their use, Sidney Rogerson, in *The Last of the Ebb*, quoted by John Terraine in his *To Win a War – 1918 The Year of Victory*, writes of May 1918, when the Germans smashed through the French and British lines and by 30th May had captured 50,000 prisoners, and taken some 800 guns:

> It was a crowning mercy that they [the Germans] had no cavalry. How many times during the retreat did we thank Heaven for this! The sight of a few mounted men in the distance would at once start a ripple of anxiety, the word 'cavalry'! being whispered and passed from mouth to mouth down the firing line. Men looked apprehensively over their shoulders, fearful lest horsemen might already be behind them. *Cavalry was the one factor which would have smashed the morale of the defence in a twinkling.* [My italics]

None of the other commanders, particularly Plumer, who of course knew the Salient well, or Rawlinson, would agree with this cavalry-led 'great thrust through' approach. They both favoured the 'bite by bite' method, but Gough accepted – some say reluctantly at first – the idea of a cavalry breakthrough, and so as a result the nightmare of Passchendaele took place, and Gough built up a reputation for ruthlessness in pressing the attacks and the resulting high casualties. Lloyd George called for Gough's removal at the end of 1917, but

Robertson and Haigh maintained their support for him.

Gough has also been blamed for the German breakthrough in March and April 1918 when his 5th Army was overrun (see 1918 below). In fairness to Gough, there was a desperate shortage of British troops on the Western Front in 1918. Lloyd George (by now Prime Minister in place of Asquith), would not release more men to Haig, particularly because of the 1917 losses. And Haig, much against his will, had been instructed to send five divisions he could ill afford to lose to Italy in 1917, in an effort to bolster the Italian effort. Haig had also been forced to reduce the size of his divisions because of the lack of new men being released to the Western Front. This reorganisation of divisions and shortage of troops caused administrative chaos just as the Germans were making preparations for their big breakthrough.*

*Additionally in 1918, Gough had been compelled to take over an extra 25 miles of ill-prepared front line trenches from the French, and his troops were dangerously over extended, when the Germans launched their massive 'Operation Michael' attack (see below, Parts 46–48, covering the 1918 German offensive).

John Toland, an American author, paints a quick sketch of Gough in 1918 just prior to the German breakthrough that is rather different from the usual one – particularly of the Australian writers. He says:

> At forty-seven, Gough was by far the youngest of Haig's military commanders. A short man with a long, lean face, he was noted for his terrier tenacity and courage. He had a rare relationship with his men, who felt he was one commander who understood the hellish life of the trenches.

Several other observations of Gough during this period; Martin Middlebrook quotes Lieutenant-Colonel M.V.B. Hill, CO 9th Royal Sussex Regiment, who comments as follows:

> He spent a day with our division and he came round with me inspecting my battalion while they were training and he said they were a good battalion. Division was very annoyed that Gough lunched with the brigade and not with them. He was a charming man but I didn't think he had too many brains.

Also quoted by Middlebrook, a Major K.S. Mason of the 16th

(Irish) Division who was the Divisional Machine-Gun Officer, describes a visit by Gough in March 1918 just before the German attack:

I was present at the Divisional Mess when General Hull told General Gough that he was unhappy about his dispositions. He wanted only one brigade in the front line. General Gough would not agree to this and said: 'I wouldn't dream of such a thing. The Germans are not going to break my line'. I saw quite a lot of General Gough during his visit and came to the conclusion that he was a very arrogant, conceited and pompous man.

General Sir Ivor Maxse, on the other hand, seems to have thought highly of Gough, and worked well with him.

Ian F.W. Beckett in *Look to Your Front* says that Sir Henry Wilson was certainly implicated in Gough's dismissal, and that Gough was also on bad terms with many at GHQ. Beckett quotes from Liddell Hart, who says Gough described Wilson as crooked, and he also criticised Allenby, Byng and Monro.

Gough was replaced by General Birdwood, and he remained unemployed until 1919. He retired in 1922.

Field Marshal Sir William Robertson (1860–1933)

Robertson was a very unusual figure, and by his military attainments, unique in Victorian times. Robertson's father was a village tailor and postmaster and his son, William, entered into domestic service at the age of 13. Four years later, when he was just under the minimum age of eighteen years, he joined the army as a private soldier in 16th Lancers. His mother was not pleased. She wrote to him, 'I would rather bury you than see you in a red coat.' The army, she said, 'was a refuge for idle people.'

Completely by his own efforts and ability, and unremitting labour and intense study, he rose to the highest rank in the army. Following ten years in the ranks he passed the examination for a commission, and when he was commissioned in 1888 it was into 3rd Dragoon Guards as 2nd Lieutenant. He lacked the independent financial means to live as a cavalry officer, but he managed to survive because his regiment was in India, and pay in India was higher than at home. Even so he could not afford to drink or smoke in the mess.

Robertson possessed a great gift for languages, and as cash awards were given by the Indian government for proficiency in languages, he mastered Urdu, Hindi, Persian, Pushtu, Punjabi and Gurkhali, engaging native tutors to teach him.

Having obtained commissioned rank his next move was to apply to attend the Staff College where, until then, no ex-ranker had attended. The entrance examination, among other subjects, required knowledge of mathematics, German or French. By rising at four or five in the mornings he studied hard before attending to his normal regimental duties, and not only did he pass the entrance examination, but he ultimately commanded the Staff College.

At the outbreak of war he was Quartermaster General to the BEF. Here, in France, in difficult circumstances – covering the arrival in France, and then the retreat from Mons to the Marne, and then move back to the north – he did a very good job in the prevailing conditions by seeing the troops were kept supplied with food, clothes and ammunition.

When he crossed the Channel to France in 1914 he was 55 years old. Stocky and powerfully built, his movements were heavy and deliberate. He had a thick moustache, prominent jaw and chin, and his eyes below heavy eyebrows were dark and penetrating. He spoke in a deep gruff voice.

Despite some opposition from Sir John French, he became French's Chief of Staff, succeeding Sir John Murray early in 1915. He was the only real rival to Haig as CIC when French was sent home in 1915, but instead, he was appointed CIGS (Chief of the Imperial General Staff), effectively then the liaison between army and cabinet. When he was appointed to this position on 23rd December 1915, he felt a profound sense of anxiety. He said he had to deal with five commanders in chief abroad, one at home, and about a dozen Allies. In addition, he had to work closely with the cabinet and other politicians, and this part of his job he disliked intensely.

Robertson is another who appears not to have had a high regard for Sir John French's generalship, and when Haig took over, Robertson as a 'pro-Westerner', supported Haig against all pressure.*

*The 'side show' Robertson really detested and considered to be an absolute waste of men, money and material, was Salonika, where the casualties of the Allied troops amounted to less than 20,000, but almost 450,000 were invalided home suffering from malaria. See below.

Like Haig, Robertson was taciturn in speech – although he wrote clearly and concisely. He was not interested in conversation, and even less interested in argument, and this made it difficult for him when dealing with politicians. His response to criticism was either a series of ferocious grunts or the blunt comment, 'I've 'eard different'. Other famous comments for which he is remembered – true or not – are: 'Get 'Aig'. And when Sir John French asked him to recall General Smith-Dorrien from command of the 2nd. Army, he said to Smith-Dorrien: ''Orace, you're for 'ome'.

To quote David R. Woodward, who edited Robertson's military correspondence:

> When Robertson was angry it was said that his countenance took on the appearance of an approaching storm. His chin would go into his collar, a second chin would appear under it, his eyes would go dark, his whole face assume a quite terrifying wooden aspect, while the hand tucked into the Sam Browne belt flapped gently like a fin. And then came a grunt like a cork out of a bottle, releasing the flow of words which he generally shot at you without turning his head as he strode by.

Field Marshall Sir Henry Hughes Wilson (1864–1922)

Wilson seems to have been a complex man in many ways, and was probably heavily influenced by his upbringing. Robertson disliked him intensely, and was horrified when Wilson was appointed to his (Robertson's) job in March 1918.

English born, althought brought up in Ireland, he was also an absolute Francophile. Whether having a series of French governesses as a child brought this about is not known, but it certainly gave him a fluent command of the French language, and he put this to good use in his own interests during the war. On a visit or visits to France before the war, in 1910, he become fascinated by Foch, and this stayed with him all his life. He used all his influence to try to make Foch supreme commander of both French and British forces.

He was another unfortunate general in his appearance. It is said he was once sent a telegram by some colleagues addressed, as a joke, to 'The ugliest man in the British Army' – and it reached him.

Wilson, who was educated at both Marlborough and Wellington, always intended to make his career in the army, but unfortunately he failed both the entrance examinations to Woolwich and Sandhurst a number of times. He finally entered the army by the back door by taking a commission in the Irish Militia. Eventually he was gazetted into the Rifle Brigade and joined the 1st Battalion in India, in 1884.

As a regimental officer at that time he appears to have been the embodiment of the Rifle Brigade. His commanding officer in South Africa describes him as having unfailing cheerfulness in the arduous conditions prevailing. Nothing affected his spirits, he had a joke for everyone, and he was equally good at his duties in the camp and in the field.

In 1910 he was named Director of Military Operations, and he strove to infuse his own sense of urgency into his colleagues in his belief that Britain would go to war with Germany, and that it was imminent and inevitable. Churchill gives Wilson credit for unfolding in 1911, 'with what proved afterwards to be extreme accuracy', the German plan for attacking France and the advance through Belgium.

Wilson had allied himself closely to Sir John French in the 'Curragh Incident', and French cannot give Wilson enough praise, saying in his book *1914*:

His [Wilson's] *magnum opus* in peace-time was done when he was Director of Military Operations at the War Office during the four years preceding the war. His countrymen have never realised, and probably may never know, the vital importance and invaluable results of the work he did there... In those many weary, anxious days we passed together during my term of command in France, I cherish a most grateful remembrance of his unfailing and invaluable help, as well as his sincere, loyal and whole hearted support. Of iron nerve and frame nothing seemed to tire him.

Having said that, Robin Neilland, in *The Great War Generals on the Western Front 1914–18* quotes an interesting passage about a note that Brigadier General Sir James Edmonds (of whom see below), sent to the librarian of the Staff College at Camberley in 1955, concerning a biography of Wilson:

The story of how Wilson left GHQ to become liaison officer at French Grand GHQ suppresses the truth. I happened to witness his dismissal. At St Omer in 1914 I was billeted – with Earl Percy and Sir Ernest Swinton, the Father of Tanks – in the house next door to the C-in-C's in the Rue St Bertin. Just before Christmas as I came out I found Sir John French and Wilson in altercation on the pavement; Henry was begging not to be sent home and French, purple in the face with rage shouted 'You have done me down every time, you imposter, and you shall not stay here; you can go and live with the d****d French you are so fond of'.

Later, Wilson's dominant trait was said to be a passion for intrigue. He himself is said to have described it as 'mischief'. This characteristic made him enemies, and even his friends were wary of him. Although he became a Field Marshal and CIGS, top field commands evaded him. To keep him 'out of mischief', he needed to be kept busy otherwise he stirred things up.

Lloyd George writing in his *War Memoirs*, in the 1930s said of Wilson:

> He had undoubtedly the nimblest intelligence amongst the soldiers of high degree. He also had the lucidity of mind and therefore of expression which was given to none of his professional rivals. It was a delight to hear him unravel and expound a military problem. For this reason he was especially helpful in a council of civilians. But he had no power of decision. That is why he failed in the field. For the same reason he was not a complete success in council.* He shrank from the responsibility of the final word, even in advice.

*Referring here to the Supreme War Council.

Wilson was the only top general to die by bloodshed. He returned to Ireland to work for the Protestant cause after leaving the army, and was assassinated by Catholic Republicans in June 1922.

PART TWENTY

Each had been born and bred in the last age; each belonged to a highly conservative profession. Their abilities and defects reflected and illustrated those of their countries... Each in turn, as commander-in-chief, bore his nation's sword at a period when the course of the war pivoted on his judgement and will.'

Correlli Barnett, *The Swordbearers.*

Allied and enemy generals involved on the Western Front

General Joseph Jacques Césaire Joffre (1852–1931)

Sir John French's first impression of Joffre, on 14th August 1914, was: 'A man of strong will and determination, courteous and considerate, but firm and steadfast of mind and purpose and not easily turned or persuaded.'

'Papa' Joffre was a dominant figure in the first part of the war. Like Robertson, he came from a poor family, his father was a cooper, and with eleven children to support. While a student, Joffre was caught up in the Franco-Prussian War serving in the artillery, and took part in the siege of Paris in 1871. Later he joined the Engineer Corps and spent most of his career abroad in Indo China, Madagascar and other parts of the French Empire. Like Sir John, he too became Commander in Chief without attending the staff college courses.

It is generally accepted that he was not a great strategist; he was an intuitive soldier, and not an intellectual one. He relied upon 'gut feelings'. Everyone who writes about him mentions he had an enormous, even gargantuan appetite, and Heaven help anyone who disturbed him after his lunch – for any reason.

177

He was also renowned for his patience, courage and lack of nerves – he was unflappable, however bad the news. His weakness was his stubborn adherence to Plan XVII (see Part Fifteen above), and slow acceptance of the German numerical superiority. He was an advocate, indeed if not *the* prime advocate, of 'attrition'. His popularity with the French government and other military leaders declined as the war progressed, and the Battle of Verdun, in 1916, brought about his downfall and subsequent 'promotion upstairs' to Marshal of France. This was the end of him as a field commander.

General Robert Nivelle (1856–1924)

General Nivelle was an artillery officer, and increasingly the war was being seen in some quarters as one in which the artillery was, or would be, the dominant factor. Replacing Joffre in December 1916, Neville had impressed everyone by his defence at Verdun, and by his innovative 'creeping barrage' tactics (the co-ordination of infantry advance and artillery support). He announced he had a plan for massive success on the Western Front using these tactics, and this would end the war. A number of senior French officers, Pétain in particular, together with the British BEF commanders, greeted his ideas with less enthusiasm than the French government. But the French government, like their British counterparts, by this stage of the war, were desperate for success. The French had suffered massive losses of troops since the beginning of the war, and with so little to show for it all.

Lloyd George was now the British Prime Minister, and he became an enthusiastic backer of Nivelle and his plan. Like Lloyd George, Nivelle was a persuasive talker, and accounts say he was an urbane, confident and charming man, with a fluent command of English – his mother was British – and he seemed the answer to the prayers of both governments at this stage of low morale and little success.

Nivelle was as unlike the gruff Robertson and the reticent Haig as you could get, and both these disliked and distrusted Lloyd George. And the antipathy was mutual. Nivelle believed that his methods – which had produced such good results at Verdun, and which, among other gains, had included the capture of 10,000 prisoners – could be applied equally successfully on a much larger scale. He said if he were to be given command of all the Allied armies – French, British and Belgian – he felt sure he could produce a victory without great loss. 'I have a formula' he announced, and Lloyd George felt that at last here was a general he could work with. He planned, successfully, to bypass Haig and Robertson and manoeuvre Nivelle into overall command.

Haig, it would appear, was not against Nivelle and his ideas initially. And he did not object to the French taking over the major role in the proposed forthcoming attack. He did not relish the idea of British troops coming under Nivelle's command, but publicly at least, he accepted this temporary transfer. Haig wanted to use his own troops for a major British offensive in the Ypres salient area (see Parts Forty and Forty-one below) where he wished to retake Messines, and then, with the aid of a sea-borne landing, push northwards and retake Ostend and Zeebrugge. (These two ports played a prominent part in the German U boat campaign which was crippling British shipping with heavy losses.)

Robertson had written to Haig earlier expressing the hope that Haig and Nivelle would be able to get together and work things out. And on 13th March 1917 Robertson wrote to Nivelle saying: 'I shall do my best to give you every assistance in your responsible task that I can give.'

Relations between Haig and Nivelle became strained when Nivelle appeared to back track on the understood – by Haig at any rate – agreement that if Neville could not achieve a breakthrough quickly by his proposed *masse de manoeuvre* then the whole offensive would be called off. Haig would then be free to deploy his troops in an attack in the Ypres Salient to clear the Germans from the Belgium coast.

After delays, not all caused by Nivelle, and with the loss of the last vestige of surprise, meanwhile the German army having quietly withdrawn to their new massive defensive 'Hindenburg Line', Nivelle's offensive finally got under way in April 1917. Unfortunately it had no greater success than the previous major offensives (see the details of the battles of 1917 below). Haig's British army had some success on April 9th in the area that Nivelle had turned over to him around Arras, where four divisions of the Canadian Corps captured Vimy Ridge. But as the battle dragged on into May, the French had obviously suffered a clear defeat, and the Allied casualties mounted to some 350,000.

Nivelle was dismissed on 15th May 1917 and replaced by Petain.

Marshal Henri Philipe Benoni Omar Joseph Pétain (1856–1951)

'They shall not pass' is perhaps the statement for which Pétain will always be remembered; the watchwords of his famous defence at Verdun in 1916. In 1917, after Nivelle's failed and costly offensive, Pétain was called, and on 15th May 1917 he was appointed head of the French army on the Western Front.

Pétain managed to rebuild the shattered morale of the French when he took charge, and he believed, at this stage of the war, in the policy of defence in depth, but the idea was still, as one source puts it, 'fundamentally alien to many French commanders'. While officially retaining his post he was subordinated to Foch.

Sadly, at the age of 83, he was recalled to head the Vichy government in occupied France in the Second World War, and after the war he was condemned to death for treason. General Charles de Gaulle commuted the sentence.

Field Marshal Ferdinand Foch (1851–1929)

As assistant to Joffre, Foch's career went into a decline when Joffre was dismissed, and from December 1916 he was relegated to a backwater of 'non jobs'. Petain brought him back as chief of general staff, in May 1917, but his experiences as co-ordinator of the Allied effort in Italy at Caporetto in the autumn gave him the prominence he really needed, and this led to his appointment as co-ordinator of Anglo-French forces on the Western Front.

In April 1918 he was officially installed as Allied commander in chief, over the head of Petain his erstwhile superior. Later, in June 1918, his command was extended to the Italian Front as well. He later expressed his views on command of national forces, and leading a unified command, to Commandant Bugnet, saying:

It is not sufficient to issue orders! It is necessary to see that they are executed; people must be watched, one must always have them under one's eye. Believe me, it the duties of a commander were merely those of giving orders, it would not be a difficult task. He must ensure they are carried out. When I commanded the Allied Armies, I always had the means of ensuring this supervision; I used to send Desticker here, Pagezy there. I kept in touch with the execution of my orders; they kept me posted. Obviously, when one has subordinates whom one trusts, they can be given liberty of action, but it is always necessary to be certain the orders are carried out. That is the whole secret... You see unified command is only a word. It was tried in 1917, under Nivelle, and it did not work. One must know how to lead the Allies – one does not command them. Some must be treated differently from others. The English are English, the Americans another matter, and similarly with the Belgians and Italians. I could not deal with the Allied Generals as I did with our own. They also were brave men who were representing the interests of their own country. They saw things in a different light to ourselves. They agreed with reluctance to the unified command; although they loyally accepted the situation, a mere trifle might have upset them, and dislocated the whole scheme. I could not give them orders in an imperative manner.*

*To me, the content and staccato style of his delivery – particularly in the first paragraph – is somewhat reminiscent, at least in translation, of the late Field Marshal Bernard Montgomery. In passing, Montgomery was with the 2nd Battalion, Royal Warwickshire Regiment, in August, 1914, as a junior officer, and as such involved in the battles of Mons and Le Cateau.

Belgian Commander-in-Chief, King Albert I (1857–1934)

Succeeding his uncle Leopold II in December 1909, Albert has been described as a cultured and capable monarch who had spent his life in the army. The army at the outbreak of war numbered, theoretically, some 43,000 men, plus reserves, but in actuality there were far fewer reserves available than the plans optimistically stated, and many units were under strength.

Albert took command of the army when Germany invaded, but his troops took up the positions in the centre of Belgium which had been allocated to them by the peacetime plan. As a result they were not available to put into operation Albert's more realistic plan which assumed the attack would come from Germany, and so placed the troops round the frontier fortresses of Lèige and Namur. When the Belgian troops were overrun he was compelled to withdraw, first to Antwerp, and then to Flanders, and eventually establishing his headquarters at Le Havre.

His overriding aspirations were for the repossession of an essentially intact Belgium, and he remained a somewhat uneasy ally by maintaining a stance which saw Belgium as a neutral nation, compelled by invasion, to fight. Collaboration by Belgian forces was therefore limited. He declined to cooperate with Joffre in 1914, and obstructed Allied plans to include Belgian forces in offensives along the Western Front, and in 1917, he encouraged proposals for a separate peace with Germany. Later, in 1918, he relented on his position and was converted to the Allied cause, and Foch confirmed his appointment, in late 1918, as commander of the Flanders Army Group, with some British and French forces under his command.

Throughout the war he had been regarded, both at home and abroad, by the general public as an unsullied hero, and his obstruction to Allied plans was generally unknown. He was mourned universally upon his death in a mountaineering accident in February 1934.

The American general – John J. Pershing (1860–1948)

Although the American troops did not really enter the battlefield until 1918 – at the second Battle of the Marne 18th July to 7th August – their leader, General Pershing, arrived in Paris with his staff on 4th July 1917. His army existed mostly on paper when he arrived. Like Britain in 1914, while America had a substantial navy her cadre of professional soldiers was small, and it was scattered over the country in forts and garrisons, and in the Philippines. And again, like Britain in 1914, the eager recruits in the USA in 1917 trained on wooden mock-ups for guns, and some would arrive in France, like the British Territorials of 1914, with only the most rudimentary instruction and training.

The French were desperate to get their hands on these fresh, innocent, optimistic and unscarred young men as support troops for their army and as the junior in the field they had assumed Pershing would fall in with their ideas and plans. They were very wrong. Pershing was determined to use the AEF as a national fighting unit, emphasising the formal position of the USA as an 'associated power' unencumbered by alliances.

Pershing won both acclaim and criticism as a commander in France, but was generally thought to have done well. He was an advocate for complete victory over Germany before an armistice, and also committed to the imposition of punitive ceasefire terms. He spoke out against the Treaty of Versailles.

He clashed with the French higher command on occasions, particularly with Foch, and Clemenceau at one stage called for his dismissal.

German generals

Helmuth Johann Ludwig von Moltke (1848–1916)

Von Moltke was the nephew of the famous Prussian field marshal of the same name, and the younger von Moltke succeeded von Schlieffen, in 1906, to the position of Chief of General Staff. Moltke tinkered with the famous 'Schlieffen Plan', and ignored its author's exhortation to keep the right flank strong. The reason for the alterations, it would seem, was because he was concerned with the French military build-up along the frontier further south.

When the Kaiser began to waver in the July crisis of 1914, and to have second thoughts about war, von Moltke told him it was too late to stop the mobilisation. Success did not follow him with the advent of war. He persisted with the flawed Schlieffen Plan long after it was no longer a valid instrument, and he came to be regarded as inept, not only because of his mistakes with the plan, but because he failed to keep contact with his subordinate commanders and remained far from the theatre of action. For a time, at a critical moment of the battle of the Marne, he issued no orders at all. In fairness, he was fighting on two fronts, and beset by communication problems. He feared a Russian attack in the east; he diverted troops from the main German invasion of Northern France; and he worried about the French in the south. Within six weeks of the war being declared he was retired and replaced by Falkenhayn.

Erich von Falkenhayn (1861–1922)

Falkenhayn was promoted to the rank of general in 1912, and at the outbreak of war he held the position of War Minister. Coming from an aristocratic Prussian background, he enjoyed the confidence of the Kaiser, and when he replaced Moltke as chief of general staff, on 14th September 1914, he combined the two jobs until February 1915. Churchill says of Falkenhayn, in his book *Great Contemporaries*:

Moltke had disappeared with the failure at the Marne, and a new chief, perhaps the ablest of German commanders, Falkenhayn directed the German armies. He still looked to the West as the scene upon which the decision would be obtained. Here were the hated French, here above all in his own words was 'our most dangerous enemy ... England, with whom the conspiracy against Germany stands and falls'.

However, because of the the eastern and western factions in Germany he was caught by opposing political, and military, polarisation. He became indecisive in his actions over the conflicting demands of the two fronts, and hesitated to commit troops decisively in one or the other theatres. Verdun proved to be his final undoing, as it had Joffre's, and this, combined with the stalemate on the Western Front, and hostility from Hindenburg and Ludendorff, resulted in his resignation in late August, 1916.

Falkenhayn lived until 1922, but when he left the high command in 1916, it was noted that his hair had turned completely white.

Erich Ludendorff (1856–1937)

The name of Ludendorff is inseparable with that of his mentor, Hindenburg. The two came together on the Eastern Front, and Churchill, who was filled with admiration for Hindenburg, said:

> Nothing is more becoming than the relations which Hindenburg preserved with Ludendorff. Certainly it was a marvellous partnership. His lieutentant [Ludendorff] was a prodigy of mental energy, cast in a military form. Hindenburg was not jealous; he was not petty; he was not fussy. He took the responsibility for all that his brilliant, much younger, subordinate conceived and did. There were moments when the nerve of Ludendorff flickered and in those moments the solid, simple strength of Hindenburg sustained him.

Following the failure of his great 1918 offensive, Ludendorff resigned from the army on 26th October 1918, and by that time, Robin Neillands, in *The Great War Generals on the Western Front 1914–1918*, states:

He was on the verge of a nervous breakdown. He entered politics in 1920 and stood as a National Socialist candidate in the Weimar elections of 1924 and served in the Reichstag until 1928. During this period he met Adolf Hitler and told Hindenburg in 1933, 'this accursed man will take our Reich into the abyss'. He [Ludendorff] and his wife had become fanatical followers of a pagan cult that worshipped ancient gods.

Some report him as being insane when he died.

Paul von Hindenburg stayed on as head of the German army until after the signing of the Treaty of Versailles. Like Ludendorff, he also entered politics, and became head of the Weimar Republic. In 1933 he gave way to Adolf Hitler, who became Chancellor of Germany.

PART TWENTY-ONE

*On doit des égards aux vivants; on ne doit aux morts que
la vérité. (One owes respect to the living; but to the dead
one owes nothing but the truth.)*

Voltaire (Francois-Marie Arouet).

Portrayal of the British troops and commanders

Lyn MacDonald, in 1998, writing the Foreword to her book *To the
Last Man*, says:

In recent years I have listened in the company of war veterans
to speeches which were kindly meant and expressed with real
sincerity but whose sentiments have caused them pain. They
keep their thoughts to themselves, for they learned self-control
in a hard school and they realised long ago how difficult it
can be to explain the concepts of service and loyalty, as *they*
understood them, to a more liberal, less reverent and perhaps
more self-indulgent generation. Moreover, they themselves have
not been impervious to the bombardment of scathing criticism
of 'the Generals', the analysis of the conduct of the war, the
re-evaluation of its worth, and the shift in perception of the
ordinary soldier from brave hero to pitiful victim. They never
saw themselves as heroes, nor even particularly brave, for they
were scared stiff most of the time, but they had some sense
of achievement in what they endured and they decidedly did
not regard themselves as victims. Now many are half convinced
they were and, worse, are half-ashamed of it.
It is hard to stand in a war cemetery among those serried

headstones with their homely, poignant inscriptions and fail to be moved to sadness, to pity, sometimes to anger, and even to conclude that such a sacrifice was futile. Looking back on the threshold of a new century as the Great War recedes into history, it is easy to believe that it was, but the generation who fought that war were neither fools nor dupes, nor sheep led bleating to the slaughter, and to pity them as such is to do them a deep injustice.

Writing in 1960, Cyril Falls, in the Preface to *The First World War*, says:

I wanted to show what the war had meant to my generation, so large a part of which – and so much of the best at that – lost their lives in it. I wanted to commemorate the spirit in which these men served and fought. The modern intellectual is inclined to look with impatience upon the ardour with which they went to war. To him it is obsolete. If so, I must be obsolete too. Looking back, the intensity – and I dare add the purity – of that spirit still moves me deeply. I speak particularly of the combatants, including leaders and staff.

Charles Edmonds (pseudonym of Charles Carrington) and author of *A Subaltern's War* writes in much the same vein as Cyril Falls. Martin Stephen quotes him as writing:

I never meet an 'old sweat', as we like to describe ourselves, who accepts or enjoys the figure in which are now presented, though it is useless – undignified – to protest. Just smile and make an old soldier's wry joke when you see yourself on the television screen, agonised and woebegone, trudging from disaster to disaster, knee-deep in moral as well as physical mud, hesitant about your purpose, submissive to harsh, irrelevant discipline, mistrustful of your commanders. Is it of any use to assert that I was not like that, or my dead friends were not like that, and the old cronies that I meet with at reunions are not like that.

Philip Warner devotes a number of passages in his book *Passchendaele* to the sentiments expressed by another author, Arthur Osburn, who served in the First World War – as a doctor in the RAMC, who was awarded the DSO, and who attained the rank of lieutenant-colonel. Osburn, apparently, began his army career as a private in the Artist's Rifles at some unstated time, and he takes the more typical 'butchers and bunglers' approach. Warner, quotes from Osburn's book (published in 1932), *Unwilling Passenger*, which says:

> The private soldier, who may be just as sensitive and as well-educated as those above him, must suffer and endure, often without knowing the object or the purpose of his exertions: that alone almost doubles the sense of uncertainty and the hardship of war. He must put up not only with the guile and fury of the enemy but with this constant uncertainty, and the failures and blunders, impatience and often contradictory orders of his officers. Because it is mainly with the 'vile body' of the rank and file that the Generals experiment, it is the rank and file that must always be the *first* to learn just how and why and to what extent each attack or manoeuvre has been a failure, the *last* to learn the extent or significance of a success. Often knowing that their efforts have failed and are merely bringing death or mutilation to themselves, they must yet continue an obviously futile attack until some officer – perhaps a boy only half their age – has convinced some other officer far from the fighting line that success is impossible... Whoever wins or loses the battle which he is ordered to fight, the economic surroundings of the average soldier at home are such that often he could scarcely be worse off than he is already even were his country defeated.

While admiring his compassion, I feel it seems unlikely that 'a boy' – presumably a junior subaltern – would be in a position to convince some senior officer, 'far from the fighting line', on the necessity of calling off an offensive. Philip Warner expresses his doubts that a British soldier would have been as well off if defeated. However, the views Arthur Osburn expresses make interesting reading, and perhaps are not what one would have expected from an officer of his rank, and that era.

However, from other comments he makes about officers, he appears to feel slighted because being a RAMC lieutenant-colonel he was not held in the same regard by senior officers as those of his rank in the fighting arms. He also felt – as quoted again by Philip Warner – that serving in the RAMC required exceptional courage, whether as officer or in other ranks, because their job meant they had to wait unarmed: 'Waiting unarmed,' said Osburn, 'is the worst penalty to which imaginative man can be subjected.'

And Osburn, says Warner, also bitterly resented the fact that his stretcher-bearers were disparagingly referred to farther down the line as 'non combatants', and that the RAMC as a whole were regarded as social inferiors by officers in certain regiments. Apparently former Eton contemporaries expressed surprise at him doing such work.

PART TWENTY-TWO

A great lesson from Kafka's diary. He wrote it during the First World War, which he never mentions. Not a single line refers to it.

Jean Cocteau. Entry in his diary dated 20th August, 1953.*

*Actually Cocteau was not absolutely correct when he wrote this because Kafka *does* mention the war, although only barely. The entry in his diary for 2nd August 1914 reads: 'Germany declared war on Russia. – Swimming in the afternoon'.

Reference material: Maps

Although so much has been written about the First World War one can experience a number of frustrations when seeking information from books, particularly in the case of maps. I have found difficulty on a number of occasions in relating text to maps, many of the maps have no scale of distances, and infuriatingly, the places named in the text which I want do not appear to be shown on the accompanying map.

In fairness, many locations of interest to the family researcher may no longer exist – tiny villages and hamlets, farms, roads and hills – places that were once familiar, and possibly of renown or dread to the troops in the vicinity. Some place names were bestowed by the British troops and so never appeared on French or Belgian maps.*

*Two years after writing the above paragraph I was still trying to locate any other references to 'Forward Cottage', 'Cross Roads Farm' and 'Hill Top Farm' all of which, as I mention, were singled out in the 3rd Rifles War Diary for 1915, and lay somewhere near La Brique, just outside and NE of Ypres. But one should not give up in one's searches because after writing of this lack of success, and after lots of searching, I was

191

delighted to find all three locations in *Topography of Armageddon A British Trench Map Atlas of the Western Front 1914–1918* by Peter Chasseaud. I found them on page 20, Fig 5, 'St Jean', and also page 14, Fig 3, 'Ypres'. Hill Top Farm, I discovered, housed an OP (Observation Post for artillery spotting) in 1915, and this could account for much of the unwelcome attention the 3rd Rifles experienced from the Germans at that time. Forward Cottage (C21b) is also mentioned in a much later battle, Third Ypres, on page 67 of Martin Marix Evans *Passschendaele and the Battles of Ypres 1914–1918*.

Searching for military units

On occasions it is not possible to find references to any military unit below division level, and frustrating though this is, with so many brigades and battalions involved on the Western Front alone as the war drew in more and more troops, perhaps this is not really surprising.*

*Part Eleven above defines and explains the composition of all these units.

Another problem that can affect a book-search for a particular regiment, or a battalion of that regiment, is that an author may wish to highlight only a particular aspect of a battle – a certain day perhaps, or a place, or a particular engagement within a battle area – and this chosen incident or location may have involved directly only one or a few of the units that were serving in the area at that time, and other units, as a consequence, are not mentioned.

Reliability of documents

It would seem that no sources of information are to be considered completely reliable. The Official Histories of the war, together with Divisional Histories and Battalion War Diaries, are described as inaccurate, and even suspect, by some writers, so too are personal reminiscences, particularly those written many years later, because of the tricks memory plays, and subsequent influences.

Douglas Haig has been accused of doctoring some of his dispatches, but Haig says in the preface to the published collection of his dispatches, edited by his private secretary, J.H. Boraston:

Compiled, however, during the actual process of the events they describe, the despatches do not pretend to be a complete and final account of the three momentous years of crowded incident and stupendous happenings with which they deal. Yet because they were put together under the immediate strain of battle, while the results of the decisions and actions they recount were still undetermined, and were issued for the information of a nation whose fate still hung in the uncertain balance of war, they possess an atmosphere of their own which gives them a definite historical importance. Moreover, they are at the moment the only available official account of a most splendid and most critical period in our national existence.

Haig himself was a victim of 'doctoring'. When his work was published in 1919, passages that criticised the government in respect to manpower and various other warnings by Haig to the government, were deleted by Lloyd George's government. The 2001 edition has however reinserted the passages concerned, and with the accompanying succinct commmment by Terry Cave on the cuts in the original edition: 'Lloyd George, no admirer of Haig'.

Referring to battalion war diaries in general, C.T. Atkinson in his preface to *The Devonshire Regiment 1914–1918* says:

It must be remembered that these diaries were compiled under circumstances of the greatest difficulty, by people who had many other duties of greater importance to attend to, and that too often, especially when there had been any specially heavy fighting, there was hardly anyone left who could give an account of what the battalion had been through, even if there had been time and opportunity to investigate things carefully. When the whole staff of a battalion got wiped out together, it is hardly wonderful if a diary became a casualty also.

Books and statistics published during the war, and those published soon after the end of the war, also have doubts cast upon them because additional, and possibly conflicting information, and or interpretations, come to light in later years. Alternatively, the closeness of the war, and the affects of personal experience and opinions, coloured objectiveness.

Letters from soldiers, particularly those published in newspapers during the war of the 'from a soldier at the Front to his parents' type, have also been accused of being untrue, or propaganda composed for home consumption, and sometimes for a cash reward.

War correspondents and censorship

Because of government censorship imposed as the war progressed, and also because some accounts of events were published for propaganda purposes for the home reader, Philip J. Haythornthwaite, author of *The World War One Source Book*, has this to say on the subject:

> Much of the 'informed comment' upon strategical matters, and indeed the dispatches of war correspondents, were dismissed or treated with scepticism by those with actual experience of the war.
>
> The following skit appeared in *The Wipers Times*, 26th February 1916, and demonstrates clearly the derision with which such announcements were viewed; the supposed author 'Bellary Helloc' was a skit on Hilaire Belloc.
>
> 'Under existing conditions, everything points to a speedy disintegration of the enemy ... let us take as our figures, 12,000,000 as the fighting population of Germany. Of these 8,000,000 are killed or being killed hence we have 4,000,000 remaining. Of these 1,000,000 are non-combatants, being in the Navy. Of the 3,000,000 remaining we can write off 2,500,000 as temperamentally unsuitable for fighting owing to obesity and other ailments engendered by gross mode of living. This leaves us 500,000 as the full strength. Of these 497,250 are known to be suffering from incurable diseases, this leaves us 2,750. Of these 2,150 are on the Eastern Front, and of the remaining 600, 584 are Generals and Staff. Thus we find that there are 16 men on the Western Front. This number I maintain is not enough to give them even a fair chance of resisting four more big pushes, and hence the collapse of the Western Campaign.'

One must say in fairness to the newspaper correspondents that in the early years of the war particularly they were not welcomed by the army commanders at all, and they suffered great frustrations trying to get to the front and see for themselves what was happening and to file reports with their newspapers.*

*The position had hardly changed since the famous war correspondent William Howard Russell attempted to file his dispatches from the front in the Crimea War. He wrote to his editor at *The Times* in June 1854 from Varna: 'I have just been informed on good authority that Lord Raglan has determined not to recognise the press in any way, or to give them rations or assistance, and worse than all, it is too probable that he will forbid our accompanying the troops.'

When trench warfare set in it became somewhat easier for the war correspondents to watch and understand how battles were progressing; however, Martin J. Farrar, in *News from the Front*, says that while the Battle of First Ypres was taking place correspondents were still kept away, and reporting restrictions were severely enforced. Reporters were liable to arrest and deportation. He mentions something in respect of reporters that nowadays looks unbelievably quaint: 'In London the correspondents listed on the official War Office registery were still waiting, with their horses and servants, to join the British army.'

Opinions and factions

The pendulum swings, fashions change, and reputations become tarnished or re-established. Heroes become villains, and vice versa. Defeats and victories are now not always what they once were, or so it would seem. And it is all too easy to expound with hindsight, and the mores of today.

Those who write, or wrote, on The Great War, often have their own, and sometimes hotly held, assessments of the people involved; and they have their own interpretations of the events they wish to portray – as of course do those who write on other historical or political matters. Acounts are affected by national, or political, or personal convictions or prejudices – and by those who wish to ally themselves with a particular faction, or school of opinion.

There is therefore a temptation for a writer to accept a statement about someone, or some event or occasion, from a source that fits neatly with his or her own sentiments – and then to quote the statement as a fact without qualifying the strength of its validity, or questioning how interpretative, selective or biased the source was. Unfortunately for the reader, these 'factual' statements tend to be written with confidence and authority, and stated, or implied, as definitive, rather than a personal view, interpretation or belief, that may or may not be valid.

Who said what?

For example, the famous quotation by Kiggell:* *'Good God! Did we really send men to fight in that?'* Robin Neillands provides a good example of the proliferation of this 'fact' about Kiggell in his *Great War Generals on the Western Front 1914–18*, where he says:

> The persistent criticism that has followed Kiggell in the years since the Great War does not relate to his professional abilities, however, but to the allegation that, two months into The Battle of Passchendaele in 1917, he visited the front, saw the conditions and, or so it is said, burst into tears exclaiming, 'Good God, did we really send men to fight in that?' Careful research, as well as enquiries among a large number of Great War experts, have failed to find any truth in this allegation, and it is most unlikely that Kiggell ever said it.

*Kiggell is also sometimes referred to as 'the highly placed officer at GHQ' in other accounts.

Philip Warner is one of the authors who gives credence to the story. He say in his *World War One a Chronological Narrative*: 'The story has been denied, but is probably true'. He does not reveal the source for this assertion, or why he believes it to be true, he merely prefaces the story: 'it was reported of Kiggell'. In another of his books *Passchendaele* Warner repeats the allegation, this time he writes it without without any suggestion of qualification, or any reservation, but as a simple statement of fact, and again with no word of his source or authority. He says:

> Kiggell, as mentioned earlier, was the officer who, seeing the battlefield some time after Passchendaele had finally been reached, broke down and wept saying: 'Good God, did we really send men to fight in this?'

The Holts, on page 22 of their battlefield guide to the Ypres Salient, also perpetuate the story under the sub-heading 'Passchaendale 31 July – 10 November 1917, ... he [Kiggell] is said to have burst into tears and cried, "Good God"' etc.

The Anthology of Armageddon helps to keep the story alive, also without any qualification, and even pads it out a bit with detail:

> The abnormal conditions [Passchendaele] were not appreciated at GHQ. *After* the battles were over, the highly placed General Staff Officer responsible for their initiation and continuance visited the battle-front for the first time. When he saw the appalling state of the ground he exclaimed: 'What! Do you mean to say that we sent men to fight in this?' and when the junior officer who was showing him around assured him that he had, he sat down by the side of the track and burst into tears!

Perhaps it is not too surprising that this oft related story originated – in print at any rate – in Basil Liddell Hart's first version of his well-known work on the First World War, then with the title *The Real War 1914–1918*, and he repeats it verbatim on page 336 of his re-worked version entitled *History of the First World War 1914–1918*, published four years later. Once again there is no record of his source. Lloyd George picked up the story and ran with it in his *War Memoirs* published three years after Liddell Hart's original work, and although he does not actually name Kiggell as 'the highly placed officer from GHQ' there is little doubt who he means.

According to Frank Davies and Graham Maddocks in their book *Bloody Red Tabs*, more information only came to light in 1958, when Liddell Hart was persuaded to name the 'highly placed officer from General Headquarters' who was the subject of the story. He named Kiggell in the January 1958 edition of the *Spectator*. Kiggell had died four years earlier. Davies and Maddocks say that the original story was passed to Liddell Hart in 1927, when he was military correspondent of the *Daily Telegraph*, allegedly by James Edmonds. Edmonds in turn is described by Professor Brian Bond as a notorious, and not always reliable gossip, and Professor Bond said it is improbable that Edmonds actually witnessed Kiggell's [alleged] outburst.

Davies and Maddocks, who have followed the story in some depth, mention that the author Dennis Wheatley in 1978 published a new version of the famous incident in which the 'highly placed officer' is named as Sir Archibald Murrey. They also introduce another officer, Brigadier-General John Davidson, who claimed the 'weeping' staff officer was himself, but he held his hands in front of his face to show he was dumb to enquiries not to hide his tears.

It would have been fascinating to have had Kiggell's comments, but we shall never know the answer now. Those who favour the 'Butchers and Bunglers' school will no doubt continue to perpetuate the Kiggell story for, if nothing else, it makes a dramatic anecdote to support their beliefs.

Lions and donkeys

A further example of unauthenticated stories is the oft-quoted comment – attributed to General Falkenhayn – of the popular perception of British generals as the 'donkeys leading the lions'. John Baynes, in his study of Maxse, states that John Terraine and others tried to track down the origin of this epithet and the use of it by Alan Clark in his book entitled *The Donkeys*. This is exactly how it is produced in my copy of Clark's book:

> *Ludendorff:* 'The English soldiers fight like lions.'
> *Hoffmann:* 'True. But don't we know that they are lions led by donkeys.'

> FALKENHAYN: *Memoirs.*

And how could anyone doubt that as authentic? Apparently it is a direct quotation from Falkenhayn's memoirs. But eventually in reply to an enquiry, although he had apparently ignored previous requests for enlightenment, Alan Clark replied: 'The quotation was given to me by Basil Liddell Hart.

'Contemptible little army'

Another accepted 'fact'. It is widely accepted that the sobriquet 'Old Contemptibles' arises from the order that General von Kluck allegedly received from the Kaiser on 19th August 1914, which read:

It is my Royal and Imperial Command that you concentrate

your energies for the immediate present upon one single purpose, and that is, that you address all your skill and all the valour of my soldiers to exterminate the treacherous English and walk over General French's contemptible little army.

It has been said that the word 'contemptible' is a mistranslation, and the order should read 'insignificant', but 'contemptible' stuck, and was adopted by the BEF.

Brassey's *Companion to the British Army* says, however, that in 1925, the matter of this alleged statement was referred to the Kaiser at Doorn, where he was exiled after the war, but he denied ever having used 'such an expression with reference to an army, the high value of which I had always appreciated'.

PART TWENTY-THREE

I try to think forward to the day when some man will try to put together the thousand and one statements of those who were witnesses of these events which at present are beyond the power of thought to compass. What will he make of them? God knows!.

Jules Romains, in *Verdun*, expressing the thoughts of one of his military characters who is writing to a civilian friend.

Well-known books on the Great War

Brigadier General Sir James Edmonds (1861–1956)

Edmunds, while being responsible overall for the compilation of the official history of the Great War on the Western Front, did not feel prevented from voicing his own personal opinions and dislikes. (See also his comments and comments on him I have mentioned elsewhere.) For example, according to Robin Neillands, Edmunds castigates Major General Sir Charles Callwell's biography of Field Marshal Sir Henry Wilson. The book was in the library of the Staff College at Camberley, and in a letter to the librarian, dated 13th May 1955, Edmunds wrote:

> You may or may not like to paste the enclosed note into Callwell's life of Wilson, I have sent a copy to the War Office library. Wilson's death makes me think that the punishments for ill doing are awarded on this earth.*

*As I mentioned, Wilson was murdered by the IRA after the war.

The author Dennis Winter in turn makes scathing remarks about Brigadier General James Edmunds *and* his official history of the war on the Western Front:

> Few official historians have had better brains than Edmunds. His staff college entry marks were double Haig's and he reckoned to be able to translate military material from any European or Asian language.

He then goes on to say:

> Only a profoundly knowledgeable man could have produced an Official History so misleading in detail and yet with a ring of plausibility which has led to a general acceptance for so long.

Winston Churchill

Among his many works Churchill wrote a three-part study of the war in 1923, *The World Crisis 1911–1918* (from which I have quoted), and between then and 1927 this study ran into some 19 impressions. In 1930 he published the work, slightly abridged, in one volume.

Churchill was a major figure on the political stage in both world wars, particularly the second, when he became Prime Minister. Although the subject of great admiration by some, he was viewed in a less than favourable light by others. In 1915, following the failure of the sea-borne attack on the Dardanelles, he resigned office. With no prospect of another cabinet post at the time he began searching for other employment, and Lord Derby, observing Churchill calling at the War Office wrote a warning to Lloyd George [his chief at the War Office]:

> If as I hope there will be a new Party formed at the end of the war which will break down the old Party ties, Winston could not possibly be in it. Our Party will not work with him, and as far as I am concerned personally nothing would induce me to support any government of which he was a member. I like him personally. He has got a very attractive personality, but he is absolutely untrustworthy, as was his father before him, and he has got to learn that just as his father had to disappear from politics, so must he.

Prose, poetry and publishers, post war

There existed in the post-war era of the 1920s and 1930s people in a section of the intellectual writing and publishing world who not only knew each other, but frequently 'took in each other's washing'. They were a small, interactive, and at times acrimonious, group, among them ex-servicemen.

Robert von Ranke Graves (1895–1985)

Graves was a product of two cultures; his father's family was Irish, and his mother's German. He was educated at Charterhouse, which he said he hated, but where he was greatly influenced by one master, the famous mountaineer George Mallory, who, in 1924, disappeared while approaching, or some believe returning from, the summit of Mount Everest.

At the outbreak of war Graves was on holiday climbing in Wales and there he enlisted in the Royal Welch Fusiliers. Like many another at this time he gained a commission on the strength of an introduction to a regiment – in his case from the secretary of the local golf club – and the fact that he had been, for a while, in the OTC at Charterhouse.

Graves appears to have been proud of holding a commission in the Special Reserve of his regiment and, as he points out, it meant he was not a temporary officer like those of the 'New Army', but held a permanent commission in the Special Reserve Battalion. After the war in the village where he lived for a while he says he was known locally as 'the captain'.

He fought in the battles of Loos and the Somme, was wounded in 1916 during the capture of High Wood and sent home to Queen Alexandra's Hospital in London. He had earned early promotion to the rank of captain, but he does not appear to have been decorated for his exploits, or if he was he remains reticent of the fact;* he says modestly that he never performed any act that he considered to be worthy of mention.

---

*In his autobiography he says that on the whole it was understood in his regiment that the award of decorations would be restricted to regular officers, and not issued to those in the Special Reserve. If accurate this seems unfair as temporary officers in his regiment were given medals, e.g. Sassoon.

Following his hospital treatment and a medical board, he went out to France again in January 1917, but was soon invalided home suffering from lung trouble (and possibly he was diagnosed with neurasthenia as well – see below). At his request, having been offered a choice, this time he was sent to Somerville College, Oxford, then converted to a hospital. On his release from hospital he was accepted as an instructor in one of the officer cadet battalions based in England, but after a couple of months of this work he became too unwell to continue and went back to Somerville again.

While he was in hospital at Oxford, Graves, like Sassoon, met and mixed with celebrities of the day, among them H.G. Wells, Bertrand Russell, Aldous Huxley, Lytton Strachey, The Morrells, Arnold Bennett and Ivor Novello, John Galsworthy and the Sitwell family.

From Oxford he was sent to Osborne Palace on the Isle of Wight, by then also in use as a hospital, and one of a number of large buildings converted to take 'neurasthenia' cases (shell shock).* This was the end of his active service career, for he was not sent back to the Western Front or any other battle area.

*Graves wrote that having gone straight from being a schoolboy into the army he had no experience of independent life and he was still, after the war, mentally and nervously organised for war. Shells used to come bursting into his bed at night, and during the day strangers would assume the faces of friends who had been killed.

In 1917 Graves escorted Sassoon to Craiglockhart hospital (another nursing home/mental hospital, see below) on the edge of Edinburgh, where he stayed a few days with Sassoon who, reluctantly, had been persuaded to go there to avoid being court-martialled for his public attack on the continuation of the war. While at Craiglockhart, Graves made the acquaintance of Dr William Rivers* who became interested in Graves' poetry and was a mentor on the psychological aspects of his literary work.

*Rivers was a specialist in psychiatric disorders and as a result of his work with 'shell shock' cases became a noted lecturer on the subject.

It was at Craiglockhart that Graves met Owen. Like Sassoon, Owen was an inmate, and neither Graves nor Owen seemed to take to each other. Graves described Owen as 'a weakling with that passive homosexual streak in him which is even more disgusting than the active streak in Auden'. As Graves, like Sassoon, had enjoyed at least a 'passive' homosexual love affair – in the case of Graves with a younger boy when he was at school – this seems rather unkind. Owen described Graves as 'a big rather plain fellow, the last man on earth apparently capable of the extraordinary delicate fantasies of his books'.

In 1929 Graves published his famous autobiography *Goodbye to All That*, and Edmund Blunden and Siegfried Sassoon were so incensed by the book that they threatened the publisher with legal action. Both had been great friends of Graves, as well as fellow soldiers and poets, but quarrels had developed over the years. Blunden had been commissioned to write a review of the book when his friendship with Graves had long vanished. He subtitled the draft of his review 'The Welsh-Irish Bull in a China Shop' and scored it with furious comments.*

*Miranda Seymour, a biographer of Graves, is of the opinion that most of Blunden's and Sassoon's criticisms were trivial and irrelevant and out of proportion to their fury. It has to be taken into account also that both Blunden and Sassoon had just published their own war experiences and Graves had been an unenthusiastic reviewer of the first of Sassoon's war trilogy.

Keith Simpson in his introduction to Captain J.C. Dunn's book *The War the Infantry knew 1914–1919* (published in 1938 and see below) goes into more detail saying:

Sassoon's first reaction at seeing an advance copy [of *Goodbye to All That*] sent to him by Blunden, was one of hysterical rage. He was furious that Graves had included an unpublished poem without his permission and had publicised intimate details about his mother and his own breakdown during the war. Because of the breach of copyright, Johnathon Cape, the publishers had to withdraw as many copies as they could of the first edition and remove Sassoon's poem. Blunden was motivated probably by envy of Graves which prompted him to encourage Sassoon's righteous indignation. In the bitter recriminations between Sassoon and Graves, Blunden was anxious to enlist the support of Dunn who was mentioned in *Goodby to All That*. In the same letter of support to Dunn, Blunden wrote of Graves that, 'it's a crying shame that a man who had been regarded as a very fine specimen of a Modern

205

Poet should now associate that title in the public mind with his latrine bucket'.

Graves confessed that he wrote *Goodbye to All That* for money at a time when he was badly off financially. And although no one has denied the book gives an authentic picture of life on the Western Front, his critics claimed that it is more a work of fiction than autobiography.

Graves wrote in the prologue to the revised 1957 edition: 'Reading the book again for the first time since 1929, I wonder how my publishers escaped a libel action.' The book, he said, was written at a time of domestic crisis, with very little time for revision. And when he had quarrelled with or been disowned by many of his friends – and had been 'grilled'* by the police on a suspicion of attempted murder – and ceased to care what anyone thought of him.

*This police 'grilling' occurred after an incident involving a small group of 'bohemians' of the post-war era. Apparently during the course of one of the regular meetings of these like-minded poets and artists, Graves' 'muse', Laura Riding, had jumped, slipped, or fallen out of a third storey window shouting 'Goodbye chaps' in a dramatic 'suicide gesture' after the quarrel among them. She was very lucky not to have been killed in the fall.

Among the supporters of *Goodbye To All That* were T.E. Lawrence, Liddell Hart, and Frank Williams. Lawrence (the Lawrence of 'Lawrence of Arabia' fame and the author of *The Seven Pillars of Wisdom* and *The Mint*), wrote to Graves in 1929 saying the book was full of humour and exactly right in its presentation of 'wounds and nerves'. Lawrence said he especially pleased by the generous portrait of Sassoon.

T.E. Lawrence suggested to his publisher Jonathan Cape, who was keen to publish a biography of Lawrence, that Graves would be a suitable candidate to write it. Graves, who was as usual desperately short of money, accepted agreeing that Lawrence would have the last word on anything written, and certain things would not be written about.

Frank Richards, DCM, MM

Author of *Old Soldiers Never Die*, and a reservist regular private soldier who served throughout the war in the 2nd Battalion of the

Royal Welch Fusiliers on the Western Front (surviving from Mons in 1914 to the Armistice in 1918), Richards says of both Graves and Sassoon that they were considerate to their men and extremely steady and cool in the line whether going out on raids or when attacks were in progress. Richards adds that Graves and Sassoon were brave young men who never shirked any duty. And Richards, in his book, can be quite scathing about any officer, NCO, or man he feels let the side down.

Neither Graves nor Sassoon claimed to feel cool but were often in state of wild fearful elation or despair.*

*Graves stated he was drinking a bottle of whisky a day by the end of 1915. This is shades of Captain Stanhope in 1918 in *Journey's End*. It is not easy to tell with Graves's 'faction' which is his real personal experience and which is descriptive of times and conditions generally.

Apparently Graves, as an act of kindness, had edited Frank Richards' book for him because he had been touched when Richards had written to him to say how much he had enjoyed *Goodbye To All That*. Richards at the same time had enclosed a copy of *his* wartime experiences and asked Graves if he thought it was worth anything. Graves did, and spent two months editing Richards's book in 1933, but said nothing about the help he had given Richards until he wrote an introduction to another edition in 1964.

Graves also persuaded Richards to write about his pre-war life in their regiment, and this was subsequently published in 1936 as *Old Soldier Sahib*.

Sir Basil Liddell Hart (1895–1970)

Hart is an interesting figure and another controversial writer.* He was born in Paris where his father, Henry Bramley Hart, was minister at the Methodist church. (Liddell was Basil's mother's maiden name but was apparently added to Basil's birth certificate at his maternal grandfather's request.)

*See also above concerning Kiggell and Ludendorff.

Despite being sickly as a child, after attending St Paul's School and while at Corpus Christi College, Cambridge, where he was not doing very well at the end of his first year, Liddell Hart managed (by dispensing with his glasses) to pass the medical board for the army. Overcoming parental opposition he obtained a temporary commission in the regular army and was gazetted second lieutenant on 7th December 1914 in the King's Own Yorkshire Light Infantry. He was despatched to Tunbridge Wells to attend a course of instruction for officers.

Despite being a renowned writer on military strategy and tactics after the war, his own front line war experiences do not seem to have been either very prolonged or particularly distinguished. He was one of the fortunate ones on the opening day of the Somme battle on 1st July 1916, as he was held in the immediate reserve cadre while the rest of the battalion went over the top. In the first three days of the attack his battalion lost 450 men, most in the first hour of 1st July.

He served three very brief spells of duty on the Western Front with the KOYLI and was sent home unwell each time; once as a result of breathing difficulties – thought possibly to be from the effects of inhaling gas while wandering around trenches – and twice either for slight wounds or the effects of accidental or other minor injuries sustained while on active service.

Alex Danchev, in *Alchemist of War*, says of Liddell Hart's postings to the Western Front:

These stints in and around the old front line varied considerably in danger but not in duration. In fact, a curious pattern emerges. Each one was very short and abruptly curtailed, and in every case a certain vagueness, or ambiguity, surrounds the curtailment.

Later, becoming an ardent follower of Fuller, Liddell Hart enlisted Fuller's aid in an attempt to transfer to the Tank Corps after the war:

Your arguments are so convincing on the tank v. the other arms as they exist, that I am fain to become a disciple... If it is not trespassing too far on the kind interest you have taken in my efforts, may I ask what are the possibilities of a transfer to the Tank Corps?

It was not to be; he was invalided in 1924 and put on half pay as a captain, His medical board reported he was said to be suffering from a moderate degree of DAH (disordered action of the heart), and previously influenza in 1918 and tonsillitis in 1919. Through influence and the good offices of a friend, Major General Sir Ivor Maxse, Liddell Hart obtained a post as assistant military correspondent, and tennis correspondent, to the *Morning Post.*

Liddell Hart mixed with the great in military and political circles, and despite his comparatively modest military experience in the war, he does not seem to be shy or retiring when dealing with them. He claimed, it is alleged, there was an occasion when he reproved an officer during a briefing of retired officers saying: 'As a brigadier* you cannot talk as you are doing to a former Chief of the Air Staff.' Not bad going for an officer who had never risen above the rank of captain and had hardly shone in the field! He was, apparently, always quite prepared to lecture his ranking superiors.

*The brigadier was Lord Carver (1915–2001), who was to have a distinguished career in the Second World War and become a Field Marshal, Chief of the General Staff, and Chief of the Defence Staff as well as the author of *Britain's Army in the 20th Century* and a number of books of military history. Created a life peer in 1977, Carver was described by Sir David Fraser, a fellow soldier, writer and historian, as: 'an highly intelligent Wykehamist, he suffered fools neither gladly nor agreeably'. Tall, austere and with a cutting tongue, it is not recorded how he responded to Liddell Hart's admonition, if indeed it was made.

In 1925 on the retirement of the renowned war correspondent Col. Repington, Liddell Hart became a fully-fledged military correspondent with the *Daily Telegraph*, and later he joined *The Times.*

He may not have had much practical experience as a soldier in the field of battle, but he became a respected theoretical tactician who delighted in war games. Interestingly, and possibly sensibly, in 1934 he declined an invitation from General Sir John Burnett-Stuart, GOC British Troops in Egypt, to take part in a series of exercises and to have the opportunity to take command of a desert column to put some of his ideas into practice. He said in his reply: 'Whether or not I succeeded or failed as a commander would be little or no gauge on my value as a critic.'

The author of some forty books and many articles, a number of them on military matters for which he was given great acclaim by some, and critical disapproval by others, his best remembered book is on the Great War. Originally titled *The Real War 1914–1918* published in 1930, it was enlarged in 1934, and re-titled *History of the World War 1914–18*, and finally renamed *History of the First*

World War in 1970. It was a very successful book for him, and is frequently quoted as an authoritative reference source.*

*The reviewer of the book in the *Western Mail* was obviously unaware of the general stance of Liddell Hart, or the controversy the book aroused. In fact one wonders on occasions if the reviewers of books actually read them. He says: 'Remarkable for its clarity and objectivity, and for analysis undistorted by professional prejudice or by bitterness over the unrecallable past.'

Professor Brian Bond, President, British Commission for Military History, 1999, writing a study of Liddell Hart in *Look to Your Front* says:

On the wider 'front' of popular opinion it must be acknowledged that Liddell Hart's unremitting efforts to propagate his interpretation of the First World War have been remarkably successful. In the 1960s his controlling hand and distinctive authorial 'voice' seemed to be omnipresent. Thus he was consultant or adviser for the BBC's celebrated *'Great War'*, Joan Littlewood's play *'Oh What a Lovely War'*, the screening of *'Lawrence of Arabia'* and the play *'Ross'*. His was the chief inspiration behind Purnell's best selling part-work series on the First World War. 'Moreover in this radical, revisionist decade it was almost obligatory to obtain Liddell Hart's approval and imprimatur for publication on the First World War. Thus he vetted the drafts of Alan Clark's *The Donkeys* and A.J.P. Taylor's irreverent *History* which depicted British Western Front generals as donkeys and the war itself as meaningless; praised Leon Wolff's poignant dirge about the Passchendaele campaign [*In Flanders Fields*] and passed an anathema on John Terraine for his heretical presumption in daring to write sympathetically about Haig.

Like Robert Graves, Liddell Hart also wrote a biography of Lawrence. Alex Danchev, writing in his biography of Liddell Hart *Alchemist of War*, mentions an occasion where Liddell Hart and his first wife Jessie were wining and dining in Mayfair, and Jessie turned to a fellow guest saying:

'T.E.L [Lawrence] thought Basil's book much better than previous books on him including Robert Graves', and wished

210

they had not been written. Her companion replied, 'that's interesting, he [Robert Graves] is my brother.'

Turning from this *faux pas* she burst in on another guest, Warwick Deeping, who was talking about a proposal to make a film of his book *Sorrell and Son* with the question 'who wrote it?'

Still, if she was inclined towards social gaffes, apparently she had in compensation a fine appearance with a small waist, and dressed well. Liddell Hart it would seem was very interested in ladies' attire and small waists. He wrote to General Sir Ian Hamilton in 1939 'on a matter of cardinal importance' (Alex Danchev reporting the occasion remarks that although Liddell Hart's letter does not survive, Hamilton's reply does or did) and Hamilton in reply to Liddell Hart said:

> It is extraordinary that you are able to turn from matters of such grave interest [the impending Second World War] to concern yourself with a subject so slight as the waist of the lovely Kattie Dennistoun.* I will make full enquiries in the much diminished circle of her friends and see if I can rake up a more convincing picture.

*Hamilton, who had been in command of the ill-fated Gallipoli campaign in 1915/16, apparently, while reminiscing on his youth, had mentioned to Liddell Hart the pretty daughters of a family friend who, he said: 'were all tall, fit and supple and they had the smallest waists in Scotland, Katty's [*sic*] being 14 inches and the others 15 inches. I have squared these circles myself and so should know.' Liddell Hart, it would seem, was agog.

Siegfried Lorraine Sassoon MC (1886–1967)

Sassoon, a renowned author of both prose and poetry, was born into a wealthy background of Jewish bankers. His father deserted his wife and died soon after, leaving her with three sons to bring up. Siegfried, like Wilfred Owen and Donald Hankey, was very attached to his mother. After leaving Marlborough Sassoon went up to Cambridge to read law, then switched to history, but left without taking a degree. Hunting, cricket, buying old books, and reading poetry were his main interests, and his mother introduced him to a literary milieu where he met Rupert Brooke.

On the outbreak of war Sassoon enlisted in the Yeomanry, and

211

then transferred to the infantry, and was commissioned into the Royal Welch Fusiliers. He joined the 1st Battalion in France where he met Robert Graves who at that time was also with the 1st Battalion. Sassoon was awarded the Military Cross and earned the nickname 'Mad Jack' for his exploits. He suffered from both trench fever and wounds. When he was home on sick leave in 1917 the famous episode of his statement of protest against the continuation of the war took place, which resulted in him being sent to Craiglockhart Hospital for Neurasthenic Officers to avoid being court-martialled (see Robert Graves above).

While at Craiglockhart hospital he linked up with Wilfred Owen after Owen had knocked on his door one day and nervously introduced himself. Owen's initial impression of Sassoon, according to Hibberd, a biographer of Owen, was of a 'handsome very tall stately man with a general air of boredom'. For his part, Hibberd says, 'Gazing vaguely somewhere above Wilfred's head, Sassoon noticed that "Little Owen", as he often referred to him later, had a slight neurasthenic stammer and was "perceptibly provincial".'

Hibberd's view is that Owen, who had spent about as much time as Sassoon in the front line, suffered far worse experiences than Sassoon. He also says Sassoon was driven by his instinct for martyrdom – both on the field of battle and at home. Be that as it may, after returning to the Western Front, and being wounded a second time, Sassoon ended the war on permanent sick leave. He converted to Catholicism in 1957 and died ten years later.

Sassoon, who uses pseudonyms in his two 'faction' books incorporating his war experiences – *Memoirs of a Foxhunting Man* and *Memoirs of an Infantry Officer* – refers to himself as George Sherston, as he does again in *Sherston's Progress*, and he names his regiment, the Royal Welch Fusiliers, as 'The Flintshires'. He calls Robert Graves 'David Cromlech'. In *Siegfried's Journey 1916–1920* he uses real names throughout.

His collection of anti-war poems, *Counter attack*, received acclaim when it was released in 1918. Bertrand Russell and other leading pacifists around him had encouraged him to play up contempt for the military leaders in his writings, and to stress the useless slaughter of the troops. When he made his statement of protest he threw away his MC – though according to Robert Graves he continued to wear the ribbon on his tunic. (Another version says it was the MC ribbon from his tunic that he tore off and threw away.) A comment on Sassoon comes from a friend of his, the Benedictine nun, Dame Felicitas Corrigan who published Sassoon's *Siegfried Sassoon: Poet's Pilgrimage* (1973). She says of him: 'Sassoon was too egocentric to be really likeable.'

Sassoon lies buried in the graveyard of a small church in Somerset in the village of Mells. Also buried here are Asquith, Bonham-Carter and Ronald Arbuthnott Knox. Sassoon had asked to be buried near Ronald Knox* at Mells.

*Knox a theologian and writer was a contemporary of Sassoon. He died in 1957, ten years before Sassoon.

Edmund Charles Blunden MC (1896–1974)

Blunden's book, *Undertones of War*, is a much more low-key and tolerant work than either the war books of Graves and Sassoon. He writes with kindness and gentleness and is at times elegiac without playing down the awfulness of it all. He, like Behrend, writes with affection for his CO. The book was first published in 1928, and sold out almost immediately. Reviews were very favourable, and a revised edition appeared in 1930. Like so many who served, the war haunted him, and apparently Sassoon maintained that of all the war poets Blunden remained the most obsessed by it.

He was born in London on 1st November 1896. His father was headmaster of a Church of England primary school. His mother on the other hand was of a family with an aristocratic background. Blunden won a scholarship to Oxford, but because so many of his friends had enlisted and were being killed, he cycled to Chichester and enlisted in the Royal Sussex Regiment. Two weeks later he was commissioned into the 11th Battalion.

Writing in 1956 in the preface of the new edition of his book, he says the book was written in Tokyo in 1924 and after, and without books and papers, but with two maps he had kept covering the regions he knew. It was written, he said, with no grander ambition than to preserve some of the multitude of impressions, and admirations of a happy battalion – happy in spite of terrible tasks and daily destruction. Some claim it is the best English book about the war. Arnold Bennett wrote: 'This book will be a classic. It cannot *not* be a classic'.

Wilfred Edward Salter Owen MC (1893–1918)

Owen was born in Oswestry on 18th March. He appears to have been a bright boy, studious and obsessed with poetry from an early age. In 1913, undecided on his future career, and having failed to win a scholarship to Reading University, he was at a loose end. After some thought he decided to go to France to improve his language skills and to try again for Reading next year. He settled in Bordeaux where he had managed to obtain a job as a part-time teacher of English at the Berlitz language school.

Hibberd, a biographer of Owen (see above under Sassoon) says that while in France Owen came very much under the influence of the French poet Laurent Tailhade whom he heard lecture at the Casino in Bagnères, met socially, and then became a friend. Tailhade introduced Owen to the poetic movements of 'Aestheticism' and its off-shoots 'Decadence' and 'Symbolism' and these bore an influence on Owen's future poetry.*

*Tailhade, according to Hibberd, had been a disciple of the leading Symbolist, Mallarmé, and a close friend of the leading 'Decadent', Verlaine. Writing to his mother about his first meeting with Tailhade, at Tailhade's hotel, Owen said: 'He received me like lover ... he quite slobbered over me. I know not how many times he squeezed my hand; and sitting down on a sofa, pressed my head against his shoulder.'

Eventually, after much deliberation while he was back on a visit in England, Owen enlisted in the army in June 1915, and after training in an Officer Training Corps unit,* he was gazetted as Second Lieutenant on 4th June 1916 to 5th Battalion, The Manchester Regiment (the regiment's training battalion).

*The Artists' Rifles (1/28th County of London Battalion).

Despite the desperate need for replacements in France following the Somme battles, Owen was kept in England to train new recruits in musketry. He was by all accounts very good and conscientious as a trainer, and in addition an excellent shot with a rifle. While engaged in these training duties he applied to join the RFC, but his CO, who was keen to retain Owen's services in his present capacity, seemed rather conveniently to have mislaid his application. Owen was eventually posted to a regular battalion of his regiment, the 2nd Manchesters, after being told initially, while waiting posting at Étaples, that he would be sent to the Lancashire Fusiliers.

He was delighted to be joining his own regiment, but by the time he joined up with them in January 1917, the battalion – which had been reduced to 6 officers and 150 men at Serre in November 1916 – was almost entirely a new unit, rebuilt with large drafts from England.

Life in the battalion on the whole was fairly uneventful until Nivelle's spring offensive in 1917 (see Part Forty-one below). To quote Hibberd again: 'It was during these nine days [the attack on the Hindenburg Line] 13th – 21st April 1917, that having had many escapes from shells and bullets, Wilfred Owen's nerve finally gave way when he was blown into the air by a big shell bursting a few yards from his head while he was asleep.'

He seemed to recover superficially, but on 1st May Major Dempster, whom Owen feared and detested, became acting CO, and on that day Owen's army file recorded, 'Second Lieutenant Owen was observed to be shaky and tremulous, and his conduct and manner were peculiar, and his memory was confused'.

After spending quite a while at the Casualty Clearing Station at Gailly, now a specialist hospital for shell-shock cases, he was sent first to the No.1 General Hospital, Étretat, near Le Havre, and then on 25th June 1917 to the Welsh Hospital at Netley, near Southampton, and finally to Craiglockhart War Hospital for Neurasthenic Officers. Here, as I have said, he met Sassoon, whom he idolised. Sassoon introduced Owen to a new world of gentlemen's clubs, intellectual gatherings of pacifists and radicals, and a homosexual circle which including poets, and publishers.

At the end of August 1918, Owen was finally drafted back to France despite the efforts of Charles Scott Moncrieff – one of Sassoon's circle – to keep him in England in his earlier job as a trainer of new troops.

Owen was awarded the Military Cross. The citation reads, 'For conspicuous gallantry and devotion to duty in an attack on 1st/2nd October, 1918'. A month later he was killed leading his company of the Manchesters in another attack across the Sambre-Oise canal on 2nd November, just nine days before the end of the war. It seems a particularly cruel act of fate that his mother received the telegram announcing his death on 11th November, Armistice Day.

Although Owen is generally highly regarded today – and is perhaps famous because of Britten's use of Owen's verses in his dramatic *War Requiem* (first performed in 1962) – Owen's poems earlier received a mixed reception from both fellow poets and reviewers. On the publication of Owen's poems after the war Henry Newbolt dismissed them as the work of a broken man, and W.B. Yeats deliberately omitted Owen from the 1936 *Oxford Book of Modern Verse*. Sassoon and Graves however, despite their rather patronising attitudes to 'provincial little Owen' as a person, both came to respect him as a poet, and commended him sincerely to others.*

*Sassoon, Graves, C.D. Lewis, Edmund Blunden and the Sitwells were involved and instrumental in the promotion and the publication of Owen's poetry after Owen was killed.

Ian Hay (1876–1952)

This is the pseudonym of the novelist and dramatist Major-General John Hay Beith who had written light-hearted school stories before the war, but his famous book, published in 1916, *The First Hundred Thousand*,* is probably the one for which he will be most remembered.

*To indicate the popularity of the book, my copy, printed in 1916, is the eleventh impression.

Read today, the rather determinedly cheerful come-what-may style, with jocular references to 'brother Bosche' and his 'amusing escapades', may strike one as very dated, but the language and sentiments expressed are quite of their time, and of course it was written before the war had settled into its long drawn out misery where no break-through seemed possible, and when daily casualty lists grew to enormous proportions.

The author states in his introductory note that the book is a record of the personal adventures of a typical regiment of 'Kitchener's Army'* and the chapters were written from day to day, and originally published from month to month. The characters, he says, are entirely fictitious, but that the incidents described all actually occurred.

*The 10th Argyll & Sutherland Highlanders. They formed part of the 27th Brigade in the 9th (Scottish) Division. All three brigades in this division were composed of 'New Army' infantry battalions.

A correspondent of Philip Warner (quoted in his *The Battle of Loos*), a Mr G.P. Keef, sent Warner an account written by a Captain Wyllie, Royal Scots Fusiliers, who had met Ian Hay. Captain Wyllie says that Ian Hay was, at the time of Loos, Captain Beith of the 10th Argylls and Sutherland Highlanders, and Wyllie had met him at Talavera barracks in Aldershot in 1914 when they were in the same Mess together. Hay/Beith was then a Lieutenant in the 10th Argylls, and Wyllie describes him as a tall dark serious man who did not look as if he had a spark of humour in his make up, but, he adds, this was far from the truth.

Ian Hay survived the war – serving for a time as a member of the British War Mission to the USA –and after the war, in addition to adapting many of his own novels for the stage, he dramatised stories by P.G. Wodehouse, a close friend of his.

Wilfrid Ewart (1892–1922)

Ewart came from a background of distinguished military forebears, and although even as a boy he was not of robust health, he served in the Scots Guards on the Western Front from 1916 to 1918. He survived the war, his wounds and his illnesses, only to die in Mexico in the most tragic and pointless circumstances soon after his friends and comrades had fallen on the battlefields.

The Times, dated January 6th 1923 reported the circumstances saying that Ewart was in Mexico City to write his book or books, having arrived from Sante Fé on 31st December 1922:

> He had reached his hotel at 11.30 pm and it is assumed, that attracted by the sound of guns firing in the street, where rowdy merry-makers were following the local custom and firing at random in the air, he leaned over the balcony of his room and was shot.

His book from which I have quoted excerpts, *Scots Guard on the Western Front 1915–1918*, was published after his death.

Henry Williamson (1895–1977)

Author of many books, he wrote among others the compelling, moving, and partly autobiographical saga *A Chronicle of Ancient Sunlight*. Five volumes in the series cover the 1914–1918 war years.

He was born on 1st December 1895, and died on 13th August 1977. Anne Williamson, a biographer, described the First World

217

War as the pivot upon which the whole of his life turned.* She said it occupied his thoughts and dominated his actions throughout the rest of his eighty years, and was the direct source for seven of his fifty books. She adds that he was a complicated man who died in loneliness despite the efforts of his family and friends. He was taken into care of the monks of Twyford Abbey and died there.

*I wrote to Henry Williamson in the early or mid-1960s to say how much I had been moved by, and engrossed in, the war-years books of his chronicle, but I never received a reply.

He joined the London Rifle Brigade in January 1914, and embarked with them for France on 4th November. He suffered from the bitterly cold and wet conditions in and around Ploegsteert Wood, and was invalided home in January 1915, and later commissioned into the Machine Gun Corps. Another author, who also served in the LRB was A.D. Gristwood, who wrote *The Somme* and *The Coward.*

V.M. Yeats (died 15th December 1934, aged 37 years)

A fighter pilot, and great friend of Henry Williamson, who appears in Williamson's *A Chronicle of Ancient Sunlight* as the character Tom Cundall, Yeats published in 1934 a novel about pilots' lives on the Western Front. This was *Winged Victory*. Williamson said of the book: 'I believe that *Winged Victory* is not only one of the best of the War books, but that as a transcription of reality, faithful and sustained in its author's purpose of re-creating the past life he knew, it is unique.'*

According to Williamson the book changed hands at five pounds a time among RAF pilots in Norfolk in the Second World War because it was the only war flying book which 'wasn't flannel'. And Yeats dedicated the book to Williamson and gives one of the main characters in the book the name of Williamson, and another as 'Tom Cundall'.

*Williamson thought that only one other ['faction'] novel was in the same class as Yeats' *Winged Victory* and that was Ewart's *Way of Revelation* (see above for Ewart's *Scots Guard*).

Author unknown

Death in the Air. War Diary and Photographs of a Flying Corps Pilot published in 1933 received a mixed reception because doubts were cast on the authenticity of the photographs – partly because other than the official reconnaissance photographs taken by an aeroplane's observer, the taking of aerial photographs was forbidden. – and also the taking of photographs in aerial combat was so very difficult in those days when the cameras were heavy and cumbersome, and shutter speeds were generally slower than today.

Shortly before his death the unknown author – of what were actually typewritten notes – gave the notes and photographic negatives to a fellow flyer under a solemn promise that the identity of the photographer and diarist would never be revealed (because the taking of unofficial photographs at the front was forbidden, and a court-martial offence).

Donald William Alers Hankey (1884–1916)

Hankey was author of *A Student in Arms*, and had first produced the book anonymously as a series of essays in the *Spectator* in 1915. These were then published in book form in April 1916. So popular was the book that by the end of 1916 it had been reprinted seven times.

Donald Hankey was born in Brighton on 27th October 1884, the youngest child of six (surviving) children, four boys and two girls. After prep school he, like his father and his three older brothers, went to Rugby, and it was while there that he learned of the death of his eldest brother Hugh, 'shot in a glorious but futile charge', killed at Paardeberg in South Africa in the Boer War in 1900.

Hugh had been a hero to all of his brothers, and he excelled in practically everything he undertook. His death lay very heavily on his mother, and she died not long afterwards. The mother had been the focus of the family, shouldering most of the day to day decisions, while the father, a somewhat remote but not unkindly figure interested mainly in theology and philosophy, remained in the background, and frequently dined alone.

Although Christianity was very important to all the family, and Donald was drawn to taking holy orders, he suffered from doubts concerning the structure, performance, and attitudes of the established church. He also had doubts on his own abilities and strengths to become a clergyman in the church.* His desire was to go to Oxford to read theology, but his father decided it would be better for him to spend some time in the army before making the decision, and the likely consequences from such a decision.

*He may have also have had doubts of another nature about himself, because in his correspondence he makes occasional cryptic comments that indicate he was at least aware of having homosexual proclivities – even if not ever actively engaged in them.

His brother Maurice was in the Marines, and Donald, at the age of seventeen, was sent to the Royal Military Academy at Woolwich, 'The Shop' as it was known, to become a gunner. He did not enjoy his time at Woolwich, but was commissioned at the age of nineteen, in 1903, into the Royal Garrison Artillery, and soon after posted to Mauritius. While there he became ill with appendicitis, but otherwise settled, at least on the surface, into the routine of garrison life abroad. However, in his second year in Mauritius he suffered from a more serious complaint described as an abscess on the liver.

While on home leave in England following his illness, his father died, and Donald felt he was now free to resign his commission and go to Oxford. At Oxford he joined what was to become the Oxford and Bermondsey Mission (the OBM) and he worked among the poor in Bermondsey running boys' clubs and giving spiritual guidance to the youths in the area.

He took time off and journeyed to Australia (his mother came from Adelaide, South Australia) to try his hand at hard physical work, and at the same time to look for suitable areas in the country for sending out boys from the slums of London to engage in farm work.*

*To me this sounds like a forerunner of the YMCA 'Big Brother Movement', a scheme of similar aims and ideals but which fell into disrepute in later years when there were reports of employers ill treating boys who had been sent out to Australia under the scheme.

Following his return to England in 1914 and when war broke out Donald Hankey enlisted in the army. He applied for a commission because he doubted that he would pass the medical for joining as a ranker, but meanwhile, on 8th August 1914, he was passed medically as satisfactory, and on 'taking the King's shilling' he was enlisted into a 'K1' battalion of the Rifle Brigade,* just beating the maximum age limit of 30 by two months.

220

*7th (Service) Battalion, the Rifle Brigade. It was actually officially formed at Winchester on 21st August 1914.

Within a week he was made a sergeant. His brother Maurice, now a lieutenant colonel in the Marines, and since 1912, Secretary of the Committee of Imperial Defence, thought Donald would make a reasonable subaltern, but not so good an NCO.

Donald went to France with the battalion in May 1915, and here he demoted himself to the rank of corporal by transferring to another company on the departure and death of his company commander whom he greatly admired,* and the appointment of his successor, whom he disliked intensely.

*This was his 'beloved captain' of the essay of the same name, and appears as chapter IV in his book.

The battalion was engaged in the Ypres Salient area and Hankey was wounded in action on 30th July, one of the battalion's 300 casualties. He was invalided back to England with a hole in his right thigh. While in England – still full of doubts, but encouraged, one suspects, by his brother Maurice – he applied again for a commission. His application was successful and he was appointed once more to the artillery, to a battery in the UK. After a brief spell here, but keen to return to France, he transferred back to the infantry. This time he joined his brother Hugh's old regiment, The Warwicks, and went into one of the regular battalions.

2nd Lieutenant Donald Hankey, 1st Battalion Royal Warwickshire Regiment was killed in action in an attack near Lesboeufs on the Somme, 12th October 1916. A few days before he was killed he wrote cheerfully to his sister Hilda saying his unit was going into action very soon, but with a premonition that he might not survive the attack for which the omens were not good.

Donald Hankey is quoted in a biography by James Kissane *Without Parade* as: 'A man with a self-effacing personality, warm and charming, yet at some level strangely unapproachable'. Kissane adds that, according to one soldier, an officer's servant: 'Lt. D. Hankey to the soldiers he led was more of a chum than an officer', and the soldier named his own son Donald as a tribute to Hankey saying: 'If he is only a quarter good as D. Hankey, I will be proud of him.'

According to Professor Kissane, Donald Hankey's brother –

221

Colonel Sir Maurice Hankey, Secretary to the Committee of Imperial Defence – received a telephone call at his office in Whitehall informing him of his brother's death in action. He listened impassively and as he replaced the telephone receiver he said to his secretary, to whom he had been dictating, 'Donald's gone'. After a moment's pause, he said, 'Where was I, Owen?'

Although Donald was hastily buried after being killed, no trace of his grave was ever found, and the only record of Donald Hankey is as one of the 72,000 names inscribed on the Thiepval Memorial* for those with no known grave who died on the Somme.

*See Part Five above.

R.C. Sherriff (1896–1975)

Sherriff was author of perhaps the most famous play ever written about the war, *Journey's End* (also turned into a novel), which achieved enormous success in both America and Britain. The play nearly failed to see the light of day as the commercial theatre managements were reluctant to stage it on the grounds that it would not make any money at the box office.* However, by the end of 1929, after it was first produced at the Savoy Theatre, fourteen companies were performing the play in English, and seventeen translations were running in Europe.

*All three acts of the play take place in just one set, a candle lit dug-out, and the whole of the play takes place during the three days before the beginning of the great German offensive *Der Kaiserschlacht* on March 21st 1918 (see Parts Forty-seven and Forty-eight below).

Sherriff had joined the army soon after the war began, and ended it as a captain in the East Surrey Regiment. The success of the play led to him being offered the chance to write film scripts as well as other plays. Among his film scripts were *The Dam Busters*, and *Goodbye Mr Chips*. The story of the play *Journey's End* was also adapted for a film called *Aces High* in 1976 and set in a RFC/RAF airfield in France instead of the play's dug-out. And the play, in its original form, is at present (in the spring of 2004), enjoying a very successful revival for a limited season at the Comedy Theatre in London's West End.

222

German authors

Erich Maria Remarque

Remarque* was author of *All Quiet on the Western Front*, a book that has been disparaged by some other ex-soldier authors, as well as by the German National Socialist regime in the 1930s, but considered by others to be the most famous (anti) war novel of its era; it was also turned into a successful Hollywood film in 1930 with Lew Ayres in the leading role.

*I understand he was actually born Kramer, but later reversed the name, i.e 'Remark', calling himself 'Remarque' he went to live in Switzerland.

Ernst Jünger (1895– ?)

Jünger was a controversial figure, who apparently 'doctored' his famous books *The Storm of Steel* (*Stahlgewittern*) and *Copse 125** by amending the later editions.

*Both at present available in reprinted translations from the publishers and military booksellers The Naval and Military Press Ltd.

He is described by Professor Thomas Nevin in his work *Ernst Jünger and Germany Into the Abyss 1914–1945* as: 'One of Europe's leading twentieth-century writers, and for a time hero of the Nazi regime in Germany, he narrowly escaped death following the assassination attempt on Hitler's life.'

He was a brave, highly decorated, and many times wounded infantry soldier and storm trooper in the First World War, and where he served throughout the war (apart from spells in training and hospital) on the Western Front opposite both French and British forces.

I must confess that I find his style and language (read in translation anyway), offputting and alien, with Nietzsche-like undertones of glory through suffering, pain and death – a 'Germanic' style of philosophy that was much in vogue for a while.*

*Neitzsche lived the latter part of his life in great pain, and following a complete mental and physical breakdown in January 1889, was confined to a mental asylum until his death in 1900. I believe, though I cannot find the book now (a biography of Neitzsche I bought many years ago – by Janko Lavrin?) that the author stated that Neitzsche suffered from hereditary syphilis.

Compared with Jünger I feel much more comfortable with Donald Hankey's description of his platoon (written in the letter mentioned above to his sister Hilda just before he was killed) when he said: 'I have a top-hole platoon – nearly all young, and nearly all have been out here 18 months – thoroughly good sporting fellows' – compared with Jünger's comments on studying *his* platoon before an attack: 'The immovable face half rimmed by the steel and monotonous voice accompanied by the noise of the front made the impression of an uncanny gravity. One perceived the man had paid out every terror to the point of despair and then had learned contempt. Nothing seemed left but a great and manly indifference.'

French authors

I regret to say that I am familiar with only two books on the war by French writers. The first the famous *Le Feu* (*Under Fire*) by Henri Barbusse that some critics feel is so unrestrainedly anti war that it loses some of its impact. The other is Jules Romains' *Verdun*, published in 1938. My edition, which I bought in 1962, is a re-issue, and it gives neither a potted biography nor a background comment about the author. My edition is also a prime example of my 'text and maps' complaint above.

PART TWENTY-FOUR

Senior officers well behind the enemy lines [sic] *seldom felt the conditions of horror, or the bitter consequences of their own orders, ignored the growing list of casualties and enforced a barbaric discipline which saw the shooting of shell-shocked soldiers.*

> John Prescott writing in 1990 in the preface to
> *This Righteous War*, by B. Barnes, and quoted in
> *Bloody Red Tabs* by F. Davies and G. Maddocks.
> Prescott, in 1990, was then as he is now in 2004,
> MP for Hull East, and he is at present the
> Deputy Prime Minister.

Portrayal of the British GHQ and other HQ staff

Prescott adopts the almost obligatory stance of those whose who wish to portray the First World War military leaders and their staffs as blundering, incompetent, mindless, callous 'butchers', and/or to ridicule them as derisive 'Blimp' type caricatures of the military establishment.

This mocking portrayal was exemplified in the stage production of *Oh! What a Lovely War* by Joan Littlewood's Theatre Workshop, and Richard Attenborough's film of the same name. But not, as far as I remember, in the two earlier radio programmes that inspired these productions – these two were produced by Charles Chilton,* and the second of the two broadcasts was narrated by Bud Flanagan, who, like his stage partner Chesney Allen, had served on the Western Front. Incidentally, and apropos of absolutely nothing except 'show business' and WWI, I seem to remember Bud Flanagan saying that by way of revenge he took his stage name from his sergeant major, a man he disliked intensely. A reciprocated feeling I gather.

*The radio programme was titled *The Long, Long Trail* and according to Valerie Grove, writing in *The Oldie* Issue 181, Joan Littlewood gave him no credit on the show, and Chilton had to go to court to get his name on the programme.

I have read that Joan Littlewood used Liddell Hart – via Raymond Fletcher* – as a reference source for her stage show. Until attending a performance at a re-issue of her show at the Open Air Theatre in Regent's Park in 2002 (after an interval of nearly forty years since I first saw the production with her Theatre Workshop cast at Wyndhams Theatre), I had forgotten the inaccuracies, the selective insertions and omissions and the crude agitprop style and content of her text in the production – splendidly performed though it was on both the occasions I saw it all those years apart, and cleverly and imaginatively presented on each occasion.

*According to Brian Bond (see above) and Richard Bryson, a significant contributor to the script of *Oh! What a Lovely War* was Raymond Fletcher. Fletcher was a journalist and later a Labour MP for Ilkeston and a self-confessed fan of Liddell Hart, and he wrote revealingly by describing the play's message as: 'one part me, one part Liddell Hart, the rest Lenin' when he delivered a three-hour overview lecture to the cast of the Theatre Workshop.

Others, such as Arthur Behrend, take a more tolerant assessment of the leaders. Writing in 1963 Behrend said:

> To those young men of today who write about the 1914–1918 war without having experienced it and who tear to shreds the reputation and professional conduct of its dead Generals, I should like to say that I think they tend to overlook the conditions of the time, the prevailing standards of military knowledge, and, most of all, the power and might of the German armies.

Philip Warner, speaking of the Somme in 1916 in his *World War One*, comments on Haig:

> Haig, usually portrayed as a ruthless automaton but in reality a man of compassion and artistic sensibility driven by a powerful sense of duty...

There are others who served in the war and who write taking an opposing view of the military hierarchy, and would support Siegfried Sassoon's poem *The General*. For example, Major General J.F.C. Fuller,* CB, CBE, DSO (1878–1966), who was an insider at GHQ, and one who had little time for Haig or the other people there. He wrote in the introduction to Leon Wolff's *In Flanders Fields*:

> He [Haig] lived and worked like a clock, every day he did the same thing at the same moment, his routine never varied. In character he was stubborn and intolerant, in speech inarticulate, in argument dumb. But he was not an uneducated soldier. Unlike so many cavalrymen of his day, he had studied war, and, strange to say this was to be his undoing, because he was so unimaginative that he could not see that the tactics of the past were as dead as mutton.

*See above also under Liddell Hart.

Fuller however has been described as a somewhat maverick figure, and one who cannot be said to be a disinterested or unprejudiced observer of GHQ. At the time he was a senior figure there in a group of officers guiding the new British tank service, and he argued strongly for mass deployment of tanks on suitable ground.*

*Although it has been claimed by a number of people that until Cambrai tanks had not been used well or in the right conditions or strength, it has also been claimed, as mentioned elsewhere, that once their initial advantage of surprise had been lost, their mechanical unreliability and slow speed and vulnerability – particularly over deeply churned up ground and deep trenches – caused them to be regarded with less than enthusiasm by many at GHQ. However, a frustrated Fuller championing tanks was not likely to have viewed GHQ with less than a jaundiced eye.

Evan Charteris,* who was GSO3 (General Staff Officer 3rd Grade) to Fuller's GSO1 (1st Grade), at GHQ said of Fuller in *Tanks*, according to Alex Danchev:

> He [Fuller] stood out at once as a totally unconventional soldier. Prolific in ideas, fluent in expression, at daggers drawn with received opinion, authority and tradition... He could talk amusingly and paradoxically on any subject. His specialities were Eastern religions ... spiritualism, occultism, military history and the theory of war ... he was an inexhaustible writer, and

from his office issued reams on reams on training, plans of campaign, organisation and schemes for the use of tanks. He was an invaluable element from a military and social point of view, but his brains would have been better utilised at GHQ galvanizing that conservative centre with advanced ideas.

I believe I am correct in saying that Fuller had little or no real practical experience as a commander in the field during the First World War, I understand he was appointed GSO2 at GHQ in 1916, and remained a staff officer for the duration of the war.

*Evan Charteris, by the way, is not to be confused with Brigadier General John Charteris. Evan Charteris had been a member of 'Souls' – a group whom Martin Stephen, in *The Price of Pity* describes as being witty, elegant men and women and at the turn of the century, mostly in their twenties and thirties, but the men already prominent in public life, and the women renowned for intelligence as well as beauty. (Julian Grenfell's mother was also a member of 'Souls' apparently.)

Brigadier General John Charteris describes a prominent characteristic of Haig that had begun and developed from his school days, that of 'aloneness'. And Charteris says:

> He was his own judge, his own taskmaster; he set the standard for himself, and he did not allow himself to be deflected by a hair's breadth from his intentions or to be swayed by the opinions of others.

Charteris describes the unvarying day of Haig and the routine at GHQ as follows:

> Punctually at 8.25 each morning Haig's bedroom door opened, and he walked downstairs [and after tapping the barometer in the hall] he then went for a short four minutes' walk in the garden. At 8.30 precisely he came into the mess for breakfast. If he had a guest present, he always insisted on serving the guest before he helped himself. He talked very little, and generally confided himself to asking his personal staff what their plans were for the day. At nine o'clock he went into his study and worked until eleven or half-past. At half-past eleven he saw Army Commanders, the Heads of Departments at General Headquarters, and others whom he might desire to

see. At one o'clock he had lunch, which only lasted half an hour, and then he either motored or rode to the Headquarters of some Army or Corps or Division. He was careful to avoid giving the Headquarters messes of subordinate units the trouble of providing meals for himself and his staff, and on days when he wished to visit a distant part of the line he used to take a luncheon basket with him in his car... Generally when returning from these visits he would arrange for his horse to meet the car so that he could travel the last three or four miles on horseback. When not motoring he always rode in the afternoon, accompanied by his ADC and his escort of 17th Lancers, without which he never went out for a ride. Always on the return journey from his ride he would stop about three miles from home and hand his horse over to a groom and walk back to Headquarters. On arrival there he would go straight up to his room, have a bath, do his physical exercises and then change into slacks. From then until dinner-time at 8 o'clock he would sit at his desk and work, but he was always available if any staff or guests wished to see him. He never objected to interruptions at this hour. At 8 o'clock he dined. After dinner which lasted about an hour, he returned to his room and worked until a quarter to eleven.

There were only rare occasions when this routine of the Commander-in- Chief's day was broken even by a minute... Haig knew the name of every army corps or Division Commander and in what part of the line they were situated. He would often test his staff by asking 'Who commands such and such a corps?' Any reference to a notebook annoyed him, and he would say: 'You ought to know that; it is so and so'.

He required those working with him to train their memories. An ADC who on his first interview for orders produced a slip of paper and pencil to take notes was abruptly told that unless he could trust his memory he would have to go back to regimental duty.

To Haig the essential method of arriving at a decision was complete knowledge and study of all the factors, and then a considered and most firmly held judgement. A decision arrived at by a conscious mental process of this nature is not easily disturbed in any man; in Haig the strongly developed self-confidence emphasised the tendency.

229

John Charteris, it has been said, very much influenced Haig. He, Charteris, is a man who today would be regarded in some quarters as a 'spin doctor'. Like Haig he became a firm believer in the theory and practise of attrition (propounded by Joffre) as the means to end the war. They both believed that as a result of these attrition policies the German army would collapse.

Haig apparently trusted Charteris implicitly. Charteris was not only a friend, he was also Haig's Director of Military Intelligence, and as such is said to have fed Haig, and the Press, with misleading information about British successes and the quality of the German soldier in the latter years of the war.

Charteris from all accounts was the opposite of Haig, smooth, urbane, and a great talker. (Woodward however refers to Charteris as being 'fat dirty and unkempt' and surprisingly ascribes this description of Charteris to Haig, but I don't know in what context.)

Charteris wrote what John Buchan* describes as a *'mémoires pour servir'* – of Haig in 1929, *Field Marshall Earl Haig*. And John Buchan incidentally is one of the few people I have come across who seems to have a good word for Charteris. He says:

> General Charteris had the privilege of serving with Lord Haig in India and at Aldershot, and for the whole of the Great War with the exception of the last two months. During the battle of the Somme I had the privilege of serving under General Charteris.

*John Buchan, 1st Baron Tweedsmuir (1875–1940). Served at HQ until 1917 when he became director of information. Author of many books including Nelson's *History of the War (1915–1919)*. Governor-General of Canada, 1935. Probably best remembered for *The Thirty-nine Steps* and *Greenmantle*.

The well-known war correspondent Sir Philip Gibbs has some pretty contemptuous mocking comments on life at Haig's GHQ at Montreuil – 'this City of Beautiful Nonsense' he terms it in his *Realities of War*.

> It seemed at a mere glance, that all these military inhabitants of GHQ were great and glorious soldiers. Some of the youngest of them had a row of decorations from Montenegro, Serbia, Italy, Roumania, and other states, as recognition of gallant service in translating German letters (found in dug-outs by the

fighting men), or arranging for visits of political personages to the back areas of war, or initialling requisitions for pink, blue, green, and yellow forms which in due course would find their way back to battalion adjutants for immediate filling-up in the middle of action.

Often one saw the Commander-in-Chief [Haig] starting for an afternoon ride, a fine figure, nobly mounted, with two ADCs and an escort of Lancers. A pretty sight, with fluttering pennons and all their lances, and horses groomed to the last hair. It was prettier than the real thing up in the Salient or beyond the Somme, where dead bodies lay in upheaved earth among ruins and slaughtered trees. War at Montreuil was quite a pleasant occupation for elderly generals who liked their little stroll after lunch, and young Regular officers, released from the painful necessity of dying for their country, who were glad to get a game of tennis down below the walls there after strenuous office work.

Lieutenant-Colonel Arthur Osburn, DSO (see also above), according to Philip Warner in his *Passchendaele*, expressed a similar and even more bitter view of these young men at GHQ:

There were many young officers, almost too good-looking and much too young, who apparently had powerful friends at court, mostly lady friends, and who became ADCs to the Corps Commanders or obtained safe staff billets with the most astonishing rapidity and persistence. There was a profusion of these bright and haughty young men in fur collars, wearing eye-glasses and smelling rather of scent and face powder, who, expensively tailored and safely ensconced in palatial chateaux, five, ten, fifteen miles from the front line, were able to eat, drink, play bridge and gossip, even about 'secret orders', not wisely but much too well. These sleek darlings, without ever having heard the whisper of a passing bullet, scorning mere mention in despatches, became miraculously decorated with foreign orders and Military Crosses, and great was the bitterness and discontent amongst the ordinary fighting soldier, wet to the hips in foul mud and generally living under conditions that no sanitary inspector would consider fit for a pig on an English farm.

231

Martin Stephen, writing of Haig in *The Price of Pity* is pretty even-handed. On the less likeable characteristics he says:

> Haig was not a pleasant man, and was adept at political manipulation and scheming. In that he was similar to Lloyd George, and had he not been so he would not have survived as commander... Haig's unpleasantness is a complete irrelevance to his standing as a commander.

Fuller's picture of Haig's Chief of Staff, General Launcelot Kiggell (1862–1954), and who is mentioned above as the 'highly placed officer' who burst into tears after seeing the conditions at Passchendaele is that of:

> A tall, gloomy and erudite soldier, he was Commandant of the Staff College when I was there in 1914, and the only thing I distinctly remember him saying was: 'In the next war we must be prepared for very heavy casualties'. His theory of war was to mass every available man, horse and gun on a single battlefield, and by the process of slow attrition wear down the enemy until his last reserves were exhausted, and then annihilate him.
>
> Within the walls of the old Vauban fortress of Montreuil where GHQ was established, Kiggell meditated like a Buddhist bhikku; revolved the prayer-wheel of his doctrines, and out of them concocted Napoleonic battles on paper, which on the ground turned out to be slaughter-house dramas. He was essentially a cloistered soldier; he never went near a battle, and – if correctly reported – only once visited a battlefield, and then long after the battle had been fought. Spiritually he was the twin brother of Flecker's Mandarin in the Golden Journey to Samarkand: 'Who never left his palace before, But hath grown blind reading great books on war.'

Dennis Winter (*Haig's Command*) on Kiggell:

> Older than his years, in constant poor health and a soldier who had never held a field command, Kiggell was always cut off from the pulse of the Army and its organisation in the field. Indeed he came to France for the first time only in January 1916.

Fuller's final dismissive comments are: 'The remaining members of GHQ General Staff were nonentities.'

Barrie Pitt, an author who pays tribute to Liddell Hart for 'reading my typescript and correcting my errors of syntax and fact', not unnaturally in these circumstances appears to be another of the 'Lions led by Donkeys' faction of the 1960s. He is given to making some sweeping statements of 'fact', but for which he appears to quote no authorities or sources in his book *1918 – The Last Act*. For example:

> Only one army commander seems to have made regular inspections of conditions at the front, and after 1914, no one in the higher ranks ever spent as long as one week living the life of the front-line infantry in the trenches. Thus the crassest mistakes had been made due solely to ignorance of local conditions.

Personally I find it hardly creditable to imagine a belief that an army commander would have made a useful contribution to the war effort by standing to on the firestep for a week with the 16th Footsloggers – and come to that would the men for one moment have appreciated his presence had he done so? I can however envisage the chaos and backlog of work that would have awaited the commander on his return to his HQ after seven days isolated in a front-line trench.

Regular fact-finding inspections of the front were carried out by the staff whose job it was to do so and report back. Haig constantly visited army, corps, and division HQs. Aerial reconnaissance flights were undertaken continuously over the front. Vast numbers of photographs were called for and studied and distributed. And regular reports of conditions were received at GHQ from battalion, brigade, divisional, corps and army HQs.

Conflicting views on GHQ

John Terraine in *The Smoke and the Fire*, quotes a colonel in the field who said:

> GHQ was simply loathed. Partly because we thought with some justification that they were completely out of touch with

233

conditions in the front line. They lived in luxury while we certainly did not.

Sir Frank Fox writing as 'G.S.O.' relates in *G.H.Q.*:

> At G.H.Q., in my time, in my branch no officer who wished to stay was later than 9 am at his desk; most of the eager men were at work before then. We left at 10.30 pm if possible, more often later. On Saturday and Sunday exactly the same hours were kept. An hour 'for exercise' in the afternoon was supposed to be reserved, in addition to meal-hours; but it was not by any means always possible. During the worst of the German offensive in the spring of 1918 staff officers toiled from 8.30 am to midnight with half-hour intervals for meals. I have seen a Staff officer faint at table from sheer pressure of work, and dozens of men, come fresh from regimental work, wilt away under the fierce pressure of work at G.H.Q.

I must confess however that to me he does rather weaken his position when he adds that compared with conditions at GHQ, regimental work was care-free and pleasant. Possibly in the quiet sectors in the summer months this could be true, but generally I doubt it – Obviously I cannot speak with authority never having spent time in either conditions.

'G.S.O.' makes the following comment on officers of the New Armies and GHQ:

> Summing up in regard to the officers of the New Armies it has to be admitted that they came below the standard of the Expeditionary Force, but not much below the standard of the Territorials.
>
> Put to the test of getting a post at G.H.Q., which was supposed to be the crowning test of efficiency, the New Army Officers did not do badly. I made a rough poll one night at club dinner. More than half the officers present were 'New Army' men. In what may be called 'specialists' branches New Army men predominated.'

John Terraine quotes a visitor to Gough's Fifth Army headquarters in 1917:

234

I have come to the conclusion that the chief fault of the people who do the staff work out in France is that they have morbid consciences, do too much themselves, and work far too long hours. Malcolm* for instance is often up at 5 o'clock to go and see some outlying division; then he is at his office for an hour before breakfast, and returns to it shortly after 9 o'clock. He is working all day, either in the office or among the divisions and goes back after dinner, remaining there until midnight or later. I don't believe that any man can work his brain safely for as long hours as this.

*Major-General Neil Malcolm, Gough's chief of staff; spoken of as an unpopular figure.

The author of the foregoing was F.S. Oliver *The Anvil of War* in 1936.

So here one has alternative pictures of HQs. Gibbs' gilded and be-medalled young men playing tennis after a leisurely lunch (and no doubt to go with this scene would also be those regular 'base wallah' officers of Sassoon's poem*) and the contrasting views expressed above.

*'If I were fierce, and bald, and short of breath, I'd live with scarlet Majors at the Base, and speed glum heroes up the line to death.'

In July 2004 I heard a man (in a broadcast late at night on Radio 4) who knew Sassoon well during the later years of Sassoon's life, and he said Sassoon told him that this poem was dashed off in a fit of rage when he discovered that an hotel, where he had booked dinner for himself and a friend while visiting Rouen, had become reserved for officers of the rank of captain or above only (Sassoon was a lieutenant). Apparently he stormed in and demanded dinner and began scribbling the first draft of the poem on the back of the dinner menu. The teller of this story also played several recordings that Sasson made for him of Sassoon reading some of his poems, and among them was this one. It was fascinating to hear Sassoon's voice.

I am sure that among the staff officers at all headquarters there were individuals who would meet the charges levelled against HQ staff. Some of them I expect were people one would loathe if one met them – particularly if one were in a subordinate capacity. But I am equally sure that there were also intelligent, sensible and experienced officers who had served in the field and who were aware of the conditions the fighting men experienced. The answer is probably that as in all organisations there were people who carried out their duties very conscientiously and effectively, and those who didn't. A final observation. On 24th January 1916, Robertson wrote to Haig:

> It was very kind of you to ask my boy to join your Staff. I spoke to him yesterday and although he very much desires to push along in his own line he feels the opportunity you offer is much too good to be refused and he therefore would be very glad to come if you still wish to have him. He is at present not in a specific appointment and therefore free practically any day you may wish to have him... I am very grateful to you for thinking of the boy.'

One can imagine that many a father would have slept more easily in his bed with the knowledge that his soldier son had a place on Haig's staff, but few would be in a position to make this happen.

The commanders; the generally perceived image

Whatever one's views or feelings concerning the treatment handed out to the Generals and GHQ, unfortunately both the 'blimp' and 'butcher' image, can come to mind rather easily when one sees contemporary photographs of them. Here they appear to be – at least when in front of the camera – grim, rather arrogant looking, stern faced, tight-lipped, bushy moustached, well fed, immaculately dressed, booted and spurred figures. It is then so easy to contrast them with the inevitable immediate mental image of the many war-time photographs of burdened weary troops slogging through rain and mud apparently to be flung forward and destroyed in yet another 'dud show' dreamed up by staff wallahs living in comfort miles behind the lines.

No doubt there *were* occasions when troops, certainly by today's attitudes, were 'sacrificed' in diversionary attacks,* or attacks that failed, or in raids aimed to 'maintain the offensive spirit', and dominate No Man's Land. But the politicians and the country as a whole wanted to see the British army engaged in attacking policies to break the German army. The French too were always keen for the British to undertake a more and more active role. The war, as mentioned elsewhere, was costing an unbelievable amount of money daily, and none of the powers wanted a stalemate. Conditions everywhere just getting worse and the nation becoming poorer with no apparent resolution of the conflict in sight. People at home wanted to see results for the price of the lengthy casualty lists published daily in the newspapers.

*Those whose units were engaged in such operations sometimes saw them in similar terms. Edmund Blunden, for example, refers to one such attack – described officially as a 'holding attack' and designed to keep German troops and guns away from the opening of the Somme offensive further south – which involved his battalion of the Sussex regiment. They were to the north, around the old 1915 battlefield area, and suffered many casualties – or as he described it – 'so the attack on Boar's Head closed, and so closed the admirable youth or maturity of many a Sussex and Hampshire worthy'. He concludes his comments with irony: 'The communiqué that morning, when in the far and as yet strange sounding South a holocaust was roaring like our own experience extended for mile upon mile, referred to the Boar's Head massacre somehow thus: "East of Richebourg, a strong raiding party penetrated the enemy's third line". Perhaps too, it claimed prisoners; for we were told that three Germans had found their way "to the Divisional Cage".'

Putting them in perspective

One must bear in mind that the commanders and staff, and the regular regimental commanders, were men born and brought up in the nineteenth century. And their attitudes to, and acceptances of, many things reflected their backgrounds and their times, and were on the whole quite different to those generally accepted by British society today.

These were men – mainly from privileged backgrounds – who were Victorian by birth, upbringing and outlook, and for whom heavy casualties were considered an unpleasant but acceptable risk when given a formidable task, and when facing a brave enemy determined to resist. And the commanders were expected to deliver the attacks to break the enemy and win the war. When this was not possible they were expected to maintain an attacking offensive posture to undermine the enemy's morale, and not to adopt a passive siege mentality.

This is in complete contrast to today's philosophy when the thought of casualties and 'body bags', and the effects of these on public opinion, causes most Western governments to vacillate over committing even small numbers of troops backed up by highly sophisticated weapons, to any action. And where a considerable percentage of the comparatively very few casualties that do occur, are down to friendly fire.

237

The senior officers between 1914 and 1918 were faced with tasks and burdens no one had previously encountered or been asked to deal with, and they were, just as we are, human beings, with human failings. As professional career soldiers, they were also haunted by the fear of being replaced and sent home, the ignominy this would bring and the effect this would have on their future careers if they argued too much or demurred too much, or seemed to be found wanting in their duties.*

*I was struck by the number of senior officers in the BEF who Sir John French 'invalided home' during the four months of 1914 – I discovered the following commanders who were sent home, although there may have been more: Brig.-Gen. R.H. Davies, 6th Infantry Brigade, September 1914; Brig.-Gen. B.J.C. Doran, 8th Infantry Brigade, October 1914; Major-General Sir Charles Fergusson, 5th Division Commander, October 1914; Brig.-Gen. G.J. Cuthbert, 13th Brigade, September 1914; Brig.-Gen. S.P. Rolt, 14th Brigade, October 1914 and Major-General T.D.O. Snow, 4th Division Commander, September 1914. Although effected in 1915 not 1914, the most famous of those 'invalided home' was the Second Army Corps Commander, General Sir Horace Smith-Dorrien, the man who at very short notice had been called upon to replace Sir James Grierson who had the misfortune to die on his way to take up his command in August 1914 – see above.

To the professional commanders of the First World War, war was generally recognised and accepted as a bloody business, not for sensitive souls, and none of the commanders was a sensitive soul, but neither was he a stranger to battle in the field, or had been accused of lacking in personal courage.*

*In the early days of 'fluid warfare' of the BEF in 1914 I came across a number of senior officers in this small force who were replaced through death or injury – apart from those I have mentioned as 'invalided' home: Major-General Lomax, Commander 1st Division, wounded; Brig.-Gen. FitzClarence, V.C., 1st Infantry Brigade, killed; Brig.-Gen. Bulfin, 2nd Infantry Brigade, wounded; Brig.-Gen. Scott-Kerr, 4th (Guards) Brigade, wounded; Brig.-Gen. Hakin, 5th Infantry Brigade, wounded; Major-General Hamilton, Commander, 3rd Division, killed; Brig.-Gen. Shaw, 9th Infantry Brigade, wounded.

With the technology and hindsight of eighty plus years it is very easy for us to be critical of those First World War military leaders. We must remember that military and political mistakes are still being made today through lack of information, conflicting and incorrect information, changing circumstances, wrong decisions, and failure to act.

Operations went very wrong in the Second World War, Korea, Vietnam, and again in the Falklands, the first Gulf War, the Balkans, Afghanistan and the second Gulf War. In all of these the availability and the means to gain information, speed of communication, means of transport and sophistication of equipment were of a standard undreamed of in the First World War.

During a recorded television interview an ex-navy man who served aboard the *Prince of Wales* when she was lost to Japanese aircraft attacks in the Second World War made the pithy comment: 'War is a history of mistakes. You just hope *you* make fewer than the enemy.' He could have added: 'and luck' after 'mistakes'. At the end of the day, there seems to be only one certainty in any war and that is, however well thought out and planned, however well prepared and detailed, once the pieces are set in motion everything will probably start to go wrong.

It is unlikely that any of my relatives who enlisted in 1914 would ever meet or see any of the exalted military leaders; or if they did, would have known what effect their deliberations and actions would have on them, or their comrades, in the years to come.

Shortage of staff officers and experienced commanders at all levels

Andy Simpson in his book *The Evolution of Victory* says that by the end of the year 1914, the BEF had taken almost 90,000 casualties mostly from the first seven divisions whose total effective strength on arrival in France had been only 84,000. He adds that when criticising the British armies on the Continent in later operations it should be borne in mind that these losses in trained officers, and especially staff officers, and whose experience would have been invaluable to the New Armies being created in Britain, were crippling (just as Kitchener feared).

The Official History referring to operations in 1915 says that there had been too few staff officers in peace time – two per Regular Division and one per Territorial Division – and only a small reserve. The only way during the war to obtain and train staff officers was to pull battle-experienced officers out of their regiments where they were sorely needed.

Philip Warner, *The Battle of Loos*, says, when discussing inexperienced 'raw' commanders and 'raw' troops (and although he is writing here specifically about 1915, the points can be taken generally on the early years of the war, and the subsequent consequences of that first rush to join the army in 1914):

239

The senior commanders, such as Haig and Sir John French, were raw because they had no previous experience in handling formations as large as the ones they were now responsible for. In wartime a man whose experience of command is based on a unit of 700 men can find himself responsible for many thousands. To command a force of up to half a million men, as a commander-in-chief could find himself doing at an early stage, he needs capable corps commanders, each responsible for some 40,000 men or more. In the divisions there was a need for company commanders, platoon commanders, sergeants and corporals. And it is not enough merely to have experience at any of these levels; some people are good with very little experience and some men are useless at any level no matter how much experience they have. In the First World War there were men holding higher appointments who were quite unfitted for them. In the first wave of expansion they had been promoted because there was no one else... During 1914, men flooded into recruiting centres for the new army ... whole regiments had been raised by patriotic citizens... Many of the recruits were valuable officer material.

PART TWENTY-FIVE

...So far as these results are due to the action of the British forces, they have been attained by troops the vast majority of whom had been raised and trained during the war. Many of them, especially amongst the drafts sent to replace wastage, counted their service by months... That these troops should have accomplished so much under such conditions, and against an army and a nation whose chief concern for so many years has been preparation for war, constitutes a feat of which the history of our nation records no equal.

An extract from a dispatch by Sir Douglas Haig,
published as a supplement to the *London Gazette*,
29th December 1916.

Inexperienced troops

As the war progressed the inexperienced troops became more welcome to commanders when attacks were being mounted. One of the reasons was that while the experienced troops were steady and knew their jobs, increasingly as time went by they were much less inclined to push forward beyond their immediate stated objectives. Repeated earlier experiences had made them wary; they would dig in and consolidate their new position rather than willingly go further to face a heavy counter attack with a strong possibility of the reserves not arriving in time, or not arriving at all.

Less experienced troops on the other hand would be more inclined to push on and advance as long as they could still do so. This is one of the reasons why the French and British commanders longed to get their hands on the eager young raw American troops when they arrived at the Front in 1918. These men were not war weary or cynical, and had the optimism and the spirit of the young men of Britain and France in 1914 and 1915.

War weariness among experienced troops

W.L. Andrews says of 1916 before the Somme offensive, that having survived through 1914 and 1915, the men in his unit began to think of the hopes of getting away from the Front for a spell. For those with the educational qualifications there was the prospect of going home for six months to take a commission course and training before returning. For those whom this hope was denied for educational reasons, the hope of getting away from the worst of the fighting was to be given jobs in the rear areas, jobs such as camp-wardens, or becoming officers' servants behind the lines, or instructors at schools at bases. Andrews said the men still did their jobs faithfully, but it was not expected that men would volunteer for dangerous duty as they used to do.

Writing in his diary in March 1918, Wilfrid Ewart records:

I hear today that I have been recommended for six months' light duty in England under a new scheme by which officers who have been out here for some time are sent home for a rest. As I have been out altogether longer than any other subaltern and have been over the top three times, it takes me first in this battalion. Whether I shall get it is another matter, as there is some idea that one has to have completed two years and I have not quite done that yet... Often I feel extraordinary weary and that they have had the best out of me I cannot look forward with confidence to any more battles.

Bert Chaney (see also below), who as an 18-year-old in the 7th London Territorial Battalion* and off to his first annual camp in August 1914, arrived in France on 17th March 1915. He was later a survivor of the battle of the Somme, and wrote (as recorded in *People at War 1914–1918* edited by Michael Moynihan):

To our minds the generals would keep us out here until we

242

were all killed, and although nobody thought of disobeying orders some of the originals grumbled at the way the war was going. We were proud of all the new guns, the new men coming out were just as enthusiastic as we had been originally, but after two years away from home we were beginning to think the war would never end. From now on the veterans, myself included, decided to do no more than was really necessary, following orders but if possible keeping out of harm's way. I have a feeling that many of the officers felt the same way.

*I assume this was 1/7th City of London Battalion, of the London Regiment, 2nd London Brigade, 2nd London Division.

Soldiers in the field attitudes to HQs

A light hearted look at the bureaucracy in the army comes from Mark Severn (*The Gambardier**), who maintains the 'Great Army Paper Game' had always existed, and could be instigated by actions from the very top, or the very bottom:

It is either up to Gunner Smith or the Quarter-Master-General to make the first move. Let us assume Gunner Smith, in a moment of absent-mindedness, consumes his iron rations under the mistaken impression that by so doing he will stave off the pangs of hunger. The crime is duly discovered by the sergeant, or No. 1 of his section who reports it to his section commander. The latter reports it to the battery commander, who then writes to the adjutant making a clean breast of the whole sordid story and asking for guidance as to how to obtain another iron ration. The adjutant, an efficient young officer who knows his job, writes 'forwarded' on it and sends it to the staff captain. It is then purely a matter of volleying it up and on through all the grades and formations until the correspondence finally reaches the august eye of the Quarter Master General. Anyone who writes more than 'passed to you please' or 'forwarded,' automatically wastes time and loses the respect of the other players by brandishing himself a novice. The QMG delivers judgement, and issues a three-page memo of instructions as to the procedures to be adopted should such an unfortunate thing

243

ever occur again. It is then passed back and the correct wording now is, 'For your information and the necessary action.' Finally the pile of papers returns to the battery commander and can go no further. Action has got to be taken. He sends for the quartermaster-sergeant and orders him to issue Gunner Smith with another iron ration out of the store. The QMS then calls his storeman to unpack the case of tin rations and give one of them to Gunner Smith. The net result is that three months after the consumption of his original iron ration, Gunner Smith, should he still be alive, is provided with another, and everybody has enjoyed a very ably conducted rally of the Great Game in the interim.

*A member of the Royal Garrison Artillery (RGA).

There were undoubtedly times when the front line troops were infuriated, or contemptuously amused, when they were sent back to rest areas, by reports of memos and instructions from division or brigade headquarters on matters such as complaints of slack saluting in the rest areas out of the line – or a need for more parade ground drilling practice; and the burnishing of steel helmets and polishing brass buttons and badges when out of the line, and so on. There was also the ceaseless demand for returns to be completed and despatched to HQs whatever the circumstances and however inappropriate or trivial seeming to those soldiers dealing with it at the time.

W.L. Andrews served for a while as Battalion Orderly Room Sergeant and his impressions of the administrative work carried out, and its importance in the life of the troops, paints a different picture of a battalion HQ. He says:

A battalion orderly-room at the front achieved dignity under difficulties. It might be housed in a stable with half the roof off. It might be crammed in a dug-out haunted by rats, where every few minutes the crash of a battery shook out the candlelights. Wherever it found shelter, it remained a centre of respect. The commmanding officer and adjutant here worked out their plans. The regimental sergeant-major here read out orders to his NCOs, and here the adjutant's busy clerks compiled the multitudinous records and returns which were as essential

244

to fighting as water-carts and gas respirators... It is astounding that we made so few mistakes, for you can imagine that in heavy fighting we, in some dim dug-out at the back of the line, were hard-pressed to check and verify reports, collate them with villainously scribbled records from casualty clearing stations, and with the help of company quartermaster-sergeants sort out the kits of dead, wounded, and sick, and send personal effects to the base for transmission home.

Although by comparison with men doing the actual fighting we were enviably safe we were by no means out of danger... Of the staff of six, I alone reached the end of the war unhurt. All the others were killed or wounded.

Attitudes to those at home

Keep the home fires burning while your hearts are yearning,
Though your lads are far away they dream of home.
There's a silver lining through the dark clouds shining:
Turn the dark clouds inside out, till the boys come home'.

> Verse by Lena Guilbert Ford and put to music in 1914
> by Ivor Novello.

Those at a battalion HQ, and those in the transport section, and anyone who was out of the line, were generally envied. On the whole though, as far as the troops were concerned, one gets the impression that their anger was mainly reserved for munition workers, coal miners and others at home now earning what soldiers considered to be large sums of money and living in comfort. War profiteers were despised generally rather than the top brass of the army who were too far removed and faceless, and not meriting the drawing of one's concentration away from the essentials.

Allied to the munition workers and miners, conscientious objectors* and trade union strikers also came in as subjects of contempt and resentment among the front-line troops.

*Ian Beckett says of conscientious objection that it received somewhat disproportionate attention considering that only 16,500 claims for exemption were made on such grounds.

Aubrey Smith is very incensed and bitter about the miners who were actually apparently drafted into the army and to his unit late in 1918:

> With such an accession to the transport strength as these new-comers [the miners] represented, the small muster of old hands became more pronounced, and it was reasonable to suppose that as soon as demobilisation started our little band would practially cease to exist, since our claims to rapid demobilisation were assuredly paramount.
>
> But exactly the reverse was the case. Foremost among the starred occupations was that of mining, and it was laid down that miners should be sent home before anybody else, irrespective of their period of service. It was incredible that these men, who had been conscripted for the most part at the fifty-ninth minute of the War, thrust into khaki and sent out as reinforcements in September or October [1918], should be the first to go home, while men who had volunteered in the first months of the War and seen years of active service remained in France to watch their departure.

Attitudes to the award of medals and decorations

Arthur Behrend (see above) relates that his colonel, Lieutenant-Colonel Thorp, who appears to have been an engaging eccentric – at least as seen from the distance of time and the written page – was amongst other things against both the taking of leave, and the acceptance of decorations of any sort. He believed a soldier should be brave at all times and so he despised honours and awards for this quality – and also on principle refused to take his leave when it came around. He had always instructed Behrend, who was Adjutant, that a 'nil return' should be sent in to Corps whenever the half-yearly recommendations were requested for names to be put forward for an award.

It so happened that the colonel had been forced to take leave, and while he was away his second in command took over. It was during this period that a demand arrived from Corps Heavies (Behrend was in the artillery), for the submission of a name of a warrant officer or senior NCO for what was described in the message as a 'French military medal'. The acting CO said that he was now commanding, and a name must be put forward. Behrend, although fearing the colonel's wrath on his return, suggested the regimental sergeant major's name because 'although he was on old woman, he was a decent chap who had done God knows how many years in the army, and anyway it was only a French thing'. So the RSM's name was duly sent in.

Six weeks later, to everybody's consternation, a French general arrived at the battery headquarters with his entourage to present the RSM with his medal, and the personnel of Brigade Headquarters were turned out in review order to do him the honours. The colonel, now back from leave, was speechless. The general presented RSM Oatley with his medal and pinned it to his breast and embraced him on both cheeks, and then, carried away by the occasion, he turned and kissed Colonel Thorp too.

'The medal,' Behrend adds, 'turned out to be the Médaille Militaire, the highest honour the French could confer on any soldier – so high that it carried a pension of I think a hundred francs a year for life. I must say the colonel took it better than I expected, because in some way it must have appealed to his primitive sense of humour. It certainly appealed to ours.'

Michael Moynihan reveals in *People at War 1914–1918* that one man, Ernest A. Atkins, 26699. B. Company, 16th Kings Royal Rifle Corps, grieved to his dying day for the medals he believed he was entitled to but never received. He claimed that although his papers gave his medical category as: 'C111. Defective Eyesight. Not to be sent abroad', nevertheless administrative army blunders put him in France and Flanders. He served, he said, on the Somme and Ypres fronts, and he believed he was put up for the VC, but he said the authorities would not officially admit he was there because of his medical category, and as a result the recommendations were never put through. (In 1918 the conditions for the award of the Victoria Cross stipulated that eye-witness accounts were not only necessary but must also be in the hand-writing of the witness, unless the man could not write or was unable to write because of wounds, in which case the account must be taken down by an officer and certified correct.)

Among my late father's possessions I came across a small folded sheet of writing paper with his writing as follows:

247

Military Hospital,
Shorncliffe,
Kent.

December 15th, 1939.
To whom it may concern,

I the undersigned consider it a great honour and a privilege
to have had my boots (army pattern) cleaned and polished,
also shirt buttons sewn on by a holder of the Victoria Cross
whose signature is below.

J.E. Holley
L/Cpl. R.A.S.C.

Signed: – J.H. Oakes,
ex 9th Lancers

Unfortunately I have been unable to trace any record of Mr Oakes
among the list of those awarded the Victoria Cross.

As mentioned earlier, Robert Graves remarked that he and his
fellow officer volunteers in the Special Reserve were told that unless
the circumstances were very special none of them would ever be
put up for a medal. These were, he said, to be reserved for the
regular officers as awards could affect their promotion prospects
later in their careers in the army.

Attitudes to, and treatment of, subordinates

Senior generals reprimanded more junior generals and had them
'degummed' or 'dégommé', or 'Stellenbosched'. On occasions a
battalion commander would be given a public dressing down by
roadside staff officers or a general as the battalion passed by and
were said to march badly or looked scruffy. 'Are you glued to that
bloody horse?' – brigade commander addressing a lieut. colonel,
the commander of a battalion, when he failed to dismount on being
addressed after saluting as his troops marched by.

On rare occasions the biter was bit. Brigadier General Francis
Aylmer Maxwell, VC, CSI, DSO & Bar (7th September 1871–21st
September 1917),* as Lt. Colonel Maxwell VC, commander of 12th
Middlesex, on the Somme in 1916, was one such. He was considered
a mixed blessing by his battalion because although he was greatly

admired by his officers and men, it was felt, quite correctly, that such an heroic figure as he was bound to be chosen to tackle the most dangerous portion of the German defences – Thiepval. Having disobeyed an order from Brigadier General Shoubridge to leave after his battalion had been relieved by the Bedfords, Maxwell stayed on to see the new CO through the attack on the stronghold. 'But,' he said, 'I paid the penalty of a dressing down by the general who is furious.' The divisional history claims that Maxwell's retort to Shoubridge was: 'What are you grousing about? I've got you another medal.'

*Maxwell was promoted and appointed to command the 27th Lowland Brigade, and just under a year later he was killed by a sniper near Zonnebeke during the Third Battle of Ypres, 1917. He lies in the Ypres Reservoir Cemetery, and the divisional history of the 18th Division wrote 'He was a mighty fighter, a man among men, and the 18th Division was proud to have its name associated with his.'

Battalion commanders in turn bawled out company commanders who could and did treat their junior officers badly – Robert Graves says new subalterns were spoken to and referred to as 'Warts' by battalion and company commanders in his regular second battalion. Senior warrant and other NCOs could be abrasively unfair to private soldiers. Often these criticisms and complaints about the treatment and attitudes of senior to junior ranks, all the way down the line were true, or at least true at times, from general commanding to lance corporal, and stories abound in all published memoirs. Burgoyne writes in December 1914:

All men like an officer who compels obedience, and it is no use punishing a man on Active Service as one does in peace time; the only thing is to hit him at once and hard, and if the men see their officer takes a real personal interest in them, as I think I do, or at least try to, well these Irishmen of mine will follow me I am sure. But I must have a month's rest to wheel them into line. I have about 70 sick in the Company, most of them with swollen feet from standing in icy cold mud and water; and really the whole Company, what with inoculation and general 'done-upness' is a 'washout' for fighting purposes till they have had a week or so of rest. But they have a tot of rum o' nights, and plenty of good food, and I don't worry them with parades... I heard one man coughing his soul out in the loft late this evening, and found him with bad bronchitis, so I brought him in to the house and got him under a pile of blankets with a drink, but as one of our servants said, if I am too kind all the Company will be getting bronchitis.

Sir William Robertson was said to at times to be rude and abrupt to both superiors and inferiors, and did not mask his contempt for ideas on military questions that differed from his own. One of his subordinates wrote: 'He had a way of slamming the door in your face while you were still speaking that endangered your nose and was disconcerting in the extreme.'

Spears (*Liaison 1914*) quotes the French cavalry proverb: *C'est le bat-flanc qui trinque* where when the colonel is out of temper he upbraids the captain, who swears at the subaltern, who goes for the sergeant, who punishes the private, who beats the horse, whose only recourse is to kick the bail at the side of his stall. Spears uses this quotation when recounting the events near the end of August 1914 when Joffre, the French CIC, blasted the French Fifth Army commander General Lanrezac for lack of determination and unwillingness to attack. Lanrezac promptly did the same thing almost immediately afterwards to General de Mas Latrie, the commander of XVIII Corps, for his faint heart and pusillanimity when de Mas Latrie called to see him to say his troops were in a state of fatigue and in need of rest. This is precisely what Lanrezac had told Joffre about the Fifth Army and had received a similar reception!

A contrary view is taken by W.L. Andrews who makes a point on several occasions in *Haunting Years* in expressing his respect and admiration for the colonels and majors, mainly regular officers who commanded his battalion at different times. Also for the RSM and other senior NCOs who were at that time mainly ex-regulars.

Chaney (above and below), a man often critical of people, says of his colonel at the battle of the Somme in 1916, where Chaney was when tanks made their first appearance. The tanks, he said, had made a mistake – or been given wrong information on the number of British trenches they would have to cross – because instead of continuing over the last one they stopped and began to pour murderous enfilading fire in the British front trench from their swivelling machine guns:

Everyone dived for cover, except the colonel. He jumped on top of the parapet, shouting at the top of his voice, 'Runner, runner go and tell those tanks to stop firing at once. At once I say'. By now the enemy fire had risen to a crescendo but, giving no thought to his personal safety as he saw the tanks firing on his own men, he ran forward and furiously rained blows with his cane on the side of one of the tanks in an endeavour to attract their attention.

Although, what with the sounds of the engines and the firing in such an enclosed space, no one in the tank could hear him. They finally realised they were on the wrong trench and moved on, frightening the Jerries out of the wits and making them scuttle like frightened rabbits.

PART TWENTY-SIX

It is more shameful to distrust one's friends than to be deceived by them.

Duc de la Rochefoucauld, 1665, *Maximes 84.*

Discord among Allies and some opinions about each other

The French view of the British – as seen by some British observers

Despite Foch's pre-war remark to Wilson that I quoted earlier, once we had entered the war the French, one gets the impression, always felt the British were not doing as much as they should or could, whether it was the British Government or their armed forces. A general sense of grievance seems to prevail. The French took the massive contribution of the Royal Navy as a matter of course.*

*Lord Edward Gleichen's *Chronology of the Great War 1914–1918*, says:

> The British fleet was mobilised and ready for action on the first day of the war and from that day onwards until the end of the war it maintained the blockade of the enemy, without which the war could not have been won, and protected the communications of the Allies.
>
> It patrolled incessantly, and in all weathers, the 140,000 square miles of the North Sea, and was in the main responsible for the protection of the entire coast of Europe from Archangel to Alexandria – a distance of 5,000 miles.
>
> In one month British warships proper travelled one million sea miles in home waters alone, while auxiliary vessels including minesweepers and patrol boats covered 6,000,000 sea miles or 250 circuits of the globe.
>
> In 1914 mine sweepers and patrol boats numbered 12; by the end of 1918 they numbered 3,714. From the outbreaks of the war until March 12th, 1919 the Navy was instrumental in transporting overseas for the British and Allied armies 23,388,228 effectives and 3,336,241 non-effectives with a loss to enemy action of only 4,394 people. Before America entered the war it fell to the British navy to deal single-

handed with the enemy's submarine campaign. Out of some 200 enemy submarines accounted for, about 150 were destroyed by British effort.'

And so the list goes on.

Sir Francis (later Lord) Bertie, the British Ambassador in Paris, wrote to Lloyd George in 1916 on the same subject:

> You must not forget that the French judge us purely on our doings on land and in France; our mastery of the sea and all that it involves is taken as a matter of course. It is assumed here as axiomatic that the sea belongs to us, and we are also supposed to draw large profits from our sea traffic. The French fully realise that coal in Paris costs 180 francs a ton, and they think the whole of this money goes into the pockets of English coal and ship owners. It is therefore supposed by many Frenchmen that we are making large profits out of the war, whereas they are bleeding to death.

In the summer of 1914 British troops would be fêted and cheered as they marched through the cobbled streets of French towns and villages. But later, it is said, French and Belgian peasants referred to the British troops as 'les autres Boches' as they were compelled to leave their homes when their small plots of land became part of the battlefields. Frank Richards remarked how incensed the French locals were when after the 'Christmas truce' in 1914 he and his comrades were going through Armentières and a group of French women were standing in their doorways spitting and shouting: 'You no bon, you English soldiers, you boko kamarade Allemange.'

Bert Chaney (whom I have quoted earlier) says of the German 1918 break-through as he and his comrades fell back through the hitherto untouched countryside, French civilians hurled insults at them and even spat at them.

General Jack, in his diary covering the retreat from Mons and Le Cateau in 1914, paints a different picture of the attitude of the local French populace based on his own experience during the retreat:

> As to the French peasantry: deeply concerned as they were about their own security, and bitterly disappointed at being left to the enemy's hands, their kindness by deed as well as

word all the way from Mons can never be exceeded. At no time did I see on their faces, or hear in their remarks, anything but pity for our men. They stood at their doors with pails of water, sometime wine, long rolls of bread and butter, fruit, just what they had. We must never forget them.

Edmund Blunden is another who speaks of the courtesy of many of the French people he came across in various places where he was billeted, and so does George Coppard, and he writes with pleasure of meeting again a lady named Maria in 1972 whom he had first met when she was a young girl in a farmhouse where he was billeted during spells out of the line during the war.

Adam Collins, as related by Bruce Lewis in *A Few of the First*, also mentions a kind hearted French lady who with only limited resources did her best to make life a little more comfortable for the British lads who were fighting so bravely for her country. She washed and repaired their clothes, gave them apples from her orchard and occasionally an egg or two despite her cottage being shelled. So it wasn't always acrimony between the locals and British troops.

William Linton Andrews relates in *Haunting Years*:

Though I got on very well with the French, they had no great opinion of the English. Joe Lee told me of a man who said to him, with comic emphasis: 'Soldat Anglais – confitures.'

Le Roy Lewis writing again to Lloyd George to complain on matters of protocol:

The Badge of the Legion of Honour is always worn by French Officers, by all military attachés, and by all officers here, except us. It appears this is done because our King objects to our wearing the Legion of Honour. The absence of this badge from our uniforms is much noticed and commented upon by the French, who imagine the reason we do not wear it is that we do not value the decoration. If you have the opportunity I should be obliged if you would speak to the King on this subject and get him to rescind his order, if indeed he ever issued one, about which fact I am not clear.

The American view of the British and French

America, possibly for historic reasons, seems to have nearly always favoured the French over the British. And although the USA grew very rich from the sale of materials and foodstuffs to Britain, newspaper and public support was generally lukewarm. At times there was a strong hostility encouraged by a very large and vocal support group of German Americans, and from the equally strong Irish lobby, especially following the 1916 Dublin uprising and the shooting of the Irish nationalist leaders.

In fact the Easter uprising in Ireland led to a major rift with the United States of America. The fifteen rebel leaders who were executed became martyrs in the eyes of the American press, and newspapers, particularly those of the Hurst owned press, began to decry the British war effort. 'Where are all the Englishmen?' demanded the *Philadelphia Enquirer*:

> The heroic figure that stands clearly revealed in this war is that of the Frenchman. 'What has become of the boasted millions of men that England has claimed to have raised?' 'There is no comparison between her sacrifice and those of gallant France ... Her [Britain's] workmen have regarded the war as their opportunity for personal gain. They have disregarded patriotism for greed. Her cabinet has been torn with dissension. Her Parliament has been in a turmoil. It has raised her armies only by the strenuous efforts and the most pitiful appeals. But when they are raised – on paper – what becomes of them?

A British view of America

John Terraine in *To Win a War 1918 the Year of Victory* quotes *The Times* war correspondent, Colonel Repington, dining at Claridge's on 4th January 1918 with 'a well known man' who said:

> America was coming on very slowly. The 4th Division was only now arriving in France, where the numbers were not over 140,000. Most Americans believed they had over half a million men in France, and would be very disgusted if they learned the truth... The Americans were not using their merchant ships sufficiently, and were leaving too many at their normal

256

commercial work. Also, the American decision not to use our plant in America for turning out rifles, 8-inch and 9.2-inch guns, etc., had proved disastrous, and America had not yet turned out a single heavy gun as she had neither the tools nor the workmen.

Lloyd George in his *War Memoirs* says the Americans would have none of our aeroplanes nor of our cannon.

They would have patterns of their own which would demonstrate to antiquated European craftsmen what could be done by a nation which had demonstrated its supremacy in machinery... The result was dismal. By the time of the Armistice half the aeroplanes in use by the American army were of French or British make. The light and medium artillery used up to the end of the war by the American army was supplied by the French. The heaviest artillery was furnished by the British. No field guns of American pattern or manufacture fired a shot in the war. The same applies to tanks ... not a single tank of American manufacture ever rolled into action in the War.

The British view of the French

The British were shouldering more and more of the burden, *and* the financial cost of the war, and were subsidising their allies. Joseph Austen Chamberlain, Secretary of State for India, and a member of Lloyd George's War Cabinet, said in 1916 (when putting forward a case that Britain could not afford conscription) that Britain was bearing the whole cost of the Allies' war. France had recently intimated that she could not pay her share of the £300 million Anglo-French subsidy promised to Russia, and furthermore, the previous week, France had asked for a £60 million loan herself, and would doubtless want even more.

A continuing source of aggravation to Sir William Robertson was the French insistence on the maintenance of a large Allied force in Salonika. To Sir William – and to Haig and the other 'Westerners' – the campaign was a complete waste of men and materials badly needed on the Western Front.

In March 1916 Robertson circulated a note to the Cabinet protesting once again at the endless stalemate on the Salonika front:

A force of more than 200,000 men has now been locked up for several months without exerting any appreciable influence on the course of the war, to the amusement of neutrals and the delight of the enemy, while a wholly unnecessary strain upon our financial and shipping resources is caused by the maintenance of a large force in a distant theatre, in which it cannot attack, is very unlikely to be attacked, and does not detach from the main theatre an adequate number of our enemies. It is time to put an end to this ridiculous situation.

Robertson wrote in a General Staff Memorandum:

I can take no responsibility. I consider the whole project entirely unsound from every military point of view.

The French, supported by Lloyd George, refused to give way. Kitchener interpreted the French attitude as an intention to extend her post-war influence in the Mediterranean. Others saw it as a result of a peculiarly French military intrigue.*

*The French commander, General Sarrail, was a radical Protestant – one of the few French military men who was not a High Tory Clerical and he was favoured by some in government circles who saw his withdrawal, had it been allowed, as Catholic interference.

So the Anglo French forces in Salonika stayed. Although Allied troops suffered fewer than 20,000 battle casualties throughout the Salonika campaigns, almost 450,000 men had been invalided out of the theatre with malaria alone by late 1918.

Le Roy Lewis wrote again to Lloyd George, this time on perhaps a more generally vexing point as far as the British army was concerned than wearing or not wearing the Legion of Honour badge. His concern was the fact that the French Government obliged the British military to pay *Octroi* duty (local customs tax) on everything they brought into their towns. It was not only resented, but it was a troublesome operation, and convoys could be held up for hours while a *douanier* made an estimate of what the British commanding officer would have to pay. Le Roy was indignant about this:

It is no argument to say that the French Army also pays these duties. The real argument is: would the Germans pay *octroi* duty if the British withdrew from France?'

James Cameron, writing in *1916 Year of Decision*, says:

> For those thinking in terms of latter-day operations the mutual isolation of the two Armies in 1916 is hard to recall, they fought as two wholly separate entities, overlapping here and there, with the minimum of co-relation, and the minimum of mutual confidence. Some aspects of this relationship would have been better suited to a pair of competitive business houses in a strictly commercial world. Not long before, for example, Haig had received a letter signed by Joffre asking, *'par voie de reciprocité'*, for a detachment of 2,000 men, in lieu of the sixty-eight heavy guns which had been left on their 10th Army front recently taken over by the British. There had also been some ammunition left over and Joffre required 'compensation' for this, in the shape of another thousand workmen! *'on peut envisager'*, wrote Joffre, precisely as one chartered accountant to another, *'les compensations necessaries sous forme.'*
>
> 'This,' said Haig, 'was altogether a very strange document for any soldier to write to another.' He told Jofre very brusquely that he was certainly not interested in the business of bargaining men and cannon. 'The truth is,' he told his diary, 'there are not many officers in the French Army with gentlemanly ideas.'

Haig's view of the Italians?

Haig, as the British C in C – and again this is according to Cameron – held no better view of the Italians than he had above of the French, although he had no direct contact with the Italians.

> He [Haig] conceived the curious view that the Italians were taking it easy and conserving considerable of their reserves in order one day to fight, of all people, the Swiss. 'The Italians,' he said, 'seem a wretched people, useless as fighting men, but greedy for money. Moreover I doubt whether they are really in earnest in this war. Many of them too are German spies.'

If he did hold these sentiments, and Cameron does not reveal his source, it is not surprising that Haig was a pronounced 'Westerner' and detested being ordered to send some of his much needed divisions to support the Italians.

The BEF in relation to the French army

The British High Command, although independent, was frequently under strong pressure from the French to undertake a more active role whether in a position to do so or not, and whether or not the British agreed with proposed French plans. And always in the background lurked the eternal conflict of national interests and positions.

Britain was fighting on French and Belgian soil, but in 1914, 1915, and early 1916, the French, with their huge armies spread over a wide area, carried by far the greater burden of the Allies' fighting and casualties (and the French were very profligate with casualties in the early years). Britain had to remember this burden when France called upon her again and again for more assistance. At the same time Britain was desperately trying to train and build up her new armies, and all the while her original and irreplaceable small force of regulars, the potential trainers of the new armies, was being decimated in Belgium and Northern France.

Anthony Farrar-Hockley says in his book *The Somme* that for the first two years of the war the French, under Joffre, had lost so many men and had expended so much ammunition that his reserves of men and munitions was running dangerously low. The numbers of troops ready in the depots fell far short of his needs. He goes on to quote Joffre:

'There was too, the prospect of handing over a greater sector of the line to the British, whose present responsibility [1915], was man for man much less than the French.'

Farrar-Hockley says in a footnote:

This was to be a bone of contention between the two allies throughout the war. The comparison was hardly a fair one; the British held a series of sectors in which the enemy were constantly active and in greater strength than in many of the French.*

Like the majority of his brother officers Joffre regarded the British Expeditionary Force as a collection of amateurs, not without courage, but largely without skill.

*See Part Thirty-four on definitions and descriptions of active and inactive parts of the line – Live and Let Live.

Soldiers' recorded opinions on those from other countries can only be taken as personal ones, and no doubt there were a whole range of opinions based on fleeting or more prolonged contacts, intuitive likes or dislikes, instant empathy or antipathy, past histories of the nations, personal experience and knowledge or lack of it of each others' language. All of these factors coloured attitudes and comments. But here are just a few.

British soldiers speaking of French troops

Aubury Smith on meeting up with French at the time of the Somme in 1916 in the Bray area:

> The French soldiers were very friendly. [Smith spoke French reasonably well it would seem, and this of course could make a world of difference when dealing with the French civilians and troops.] We were apparently on the right of the British line where it joined the French and were evidently destined to see a good deal of our allies. What pleased me was their freedom from outward show and eyewash.* Their wagons were old and their harness did not appear ever to have been washed; it certainly might have been softened somewhat, but the fact that the steelwork was rust spoke a great deal for their intelligence. Were they any wit the less useful as transport units because they did not care a rap about their brass and steel? On the contrary their transport work was magnificent.

*Smith, as is apparent, was not keen on 'spit and polish'. In fact he seems almost obsessed by the use of it, and can't bear it. It occurs quite often in his narrative, and unfortunately for him, as a member of the battalion transport a lot of time was spent on the horses' accoutrements when out of the line. His admiring view of the French therefore might have been coloured – just a little!

American soldiers on the British

Philip J. Haythornthwaite quotes: 'The Imperial Hotel, St Anne's, June 1918' (*The Return*, pp. 5–7, 7 June 1918):

> Replying to a British toast of welcome to 'The Army of America', Lieutenant Armitage of the AEF spoke of and for the US Army: 'Before the war they [the American troops]

were a mere handful, and were somewhat looked down upon, as a rule, by American people, as being a group of wasters, loafers, who did nothing but drink cocktails ... [now] political power, wealth, social position has absolutely no influence. The selected draft in America has swept in all men and equally distributed the burdens of our country [upon men] who are itching to get over here and stand side by side with you in the game you have played so well... when this terrible struggle is over, there will be bound together by bonds of personal friendship that can never be broken, the two great Anglo-Saxon nations of the world... No one realizes better than we do now that only the magnificent resistance of the British and French Armies and the eternal vigilance of the Royal Navy has kept our own dear shores free from invasion ... we not only thank you, but with that we give the offer of our lives, of our fortunes, and everything we have, everything we are, and everything we hope to be.'

Expressing somewhat different sentiments, William T. Scanlon, in *God Have Mercy on Us*, describes meetings between American and British troops in 1918:

Then we would remind them how we had knocked hell out of them during the Revolution. We would keep it up, as long as they were in sight. Usually the English soldiers would try to be a little sociable at first, but not us. Our vocabulary of coarse words was never put to such a task as when we met the Limeys. Three, four, and more dimensional cuss words were the rule.

Another opinion from an American, a Major Garretson, serving in the British Sector of the front in July 1918 in a training establishment behind the lines (as reported by Malcolm Brown):

On the 4th July the whole of France and England made a gala day of it, and indeed it was a curious privilege to be in a British Army Service School and hear British officers toasting the United States for the courage it showed 150 years ago in insisting on personal liberty, and fighting a mad German Prince [i.e. King George III] to get it. It may be said to the Britons' credit, there was never a word of regret about lost territory or anything of the sort, which is quite remarkable when you think of the Briton's love for empires beyond the seas.

British soldiers' comments on American soldiers

Wilfrid Ewart, while waiting on Abbeyville railway station for the Paris train in June 1918, and looking about him at the different soldiers on the platform, describes the Americans there as:

Lithe and slim, rather like keen commercial travellers, with nasal voices, odd cynical faces, and an air of being perpetually .amused.

Ernest Atkins (see below) says:

They [the Americans] were quite inexperienced and there was lots of faults with their equipment. They had silk socks, and this caused sore feet. Their gaiters soon lost their buttons and gaped open – lots of our fellows sold them half their puttees for twenty francs. Their breeches were too tight at the knees and although they were smart, their knees were soon through.

Bert Chaney, on the only time he met up with American troops, in 1918:

The 33rd Chicago Regiment came under our special care, to be carefully initiated into the mysteries of war, but they had so much swank and bounce, they knew all there was to know, that I am afraid we did not take to them at all. Besides carrying rifles they also wore automatic pistols. They took one look at our revolvers and told us we looked like a bunch of cowboys with such out-of-date weapons, and we retorted by saying they had no idea how to carry a rifle properly. They were continually showing off their prowess by drawing their automatic pistols from their holsters as fast as possible and twirling them round and round their trigger fingers. They were an uncouth, uninhibited, extrovert mob, never alluding to their regiment as the Thirty-third but always as 'de Dirty Turd Chicago Boys'.

263

Aubrey Smith notes a brief encounter of his first sight of American troops in 1917, after his unit was withdrawn from Passchendaele:

As we travelled onwards into the desolation with this immense plain on either side of us, the firing line got farther away as it bent south-eastwards, but we passed several back area hutments and camps. One of the latter was occupied by Americans, who clustered round when we happened to stop [the train] and an exchange of pleasantries followed, each army summing up the other's characteristics. These Yanks wore forage caps, smart khaki uniforms and green canvas gaiters, utterly unsuited for mud; still they would live and learn. It was rumoured that their first division would not be fit to be put in the trenches till about the end of the year, and, in view of their considerable distance from the firing-line, Mac imitated an American twang and called out; 'Waal, I guess there's no war at all!' The Yanks laughed and seemed to appreciate the thrust.

British soldiers' views on Canadians

Norman Ellison writing on 5th June 1915:

The Canadians are fine fellows and the most independent lot I have ever struck. For instance a batch went 'up the line' tonight and before they left, they were paraded before the CO for the customary speech wishing them 'Good Luck'. Now a CO's parade in the British army is about the most solemn and formal function there is, but these boys do not care tuppence about army etiquette and formalities. On roll-call instead of the usual 'Here Sir', it is 'Sure' or 'Right here' or 'That's me'. When the CO had spoken to them they started cheering and one fellow shouted out quite loudly 'Waal – he's a bloody good scholar, anyway' in the broadest Canadian accent.

During September and October 1915 Aubrey Smith was learning the arts of the battalion transport section with the LRBs, and part of their duties was to help unload troop trains. He says:

It was fun detraining the Canadians, who had far less of the

264

'Brasso' and dazzling appearance than Kitchener's men. They did not mind how they got the vehicles off the train or who gave orders, nor did they attempt to dress their mules by the right, when they had got them in the yard. The men showed rather an inclination to explore the village and it was some time before they could be collected together to march off.

Criticism of opinions expressed by some Canadian and Australian writers about the British

Robin Neillands, while praising the qualities of the Dominion troops, at the same time attempts to balance the criticisms made by some of their military historians of the British leadership and British troops. He says, in his study of the generals on the Western Front, *The Great War Generals on the Western Front 1914–1918*:

> ... they were good troops, well trained, well led, highly motivated. Without these qualities no unit can do well in war, but this has been overshadowed in the last twenty years by a swelling chorus of self-regarding praise, orchestrated in Canberra and Ottawa, and although to a lesser extent, in Wellington, growing in volume as the veterans of the Great War have died, and dedicated to the notion that the soldiers of Canada, Australia and New Zealand were, stronger, braver, more intelligent, and better led, than the troops provided by the Old Country. In fact few of the Great War veterans from those countries would have supported that allegation... Much of this comment can be accounted for by patriotism and a natural pride in the exploits of the national army in the Great War – or by attempts to bolster growing republican sentiment in those countries. It is, however, regrettable that some historians in Canada and Australia have attempted to elevate the considerable exploits of their Great War forebears by denigrating the actions and courage of their British comrades-in-arms.

British soldiers' views on the Portuguese troops

During the war Portugal mobilised about 100,000 men, and suffered some 21,000 casualties, including more than 7,000 fatalities. The two divisions of the Portuguese Expeditionary Force on the Western

Front were not regarded highly by the British troops (see 1918 below). Known by their several nicknames, 'The Pork-and-Beans', 'The Geese', and 'Gooses', they were generally considered to be dirty in their trenches, and unreliable in the line.

In defence of the Portuguese troops however, when Portugal entered the war in 1916, there was a 'pro-Allies' government in power. Later the government changed and the troops in France received little support or encouragement from official circles at home in Portugal. It has been said that the majority of their officers, certainly their senior officers, spent most of their time in Paris rather than in the line with their men. Leave for the troops was very poor, pay haphazard and they had no particular cause to fight for. In these circumstances it is not surprising that their morale was low.

Michael Moynihan (*People at War 1914–1918*, see above) quotes veteran, Ernest Atkins, on the Portuguese:

> We did not take them very seriously. In fact when we met a regiment at a station and exchanged cigarettes with them, we noticed that they took theirs out of their gas masks. On looking inside we found they had no gas masks in the container. We never knew whether they had not been given the inside part or if they had thrown it away to make room for cigarettes and oddments.

An impression of the Australians

Chaney, again via Moynihan, and talking about some Australians he came across in the spring of 1918 during the big retreat:

> Like most Aussies of that period they were quite mad, were the roughest of the rough, had no discipline at all but were among the finest fighters in the line. At Villers Bretonneaux, here we had been rushed to hold the line, they left the trenches altogether whenever Jerry opened up a heavy bombardment, while our orders were to stand and hold and put up with it. We did not think much of them at that time, even though they said they would be back later. The big blowers, we thought, all talk and no guts. But as soon as the shelling finished and it became dark, back they came. Leaving their rifles in the

266

trenches they drew their bayonets from their scabbards and with a 'How about it digger?' and an answering 'Righto, matey' they climbed over the top and disappeared into No Man's Land.

It seemed hours later when they scrambled back into the trench, wiped their bayonets on the sandbags, grinned all over their faces and resumed trench duty as if nothing had happened. If we asked them what they had been up to, their answer was invariably 'Just had ourselves a barney, matey'. Of course there was one draw back to all this. Jerry would get mad at whatever they had been up to and slam us with everything, and once again we crouched, taking it all while the Aussies quietly flitted away with a casual 'Be seeing you, digger.'

Alan Moorehead quotes Compton Mackenzie as saying of an occasion in Gallipoli:

He [Compton Mackenzie] overtook Lieut.-Colonel Pollen, Hamilton's military secretary, who was talking to three Australians all well over six feet tall. Pollen who had a soft, somewhat ecclesiastical voice, was saying, 'Have you chaps heard that they've given General Bridges [Australian Divisional Commander] a posthumous KCMG?' 'Have they?' one of the giants replied. 'Well that won't do him much good where he is now, will it mate?'

There was a little resentment among British troops concerning the Australians because the Australians – like the Americans in WWII – were paid much more than the British soldiers, and able to 'throw their weight around', and in addition the Australians were able to get away with behaviour that would have had the British private almost permanently up on a disciplinary charge.

The New Zealand Division

A tribute to the New Zealand Division is paid by Arthur Behrend, who was adjutant of a heavy artillery brigade working closely with the New Zealanders in March 1918:

We admired them more than any other Division we had

previously met, and not only because we knew them better. They accepted us too, and in a matter of days they looked upon us as their private heavy artillery. Except when they were out of the line we were in daily contact with them till the end of the war – and with battalion and even companies as well as their Divisional and Brigade headquarters. I cannot recall a single occasion when either side let the other down. For us, bearing in mind that Heavy Artillery Brigades were Corps troops, it was a novel and stimulating experience, and I have no doubt we shot all the better for it. For no words of mine can convey to the layman the feeling of heaven which an artilleryman knows when the Division he is supporting is a good one, and of all the good and very good Divisions of the British army I would rate the New Zealand Division high among the highest.

PART TWENTY-SEVEN

Entrenchments ... owing to further advance being impossible, the efforts of the attacking forces must be limited temporarily to holding ground already won. The advance must be resumed at the first possible moment.

Manual of Infantry Training, 1914.

Fighting the static war

Major-General Fuller, the military strategist and historian already mentioned, relates a fascinating observation from a source I have not been able to trace. He says:

> The only man who accurately forecast what would happen in 1914–1918 was a Polish banker, M Bloch of Warsaw, who in 1899, wrote in his book *Is War Impossible?*: 'The war, instead of being a hand-to-hand contest ... will become a kind of stalemate... Everybody will be entrenched in the next war. It will be a great war of entrenchments. The spade will be as indispensable to the soldier as his rifle... All wars will of necessity partake of the character of siege operations... Your soldiers may fight as they please, the ultimate decision is in the hands of famine... That is the future of war ... the bankruptcy of nations and the break up of the whole social organisation.

An incredibly accurate forecast of events. And I have little doubt that if anyone in military circles at the time had read them, he dismissed them. The Boer War was a mobile hit and run defensive

269

guerrilla war by the defenders, and a chasing one by the attackers. The general considered opinion in military and political sources in pre-war Britain was that if a war occurred on the continent it would mobile and of short duration – whichever way it went. As a result British troops suffered from a serious shortage of guns and shells for artillery bombardments for the first three years, and often what they had was of poor quality, and/or with shrapnel shells at the expense of too little high explosive. Much of the artillery ammunition came from the USA as Britain, in comparison with the French and Germans, had only a tiny armaments industry and could not keep up with the voracious appetite of the guns for more and more shells.

The front lines

Following the so-called 'race to the sea' in 1914 when both sides sought unsuccessfully to outflank each other, the front lines were set almost without significant change for four years. Apart from Second Ypres in 1915, and the costly attack on the French at Verdun in 1916, all the time the German army fought on two fronts, it was, after 1914, generally prepared to defend and hold the ground it had initially gained in the west rather than mount large offensives.

Defence and attack on the Western Front

Once Germany had accepted she was in for a prolonged struggle on two fronts – Russia in the east, and France and Belgium in the west – the German army, as the invading force occupying both French and Belgium territory, dug in on the Western Front. The German army, invariably choosing and holding the commanding ground, was therefore able to be prepared to adjust its positions with a view to the most effective defence and counter attack.

Generally speaking, the German philosophy was, as it is alleged the famous German pilot Manfred von Richthofen, instructed his pilots – 'let the customers come to the shop.' So, for most of the war after Verdun in 1916, the German forces were content to sit behind increasingly well devised in-depth and immensely strong defensive lines – waiting either until the war in Russia was over, or at least until German troops could be diverted from the Eastern Front to reinforce their Western Front troops, and then mount a major offensive.

With German forces entrenched on Belgium and French soil the onus therefore was always on the French and British to take the offensive, but the Allied army commanders were embedded in a war where, until 1918, German defences always appeared stronger than British or French attacks.

Despite detailed planning and massive preparations, attack after attack by French and British troops failed to gain significant ground or break through to open country. The Western Front became to be referred to bitterly by the troops as 'the sausage machine' where men and animals were slaughtered and churned into the ground with little or no gain to show for their sacrifice.

Following years of grinding heavy losses, the French army finally mutinied in 1917 after Nivelle's failure to make his promised great break-through, and they refused to go on the attack any more (see 1917 below) and the British army had to take over even more and more of the front lines and was stretched to breaking point.

The 'shell scandal'

As I have said, the pre-war British munitions industry was small and in private hands and never envisaged as supplying the massive amount of ammunition that it transpired would be required.

A report in *The Times* on 14th May 1915 by Colonel Repington claimed that the BEF's initial failure in the Artois Offensive was caused by a serious shortage of high-explosive artillery shells. The ensuing political and public uproar fatally damaged the government, and a coalition government was formed to replace it.

Every personal account of the front lines in the early war years in Flanders and France speaks of the suffering of the British front line troops from intensive shelling by the German artillery. This was aggravated by the chronic lack of the retaliatory power of the British guns that were not only few in number in comparison, but outside the times of their attacking bombardments were frequently rationed to a few rounds a day.

A consequence of the shell shortage was that the British infantry had no option but to dig in as much as possible and crouch and

271

take it without the power to retaliate; but in the latter part of 1914, and through 1915 especially, the British casualties were severe from shelling. The trenches in 1914 and 1915 in Flanders were very rudimentary, narrow, deep in slimy mud, and because of the water table and the opened flood gates by the Belgians when the Germans invaded, it was impossible then to dig more than a foot or two without reaching water. Defences were mainly sagging breastworks of mud and sandbags easily obliterated by shelling. Aubrey Smith writes of Second Ypres of 2nd May 1915:

> In the afternoon of Sunday, the artillery fire which had been increasing in volume, swelled up into a regular barrage. No 15 Platoon had several direct hits on their trench and I don't know what happened to the other Platoons beyond them. Soon after 5 o'clock having no officer or senior NCO unhit, and no stretcher-bearers they sent along to Corpl. Miles to come and bandage, among others Webb – who had a leg blown off. Some minutes later poor Miles returned, very pale and blood stained. He squatted in his corner of the trench. 'God! Isn't this awful', he said. The intensity of the fire had increased still more.

Worn gun barrels and poor ammunition were two very contributory reasons for casualties caused by 'shorts' or friendly fire.*

*Unlike the outcry over the death of some British troops caused by the American planes in the first Gulf War, 'friendly fire' seems to have been recorded philosophically more or less as a matter of course in the First World War. And in the Second World War British pilots frequently remarked how the guns of the merchant ships in convoys opened fire on them when their aeroplanes approached to begin their convoy protection duties.

When the 'shell scandal' died down it still left the problem of the great shortage of shells that had constantly bedevilled the British since they arrived in France. Staff calculated that the munitions required to mount an attack over ten kilometres of enemy front would be 360,000 rounds for heavy artillery and 1,000,000 for field artillery. It would also be necessary to have as minimum 80 heavy howitzers, 80 heavy guns, 200 field guns and 150 trench mortars.

Early in 1916 Lloyd George at the Ministry of Munitions wrote to a correspondent who had received a letter from the front from a friend complaining about the high incidence of dud shells:

Your informant is quite right; the Hadden and Von Donop fuse which I inherited, and was compelled by the terms of my office to manufacture, first of all burst prematurely; then to obviate that a delay action was introduced and the shell would not burst at all. Du Cane and his men have now invented another fuse, but it will take time to manufacture it.

Shrapnel, a British innovation designed by Henry Shrapnel in the previous century, was really intended for open warfare where its effect could be devastating, but generally it was ineffective against barbed wire and the deep defensive positions of the entrenched enemy. (A shrapnel shell was a hollow metal canister containing very small round lead balls with an explosive charge below them designed to explode in the air propelling the charge forward and downward.) Richard Holmes in *The Western Front* quotes a medical officer who remembered its effects:

A young gunner subaltern was on his way to observe a machine gun position. Just as he got outside my door a shrapnel shell burst full in front of him. The poor fellow was brought in to me absolutely riddled. He lay in my arms until he died, shrieking in his agony and said he hoped I would excuse him for making such a noise as he really could not help it … he was a fine looking boy not more than nineteen.

The shells received from German artillery were referred to by nicknames sometimes from their appearance after exploding, or the sound they made approaching i.e. 'woolly bear' (the resulting smoke from any big German HE shell or a small HE shell bursting with black smoke). 'Plum pudding' from the shape of a trench mortar bomb; 'whizz–bang' the sound of a light shell fired from one of the smaller artillery guns (German 77 mm) which arrived as soon, if not sooner, than heard.

British artillery

Artillery was divided into two main groups, the first was a combination of the Royal Horse Artillery (RHA), and the Royal Field Artillery (RFA), and was known as the 'Field Artillery', and the second was the Royal Garrison Artillery (RGA). The latter had a variety of heavy, siege, coastal defence and mountain artillery. Both groups employed 'guns' and 'howitzers'.* Heavy guns were difficult to bring up to support the infantry in an attack, particularly in muddy conditions.

*'Guns' included those weapons with long barrels and had a great velocity on a low trajectory. 'Howitzers' fired their shells at a much steeper angle (high trajectory) and were particularly useful and suitable for the destruction of trenches and blockhouses.

The lack of heavy guns, the continuing poor quality of the ammunition, and the preponderance still of light artillery and shrapnel over high explosives, bedevilled the preliminary barrage on the Somme in 1916 as it had done in the earlier battles. And once more despite the incredible intensity of the barrages the barbed wire entanglements remained uncut, and the deep subterranean shelters built by the Germans proved impregnable. This was particularly true where the 'live and let live' principle, however understandable and welcome at the time, had allowed the Germans on the Somme prior to the 1916 summer offensive to build such massive and deep underground defences undetected and unopposed – especially in the previously held French sector of the line. Infantry adopted a formation known as 'artillery formation' to present a minimum target when attacking. Platoons and sections formed loose columns four abreast to enable them to extend into a thin line as necessary.

Peter Simkins, in *Chronicles of the Great War*, says that in the second half of the war considerable improvements and refinements in artillery techniques helped to resolve the tactical dilemmas the big guns had caused – i.e. the increasing weight and intensity of the bombardments before an offensive, which also lasted longer as the trench systems of the Germans became stronger and deeper, had not only negated any possibility of surprise, but also created landscapes of craters and mud making it doubly difficult to send reinforcements and guns forward rapidly enough to exploit local successes.

He instances the British introduction in 1917 of the instantaneous '106' percussion fuse (see Lloyd George's comments above when he was Minister of Munitions) an advance which made it made it possible to cut barbed wire efficiently without cratering the ground.

Other advances Simkins listed were accurate location of enemy batteries by means of sound ranging and flash-spotting; the extensive

274

use of topographical survey work and detailed battlefield maps prepared with the aid of air photography, and 'calibration', whereby the idiosyncrasies of each individual gun were taken into account when drawing up a fire programme. All these developments of predicted fire helped to eradicate the need for the registration of targets by preliminary shooting, and surprise and precision could be achieved at the same time to unlock the trench stalemate (see the German offensive in March – April 1918 below).

The machine gun

Martin Marix Evans in his *The Battles of the Somme* says of the static war that it was something the generals on both sides had been unprepared for. There was, he says, largely an experience of wars of manoeuvre, of battles against relatively unsophisticated opponents in which they employed combinations of infantry and cavalry movement. He continues:

The impact of new weapons on military thinking was still superficial although the immediate practical use of such weapons was understood. They had at their disposal artillery of a power formerly undreamed of; Light and medium field guns, heavy howitzers, and even huge Naval Guns mounted on railway trucks, capable of firing immense shells with uncanny accuracy for many miles... It was, however, the invention of an American (though he became a naturalised British subject), Hiram Maxim, that made the trench system so easy to defend.

He devised a gun which harnessed the recoil automatically to eject the spent cartridge, chamber a new one, close the breech block, and fire the weapon. From this the British developed the Vickers medium machine gun, the Germans the Maxim, and the French the St-Étienne.

In 1914 there were two Vickers machine guns allocated to each British infantry battalion. It was a heavy weapon and difficult and cumbersome to move about as a defensive weapon. The tripod was the heaviest part weighing some 50 lbs. The gun itself weighed 28 lbs without the water needed to keep the weapon cool. Properly set up, it has been claimed, the rate of fire could be well over 400 rounds per minute, and in the right hands up to 600, and when the gun was firmly fixed on its tripod there was little or no movement to upset its accuracy. It was a water-cooled weapon and so could fire continuously for long periods. Heat engendered by the rapid fire soon boiled the water and caused a powerful emission of steam. This steam was condensed by passing it through a pliable tube into a canvas bucket of water. By this means the gun could continue to fire without a cloud of steam giving its position away to the enemy.

It was generally operated by a six-man team. Number One in the team was the leader and fired the gun. Number Two controlled the entry of ammunition belts into the feed block. Number Three maintained a supply of ammunition to Number Two. And Numbers Four to Six were reserves and carriers. All the members of the team had to be able to perform all the tasks of assembling and operating the gun and taking over any position as circumstances dictated. Later the Lewis gun, a much lighter weapon, proved very valuable in the trenches.

The machine gun as a weapon had great fire power – the Vickers firing 450 to 600 plus rounds per minute, about 30 or more times the fire power of a rifle, and was comparatively a cheap source of power. Sir Eric Geddes related:

> I told K [Kitchener] that rifles and machine guns were the same as shillings and pounds: that nine rifles were equal to a Lewis Gun and thirteen rifles to a Vickers machine gun.

It was said that by removing cartridges from the ammunition belt, opposing machine gunners were able to rap out an exchange of rhythms such as 'MEET me DOWN in PICC-a-DILL-y', and the response, 'YES with-OUT my DRAWERS ON'.*

*A number of German soldiers spoke English; some had worked in Britain before the war, particularly in London, as waiters, and some performed with the German bands that toured the country. A joke among British troops in the early days of the war was that if you called out from the front line across to the German line 'Hey Fritz' a dozen heads would bob up replying, 'coming sir!'

Dr Stephen Bull (see below) says the Germans developed: 'Arguably the world's first effective sub-machine gun, the "Maschinenpistole 18" a *Kugelspritz* or "bullet squirter" firing 32 rounds of 9mm pistol ammunition from a "snail" magazine – first developed for the P08 pistol – on full automatic, and it was capable of causing havoc in the confines of a trench. Fortunately for the Allies the MP18 would see only a very limited distribution before the end of the war.'

The rifle

The British 303 Lee Enfield with a 10-round magazine was considered a good weapon. Its drawbacks were that it was relatively expensive and complicated, and it needed frequent cleaning to operate effectively. The constant dirty conditions in the trenches combined with bad weather meant great care was needed to protect it.

During an attack an infantryman was expected to carry 170 rounds of ammunition – among other items such as rifle, bayonet, grenades, shovel, wire cutters, empty sandbags, gas mask, full water bottle, medical kit, mess tin, iron rations etc. The whole lot weighed over 30 kg.

PART TWENTY-EIGHT

Ad hoc piecemeal planning to overcome the problems were evident in August 1916. The Fourth army ordered eighteen miles of track, five locomotives and sixty wagons to relieve congestion on its roads, but a larger response was needed as the volume of British military traffic which left the French ports doubled in 1916.

Keith Grieves. An extract from his study
The Transport Mission to GHQ 1916.

The enlargement of the British army and the logistics involved

The British armies in France had become as huge as Kitchener envisaged and of a size which had never been seen before. They covered a vast area with a density and complexity never previously encountered, and none of the generals, or their staffs, had experienced or been trained to handle this, or the kind of warfare that developed. (Wellington could have galloped from one end of his command to the other at Waterloo.)

As an example of numerical increase, by the end of the war there were something like 300,000 civilian Chinese labourers, mainly recruited from Hong Kong, employed by the British army, 100,000 or more of these were in France. Overall that means three times as many civilian Chinese labourers in 1918 than the whole of the original British army force that landed in France in 1914.

Road transport

There were the complexities of supplies and logistics to be overcome, and having to use mainly nineteenth-century means of transport in a twentieth-century war further complicated matters. Although motor transport was increasing, at the outbreak of war in 1914 the army had few motor vehicles in service. A catalogue of MT vehicles in the entire British army in 1914 shows: 124 lorries, 45 cars, 15 ambulances, 24 motor cycles, 7 petrol tractors, 57 steam tractors, 188 wheeled trucks, 18 workshop trucks, and 29 miscellaneous vehicles. A total of 507 (and this includes those overseas).*

*Source *Army Service Corps 1902–1918, Annex 1.* By Michael Young.

It was still a horse-drawn army. For example the composition of an ASC (Army Service Corps) divisional train was: 26 officers, 4 warrant officers, 42 sergeants, 67 artificers, 4 trumpeters, 523 rank and file, 62 riding horses, 597 draught horses, 17 carts, 127 waggons, 4 motor cars and 30 bicycles.

Another revealing statistic, provided by the *Official History* and referring to the end of July 1916 during the battle of the Somme, states that a 24-hour census of traffic was recorded at Fricourt, and during this time there passed by:

> 26,536 troops, 568 light motor cars, 617 motor cycles, 813 motor lorries, 1,458 six-horse waggons, 568 four-horse waggons, 1,215 two-horse waggons, 515 one-horse carts, 5,404 riding horses, 333 motor ambulances and 1,043 cycles.

One should bear in mind that with so much horse and mule transport an enormous amount of fodder was required, and this too needed to be transported.

An overly optimistic picture of the quantity and quality of mechanised transport in 1914 is given by Mr H.C. Lafone, editor of *The Light Car*, who writes authoritively:

> But while it is not correct to say that the great war now in progress has witnessed the *début* of mechanical transport in campaigning, we may truthfully state that this is the first occasion on which horse-drawn vehicles in warfare have been

superseded on a grand scale; and further we are now afforded an opportunity of noting the capabilities and limitations of vehicles designed to a specification laid down by men who have made a study of the special characteristics requisite in a vehicle employed to supply the needs of troops on active service.

Even in the Second World War, the German army – one of the most up-to-date and mechanised of armies of its time – in the early years of the war still used a considerable amount of horse transport, particularly on the Eastern Front as old newsreels will testify. And Robin Neillands (*Great War Generals on the Western Front*) actually states figures:

It is worth noting that the technologically very advanced German army of the Second World War still relied largely on horses for its transport; in 1945 it had some 2 million of the animals in service.

He does not give the source of his information as far as I could see, but there seems little reason to doubt its accuracy. Antony Beever, author of *Stalingrad* also comments on the very large number of horse-drawn vehicles at the outset of the Russian campaign in 1941 where, he says, over 600,000 horses were used to tow guns, ambulances and ration wagons, and with the bulk of the German infantry divisions on their feet, the overall speed of advance was unlikely to have been much faster than Napolean's Grande Armée in 1812.

Rail transport

Rail transport was vital, and because the French railway system could not cope with the strains put upon it, the British army brought over to France a large number of railway engines and rolling stock. By early 1917 there were more than 500 engines and 20,000 waggons serving under War Department control on almost 1,000 miles of British track in France.

Communications

Communications between the high command, field commanders, and the troops in the field, were very primitive by today's standards. Telephone wires quickly became cut during an attack, and signallers were frequently killed as they attempted time and again to repair the breaks in the telephone lines under a barrage of shellfire. The telephone wires were used for both Morse code and speech transmission, and the early wireless transmitters and receivers together with their associated power supplies equipment were far too cumbersome and vulnerable to be successful in the front line trenches or forward areas in a battle.

Once an attack or a battle had begun, most of the communication on the ground to and from the front line and battle area was by runner, and many runners were killed or wounded before they were able to deliver their messages. Those who got through, often in appalling conditions, frequently took so long that when they did, the information they carried was no longer valid or gave any idea of the true picture of the current position.

A battalion runner, Private Arthur Wrench, 1/4th Seaforth Highlanders describes life as a runner on the Somme in 1916 having just arrived there in late July. He had been instructed to find the Colonel who was somewhere in the old German second line trenches, and to ask him for any information for the General's orders:

It was a terrible journey, especially when I did not know where I was going, and it was pitch dark, except for the flashing of the guns which seemed to be everywhere, barking out all around me so that it was impossible to hear the German shells coming. This bombardment was Hellish, to tell the truth about it, and it was almost maddening as I groped my way, hopelessly lost among battery after battery of artillery in action, and further forward among old trenches into which I stumbled. After a while I spotted a gleam of light away down in an old mine crater or something. In this shelter were some Seaforth signallers so they gave me fuller instructions how to get to their HQ so I continued on as it began to get daylight, and soon I began to be chased backwards and forwards along some old shallow trenches, obviously German ones at one time.

Every time I stood upright or got out, I was shot at by

some damned German, and I couldn't find a soul about anywhere. At last I came upon the first man in the line here, and he told me that the colonel had passed along this way just ten minutes earlier. So I went on while the awful uproar of the battle was now quietened, and soon I overtook the colonel. It was now long after sunrise. In fact it was exactly 6 o'clock by my watch as I asked him the question I had set out to do which he replied with a shake of his head, and said, 'No, I have no information for the General's orders'.*

*Recounted in *The Imperial War Museum Book of the Somme* by Malcolm Brown.

In August 1914, communications were equally difficult to establish and maintain, although for different reasons. While Sir John French, the BEF Commander in Chief, was out and about visiting his two corps to see things for himself, and addressing his troops, his Corps Commanders were searching for him. In addition, staff and liaison officers from both French and British armies were trying to find one or more or all of the above, as well as each other. One can only think how invaluable a mobile phone or two would have been.

PART TWENTY-NINE

By 1916 the British could no longer afford the manpower luxury of having the cavalry uncommitted to the daily warfare and casualties of the trenches and so the 3rd Hussars formed an Infantry Company of 8 officers and 300 men to serve in the trenches and later a machine gun squadron.

Extract from *The Queen's Own Hussars Tercentenary Edition 1685–1985.*

Horses and mules, and the part played by other animals

There had been few or no scruples about sacrificing horses and mules in the general carnage of war. Some improvements in animal welfare had taken place following the Boer War when there had been an outcry over the cruel and unnecessary sacrifice of animal lives during that war, and where over 300,000 horses and 50,000 mules died, frequently through illness and neglect.

As a result of this concern a parliamentary committee in 1903, approved the formation and appointment of the Army Veterinary Corps with a consequent improvement in the physical well being of these animals, at least while they were out of the firing line.

Sir Frank Fox (author of the book *G.H.Q.* by *'G.S.O.'* mentioned above), was proud – and one hopes justifiably so – of the record of the treatment of animals of the British army during the war:

No two officials at GHQ had a better right to be proud of their departments than the Director of Veterinary Services (Major-General Moore) and the Director of Remounts (Brigadier-

285

General Sir F.S. Garratt). These two were responsible for the welfare of the half million animals of the BEF, and there was never a collection of war animals that had a better time.

Whether the animals appreciated the good time they had we shall never know, but it was reported that during the retreat of Mons and Le Cateau in 1914, when casualties were heavy on both sides, particularly among the British troops that failed to receive the order to withdraw and some 8,000 men were lost, it was not only the men who suffered. The great Clydesdale horses commandeered from brewers' drays and railway vans strained and gasped and worked until they dropped, and then they were shot so they did not fall into enemy hands.

Michael Gavaghan in *Le Cateau, 1914* says that such was the military reliance on the horse that over 120,000 horses had been rounded up in the twelve days after war was declared. He continues:

> The requirement in horses had been calculated on the assumption that the whole of the BEF and the whole of the Territorial Force would be mobilized, and that an initial three months 'supply to replace casualties would be necessary'. This made made a total of 165,000 horses, the peace establishment was 25,000, with a registered and subsidised reserve of another 25,000. The remaining 115,000 were obtained by impressments under a decentralised scheme. By November 1918, the number of horses and mules had risen to 735,409, and 56,287 camels, bullocks and donkeys had joined up. By the end of the war 529,564 horses and mules had died, been sold, destroyed, missing or cast. A further 1,500 had been drowned at sea.

'G.S.O.' says that after the Armistice when the British army was disposing of its surplus horses everybody rushed to buy them:

> Prices touched a truly extraordinary level. The unhappy taxpayer amid all his burdens saw a golden stream flowing into the treasury, because his Army was a humane, conscientious and skilful horsemaster. The military advantage to transport through keeping the Army's animals fit and well is so obvious that it need not be dwelt upon. The advantage to the *morale* of the men is not so generally appreciated, but none the less real. It

286

helped to keep our men in good heart that the animals who worked with them, and for them, were in good heart and condition. To British men with their fine tradition of humanity to animals it would have been demoralising to have seen their brutes hungry and suffering.*

*The Countess of Ranfurly, writing in her diary in 1940, recollects that her father told her that British horses left behind in Palestine after the First World War were neglected and ill-treated. She mentions this because her husband's regiment, a Yeomanry unit, the Notts Sherwood Rangers, had been sent to the Middle East theatre in 1940 as cavalry taking their horses with them, but later that year the regiment was to become mechanised (after a spell manning coastal guns) and the horses were to be sent to a Remount Depot. She adds: 'We feel frightful – so many of them are hunters and part of our families. It is so sad that these lovely animals will never again graze in England's green fields. We feel like traitors to have brought them here and now must leave them behind.'

K.W. Mitchinson (see Pioneers below), also writes that in the Great War transport sections in all divisional arms had a deep affection for their animals. These troops worked hard to improve the welfare of the horses and mules by constructing hard standings and covered stabling. He says also that casualties to the animals were often grieved over as deeply by the troops as death and injuries among the men themselves. I cannot recall seeing a mention of this compassion elsewhere. To be fair though, Aubrey Smith, who was in the LRB's transport section, and frequently expresses his frustrations and exasperation and annoyance with the horses, says:

The wants of man are of secondary importance to those of beast. A driver's primary consideration was for his horses, for on those poor dumb brutes fell the heavy burden of the day's work and they relied faithfully on their masters giving them drink and oats as soon as possible at the end of the journey. Never in my experience did a transport man – however weary or hungry he might be – defer his horse's meal in order to satisfy his own wants, and these were pressing enough at times.

At the outbreak of war army officers from, or under the orders of, the Army Service Corps Remount Service, rode round the countryside requisitioning horses for the army. The owners were paid a set sum and told they could buy them back after the war. The effectiveness of the pre-war Registration Scheme that had been introduced to obtain 14,000 horses by compulsory purchase on the outbreak of war was well illustrated by 1914 when it obtained ten times that number. Despite this there was a shortage of suitable horses. One of the reasons put forward was that because of the general increase in mechanical transport the breeding of horses was adversely affected. The breeds considered most suitable for the military for transport were Clydesdales, Suffolks, Welsh cart horses and Percherons.

Remount officers were sent as far afield as America, New Zealand, India and China as well as European countries. Siegfried Sassoon while writing of his time at the Fourth Army training school in the spring of 1916, recalls one day when:

> I observed one afternoon when we were on our way to a 'demonstration' at the Army Bombing School hundreds of light and heavy draft horses were drawn up along a road for an inspection by the Commander-in-Chief. The horses, attached to their appropriate vehicles and shining in their summer coats, looked a picture of sleekness and strength. They were of all sorts and sizes but their power and compactness was uniform. The horse-hood of England was there with every buckle of its harness brightened. There were nor many mules among them, for mules were mostly with the Artillery, and this was a slap-up Army Service Corps parade, obviously the climax of several weeks' preparation. I wished I could have spent the afternoon inspecting them.

Dogs

Dogs served as well, and were employed as guard dogs, messengers, sentries and first aid auxiliaries. They were also intended to deliver messages, getting through trenches where men were unable to and under intense enemy fire, but I have not come across any success stories of this aspect of their tasks in the field. Many dogs were trained at the War Dog School in Shoeburyness formed by lieutenant Colonel E.H. Richardson.*

---

*A particularly repellent form of using dogs in war occurred in the Second World War when according to Antony Beever:

> Several German panzer divisions also encountered a new form of unconventional weapon during this fighting. They found Russian dogs running towards them with a

curious-looking saddle holding a load on top with a short upright stick. At first the panzer troops thought that they must be first-aid dogs, but then they realized that the animals had explosives or an anti-tank mine strapped to them. These 'mine-dogs', trained on Pavlovian principles, had been taught to run under large vehicles to obtain their food. The stick, catching against the underside, would detonate the charge.

One would like to think that such practices would outrage the mind these days, but quite recently the Americans were apparently seriously contemplating training mine or explosive carrying dolphins as a weapon against submarines. The dolphins, it was argued, would not be detected as a threat by enemy listening devices aboard the submarines and so would be able to deliver their attacks.

Birds

Carrier pigeons were also used to carry messages – or were they? Well, actually no, according to Mr A.H. Osborne, editor (in 1914), of *The Racing Pigeon*, for he writes in an article entitled *Pigeons for Sport and War*:

> The public often see statements about 'carrier' pigeons, and have a very wrong perception of their capabilities. The 'Carrier' is really an incorrect name of the birds that are used for war purposes, or for carrying messages. The Carrier is a big-wattled pigeon, and its chief value is due to the æsthetic shape of its beak, but it has no capacity for flying or carrying messages.

Albert Chaney, already a 'Saturday Soldier' when war was declared and who kept a journal *A Lad Goes to War* (see above and below) is quoted by Michael Moynihan concerning his experience of carrier pigeons and dogs during the German break-through in March 1918. Chaney was a signaller, and all the lines were down, and the Aldis lamps (lamps for signalling Morse code) were unable to penetrate the mist.

> I scribbled two similar coded messages on the special thin paper provided, screwed them up and pushed them into little containers which clip on to the pigeons' legs. I and one of the boys, each carrying a pigeon, crept up the steps, pushed the gas blanket to one side and threw our birds into the air. Away they flew. We watched them as they circled round a

couple of times and then, like divers, they swooped straight down and settled on top of the dug-out. We retrieved them and tried once more but those birds refused to fly in the mist. They had been trained to fly direct to their loft and would not start until they could see it.

So down to the dug-out again to write another message and put it into the small pouch attached to the dog's collar. Leading it to the entrance I gave it a parting slap on the rump, at the same time shouting firmly 'Home boy! Allez!' I watched it for a minute or two as it trotted off, then dropped the gas blanket back in position. Even while we were still sighing with relief a wet nose pushed the blanket aside and in crawled the dog, scared out of its wits. All our efforts could not budge him ... we eventually took the message from his collar, put it on the other dog and tried to send that one on his way... He would not even move... So ended all our wonderful preparations for keeping communications going during the attack.

Even if the pigeons or poor frightened dogs had gone it would all have been a wasted effort as the RE signallers at the other end had already been overrun and killed or captured.

Animals as pets and mascots

As always with British troops (and I stress that throughout where I use the term 'British' this embraces the 'Imperial troops' as well) many units had pets. There is an endearing story from a Private Durham of the 3rd Canadian Cyclists in a letter home in 1916 (recorded by the Imperial War Museum). He says:

> There is a trench cat, a strict neutral, we call him Wilson* because we found him asleep on a haversack with a rat rifling the contents! 'Too Proud to Fight.' He walks across No Man's Land at will and knows the meal times on both sides.

*The reference to the American President Wilson and 'too proud to fight' comes from the remark that Wilson made when opinion – both in Europe and the USA – was being expressed that America should enter the war after the sinking of the *Lusitania*, aboard which vessel were American citizens. There was, he said, 'such a thing as being too proud to fight'.

Soldiers and dogs always get together given the chance. I remember my father recalling fond memories of various dogs that had attached themselves to his regiment overseas during the First World War, and also reading of the heart-rending howling of the dogs that had to be left behind at Dunkirk in the Second World War. One hopes they soon became friends of the victors. *The Times* correspondent in France wrote in 1917 that many men adopted local strays as pets. 'It is the dogs, who enlist the men's sympathies more than anything else. Like frightened children, they join the ranks, nestling down by the side of the men for warmth and protection.' The National Canine Defence League fought hard to protect dogs during the war and was the instrument in getting the War Office to drop the idea of using dogs to draw guns at the front.

Captain Wyllie, who is mentioned elsewhere, records that in the midst of the battle at Loos he was sheltering in a captured German trench when out of a small hole in the wall a field mouse peeped out at him. He says it had obviously been a pet of a German soldier who had been located in the trench for some time as there was a distinct track along a narrow ledge leading from the hole. He continued:

> I put my finger forward and the mouse approached and let me stroke its neck and chin and as the little creature had obviously been a long time without food or water, I gave it a nibble from one of my biscuits and a drink of water from the tip of my finger which I dipped into my water bottle. It would seem that the Hun and British were friends alike to the field mice and I trust this should be true.

Earlier in the century Frank Richards recalls his regiment's mascot, a goat:

> Our next station was Agra, about three hundred miles' march from Chakrata. On the day we arrived at Meerut, where the Battalion had to do ten day's manoeuvres before continuing with the march, the Goat died. I think it was old age, for he had been with the Battalion since he joined it eight years before, at Malta, or it may have been Crete. Every man in the Battalion was genuinely sorry that the wicked old rascal had gone West, but the vegetable-wallahs [whom the goat used to

291

butt from behind and steal their wares] were mighty relieved; they did not say much but they walked around the camp with a jauntier air than what they had done when he was alive. He was buried underneath the big tree where they hanged the rebels during the mutiny. If he could have spoken I have no doubt he would have chosen the same spot for his last resting-place. It was only a few yards from the little tent he used to stay in, from which he had many times broken loose to trail the vegetable-wallahs.

The old Bacon-Wallah [nickname of one of the Battalion soldiers] was present at the burial and informed us that if his family carried out his last wishes he also would be buried under that same tree. A large cross was put on the Goat's grave, giving full particulars of his service. Three years later I paid a visit to Meerut and found the grave in beautiful condition; one of the men of the Battalion that was encamped there told me that more work had been done on the Goat's grave than on all the soldiers graves in the cemetery put together. A kind of unwritten law existed among the troops in India that the graves of regimental mascots or of men buried outside the cemeteries should always be well cared for... The old Bacon-Wallah was very much alive on this visit and pronounced a eulogy on the Goat in these words:

'He was a royal beast and I held him in sincere admiration. He could not read or write, but neither can many of us, and in one respect he put every man of his regiment to shame: That Goat knew better than any one of you how the natives of this country should be handled.'

I never again visited Meerut after that, but I have often wondered whether the old Bacon-Wallah is buried under the tree – even if he had been granted permission by the authorities it is extremely doubtful whether his children would have allowed him to be buried alongside the Goat, though the Goat was clearly his kindred spirit.

PART THIRTY

I adore War. It's just like a big picnic without the objectlessness of a picnic.

Taken from a letter dated 24th October 1914,
written by The Hon. Julian Grenfell, DSO Captain,
1st Royal Dragoons. Wounded 13th May 1915.
Died of wounds 26th May 1915.

The 1914 campaigns

There are quite frequent references to the feeling of unreality of war in those early hot summer days following the arrival of the British troops in France. The blistering heat, sore feet, thirst, and the constant pounding along the cobbles in the towns and the dust on the roads, occupied the attention of the troops more than the concern of actual sound and fury of arms. I must confess to be very taken by the following incredulous outraged roar from a senior reservist NCO – allegedly made to his officer in the opening round of the company's first brush with the enemy: 'Look out sir! THEM BUGGERS IS USING BALL!!' (i.e. live ammunition).

Not everyone had the same feelings of unreality in those early days. A Major A. Corbett-Smith wrote concerning the retreat from Mons – as quoted by Philip J. Haythornthwaite:

One man, a bugler in a county regiment, little more than a child in years, went raving mad as he staggered across a trench and fell dragging with him a headless Thing which still kept watch with rifle against shoulder. His shrieks, as they pulled

293

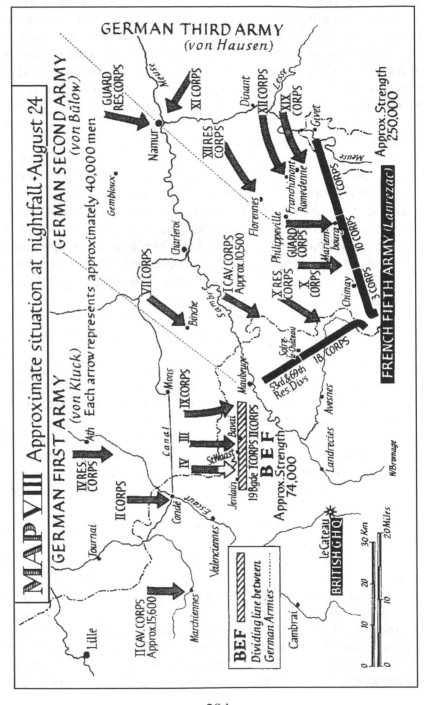

MAP VIII · Approximate situation at nightfall · August 24

GERMAN THIRD ARMY
(von Hausen)

GERMAN SECOND ARMY
(von Bülow)

GERMAN FIRST ARMY
(von Kluck)

Each arrow represents approximately 40,000 men

GUARD RES. CORPS

XI CORPS

XII CORPS

XIX CORPS

XII RES. CORPS

VII CORPS

I CAV. CORPS
Approx. 10,500

X RES. CORPS

GUARD CORPS

X CORPS

I CORPS

10 CORPS

3 CORPS

18 CORPS

53rd & 69th Res. Divs

FRENCH FIFTH ARMY (Lanrezac)

Approx. Strength 250,000

IV RES. CORPS

III CORPS

IV CORPS

IX CORPS

II CORPS

II CAV. CORPS
Approx. 15,600

19 Bgde I CORPS II CORPS

B E F
Approx. Strength
74,000

BRITISH GHQ

Meuse
Meuse
Lesse
Meuse
Sambre
Canal
Escaut

Namur
Gembloux
Charleroi
Binche
Dinant
Givet
Florennes
Philippeville
Mariembourg
Franchimont
Romedenne
Chimay
Solre-le-Château
Maubeuge
Bavai
St Waast
Jenlain
Mons
Condé
Valenciennes
Marchiennes
Lille
Tournai
Ath
Avesnes
Landrecies
Cambrai
le Cateau

BEF ▨▨▨
Dividing line between
German Armies ----

0   10   20   30 Km
0   10   20 Miles

W. Bromage

the two apart, ring even now in my ears. He died that night, simply from shock after the awful tension of the day.

Mons and Le Cateau

While the BEF was moving up on 22nd August 1914, Sir John French still believed he was taking part in a general advance, but the French Fifth Army, under General Lanrezac, had been fought to a standstill around Charleroi. By the 23rd Sir John had his doubts about any further forward moves, and conscious of Kitchener's instructions about the use of the BEF, he declined the request of the French army to attack the right flank of the Germans facing the French. He agreed however to hold his ground for 24 hours before joining the retreat as the French fell back. The British troops became overwhelmed by artillery fire, and despite repulsing many attacks, they were over stretched and in danger of being outflanked.

Philip Gibbs reported for the *Daily Chronicle* on seeing British casualties for the first time while he was at a French railway station:

> At a French junction there was a shout of command in English, and I saw a body of men in khaki, with Red Cross armlets, run across a platform to an incoming train from the north, with stretchers and drinking bottles. A party of English soldiers had arrived from a battle at a place called Mons... I saw a number of 'Tommies' with bandaged heads and limbs descending from the troop train. Some of them hung limp between their nurses, their faces, so fresh when I had first seen them on the way out, had become grey and muddy, and were streaked with blood. Their khaki uniforms were torn and cut.

Sir John had been told that the 4th Division was being sent to join him and meanwhile he converted the lines of communications troops to form into the 19th Brigade under the command of Major-General J.G. Drummond. This brigade was composed of 2nd Royal Welch Fusiliers, 1st Middlesex, 2nd Argyll and Sutherland Highlanders, and 1st Cameronians.

Smith-Dorrien was worried about the position of his II Corps, and with good reason. His 3rd and 5th Divisions were stretched across 20 miles of very difficult country around Mons – a mining area with pitheads, slag-heaps, and a railway line for carrying coal to the main line – far from ideal for a defensive engagement.

The town of Mons in 1914 had a population of some 28,000 people, and consisted mainly of rows of miners' cottages fronting on narrow cobbled streets. The area was not a very prepossessing one with a sprawl of drab mining villages surrounding it, and the Mons-Conde Canal was crossed by eighteen bridges, some road and some rail. There were also lock gates.

The canal, running almost directly east to west, was to be the front line area on 23rd August. Smith Dorrien had too few engineers and too little explosives to demolish the bridges and block the roads, and his troops had time only to scratch holes in which to lie in for cover, and to barricade the streets they used furniture from the cottages.

Orders for a withdrawal for the BEF were given on 24th August at 1 am. The two Corps commanders were told to sort out the details between themselves and to hold a line running east to west through Bavay. The British troops were exhausted. Most had had no food for 24 hours and less than two hours' sleep.

Supported by massive artillery fire the German troops pressed forward. General Allenby, it is said, rode up and ordered the 2nd Cavalry Brigade to charge the guns. Whoever actually initiated the order, and opinions differ, the result was that the 9th Lancers and 4th Dragoons charged until they ran into wire – not barbed wire placed by the enemy but existing wire – and heavy fire from the German guns. The cost of the charge was high with 250 casualties among the Dragoons and Lancers. The Cheshires and Norfolks gave the cavalry covering fire, but when the order came to withdraw the Cheshires never received it, and fought on to 6.30 pm when the survivors were forced to surrender.

On the night of 25th August the HQ of the BEF was established at St Quentin, and Sir John French issued orders that the retreat from Mons should continue on 26th for a further ten to fifteen miles south-westerly. Unfortunately neither I nor II Corps were in a position to assist each other if and when they were attacked.

When Sir John decided to pull back as the troops of the French 5th Army were going to leave his flank exposed as they were forced to withdraw, his exhausted troops were trying to catch a few hours' sleep. Wounded were being evacuated and the Quartermaster-General of the BEF, Major General Sir William

Robertson, was grimly trying to organise the essential food and supplies of all kinds, and staff officers worked feverishly making plans for the withdrawal.

General Jack, reported by John Terraine, says in his diary of this time of the retreat from Le Cateau:

After leaving the Argylls at Honnechy in order to seek brigade headquarters I was too exhausted to remember details clearly till the 28th ... a large number of valises and entrenching tools were absent having been lost in action or thrown away by order or otherwise; all troops, however, had their arms, besides the residue of their ammunition. The officers were afoot, many of them carrying one or two of their men's rifles. The chargers bore equipment or exhausted soldiers, and towed a man hanging on to the stirrup on either flank. Transport vehicles gave similar assistance... Here and there in this ghastly queue marched a fairly solid company, platoon or section. Abandoned equipment littered the roadside; at intervals waggons had been left for lack of teams.

... During the morning things began to improve. Staff officers at road intersections disentangled the medley: '3rd Division on the right of the road, 5th Division on the left, 4th beyond the 3rd.' There the different regiments were sorted out and formed into companies. Ammunition and rations, previously dumped by the transport, were issued... The distance marched from Le Cateau was about 44 miles, the weather hot, and the men had had practically no proper meal or rest for thirty-six hours or more. Colonel Robertson estimated that the Cameronians covered fifty-seven miles in that time... The men urgently required rest, proper meals, and a wash. Their feet are terribly raw from seven days' marching and fighting, with no chance to remove their boots... There was however no repose for the battalion quartermasters nor for my office as the tale of deficiencies in stores and equipment is staggering, necessitating the making up of long indents in triplicate for replacements.

My regiments in 1914

The Rifle Brigade

Battle honours 1914: 'Le Cateau', 'Retreat from Mons', 'Marne', 'Aisne', 'Armentières'.

The First Battalion

The Regimental birthday was 25th August, and on that day in 1914 the 1st Battalion marched into its first action, two days after its arrival in France. The battalion had arrived just too late to take part in the battle of Mons but was thrown in with the rest of the 4th Division as the retreat continued through the battles of Le Cateau, the Marne, and then the stand on the Aisne.

When the 4th Division under Major General Snow had arrived it was placed, together with Allenby's Cavalry Division, under Smith Dorrien's Command. The 4th Division had no 'cookers' (field kitchens) and so no means of providing proper meals, and the cavalry had been scattered and was in need of rest.

The heat was intense, and the troops were desperately tired, and many had not been properly fed for days, and although Robertson had started to stockpile supplies on all roads south, much of the meat was beginning to rot in the heat of the sun.

The order was given to the battalions of II Corps 'we stand and fight'. And there they stood. The three divisions of II Corps, plus artillery of 220 guns awaited the attack of seven German Divisions, with over 500 artillery guns.*

*One source however claims that not all the German Divisions were actually in a position to attack as Von Kluck's eastern corps was too far out of position, and two western corps were trying to outflank the BEF.

II Corps had a small addition of French troops – General Sordet's cavalry corps, who took their place on the left of the II Corps. The French cavalry had ridden over forty miles to cover the left flank and were a very tired but very welcome addition.

For the artillery it was probably the last of the 19th-century-type battles. The British guns were lined up as though they were at Waterloo and in most cases the opposing batteries could see each other. The German artillery opened fire at dawn on 26th August 1914, and firing with rifles from shallow trenches the British troops

298

were able to restrict the German army to a slow advance, and by evening the British troops were able to begin – considering the circumstances – an orderly and organised withdrawal. Inevitably units became mixed up.*

*In passing, and to illustrate the confusion that can occur in the midst and aftermath of engagements, and with the consequent difficulties of presenting an accurate picture of what is happening and casualty figures at the time; John Terraine, writing in his book *Mons The Retreat to Victory*, quotes the recollection of 'an officer' – who in 1914 met a group of weary, footsore soldiers on the road after Le Cateau, and asked them who they were:

'Sole survivors of the Blankshire Regiment, sir. All the rest got done in yesterday. Not a soul except us alive.'

'All right. Keep straight on for a couple of miles or more and you will find three or four hundred other sole survivors of your regiment bivouacking in a field.'

The officer quoted above, was actually named Baker-Carr and he later became a distinguished tank commander and a brigadier general. At that time of the incident quoted he was serving as a volunteer chauffeur to officers of the Headquarters Staff.

For further examples of units becoming mixed in the course of a battle see the 8th Devonshire's War Diary at the Battle of Loos below, and the 'Grimsby Chums' and Royal Scots above in Part Four.

Le Cateau, 4th Division, 11th Infantry Brigade

The task of the 11th Brigade at Le Cateau was to act as rearguard in the retreat from Mons after the tail of the 3rd Division had passed through. The rear party of the brigade was still coming in at 6 am, and the last in was 1st Battalion of the Rifle Brigade. After holding off an attack from the north, the 1st Rifles closed upon the main body of the brigade and in its withdrawal suffered its first casualties.

At the end of this rearguard action the 1st Rifles were directed into a sunken road between Beauvois and Ligny, and this quickly became the front line trench when the other battalions were driven back. The 1st Battalion Somerset Light Infantry took position on the Rifles' left, and to the left of them, in the area of the railway line, were the 1st Hampshires. Behind the 1st Rifles and the Somersets were the 1st East Lancs.

When the advancing enemy appeared the riflemen gave such a display of rapid fire that the German troops took it for machine-gun fire. It happened to be the anniversary of the Battle of Crecy, and the men of 1914 gave as good account of themselves with their rifles as the bowmen at Crecy did in 1346 with their longbows.

The 4th Division received orders to retire at 5 pm. The 10th

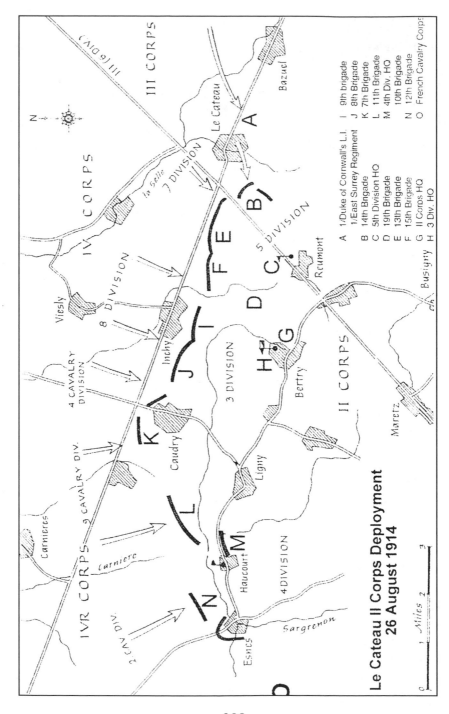

**Le Cateau II Corps Deployment
26 August 1914**

Miles

A 1/Duke of Cornwall's L.I.
  1/East Surrey Regiment
B 14th Brigade
C 5th Division HQ
D 19th Brigade
E 13th Brigade
F 15th Brigade
G II Corps HQ
H 3 Div. HQ
I 9th brigade
J 8th Brigade
K 7th Brigade
L 11th Brigade
M 4th Div. HQ
N 10th Brigade
N 12th Brigade
O French Cavalry Corps

Brigade this time being given the task of rear guard. The 11th Brigade reached Elincourt that night and was able to rest there.

In the twelve days of the retreat, the 1st Rifles covered 156 miles, 146 of them on foot.

5th Division, 14th Brigade, Duke of Cornwall's Light Infantry

Battle honours 1914: 'Mons', 'Le Cateau', 'Retreat from Mons', 'Marne,' 'Aisne' 'La Bassée' 'Armentières'.

The 5th Division was commanded by Major General Sir C. Fergusson, Bart. And the 14th Brigade by Brig. Gen. S.P. Rolt. The 14th Brigade consisted of 2nd Battalion The Suffolk Regiment, 1st Battalion East Surrey Regiment, 1st Battalion Duke of Cornwall's Light Infantry and the 2nd Battalion The Manchester Regiment

1st Battalion Duke of Cornwall's Light Infantry: Mons and Le Cateau

They were soon involved in battle after their arrival in France starting on 23rd August at Mons, and it is recorded that on 24th August, the battalion was almost completely surrounded, and sustained heavy casualties.

Peter H. Liddle, writing in *The Soldier's War 1914–1918*, describes the feeling of the unreality of the war (mentioned above) in August 1914, by quoting from a letter written by Captain A.N. Acland, Adjutant of 1st Bn. Duke of Cornwall's Light Infantry, to his wife following the setting up of their outposts on the canal at Sardon to await the arrival of the advancing German troops. These appeared on 23rd August in small patrols, but then at 4 pm:

> They arrived in a large solid mass on the road we were holding on the far side of the canal and proceeded to march up to a point we had carefully ranged on... They deployed quickly on either side of the road and came on quickly.

The advanced companies of the 1st Cornwalls had been ordered to retire in the face of a strong attack, and withdrawal began. The canal bridge was blown, a stand was made at the neighbouring river bridge and that was blown too, after which retirement to the village, not inappropriately named Dour, was carried out.

Acland continues:

301

I can't quite describe my feelings through this show, but I somehow don't believe it dispelled the odd idea that we were on some big sort of manoeuvres, which had idiotically been with me since we started from the Curragh. The burst and hum of the shrapnel surprised me and the bullets made me duck my head – I won't say I was not frightened, but I'm sure I was but don't think I knew it.

The general withdrawal was ordered, and covered by 2nd Manchesters, the battalion fell back from the Mons-Conde canal. The Cornwall's War Diary records that no longer were the British troops greeted with cheers, but tears and mourning, and streams of people of all ages fleeing for safety crowded the roads.

The battalion covered the retreat of 14th Brigade at Bavi on 25th August, and at 6 pm moved to positions just east of Le Cateau. The men were in bivouacs* in a field at the fork road on SE outskirts of the town, and drenched to the skin by an outbreak of a rainstorm they finally received rations for the first time since 8 pm the previous night. The battalion covered the retreat of the 5th Division and moved back to the Aisne and crossed it on 30th August.

*Bivouac was a makeshift tent to hold a few men. It usually consisted of waterproof sheets supported by a central ridge pole about 3 feet above ground, sometimes just a sheet or sheets supported by the cover of a hedge. Also used loosely for any temporary cover from the weather.

The 5th Division held the main canal line, and the 3rd Division held the right of the front, and this included the town and the salient to the north-east where the canal runs round the town into the river Sambre.

The 5th Division had not suffered so badly on 23rd August, with losses of less than 400, but when the withdrawal began, as General von Kluck began his enveloping movement, they did not get off so easily. Fergusson found himself contending with three German divisions. When the 3rd Division on his right began to slip back he gave orders to the 13th and 14th Brigades to do the same.

In this sector the fight continued with mounting fury for six hours before the German army could make any impression on 13th and 14th Brigades. The 11th Battery, RFA, frequently firing at point blank range to support the Suffolks, was subjected to intense punishment, and by 10 am the battery had lost all its officers, and only one gun could still be manned.

Not long after mid-day Fergusson informed Smith-Dorrien that in his view the retirement should begin. What remained of the Suffolks, and their supporting detachments of the Argyll and Sutherland Highlanders, were the first to be overwhelmed. The Suffolks, having been fighting for nine hours, were now outflanked from the front, right flank, and the rear. The Cornwalls and East Surreys carried out a covering role, and as II Corps retired there was considerable congestion, and units were scattered and broken up.

Withdrawal

To give some idea of the problems of organisation involved in the withdrawal, the space required (in peace time) by an infantry brigade on the march was two and a quarter miles, and seven miles for an infantry division. An artillery division took up five miles, the ammunition another mile and a half, and the field ambulances and divisional trains another mile and three quarters.

An Anthology of Armageddon quotes an author as follows on the effects of long forced marches:

> The unvaried testimony of the soldiers was that every one at times slept on the march. They passed through villages asleep. When sleep deepened and they began to reel, they were awakened by their comrades. They slept in water, on stones, in brush, or in the middle of the road as if they had suddenly fallen in death.

Peter Liddle again quotes Capt. Acland of the 1st Cornwalls on the utter physical weariness of the long marches on the retreat from Mons:

> At every halt we *all* slept. The men were so dead asleep that we officers had to shake them to wake them. For many miles Hammans and I walked arm in arm to keep us from rolling too much like drunken men.

303

The strain begins to show in the high command

The stresses of the times produced an angry exchange between Sir John French and his 1st Corps Commander, Sir Douglas Haig. Haig had been asked by Lanrezac if he would give effective support to the French 5th Army in an attack. Haig, who had received a report from a British airman that German forces had been observed advancing fast south-west of St Quentin, passed the airman's report to Lanrezac and said he was anxious to cooperate with the attack. He was however aware that his infantry needed a few hours rest and he sent word to GHQ to that effect. He added he could offer Lanrezac the support of his artillery and machine guns if GHQ approved. Sir John French replied: 'No active operations of any arms except of a defensive nature will be undertaken tomorrow'. The French fought the battle of Guise the next day with no support from the BEF.*

*For a much fuller account of these events see *Liaison 1914* by Edward Spears who was an eyewitness to most of the fateful decisions, made between Mons and the Marne.

French sent a peremptory message the next day to Haig:

Please be good enough to inform the C in C how it is that any confidential promise of support by I Corps was made to General Lanrezac or why any official exchange of ideas was initiated without authority from headquarters.

Haig replied with a curt and stinging snub to Sir John French:

I do not understand what you mean. I have initiated no exchange of ideas. GHQ not having secured from the French roads for the retirement of my corps, I had for my own safety to enter into relations with the nearest French force on my right. As far as possible I have maintained touch with the left of these French troops – and due to the presence of this corps [Haig's corps] their left has been protected ever since we left Maubeuge. My corps still protects their left, and if the enemy advances from St Quentin southward I shall have for my own safety to deploy guns etc., without asking authority from GHQ ... I therefore beg you will not give credit to such allegations as

304

Field Marshal Earl Kitchener of Khartoum.
Photograph courtesy of the
Imperial War Museum, London. (Neg: Q 08742)

Field Marshal Sir William
Robertson with the French
commander Marshal Foch.
Photograph courtesy of the Imperial War
Museum, London. (Neg: Q 34843)

Chateau Wood, 12th October 1917.

Photograph courtesy of the Imperial War Museum, London. (Neg: E (Aus) 1220)

Battle of Pilkem Ridge 31st July - 2nd August 1917. Carrying a wounded man near Boesinghe 1st August 1917. Photograph courtesy of the Imperial War Museum, London. (Neg: Q 5935)

Water cart stuck in mud at St. Eloi, Pilckem Ridge, 11th August 1917.

Photograph courtesy of the Imperial War Museum, London. (Neg: Q 5943)

Troops blinded by tear gas waiting outside an advanced dressing station near Bethune, 10th April 1918.

Photograph courtesy of the Imperial War Museum, London. (Neg: Q 11586)

General Sir Hubert Gough

Field Marshal Sir Henry Wilson

Rifleman Alfred Watts, 3rd Battalion
The Rifle Brigade, 1914.

Sergeant Cecil Henry Westlake (2nd from left, middle row) 1/5th Duke of Cornwall's
Light Infantry, 1917 or 1918.

Private Joseph Edward Holley, 1/1st
Kent Cyclist Battalion, 1914
(the standing figure).

Lance Corporal Horace Westlake,
8th Battalion The Devonshire Regiment,
1914 or 1915.

the one under reference without first ascertaining whether it is true or not.

French apologised to Haig after Haig drove angrily to see him the next day. Sir John did not trust Lanrezac and feared that he would wantonly expose the British troops. He was aware of being dangerously pressed by the advancing Germans, and also aware of not being in Joffre's (the French CIC's), confidence, and not able to see the whole picture. He was also conscious all the time of the anomalous position of the BEF – a force autonomous, not subordinate, but still a unit in the French plan, and dependent on French communications. And all the time in his mind's eye his order from Kitchener: *'The greatest care must be exercised towards a minimum of losses and wastage.'*

One cannot but feel for Sir John French whether one likes him or not (and his treatment of Smith Dorrien later, and his comments in his book of 1914, make it difficult to defend him). He was sixty-two years of age, and had recently suffered a severe heart attack, and was under doctor's orders to go carefully. Murrey, his chief of staff, had collapsed on the critical day of Le Cateau, and as I have said, Grierson, his designated II Corps Commander, died on his way to take up command and Grierson's replacement, Smith-Dorrien, was the man he disliked intensely.

On 30th August he telegraphed to Kitchener that he was thinking of pulling the BEF behind the Seine because, he said: 'My confidence in the abilities of the leaders of the French army to carry this campaign to a successful conclusion is fast waning.' The receipt of this missive caused consternation in Whitehall.

Eventually, after a visit by Kitchener (a visit that did not start well because Kitchener arrived in uniform, and the uniform of a Field Marshal at that, which made French feel he was being deliberately outranked), there was a conciliatory letter from the Prime Minister, Asquith. This was followed by the departure of General Lanrezac, who was dismissed by Joffre, the French CIC, from command of the French Fifth Army, and his replacement by General Franchet d'Esperey. Sir John then cheered up.

On 4th September, Sir John was invited to a meeting with Joffre and d'Esperey at which Joffre said he had come to thank Sir John personally for his readiness to cooperate in an action on which might depend the fate of Europe. 'The time for retreat was over,' he said, adding that 'tomorrow a new war would begin. Those who could not advance would stand fast, and die if necessary *sur place*. Not another metre of withdrawal!'

Sir John, quite overcome turned to an interpreter and exclaimed: 'Damn it, I can't explain. Tell him that all men can do our fellows will do. But tell him that my forces can't be ready by six: we'll have to make it nine.'

The Marne and the Aisne

Here, on 5th September, the BEF, back beyond the river Marne, and supporting the French, halted the German troops, and counter attacked from 7th–10th September.

The end of the mobile war

The Germans retreated and then dug in as they reached the river Aisne (12th–15th September). From this moment the war of movement really ceased and began to shape into the trench warfare of the Western Front of the next four years. The war diary of the 1st Rifles records on 22nd September, when the battalion returned to the front line after relieving 1st East Lancs, that the front was now covered with spiked sticks and barbed wire entanglements.

The Devonshire Regiment

Battle honours 1914. 'Aisne', La Bassée', 'Armentières'. Neither of the regular battalions was engaged in the opening battles of 1914 (the battles of Mons and Le Cateau).

3rd Division, 8th Brigade, 1st Battalion Devonshires

When the battalion was reunited it marched 16 to 17 miles a day in the wake of the BEF by Doué, to Sarcy on 11th September, Monthiers on the 12th, when they took their first German prisoner, a straggler. Then to Oulchy La Ville and arrived at Braine

306

on 14th. September. Here the battalion spent a very uncomfortable night in pouring rain. On 15th September, the Devons joined the 8th Brigade as part of the 3rd Division (replacing the 1st Gordon Highlanders who had had three companies cut off and captured at Le Cateau), and took over reserve positions on western side of the Vailly–Jouy road. They moved forward to the front line the same day.

The 8th Brigade had a rough time as the Germans counter-attacked. The Devons having just arrived were the only unit in the brigade at full strength, and the only battalion to have any machine guns. After holding the front trenches (although they were really only hastily dug joined holes) for 10 days, the battalion was withdrawn to Courcelles to rest. Casualties amounted to nearly 100 with 60 men sick.

Transfer to 14th Brigade, 5th Division

On September 29th, the battalion received orders to transfer to the 14th Brigade, 5th Division to replace the 2nd Suffolks, another battalion that had almost been annihilated at Le Cateau. They joined the Fifth Division, commanded by Lieut. General Sir Charles Fergusson, on September 30th. The 14th Brigade at that time was under the command of Brigadier-General Rolt. The other battalions in the brigade were: 1st East Surreys, 1st Duke of Cornwall's Light Infantry, and 2nd Manchesters.

Rifle Brigade, First Battalion

The battalion began to advance on 6th September, and crossed the Aisne at Vemzel during the morning of 13th. An officer of 'A' Company records that the bridge had been destroyed by the enemy, and the men had to cross one at a time by a single girder.

The battalion advanced to Ste. Marguerite and dug in, and here the war diary records another laconic entry concerning friendly fire:

'A' Company in a wood on the Maubeuge road came under shell-fire from guns at close range. The British artillery under the impression that 'A' and 'B' Companies who were in the process of being relieved by 'C' and 'I' Companies were

307

German troops. Casualties that day were 13 officers wounded, 4 other ranks killed, 33 wounded, 6 missing.

The battalion was relieved by 1st East Lancs on 19th September, and moved back to reserve positions.

Rifle Brigade, Third Battalion

At 4.30 pm on 21st September the 3rd Battalion crossed the Aisne at Bourg and relieved the 1st Bn. Royal Berkshire Regiment in the trenches. Over the next 24 hours they suffered their first casualties with 7 other ranks killed, 1 officer, 21 other ranks wounded, and one man missing.

Four days later, 'D' Company attacked the enemy line at 4.15 am on 25th September, and came under heavy machine gun fire. Only small parties reached the German parapet and the company lost 3 other ranks killed, 1 officer and 26 other ranks wounded, and 1 officer and 23 men missing.

Duke of Cornwall's Light Infantry, 1st Battalion

They crossed the Aisne on 13th September, and marched on to Ste. Marguerite. The battalion took part in the attack on Chivres on 14th but heavy machine gun and rifle fire drove them back to Missy. Three officers were killed or mortally wounded, two other officers wounded, and 145 other ranks were killed or wounded. Heavy shell fire forced them to the west of the village on 15th, and later they fell back to Ste. Marguerite in reserve. On 20th they relieved 2nd Manchesters in the forward trenches, and in turn were relieved by 1st Bedfordshires on September 24th.

von Moltke replaced

As the battle of the Aisne slowly crystallised, the German Commander in Chief, General von Moltke, overcome by the failure of his blitzkrieg, was replaced by General Erich von Falkenhayn.

PART THIRTY-ONE

*No one foresaw what the war was going to develop into,
its horror, its duration, its dreariness. No one foresaw
trench warfare, and it occurred to none that the day of
the mighty manoeuvres of armies in which cavalry, artillery
and infantry combined in grandiose operations was over
for ever.*

*Looking back, I am deeply thankful that none of those
who gazed across the Aisne on September 14th [1914]
had the faintest glimmering of what was awaiting them.
They were untroubled by visions of mud and soaking
trenches, nor were they borne down in despair by a vision
of years of misery ahead.*

*There was nothing to show them that the most dramatic
period of the war was over, and that between them and
the victory they believed awaited them across the river,
stretched four weary years of stalemate on the western
front.*

Major-General Sir Edward Spears, *Liaison 1914.*

The British Expeditionary Force ordered north

After the battle of the Aisne, Sir John French, still concerned about
the safety of the Channel ports, moved the BEF to the Sector of
Ypres, and to its original position on the left of the French line.

1st Devons in Flanders

So, on 1st October, as part of the II Corps, the 1st Devonshires
began the march westward for the departure from the Aisne and

for the transfer of the BEF to Flanders. Later the companies of the 1st Devons were split up and took part in the battle of La Bassée (10th October–22nd November 1914), and Armentières (13th October–2nd November), where under heavy shelling they suffered a number of casualties.

The battalion was heavily involved in fighting throughout October. For a while the Devons had been held as divisional reserve, and the companies pushed out to help where and as necessary. By 26th October they had suffered nearly 250 casualties and received a special message of congratulations from the corps commander, Smith-Dorrien, for their efforts.

The Fifth Division was now replacing the cavalry on the line opposite the Messines Ridge, and the Germans attacked very strongly around Givenchy and Festubert on 29th October. German losses were heavy and it was estimated that between 600 and 700 were lying dead in front of the trenches. Following heavy fighting alongside the Gurkhas the battalion was relieved and arrived to rest after three weeks of almost continuous fighting. They rejoined the 14th Brigade on 1st November at Lestrem (now under the command of Brig.-General Maude – Rolt having been invalided home on 23rd October).

The Rifle Brigade in the ordered move north

On 7th October 1914, the 1st battalion having been relieved by French troops from its trenches above Ste. Marguerite, moved north to Estrees St Denis, a march of sixty miles. The march from the trenches was the most severe ordeal through which the men had yet passed. The spell in the trenches following on the exertion of the retreat and the advance had weakened them, and it was only by sheer driving that they could be kept going. Directly there was any slackening of pressure men fell out right and left and lay where they fell.

At the end of October Captain Bridgeman noted that the battalion had marched 330 miles since its arrival in France on 23rd August. When the BEF was ordered north to take up its original position on the left of the French, the battalion went to Armentières. It would suffer heavily. By the end of 1914 the battalion casualties were 7 officers killed, 15 wounded, 2 taken prisoner, 144 other ranks killed, 318 wounded, 350 missing.

In keeping with the orders for the BEF, the 3rd Rifles also moved to the left of the Allied line in early October 1914. The 3rd Battalion endured an appalling march similar to the 1st Battalion and during the same period, when it was withdrawn from Soupir and after a fifty-six mile march to Compiegne, was despatched by rail to St Omer area, detraining at Blendecques on 11th October at 5.30 am. From there it marched to Arques and billeted, moving on to Hazebrouck on 12th October by motor bus.

1st and 3rd Rifles at the battle of Armentières, 13th October–2nd November 1914

The First Battalion as part of 4th Division, and the Third Battalion as part of 6th Division, were advancing side by side with the 6th on the right and the 4th on the left. But whether it was because the 4th Division found a greater difficulty in disengaging from the Aisne, or because the troops were wearier, or because the French transport facilities were inadequate, the 4th Division began the operation a day behind the 6th Division and never caught up. As a result the 4th were unable to provide vital help to the 6th Division when required and expected.

The 6th Division found that Meterenbeque was strongly held, and because of the poor weather conditions the divisional artillery could give no assistance. The 1st Royal Warwicks however, despite fog and rain, after a smart combination of fire and field craft occupied the position, and two companies were working their way forward into the western end of Meteren as the commander of the 4th Division appeared.

The frontage of the 17th Brigade attack on 13th October was from the Hazebrouk-Bailleul railway to the Trazeel-Meteren road. The North Staffordshires were attacking on the right between the railway and the road running east and west immediately north of Merris, and the 3rd Rifles on the left – supposedly in touch with the 4th Division. The weather was poor and visibility bad. There was no sign of the 4th Division, and there was little sign of the promised artillery support.

A senior officer who was present reported the 3rd Rifles, as though on manoeuvres, moved out in small columns under the German shellfire, and then extended and advanced by alternate rushes (artillery formation). Despite vigorous opposition and the heavy going, and despite the inadequate artillery support, the attack was steadily and successfully pressed home. By 2.30 pm the Rifles HQ were in Oerberdoen Farm at the crossroads immediately north of Merris and all four companies were pushing their way up the slopes of Hill 40 – the important high ground above the village to the north-east. In the absence of the 4th Division, the Leinsters, who had been held as brigade reserve, plugged the gap. On the right the 18th Brigade had been unable to keep pace with 17th Brigade having also encountered heavy opposition.

This action on 13th October cost the Third Battalion three officers, including the Colonel, and seventy-six NCOs and riflemen killed or wounded. Major Lord Henniker assumed command.

The Third Battalion's part in the battle of Armentières on 18th October followed their attack on Hill 40 on the 13th. They had been moved up by lorries following a report that German cavalry were present, but when the battalion arrived they found that if the information about the cavalry had been correct, the enemy meanwhile had been dispersed by British cavalry, and instead of a battle the battalion received its first pay since its arrival in France. Unfortunately there was nowhere to spend it.

Throughout the remainder of the year both 1st and 3rd battalions were engaged in operations mainly to keep the enemy away from the main battle now raging to the north.* The Third Battalion had been lent to 16th Brigade on 24th October, and when it returned to 17th Brigade on 16th December, it took over trenches near La Chapelle d'Armentièrs and into the stationary warfare that was to dominate the future.

*This battle became known as 'First Ypres' and lasted officially from 10th October to 22nd November.

On 16th November 1914, the 2nd Battalion suffered its first casualty with the death of Acting Corporal Green from bullets coming through the loopholes in the trenches. The War Diary notes that not only were civilians in the forward area, but in front line positions!

Lord Reith, writing of the Armentières area in the latter part of November 1914, where he had just arrived as Battalion Transport Officer with 1/5th Scottish Rifles (Cameronians), said the sector where they were was extraordinarily quiet at the time. 'Two or three days would pass without even a crack of a rifle, but nevertheless a brooding feeling that anything might happen at any time. Awful things might be happening close by up Houplines way' (where 1st Rifles were, or had been very recently).

The 1/5th Scottish were now part of 6th Division, the same division as the 3rd Rifles, but in a different brigade.*

*They formed part of the 19th Brigade, together with the 1st Cameronians, 2nd Argyll and Sutherland Highlanders, 1st Middlesex, and 2nd Royal Welch Fusiliers. (See Frank Richards, Royal Welch Fusiliers, see above for his comments on the 1/5th Scottish Rifles.)

Ploegsteert (Plugstreet)

The 1st Battalion Rifle Brigade at Ploegsteert, like all the battalions of 11th Brigade, had a bad time in December. On 19th December, together with 1st Somersets, and 1st Hampshires, they had moved across the mud of No Man's Land of Plugstreet Wood to attack a heavily defended German strong point known as the 'Birdcage' (because of the surrounding barbed wire). The attack by the 11th Brigade was a failure. The enemy wire was unbreached and the attack cost over 250 men. A member of the 1st Battalion Rifle Brigade describes this attack thus:

The advance began at 2.30 pm, and almost immediately a Colonial friend in front of me was killed. The German infantry shooting was good, the bullets were singing past our ears, and unfortunately nearly all of us were without cover. So we had to lie down and trust to the Omnipotent taking care of us.

The wounded began to straggle past us; most of them had been relieved of rifle and equipment, some hardly able to walk, and others groaning in agony; in the fading light it struck our hearts with sympathy for these brave men. Some of my party crawled up to one boy and tried to carry him through; he was hit in the right shoulder. They were unfortunately unable to carry him far; his groans were pitiful; then they stopped, our two men returned – the boy had passed away. Then another voice was calling. He was found and brought in.

In the meantime it was getting quite dark, so we were but few left. Our call had not come, and we seemed to be in a perilous position. After enquiring from the firing line we could not get any positive orders, so I gave the advice to make for

313

our trenches and make further enquiries there. This was an ordeal too, for we were falling over bushes and into ditches.

I brought my friend's rifle back as he was forbidden to return after carrying my Colonial friend, who died a few minutes after leaving us. In the dark I was calling to the others when my pal heard my voice, and we were glad to find one another again. We got back to our trenches safely, only to find Captain Morgan-Grenville was killed and also Captain Prittie who was in command of the Rifle Brigade attacking force.

One of those killed in the abortive attack by 1st Battalion of the Rifle Brigade on 19th December 1914 was Rifleman Reuben Barnett. He was 15 years of age, and his body lies in Rifle House Cemetery in Plot IV, E10.

Plugstreet was not really a main point of attack, as this action was designed to help relieve pressure on the French by preventing German troops in the Plugstreet sector sending reinforcements to take part in the attack on the French in Artois.

This area is also of particular interest because two future British Prime Ministers, Winston Churchill and Anthony Eden, *and* the future German leader Adolf Hitler, fought around here.

There existed in those early war years a brewery that became the bath-house used by the Rifle Brigade and others, and it is quite possibly the one Alfred Watts mentions in his letter below. It stood outside of the village and on the road to Armentières, close by the London Rifle Brigade Cemetery, and also close to the place where Churchill, by now an ex-cabinet minister who had become a battalion commander, had an office in a convent or hospice when he was out of the line.

Churchill, with no prospect of government office, had requested to be posted to the front as a soldier (he had of course held a regular army commission in the cavalry when he was gazetted from Sandhurst before the Boer War, and before becoming a journalist and entering politics). After leaving the Cabinet in 1915 following the ill-fated Dardanelles campaign, he served for a little while with the Grenadier Guards at Neuve Chapelle, and then was posted as a Major to take command of a 'New Army' battalion, the 6th (Service) Battalion Royal Scots Fusiliers, 9th (Scottish) Division. He was soon promoted to Lieut. Colonel. It is said he was originally intended to get a brigade but politics interfered.

314

Whatever views were held about him as a politician – and I have mentioned Lord Derby's – I have yet to read anything other than praise for Churchill as a commanding officer. He seems to have been genuinely liked and admired by all ranks for his boundless energy and concern for the welfare of his men. He was also regarded as courageous, and delighted his men by personally guiding visiting dignitaries into the danger areas.

Anthony Eden, served at Plugstreet with 21st Battalion King's Royal Rifle Corps in April 1916 as a platoon commander. (See also below, Flanders 1917.)

Adolf Hitler (20.4.1889–30.4.1945) although not actually at Plugstreet Wood, was close by serving at Messines in the winter of 1914, just before he was awarded the Iron Cross, 2nd Class, at Bois Quarante Wytschaete. Later in the war he was awarded the Iron Cross 1st Class, and this was apparently an unusual award for a corporal.

Hitler, has been accused of avoiding his military (conscription) service in 1913, but in August 1914, he addressed a formal petition to King Ludwig III of Bavaria asking to be allowed to volunteer, although of Austrian nationality, for a Bavarian regiment. The reply granted his request.

Hitler records in *Mein Kampf*: 'I opened the document with trembling hands; no words of mine can describe the satisfaction I felt... Within a few days I was wearing the uniform which I was not to put off again for nearly six years.'

He was enrolled in the 1st Company of the 16th Bavarian Reserve Infantry Regiment, known from its original commander as the List Regiment. (Rudolf Hess was also a volunteer in the same regiment.) On 21st October 1914 they entrained for the front and after a two day journey to Lille they were sent up the line as reinforcements for the 6th Bavarian Division of the Bavarian Crown Prince Rupprecht's VI Army.

Hitler's first experience of fighting was in one of the fiercest and most important engagements of the war, the First Battle of Ypres. For four days and nights the List Regiment was in the thick of the fighting round Beclaere and Gheluvelt. Hitler said in a letter to his old landlord that when they were pulled out of the line the regiment in those four days had been reduced from 3,500 to 600, and the four companies had to be broken up.

Hitler served throughout the war as a runner (*meldeganger*). In

1915 he was at Neuve Chappelle, and in 1916 on the Somme. On 7th October 1916 he was wounded in the leg at Bapaume, and sent back to Germany for the first time in two years. He returned to the front in March 1917 and promoted to Lance Corporal. His regiment was engaged at the battles of Arras and Third Ypres, and the spring of 1918 saw him and his regiment in the last German offensive. In October Hitler was caught in a British gas attack at Ypres, and he finished the war in hospital at Pasewalk, in Pomerania.

Despite being a very experienced and long-serving soldier there is no evidence (that I have seen) that he applied for promotion – either to the rank of an NCO or for a commission. Alan Bullock in his book *Hitler A Study in Tyranny* said he was regarded as a strange fellow by his comrades:

> He did not care about leave, received no parcels or letters from home. He was silent when others grumbled about the time they had to spend in the trenches, or the hardships they endured. He frequently sat silent with his head in his hands in deep contemplation and none could arouse him from his listlessness.

In 1935, Churchill wrote of Hitler:

> We cannot tell whether Hitler will be the man who will once again let loose upon the world another war in which civilisation will irretrievably succumb, or whether he will go down in history as the man who restored honour and peace of mind to the great Germanic nation and brought it back serene, helpful and strong to the forefront of the European family circle. It is a mystery on which the future will pronounce. It is enough to say that both possibilities are open at the present moment.

Today we know what the future pronounced, and it was unfortunate for us all.

2nd Devonshires move to Flanders

Before daybreak on the morning of 11th November, the 2nd Devons found themselves on their way up to the trenches to relieve two

316

battalions of 13th Brigade who were under orders for the Salient.

Following the rest of 23rd Brigade's arrival, the division adjusted its line with the 23rd taking over trenches NW of Neuve Chappelle with the 2nd Devons on the left of the brigade's line. As with the other units coming from overseas the Devons felt and suffered the cold badly in the waterlogged trenches, and there were many case of frostbite. The Devons occupied the same trenches for the next couple of months in extremely wet weather, and it was impossible to keep the trenches dry as they filled with water faster than they could be drained.

The 8th Division suffered high casualties because the German lines were very close and in more than one place enfiladed those of the British. The Germans kept up heavy rifle and machine-gun fire, and they also held the dominating Aubers Ridge artillery positions and observation. The communication trenches were usually flooded and then it was impossible to approach the front trenches except above ground.

Autumn and winter 1914

The fine hot summer weather deteriorated into a cold wet and blustery autumn as the leaves fell, and dust began to give way to mud. Then winter. The bitter chill of an icy winter took its grip and toll on the soldiers on the Western Front as they shivered and suffered from frostbite, bronchitis, pneumonia, and the new infections of 'trench feet' and 'trench fever'.

'Trench fever' epidemics were common.* It had some of the symptoms of influenza and some of those of typhoid. It was not until 1918 that its cause was traced to an organism transmitted in the excreta of the body louse. All the troops were lousy, and despite all attempts to rid themselves of the lice by the washing and fumigation of their clothes at every opportunity when withdrawn from the front, as soon as they returned to the line they were lousy again.

*The war correspondent Sir Philip Gibbs suffered from the disease and towards the end of the Somme battle in 1916 he was taken to hospital at Amiens. He writes of this occasion: 'When I was carried in on a stretcher the rosy-cheeked young orderly, after taking my temperature and feeling my pulse, said "That's all right. You're going to die." It was his way of cheering a patient up.'

317

The outlines of the war as it would be for the next four years began to take a rudimentary shape in the icy ground as the hastily dug muddy, freezing connecting holes were becoming shallow trenches, with protective breastworks and tangles of barbed wire. It was realised now that it would not be 'all over by Christmas' after all.

As the weather became harsh, and all the soldiers suffered, it was again particularly hard on the 2nd Battalion of the Rifle Brigade, and the 2nd Devons, and those other battalions of regiments who had been recalled from the tropics. And of course the troops of the Indian Brigade who felt the cold intensely.

On 22nd November, 44 men from the 2nd Rifles were sent to a field ambulance suffering from frostbite in the feet. Trenches were full of freezing mud and water. Seventeen degrees hard frost was recorded for two nights and the men's wet boots froze to their feet. A battalion cemetery was formed in a field behind the HQ at Fauquissart. Sheepskin coats were issued and white sheets for patrol work in the snow.

1st Devonshires

The battalion suffered a very dispiriting winter from November 1914 until the spring of 1915. The regimental history, quoting the battalion diary, says that although there were frequent exchanges of rifle fire on both sides, not mere sniper fire, the serious shell shortage restricted the British 18-pounders and field howitzers to five rounds a day. This precluded any major operations although the division held this sector for nearly two months before the British authorities finally abandoned all hope of an offensive, and concentrated on making the defences proof against attack. The state of the ground and the weather would really have prohibited any attempt of an attack anyway, and as always the Germans held what little high ground there was.

As the weeks went by heavy rain turned to sleet; the trenches were always falling in, and the problem of drainage was almost insurmountable. The liquid mud rather than water completely defied the pumps, and the men had to spend hours at a time knee-deep and even waist deep in this awful stuff and could barely stagger away when at last relief came. The exhausted troops had then to grope their way back to billets over ground behind the trenches which was already pitted with shell-holes full of water.

For the Devons, in common with the other troops manning the line, the mere maintenance of the front line was a tremendous strain, and the troops also had to dig a support line, and to make communication trenches. Even when nominally 'resting' they had to provide parties for work on roads that were unsuited for the increasing number of motor lorries now appearing on the scene.

2nd Devonshires

The 2nd Devons took over trenches opposite Messines Ridge on 12th November, and while in the trenches during this bitterly cold month 54 men were sent to hospital suffering from frostbite. On 18th December, companies of the 2nd Devons, supported by 2nd West Yorks and units of the Royal Engineers, were engaged in an attack around Neuve Chappelle, at the Moated Grange which lay in No Man's Land. Stopped eventually by barbed wire, and after losing many men, the remaining Devons held on to the captured trench until relieved by the 2nd West Yorks, one of whom, Lt. Neame, was awarded the VC when the Germans counter attacked on 19th December.

Christmas 1914

At home the week of Christmas brought in a rush of freakish capricious weather; for days southern England was covered in a thick and choking fog, followed by furious gales and blizzards, and then, as in Belgium and France, a terrible cold descended on the country.

The last horse tram car service in London, from Tower Bridge Road to Rotherhithe, closed, and a London pantomime brought a cheerful chorus that soon would be spread to the troops all over France, particularly in the bath houses: *'Here we are, here we are, here we are again.'*

The Christmas Truce

The Rifle Brigade

The unnamed author of the letter about the 1st Rifles attack on the Birdcage also wrote about Christmas Eve:

To-day we are washed shaved, and our rifles and swords* as clean as possible. Headed by the bagpipes we were marched off to a big laundry and had warm baths. The bagpipes caused great excitement among the inhabitants; the boys and girls danced to them as we marched along. Our Christmas Eve consists of three candles in different parts of the room, some of us are writing, and a small group playing cards. Others are trying to get warm, stepping to a mouth-organ very well played.

*In the Rifle Brigade bayonets were always referred to as 'swords'.

Captain Bridgeman of the 1st Rifles reported that a document from the Germans opposite handed to a stretcher bearer while he was collecting identity discs in No Man's Land proposed a formal armistice on 31st December. Bridgeman explained that the battalion was not empowered to make arrangements of this kind. However on Christmas Day both the British and German troops entered No Man's Land and collected their dead without hindering each other.

The 2nd Battalion The Rifle Brigade

The Battalion Diary notes the informal truce over Christmas saying there was no firing on either side until sniping began again on 28th. It also comments that December saw the bitterly cold weather continue and in addition mud made the rifles impossible to fire.*

*See earlier comments on the the British rifle, the 'SLE' (Short Lee-Enfield, 303 with a 10-round magazine).

The 3rd Battalion The Rifle Brigade

War Diary records:

On December 15th we left the 16th Infantry Brigade and returned to the 17th Infantry Brigade commanded by Brig. Gen. Doran, and went into new trenches at Armentières, on the line we had retired to during the fight on 17th October. Here we did another 34 days without being relieved.

Christmas in the trenches will always be remembered by the Battalion as a day of perfect peace during which, by mutual consent, both sides declared a truce. There were many interesting features on this Christmas Day not the least of which was a German juggler who drew a large crowd of Riflemen and Germans in the middle of No Man's Land.

The following is part of a letter from Sergeant A. Lovell, A Company, 3rd Battalion Rifle Brigade, to his parents at Walthamstow as recorded in *The Rifle Brigade Chronicle 1914*:

Christmas Day, 1914. My Dear Parents, Christmas Day! The most wonderful day on record. In the early hours of the morning the events of last night appeared as some weird dream – but to-day, well it beggars description.

You will hardly credit what I am going to tell you; but thousands of our men will be writing home to-day telling the same strange and wonderful story.

Last night as I sat in my little dug-out, writing, my chum came bursting in with: 'Bob! Hark at 'em!' And I listened. From the German trenches came the sound of music and singing. My chum continued with: 'They've got Christmas trees all along the top of their trenches! Never saw such a sight.'

The Devonshires

I can find no mention of the Christmas truce for the 1st Devonshires although they appear to have been in the line having relieved the 2nd Duke of Wellington's, and the 1/9th London, in the trenches on 23rd December.*

*The history of the Devonshire Regiment 1914–1918, referring to the 1st Battalion at this time says that General Maude, Commander of 14th Brigade, expected much from his battalions as his section of the line had to be a model, and a tremendous amount of work was needed to satisfy him. No sooner had a piece of the line satisfied 14th Brigade requirements than the brigade would be relieved, spend a few days in billets, and then be given a new section of the line which was invariably found far below the Brigadier's standard, and the battalions would have to dig an entirely new line. This involved strenuous work sapping out and connecting up sap-heads (saps were deep narrow trenches or tunnels extended forward into No-Man's Land beyond the front-line trenches).

2nd Devonshires

On Christmas Eve the battalion relieved 2nd Scottish Rifles in the

321

front line. The War Diary records that 'on 25th December, the Germans got out of their trenches and came towards our lines. Our men met them and they wished each other a Merry Christmas, shook hands and exchanged smokes. Sniping began again about 7.30 pm.'

Duke of Cornwall's Light Infantry

Unlike the Rifle Brigade and 2nd Devonshires, the War Diary of the 1st Battalion DCLI does not mention the Christmas truce as the battalion had been relieved during the night of 17th. The regimental history says the 1st Battalion came out of the front line plastered from head to foot with mud and presenting a sorry sight after holding the fire-trenches for a fortnight.

They spent Christmas day in billets at Dranoutre, each man receiving the Christmas gift from Princess Mary, and a Christmas card from the King and Queen. They returned to the front line on 29th December to relieve the 2nd Manchesters just south east of Wulverghem. The final entry of the Battalian Diary for 1914 reads: 'At midnight the New Year was ushered in by three hearty cheers.'

The 2nd Battalion had only arrived in France on 21st December at Havre, and formed part of the 82nd Infantry brigade, 27th Division – a division made up of regular infantry battalions which were not in the United Kingdom at the beginning of the war – and they brigaded with the 1st Royal Irish Regiment, 2nd Royal Irish Fusiliers, and the 1st Leinster Regiment. The Cornwalls marched to Wardrecques (about 3 miles from Arques) where they billeted in two large factories.

Other references to Christmas 1914

Burgoyne (see above) records in his diary for Christmas Day:

> Hard frost last night. There was a bright moon and a lot of musketry fire, and as we are within rifle shot of the German lines [they had just gone into the reserve trenches] we were kept rather on the *Qui Vive*. At midnight our guns fired 21 rounds and the French cannonaded up to day-break when a thick fog came down and all firing ceased, with the exception

322

of an occasional shot. Some fools in the HAC* stood on the parapet on Xmas morning, I hear, and sang 'Auld Lang Syne' and the Hun let a volley rip into them; and a little later that day, some of the officers were out of their lines talking to the Germans. But there are very strict orders against this sort of thing.

*I am almost certain this must have been the Honourable Artillery Company, 1/1st Battalion, as they were also part of 3rd Division and fighting as infantry.

My regiments as 1914 ends

Rifle Brigade

Three of the four regular battalions of the Rifle Brigade were now settling into trench warfare. The First Battalion as mentioned above at Ploegsteert ('Plug Street'or 'Plugstreet' to the troops), the Second Battalion at Fauquissart, opposite the Aubers Ridge, the Third Battalion at Armentières (Porte Egal Farm). The newly arrived Fourth Battalion with the 27th Division was back at St Omer digging reserve trenches. Basil Harvey, *The Rifle Brigade*, says:

Christmas saw the three Rifle Brigade Battalions in the line taking part in the truce, when they met the enemy in no-man's land. By then three officers and 120 Riflemen were all that remained of the 1st Battalion.*

*When the battalion landed in France on 23rd August, the combined total of officers and men was 981.

The war diary of 3rd Rifles reads:

...we spent the next five months in this same line. Although it was looked upon as a quiet bit of the line by other people we had our share of casualties averaging 4 a day while in the trenches. Quite frequently we had a severe shelling from the German 5.9 howitzers and it was seldom that our own shell allowance ran to more than twelve 18 pounders a day in retaliation.*

*See earlier comments concerning shell shortages in the BEF.

323

The diary adds that the medical officer would come up to the front line trenches several times a day through a communication trench (this was a trench running from the front line back to battalion HQ) with two feet of water in it. He eventually had to go sick with a bad lung.

DCLI

By the end of 1914 both the regular battalions of the Duke of Cornwall's Light Infantry were in France. The 1st DCLI had been engaged in actions throughout October and November in 1914 and it won its first VC when Bandsman Thomas Edward Rendle was awarded the medal for attending the wounded and rescuing men who had been buried alive from the trenches while under shell fire.

The 2nd DCLI, like the 4th Rifles, had only arrived in France just before Christmas and was also becoming acclimatised and settling in as part of 27th Division.

Devonshires

1st Battalion ended the year still trying to satisy the demands of General Maude for perfect trench systems. The General wrote enthusiastically that the battalion was in splendid spirits; whether the battalion would have echoed his sentiments is not recorded, but they carried on digging and sapping until the end of January 1915 when at last they were allotted their own divisional frontage, and the General was pleased with their efforts. 'The line is four times as strong as when we took over.'

The 2nd Battalion as part of the 8th Division had seen heavy fighting and suffered large casualties in November and December around the Moated Grange farm where they had to keep the Germans busy to prevent them sending troops to support those where the French were attacking north of Arras.

PART THIRTY-TWO

Select a flat ten-acre ploughed field, so sited that all the surface water of the surrounding country drains into it. Now cut a zig-zag slot about four feet deep and three feet wide diagonally across, dam off as much water as you can so as to leave about a hundred yards a squelchly mud; delve out a hole at one side of the slot, then endeavour to live there for a month on bully beef and damp biscuits, whilst a friend has instructions to fire at you with a Winchester every time you put your head above the surface.

Bruce Bairnsfather, a subaltern in the Royal Warwicks and creator of the famous 'Ole Bill' and 'Young Bert' cartoon characters, describing conditions in the front line trenches in the first part of 1915, as related by Charles Messenger in volume two of his *For Love of Regiment*.

The fortunes of the regiments in 1915

The regulars become spent

The heavy losses of 1914 and early 1915 drained the BEF, and one source claims 30,000 men a month, every month, would be needed to bring the BEF up to strength.

The 'Old Contemptibles', the soldiers of the pre-war regular army, fighting continuously since August 1914, were almost gone. The men of its famous regiments had fallen and bled and died at Mons, Le Cateau, The Marne, The Aisne, La Bassée, Messines, Armentières, and First Ypres in 1914, and would continue to do so at Festubert, Neuve Chapelle, Second Ypres, Aubers Ridge, and finally Loos in 1915. And here the original BEF would really cease

325

to exist, and here too would see the departure of their commander in chief, Sir John French.

The first verse of Ernst Lissauer's *Hymn of Hate* composed early in the war read:

> French and Russian they matter not,
> A blow for a blow and a shot for shot,
> We love them not, we hate them not,
> We have but one and only hate,
> We love as one, we hate as one,
> We have one foe and one alone.
> Come let us stand at the Judgement place,
> An oath to swear to, face to face,
> An oath of bronze no wind can shake,
> An oath for our sons and their sons to take.
> We will never forego our hate,
> We have all but a single hate,
> We love as one, we hate as one,
> We have one foe, and one alone
>   ENGLAND

The changing composition of the BEF

So, as 1915 began, increasingly the drafts from home to the regular battalions were being made up of inexperienced newly trained recruits together with a handful of returning ex wounded regulars. More battalions of the territorial force were transferred from lines of communication troops to become front line soldiers, and as the year ended Kitchener's 'New Army' prepared to take over from the regulars to continue the struggle on the Western Front for the next three years, until finally the gaps in all the infantry regiments would be filled with conscripts.

The British High Command desperately wanted 1915 to be a time to re-group, train, and to bring to the Western Front those urgently needed replacement divisions of fresh untried 'New Army' troops, and give them a chance to get acclimatised to front line conditions. Massive increases in artillery and shells (reliable shells) were paramount needs too.

'The Front' was taking its future shape as fortifications and trenches were being seen as permanent features. The shortage of artillery and shells were worrying to all concerned. Time was needed, but it was not going to be available as the spring of 1915 found the BEF, despite the initial wishes of the commanders, engaged in several operations. These, although smaller and of shorter duration by the standards of later battles, nevertheless continued to further the losses of experienced troops and to drain resources.

These smaller engagements cost the BEF some 26,000 casualties in addition to the usual daily losses in the trenches in other areas where no major battles were undertaken but where the areas were still regarded as 'active'.

1st Battalion Rifle Brigade

In first four months of 1915 when not engaged in its front line duties as part of 11th Brigade of the 4th Division, the battalion rested at Ploegsteert and Armentières.

3rd Battalion Rifle Brigade

Soon after his arrival in France with the draft replacements on Tuesday, 29th December 1914, the first of my soldier relatives, Rifleman Alfred Watts, joined his regiment, 3rd Battalion The Rifle Brigade, at Armentières and became a member of B Company.

On the same day the Colonel, Lt. Col. R. Alexander, who had been wounded earlier and just returned to the line was hit again, and he died in Bailleul Clearing Station three days later.

In early January 1915 Alfred Watts wrote the following letter to his younger sister Alice, who it seems was either a bit dilatory in writing, or her letters had only just reached him.

Note address,

> January, 1915.Friday,
> B Coy.
> 3rd Battalion,
> Rifle Brigade,
> 6th Division,
> BEF.

Dear Alice,
Have just received your letter which was forwarded from the base. It was about time you sent a letter although I know it

is a nuisance. I often say to myself I'll never write any more letters, but bless 'yer 'eart' I still do it.

So the Mitcham town guard gave you a treat eh? Well we are going to give the Germans a treat later on. I'm going to have my first experience in the trenches this weekend. We are about two miles from our trenches and there are eight of us in this empty house. What a hole! I wish you could see us.

Last night at about 9.30 pm we thought Xmas had come. The shells lit up the room, and the old windows rattled and it was grand. The people round here don't take any notice and they are happy to know we are here.

The Germans were in this place some time ago but they are further away now. Whilst I am writing this letter the Germans are trying to bring down one of our aeroplanes. The shells explode in the air and they look like kites. It is very interesting to watch it, and our flier doesn't seem to worry much although the shells are all around him.

Our company went and had a hot bath this morning. I needed it. There were ten of us in a large tub containing about 5ft of hot water. After our bath we had clean clothes and 'here we are, here we are here we are again.*1

Thank the girls for their kind wishes and my regards to Beattie, Daisy and Lil. So Maude went to Sheerness [the Rifle Brigade's 5th and 6th training battalions at Sheerness on the Isle of Sheppey] to see old Parker? I haven't had time to write to him but he'll soon be out here. My best wishes to Maude and tell her that when Parker comes out here he's coming for a holiday – Perhaps.

It's money for treacle and every time you get a bulls eye you get a packet of fags or a tin of Keetings, which is what one needs.*2

Yes, I've seen the boxes that you mentioned and I could have sent one or two home if it was possible to do so, but as I have already informed you that what we could do and what we're allowed to do are two different things.*3

Yes, the watch is all right and keeps good time. I'm the only one with a watch so you can bet your last shilling it's handy. The mirror too will soon be worn out by the way it is used. We shave as often as possible for cleanliness sake.

To get to this place we had a 24 hour train journey right

through France and then a march of about 12 miles. One of the boys was a bit unwell and to save him from falling out I carried his pack the last mile or so and it nearly crippled me. I was dead beat and I never want that feeling again.*⁴ But now I'm like a young racer that's favourite for the race. I'm IT with a capital 'I'. Don't you worry about me looking after myself. I'm not going to have my clock spoilt for fun. I'm going to keep smiling as that's the best thing to do, especially out here. Once your thoughts get the better of you you're whacked as far as feelings go.

I'd like to be home, but not while the war lasts. I'll appreciate everything when I do come home – 'What ho the Benedictine'! Au revoir and love to all.

Your Affect. Brother
Alf.*⁵

*¹ See the reference to the London Christmas Pantomime show, and my guess above of the location of the bath house.

*² I'm not sure of this reference. It could be literally a bull's eye in rifle shooting as the Rifle Brigade always kept up its marksmanship with constant competitions and practice whenever possible when out of the line (see below) but I don't know what he means otherwise. 'Keetings/Keatings' was (and maybe still is) a flea powder.

*³ 'The boxes' were gifts sent by The Princess Mary to the troops at Christmas 1914 continuing the tradition started by Queen Victoria in the Boer War. The box was an embossed brass tin containing a mixture of cigarettes, pipe tobacco, chocolate and a greeting card. The King and Queen sent a postcard bearing pictures of themselves and with the inscription 'With our best wishes for Christmas 1914. May God protect you and bring you home safe. Mary R and George R'.

*⁴ No wonder he was tired out. Remember an infantry pack weighed 80 lb (36 kg) and Alfred was carrying two of them towards the end of a 12-mile march after spending 24 hours being shunted all over France in a train in very crowded and uncomfortable conditions. No padded seats, and often no seats. Troop train trucks usually bore the sign '8 Chevaux ou 40 Hommes'.

*⁵ He never saw any of his family again.

Battle of Neuve Chapelle 10th–13th March 1915

There were two factors that brought about this battle. One was the pressure from the French High Command for the BEF to join with the French attacks that Joffre was planning to reduce the salient extending from Arras to Rheims. The second was to prove the 'British fighting spirit' to the French to counter the criticism from them that the British were not pulling their weight.

Joffre intended the attack at Neuve Chapelle to be a part of a combined Anglo French effort, but this was dependent on the British taking over French positions held by two corps north of Ypres. Sir John French found himself in an awkward position. The British government had already decided to land an expedition to attack the Turks in the Dardenelles, and had earmarked troops for this, and in addition the 29th Division, the last to contain mainly regular battalions, was to be sent to Salonika in northern Greece – see above.

Sir John now had no troops to spare to relieve the French. As a result, and no doubt angry, Joffre decided to abandon the combined assault. In the circumstances Sir John felt obliged to go it alone, but now of necessity to reduce the scale of the attack from that originally envisaged.

Sir John was not only anxious to show his allies that he was willing and able to mount a substantial attack on his own, but he was also concerned about the condition of Haig's First Army. This was badly placed in inadequate trenches and unsuitable terrain enfiladed by fire from the enemy. However Haig said the decision to attack at Neauve Chapelle/Aubers Ridge was because his troops were better than Smith Dorrien's, and Sir John French 'could never be sure of getting satisfactory results from SD'.

The 7th and 8th Divisions

The battle of Neuve Chapelle was to be fought by Haig's First Army, IV Corps, commanded by Rawlinson, using the 7th and 8th Divisions, together with the Indian Corps. The 7th Division was commanded by the redoubtable Major General Thomson Capper. The commander of the 8th Division was Major General Francis Davies, who would be blamed, unfairly it would seem, by Rawlinson for failure to push forward at a critical point on 10th March.

Included in the plan for the 8th Division were the 2nd Devons as part of the 23rd Brigade, and 2nd Rifles as part of 25th Brigade.

The 27th Division, of which the 4th Rifles and 2nd DCLI were members, would be involved at the action of St Eloi 14th–15th March, as part of V Corps.

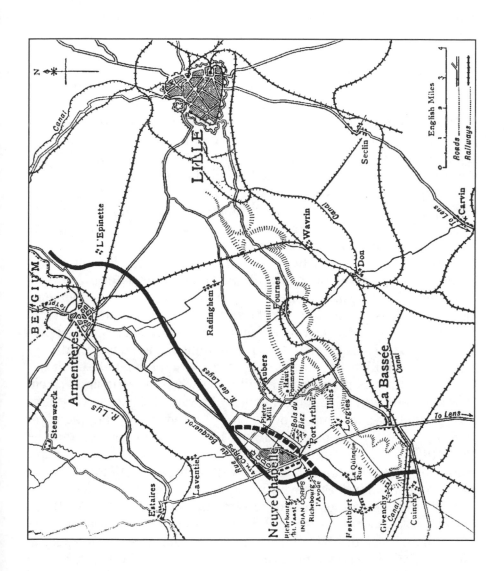

Neuve Chapelle was a tiny farming village in 'French Flanders' (the Artois) some nine miles south west of Armentières. There was inevitably a church, and there was also a brewery and some scattered houses. The village in itself had no strategic purpose, but the ground of Aubers Ridge did. The positions held by the German forces formed a salient around the area, and the final and scaled down British plan was to attack and capture the village, and then to form a defensive line below the crest of Aubers Ridge.

If successful the plan would provide dry ground secure from observation, and also suitable to serve as a jumping off point for a future attack, possibly taking the town of Lille, an important rail junction at present twelve miles behind the German lines.

Aubers Ridge lay within a mile to the east of the village. Like the village, it formed part of the German defences, and despite being only thirty-five metres at its highest the ridge enabled the enemy to see over all the British positions.

To carry out the objectives, the plan was for the British troops to deliver a short but violent artillery bombardment followed by a powerful infantry assault. Speed and surprise were the key elements of the attack because although the British forces had superiority in numbers initially, the Germans could bring up reserves to support quickly, and also appeared to have unlimited supplies of artillery ammunition unlike the British with their strictly limited supplies.

The weather, as it always seemed to be when the British attacked, was atrocious; unsettled, bitterly cold with rain and occasional snow. The ground was soft and difficult to operate in and during the night before the attack it froze. The 2nd Devons from Egypt, and the 2nd Rifles coming from India, and of course the Indian Corps, must still have been feeling the weather to be particularly harsh after tropical climes as they shivered and waited to attack.

William Linton Andrews wrote that his battalion, the 1/4th Black Watch, was attached to the 2nd Black Watch regulars who were at that time part of the Indian army Division, the Meerut Division, at Neuve Chapelle. A young runner of 2nd Black Watch shared a dug-out with him, and the lad shivered all the time and stammered 'It's not that I am afraid Corporal, it's the c-c-cold. We've only come lately from India. I'm all right chum, but I just c-c-can't help it.' Andrews said snow swept down upon them in the flooded trenches, and they grew colder and colder and he never thought he could be so chilled and still live. It was a biting torture of the body.

Haig and Rawlinson had planned the battle meticulously, and it was to be the blueprint for all other major Western Front battles to come. Models of the battleground were constructed and the troops rehearsed well. Aerial photographs were taken of the enemy lines and maps prepared for the artillery bombardment. The guns were placed without the enemy being aware of them by registering targets a few at a time. The attacking battalions were moved up to their jumping off positions by 4.30 am and the barrage started promptly at 7.30 am with devastating effect.

The 25th Brigade got off to a good start as the barrage lifted just after 8 am moving on as the troops rose from their trenches and advanced across the muddy fields. The wire had been broken, and the leading battalions passed through the German front line and into the support positions. Losses had been comparatively few, and the support troops passed through and the village was occupied shortly before 9 am.

The 2nd Rifles had passed through the two leading battalions of the attack (2/Lincolns and 2/Royal Berkshires) as planned and met up with the 2/3rd Gurkhas in the village. The 2nd Rifles, as related in Gordon Corrigan's *Sepoys in the Trenches*, 'gave the Gurkhas three rousing cheers'. The first Victoria Cross of the battle was won by Rifleman Gobar Sing Negi, of the 2/39th Garwhal Rifles, who was killed in the engagement leading a bayonet charge driving back the enemy until they were forced to surrender.

It was at this point that a real breakthrough looked more than possible. The 2nd Rifles and 1st Royal Irish Rifles had accomplished their tasks, and Geoff Bridger in *The Battle of Neuve Chapelle* quotes a letter from Lt. Pennefather, D Company, 2nd Rifles, who writing to a fellow officer says:

We then arrived at the other side of the village and joined up with the Indians on our right, and our job was finished since we had broken a gap in the line and could have gone to Berlin, at least if there had been anyone behind.

The commander of the 2nd Rifles, Lt. Col. Stephens, confirms this, saying there was nothing to stop him advancing, and sought

333

permission from his Brigadier-General, A. Lowry Cole. Stephens felt the Germans were shaken and disorganised and there was no reason not to pursue them. His request to spearhead an advance was refused because the policy called for a coordinated broad frontal approach by the two brigades, and unfortunately the 23rd Brigade had run into trouble and had not arrived.

23rd Brigade

The reason for the hold up was caused, at least initially, by the late arrival of two howitzer batteries from England. This resulted in a section of the German line still operating effectively as the batteries had not been able to register their targets before the attack started. The attacking wave of the leading battalions of 23rd Brigade – 2/Scottish Rifles and 2/Middlesex, on the left of the 25th Brigade – were virtually wiped out, as they ran into uncut wire and machine gun fire.

2nd Devons

Brigadier-General Pinney, commander of 23rd Brigade, after consultations with Davies and the commanders of 2nd Middlesex and 2nd Devonshires, ordered the Devons, together with two companies of the 2nd West Yorks, to go to the aid of the 2nd Scottish Rifles as they were in a better position to continue the attack than the pinned down 2nd Middlesex.

Second Lieutenant George Clinton Wright of the 2nd Devons showed great gallantry and was said to be recommended for the VC. He was killed while giving support to the beleaguered Middlesex. The award was not approved.*

*It has been claimed that a Victoria Cross was more often awarded if the battle was successful, but I don't know if this is correct.

The Indian Division

As the bombardment in front of 23rd Brigade had not been entirely successful, elements of the Indian Division also ran into trouble. The wire had not been cut by the initial bombardment, and hidden machine guns were still operating as deteriorating weather conditions had hindered, and in places prevented, the aircraft observations. The Garhwal Brigade ripped at the barbed wire and hacked their way through. This brigade met with mixed fortunes. The 1/39th Garhwal Rifles lost direction early on in the attack and became isolated from their nearest comrades 2/Leicesters and all efforts to relieve them met with costly failure.

The attack continues – without success

This first day was really the only one where the breakthrough could have been made. After that, with the element of surprise having gone, the Germans rallied and were able to bring up their reserves and reinforced the line with six battalions the following day.

By the late afternoon of the 12th March, it became clear that Capper's 7th Division was in no position to take part in any proposed coordinated attack with Davies's 8th Division, and the 8th now had to push ahead alone.

The Irish Rifles and 2nd Rifle Brigade, on the 25th Brigade's southern sector, launched an attack, but they were cut down as they left their trenches. 'C' and 'D' companies of the 2nd Rifles made a second abortive attempt and two men volunteered on a suicidal mission to cut a path through the unbroken barbed wire.*

*These two men were CSM Harry Daniels, and Acting Corporal Reginald Noble who were each awarded the Victoria Cross for their heroic efforts. Both were wounded, Reginald Noble mortally so and he died the following day. Daniels, more fortunate, recovered from his wounds and later commissioned and awarded the MC, he became a Lt. Colonel. He died on his birthday in 1953.

23rd Brigade deployed the 2nd Devons and the 2nd Scottish Rifles. Their orders were to force their way through to the Piètre Road, but both battalions had suffered such severe casualties already, and they were so tired from lack of sleep and battle fatigue that whenever they halted they collapsed into a sleep akin to death. They had been fighting non-stop since the early morning of 10th March, and not long before midnight of the 12th March they ran into an insurmountable barrier of a thorn hedge reinforced with barbed wire. The troops on either side were also halted in their attack.

335

The battle ends

At the end of three days the drive had petered out. The Germans had made an abortive counter attack and suffered heavily, but overall losses were about equal and it was realised the situation was hopeless, and the attack abandoned.

The actions in the area

There were really three battles of the Neuve Chapelle area. The first against the village, the second a little later against Aubers Ridge 9th May and the third at Festubert 15th to 25th May.

The post-mortem

Communications between the units in the front line and Haig's HQ often took hours, and there had to be a lot of guesswork by the staff as information was often conflicting as well as long delayed. The prevailing weather conditions prevented aerial reconnaissance most of the time, and there were the shortages of artillery ammunition. Inevitably faulty information led to faulty orders being issued.

As mentioned above, Sir John French blamed Rawlinson for not throwing in his reserves at the critical moment on the first day of the battle, and Rawlinson in turn blamed the 8th Division commander Major General F.J. Davies for failing to advance immediately after the capture of the village. Rawlinson wrote to Kitchener:

> It was I think our failure to press forward rapidly in the first instance that prevented us from gaining more ground, and for this I am afraid Davies is to some extent responsible though he was not very well served by one of his Brigadiers. Then again on the second day he did not direct his leading brigade on the right objectives with the result that the Indians were somewhat exposed on their left flank, so after talking the matter over with Douglas Haig I have asked for him to be replaced.

Later, under pressure, he withdrew the criticism and admitted responsibility. By now the main attention was being directed further north.

336

2nd Rifles. Fromelles

Ray Westlake, in an article in *The Great War Magazine* September 2003, says that the records of the 2nd Battalion of the Rifle Brigade note that from the period 1st April to 8th May, 1915 they occupied trenches in front of Sailly and when out of the line they were billeted on the Rue Tilleloy, Rue du Quesness, Rue Bataille, in Sailly, Fleurbax and Bac St Maur. He continues:

> During the evening of 8th May, the Battalion moved forward to its assembly positions, suffering a number of casualties from friendly fire as British artillery shells fell short among them.
>
> At 5.40 am the next day, the first line advanced towards Fromelles and successfully took the enemy's trench opposite. The second line followed on behind and whilst in the captured position both lines suffered severe losses due to machine-gun fire from both flanks. The attacks on their right and left had not succeeded and thus left them exposed to the enemy.
>
> With all company officers either killed or wounded, what remained of the Battalion held on to its meagre gains, eventually retiring around 5 am on 10th May, with a total strength of just 2 officers and approximately 195 men. The Battalion's total casualties amounted to 77 killed, 340 wounded and 212 missing.

Comments on Fromelles

Lieut.-Col. A. Kearsey in *1915 Campaign in France* says of this battle:

> The reasons for our failure at Fromelles and Rue de Bois on May 9th and for more encouraging results at Festubert between May 15th and 25th are clearly brought out. One main reason appears to have been that we had to postpone our offensive operations after the Neuve Chapelle battle, and then until May 9th the Germans turned their light field defences into semi-permanent fortifications. We had not a sufficient quantity of effective heavy H.E. shells to destroy them.
>
> In addition to our inadequate supply of H.E. and gas ammunition, our armament was not sufficient. Many of the

337

New Army divisions had not got their complement of guns and we could not distribute half as many guns per mile of front as the French could. For our continuous sixty hours' bombardment on May 13th, 14th and 15th, we had 121 howitzers, varying from fifty-four 4.5-inch to two 15-inch howitzers. We also had 312 guns varying from four 6-inch to sixteen 15-pounders.

Much of the ammunition, however was faulty, and, owing to the wet, misty weather, observation of fire was difficult; nor could the explosion of the bulk of the H.E. shells be seen, owing to the sodden condition of the ground on May 13th and 14th.

It would seem that once again much of the British difficulties stemmed from the oft quoted complaint of lack of heavy calibre artillery, poor quality artillery ammunition and worn gun barrels.

2nd battle of Ypres, 22nd April–25th May, 1915

The 22nd of April was a lovely spring day. Liddell Hart describes it as follows:

The sun was sinking behind Ypres. Its spring radiance had breathed life that day into the dead town and the mouldering trench lines which guarded it. A month hence the town would be a shell with all the eerie grandeur of a greater Colosseum.

Another description of the beginning of the end of the city is from an observer of the occasion, J.H. Morgan who writes in *Leaves from a Field Notebook*:

The dreaming beauty of the distant city almost persuaded us that we were the victims of a gigantic illusion. But even as we gazed the city acquired a desperate and tragic reality. Voices of thunder awoke behind the ridge, the air was rent like a garment, and first one cloud and then another and another arose above the city of Ypres, till the white towers were blotted out of sight. A black pall floated over the doomed city, and from that moment the air was never still, as a rhythm of

German shells rained upon it. The storm spread until other villages were involved, and a fierce red glow appeared above the roofs of Vlamertinge.

Norman Ellison in *Remembrances of Hell* describes his experience in the opening stages of the bombardment of Ypres:

High above our heads we heard the passage, like the rumbling of a railway train, of enormous 17 inch howitzer shells. As they burst amongst the buildings of the town, reddish clouds of brick-dust, hundreds of feet high, shot into the air and slowly expanded into a heavy pall over the doomed place. The damage caused by these large shells was enormous. A few weeks later I was with a party in Ypres looking for unbroken mirrors to cut up into periscopes. The streets were pocked with shell craters forty feet across and as many feet deep. Whole rows of houses had collapsed like a pack of cards; many had the whole façade torn off to expose the interior floor by floor, like some tragic doll's house with a hinged front.

Gas

At 5 pm on 22nd April a resounding crash of artillery gunfire broke out from the German lines and shells crashed down on Ypres and the surrounding villages, many of the latter untouched until then. The battle had opened bringing with it a greenish yellow fog changing to a blue white mist swirling into the trenches held by Algerian French colonial troops. These troops, coughing and choking, fled back from this unknown agency. They left behind them a gap in the front over four miles wide filled only by the dead and dying suffocating in agony from the chlorine gas. For this is what it was.

To the south flank of the gap, packets of troops from the Canadian Division together with French troops were rushed to try to fill some of the empty space, but there were gaps of between 1,000 and 3,000 yards still unfilled. The Germans, having had complete success with this surprise attack, failed to exploit it by advancing only a couple of miles and then inexplicably stopping when they could have gone right through to Ypres only four miles from their lines.

Liddell Hart says Falkenhayn, the German commander, merely

wanted to try the gas as an experimental aid to an attack which itself was merely a cloak to his projected blow against the Russians, and he was not particularly concerned whether the salient was erased or not.

Cyril Falls (see below), in *The First World War*, takes a different view, and says the Germans followed up for two miles and then ran into their own gas and halted, and by dawn the next day, 23rd April, the British had strung out battalions from three divisions to fill the gap, albeit only very thinly.

Second Army

The 4th Division engagements between 24th April and 4th May were officially known as the battle of St Julien, and also engaged were the 27th Division (2/DCLI and 4/Rifles). Both divisions were again at the battle of Frezenberg 8th–13th May, and the battle of Bellewaarde 24th–25th May 1915.

4th Division. 1st Rifles

The 1st Rifles had been moved to Poperinghe on 24th April, in preparation to advancing to take part in the battle. On the way to Poperinghe, at Hazebrouck, the train of the 1st Rifles drew level with another on board which were the territorials of the The London Rifle Brigade, also moving towards the battle, and understandably very apprehensive. Aubrey Smith records this meeting as follows:

> To our great delight we found a trainload of the 1st R.Bs [Rifle Brigade] alongside us, so that the 11th Brigade was evidently on the move and we were not an isolated unit being withdrawn from the 4th Division as we had feared. 'Cheerio LRBs,' was their greeting, 'we're in for it this time all right'. And somehow one felt it didn't matter if we were, so long as we had these cheerful regulars with us.

Smith said that later on their arrival that same afternoon:

> ...we stepped out on to the platform at Poperinghe* and threaded our way in single file over the prostrate bodies of wounded French and Algerian soldiers, who were probably

waiting for a train to take them away. They were the ghastliest sight we had yet seen, some being blind, others limbless and most of them looking pathetic in the extreme.

*Poperinghe, or 'Pop' to the troops of the BEF, was a favourite quiet spot at that time just out of range of all but the very largest of the German guns in the Ypres Salient area. It was to become famous for the 'Toc H' club haven, 'Talbot House', run by 'Tubby' Clayton (incidentally it is not only possible still to visit the club today, but to stay there). Although the town was never shelled seriously, and civilians lived there all the time, it was subject later to bombing air attacks when the Germans tried to smash the vital railway station.

From Poperinghe the 1st Rifles marched to billets near Busseboom, and then to Vlameringhe on the 25th, and moved forward by marches to St Jean and positions near Fortuin. They held the line under constant shellfire without sleep, barely any food, and in cold rain, and with the rudimentary trenches a morass of slimy mud. On 28th April they dug in on the northern slopes of Hill 37. In the five days from 25th April to 30th April their casualties were 253 killed, wounded or missing.

They withdrew to bivouacs south-west of Elverdinghe and were back in the line at Mouse Trap Farm on 9th May where they again held position under heavy shellfire. The enemy attacked on 13th May, and the resulting casualties from this attack were 2 officers and 130 other ranks. After relief the battalion carried out further tours of the front-line, and the casualties during the month of May were 5 officers and 395 other ranks. (These casualties were of course in addition to those 253 above for the last week in April.)

27th Division

The 4/Rifles served in the Sanctuary Wood and Bellewaarde Wood area during May and June, and like their sister battalion 1/Rifles above they suffered heavily. The battalion records note that for the period 22nd April to 14th May the 4th Battalion's casualties were 116 killed, 606 wounded, 46 missing. At the end of May they moved by stages to the Armentières sector.

Conditions were the same for all the troops desperately holding the Salient at that critical time. Few in number, and with no reserves available, mixtures of units were moved from one section of the front line to another as the German attacks dictated. To give an idea of the confusion and difficulties the troops and their commanders faced, Lyn MacDonald (*1915 The Death of Innocence*) states that the 4th Division alone were attached to six different divisions under five different commands in five different sectors. The Salient, as I mentioned above, meant that the German troops could not only see the entire area back beyond Ypres towards Poperhinge, but could pour enfilading artillery fire onto the British lines and the town of Ypres from three sides.

Duke of Cornwall's Light Infantry. Ypres 1915

Battle Honours: 'Ypres 1915', 'Gravenstafel', 'St Julien', 'Frezenberg', 'Bellewaarde'.

On 4th January 1915 the 1st Battalion moved to Bailieul, and when they marched through on 7th January they met up with their 2nd Battalion. On 16th January 1915 they moved to trenches south west of Messines (a place to become famous in 1917) and spent the time until late March on tours of duty in the trenches around Kemmel.

They stayed in Flanders where they took part in the 2nd Ypres battle (1st battle of Ypres was in October-November 1914) and were involved the fighting around Hill 60 between 17th and 22nd April 1915. They came out of the line on 22nd April and returned later just north of the Ypres-Comines Canal and stayed in the same sector throughout the months of May and June.

2nd Battalion began the new year of 1915 with tours of duty in the St Eloi sector trenches, and suffered casualties in various attacks and retirements during February and March. In April the battalion was directly engaged in the 2nd Ypres battle and suffered the loss of three 2nd Lieutenants and 46 other ranks killed, 7 officers and 216 other ranks wounded, and 6 missing. On 29th April they moved into dug-outs at Sanctuary Wood. May and June found them at Armentières, Houplines and Le Touquet.

PART THIRTY-THREE

'He was very upset, this poor soldier,' Nellie, [my mother] said, 'he had wanted to help Alf. When he finished telling us what had happened he pulled from out of his pocket a few small personal effects of Alf's together with his cap badge – still with dried mud on it. He put them on the table in the kitchen. We looked at them. It was such a shock. That was all that we had left of Alf.'

Nellie Holley (née Watts] recounting the description of her brother Alfred's death in Flanders in 1915, brought to the family by a comrade.

Flanders 1915 in the aftermath of Second Ypres

Even when historians declared these (pre Loos) 1915 battles had been officially ended, the Germans were still shelling the British line heavily in Flanders in June, and the 3rd Rifles like the others in the area were having an unpleasant time.

3rd Battalion The Rifle Brigade, typical daily activities and casualties in early and mid 1915

The war record of the 3rd Battalion of the Rifle Brigade during 1915 is no doubt similar to those other regiments not actually engaged in major battles but serving in an 'active' part of the line. As the battalion continued its front line routine of duties the record is one of a steady toll of daily casualties, draft replacements, and the training of attached inexperienced troops (see the LRB with the 1st Rifles above). From *The Rifle Brigade Chronicles for 1914–1915*:

343

WAR-RECORD OF 3RD BATTALION.
1915.
ROLL OF OFFICERS ON 1 JANUARY

Lieut.- Col. Lord Henniker, Commanding.
Captain F.H. Nugent, 2nd in Command [from 5th Jan].

'A' COMPANY.

Captain C.F.T Swan
Lieut. Hon. N.G. Bligh
Lieut. H.S.C. Peyton
2nd Lieut. T. O. Jameson
2nd Lieut. R.M. Kirkpatrick

'B' COMPANY.

Captain R.G. Hopwood
Lieut. M Alexander
2nd Lieut. Hon. M.T. Boscawen
2nd Lieut. R.O. Skeggs

'C' COMPANY

Captain. R. Piggot
Lieut. Hon. T.G.B. Morgan-Grenville
2nd Lieut. W.H. Beever
2nd Lieut. F.H.J.Marshall

'D' COMPANY.

Captain H.S.C. Richardson
Lieut. J.T.W. Reeve (acting Machine-gun officer)
2nd Lieut. A.E.P. Ellis
2nd Lieut. J. H.. Smith
2nd Lieut. J. Crawford-Kehrman

Adjutant:	Captain Hon. C.H. Mersey-Thompson
Quartermaster:	Hon. Lieut. L. Eastmead.*
Transport Officer:	Lieut. E.R. Kewley*
Medical Officer:	Lieut. L.C. Somervell
Chaplain:	Rev. N.S. Talbot

*See below when by end of war Lt. Eastmead was a Captain, and Lt. Kewley was Lt.-Col. and commanding the battalion. These were the only two officers left of those who sailed to France in 1914.

6 January – Corporal H. W. Simpson promoted 2nd Lieutenant in 'D' Company. [Wounded 1st February].

7 January – after only two days' rest, we took over a bad bit of trenches full of water near HOUPLINES for two days.

12–16 January – 2nd Lieutants J. Simmons ('A') and R. D. Trotter ('B') posted.

Lieutenant Godolphin Osborne rejoined, and became Machine-gun Officer again.

20 January – Brigadier-General G.M. Harper, C.B. DSO took over the **17th Brigade**.

24 January – 2nd Lieutant Crawford-Kehrman killed.

30 January – 2.30 pm Battalion inspected by Major-General Keir, commanding 6th Division, who expressed his appreciation of the turn-out and the appearance of the Battalion, and his great satisfaction with the manner in which it has always performed its duties.

1 February – Reinforcement of fifty men under 2nd Lieutenant P.G. Mayer ('C').

3 February – 2nd Lieutenant Simpson wounded [promoted from Corporal 6th January]; 2nd Lieutenant Jirkpatrick sick, but after a short time reurned to duty. Riflemen Bristow and Holton crawled close to the German trenches, returned for hand-grenades, and crawling through the German wire threw them and scattered a German working party. They subsequently received D.C.Ms. [See my comments elsewhere on naming ORs in war diaries.]

10 February – Captain Godolphin Osborne severely wounded [he died on the 25th]. Lieutenant Reeves became Machine-gun officer again.

16 February – Reinforcement of seventy-five under 2nd Lieutenants W.G.K. Boswell ('C'), E.M. Winch [mortally wounded 5th March] and V. Herbert-Smith ('D') [also killed in March].

18–21 February – and 22–28. Two companies of a Canadian regiment were attached to the Battalion; for two nights they were split up among the platoons; on the third they worked in their own platoons, each under a Rifle Brigade Officer.

5 March – 2nd Lieutenant Winch mortally, and the Rev. N.S. Talbot slightly wounded. For his work during the winter the latter was afterwards awarded the M.C.

20 March–1 April 2nd Lieutenant V. Herbert-Smith killed [joined battalion 16th February]. 2nd Lieutenants E.W. Armstrong ('D') and R.C. Bridgeman ('D') joined.

2nd April – Captain Pigot handed over 'C' to Captain Meysey-Thompson and succeeded him as Adjutant. About this time detachments of the Royal Warwickshire and Gloucester Regiments (T.F.) (48th Division) were attached, one platoon

345

to each Company for two days or so at a time. A Corps Horse Show was held.

21st April – 2nd Lieutenant Ellis wounded.

28th April – 2nd Lieutenant F.E. Young, 6th Battalion (S.R.) ('D') joined the Battlion from the 1st Battalion K.S.L.I., to whom he had been attached for several months.

2nd May – The first appearance of gas at Ypres. Within an hour or two we had all been issued respirators, roughly made by the seamstresses of Armentières under the directions of the Quartermaster. A succession of improved patterns followed.

11th May – Captains Nugent and Bligh and Lieutenants Boswell and Young sent to the 2nd Battalion to replace casualties at Fromelles on the 9th.

17th–31st May – Captains Peyton, Reeve, Lieutenant Beever and 2nd Lieutenant invalided to England. Captain Alexander became Machine-gun Officer.

During these five months there was a continual wastage; forty-seven NCOs and men were killed and 111 wounded; but the numbers were well kept up by constant small drafts, and on 31 May the strength of the Battalion was twenty-two officers and 1,036 other ranks. We did not always occupy the same trenches; sometimes the Germans were 600 yards off, sometimes only 100.

1st June – Battalion relieved by 1st Battalion Argyll and Sutherland Highlanders and 1st Battalion Royal Scots, and proceeded via Bailleul and Poperinghe to Ypres, reaching trenches **N.E. of La Brique** on 5th June; these were well-designed, and some way from the Germans, as two re-entrants faced each other here, but required a great deal of work.

...During the month [June] our Artillery was short of shells and could give us little support. Vlamertinghe church was destroyed by fire except for a big Calvary on the outer wall of the tower. We had three weeks on end in the trenches.

...During these two months the Battalion had three tours of the trenches north-east of La Brique and St Jean – 5th to 25th

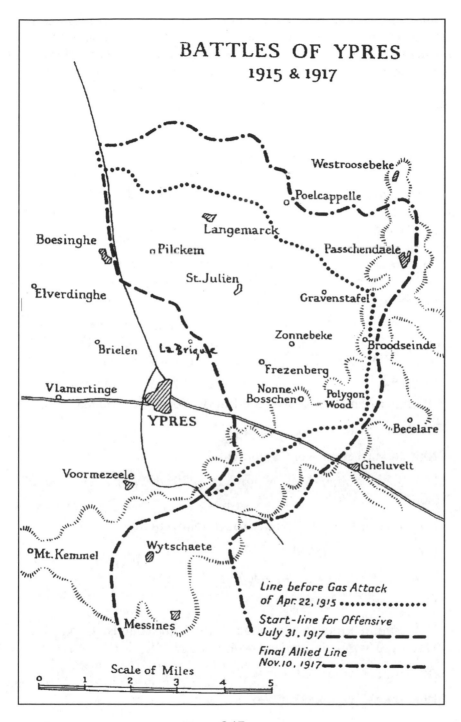

BATTLES OF YPRES
1915 & 1917

Westroosebeke

Poelcappelle

Langemarck

Boesinghe

Pilckem

Passchendaele

St. Julien

Gravenstafel

Elverdinghe

Zonnebeke

Broodseinde

Brielen

La Brique

Frezenberg

Vlamertinge

Nonne
Bosschen

Polygon
Wood

Becelare

YPRES

Gheluvelt

Voormezeele

Mt. Kemmel

Wytschaete

Messines

Line before Gas Attack
of Apr. 22, 1915 ···············

Start-line for Offensive
July 31, 1917 ▬ ▬ ▬ ▬

Final Allied Line
Nov. 10, 1917 ▬·▬·▬·▬

Scale of Miles

0   1   2   3   4   5

June, 11th–19th July, and 27th to 3rd August, going out in between to billets in the woods north-east of Poperhinge... During the periods in billets large digging parties of 400 to 600 men had to be found nearly every night.

The War Diary for 3rd Battalion Rifle Brigade gives more details of casualties.

At the end of May (1915) we left Armentières arriving in the Ypres Salient on June 4th. On 7th June Lt. Col. Lord Henniker went home and Capt. Pigot commanded the Battalion.*

*One wonders what lies behind that cryptic entry concerning the colonel.

Four new replacement subalterns joined on 4th June, and on 5th June at 4pm the Battalion relieved the Seaforth Highlanders and East Lancs in the trenches.

6th June, Capt. The Hon C.H. Meysey Thompson was wounded, together with 18 other ranks, and 2 other ranks were killed. (Captain Meysey Thompson died of his wounds at Bailleul on 17th June).

7th June, 1 man was wounded and 1 died of wounds.

8th June, 3 men were wounded.

10th June, 3 men were wounded.

11th June 5 men were wounded [Alfred Watts was one of them].

13th June, Lt. Mayer wounded, 1 man killed.

14th June, 2 wounded.

15th June 2 killed 5 wounded.

16th June, 6 wounded.

17th June 6 killed 6 wounded 1 died of wounds, Capt. Hon. Maysey Thompson died of wounds.

18th June 2 wounded.

19th June 1 wounded.

So during the two weeks of taking over the front line trenches in this 'active', but comparatively quiet part of the Salient, the battalion suffered a steady stream of casualties. They held the line here until the German flame thrower attack in August at Hooge when the 3rd Rifles were pulled out and sent over to reinforce the British counter-attack. The occasion was described in the *Chronicles of the Rifle Brigade* thus:

> On 26th July, the Germans made their flame attack against the 14th Division at Hooge. The 6th Division were taken out of the line at the beginning of August and counter-attacked at Hooge on 9th August, regaining our original ground. For this attack the 17th Brigade was in Reserve, going into the line on 13th August to consolidate the trenches. This was not a pleasant job; the trenches had ceased to exist after our heavy bombardment of 9 August, and corpses of three or four fights during the previous month were lying about everywhere... On 11th August 575 men were lent to the 16th Infantry Brigade for carrying digging out, and bringing in killed and wounded from the 'crater' at Hooge.

They returned to continue their tour of duty at La Brique on 27th August with the rest of the 17th Brigade. Their casualties in other ranks during the three month period were 40 killed and 134 wounded. The battalion strength on 31st August 1915 was 24 officers and 764 other ranks.

On 14th October they were transferred: 'much to our regret' to the 24th Division in place of the 6th Division. On 20th October after two very muddy tours of the trenches about 2½ miles north-east of St Eloi, the battalion went into reserve with the rest of the 24th Division for five weeks, being relieved by the 3rd Division. They marched by stages some 42 miles into permanent billets at Norteulinghem about 10 miles north-west of St Omer. *The Chronicles* record:

> This was the first rest the Battalion had had since the beginning of the war. A lot of training was done during the five weeks, and various inter-Divisional competitions at musketry and football were arranged, nearly all of which the Battalion won.

The casualties for the period September to December 1915 were 36 NCOs and men killed and 102 wounded, making a total for the year of 123 killed and 347 wounded. A grand total of 470 casualties during the time that the battalion was not engaged in any battles. The pattern and routine of static trench warfare had emerged along the whole of the Western Front.

The main danger times in the trenches in the active sectors were generally regarded as dawn and again at dusk. The British lines often faced into the east and the early morning sun. All the soldiers in the front line 'stood to' at dawn. And often accompanied this by the 'morning hate' of rifle and machine gun fire aimed at the enemy trenches on the off chance of a possible attack or catching a last-minute return of enemy working parties in No Man's Land.

When 'stand down' was given, troops prepared their breakfasts while a few were detailed to be on stand by sentry duty with loaded rifles. They did not peer over the top of the trench standing on the fire step, because of the almost certainty of a bullet in the head from an alert sniper. The enemy was observed either by periscope, which again could get a bullet through it, or loopholes guarded by a thick metal plate covered in sacking to prevent the metal reflecting. The daylight hours in the front line trenches, as described below, were given over to routine 'housekeeping' chores for those not on sentry duty.

Dusk saw a repeat of the morning 'stand to' and then groups of soldiers would be detailed for two hours sentry duty on the fire step while others were despatched to the rear to collect rations and water and ammunition. Others would be formed into working parties in No Man's Land to patrol and man listening posts in shell holes and forward saps; or carry out the never-ending tasks of repairing the wire and parapet.

Front line troops were, whenever possible, relieved at night. The incoming troops were frequently laden with trench stores including food, ammunition, picks and shovels, duckboards, rolls of barbed wire, corrugated iron sheets as well as their own weapons.

When the weather was bad the rain and glutinous mud could make it many hours for the troops stumbling and cursing in the dark, and under the threat of enemy machine gunners and artillery fire, to reach their appointed stretch of the assigned trench. They got sucked into the mud, sometimes waist deep in the damaged and narrow communication trenches. They tripped over broken

350

telephone wires, caught their feet in drainage holes, and sometimes their guides got lost.

Tours of trench duty varied according to the circumstances of the time, including the number of units available to rotate, and the quietness or otherwise of the line in the area. (The War Diary of 3rd Rifles reads laconically in December 1914 that they did 34 days without being relieved.)

Sniping

In addition to the artillery attacks in the 'active' sectors there was the constant danger from snipers, and, as the war went on, these activities became more sophisticated. To me, and I appreciate that it is probably quite illogical, I find the whole aspect of sniping particularly repellent. A successful sniper was a soldier who had the mentality and characteristics of a hunter/sportsman; someone prepared to hide patiently for hours to lie in wait for an unsuspecting target and then kill from concealment. For the sniper the 'trophy' was an enemy soldier, but not an enemy soldier approaching with lethal intent, or returning fire; a sniper attempts to kill anyone who moves – a figure going towards the latrine behind the line, or just standing to stretch in the sun, or one moving from one part of the trench to another as he goes about some domestic chore. One moment alive and unsuspecting, the next moment: 'It is with regret that I have to inform you of the death of … while engaged on active service.'

I can appreciate that if one *has* to be killed in a war, then a bullet in the head, quite unexpectedly out of the blue, is no doubt the least fearsome of deaths a soldier can contemplate. Especially if compared with those dying slowly in agony in No Man's Land between the lines sometimes lasting for days, or to be wounded and weighed down by equipment slowly drowning in mud while comrades are unable to extricate or even stop to help; or even being terribly wounded and spending the rest of life in pain and chairbound. But it is the cold-blooded act of the sniper that really repels me; the act of the assassin.

The early snipers were sometimes officers with pre-war game hunting experience and who provided their own 'big game' hunting rifles fitted with telescopic sights. Other-ranks snipers were selected from marksmen and to whom special training in the art of sniping was given. Dr Stephen Bull says much of the specialist training for British snipers was initially provided by the Lovat Scouts, a unit raised from Highland gamekeepers and deer stalkers.

The number of snipers per battalion varied from eight to twenty-four as the war progressed and sniping, as in all other aspects of trench warfare, developed into a specialised role with sophisticated equipment. Special clothing and a powerful telescopic sight became the norm, and for the British soldiers cunningly concealed hides and observation posts were constructed by the Royal Engineers.

My first soldier relative departs from the story

Seven days after the 3rd Battalion Rifle Brigade arrived at the front line north-east of La Brique on 4th June, 1915, Alfred Watts became one of the casualties,* and died of his wounds on Friday 11th June.

*He is not listed by name in the Battalion War Diary as it seldom mentions the names of other ranks. If they are mentioned it is, as I have said, usually for an award that has been given, or a mention for a specific deed, but not when listing casualties.

I can only surmise the sequence of events when Alfred Watts was fatally wounded. I am almost certain it would have been some time after 'stand down' in the morning when he, like the other members of his platoon and section not engaged in sentry duty on the fire step, having cooked and eaten their breakfasts* would have been detailed by the sergeant to clear up the trench. These were the never-ending chores of filling sandbags, draining the trench, replacing duckboards, repairing and rebuilding the parapet and parados, shoring up the sides of the trench damaged by previous artillery fire, sanitary duties (digging latrines) and cleaning up generally. Those not detailed for chores would clean their equipment and rifles, or attemp to de-louse their clothing ('chatting' it was called) and write letters or cards to home.

*Breakfast was often bread dipped in bacon fat, or a little fat bacon on a hunk of bread.

Throughout the day work would be interrupted by the sudden unholy scream of an approaching shell, or the shouted warning of 'Minnie coming' as the wobbling approach of a minenwerfer was spotted, causing the riflemen to dive for any possible cover. On one of these occasions Alfred would possibly have heard a great crash and felt an almighty blow in his arm and shoulder as he was thrown back, dazed by the noise and with the onset of agonising pain, and the realisation he had been hit. With the cry 'stretcher bearers' passing down the trench those of Alfred's mates finding themselves unscathed would have hastily checked him and the others who had been wounded, and where possible applied a field dressing over the most obvious wounds, while waiting for the arrival of the stretcher bearers* and listening for the approach of another salvo.

*Each British infantry battalion had 16 stretcher bearers on its strength, but the number would be increased to double or more before a major attack, and many more were needed in places like the Salient in 1917 where up to six or eight men were needed to carry a wounded man on a stretcher through the glutinous mud and slime. In many regiments members of the battalion band usually doubled as stretcher bearers, but not in all.

Those wounded able to walk would make their way as best they could, confused and stumbling, back down the communication trench to the Regimental Aid Post. Alfred hit in both shoulder and arm would have been lifted on to the stretcher to the encouragement of: 'All right mate, stick it, we'll soon have you there, that's a blighty one if ever I saw one. You'll be home in no time.'

And so, in and out of consciousness as his stretcher was manhandled to the Battalion Aid Post,* he and the other wounded would be examined as soon as possible and then taken a little further back to the Field Dressing Station to be properly bandaged and tagged for the Field Hospital or Casualty Clearing Station.

*The Battalion or Regimental Aid Post was where the battalion medical officer and his orderlies would diagnose the wounds, give injections and apply or change dressings and bandages, and give whatever aid they could within the very limited facilities on hand. Most likely it would be located in a cellar or a dugout in the support or reserve lines.

From the aid post the way back would be first by stretcher bearers, then horse-drawn or motor ambulance of the field ambulance unit by relay and collecting posts to the advanced and main dressing stations. Here too the priorities of the medical teams would be the temporary treatment and classification of wounds, and carrying out amputations and other emergency operations if vital – and if the facilities existed.

W.L. Andrews speaks of his battalion's dressing station during the battle of the Somme:

Dear old Major Rogers had his dressing-station there, and in fourteen hours of unbroken work, under continuous shell-fire, he dressed over 400 wounded men. A Catholic padre, Father Northcote, helped the wounded and comforted the dying, until a shell splinter knocked out an eye. This priest was loved by us all, and as much by the most hopeless atheist as by the most fervent Catholic. He returned to the brigade as soon as he could leave hospital.

From the dressing stations the wounded were transferred to the casualty clearing stations where most of the initial surgery was conducted. If possible there was one dressing station for every division, and they were sited seven miles or so behind the lines preferably or ideally with a railway siding at hand. Those who had survived this far, but required further treatment or convalescence, would, depending on the location, be sent back by train or barge to a base hospital and thence – if it was deemed suitable – to England.

I don't know if Alfred made it as far back as the casualty clearing station alive. These places were only able to offer surgery of a pretty basic nature anyway. One must remember too that there were no antibiotics then, and blood transfusions generally were rare anywhere before 1917.

One of Alfred's comrades later called on Alfred's parents, and my mother, at that time a girl of fourteen, remembered the occasion well. 'He was such a nice man,' she said. 'He had been wounded in the jaw, and was with Alf [at the dressing station or casualty clearing station].' At some stage Alf, in great pain and going in and out of consciousness, said to this man, 'My bandages are too tight'. No medical staff were on hand at the time but he apparently managed to loosen his dressings a little. 'Unfortunately,' my mother said, 'the wound must have been very severe and deep because Alf immediately started to bleed profusely. The other soldier was in a dreadful state, he couldn't staunch the flow of blood, and he couldn't speak or call out to attract attention because of his broken and bandaged jaw. So Alf quickly bled to death before anyone could attend him.'

354

Alfred's parents had of course received the news of his death before the convalescent rifleman visited them. The standard letter of the time was *Army Form B. 104–82B* and with it a formal message of sympathy from the King and Queen which read:

The King commands me to assure you of the true sympathy of His Majesty and The Queen in your sorrow.

He whose loss you mourn died in the Noblest of causes. His Country will be ever grateful to him for the sacrifice he has made for Freedom and Justice.

Secretary of State for War

Alfred Watts lies in La Brique Military Cemetery No. 2, on Pilkemseweg. It is possible to step straight off the pavement over a little kerb wall directly into the cemetery which was opened in February 1915, and used until March 1918. It stands on the site of, or close by, what in Alfred's time was either the Regimental Aid Post or the Casualty Clearing Station at La Brique. So his final journey was quite a short one from where he was fatally wounded.

On the opposite side of the road is La Brique Military Cemetery No. 1. Both the cemeteries are small ones and lie opposite each other on what is now a quiet residential road. There are 847 graves in No. 2 cemetery; No. 1 is much smaller with 90. There are trees around, and the road has little traffic. I don't know why, but I find this strangely comforting.

Alfred lies alongside other comrades of the Rifle Brigade who died around the same date. His headstone is of course the standard one. At the top, in the centre of the face of the stone is the Rifle Brigade Badge. Directly below this carving begins the inscription 'Z/2411 Rifleman'. Below this, 'A WATTS'. Below again, 'THE RIFLE BRIGADE'. And beneath '11TH JUNE 1915, AGED 27'. Below again, centrally placed is the large cross (Jewish soldiers have a star). At the very bottom, just visible at ground level an inscription 'GONE BEFORE'.

A little way behind Alfred Watt's grave is another Rifle Brigade soldier's headstone, one that is very slightly different from the others although at first glance it looks the same. It starts the same way with the regimental badge, and below 'S/107 Corporal'. Below

355

that 'A.G. DRAKE' followed by the two letters 'V. C'. Below that 'THE RIFLE BRIGADE' and below that '23RD NOVEMBER 1915 AGE 22' and below that in place of the normal cross there is a large cross, the Victoria Cross.*

*Alfred George Drake was a corporal in the 8th Battalion of the Rifle Brigade. He was from Stepney in the East End of London and born on 10th December 1893. The 8th Battalion was occupying the trenches at La Brique (where the 3rd Battalion had been in the spring of 1915). He was one of a patrol of four in No Man's Land reconnoitring towards the German lines (one officer, Lt. Tryon, one NCO, Drake, and two riflemen). The patrol was discovered when near the enemy who opened fire with rifles and machine guns wounding the officer and another member of the patrol.

Drake sent the remaining man back with the wounded rifleman and he stayed with the officer who was too badly wounded to be moved. Drake, although hit repeatedly, continued to dress Lt. Tryon's wounds regardless of the enemy fire. Eventually a rescue party discovered them. The officer was still alive, although unconscious. Drake, riddled with bullets, was dead by the side of his officer.

Personally, I find one of the striking features of the war cemeteries in both France and Belgium, is that I have never seen any signs of graffiti, vandalism, desecration or damage anywhere in these cemeteries or memorials. And they are easily accessible twenty-four hours a day to anyone. I dread to imagine what they would be like here in the same circumstances.*

*Alas! What I have written above seems no longer to be the case for in an article accompanied by a photograph, and dated Wednesday, 30 July 2003, *The Times* reports:

Gravestones of 45 British, Canadian and New Zealand First World War soldiers lie broken at St Aubert cemetery near Cambrai in northern France. The damage was discovered on Monday.

Peter Francis, spokesman for the War Graves Commission, said: 'It looks like a completely mindless act of vandalism'. St Aubert police said: 'We do not believe the vandals were motivated by any religious, racial or nationalistic feeling. An investigation has been launched but we do not have any leads'. The vandals had burnt the visitors' book at the entrance to the cemetery which contained the graves of 435 Commonwealth soldiers who lost their lives between 1917 and 1918... In April the graves of British soldiers in Etaples cemetery, near Boulogne, were effaced with swastikas and slogans denouncing the Iraq war. President Chirac sent a letter of apology to Britain.

And again, on 2nd August 2003, in *The Times*:

French gendarmes blamed bored, drunken youths yesterday for a spate of attacks on Commonwealth war graves in northern France. The gendarmerie is planning to step up patrols after headstones and crosses were smashed at the First World War cemetery at Aix-Noulette outside Lens in the third such incident over the past ten days.

The attacks have dismayed the Commonwealth War Graves Commission and infuriated French government ministers. Detectives said the vandalism was part of a pattern witnessed in recent years at weekends and during school holidays.

2003 seems to have been the year for desecration as once again *The Times*, on Wednesday 3rd December 2003, reported another instance. The difference this time is that there appears to be no political motive or straightforward vandalism. Under the heading 'Thieves steal British war grave headstones "for garden ornaments"' the article said: 'Headstones stolen last Friday night from Hiberts Trench Cemetery at Wancourt, next to the A1 motorway, between Paris and Lille, were, the police in Arras concluded, stolen to order for garden ornaments – or for propping up caravans! A CWGC spokesman said they will cost £300 each to replace.' (The spokesman said the headstones are made from Portland stone – so it would seem they have discontinued the experiment I mentioned above of using the Italian stone, and returned to Portland stone.)

PART THIRTY-FOUR

In their accounts of trench war, combatants distinguish between quiet or cushy sectors of the front line and active sectors where aggression prevailed. 'Cushy' was a term used to describe any comfortable state, but especially those sectors where the reciprocal violence of enemies was small in volume and perfunctory in performance. On a cushy sector, life was relatively safe, tolerable, even comfortable, and greatly contrasted with life on an active sector, where continuity and zeal marked the fighting.

Tony Ashworth, *Trench Warfare 1914–1918*
The Live and Let Live System.

Active sectors

People tend to imagine that casualties occurred mainly during the big set-piece battles, but Alfred Watts died in a typical pattern of casualties in an 'active sector' of the front line where the majority of daily casualties were outside the major battle dates. These dead and wounded were mainly the result of artillery fire of some kind – high explosives from howitzers, trench mortars and minenwerfers, and sometimes the quieter 'plop' and hiss from gas shells.

Sniper fire was another constant hazard, not only in the front line, but also for the unlucky in the support area behind the front line trenches. There were many casualties, including deaths, from 'spent' bullets that had passed over the tops of the front line parapets and hissed and spun their way up to a mile behind the line to 'safer' areas.

Another description of life in an 'active' part of the line when

359

no battle was being engaged, and the way casualties were sustained during those times, was discovered by a Mr C.A. Blofield in a letter he found when clearing an old cottage. He said the faint pencilled writing made it almost illegible and he nearly threw it away with other unwanted items. Fortunately he examined it more closely and realised it was a letter from a wounded soldier (another Albert) to two aunts written from somewhere in France in the Great War. Mr Blofield kept the letter and researched the family. The letter and the results of his research were printed in the December 2000 Newsletter of the Dacorum Heritage Trust. Here is the letter:

A.P.O. station 13, France.

My Dear Aunts,

The Boche got me on the 21st and I am at present hung up at the above address. I was sitting in the barn in which we were billeted, quite calm, inoffensive and doing nothing to anybody when along came some of Fritz's heavy shrapnel and whizzbangs, one of which exploded on the top of our billet and sent a piece of something or other down on my napper. Of course, I did not stop long in that barn and got down into the cellar below it and then discovered that my head was bleeding. One of the stretcher bearers in the battalion bandaged me up forthwith and I was bundled off to the dressing station, whence I was motored to another place about four miles away and dressed again. In the afternoon I was whisked off to a clearing station where they put me under gas and examined it thoroughly to see if there was any shrapnel inside. Finding none, they sent me back to the tent and yesterday they put practically all who were there into a train (the Princess Christian Hospital Train by the way), and sent us off to the above address. Do not be anxious over me for I shall soon be all right, as I was always rather lucky. I had just got everything cleaned up ready to go on parade for rifle inspection and I had taken every spot of dust off my rifle and had just sat down for a rest when Fritz thought he would improve the shining hour and the look of our barn by sending us some souvenirs. He sent us some over a eight o'clock the same morning and one of our sergeants got his leg broke and pretty badly scratched all over. My lot came over at 10 o'clock.

We came out of the trenches on Tuesday night and our friend sent us a parting gift by putting a whizzbang on the side of the communication trench just about five yards in front of the leader. I can tell you we did skip past that point, no stopping to consider matters. To go back to Monday, we were out on ration party when our blokes decided to give them some gas. Well we had got our rations: I had got two bags of bread and we were just getting back to our dug-out when the fun began. Heavies, shrapnel, whizzbangs, trench mortars, rifle grenades, bullets and old Harry himself came by,* and to cap the lot, it started to rain. We took what shelter we could and arrived at the dug-out about an hour later than we should have done. In spite of all the gifts our friends over the way had showered on us, not a man was hurt, unless I say an officer who was injured slightly in the heel owing to one of his men displaying excessive haste in going up a trench with his bayonet fixed, but then some people always are in such a hurry. Well as I hope I have made you see by this letter, I am not at all bad in myself and I am very hopeful of the little place healing up all right and being up yonder with my pals again. I do not think I have much more to say at this time and I hope you are quite well. Goodbye and God bless you all at home. Remember me to all.

Your affectionate nephew,
Albert

*Despite suffering from a shortage of artillery and shells at the time, the presence of British artillery units and their activities were not always welcomed by the infantry in the front line because any non requested artillery fire from the Royal Field Artillery invariably brought a retaliatory response from the German artillery directed at the British front line.

Mr Blofield continues:

Sadly Albert's luck didn't hold. At some stage after this letter he was transferred to the 19th Manchester Regiment and was killed at Arras on 23rd April 1917. He has no known grave. Of the five brothers who went to war, two were dead, one so badly shell shocked that he never led a normal life again, and one so badly wounded that he walked with difficulty thereafter.*

*Shades of the Newfoundland Goodyear family mentioned earlier.

The weather around Ypres continued to be miserable in the summer of 1915 adding to the dreariness of life for the troops in the Salient. Norman Ellison,* writing in June 1915, the time Alfred Watts was killed in the line near La Brique, and entrenched a mile or two to the south east, at Zillebeke Lake, near Hill 60, said:

> The battalion found that perhaps one-tenth could find accommodation in the dug-outs, yet cover from the ever threatening rain and, more important, from shell fire was of the utmost urgency. [They were close to 'Shrapnel Corner'] they proceed to dig themselves in and before nightfall were safely tucked away in a series of shallow holes roofed with ground-sheets, sandbags, corrugated iron or whatever could be scrounged at short notice, each holding two or three men.
>
> For nearly two months they were to remain, unrelieved in this cramped and comfortless spot, unbathed, never undressed and from Colonel downwards inexpressibly lousy. The top of the bank was under direct enemy observation from Hill 60, barely a mile distant, and during daylight our sentries kept constant watch for aeroplanes... At night a patrol saw that no chink of light showed from carefully shaded candles.

*Norman Ellison (1893–1976) was a writer, broadcaster and naturalist, and he kept a diary of his war years in Flanders and France where he served with 1/6th (Rifle) Battalion, The Kings Liverpool Regiment. The diary was edited and published in 1997 by David Lewis under the title *Remembrances of Hell*.

Although the battle of Second Ypres was over by the late spring/early summer of 1915, sporadic fighting continued throughout 1915 and 1916 in the Salient until the full-scale battle of Third Ypres in 1917.

'Quiet' sectors

Some areas were regarded almost as rest areas at times, and where and when possible these were the sectors in which new untried units were introduced to the front line. Outside of the actual battles, much depended on the 'live and let live' philosophy of the opposing units. Edmund Blunden says: 'our future in short depended on the observance of the "Live and Let Live" principle, one of the soundest elements in trench war. G.S.O. paints an almost idyllic picture of life in a quiet sector:

Behind the parapet it was almost as safe – and on dry days as pleasant – as on a marine parade. A solid fortification of sandbags, proof against any blow except that of a big high-explosive shell, enclosed on each side with a walk, drained, paved, lined with dug-outs, in places adorned with little flower beds.

PART THIRTY-FIVE

A more unpromising scene for a great offensive battle can hardly be imagined.

Official History France and Belgium, Vol. 2, 1915.

LOOS, the unwanted battle, 25th September–8th October 1915

The French pronounced it as 'Loss' but to the British troops it was always as 'lose' or 'looze'. The battle stemmed from a French call for a substantial British contribution to a further French offensive in 1915. The French planned to attack once again in the Artois and Champagne areas.

A number of proposals had been put forward and rejected for the British participation in this offensive. In cold-blooded terms the required British action was seen by the French CIC, General Joffre, as a subsidiary effort to the main French attacks, and purely for the purpose of containing a large number of German troops who otherwise would be free to counter the French offensive.

Joffre played down the British objections that the terrain he had selected for them was unsuitable for an attacking battle. He told them confidently, and reassuringly, that they would find particularly favourable ground between Loos and La Bassée, but the British, having had to take over the ground from the French troops, thought otherwise. Haig, whose First Army had been allotted the Loos sector, and Rawlinson, Commander of IV Corps, whose front covered the most exposed positions, viewed the prospect of a battle here, and at this time, with gloomy foreboding.

Sir John French too was not happy with the plans, but at the same time he was conscious of the pressure on him to assist the

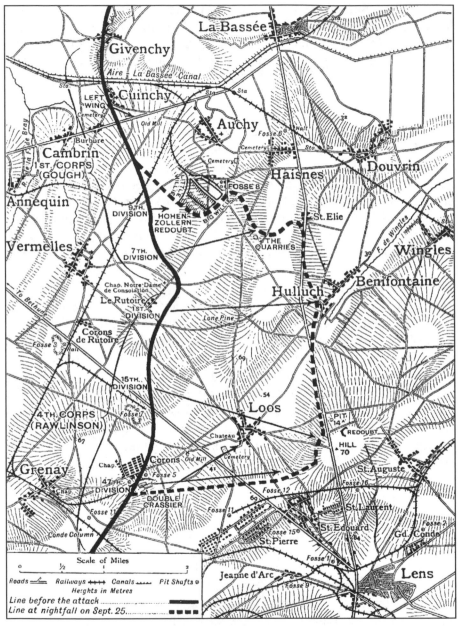

The Main Attack: map showing approximately the battle-lines of the First Army under
Sir Douglas Haig at daybreak and at nightfall on 25th September 1915

366

French forces. Kitchener, it would appear, actively instructed him to support Joffre in this attack, seeming to forget his previous strictures to Sir John to conserve the BEF wherever possible. No doubt too French also remembered his unpleasant task of telling Joffre he could not give him the required support for the original plans for the attack at Neuve Chapelle earlier, and it would be even harder now once again to refuse to help the French troops when called upon to do so.

The lack of artillery and the use of gas

The British troops were still without sufficient artillery pieces and ammunition to be able to nullify the expected response from the Germans when the British attack began. Shrapnel, the main type of shells available, would be ineffective against the German thick barbed wire defences, and so Haig was forced now to consider the use of gas* as the only alternative to the intense preliminary bombardment he wanted but was not able to deliver.

*The code name for gas was 'Accessory No. 1' (see below in the War Diary of the 8th Devons).

Gas had never been used by the British, and apart from any objections to using it on ethical grounds, they had no means of delivering it apart from releasing the gas from cylinders. This method of releasing the gas was untried in the field, and in the event would prove to be ineffective, and as the moment of the attack loomed, the light breeze died away completely, and in some cases even reversed direction back towards the British front line.

The terrain; a recipe for failure

The long gently upward sloping ground without suitable cover for the attacker invited disaster. And, if that wasn't enough, parts of the area were littered with mine workings and slag-heaps. These both hindered the attackers, and at the same time provided observation for the defenders – and, inevitably, the German troops held the high ground, completely overlooking the British positions. Finally, once again, the weather preceding the offensive was awful, and the hard chalk ground was very difficult to dig.

Despite all these contrary indications for success, here again, as at Neuve Chapelle in the early stages, in places the British would actually break through the German line capturing about 8,000 yards of German trenches, and penetrating up to two miles of territory.

47th London (TF) Division

Patrick MacGill, a professional writer before the war, served as a stretcher bearer with 1/18th London Irish Rifles,* part of 141st Brigade, of the 47th London (TF) Division.

*This battalion, formed on 4th August 1914 as part of 5th London Brigade of the 2nd London Division, landed at Havre in March 1915. The formation became part of 47th Division on 11th May 1915.

The brigade consisted of the following elements of the London Regiment: 1/17th (County of London) Battalion (Poplar and Stepney Rifles), 1/18th (County of London) Battalion (London Irish Rifles), 1/19th (County of London) Battalion (St Pancras), 1/20th (County of London) Battalion (Blackheath & Woolwich).

MacGill describes the prelude to the battle and the opening attack in his book *The Great Push* first published in 1917, and mainly written at the scene of the action, with the last chapter written in hospital at Versailles where he was recovering from wounds he received at Loos.

MacGill's battalion had already seen action at Aubers Ridge and Festubert and by the time of Loos could be regarded as seasoned troops. They kicked a rugby football ahead of them as they went over the top, and further to their left were the East Surreys who would imitate them and kick footballs ahead of them on the first day of the Somme the following year.

The Irish Rifles stood next to the French in the line at Loos and prior to the battle of Loos MacGill recounts:

Night after night we went up to the trenches and performed our various duties. Keeps and redoubts were strengthened and four machine guns were placed where one stood before. Always while we worked the artillery on both sides conducted loud voiced argument; concussion shells played havoc with masonry, and shrapnel shells flung their deadly freight on roads where the transports hurried, and where the long-haired mules sweated

368

in their traces of the limbers of war. We spoke of the big work ahead, but up till the evening preceding Saturday, September 25th, we were not aware of the part which we had to play in the forthcoming event.

An hour before dusk our officer read instructions, and outlined the plan of the main attack, which would start at dawn on the following day September 25th, 1915:

'In co-operation with an offensive movement by the French 10th Army on our right, the 1st and 4th army corps were to attack the enemy from a point opposite Bulley-Grenay on the south to the La Bassée Canal on the north. We had dug the assembly trenches on our right opposite Bully-Grenay; that was to be the starting point for 4th Corps – our Corps. Our Division, the 47th London, would lead the attack of the 4th army corps, and the London Irish would be the first in the fight... Five minutes past six our guns would lengthen their range and shell the enemy reserve, and at the same moment our regiment would get clear of the trenches and advance in four lines in extended order with a second's interval between the lines. The advance must be made in silence at a steady pace.

'Stretcher-bearers had to cross with their companies; none of the attacking party must deal with the men who fell out on the way across. A party would be detailed to attend the wounded who fell near the assembly trenches... The attack had been planned with such intelligent foresight that our casualties would be very few. The job before us was quite easy and simple.'

The 47th Division gained all its objectives, but lost 1,200 men in the first phase of the attack.

7th Division

Commanded by Major General Sir Thomas Capper KCMG, CB, DSO (see also the battle of Neuve Chapelle above) this division did not exist before the war as it was formed from three regular battalions still in Britain, plus others brought back from overseas. The division arrived in Bruges on 7th October 1914, and the author, military historian, and later military correspondent for *The Times*, Cyril Falls (see below) regarded the 7th Division as one of the greatest fighting formations Britain ever sent to war.

369

The 7th Division was part of I Corps, together with the 2nd and 9th Divisions, and the 7th Division's area for the battle of Loos was to be the northern part of Hulloch and Cite. A glimpse of the 7th Division at Loos is described in *A Generation Missing* by Carroll Carstairs:

> Soon it began to rain, a thin persistent rain. To make matters worse the 7th Division, relieving the 9th, appeared, coming up the trench meeting the wounded coming down, the congestion became terrible. There was no room for me, and I and my signallers continued laying the wire on top of the trench, although the chances of the wire getting cut or, incidentally, our getting hit was greater. Up the trench I kept pace with the 7th regular Division – jaunty, doughty Cockneys who scoffed with grim but good humoured sarcasm at the failure of Kitchener's volunteers, and who felt a kind of pride that they, the regulars, should have been needed... Poor devils; little did they reckon on the morrow's massacre that awaited them – I think of them still, cocky, and sure, and ready to tackle what they considered was their own professional job.

The 7th Division were away to the left, north of MacGill's 47th Division, and between them were – directly on the left of the 47th – the 15th Division, then the 1st Division, and on their left the 7th Division. (North and to the left of the 7th were the 9th and 2nd Divisions, and on the northern side of the La Bassée canal, at Givenchy were the Indian Corps.)

The opposing trenches lay some 200 to 400 yards away. Principal coal mines were '*fosses*' and auxilliary shafts '*puits*'. Both had winding gear towers rising to an elevation of a hundred feet, and of course were used by the Germans for observation. One structure, a double pit-head, because of a vague resemblance, was given the name of 'Tower Bridge' and this gave the Germans a wonderful observation platform. The small British guns, 18 pounders, made no impression on it, but when it did fall into British hands the German 5.9s made short work of it.

It is here, at Loos, just prior to the opening day of the battle, that my second soldier, Horace Westlake, and his comrades of the 8th Devons, enter my story.

370

8th 'Service' Battalion, The Devonshire Regiment at Loos, September 1915

When the Guards Division was formed, the 8th and 9th Devonshires, members of Kitchener's 'New Army', replaced the Guards Battalions in the 20th Brigade of the 7th Division. The Devons did not arrive in France to join the rest of Brigade until 4th August 1915, so they had only been in France a few weeks before the battle.

The 20th Brigade, under the command of Brigadier-General Hon. J.F. Heburn-Stuart-Forbes-Trefusis, now consisted of 2nd Borders, 2nd Gordons, 1/6th Gordons (TF), and the 8th and 9th Devons (Service) battalions – a mixture of regular, territorial and new army battalions.

Both the 8th and 9th Devonshires were raw inexperienced troops, but they were well led and full of courage and confidence. For the coming battle the 8th Devons were placed opposite the German position of Breslau Trench with the Fritz Redoubt to the right of Breslau as the Devons faced. The latter (Fritz) redoubt was opposite the 2nd Gordons who were to the right of the Devons. The Gordons also faced Gun Trench. To the Devons left were the 1st South Staffs facing a German strongpoint called the Pope's Nose Redoubt. To the left of the 1st South Staffs were the 2nd Royal Warwicks.

The Devons were lucky in that they had these regular battalions on each side of them, and that must have been a comfort to them as they faced the conflict ahead even though, by now, a number of the troops in the regular battalions were draft replacements for the original dead and wounded 1914 regulars and reservists.

The War Diary of the 8th Devons

The diary records that on 23rd September they left their billets at Verquignuel at 6.30 pm for Vermelles ready to go into the trenches at 9.15 pm on 24th:

> 'C' Company were in the new front and headquarters companies in the old front line. The trenches were very muddy and bad to move about in. Captains Roberts and Jordan, Lt. Sheepshanks and 2nd Lieuts. Pepys and Drew were left behind with the transport as reserve of officers.

The diary, for the opening of the battle in the early morning on 25th September, reads as follows:

As soon as our guns started the intensive bombardment the German guns, scenting what was in the wind, replied with heavy and light artillery, and caused some casualties though not many. On the signal being given 'C' 'A' and 'D' companies seemed to all go forward together in one line, this happened probably because 'A' and 'D' companies started too soon. The result was great crowding towards the gaps in the wire, and a consequent increase in casualties, most of which occurred just outside or in the midst of the wire in front of Breslau Trench.

It is more than likely that the gaps in the wire were not caused by the British shelling, but by the Germans deliberately making gaps behind which they would have positioned machine guns lined up ready to rake the attacking troops as they came through. The War Diary continues:

Another result of the excessive speed with which the attack started was that the front three companies seem to have caught up 'Accessory No 1' and casualties occurred from the effects of this.

To have had any chance of success the gas needed a breeze to blow it towards the German trenches. The gas cylinders were turned on at 5.50 am. What little breeze there was proved fitful; on the right sector it drifted slowly over the German lines, on the left it drifted back into the British trenches. The War Diary continues:

During the advance from our own trenches to the Breslau Trench every officer save three was either killed or wounded. Col. Grant shot and killed, Major Carden shot and killed, Captain Kekewich shot through the head and dying soon afterwards. Lt. Windle, Lt. Carver, and Lt. Ashcroft all killed. The first and last named by bullets, and Lt. Carver by a shell and Lt. Dobson apparently killed by 'Accessory No. 1' in the Breslau Trench. Capt. James wounded, shot in the stomach, Capt. Pryn, wounded, shot six times in the ankles and legs. Lt. MacMichael arm broken by a shell, 2nd Lt. Nixon wounded shot in the leg and arm. 2nd Lt. Bridson wounded, shot in the stomach. 2nd Lt. Gracroft taken to hospital suffering from the effects of 'Accessory No. 1'.

As soon as the attack reached the Breslau Trench the few Germans there put up their hands and surrendered. The attackers then bore to the SE and crossed Hulluch Road. No opposition was met with and Gun Trench was reached. The German gunners put up their hands and surrendered and so the battalion captured four field guns. These guns by their overheated state bore witness to the intensity of the German artillery fire. The charge towards the guns was led by Sgt. Northam of 'A' Company, and '8th Devons' was chalked upon them.

It was still only 8 am and the diary continues:

Then the advance proceeded to the cross roads west of Hulluch. The Battalion here was about one hundred strong* in charge of Capt. Gwynn and 2nd Lt. Trott. All the machine guns were gone – two knocked out in the first advance and the other two seem to have been lost on the outskirts of Hulluch owing to a section getting too far forward and getting cut off.

*The battalion strength was now down to about half the strength of a company. The battalion at full strength would have had in the region of 850 men or more.

Here, at the cross roads, the 8th Devons were stopped after that tremendous advance including the capture of four field guns in the face of heavy artillery and machine gun fire. Remember, these were raw troops who had never been in a battle, and who had lost all their officers but three; and out of a battalion strength of something in the region of 900, were at this point at the cross roads down to 100. Back to the War Diary:

No advance from these cross roads was possible during the day for two reasons: (I) at first the artillery was still firing just beyond our position and (II) no troops came up to reinforce.*

*See my comments below concerning the whereabouts and what had happened to the reserve troops.

So the battalion dug in just west of road with their right on the cross road. The 2nd Gordons were on the right and no one at all on the left. At this place Sgt Northam mentioned above was killed by a sniper. [He was the man above who led the charge to capture the field guns.] At this time there seems to have been very few of the enemy in *Hulluch or Cité St Elie and lack of support alone kept the German line unbroken* [my italics].

All day this position was held and at 6.15 pm ration parties started off to draw rations at cross roads Chappelle Nr. Dame de Consolation. At about 9.30 pm the enemy coming from Cite St Elie got behind our position in estimated strength of a company, [200 men or so] and the first known of this was the interception of the ration parties. A retirement was then made to Gun Trench in the course of which many losses were sustained owing partly to rifle fire and bombing by the enemy, and partly due to rifle and machine gun fire from the Bedfords in Gun Trench who in the dark mistook friend from foe. [See comments on 'friendly fire' elsewhere.]

The circumstances stated so calmly in the War Diary, can barely be imagined now. The Devons having advanced so far, and waiting for the reinforcement by the reserves that never arrived, found themselves counter-attacked by a heavier force. And with darkness descending they retired back to their earlier advanced position only to be met with heavy fire in their rear from British troops (the Bedfords of the 21st Brigade who obviously had no idea of the Devons' whereabouts and in the poor light mistook them for the enemy counter-attacking).

Back to the diary again:

Here Capt. Gwynn and 2nd Lt. Trott who had led so gallantly during the day were both wounded, and CSM Bryant who had prevented panic setting in was stunned by a German bomb when attempting to rescue Sgt. Hansford who got cut off in retirement. The remnants of the battalion occupied Gun Trench and there dug themselves in finding the 2nd Borders on their left on Hulluch Road, and 6th Gordons on the right. Mixed up in the battalion were many of the 9th Devons and a few other units. There was no more infantry action during the night.

374

During the course of the evening R.Q.M.S. Davey* was on the Hulluch Road with ration wagons about half a mile from the firing line when he met some men of another unit flying in disorder. Borrowing a rifle and bayonet he rallied them; led them back to the firing line and stayed there until the arrival of a staff officer.

*For this action he was awarded the French Médaille Militaire.

Sept 26th. During the night Gun Trench was improved and by daybreak it afforded sufficient protection from rifle fire.*

*One must remember this trench was a captured German one, and would have been facing the wrong way for the British troops now holding it.

The position was now as follows: from Hulluch Road to two hundred yards south were the 2nd Borders about 250 strong, then a mixture of 9th and 8th Devons, the latter about 50 strong with no officers, and on the right were 1/6th Gordons.

At about 530 am the reserve officers Capt. Roberts, Capt. Jordon, Lt. Sheepshanks, 2nd Lt. Drew and 2nd Lt. Pepys joined the battalion in the trench. Captain Roberts took command. The rest of the day was passed in the trench as verbal orders were received from Brigade about 8 am to hold on. There was no infantry action: the German guns were active but did not shell us at all. Very likely they did not know where we were. There was a little sniping, but most disconcerting was the unaimed fire and stray bullets coming from the direction of *Foss 8*, which was practically 'reverse fire'. Owing to this one man was shot through the back of the head and killed.

Our guns were very busy shelling Cite St Ellie and *Puits 13*, and this was a pleasant spectacle. We were relieved by 2nd Royal Scots Fusiliers, [from 21st Brigade] at 10 pm and received orders to occupy Curley Crescent. Found this occupied by 2nd Gordons and reported this to S.C. who told us to get in where we could. Eventually got into the old support line with right on Hulluch Road and left on Chappel Alley.

Sept. 27th, 28th and 29th. Restored organisation as far as possible. *Battalion now 130 strong* [my italics] as many stragglers came in and about 50 men had spent yesterday in trench north of road. Spent three very uncomfortable days: all ranks very tired and very dirty and weather was very bad. There was continuous fighting for *Foss 8* and also below the Loos ridge, the first of which could be plainly seen. German artillery was very active indeed, and they had got up some of their bigger guns.

At 7 pm on 29th September [orders] to billets but these immediately cancelled by an order 'to stand to arms and be ready to move at once'. Then verbal orders we were to move up to the front line and ready to attack to the north as Hohenzollern Redoubt had been retaken. So moved up to New Front Line.

Again one can barely imagine how this remnant of the 8th Devons must have felt. They had had no rest since 23rd September – if they got any then. The weather was vile, they had advanced into a murderous barrage of fire at dawn on the 25th, caught by their own gas and cut to pieces by shell and machine-gun bullets. Undeterred they had advanced and captured enemy troops, trenches and field guns. Held up awaiting reinforcements that never came, they were counter-attacked by outflanking enemy troops, and as they withdrew they were fired on by another British unit and suffered more casualties. They were then set to work all night consolidating their new previously captured trench, and stuck it out still without rest and probably with little or no food or drink. Finally, six days after their dawn attack on the 25th, getting the word they were to be withdrawn and rested, and no doubt overwhelmed with relief at the prospect, they were immediately told no; instead they were going to sent back in the line again to advance in another attack against an enemy who had now fully recovered, and who had brought up reserves of fresh troops and artillery.

Then, and I can imagine barely daring to believe their ears, they were told that it was a mistake, and they were to march back to Beuvry, where they arrived about 2 am.

The final comment in the diary reads:

Draft of 50 men arrived on September 28th and these men very tired and could hardly march the distance, but all ranks the same.

The reserves

This time, at Loos, there *were* reserves available, but the tragedy lay in that they were held too far at the rear. These troops, as they moved up from their distant reserve lines, were hopelessly delayed by massive traffic congestions, and their guides losing the way in the dark. Marching all night, without food and water, the 'fresh' reserves arrived 24 hours late; hungry, thirsty, and exhausted. They were too late to reach the forward positions in time to take over the offensive from the tired, terribly depleted, attacking first wave (among whom were the Devons); and as a result the Germans were able to re-form and counter-attack.

The reserve divisions selected for this vital part of the battle were completely inexperienced, untried and newly arrived in France – men of 'Kitchener's New Army', the 21st and 24th Divisions. Later, to strengthen these divisions with seasoned troops, regular battalions were inserted, and. among those were the 3rd Rifles, transferred from the 6th Division to the 24th Division in October 1915 following the battle of Loos.

Summing up

The result was that the Germans, as at Neuve Chapelle, although surprised and in places overwhelmed by the initial British breakthrough, were now, thanks to the delay in the arrival of the British reserves, able to rally and counter-attack, and when the British reserves finally arrived at the front – in chaos and bewilderment – they staggered forward into a deadly barrage of hissing machine-gun bullets and screaming exploding shells.

Exact battle casualty figures are almost impossible to confirm. The generally accepted figures are that the British losses were in the region of 60,000, and most of these in the first twenty-four hours. The Germans about 20,000, and the French, in their two sectors, in line with their reckless expenditure of men, some 143,000 in the Champagne area and 48,000 in the Artois area.

Philip Warner in *The Battle of Loos* says the riflemen went into action carrying 200 rounds of rifle ammunition, 3 sandbags, an iron ration and an extra ration of cheese.

As always there were mixed fortunes, and other regiments suffered equally badly in different parts of the line. But here for a while I shall leave those exhausted and decimated 8th Devons. I hope they were able to rest in their billets. Horace Westlake, like so many of his comrades that September, never made it to the billets at Beuvry or anywhere else. As they went over at 6.30 am 'Zero Hour' there were many casualties right away. The Germans manning the parapet at Breslau Trench were firing into the advancing Devons with rifles, machine-guns and with artillery supporting.

Unluckily the 22nd Brigade on the left had come across much uncut wire, particularly about the Pope's Nose, just north of the Slit; and neither the South Staffs nor the Royal Warwickshires could force their way in. The Borderers were diverted to assist the 22nd Brigade by bombing along the German trenches from the flank, and the Devons pushing forward lacked the support they might have had, and it is more than likely Horace was killed in this opening phase of the battle like his colonel and most of the officers, and so many of his comrades.

At any rate, some time during the day, after the whistles sounded, and they climbed out and went 'over the top' into No Man's Land on 25th September, soon after dawn, twenty year old Horace was killed. No trace of him was ever found, and he now exists, as I said earlier, only as a name, inscribed on a tablet on panel 35 to 37 at the Loos Memorial, Pas de Calais, France.

One officer sent out as a replacement to the 8th Devons, just after they were pulled out of the line, said he was given command of No. 1 Platoon, 'A' Company. The platoon consisted of a sergeant and three men.

The official History of the Devonshire Regiment in the Great War is quoted as giving the casualty figures for the 8th Devons at Loos as 19 officers and 620 men.

The Loos memorial

There are lots of names on the memorial panels that commemorate 20,000 officers and men. The panels stand at the side and back of what was then known as 'Dud Corner' Cemetery, on the site of a

German strong point – The Lens Road Redoubt, captured by 15th Scottish Division on 25th September 1915.

Those 20,000 names are the names of those who have no grave. The panelled wall is about 15 feet high, and behind this wall are four small circular courts, open to the sky where the lines of tablets are continued. Between these courts are three semicircular walls or apses, two of which carry tablets, while on the centre apse is erected the Cross of Sacrifice.

In this cemetery, of which the Memorial panels form a part, in addition to the 20,000 names on the panels there are the identified graves of 1,700 officers and men, nearly all of whom fell at the battle of Loos.

The commander of the 7th Division, Major-General Capper, also died at Loos, shot through the lungs, he died in number 6 Casualty Clearing Station the following day. He lies in Lilliers Communal Cemetery.

A description of the event is quoted in *Bloody Red Tabs* by Davis and Maddocks, from a letter written by Captain E.P. Bennett, VC, MC in May 1926:

Suddenly we were faced with the German front line trench. Far too wide to get across, and we had to drop into it. Colonel Lambton [CO 2nd Worcesters, Bennett's battalion] sorted us out into companies and again gave the advance. Unfortunately, the trench was very deep and there were few places where we could get out. The result was the battalion streamed by as best it could. The rifle fire was hot and we were coming over, necessarily, in small numbers at a time as I ran across I overtook General Capper running with our men. He was actually joining in the assault. He must have been shot almost immediately as I did not see him again.

The departure of Sir John French

It has been said that a lot of lessons were learned at Loos. Sir John French was sent home, blamed for keeping the reserve troops too far back and under his control instead of giving them to Haig, his 1st Army commander. Haig got French's job, and French ever after regarded Haig with enmity.

Haig's first big battle induction as Commander In Chief of the British Expeditionary Force would come next year. A battle with a name that still send shivers through British military history; the 'battle of the Somme'.

Elsewhere in 1915

1/5th Battalion Duke of Cornwall's Light Infantry

The battalion moved to Newquay and Falmouth for training during 1915, and it was here they were converted to a Pioneer Battalion.

The 1/1st Kent Battalion

The second battalion of the Kent Cyclists, formed in 1914, took over the coastal patrols of the original 1st Battalion when the 1st Battalion was readied for overseas service. The 1st Battalion now became the 1/1st Battalion and the 2nd Battalion the 2/1st Battalion.

At Chiseldon Camp, on the Marlborough Downs in Wiltshire, in November 1915, the 1/1st Battalion had its bicycles removed and was re-formed as non-cycling infantry.

Rumour and excitement ran high as the battalion wondered to which theatre of war it would be sent as they were now joined by three other former cyclist battalions to form a brigade: the 1/25th London Regiment, the 2/6th Royal Sussex Regiment and the 1/9th Hampshire Regiment.

The harsh autumn and winter weather made Chiseldon a bleak sea of mud, and the Kents suffered in the conditions along with the other Territorial and K1 and K2 units training all over the country. However, they were fit and young, and still keen and not discouraged.

Soon after arrival at Chiseldon the 1/1st Kents together with the rest of the new brigade were inspected by a general who, my father told me, did not seem over impressed by them. The battalion, like the others, up to that time had not been together as a battalion to train as normal infantry because they had spent all their time bicycling on coastal watch and patrolling duties, and in consequence experienced little or no formal infantry training.

The inspecting general decided the brigade was not ready for overseas frontline duties, and instead it was given intensive training.

380

This included long route marches carrying a full pack, using portable cookers to prepare hot meals on the road, taking over and leaving at night the vast network of trenches dug in the chalk of the Marlborough Downs, and field firing exercises on the ranges.

As a matter of interest, Philip Warner records in his book *The Battle of Loos* that there was one member of the 1/1st Kents on the Western Front in 1915, and he had taken part in the battle of Loos.

This was a Mr A.B. Swaine, a member of the Kent Cyclist Battalion pre-war who in October 1914, when the Army Cyclist Corps was formed, did a temporary transfer for three years into the regular army. He, together with about 100 others drawn from various Cyclist Territorial units, gathered at the White City in London, re-fitted and were despatched to France in mid November 1914. Arriving at Hazelbrook [*sic*] (Hazebrouck?) they joined a number of regular troops from different units, and were divided into companies of cyclists, with one company being attached to a division. Mr Swaine was sent to the First Division where except for about a dozen 'Transferred Territorials' all his fellow cyclists were regulars. He was erroneously reported missing and killed at Loos after he crashed his cycle into a shell hole while he was suffering the effects of gas.

In 1917 he was returned to England and commissioned into the Buffs (the East Kents). Strangely enough he then spent the rest of the war on the North West Frontier where his old regiment, the Kent Cyclist Battalion, were serving! He does not say in his letter to Philip Warner whether he met up with them or not.

Exit 2/DCLI and 4/Rifles

On 27th November 1915, both the 2nd Battalion DCLI and 4th Battalion The Rifle Brigade, as part of the brigades despatched so reluctantly by Sir William Robertson for Salonika, embarked at Marseille, and so to the sickness of malaria and other illnesses that decimated the troops in that theatre of war.

Christmas 1915

There was no general reintroduction of the unofficial fairly widespread truce of 1914. The commands of both sides were anxious to see it did not happen again, but I have seen two written accounts of a local 'truce' at Christmas 1915. *The Times* obituary column of Saturday 28th July 2001, recording the death of one of the last of the 'Great War' veterans says:

As a private soldier in the Royal Welch Fusiliers in northern France in 1915, Bertie Felstead was a participant in one of the strangest episodes of the First World War – the second 'Christmas Truce' between the warring sides.

This was the last of such spontaneous effusions of goodwill, and though not as extensively observed as that of 1914, December 25th 1915, did, nevertheless, witness scenes of extraordinary fraternisation between enemies who had by then been locked in battle for more than 15 months.

It began on Christmas Eve at Leventie to the west of Lille, where 15th battalion Royal Welch Fusiliers was holding the line. As the night drew on, sounds of merrymaking and singing were heard from the German trenches. Shouts of 'Merry Christmas Tommy' were answered from the British trenches with 'Merry Christmas Fritz', and then the Germans did their foes the courtesy of singing All through the Night. The Welshman replied with Good King Wencelas and followed this up with a selection of other carols from their well-stocked male-voice choir repertoire.

Then, as dawn came, in the words of Felstead seventy years later: 'Human nature being what it is, feelings built up overnight and so both sides got up from their front line trenches to meet halfway in No Man's Land'.

Arming themselves with pieces of sausage, tinned coffee, sauerkraut and cigars, the German 'field greys' of the Bavarian reserve infantry regiment opposite surged from their trenches to meet the khaki-clad opponents at the small willow-lined stream which wended its way through the middle of 'No Man's Land'. There, they exchanged their produce for cigarettes, tobacco, bully beef and biscuits, brought out from their lines by The Royal Welch Fusiliers.

382

This barter having taken place, the peaceable spirit became infectious. Mingling in a haphazard throng, men slapped each other on the back, pumped each other's arms with handshakes, kicked a ball about and wished each other the best of the season in a mixture of English, French and German. It was universally agreed that the war was 'no bon'.

'Of course, we realised that we were in the most extraordinary position, wishing each other Happy Christmas one day and shooting at each other the next,' recalled Felstead, 'and we sheltered each other. No one would shoot at us while we were all mixed up.

This strange truce was not permitted to last long. After less than half an hour a staff officer accompanied by a sergeant major appeared yelling 'You came here to fight the Huns, not to make friends with them.' The Welsh infantry reluctantly returned to their lines, upon which the British 18-pounders loosed off a salvo at the German trenches.

Albert Felstead was born in Hertfordshire in 1894, and in January 1915 volunteered for The Royal Welch Fusiliers, with whom he was to serve on the Western Front and in the Balkans. In 1916 he fought in the Battle of the Somme, receiving a 'blighty' wound which put him hospital for a period. He took part in the campaign in Salonika before being finally invalided home with malaria in 1917. He died on 22nd July, 2001, aged 106.

There is another independent account of this same episode quoted in *Anthology Armageddon* from *Up at Mamentz* by Llewellyn Wyn Griffith, who describes the enforced ending thus:

An irate Brigadier came spluttering up to the line, thundering hard, throwing a 'court martial' into every other sentence, ordering an extra dose of militant action that night, and breathing fury everywhere.

Wilfrid Ewart also witnessed this last Christmas meeting of the two sides. Serving with the 2nd Scots Guards, he recorded the events of that Christmas morning of 1915 as follows:

Between the irregular lines of the trenches, with their jumbled white sandbags and untidy earth parapets, is a stream marked by a line of twisted brown willows bent to every conceivable grotesque shape. The stream runs down the middle of No Man's Land, which is itself a place of coarse grasses hiding little mouldering heaps of grey and khaki – the slain of Festubert, of Neuve Chapelle, and late September (heaps of old clothes or fallen scarecrows, they look like), of knobs and unexpected pits, of earthy holes and water-logged ditches. And here our men meet the Germans.

So soon as it grows light this morning, we start peeping at each other over the top of the parapet ... calling across to each other. And presently, at about 7.50, a German stands up openly on the parapet and waves his arms. He is followed by two in field-grey overcoats and pill-box caps. Then they come out all down the line, stand on the parapet, wave, shout, and finally swarm forth from their trenches on either side.

A British sergeant is shot dead almost at the outset, as he stands on the parapet. But this makes no difference. It must be an accident. The supreme craving of humanity, the irresistible, spontaneous impulse born of a common faith and a common fear, fully triumph.

And so the grey and the khaki figures surge towards each other as one man. The movement has started on the right. It spreads like contagion. Only we officers, the sentries, and a few non-commissioned officers remain in our trench. The men meet at the willow-lined stream; they even cross it and mingle together in a haphazard throng. They talk and gesticulate, and shake hands over and over again. They pat each other on the shoulder and laugh like schoolboys, and leap across the little stream for fun. And when an Englishman falls in and a Bosche helps him out there is a shout of laughter that echos back to the trenches.

The Germans exchange cigars and pieces of sausages, and *sauerkraut* and concentrated coffee for cigarettes, and bully-beef and ration biscuits and tobacco. They express mutual admiration by pointing and signs... We shout 'Hullo Fritz!' 'Good morning Fritz!' 'Merry Christmas Fritz!' 'How's your father' 'Come over and call!' 'Come and have breakfast', and the like amid roars of laughter... So for ten brief – all too brief – minutes there is peace and goodwill among the trenches on Christmas Day... Two officers from the Ninety-fifth Bavarian Reserve Infantry Regiment in black accoutrements and shiny field-boots come out and say 'You will have five minutes to get back to your trenches before our artillery will open fire'. And it does... A common brotherhood of suffering – or is it an act of God, or just human curiosity? – has united Englishman and Bavarian in fraternity on the battlefield this grey Christmas morning which no one on either side who has taken part in this quaint scene will ever forget.

The year ends

At the very end of 1915, General Sir William Robertson, now CIGS, was appalled by what he found at the War Office, and in the Government, and grimly set about trying to put things right, as he saw it. On 31st December 1915, reports David Woodward, Robertson, now just installed as Chief of Imperial General Staff, in London wrote to the new Commander of the BEF in France, General Sir Douglas Haig:

PRIVATE   War Office.

I have gravely neglected you but I have been very busy. I have spent nearly two hours discussing with K [Kitchener] the Command in Egypt. Result today is that he has gone to the Prime Minister proposing 2 Commanders and taken my written protests. What will be the outcome I do not know, K says he will resign if his proposal is not adopted... I am just sending a War Office letter telling you what big guns you may expect to get in the next 3 months. L George has also promised to tell me our prospects as regards ammunition. You should economise 6 inch Howitzer ammunition and you ought to send home at once any of those Howitzers requiring repair. He tells me he can repair them in 2 months.

I hope to tell you soon what you may expect in the way of New Divisions and 2nd line Territorial Force Divisions. It is a difficult problem to solve. One division wants men; another rifles, another breeches etc. Therefore it is not easy to say which will be ready first or when. I am kept hard at it by many matters which ought to have been settled months ago. There is a dreadful need of superior control of the war and our money though plentiful has its limits. There has been no coordination of the different departments. K has been working up to 70 Divisions. L.George has ordered material for 100 Divisions. The Chancellor of the Exchequer did not till yesterday know of either of these things! Now he says the money will not run to it and I do not think it will. Clearly he cannot do impossibilities and the Government must decide what force they will maintain. There is great waste going on. The want of a military plan has led to a very great expense in sea transport for instance. No less than 17 fat mounted Brigades have for long been allotted to Home Defence. Although more than 100,000 men are on the Home Defence order of battle. Of course they are not nearly all efficient, but they count as men. In many ways we are using our resources in the worst possible way. We have heaps of men as it is, but there is no intelligent plan for using them. What I am now aiming at is to find what number of men we can raise and pay for, then what we need for Home Defence; then the remainder will be for you I hope. I wish we could get away from Salonika but so far the French hold us there. Rub this in every time you see Joffre.

I am doing all right on the War Committee but it is difficult to keep one's temper. At the last meeting Balfour weighed in with a proposal that as the Western Front was so strong we should transfer all possible troops to co-operate with Russia on the Eastern Front! Words failed me and I lost my temper.

James Cameron's view of 1915 – written from his own perspective in 1962 – was that it was not the 'shell scandal' that brought down the Liberal Government of Asquith, but the furious dissent in the Admiralty between the First Lord, Winston Churchill, and the First Sea Lord. Admiral Fisher. He claims their actions forced into existence a coalition government, and they departed from the scene. He adds:

For a year past [the year of 1915] Britain had conducted a war through an Administration torn with conflicting aims – A War Minister bent on a decision on the Western Front, A First

Lord seeking victory in the Dardanelles and Constantinople, a Colonial Secretary occupied with East Africa, a Secretary for India conducting his own private campaign in Mesopotamia, a Chancellor of the Exchequer anxious to divert attention to the Balkans, a Prime Minister who wanted – no one could determine what, unless it was a quiet life.

And for good measure:

Sir John French, The C.-in-C., had himself just had gone out with the tide as the old year ended – Haig had at last contrived to unseat him, after a calculated campaign of undermining... Haig, the impeccable, experienced, distinguished, ambitious, unscrupulous, insensitive and cunning country laird and professional soldier, valiant in war and resourceful in private life, became Commander in Chief of the British Armies in France.

And should our allies should feel smug about our shortcomings, Cameron throws in:

The Czarist lords of Imperial Russia – where Falkenhayn's breakthrough had already cost 2,000,000 men – observed the disintegration of their enormous Armies and knew, rightly that nothing could follow defeat but revolution. Italy had just been persuaded to join the War by the offer of rich prizes at the expense of Austria-Hungary ... Serbia ... was already scattered in defeat.

PART THIRTY-SIX

Virtually all Europe was locked in a tangle of dimensions unprecedented in any sort of experience. More than that it was becoming terribly clear that nothing whatever – no sudden victory, no one-sided disintegration or defeat – could extricate the continent from this murderous deadlock; there was no conceivable end but the grinding process of attrition, for how long no one could tell.

James Cameron, *1916 Year of Decision.*

1916

Britain

1915 had been a depressing year for the British and French, and 1916 was not going to be any better. Much of the attention at home in political circles in early 1916 was given to the advisability, practicality, and the cost, of introducing some form of conscription.

Despite the greatly increased number in the two armed services (if the Indian and Dominion troops were included the number was in the region of five million men) still more men were needed. On 4th January Lord Derby reported that out of some five million men of military age not already in the forces, over half had offered themselves for enlistment or attestation. The remainder, including some 650,000 single men unattested and unstarred, justified the action of compulsion.

Mr W.M. Hughes, the hard of hearing Australian Prime Minister, was in London complaining about the mismanagement of manpower, and at the same time he wanted to know why Australia had not been asked to do more.

Following the death of Kitchener, the big question was who would replace him as Secretary of State for War. Lord Lansdowne, a one-time Foreign Secretary earlier in the century, now in the current Coalition Government as Minister Without Portfolio, took a very gloomy view in November 1916. He saw the only way out of the intolerable impasse was a negotiated peace. Among the points he made, he said:

> The financial burden which we have already accumulated is almost incalculable. We are adding to it at the rate of over £5,000,000 per day. Generations will have to come and go before the country recovers from the loss which it has sustained in human beings and from the financial ruin and the destruction of the means of production which are taking place.

Mainly though, for the people at home, the year would be remembered as the year which saw the death of Lord Kitchener, the only major sea-battle of the war, and most of all, 1916 would be remembered as the year of the battle of the Somme.

France

There was also an air of pessimism in certain quarters of French government circles. Monsieur Thomas, the French Minister of Munitions, was unhappy about the state of the Russian war machine, and said in a letter to Lloyd George:

> if that unhappy country [Russia] had the least notion of what organisation means the results would be nearly as great and the output as important as in France at the present time.

He expresses other concerns; the old familiar feeling, spoken or unspoken, about the commitment or lack of it from Britain:

> Our people think that the British are in a state of inaction, that they are accumulating enormous forces, but the efficiency of them has not been tested. Not much would be needed to undermine French confidence in British co-operation now.

For the French, the most remembered feature of 1916 would be

390

the battle of Verdun. This would prove to be the longest and most costly battle in terms of casualties for the French. It began on 21st February, and lasted until 18th December 1916, and would see the downfall of both the French and the German commanders – Generals Joffre and Falkenhayn.*

*As always, stated casualty figures vary, but it is I think generally accepted that the combined casualties for both sides reached over 700,000.

The fortunes of my regiments in 1916

1st Devonshires and 1st DCLI

Following the decision at the end of 1915 to transfer some of the seasoned battalions of the regular army to the New Army, there were changes in the 5th Division. One of these changes, on 12th January 1916, saw the 1st Devons, and 1st DCLI, no longer being part of the 14th Brigade, but becoming members of the 95th Brigade, in 5th Division. As a result of this change they would be sent to Italy in 1917 as one of the divisions reluctantly released by Haig to assist the Italians (see above).

1/1st Battalion Kents

Perhaps Robertson's sorting out at the War Office was beginning to have an effect because at Chiseldon the word came at long last, the Kents, with the rest of their brigade, were to embark for overseas – for East Africa, and some kit was issued marked '4th East African Brigade'.

Then, in the best army tradition, this order was cancelled and the kit withdrawn. Next the word was 'Egypt' then 'France'. Finally it was definite, they really *were* going somewhere at last. And here the gods of fortune and war smiled on the brigade, for the brigade was bound, not for France – and slaughter to come on the Somme – but now, numbered as the 44th Infantry Brigade, for India, where they were to relieve a regular army brigade who were destined for the campaign in Mesopotamia and the horrors that would await them there.

The major part of the territorial brigade, 1/25th London Regiment, 2/6th Royal Sussex Regiment and 1/9th Hampshires, sailed from

Devonport aboard the White Star liner *Ceramic* after taking train from Chiseldon between 1st and 3rd of February 1916. The Kents followed and sailed from Devonport aboard the P&O Branch Line ship *Benella* on 8th February. Sailing via Suez the Kents arrived at Bombay on 2nd March, 1916.

Cyril Bristow in his history of the Kents, *The Kent Cyclist Battalion*, relates that the brigade was sent to Bangalore in Southern India for further training where it became a unit of the 9th (Secunderabad) Division of the Indian army. Conditions were pleasant at Bangalore, the climate was a reasonable one with a mean temperature of 76 degrees Fahrenheit, and the rainy season was confined mainly to the months of October and November. Parties of platoon strength enjoyed various excursions as they became acclimatised.

The Kents however would discover that for the troops who were not sent away to the hills at the end of March, the heat on the plains would become so intense as to be unbearable. The day-time temperatures in the cantonments stayed between 116 and 120 degrees Fahrenheit or more, and even at midnight temperatures of 109 degrees were not unusual. In these conditions parades were discontinued between seven thirty in the morning and sunset apart from a short parade before breakfast and an occasional one after sunset. Life was, or would be, very different in Europe for my other battalions in 1916.

The 1/5th Duke of Cornwall's Light Infantry (TF) in 1916

In April 1916, the Cornishmen, now transformed into a pioneer battalion, found themselves attached to the 61st (2/South Midland) Division at Tidworth preparing to go to France, and this seems an appropriate point to explain and define the pioneers.

Pioneer battalions

The concept of the pioneer battalions was a very good one, for although infantry battalions for some years had their own pioneer sections, with the onset of trench warfare at the end of 1914 the opposing forces were compelled to throw up defences as a protection against incoming artillery shells, machine gun and sniper rifle fire, as well as possible assaults by attacking infantry. But neither the

392

infantry nor the Royal Engineers could cope adequately with all these extra tasks in addition to their normal and already increasing onerous duties.

As General Sir Hugh Beach said in the Foreword to K.W. Mitchinson's book *Pioneer Battalions in the Great War* there was a huge demand for manpower with a basic training as infantry, but with special skills and aptitude for earthwork. Hence the idea of special 'pioneer' troops of battalion strength. Ideally fifty per cent of a pioneer battalion was expected to be men used to working with a pick and shovel, the other half to possess recognised artisan trades.

Their formation

In December 1914 the War Office announced a decision to create and post a pioneer battalion to each division of the new armies then forming in Britain. Pioneer battalions were to be strong numerically – 24 officers and 860 men being a typical establishment.

In practice the day to day work of the pioneers concentrated on the 'domestic chores' of trench life, shoring, revetting, building dugouts, overhead cover and shell-proofing. In addition they were sapping, mining, building trackways for men and animals, guns and vehicles. They also engaged in tunnelling and the rendering habitable of flooded shell holes in seas of mud.

They were to work for the most part in detachments, responding to the instructions of the Commanders of the Royal Engineers of each Division. The pioneers' special skills were recognised by a rate of pay of 2d a day more than their infantry equivalents, but substantially less than the Royal Engineers. They were supposed to receive special training, but not all did.

In addition to building protective breastworks, trenches dugouts and communication trenches, the pioneers made new roads, felled trees, and constructed bridges. Additional camps had to be built, gun emplacements laid, wire obstacles placed, railway embankments constructed and extra tracks laid.

Selection

The selection of a battalion as a pioneer unit seems to have been somewhat arbitrary to say the least. Battalions were given no choice as to whether they wanted to become pioneers or not. It was possible however, sometimes, to exchange into another battalion, particularly if the nominated pioneer battalion was short of the skills required, so the vacated pioneer places could then be filled by other men who had the necessary skills and experience needed.

At any time from their formation the pioneers could be called upon to drop their picks and shovels and grab their rifles to fight as ordinary infantrymen, and they often were.

General Beach continues by saying that although living conditions and the incidence of casualties were less severe in pioneer battalions than in normal infantry battalions, they were at times horrific enough. In 1918 a pioneer battalion fighting on the front line sustained 50% casualties in one week and was awarded one VC, one DSO, four MCs, one DCM, and nine MMs.

The 1/5/DCLI were selected as pioneers because many of its members were used to manual work – Cornwall of course was famous for its clay works and tin mines; many other pioneer battalions had large contingents of coal miners.

The pioneers of all divisions in the 'New Army' when they arrived in France in 1916 had to acclimatise to new surroundings, and the excitement of being overseas. Mitchinson says that 'Route marches were undertaken to harden feet, build esprit or simply to fill time.' Early in 1916 the 9th North Staffs were passed by General Haig's staff car. The men were amazed to see Haig get out of his car and take the salute as the battalion marched past.

The pioneer battalions, or at least some of them – including 1/5 DCLI – unlike most infantry battalions (see 3rd Rifles above), in their war diaries not only record the names and regimental numbers of their casualties, but also note the circumstances in which the men were killed or wounded.

The 1/5 DCLI go to France

As the pioneer battalion of the 61st Division (South Midland), the 1/5th Battalion (TF) Duke of Cornwall's Light Infantry arrived at Le Havre on 22nd May 1916, Here they experienced an outbreak of German measles that resulted in a regular flow of Cornishmen to hospital in June and July.

But soon after their arrival in the Laventie area they were seen, as a chronicler wrote, 'working furiously for their comrades of the

61st Division', and that from every part of the Divisional front the 1/5 DCLI would be seen like ants for ever busy in repairing, constructing and carrying.

Difference between the pioneers and the Labour Corps

The pioneer battalions of the infantry should not be confused with another body which, in a way, carried out similar duties to the pioneer battalions, but these were not expected – at least officially when they were created – to be in the line of fire, and not to fight as infantry as were the pioneers. This body was the Labour Corps.

The Labour Corps

Created in 1916, as a result of shortage of man-power, the Labour Corps consisted of men who were unfit for actual duty in the line, and who would carry out what were loosely described as 'garrison duties' in the back areas, thus releasing fighting troops.

Roger Pocock, author of *Chorus to Adventurers*, commanded a Labour Company in France. He says:

> For young and able-bodied men it was their right to serve in the fighting line, but for us of the Labour Corps, the aged, the disabled, the wreckage of the army and of the nation, it was a privilege to be allowed within the danger areas. The coloured men of the Labour Corps were young, with thrice our strength, but they were not permitted as we were within the range of shells. Almost every man in my five hundred had been disabled, or claimed some mortal disease and gloried in it. We were an amazing mixture of volunteers up to seventy years of age, of conscripts drawn from sedentary life, of Jews from the slums, and gypsies from the highways, roughs, tramps, company directors, public entertainers, pavement artists, navvies, rich, poor, destitute, but all of us rated unfit. Nobody as yet seems to have thought it worthwhile to tell the story of the dregs of England put to the test of war.

Pocock adds that on their arrival in France at Boulogne they did not care much for the 'well decorated base wallahs with no manners' who sent them off to join the Second Army – without apparently informing anyone they were coming. They arrived at their destination after a three mile march to their accommodation to find a barn with snow driving through it driven by a gale, with no fuel, food or blankets. Two men died in the night.

Eventually, after Pocock had ordered two officers to stop and plunder any vehicles for supplies, he tramped through the blizzard to Hazebrouck found a telephone and blistered the ears of the staff officers. Following this event they were soon moved to what he described as the finest camp in Flanders, an evacuated POW camp –evacuated because the German government objected to its nationals being under shell-fire, and threatened reprisals upon British captives.

A medical inspection invalided ten men to Britain, and the rest began their labours of unloading trains, building light railways and mending roads while the shells screamed overhead towards Poperinghe and made the road untidy. Steadily, he said, the invalids gained strength from outdoor living, good food, and moderate labour. They watched processions of German prisoners, to whom they would give all their cigarettes. Interest in the army led to pride in the service, eagerness to help, a sporting rivalry between platoons, and the discovery that the 178th Labour Company was not to be beaten by any sort of unit in the field.

A 1916 naval digression – Jutland

Given the continual striving to maintain pre-eminence in naval matters it is disconcerting to find that in the only large-scale fleet battle of the war – the battle of Jutland in 1916 (31st May – 1st June) although the British navy could claim a psychological victory as the German navy never offered battle again, the engagement revealed important deficiencies in the British navy in terms of signalling, accuracy of gunnery, poor quality shells, range finding, armoured protection and safety design.

Cyril Falls quotes Admiral Beatty who having lost two ships and with his own flaming beneath him, said to his Flag Captain: 'Chatfield, there seems to be something wrong with our bloody ships today. Turn two points to port' [two points nearer to the enemy].

The British losses in vessels at Jutland were three battle cruisers, *Queen Mary*, *Invincible*, *Indefatigable*, three armoured cruisers, *Defence*, *Black Prince*, and *Warrior*, and eight destroyers, *Tipperary*,

Ardent, *Fortune*, *Shark*, *Sparrowhawk*, *Nestor*, *Nomad*, and *Turbulent*. The Germans lost two dreadnaughts including the *Lutzow*, one battleship, one battle cruiser, four light cruisers and five destroyers.*

*The quoted losses in officers and men vary a little according to the source used. One says for the British 6,097 were killed (including two Rear Admirals), and 177 prisoners; the Germans 2,545 killed and no prisoners. James Cameron in *1916 Year of Decision*, gives different figures – British casualties 6,945, German 3,058. John Terraine in *The First World War 1914–1918* gives the figures as British: 6,097 killed, 510 wounded, German: 2,551 killed 507 wounded.

As an aside, armoured protection and safety in design would continue to be a problem for British naval architects in later years also. British capital ships in the Second World War seemed to sink in action, or blow up much more readily than their German counterparts, that on the whole, endured much heavier pounding before succumbing to intensive attack both from the air and sea. Again, in the Falklands War, British type 42 destroyers suffered badly from design faults with toxic and flammable materials being used in the fittings, and it was reported, lack of suitable weapons to deal with the Argentine air missile attacks.

PART THIRTY-SEVEN

I have many times asked myself whether there can be more potent advocates of peace upon earth through the years to come than this massed multitude of silent witnesses to the desolation of war.

> King George V, in 1922, referring to the massed
> war graves of The Great War.

The battles of the Somme, 1st July–18th November 1916

The Somme terrain

The area was really a vast prairie with the waterways of the rivers meandering gently through, and with small villages and extensive farm lands that were of no real strategic value. Unlike Flanders, the Somme region held no Channel ports, no U-boat bases, no rail centres, no large towns and no major roads to provide for the massive transportation of men and supplies necessary for a decisive breakthrough.

For the French the area had long been a quiet sector and the Germans had found plenty of time to consolidate their defences into a number of almost impregnable strong-points, and very deep trenches – as the British would find to their cost. Malcolm Brown describes the area as a 'vast linear fortress constructed by the Germans during the long period of relative quiescence before the battle.'

Why the Somme?

Before the German attack at Verdun, Joffre had wanted a combined

French/British attack to take place in the spring of 1916 astride the Somme. The general consensus as to why he proposed that the battle should take place in this area is that the French wanted the British to be heavily involved in 1916, and the Somme area of Picardy was where the French and British armies came together.

French pressure

However, once the German offensive at Verdun was under way and the French troops committed to the battle in great numbers, the French were not in a position to play a major role in a combined Anglo French attack. In fact, they needed a British army to attack on the Somme in full force to take the pressure off at Verdun, and the French wanted this now a mainly British attack, to take place on 1st July. The British had planned to attack on 29th June.

Political pressure – the Balkan element

Looming in the background too was the likely advent of Roumania into the war, and the demands she was making on the Allies if this event was to come about. Government pressure was increasing on Haig to keep German forces fully engaged on the Western Front to prevent troops being sent to the assistance of her partners in the Balkans – or to strengthen the Eastern Front where the Russians were in trouble.

The Somme area before the offensive

Wilfrid Ewart, having just arrived in the region from the hated Salient around Ypres, described the Somme area in tones of wonder and delight as his battalion of Scots Guards marched towards the battle to take their place in the line some miles ahead:

> What a different country, this, from the flat, closely cultivated small-holdings of Belgium! Rolling hills, crowned with woodland and scored high leafy hedgerows, stretched away into distances infinitely dim and blue. It was God's own country this night. Not less wonderful because of the harvest which, more forward here than further north, was strewn about the hillside fields and valleys in a wealth of stooks and sheaves... Evening stole

on, the rooks rose from the fields and wended their homeward way; from the grey village churches, hidden in combes and clefts, came the sound of bells. In this late summer scene there could be found no jarring note, but as the long, snake-like column [of troops] mounted the last rise one divined a panoramic study of blue and gold untouched, unsullied by a hint of war.

The war correspondent Sir Philip Gibbs wrote of the Somme in 1915, when the countryside, even in the front-line area, was green and still fairly unspoilt because a strange kind of truce existed between the Allies (see 'live and let live' above):

The village of Curlu was actually beyond our Front Line, and was a kind of outpost in No-Man's-Land, within 500 yards or so of another village held by the Germans in advance of their own front line. Between these two villages was a thicket of silver birches and willows, half of which belonged to us and half to the enemy. By tacit understanding on both sides, neither of these villages was shelled.

Our officers – they were Loyal North Lancashires* – used to go to bed every night in their pyjamas. I had a meal with them there, and they told me of this strange truce inherited from the French. They were all for it. One of them took me into the thicket, telling me not to speak or cough. Stealing through the trees, we came on two men dressed in green with green veils over their faces, and green gloves. Beyond them if we had walked a few yards we should have bumped into German sentries. Occasionally there was an exchange of shots in the thicket, and sometimes a real fight, but as a rule there was peace and as a token of pax each side retired behind a wicker gate which was then shut. From the Front line behind I looked into both villages and saw German soldiers moving about in theirs and – fantastically strange! A woman wheeling a perambulator. This state of things lasted until the Battle of the Somme when both villages were blown off the map.

*Formed from an amalgamation of the 47th and 81st Regiments of Foot in 1881.

The battle: Preliminary barrage

After immense preparation the barrage began on 24th June 1916 – the infantry attack was then still planned for the 29th June. The gunners' daily routine began each morning when they fired a concentrated barrage for eighty minutes using every available gun, and for the remainder of the day a continuous, but steadier barrage was fired. The plan was that on the morning of the actual attack, the opening morning period of the barrage would be reduced to sixty-five minutes so the infantry could go across while the Germans were expecting a further fifteen minutes of shelling.

At night half the guns rested, but the barrage was supplemented by heavy machine-gun fire harassing the enemy's rear areas to hinder supplies coming up to the front. Initial reports of the bombardment were encouraging. Great gaps had been found in the wire in the Fricourt salient area, and raiding parties had passed through these on several nights to find portions of the enemy trenches unoccupied. East of the Ancre however observers could see that many of the original belts of barbed wire, some as deep as 40 yards, had remained uncut. North and south of Thiepval the enemy was reported as very vigilant and raiders made no progress against the defences.

Aspects of the preliminary barrage

Most of the heavy batteries the British were using had been loaned by the French. Foch had lent Rawlinson's Fourth Army sixteen 220 mm howitzers, twenty-four 120 mm guns and sixty of the famous quick-firing 75s disposed to shoot gas shells – of which, as yet, the British had none.

This continuous artillery pounding of the enemy lines, while generally giving heart to the British troops (who for so long and so often had been on the receiving end of shelling when their own guns had been strictly rationed in terms of rounds allowed to be fired) also had an adverse effect. The gun barrels became worn and aim unreliable, and as a consequence more 'shorts' fell, resulting in British casualties. And still the ammunition was of poor quality, and we had nowhere near enough heavy calibre guns.

General A.H. Farrar-Hockley (writing in 1964, and at that time a colonel), says in his book *The Somme* that Haig was apparently still worried about the coming attack despite all the preparations and the increase in artillery compared to that available at Loos. There was the vulnerability of the Fricourt salient, and Montauban spur, which he feared were underestimated by the Fourth Army.

For whatever reasons the more worrying aspects of the state of German defences did not seem to have reached Rawlinson. His diary for the night of 30th June 1916 records: 'The artillery work during the bombardment, and the wire cutting has been done well except in VIII Corps, which is somewhat behindhand.'

Farrar Hockley says of Haig at this time:

Haig seems to have been in ignorance of the true picture. He wrote in his diary: '*Friday, June 30*. The weather report is favourable for tomorrow. With God's help, I feel hopeful. The men are in splendid spirits. Several have said that they have never been so instructed and informed of the nature of the operations before them. *The wire has never been so well cut* [my italics], nor the artillery preparation so thorough. I have seen personally all the Corps Commanders and one and all are full of confidence. The only doubt I have is regarding VIII Corps (Hunter-Weston) which has had no experience in fighting in France [having come from Gallipoli] and has not carried out one successful raid.'

Was Rawlinson aware of the problems of uncut wire? Haig himself had issued instructions that the methodical bombardment should be continued until the officers commanding the attacking units were satisfied that the obstacles to their advance had been adequately destroyed. This intelligence could only be delivered to HQ through the chain of command, and it is possible there was on this occasion, as on others, some 'selective editing' before it reached the top. Some commanders had a reputation for being overly pessimistic while others more buoyant and confident in their expressions. Unenthusiastic commanders ran the risk of being sent home ('Stellenbosched', 'degummed').

Richard Holmes, in *The Western Front*, says that while Haig was convinced the wire had been cut, Rawlinson was less confident, as were some of his corps commanders, and yet, according to Holmes again, Rawlinson's Fourth Army HQ specifically warned that:

> All criticism by subordinates ... of orders received from superior authority will, in the end recoil on the head of the critics.

This warning quoted by Holmes has obviously been extracted from a longer passage, and the original context is not clear. But whatever reservations were felt and not uttered, or uttered but not passed on, in the chain of command in the field, it would have taken a very brave/foolhardy man to try to put a hold on 'the big push' at this stage, especially with the increasing calls from the French military for pressure to be taken off them at Verdun, and the political pressure from the British government. A.H. Farrar-Hockley continues:

> It must be regretted that the commander-in-chief had not made searching enquiries into the reason for the failure of 'Hunter-Bunter's' [Hunter-Weston's] command.

The start of the offensive was postponed to 1st July, and this pleased the French as it was the day they wanted originally for the British attack to fit with their own plans.

Could Rawlinson command his army effectively with corps pushing open flanks in different directions and several others moving out into open country? An intermediate HQ at least must be available for the mobile elements. Haig decided this would be called 'HQ Reserve Army', and Gough should be the commander.

The British troops

There were 18 Divisions of which 14 would attack in the first line. Of these, eleven divisions were from Kitchener's Army or the Territorial Force – the volunteers of 1914; with hardly a conscript in the ranks. Churchill described them as:

> A young army, but the finest we have ever marshalled; improvised at the sound of the cannonade, every man a volunteer, inspired not only by love of country but by a widespread conviction

that human freedom was challenged by military and Imperial tyranny.

A differing view comes from an Australian historian, Dr C.E.W. Bean, in *Anzacs to Amiens*, who says of the British:

The Australians never forgot the English Staff [after Pozières] which sent them there, nor their mates killed, nor the New Army Divisions which had failed them so often on their flanks...

General Sir Ivor Maxse* was one of the those who had direct experience of the training of some of the New Divisions, and Malcolm Brown quotes as follows from Maxse's battle report:

The New Divisions can be relied upon to do as well as the old ones provided they understand what is required of them, and they do even better when they are also given reasons for dispositions... We took into our confidence the sixty-four section commanders of all battalions, gave them the *reason* for their positions in our forming up trenches and drilled them to move from their positions direct to their objectives in the enemy lines. Thus all ranks started with some idea of what they were to do, a conviction their pals also knew what to do, and a complete absence of any fear of being left in the lurch by them.

Maxse fought on the Somme at Thiepval and the Schwaben Redoubt, and a view of him in 1916, reported by Martin Stephen in *The Price of Pity*, from *Tales of Old Soldiers* by Tom Quinn, says:

The problem was on both our flanks where the fighting was ferocious. That's where they got the worst of it, and all the time General Maxse – he was only 5ft 6in tall and his equerry was 6ft 3in – watched the battle through his field glasses. I remember he came to see us. 'Good morning gentlemen,' he said. 'Damned good show.'

Maxse, though highly regarded, was not popular with everyone and when he had Sir Thomas Jackson 'degummed' after the failure to

405

take the Schwaben Redoubt, a private soldier, Robert Cude, who was a battalion runner with the 7th Buffs wrote in his diary, as quoted by John Baynes:

> Brigadier General Jackson is relieved of his command and returns to England. For what – being a human man. He will carry with him the well wishes of the whole brigade and we can never forget the man who would wreck his career rather than be a party – however unwilling – to the annihilation of troops under his command. What would the Brigade like to do with General Maxse, the man with a breast full of decorations – not one earned!'

*Sir Ivor Maxse (1862–1958), retired in 1926 having served in the army since he was commissioned into the Royal Fusiliers in 1882. He transferred into the Coldstream Guards in 1891. By all accounts he was an able commander with outstanding talents as a trainer and tactician. He served with the 1st Guards Brigade in 1914 as Commander 1st (Guards) Brigade, and was responsible for the raising and training of the 18th (Eastern) Division. In January 1917 he became GOC XVIII Corps.

Denis Winter quotes Liddell Hart as describing Maxse as:

> Difficult to argue with as he always wants to do all the talking bubbling over with fiery energy. Brilliant surface cleverness. Possibly not very deep but seizes points fast. Red hot enthusiast for efficiency. Likes people who show they are not afraid of him.

John Baynes (*Far From a Donkey*) describes the first meeting between Maxse and the young Brigadier-General Bernard Freyberg VC:

> Maxse's first words to Freyberg after they met were, 'I hate you bloody gallant Brigadier-Generals – what the devil do you know about training men?' Maxse had a disagreeable technique for imposing his will, but militarily he was extremely able, and the well trained New Zealand Division of the Second World War owed much of its excellence to the methods devised by General Maxse and taught to Freyberg in 1917.

Early in the evening on 28th June, the officers of the 9th Kings Own Yorkshire Light Infantry were called to their battalion HQ for a last drink before the 'Big Push', and Lt. Lancelot Dykes Spicer sent his parents an account of the gathering – reported by Alex Danchev in *Alchemist of War*, and in Malcolm Brown's *Imperial War Museum Book of The Somme*:

> We assembled, glasses were put into our hands, drinks were passed around and we drank quietly to one another – everyone was naturally feeling strained. The Adjutant and the Second in Command were away on some course, so the Acting Adjutant, Keay, was in charge. Lynch [the Commanding Officer] came into the room and was given a glass. Keay went up to Haswell, the senior captain, and said quietly to him 'I think you should propose the CO's health!' 'I'm damned if I will,' said Haswell (I was standing just by and heard the conversation). 'I don't wish him good health and I am not prepared to be insincere on this occasion.' 'You must,' said Keay – 'I won't,' said Haswell. For a few minutes they argued, and then Haswell stepped forward and raising his glass said:
>
>   'Gentlemen, I give you the toast to the King's Own Yorkshire Light Infantry, and in particular the 9th Battalion of the Regiment' – slight pause – 'Gentlemen, when the barrage lifts' ... We emptied our glasses and were silent.

Apparently Liddell-Hart's version describes the episode following the CO's entrance as:

> ... Struck by a happy thought, H-[Haswell], raised his glass and said, 'Gentlemen, when the barrage lifts'. The inspiration appealed to us all, the breach that had torn the battalion was forgotten, and after the toast had been drunk, all linked arms, forming a circle round the table, and sang 'Aud Lang Syne'.

Captain Haswell was among those killed on 1st July. His moving words however lived after him, and from 1921, until some time in the 1980s, they were quoted under the name of the battalion in the 'In Memoriam' column of *The Times* on every 1st July.*

In 1987 Gerald Gliddon published a book – a topographical history of the battle of the Somme – and chose for his title *When the Barrage Lifts* – I presume this was in memory of Haswell and the many thousands of others who died when it did.

Malcolm Brown also records a letter another member of the KOYLI, in a sister battalion, the 8th Battalion, 2nd Lt. Percy Boswell wrote to his parents on the 30th June 1916 before he went over the top at 7.30 am the following morning:

> I am just writing you a short note which you will receive only if anything has happened to me during the next few days.
>
> The Hun is going to get consummate hell just in this quarter and we are going over the parapet tomorrow when I hope to spend a few merry hours in chasing the Bosche all over the place. I am absolutely certain that I shall get through all right, but in case the unexpected does happen I shall rest content with the knowledge that I have done my duty – and one can't do more.
>
> Good Bye and with the Best of Love to all from
> Percy.

He was killed in the first few minutes of the attack.

The effective strength of the battalion would have been about 800. The 8th KOYLI's casualty list the following day, 1st July 1916, was 21 officers and 518 men.

The battle engagements

The military historian Captain (later Brigadier) E.A. James divides the Battle of the Somme into a number of separate engagements and specific attacks involving the Third, Fourth and Fifth Armies.

He breaks these down further into Corps and Divisions giving a total of 54 infantry divisions.* This, according to Ray Westlake, embracing some 616 infantry battalions plus those of the Royal Navy Division and two cavalry divisions.

*According to Cyril Falls, British divisions engaged numbered 55, and these included 4 Canadian, 4 Australian, and 1 New Zealand. The French had 20 and the Germans 95.

The Somme battles begin: my battalions' locations

The Duke of Cornwall's Light Infantry

The 1st battalion, now part of the 95th Brigade of the 5th Division, instead of the 14th Brigade, reached the battle area in mid-July. The 2nd Battalion was no longer in France having sailed from Marseille to Salonika and arrived on 5th December 1915. The 1/5th would not reach the Somme area until they left the Laventie sector on 28th October, arriving Bonnières on 6th November, then via Beaumetz and Martinsart Wood, to dug-outs between Contalmaison and Pozières on 17th November, and so, fortunately for them, they were not really engaged in the Somme battles of 1916.

The Devonshires

The 1st Battalion Devonshires, like the 1st DCLI, were now also part of the 95th Brigade, 5th Division, and also moved into the battle area in mid-July. The 2nd Battalion Devonshires, still part of 23rd Brigade, 8th Division, were involved in the Somme offensive from day one. 8th Battalion Devonshires would also be heavily engaged on the Somme in 1916.* As part of the 7th Division, 20th Brigade, they too went over the top on the opening day and it is unlikely that any of Horace Westlake's comrades of the 8th Battalion who survived Loos, would, if they came out alive, be unscathed.

*The 8th Devons, as part of the 7th Division, shared the honour of being in the only division asked to make three attacks in July. How much this honour was relished by the division is not recorded.

The Rifle Brigade

1st Battalion Rifle Brigade would be involved from day one of the

409

battle as part of the 11th Brigade, 4th Division. 2nd Battalion Rifle Brigade, 25th Brigade, 8th Division, also went over on 1st July – at Ovillers south west of Pozières. 3rd Battalion Rifle Brigade, as part of the 17th Brigade, 24th Division, began their Somme experiences when they attacked Guillemont Station on 18th August, in the battle for Guillemont – one of the many horrific 'battles within a battle' taking place on the Somme. They continued fighting in the area until the 24th Division was pulled out of the Somme fighting to reach the front line at Vimy Ridge on 12th September. As with Horace Westlake, it is unlikely that any of Alfred Watts' surviving comrades of 1915 would come through the Somme.

British casualties on 1st July

As in all the WWI battles, the quoted statistics of casualties for the 1916 Somme engagements vary according to your chosen source. A generally accepted guide for the first engagement of that opening day on 1st July 1916 is that the best part of 60,000 of the British (and this term always includes the Imperial) troops who, as the whistles blew and the barrage lifted, rose out of their trenches from 7.30 am onwards, were recorded as dead, wounded or missing by the end of the day. It is hard to visualise those casualties for one day's fighting. What would 60,000 men look like? Major and Mrs Holt in their Somme Guide describe it as:

> If these sixty thousand men passed by in a single column, spaced an arm's length apart, they would stretch for a distance of 30 miles.

The German preparations

Dr Stephen Bull states that the 1916 German 'Construction of Field Positions' manual *Stellungsbau* describes the preparations as consisting of major strong-points and 'holding on' points that could be gradually linked and locked together to form new lines of defence. Dummy positions would be used to mislead enemy airmen. Lines were to be laid out so that forward positions overlooked the enemy and aided artillery observation. Further back, trenches housing the main garrisons were on the reverse slopes unseen by the enemy... Machine gun positions were to form the framework of the line, a

410

minority of them placed well forward, with surprise increasing their potency. Trench mortars were best placed in their own pits, not in the main trenches, so as to be out of the likely enemy bombardment zone.

So despite the British months of meticulous planning, the weeks of practice, the reams of instructions, the massive build-up of supplies and equipment, the aerial surveys and mapping for the attack, and the incredible barrage which it was believed very few enemy troops could survive (and those who did would be so stunned and demoralised that they would be incapable of offering immediate resistance) the Germans were ready and able to wreak devastating havoc on the advancing British troops. Dr Bull goes on to state:

> The German wire – which had sixteen barbs to the foot – was secured to crossed irons or corkscrew supports making thick webs about four feet high and thirty to forty feet across; these were supported by trip wires, low entanglements and iron spikes or 'calthorps'. Although the British bombardment on the Somme had been massive it had been lacking in important respects. Its duration had ruined any element of surprise, and its wire-cutting potential had been overestimated. Worse, although just over 2,029 guns had been deployed, only 452 were 'heavies' capable of dealing with deep bunkers. This was a smaller proportion of heavy artillery than the Germans had managed at Verdun.

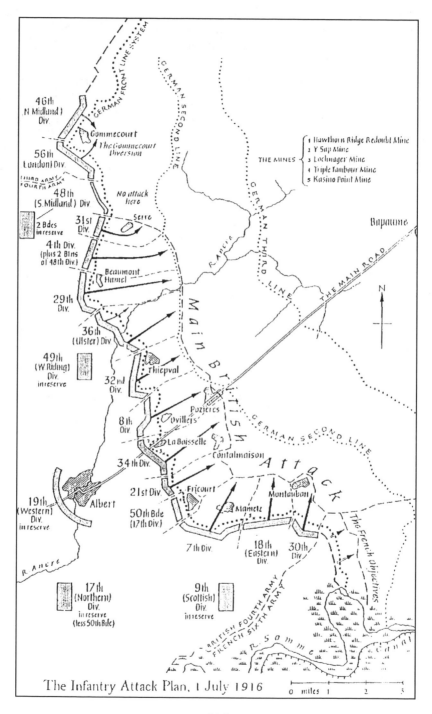

The Infantry Attack Plan, 1 July 1916

PART THIRTY-EIGHT

If you want the old battalion
We know where they are,
We know where they are,
We know where they are.

If you want the old battalion
We know where they are
They're hanging on the old barbed wire.

We've seen them, we've seen them,
Hanging on the old barbed wire.
We've seen them, we've seen them
Hanging on the old barbed wire.

Song *The Old Barbed Wire*. Origin unknown.

How my regiments fared

The Divisions

To follow the progress of such an intimidating number of troops and units as those that took part in the battles is way beyond my self-appointed terms of reference, but there are still books available, and still being written, on all aspects of the Somme engagements – both in 1916 and 1918 – for anyone who wishes to examine the battles in detail.

Nearly all of the battalions of 'my' regiments were heavily engaged, and although one battalion arrived late on the scene and played a minor role compared with others, and one was far away, even so it has been quite a task to disentangle my units from the many. Because it is easier, I have taken them by divisions – in date order where possible.

The Fourth Division, 1st Rifle Brigade, Beaumont Hamel

The 4th Division were on the left of the 29th Division facing towards Redan Ridge. Beaumont Hamel, described by Gerald Gliddon in *When the Barrage Lifts* as the third largest village on the Somme, having some 160 houses and a system of caves and underground passages which had been excavated in order to obtain hard chalk for building purposes. He says that after the battle John Masefield described the village as unrecognisable by its former occupants.

General A.H. Farrar-Hockley, says of the area that Beaumont Hamel was four miles south of Gommecourt, halfway up between spurs where two main spur lines ran down in rough parallel south-east towards the Ancre. He continues:

Of all the corps tasks undertaken that morning, General Hunter-Weston's was the most difficult [VIII Corps]; for whichever way he tackled it, the ground lay overwhelmingly in the enemy's favour and none of the approaches Hunter-Weston could adopt as an attractive proposition.

The trenches were closer than at Gommecourt:* about 500 yards at the greatest interval – chiefly opposite Beaumont Hamel and to the south – from 150–250 yards in the north. Those of the Germans were deep and well revetted, their tops meshed with barbed wire against trench raiders. Few of the chalky parapets were visible to the British; the trench line lay for the most part on reverse slopes on either side of the spurs, except behind Beaumont Hamel and below Serre where the fire positions rose in terraces on the enemy's forward slopes... The protection lay, as ever, in the dugouts, deep and dry, constructed through the quiet [inactive 'quiet' months of French occupation] of late 1914 and the whole of 1915.

*Gommecourt. This battle was planned as a subsidiary attack aimed to keep the German army guessing where the main thrust of the offensive would be, and to take the pressure off the 4th Army. The London Rifle Brigade, 1/5 Battalion (see Aubrey Smith above, in 1915) were no longer with the 1st Battalion of The Rifle Brigade, or part of the 11th Brigade, 4th Division, but were now in the 56th London Division, and taking part in the Gommecourt diversion. The Londoners suffered heavy casualties. In two hours they had taken almost every one of their objectives, but later running desperately short of ammunition, and signalling again and again: 'SOS Bombs', reliefs and supplies could not get through to them, and they were gradually overwhelmed. The last survivors, hiding in shell-holes finally made it back after darkness fell. A.H. Farrar-Hockley says of them and the Gommecourt experience:

> Their task had not been to capture Gommecourt, perhaps the strongest position in the Sector, but to divert upon themselves 'the fire of artillery and infantry which might otherwise be directed against the left flank of the main attack near Serre'.
> They had certainly achieved this end. In view of the task of their comrades to the south, it was as well they had.

The Brigades in the 4th Division

The 11th Brigade, with the 1st Rifles alongside the 1/E.Lancs, 1/Hampshires and 1/Somerset L.I., was composed entirely of regular battalions, but the original ranks would be well depleted by now, and at the opening of the battle how many of the troops were the original regular soldiers is open to conjecture.

11th Brigade

The 1st Rifles were to open the attack on 1st July together with the 1st East Lancs, and with the 1st Somersets to follow in behind the 1st Rifles. The 1st Rifles and East Lancs immediately came under murderous rifle and machine-gun fire from both flanks as they 'went over the top' – the East Lancs from the Ridge Redoubt strongpoint and Beaumont Hamel, and the 1st Rifles from the Quadrilateral and the Ridge Redoubt. The German wire here, as in so many other places, had remained uncut despite the intense artillery barrages of the previous days.

To get an idea of the extent of the involvement of the 11th Brigade on 1st July, the Brigade's commander Brigadier-General Bertie Prowse CB, DSO was killed that day, and all of the four battalion commanders were casualties; three killed and the fourth wounded. According to Captain G.A. Prideaux of the 1st Somerset Light Infantry (quoted in *Bloody Red Tabs* by Frank Davies and Graham Maddocks):

> At about 9.45 am the General [Prowse] decided to move his HQ into the German front line, thinking it was cleared of all the Germans. Just as he was getting out of our front line

trench, near 'Brett Street', he was shot in the back by a machine gun in the 'Ridge Redoubt, and died that afternoon.

Another member of the 11th Brigade, Lieutenant G.A Robinson MC, 1st Rifle Brigade, writing to the official historian in 1930, said:

Brigadier-General Prowse gave me orders to open the brigade ammunition dug-out that had been blown in. Immediately afterwards he was mortally wounded while assembling men of the Seaforth Highlanders in our front-line trench. Brigadier-General Prowse showed great gallantry in his efforts, ignoring the great breaches in our parapet, exposing himself to great danger.

Lieutenant-Colonel W.A.T.S. Somerville DSO, Brigade-Major, 11th Division at the time wrote:

2 enemy machine guns opened from Ridge Redoubt. These guns – to my mind – were the main cause of the failure of the 4th Division attack in the northern sector. The redoubt was never taken, and was strongly held throughout the morning.

The Rifle Brigade managed to bomb their way to their objective, and the following description of this attack is given by CSM Percy Chappell of the 1st Somersets in Martin Middlebrook's *The First Day on the Somme*:

The 1st Rifles were held up at the German wire and an indecisive bombing fight was taking place. Suddenly a Rifle Brigade officer stood up and shouted 'Come on, lads. Let them have it!' And the whole line rose and charged the enemy trench. This resolute action made the Germans bolt and freed the Somersets from being pinned down in the open.

Unfortunately the 1st Rifles were later bombed out in their turn, and by now being so weak in numbers (their casualties had amounted to 474, about half their effective strength) they were relieved the next morning by the 1st Irish Rifles.

After their relief the 1st Rifles, together with the rest of the remnants of their brigade, were moved to other parts of the area, and then sent to the Ypres sector for a spell as this was now regarded as 'quiet'. They returned to the Somme with the rest of the 11th Brigade on 16th September for further training before being sent into action again, this time east of Lesboeufs, on the northern slopes of Morval Spur, towards Le Transloy, on 17th October. Here, in two days, they suffered a further 261 casualties.

They moved on to Guillemont, the scene of the 3rd Rifle's earlier battle (see below 24th Division) but now in British hands, and attacked at Boritska Trench on 23rd October. Their casualties on 23rd October amounted to a further 122. Then, relieved, they moved to Trônes Wood, and by stages departed the Somme battle area.

The battle for Beaumont Hamel still dragged on until mid-November (as part of the 'battle of the Ancre'). Troops from both sides lost thousands of men as attacks were mounted and failed, until finally, on 13th November, the 152nd Brigade of the 51st Division, at 5.45 am, led by the 5th Sutherland Highlanders, through dense fog and uncut wire, began the final assault. In the evening they were through Beaumont Hamel and consolidated the final objective taking 600 prisoners out of the 1,700 captured.

Guillemont. 24th Division

Guillemont was described by Liddell Hart as 'a shambles of horror', and the way to it from Trônes Wood, said Gerald Gliddon, was 'down a slope, up another slope, now only a few hundred yards of farm road, yet in July and August 1916 it seemed an infinite distance'.

The German shelling of the British forward positions had been persistent throughout the latter end of August, and the weather bad. On 27th August, when a further attack was planned, work became extremely difficult owing to hostile shelling (a lot of which were gas shells), and the trenches became waterlogged and deep in mud.

3rd Battalion, The Rifle Brigade, Guillemont Railway Station

The 3rd Rifles had not moved down to the Somme area until 12th August and were in reserve just to the west of Guillemont from 12th to 14th August. Heavy rain fell on 15th August and an artillery

417

officer, Lt. Page, described conditions as 'very unpleasant in the hot August weather with many unburied corpses'.

On 18th August a new attack began at 2.45 pm on a broad front and the objective of the 3rd Rifles was Guillemont Station. The station, lying on a light railway just outside and to the north of the village, had become a tactical feature of some importance. Up to zero hour there had been a sustained bombardment of the German positions for almost 24 hours. The sound was described by one gunner back in Maricourt:*

Exactly to the second hell broke loose, and thousands of guns went off at the same moment. Never have I heard anything like it, or could have imagined such noises possible. It is quite impossible to describe to people who have not experienced it. It actually hurt, and for a time I felt as if my head would burst.

*Source, Michael Steadman *Guillemont.*

He retired below to the telephone-pit which had been dug 20 feet down into the solid chalk.

There matters were almost worse, the noises were not so violent, but the vibration was so great that at first I thought my heart was going to stop from being so jolted. If one could imagine the vibration of the screw [propeller] of a ship intensified a thousand times it might give some idea of my sensations.

Michael Steadman writes:

By far the most significant advance of the day was achieved by the men of the 3rd Rifle Brigade on the northern, left side of the attack upon the village.

The Rifle Brigade men north of The Quarry advanced with the greatest speed to take a number of German prisoners from the devastation at the Station. This battalion managed to capture a section of the Waterlot Farm road to the north-west of the station where they joined up with soldiers from the 8th Buffs who had advanced successfully into the area of ZZ Trench, west of Ginchy.

On 21st August the 8th Buffs and 3rd Rifles again scored a success by taking the greater part of ZZ Trench leading into the northern part of the village.

The casualties suffered by the 3rd Rifles on 18th August were 225 at Guillemont Station. 'D' Company were engaged in an attack on 21st and all the officers and three-quarters of the assault members were lost. The remainder consisting of 23 men under a sergeant held the gains until relieved after dark. On 1st September they attacked on Orchard and Tea Trenches and suffered a further 211 casualties.

On 24th August the 24th Division was relieved by the 20th Division. And by stages the 3rd Rifles moved to the front line at Vimy Ridge on 12th September.

The 5th Division, 1st Duke of Cornwall's Light Infantry

The 1st DCLI, 95th Brigade, of the 5th Division, as with the Rifles in the 24th Division earlier, also had its share of the Guillemont killing ground. The Cornishmen were involved in the final stages of the battles for Trônes Wood and Guillemont. Michael Stedman in his study *Guillemont*, comments on the enormous number of infantry and supporting units that were drawn into the battles. He says in his introduction:

> ... it therefore proved impossible to name anything other than a proportion of those myriad battalions who came and were swallowed, their men fixed forever into the terrible black hole which Guillemont became.

The weather improved greatly in the first two days of September, and the British attack, led by a bombardment, got under way. The barrage was to be a rolling barrage – advancing at a rate of 50 yards a minute – and the orders for the troops of the 5th Division, which was to attack on the right wing, were to keep as close as possible to within 25 yards of the curtain of fire. This must have been a hair-raising experience that required steady nerves knowing the risk of 'shorts' and worn artillery gun barrels. Captain A.K. Totten of the 1st DCLI, 95th Brigade, was awarded an MC for his bravery during the attack.

419

When the men of the 95th Brigade reached the top of the slope to the north of Wedge Wood they could look down upon the devastion which was Guillemont village. The village of Guillemont, or what had once been the village, finally fell as a result of very fierce fighting between 3rd and 6th September to the 20th Division.

A Sapper officer, Lieut. P.F. Story of 96th Field Company, Royal Engineers, 20th Division, wrote home on 10th September (as quoted by Malcolm Brown):

It [his news of the capture of Guillemont] is now about a week old, that we, as a division, took Guillemont. My brigade was on the right. We have all been very congratulated on the result, as we sappers played no small part in the affair; both Brigadier and Divisional general have been most laudatory in their congratulations and thanks. Casualties, alas, pretty high, two officers wounded, and some forty-one men in the company. We fairly pasted the Boche – some six hundred prisoners and a large number of killed and wounded. My orderly, alas, was badly wounded at my side by a whiz bang, which sent me head over heels, but I am thankful to say I came through unscathed, but dead beat to a turn. Three nights without a wink of sleep would in the ordinary way seem an impossibility, but I've done it.

The Boches were good specimens, mainly of the 73rd Fusilier Regiment (Prussians)... The prisoners fraternized fairly well with our men, and carried back many a wounded man; they were very good stretcher-bearers.

Guillemont was blotted right out, not one brick standing on another – nothing but a sea of crump* holes of all sorts and sizes; it was very difficult moving about in the dark. The fight itself went through without a hitch, the real bad time comes when you are consolidating and have to face the counter-attack with its heavy shelling, but we managed to get consolidated early, and were able to defy the Boche. We are resting at the moment and feel we deserve it. Our General came today, and inspected us, pouring out many kind words.

*Shell.

Geoffrey Mallins, the official War Office photographer said after the final capture of the village (as quoted by Gerald Glidden):

420

Before the 25th September attack the village of Guillemont did not exist, in fact, it was an absolute impossibility to tell where the fields cnded and the village began... It was one of the most awful specimens of the devastated track of war that existed on the Western Front. The village had been turned by the Germans into a veritable fortress; trenches and strong-points bristling with machine guns commanded every point which gave vantage to the enemy.

5th Division, 95th Brigade, Longueval – Delville Wood area: 1st Battalion Devonshire Regiment

Gliddon describes the village of Longueval as the gateway to Delville Wood. The German trench line skirted the south of Longueval and then turned south-east in the direction of Guillemont.

Like the 1st DCLI, the 1st Battalion of the Devonshire Regiment were also part of the 95th Brigade. The Regimental History records that the 5th Division had started for the battle area on 14th July, moving by Herissart and Becordel Bécourt, reaching Montauban on the 19th and that night began relieving the 3rd Division between Longueval and High Wood, an area northwest of Guillemont. The history continues:

The 95th Brigade went in on the right, S.W. of Longueval, with the 13th on its left, the 1st Devons being in reserve near Montauban. At that moment the southern half of Longueval was in British hands, together with the S.W. portions of Delville Wood, but the situation in this quarter was exceedingly obscure and changed constantly as each side in turn attacked and counter-attacked. Even when no attack was in progress there was constant shelling, the front line trenches were nothing better than the hastily-dug line where earlier attacks had been brought to a standstill, they had usually to be approached over the open, so ordinary reliefs and the carrying up of rations and ammunition were often attended with severe casualties.

The 95th Brigade went in on the night of the 22nd–23rd July, and despite early successes they were pushed back almost to Pont Street, the starting point, just west of Longueval. On the night of 23rd the 1st Devons relieved a mixture of units mainly East Surreys and DCLI.

The Devons were faced with the task of consolidating the trenches, and rescuing the numerous wounded who were lying out in front, and all the time the British trenches were subjected to heavy shelling. After stopping a determined German attack on 24th July they were relieved on the 25th, going into support. They suffered 100 casualties, and one of the fatalities was a Lieut. Tomlinson, promoted in the field, who for a time had been acting Adjutant.

The relief of the whole division began on the 29th and, in the words of the Devons History, 'Then proceeded to Abbeyville to recuperate, replenish its shattered ranks, and prepare for another turn in the great struggle.'

The Devons, with the rest of the 5th Division, were back in the trenches on 26th August. As part of the 95th Brigade the 1st Devons were involved in the attacks around Leuze Wood, some one and a half miles east of Guillemont. Although suffering heavy casualties the Devons were lucky in the proportion of wounded to killed and missing. The Devons were relieved by a battalion from the 16th Division on the 5th September, and withdrew to a bivouac near Bilton Farm. Congratulations were received from both the Corps Commander, General Morland and the Brigadier, who said of the 95th Brigade that they had advanced over a larger front and to a wider depth than any other brigade during the whole war.

The 7th Division, The 8th Battalion, The Devonshire Regiment, Mametz

The 8th Devonshires, still part of the 20th Brigade as they had been at Loos in 1915, were in support on 1st July behind their sister battalion 9th Devons and 2nd Gordon Highlanders. The right-hand advancing battalion was the 2nd Gordons, attacking down the valley close to the railway line. Gerald Gliddon describes the area as follows:

The village of Mametz is four miles east of Albert on the D64 Fricourt-Guillemont road... It was formerly a railway halt on the line from Albert to Peronne... Before the war with about a 120 houses Mametz was about the fifth largest village in the area. It was the objective of the 7th Division for the 1st July.

A particularly well placed machine-gun was in 'Shrine Alley' to the south-west of Mametz, and it had a clear field of vision and fire that included Mansell Copse. There was also a steep bank with undergrowth full of dug-outs which was also known to be a potentially very dangerous spot.

The 9th and 8th Devons, on the left of the Gordons, were to join up with the Gordons from the reserve. The 2nd Gordons advanced and were cut down by the machine-gun fire from 'The Shrine'* (the crucifix in the village cemetery), and then the 8th and 9th Devons were in turn caught by the same machine-guns. These circumstances were predicted by Captain D.L. Martin of the 9th Devons when he viewed the position, and feared the worst. Sadly he was one of the first to fall.

*In October 2000 I stood on the site of this attack of the 1st July, and looked from the Copse across to the German line, and then walked to where the Germans would have looked down as they waited with machine-guns at The Shrine. As the British troops climbed towards them, they opened a devastating fire. Even after all these years I found a number of spent .303 cartridges and any number of shrapnel balls just on or just under the surface of the ground at the German position.

The casualties were heavy and both the Gordons and 9th Devons were brought to a halt. 'B' Company of the 8th Devons moved forward at 10.30 am to fill the gap that had developed between the Gordons and 9th Devons, and the Gordons were now not in touch with the Devons, although they were with elements of the 91st Brigade. 'B' Company of the 8th Devons too were forced to take cover (in the hollow of Fricourt Road) and were not able to move again until 4 pm. All the officers became casualties and Company Sergeant Major Holwill took over command.

'A' Company of the 8th Devons pushed forward but also came under heavy machine-gun fire near Mansel Copse and was checked. 'C' Company were given orders to move forward from the reserve trench to reinforce the line near Hidden Wood, but its leading platoon lost so heavily as it crossed No Man's Land near Mansel Copse that Lieut. Savill, the platoon commander, decided wisely to move further left to gain a little ground cover from the machine-gun fire and they reached Hidden Wood without further loss. All the companies were moving forward again and all the objectives were taken, clearing the deep dug-outs in Danzig Trench and moving to Hidden Wood and Orchard Trench.

423

By about 6 pm all the division's objectives had been secured. The 9th Devons had more casualties than the 8th on this opening day of the battle of the Somme with only one officer out of 18 not hit, and 8 of them killed. 141 men were killed, 55 missing, 267 wounded. Total 463 out of the 775 who started. The 8th suffered 3 officers killed and 47 men killed or missing, 7 officers and 151 men wounded.

The War Diary records that on 4th July the dead of the 8th and 9th Devonshires were buried in Mansel Copse. This is a pretty little cemetery, named after an officer of the Devons, and lies up a pathway and set among the trees of the Copse. A stone plaque outside the cemetery entrance gates reads: 'The Devonshires held this trench; The Devonshires hold it still'.

The 8th Devonshires were in action again on 14th July at Bazentin Le Grand Wood. The War Diary records:

Leading wave crept forward into no man's land during bombardment and at zero hour (3.25 am) were within 25 yards of the enemy's line. First objective entered at 3.26 am – second taken by 3.45 am – patrols cleared NE side of wood. Relieved and to White Trench on 15th July. Casualties 171. To assembly positions south of High Wood on 17th July. In action 20th July, attacked 3.15. am *Many casualties from British artillery firing short* [my italics]. Casualties 201. Relieved 11p.m by 14th Royal Warwickshires.

They were in action again between 3rd and 7th September at Mametz and Montauban and Ginchy, once again with the 9th Devons and 2nd Gordons. After being relieved, by stages of marching and train northwards, at long last they reached a quiet sector, ready to go into the line between Armentières and the Douve, where the 7th Division relieved the 19th Division. Here they spent six weeks of peace and quiet in a line that had not altered since it had been established by the 4th Division in October 1914.

Despite a raid or two, casualties were very light for them in this sector, and they were back to the Somme in the later part of November and into December. And interestingly here their patrols brought in a number of German prisoners on four successive days. The Regimental History says these prisoners seemed far from sorry to be taken.

The 8th Division, 2nd Devonshires, Ovillers

One of the 8th Division's first assault troops were the 2nd Devonshires whose task it was to attack in the formidable sector north of La Boisselle past Ovillers. Both 23rd and 25th Brigades were together again in the line as they were at Neuve Chapelle and Loos – along with the 70th Brigade.

Gerald Gliddon, again in *When the Barrage Lifts*, quotes the following poem by Ivor Gurney* when he passed through in November after the battle:

> As I went up by Ovillers
> In mud and water cold to the knee
> There went three jeering, fleering spectres
> They walked abreast and talked to me

*See under 'shell shocked'.

As part of 23rd Brigade, with the 2nd Middlesex alongside them as the other assault troops, the 2nd Devons story was very similar to that dreadful 1st July day for so many regiments. They were in their assembly trenches on the evening of 30th June, and had been waiting in readiness for several hours before the tremendous barrage opened up at 6.25 am. The dawn broke fine but misty and the concentrated violence lasted for an hour, and seemed to be doing great damage, for hardly any reply was made from the German trenches.

When the guns lifted on to the German second line at 7.30 am the Devonshires 'A' and 'B' Companies dashed forward and were within 100 yards of the enemy's front trench when they were suddenly caught in a tornado of fire from the front and both flanks. Despite this, 'C' and 'D' Companies went forward without faltering, hard in the wake of the leaders. The morning mist, and the smoke and dust, made it hard for those still in the British trenches to make out what exactly had happened. At first it looked as if the waves were lying down intact in No Man's Land, but then it was realised that they were lying still because they had been shot down wholesale and were practically all casualties. Only a handful of the Devons reached the German trenches.

The first wave of the 2nd Middlesex who went over with them were caught immediately by even heavier machine-gun fire, and again suffered serious losses, and like the Devons ceased to exist. Some 200 men – the survivors from all the attacking waves of all ranks made up from both regiments – got into the first line trenches and penetrated into the second but suffered half their number in casualties and were forced back to the German front line.

Here, under the leadership of Major H.B.W. Savile, an attempt was made to consolidate; but though three and a half companies of the 2nd West Yorkshires were sent forward in support of the brigade attack, No Man's Land had become a death-trap, and except for a few men who joined Major Savile's men, none lived to reach the German lines.

About noon the barrage was brought back to the German front lines and this enabled the survivors and some of the wounded to crawl back to their lines as the day and evening wore on.

The 2nd Devons sustained 431 casualties, and four days later the remnants of the battalion entrained for Longeau for transfer to the First Army, and three months respite from the Somme.

8th Division, 2nd Rifle Brigade, Ovillers

In the 25th Brigade of the 8th Division, the 2nd Rifle Brigade – together with 1st Royal Irish Rifles – were being held in reserve for the attack. The first assault troops would be the 2nd Berkshires and 2nd Lincolns.

The 2nd Berks assault troops were immediately met with intense rifle and machine-gun fire and only a small party made it to the German trenches. They were too few to hold it and were eventually bombed out.

The 2nd Lincolns met a similar reception and after a very hard fight captured about 200 yards of German trench. Gradually their precarious position became untenable, and about 9 am the remnants fell back as best they could to the British front line.

The Lincolns' colonel made an effort to renew the attack with the support battalion of the Royal Irish Rifles, but by this time the hurricane of machine-gun and rifle fire sweeping across front and flank across No Mans Land made the attack impossible to sustain and by 10 am the colonel had only about 30 men.

Both 1st Royal Irish Rifles and the 2nd Rifle Brigade in reserve had moved forward meanwhile in support of the two leading battalions. Apart from the leading company of the Irish Rifles who made it to the second line of the German positions, the remainder of the Irish and 2nd Rifles suffered so badly on their way to their own front line from the heavy and accurate barrage the enemy was then putting up against our forward positions, that progress was impossible.

With the wrecked condition of the British trenches, in addition blocked by the dead, and with the wounded trying to make their way back together with stragglers from the assault battalions unable to advance, the obstructions were such that the 2nd Rifles were ordered to remain *in situ* until a decision could be made regarding its employment.

Things went better for the 70th Brigade at first, and the assaulting battalions of the 8th KOYLI and 8th Yorks and Lancs had comparatively few casualties on their first dash except on the left from concentrated machine-gun fire. The German wire was completely cut and within a few minutes the first German trench line was captured along the whole front of both battalions.

As the battle progressed however, the Germans were able to bring yet more heavy machine-gun fire to bear, at the same time laying down a concentrated barrage of artillery fire behind the British front-line so that the supporting battalions were unable to progress. One company lost 50% of its effectives before leaving its assembly positions. By 10 am all communication with the troops of the 70th Brigade in the German trenches had been completely cut off. The 8th Division was so shattered that it had to be relieved by a fresh division.

29th Division, Newfoundland Regiment

Although not containing any of my battalions the 29th Division had amongst its brigades the 88th, in which served the Newfoundland Regiment I referred to earlier. It seems appropriate to mention their exploits on the Somme where they were again part of Hunter-Weston's command as they had been at Gallipoli. A.H. Farrar-Hockley says that Haig was prejudiced against all who had been in the Dardanelles campaign. I have no idea if that was so or not, but the 29th were referred to by some as 'The Incomparable 29th Division'.

At 5.15 am on the 1st July all ranks stood to. At 7.20 the assault companies climbed from their trenches, some aghast to find the barrage had already lifted ahead of them. The great roar went up as the mine under the Hawthorn Redoubt was exploded, and two companies of the 2nd Royal Fusiliers (86th Brigade) ran forward to take possession of the crater. But already German machine-gunners were there and armed with two machine-guns to hold them back. By 7.25 am the Germans were up manning their broken defences, and all was going very wrong for the whole of the 86th Brigade. The 1st Lancashire Fusiliers were caught as they rose up out of their trenches and shells fell amongst the support companies. The 16th Middlesex and 1st Royal Dublin Fusiliers behind could see that the wire ahead was largely uncut and hung with bodies. The few gaps in the wire were piled with dead. All that were left of the Royal Fusiliers battalion were 120 men.

All the 87th Brigade were caught – 2nd South Wales Borderers, 1st Royal Innskilling Fusiliers, 1st Border Regiment, 1st KOSB. The two leading battalions of the 88th Brigade were 1st Essex and 1st Newfoundland. The Essex could not reach No Man's Land because of the endless relays of wounded in every trench, and deep shell-holes, and further forward by the pile of dead bodies.

The Newfoundlanders were ordered on alone. They had to advance in the open until reaching the forward shell craters. At 9.05 they rose and marched forward in open ranks into sustained machine-gun fire. They would not halt but with determined gallantry carried on over the long open approach. In all, 26 officers and 658 men fell.* Some minutes later three companies of the Essex emerged and advanced as gallantly but also fell, just inside the enemy line. 'Thus,' said Hockley-Farrar, 'ended the assault of the 29th Division. The Corps [Hunter-Weston's] lost 14,000 officers and men that day.'

Peter Liddle in his *Testimony of War* has photographs of excerpts of a diary kept by a William Strang (later Lord Strang). Strang, at the time a 2nd Lieutenant in the 4th Worcesters, who were also part of the 88th Brigade, wrote in his diary on July 18th:

The Newfoundland relieved us in the trenches and are now back here in billets. The whole brigade is now here. The Newfoundland men have suffered as much as any battalion on July 1st, and they went forward as on parade. It was a splendid sight they made. The Essex seem to have done rather lamentably. The Borders have two officers unhurt... The KOSBs and the SWBs and the Inskillings all suffered terribly. The Fusilier

Brigade, no less – the 16th Middlesex seem to have done well – fought well for the crater on the Hawthorne Redoubt, but obliged to retire. De Lisle [Maj. Gen. H de B. de Lisle] had the chance to rest his Division but refused: he would fight on. He is reputed to have said that when he has done with the 29th they will go home in a taxi-cab. People began to call him 'Butcher'.

The Newfoundland CO saved us [he] went to [can't read the name looks like Caley] and told him it was murder to send any more battalions forward.

*Again figures vary from source to source. David Parsons' *Pilgrimage* gives the following for the Newfoundlanders:

The best numbers available indicate that 790 officers and men went over the top on July 1. Of these, 272 were killed, died of wounds or were missing and presumed dead. There were 11 officers and 427 men wounded. A total of 710 killed or wounded of the 790 present.

According to Sir Arthur Conan Doyle in his account of the opening of the battle extracted from his *The British Campaign in France & Flanders 1916*, The Corps Commander, Hunter Weston, visited the Newfoundland survivors the following day and said: 'To hear men cheering as they did, after undergoing such an experience, and in the midst of such mud and rain, made one proud to have command of such a battalion.'

PART THIRTY-NINE

The final British attack in November was a particularly heavy blow... From the middle of November onwards we awaited with great anxiety the further attacks on the Somme and at Verdun which our invasion of Roumania was likely to provoke... I was greatly impressed with the seriousness of the position by a tour which I took of the western front in the middle of December.

Ludendorff, *War Memories.*

Robertson and Haig under pressure to keep attacking on the Somme

On 29th August 1916, Robertson wrote to Haig:

I spoke to Lloyd George about this [complaints from the French that Haig was going too slowly on the Somme] the other day, and he repeated what he has said so many times lately that he thinks you are playing absolutely the right game, and doing your job in absolutely the right way ... all the War Committee think the same. Briand told Asquith last week that he was delighted with what you had done on the Somme. Of course we all know that for many reasons you should get going on a big scale as soon as you can, but we also know that it is useless going off before you are properly ready.*

*Is there a hint here to Haig to step things up and make more progress?

...The gist of the information I get is that the French seem

431

to think that the operations will necessarily soon come to a standstill because of the winter. I fail to see why this should be so. In 1914 we fought up to nearly Christmas and this year the Germans attacked Verdun in February. I think you will agree with me that we must keep up the pressure without ceasing, winter or no winter, so far as the weather will permit.*
– If we do not do this the Germans will be taking troops over to the Eastern Front and Alexeieff** is already beginning to call out.

*Again a touch of the spur it seems. Robertson himself is obviously under some pressure from the politicians and the French.
**I presume this is General Mikhail Vasilevich Alekseev (or Alexeyev, or Alexeev). The spelling of his name varies from author to author.

Robertson continues with, it seems, some irritation:

... It seems to me ridiculous that the French should talk of Verdun falling. I imagine we have had quite as hard a task at Ypres as the French have had at Verdun, and Ypres has not fallen and will not fall. Such dissatisfaction as there may be is due to Joffre and Castelnau* I believe. In any case you do what you think best and I will see that the support you now have here continues. I hope the Tanks will prove successful. It is rather a desperate innovation.

*Joffre's chief of staff with special responsibility to oversee the defence of Verdun.

Winston Churchill takes a similar view to Robertson with regard to the use of tanks at this time, but he is particularly concerned with revealing the weapon too soon. He writes:

The increasing sense of dominating the enemy and the resolute desire for a decision at all costs led in September to a most improvident disclosure of the caterpillar vehicles. The first of these had early in January been manoeuvred in Hatfield Park in the presence of the King, Lord Kitchener and several high authorities. Lord Kitchener was sceptical; but Mr Lloyd George was keen, and the British Headquarters mildly interested. Fifty of these engines, developed with great secrecy under the purposely misleading name of 'Tanks' had been completed.

They arrived in France during the early stages of the Battle of the Somme for experimental purposes and the training of their crews. When it was seen how easily they crossed trenches and flattened out entanglements made for trial behind the British line, the force of the conception appealed to the directing minds of the Army. The Headquarters Staff, hitherto so lukewarm, now wished to use them at once in battle. Mr Lloyd George thought this employment of the new weapon in such small numbers premature. He informed me of the discussion which was proceeding. I was so shocked at the proposal to expose this tremendous secret to the enemy upon such a petty scale and as a mere makeweight to what I was sure could only be an indecisive operation that I sought an interview with Mr Asquith, of whom I was then a very definite opponent... I thought I had succeeded in convincing him. But if this were so, he did not make his will effective; and on September 15 the first tanks, or 'large armoured cars' as they were called in the Communiqué, went into action on the front of the Fourth Army attacking between the Combles ravine and Martinpuich.

According to John Terraine, Haig was very enthusiastic about the tanks and in the autumn of 1916 sent his deputy chief of staff to London to press for 1,000 tanks. This sits strangely with the image often portrayed of Haig as the traditional blinkered 'nothing will ever replace the horse' cavalry man.

General Jack indicates the extent that pressure was applied to the Germans even when no major attack was being mounted. His diary entry of 3rd September when his 2/West Yorks had relieved 2/Rifle Brigade in the Vermelles area on 1st September reads:

...the Rifle Brigade had just lost heavily in a full battalion raid on the German line, the operation being covered by a powerful artillery barrage – perhaps rather short of howitzers. I think that the attack should have been cancelled or the infantry numbers reduced, because on the preceding night an R.B. patrol had become missing, and it was fair to assume that the enemy had captured it and possibly obtained some hint of the plan from the men, unintentially, or from notebooks with them. The Germans withdrew from their trenches beforehand, and on arriving in them the raiders were met by very severe shell fire

433

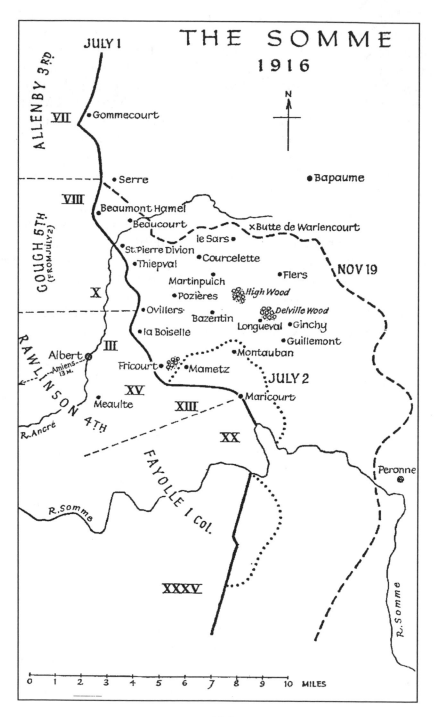

THE SOMME
1916

N

JULY 1

ALLENBY 3RD

VII •Gommecourt

•Bapaume

•Serre

VIII

GOUGH 5TH (FROM JULY 2)

•Beaumont Hamel
•Beaucourt
×Butte de Warlencourt
le Sars•
•St.Pierre Divion   •Courcelette
•Thiepval
•Flers   NOV 19
Martinpuich•
X   •Pozières   •High Wood
•Ovillers•   •Delville Wood
Bazentin•   Longueval •Ginchy
•la Boiselle   •Guillemont

RAWLINSON

Albert⊗ III
Amiens 13 M.   •Montauban
Fricourt•   •Mametz
XV   JULY 2
•Meaulte   XIII   •Maricourt
4TH
R.Ancré   XX

FAYOLLE I Col.

Peronne
⊙

R.Somme

XXXV

R.Somme

0 1 2 3 4 5 6 7 8 9 10 MILES

while machine guns swept No Man's Land, thus blocking the retirement. The operation was a failure, the R.B. casualties being 11 out of the 22 officers together with a large proportion of other ranks...

SEPTEMBER 10TH ... The Rifle Brigade dead lie all over No Man's Land, some of them hanging on the German wire which they were trying to cut or surmount when killed; among them one whom I knew is easily recognisable.

The stench from the older corpses in our parapets is sickening in places; it has been reduced somewhat by sprinklings of chloride of lime, and for me by a smelling salts bottle given years ago, by an old aunt without any thought of this purpose.

Reviewing the Somme battles of 1916

The Battle of the Somme officially ended on 18th November. British losses were around 420,000 and the estimate of German losses vary between 400,000 and 600,000 or more. Based on the Holt's calculations, the single column of the British casualties – dead, wounded and missing – marching by would stretch for 210 miles.

Major R.S. Cockburn, a volunteer of 4th August 1914, sums up his view of the battle of the Somme (as quoted by Malcolm Brown in *The Imperial War Museum Book of The Somme*):

Ypres was bad, but the Somme was worse. There were far more dead on the Somme. At times you lived with the dead. You could speak to them at night, as I have done without knowing they were dead, propped up as they sometimes were at the side of a trench. You stumbled over them, kicked their arms or feet, trod on bits of them, and the air you breathed was foul with them ... ask anyone what Trônes Wood was like at the end of august 1916, or if he was not sick (or nearly so) on going over any battlefield on the Somme. Half a head here; battered and black swelling things in shell holes; torn remnants of bodies scattered by death all over that hellish ground; your best friend blown to pieces by something which (let us hope) he never saw or heard coming.

Strategists, historians, and writers interested in the period generally

435

will no doubt continue to prod and probe the 1916 Somme campaign; apportioning praise, blame, and condemnation in accordance with their personal views and conclusions.

Richard Holmes blames at least some of the Somme failures on the differing expectations of Haig and Rawlinson. He complains that Rawlinson's handling of the battle after the first day was that:

> He behaved like the corps commander he had been, not the army commander he was.

Sir Douglas Haig, in his dispatch dated 23rd December 1916 as published a few days later in *The Times* appears fairly content with the result. He wrote:

> The objective of the offensive was threefold: (1) To relieve the pressure on Verdun. (2) To assist our Allies in the other theatres of war by stopping any further transfer of German troops from the Western front. (3) To wear down the strength of the forces opposed to us.

At the close of the dispatch, affirming that all three objectives had been achieved, he stated (as reported by Malcolm Brown):

> Any one of these results is in itself sufficient to justify the Somme battle. The attainment of all three of them affords ample compensation for the splendid efforts of our troops and for the sacrifices made by ourselves and our Allies. They have brought us a long step forward towards the final victory of the Allied cause.

Others take a different view, R.B. Gardner among them (*The Big Push*) who claims of the defenders of Haig's Somme offensive:

> Mostly military men, some of them ex-staff officers, they have appeared at times something like an unorganised conspiracy to protect his reputation. They realise that the present decade [1960s] is a vital one in the final assessment of the man; that the present judgement is likely to be the one handed down to history.

He continues, rather patronisingly:

> It was not of course, Haig's fault that he had grave shortcomings as a military commander, it was the fault of a society that put him, the man he was, in the position it did.

Some sources claim that despite the British casualty list and the lack of any significant ground gained, Haig's third point is valid, and the German army was never the same again after the pounding it suffered on the Somme and the losses sustained at Verdun. The History of the German 27th Division *Die 27 Infanterie Division im Weltkrieg* gives credence to this view:

> In the Somme fighting of 1916 there was a spirit of heroism which was never again found in the division, however conspicuous it [the division] remained until the end of the war... The spirit of the men in 1918 had not the temper, the hard bitterness and spirit of sacrifice of their predecessors.

Churchill quotes Ludendorff writing in his war memories of the 1916 British/French offensive:

> The Entente troops worked their way further and further into the German lines. We had heavy losses in men and material. At that time the front lines were still strongly held. The men took refuge in dugouts and cellars from the enemy's artillery fire. The enemy came up behind their barrage, got into the trenches and villages before our men could crawl out from their shelter. A continuous yield of prisoners to the enemy was the result. The strain on physical and moral strength was tremendous and divisions could only be kept in the line for a few days at a time... The number of available divisions was shrinking ... units were hopelessly mixed up, the supply of ammunition was getting steadily shorter... The situation on the Western front gave cause for greater anxiety than I had anticipated. But at that time I did not realise its full significance. It was just as well, otherwise I could never have had the courage to take the important decision to transfer still more divisions from the heavily engaged Western front to the Eastern in order to recover the initiative there and deal Roumania a decisive blow.

Ludendorff's *War Memories* as quoted by Winston Churchill is also quoted by Charteris as follows:

> The strain of this year [1916] had proved too great; the endurance of the army had weakened; we were completely exhausted on the western front... In spite of our victory over the Roumanian army* we were definitely weaker as regards the position as a whole... September was an especially critical month: it was not made easy for us to embark on any operation against Roumania.

*Churchill wrote of Roumania:

> Jubilation at the accession of a new Ally was still resounding through the French and British Press when startling news arrived. On September 1, Mackensen – [Field Marshal August von Mackensen] invaded Dobruja. On September 6, with the Bulgarian army and German howitzers he smashed the Danubian fortress of Turtuurkai and captured 25,000 Roumanians and 100 guns.

Perhaps the opinion expressed of the German troops in the history of the German 27th Division after the Somme could also be said of the British army, for from now onwards, a dour determination to stick it out at all costs after all the losses and suffering that the front line troops had endured in 1916, had replaced the optimism, enthusiasm, and the certainty of a victory soon to be gained, of the earlier years.*

*See the comments of Wilfrid Ewart and Bert Chaneyon in Part Twenty-five which lend support to this view.

Either way, despite the horrific battles and casualties of 1916, both British and German troops fought hard and unwaveringly in 1918 right to the end, but the arguments continue as to how much the struggles of 1916 contributed to that end. A personal and measured conclusion is expressed by Cyril Falls in his *The First World War*:

> The French fought finely on the Somme, but after the first short phase it was largely a British battle. From the British point of view this battle was fought in the wrong place – where there were no strategic objectives – and at the wrong time – before sufficient resources had been gathered. The lack of heavy artillery on and before 1 July was a main factor in the failure of that

438

day. The British started with one heavy or medium gun or howitzer per 57 yards, as against the French scale of one to twenty. On the British front the deep [German] dug-outs were nearly all intact after the bombardment, whereas on the French a considerable number had been destroyed. Defective ammunition – 'dud' shells which did not explode – added to the trouble. It would be absurd to argue that there would have been a break-through, perhaps even that the battle would have been a satisfactory one but for these handicaps, but it would certainly have been more successful. This was an offensive on a front undisturbed for nearly two years, on which the defender had worked like beavers, very different from the half-dug trenches at Verdun a legacy of slackness and over confidence.

The British tactics in the main were clumsy, lacking the skill shown by the Germans at Verdun – the evidence of study and German comparisons between British and French troops point to the same conclusions here. The British army was, as pointed out, largely an amateur force and its tactical instructors were too stiff and conventional. Yet for determination and devotion the army that fought on the Somme has never been surpassed. Many Germans, foremost among them Ludendorff, have borne witness to the weight of the blows delivered on the Somme and their effects upon the defending German forces... Only high hearts, splendid courage, and the enormous endurance of the flower of the nations of which the British and French Empires engaged could have won the results attained. Only wonderful powers of resistance by the Germans could have limited them to what they were.

Leon Wolff, the author of *In Flanders Fields*, comments:

...and when the offensive had dragged to its weary end in November 1916 only a few square miles of worthless tortured ground had been captured, while the losses of 538,000 troops on the part of the Central Powers compared to 794,000 of the Allied attackers. After this blood-bath a plaintif cry went up: 'No more Sommes!'

There is a vivid and moving description of the conditions in the final stages of the Somme in November 1916:

The ground, sodden with rain and broken everywhere with innumerable shell-holes, can only be described as a morass, almost bottomless in places: between the lines and for many thousands of yards behind them it is almost – and in some localities, quite – impassable. The supply of food and ammunition is carried out with the greatest difficulty and immense labour, and the men are so worn out by this and by the maintenance and construction of trenches that frequent reliefs, carried out under exhausting conditions are unavoidable.

In the front trenches there had been no opportunity to provide adequate cover against either fire or weather. Between the front and reserve positions on the reverse slopes of the Bazentin Ridge – Ginchy, Guillemont, Longueval, the Bazentins, Pozières stretched a sea of mud more than two miles in extent, and the valley of the Ancre was a veritable slough of despond. Movement across these wastes was by way of duckboard tracks which, exposed as they were to hostile shellfire and the disintegrating action of the mud and rain, could only be maintained by arduous and unending labour. Stretcher bearers, with never less than four men to a stretcher, made the journey down from regimental aid posts through mud which no wheeled carrier could negotiate.

Who penned those words? According to Philip Warner in his chronological narrative *World War One*, they were written by Sir Douglas Haig.

1st Devons' post Somme battles

The experiences of the 1st Devons during the aftermath of the Somme were probably pretty typical of all the troops manning the area prior to the German retreat to the Hindenburg Line. The regimental history records that the whole front was marshy and water-logged and in many places the line was held by detached posts which were 'islands' in the water. Nearly everywhere breastworks had to be substituted for trenches. It was, it said with quiet understatement, 'a dripping Autumn'.

A more graphic description is given by John Terraine, who quotes Sidney Rogerson's* account of the conditions in that November and December on the Somme. The dominating feature of trench life at this time was mud. Rogerson says:

> ...mud which was unique even for the Somme. It was like walking through caramel... No one could struggle through that mud even for a few yards without rest. Terrible in its clinging consistency, it was the arbiter of destiny, the supreme enemy, paralysing and mocking English and German alike. Distances were measured not in yards but in mud.

Terraine adds that in this glutinous morass Rogerson, inspecting the short front of the two forward companies 2nd West Yorks he commanded, found 'that the round of a few hundred yards had taken over two hours of strenuous walking'.

Twelve Days, published 1933.

Rogerson also pays a tribute to the then Lieut.-Colonel J.L. Jack, whom I have quoted quite frequently. Jack had taken command of the regular battalion the 2nd West Yorkshire Regiment in August 1916, and he provides perhaps a not often recorded or acknowledged picture of a good and concientious commanding officer in that vile autumn/winter of 1916/17.

> Jack, as was his custom, visited the front line every day, each visit taking him not less than four hours. On one occasion he was accompanied by Brigadier-General Fagan. How long it took the Brigadier to come up from still further in the rear can only be conjectured, but the very fact that he was absent from his headquarters for many hours should be some answer to those who demand to know why general officers did not put in more frequent appearances in the front line.

The British Commander's proposals post Somme battles

Haig wrote in his dispatch dated 31st May 1917:

My Lord,
    I have the honour to submit the following Report on the

441

operations of the British armies in France from the 18th November, 1916, to the commencement of our present offensive.

1. My plans for the winter, already decided on at the opening of the period under review, were based on several considerations:- The enemy's strength had been considerably reduced by the severe and protracted struggle on the Somme battlefields, and so far as circumstances and the weather would permit it was most desirable to allow him no respite during the winter.

With this object, although the possibilities were limited by the state of the ground under winter conditions, I considered it feasible to turn to good account the very favourable situation then existing in the region of the River Ancre as a result of the Somme battle.

Our operations prior to the 18th November, 1916, had forced the enemy into a pronounced salient in the area between the Ancre and the Scarpe Valleys, and had obtained for us greatly improved opportunities for observation over this salient. A comparatively short further advance would give us complete possession of the few points south of the Ancre to which the enemy still clung, and would enable us to gain entire command of the spur above Beaumont Hamel. Thereafter the configuration of the ground in the neighbourhood of the Ancre Valley was such that every fresh advance would enfilade the enemy's positions and automatically open up to the observation of our troops some new part of his defences. Arrangements could therefore be made for systematic and deliberate attacks to be delivered on selected positions to gain further observation for ourselves and deprive the enemy of that advantage. By these means the enemy's defences would be continually outflanked, and we should be enabled to direct our massed artillery fire with such accuracy against his trenches and communications as to make his positions in the Ancre Valley exceedingly costly to maintain.

...In addition to the operations outlined above, preparation for the resumption of a general offensive in the spring had to be proceeded with in due course. In this connection, steps had to be taken to overcome the difficulties which a temporary lack of railway facilities would place in the way of completing our task within the allotted time. Provision had also to be made to cope with the effect of winter conditions upon work

442

and roads, a factor to which prolonged frost at the commencement of the present year subsequently gave especial prominence.

Another very important consideration was the training of the forces under my command. It was highly desirable that during the winter the troops engaged in the recent prolonged fighting should be given an adequate period out of the line for training, rest and refitting. Certain modifications of my programme in this respect eventually became necessary. To meet the wishes of our Allies in connection with the plan for operations for the spring of 1917, a gradual extension of the British front line southwards as far as a point opposite the town of Roye was decided upon in January, and was completed without incident of importance by the 26th February, 1917. *This alteration entailed the maintenance by British forces of an exceptionally active front of 110 miles, including the whole of the Somme battle front and, combined with the continued activity maintained throughout the winter, interfered to no small extent with my arrangements for reliefs* [my italics].

PART FORTY

We're 'ere because we're 'ere
Because we're 'ere because we're 'ere;
We're 'ere because we're 'ere'
Because we're 'ere, because we're 'ere.

Sung sardonically by the troops to *Auld Lang Syne*

1917 – the new year begins

As dawn lightened the skies of northern France and Flanders, flurries of snow and sleet eddied across the landscape of frozen mud, ice-rimmed shell holes, barbed wire entanglements and dead bodies of men, mules, and horses. Above, the leaden skies offered no comfort, and the weary, frozen, shivering troops looked towards another year of endless war; a year that in the event would bring even more horrors, and add an even more ghastly aspect to that already tortured and desolate land.

According to Leon Wolff, on the stroke of midnight, somewhere in the dread Salient around Ypres, a solitary artillery gun roared an erratic seventeen rounds. There was no response from the German lines. Thus, in Flanders, was 1917 heralded to the Western Front.

The first entry for 1917 in Lord Edward Gleichen's *Chronology of the Great War 1914–1918* for the Western Front reads:

1st January 1917. Normal activity proceeding. Sir Douglas Haig promoted to Field Marshal.

445

Robertson writes to Lloyd George

On 6th January the CIGS, Sir William Robertson, while he was attending a conference in Rome, wrote to the Prime Minister, Lloyd George, concerning the continuing thorn in his [Robertson's] side, Salonika. As ever he was infuriated with the French on the matter, and with what he was sure was Lloyd George's support of them:

> I don't know what effect Mr Briand's [the French Prime Minister's] oratory may have upon you in regard to this wretched Salonika business, but it seems only right and fair to you that I should tell you *now* that I could never bring myself to sign an order for the despatch of further British Divisions to Salonika. I tell you this as a friend (I feel sure you will not mind) and I sincerely hope I may not be compelled to say it to you as Prime Minister. I don't *think* I will, but not being quite sure that you realise how strongly I feel on the matter I think it best to tell you before it may be too late.

Haig wishes to return to his Flanders campaign to break deadlock on the Western Front

At first glance Lloyd George may well have been delighted by receiving this ultimation, for here, at last, was the chance to force the issue and get rid of Robertson. Unfortunately, heading as he did a coalition government, he needed the support of the Tory party members to survive, and they on the whole were 'Westerners' and supported Robertson and Haig. Leon Wolff aptly summarises the position at the beginning of 1917:

> From the northern border of Switzerland to the Belgium coastline near Ostend a scribbled line of entrenchments stretched south-east to north-west for 350 miles, dividing the French, Belgians and British from the Germans and Austrians in opposition. This complex system of trenches and dug-outs, behind which were more trenches and dug-outs, existed in a combination with dense whirls and loops of barbed wire, thousands of armoured machine guns (that new and utterly frustrating 'concentrated essence of infantry'), and various other new and old methods of defensive warfare.

Now there was little scope for the brilliant commander, for the Hannibal-like manoeuvre, for the cut and thrust of traditional warfare waged by artful foot soldiers and speedy cavalry. There was no flank to be turned, unless some miracle the mountains and the sea could be mastered by forces of decisive size. With no way to go round, with no way of crashing through, with no generals or statesmen sufficiently subtle to find another key that might turn, both sides settled down in despair and frustration to a mutual siege. Neither could enforce its will upon the other; and since folklore of the times excluded any settlement other than military the war went on in its fashion.

Haig's wish had been to continue punishing the German armies on the Somme throughout the winter of 1916 because of their exhausted state, and to prevent them being in a position to recover to mount an attack in the coming spring. He wanted to mislead them into thinking he planned another Somme offensive, but in reality, for 1917, he was aiming to attack in Flanders, with particular reference to capturing the U-boat bases from which these craft were causing such great losses to our merchant ships, and the vital supplies they carried.

According to Lloyd George's *War Memoirs*, in November 1916 Asquith's government concerned about U-boat attacks from German bases on the Belgian coast, had informed Robertson:

There is no operation of war to which the War Committee would attach greater importance than the successful occupation, or at least deprivation to the enemy, of Ostend, and especially Zeebrugge.

Edmunds, in his short official history, also stresses the view of Admiral Jellicoe on the need to occupy the coast before winter. The admiral, Edmonds says, had emphasised the fact that the British would be unable to continue the war in 1918 owing to the lack of shipping unless we could clear the Germans out of Zeebrugge before the end of the year.

Not surprisingly perhaps, Major General Fuller dismisses this explanation with contempt, saying:

The reason Haig wanted to fight in Flanders was that this

447

region had become an obsession with him, and to force the Prime Minister's hand Admiral Jellicoe was roped in to say that, because of the U-boat menace 'if the Army cannot get the Belgian Ports, the Navy cannot hold the Channel and the war is as good as lost'.

Haig knew this was bunkum... He did not fight at Ypres for submarine bases or for the French; he fought because he was confident of victory. He did what Napoleon said was the worst thing a general could do – paint an imaginary picture of a situation and accept it as real.

However, Cyril Falls says of the time of Nivelle's planned 1917 offensive:

Both [Britain and France] were about to launch great offensives, that of the British starting three days after the American proclamation of war against Germany. On the other hand, aid in the sea war was vital. The losses from submarine attack had become disastrous and horrifying. The statesmen and the naval staff officer in Whitehall, looking at the monthly totals of sinkings so carefully hidden from the public, could tell at a glance that they pointed to inability to fight on, starvation, and surrender. There was no argument about it. It must come if this went on.

Martin J. Farrar in his *News From The Front* however supports Fuller on the usefulness of the U-boat ports saying:

Everybody except Haig, it would seem, was opposed to an Ypres offensive, which included his own generals and his French Allies.

...Haig exaggerated the importance of capturing the ports of Ostend and Zeebrugge, which the British army only needed in order to advance 30 miles from their present position. These were thought to be the main German U-boat ports for the area, which simply was not true.

America in no position to help

On the subject of the American declaration of war, Falls says of America in June 1917:

> Not a single division existed, though the total numerical strength was considerable. The equipment shortage was far more serious. This extended even to rifles... There were virtually no aircraft or pilots worthy of the name.*

*There were a handful of American pilots in the French airforce, and in April 1916 the Escadrille Lafayette was formed under a French Commanding Officer with seven American pilots. The RFC and the RNAS also had volunteer American pilots before the USA entered the war.

The campaigns of 1917: Nivelle takes command of both British and French forces in France

General Joffre, after the failure at Verdun and the inconclusive outcome on the Somme, was removed and appointed Marshal of France, and General Nivelle replaced him on the Western Front.

At the Calais Conference of Monday 26th February 1917, Lloyd George and Nivelle 'connived', it is said, a plan that would give Nivelle authority over the British Armies in France: 'For all matters connected with the conduct of operations, the plans and their execution, the strength and boundaries of the various British armies, and the allocation of supplies and reinforcements.' Robertson was stunned and could not believe these proposals had been put forward, and he promptly threatened resignation. Lloyd George backed away and agreed the proposals went too far. Further discussions followed and the proposals were watered down to one which bound Haig to obey the French C-in-C's orders for the forthcoming offensive only. Haig, needless to say, was not happy with the plans. The King wrote to Haig early in March:

> The King begs you to dismiss from your mind any idea of resignation. Such a course would be in His Majesty's opinion disastrous to his Army and to the hopes of success in the forthcoming struggle.*

*Edmonds, *Short History of World War One.*

449

Haig, however reluctantly, now accepted what would in effect be the temporary relinquishment of his command of British units in the area of Nivelle's planned offensive, and was prepared to put on 'hold' for a while his own preparations in Flanders.

With the promise of a quick decisive breakthrough in early 1917 on the Western Front, Nivelle had the full support of Lloyd George and the French Government. And the scene was set for Nivelle's great offensive.

The German withdrawal to the 'Hindenburg Line'

Unfortunately for the Allies in general, and Nivelle in particular, the Germans after the Somme battles had decided to shorten their line by some 25 miles to recover and re-group, and to free more troops for the reserve.

In 'Operation Alberich' they withdrew to specially prepared defensive positions named by the British the 'Hindenburg Line'. This was not a line of trenches in the conventional sense, but a series of linked fortified positions (*Stellungs*), and each had its own intricate system of mutually supporting strongpoints festooned with barbed wire, trenchworks and firepower. In front of these, as they withdrew from their 1916 Somme positions, they operated a devastating 'scorched earth policy' destroying villages, woods, roads, railway tracks, bridges, and pretty well everything in their path to their new positions.

Andy Simpson in his *The Evolution of Victory* says the British were slow to realise that the withdrawal would happen, the pursuit was not as vigorous as it might have been, and the skills of open warfare were not great in armies that had spent two and a half years ensconced in trenches. Simpson, to illustrate his contention, quotes Lt. Col. Fraser-Tytler's *Field guns in France*, who, because of the silence from the German artillery became convinced that the enemy had departed from his part of the front. He went off to explore, and if his assumptions were correct, to establish a visual signalling in a German strong point called 'The Block House':

> I got through our barbed wire without difficulty, in fact in that section it would not keep a chicken in, but while crossing No Man's Land the company on the right opened brisk but inaccurate

450

rifle fire on me. They were evidently in blissful ignorance of the morning's happenings [the absence of the Germans].

I reached 'The Block House' at last and found that our people had only just occupied it. They were a new Third Line Division just out, and seemed to be chiefly employed in collecting souvenirs in the intervals of taking cover from the intermittent fire from our lines. A message was sent back visually to request the company to stop firing at us, and then some young officers turned up and asked me to point out their positions on the map, as even in that short distance they seemed to have lost their bearings. As they all had revolvers at full cock there was a short interval for necessary precautions before I felt inclined to start my map-reading class.

...Next morning, the 19th March, Major Sarson, myself and my reconnoitring officer Wilshin, went mounted to try and get in touch with the enemy and to find out if it was possible to get the guns along to a certain valley. The roads and bridges across the trenches were being repaired with great energy, but in every road, and especially at cross-roads, there were 20-foot deep mine craters, so it was not easy to scheme out a way to advance. The Hun had, besides, left every sort of booby trap... The R.E. however did wonderful work in spotting quickly all these toys, and I did not hear of a single casualty.

After a gallop of over 4½ miles they at last encountered rifle and machine-gun fire and their trip ended. The Lt. Col. concluded his observations by saying:

The hinterland is certainly a wonderful sight. Only the grass is left, that had proved too much for the Hun to destroy or to remove, but every village is razed to the ground, every tree cut down and the roads blown up. I noticed a few willow trees still standing, but nearly all the hedges are levelled, and the rails and sleepers are gone from the railway tracks.

8th Division

Patrols of the 2nd Devonshires in February 1917 found the Germans still very much in evidence despite rumours they were falling back on Gough's Fifth Army front. The patrols the battalion pushed out each night found the enemy still in position, and when after four days in the line they went back into Divisional reserve, the Germans had shown no signs of departure. Other units of the 8th Division took over 200 prisoners and inflicted heavy losses on 4th March in the area near Bouchavesnes. So perhaps there was more activity in early 1917 than Andy Simpson's source observations would imply.

J.L. Jack's diary records that on 13th March his 2/West Yorks took over 1,000 yards of front line from the 2/Middlesex in vile weather, and while preparing to raid the German trenches the following night they saw the usual Very rockets going up over the German trenches and heads moving about in an advanced sap. Later that night a message was received to say that the Guards raid on his immediate left had been repulsed. So obviously on this part of the 8th Division's front the Germans were still very much in evidence. However, the next day the Guards occupied the German front line without opposition. This, Jack said, was astounding news, and at 8 o'clock his men moved across No Man's Land and occupied German trenches on a half mile front, with the Devons on his right, and the Guards on his left. He adds that from a captured German order it appears the British patrols entered the German trenches only one hour after they had been vacated.

On the 19th March, Jack says:

At 6.45, preceded by scouts, the five companies [this included the headquarter's company as well as the four rifle companies] in full marching order of dress which we had not worn in action for years, plus additional ammunition, file forward at a hundred paces intervals followed by our chargers with buff browbands, rosettes, headropes and girths, the pack animals with ammunition, tools and half water ration, we cross our old trench line and the shell field of No Man's Land where until a few days ago none could show his nose and keep his skin whole.

After living like moles for two and a half years with no view beyond the trench ahead, the effect of advancing in the open acts like a tonic on all ranks; there is a cheer as we file through the pickets of another regiment in the late German lines.

To support Andy Simpson's comments above, an entry in Jack's diary for 27th March reveals that General Grogan at Brigade HQ [where Jack had been summoned for a meeting] said quietly as Jack was departing that Higher Command was dissatisfied with the 'lack of push' of the infantry. Jack was incensed by this as he had received anxieties about the West Yorks being so far advanced, and then the enforced daily placing of almost all of his men on defence work!

Basil Harvey reports that on the advance on the Hindenburg Line on 30th March, three battalions of the Rifle Brigade (2nd, 10th and 11th battalions*) were in the line side by side – a rare or unique occasion – and took Desart Wood.

*The 10th and 11th were 'New Army' (Service) battalions, both formed at Winchester in September 1914, and became part of 59th Brigade, 20th Division

Nivelle

Although Nivelle had strong support from the politicians of France and Britain, a number of senior French officers were less than enthusiastic about his plan, and what support he had from the military grew more lukewarm as time progressed. This seemed to push Nivelle almost to a frenzy of confident predictions on the successful outcome of his offensive. On learning of the German retreat to and regrouping on the 'Hindenburg Line', Churchill quotes a communiqué or directive to the British armies under Nivelle's control:

G.Q.G.,
March 6, 1917.

Direction for the Marshal.

The retirement of the enemy on the front of the Fifth British army constitutes a new fact, the repercussion of which upon the joint offensive of the Franco-British Armies must be examined.

So far the retreat of the Germans has only been carried out on the front of the Fifth British army. It will perhaps be extended to the region of the Somme and the Oise. But in any case there

453

is no indication which would allow us to suppose that the enemy will act similarly on the front of attack of your Third [Allenby] or First [Horne] Armies, any more than on that of the G.A.R [the French Reserve Group]. On the contrary, the so-called Hindenburg position is so disposed that the directions of our principal attacks, both in the British and the French zones, are such that they will outflank it and take it in reverse.

In this respect the German retirement may be entirely to our advantage, even if it becomes general; and on this assumption I base a first decision, which is not to modify in any fundamental way the general plan of operations already settled, and in particular to stick to the date fixed or the launching of our attacks.

It must, however, be admitted that all our operations cannot be carried out in the way arranged, and I will therefore examine in succession the attitude to be adopted on the front of the British Armies and of the G.A.N.

Germans capture Nivelle's battle plans

Churchill continues by saying that General Nivelle, in his desire that all ranks should comprehend the spirit of his plan, circulated various documents of high consequence among the troops in the line. The imprudence of this, Churchill says reprovingly, resulted in the famous staff memorandum of 16th December being captured on 3rd March by German troops in a trench raid by members of Crown Prince Ruppprecht's Division. The Crown Prince wrote that the memorandum contained matters of extraordinary value.

Armed with this invaluable information, and a later capture by the 10th Reserve Division of the order of attack of the French Fifth Army (with the French Army units mentioned by name) the Germans were able to prepare and improve their defences, and a whole army interpolated between the Seventh and Third armies.

Machine-guns, artillery, battle-planes, intelligence service and labour battalions flowed in a broad stream to the threatened front. Churchill added, [and] the relief gained by the Germans in the shortening of their line through their retirement from the salient enabled ever larger forces to be concentrated opposite the impending French attack.

To add to Nivelle's woes, the Briand Government fell, and having become aware of the increasing lack of enthusiasm among his military chiefs, Painlevé, the new French War Minister, made approaches to Nivelle expressing concern over the wisdom of his ambitious plan. Nivelle would not hear of any scaling down. His plan would win the war. He replied:

> [just seizing territory would be] a poor little tactical victory. It is not for so meagre a result that I have accumulated on the Aisne one million two hundred thousand soldiers, five thousand guns and five hundred thousand horses. The game would not be worth a candle.

Robertson to Lord Esher

An interesting letter from Robertson to Lord Esher in Paris on 14th March 1917 (marked 'Private' and with a request for Esher to burn it after reading it) shows that Robertson was getting fed up with the 'back-biting' and 'sniping' between some members of the British and French authorities – civil and military – at this time. He writes:

> I am aware that the French are difficult people to do business with, and I daresay that they think we are too. The point everyone must bear in mind is that we must get on with them whether we like them or not and that it is impossible to get on with them unless they are trusted to some extent to play the game. No agreement, no Conference, no anything is of the slightest use without some approach to mutual confidence. I daresay the French place little trust in us, but unfortunately it is true too that some of our people place no trust in the French. This wretched state of affairs must cease if anything is to be done, obviously. It is impossible for me to support my people in France if they will persist in thinking that no good can possibly come out of any Frenchman.
>
> We here are perfectly prepared to leave Nivelle and D.H. [Haig] to work out their differences between themselves, if they will but do so.

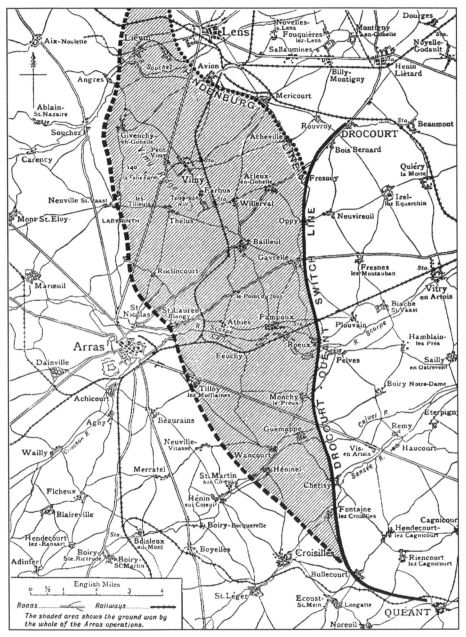

The battlefield of Arras: map showing approximately (by the shaded portion) the ground won by the British armies up to the Hindenburg Line, and its switch-line between Drocourt and Quéant, in the battle of Arras

PART FORTY-ONE

'He's a cheery old card,' grunted Harry to Jack
As they slogged up to Arras with rifle and pack.
But he did for them both by his plan of attack.

From Siegfried Sassoon's *The General – Counter*
Attack and Other Poems.

Nivelle's 1917 Allied spring offensive: Arras

The British part in Nivelle's grand offensive, Arras, was to be undertaken by General Horne, the First Army, and General Allenby, the Third Army, and timed to start six days before the French launched their attack. The First Army was to capture Vimy Ridge, near Lens and the 1915 British battle grounds. The Third Army would attack on a line south of Vimy to south of Arras.*

*The British front for the attacks extended about 12 miles in length according to Andy Wilson, 20 km according to Pope and Wheal, and Haig, see below, talks of 20 miles.

The assault began at 5.30 am on 9th April, and as for the French attack a week later, the weather, as it had been so often for the British attacks, was vile; biting cold and with flurries of snow.

For five days the artillery had blasted the German positions. There were gains of more than three kilometres on the first day, and the Canadian Corps, part of General Horne's army, took the long disputed stronghold of Vimy Ridge at a cost of some 14,000 casualties. Further south, two days later on 11th April, Gough's Fifth Army launched an attack around Bullecourt that did not go well, and the Australians suffered their worst day's losses.

457

4th Division

The 1st Battalion, Rifle Brigade, still part of 4th Division and the 11th Brigade, were in action against the village of Fampoux, and captured a position known as the 'Hyderabad Redoubt'. On 9th April two companies of the 1st Battalion captured an eclectic collection comprising a general and his staff (a total of ten officers), thirteen other ranks, three heavy howitzers, a travelling kitchen, a machine gun, telephone equipment, documents, maps and orders.*

*Among the battalion's casualties of 2 officers killed, 4 wounded and 123 other ranks killed, wounded or missing, during this engagement was Captain Bridgeman who I mentioned above at the 1914 Christmas truce. He was one of the four wounded officers and must have been one of the few survivors from 1914 still with the battalion Very few of the original 1914 regular junior officers in any regiment can still have been in the front line by 1917, let alone in the same regular battalion of their regiment. Many were promoted and transferred to 'New Army' battalions to lend their expertise and experience, and many of these were killed. I hope Bridgeman made it to the end of the war.

The Rifle Brigade Regimental History reports that the 1st Rifles:

Reached and held the furthest point of the whole British advance. It was a great day full of excitement and interest and was chiefly remarkable for the utter demoralization of the Boches and more especially for the extraordinary way in which the advances were made exactly to time, according to the time-table laid down; it seemed far more like one of the many rehearsals than one of the greatest battles of the War.

Progress was slower against the completed Hindenburg Line installations south of the river, and repeated attacks in freezing conditions against increasing opposition failed to make significant progress. The weather continued to add to the misery of the troops – the London Scottish reported that when they were relieved on 11th April by the Queen's Westminsters, they marched back through a blinding snowstorm.

Haig halted British attacks on 14th April to await news of the French offensive.

The French attacks

On 8th April, Haig wrote to Robertson:

> I hear Nivelle has had trouble. Some of the French Government wished to forbid the French offensive altogether; but Nivelle gained the day. I think this indicates the instability of purpose of our French Allies! And if anything goes wrong Nivelle will disappear.

For the French, the offensive started on the morning of 16th April. Icy rain turning to sleet met the French soldiers going forward in yet another attack destined to fail. There was no element of surprise, and Nivelle's creeping barrage tactics, so successful on a smaller scale at Verdun, were not effective. The Germans knew practically everything of the attack plans from the captured documents and prisoners, and were as a consequence well prepared.

Nivelle dismissed

Richard Holmes describes the end:

> Nivelle refused to recognise failure. He ordered more attacks in the face of evident catastrophe and then tried to blame subordinates. By the time the battle formally ended on 9 May the French army had suffered about 100,000 casualties. When he told Micheler, commanding one of his army groups, that he should be trying harder, Micheler rounded on him. 'You wish to make me responsible for this mistake: me, who never ceased to warn you of it. Do you know what such an action is called? Well, it is called cowardice.'

According to Holmes: 'Nivelle reeled like a drunken man as he walked to his car.' Whether he reeled or not to his car, he was finished as a commander.

Mutiny

On 29th April, at Châlons-sur-Marne, one French battalion refused to go back into the line. The ringleaders were arrested and four of them were shot, but the damage was done and the mutiny by the French army had begun. Once more a call was sent for Pétain, and on 17th May he took over as commander in chief of the army. He assured officers who acted with vigour and energy to suppress the mutiny of his full support. At the same time he promised the soldiers there would be no major attacks; any attacks were to be conducted economically with infantry, and a maximum of artillery. Leave was increased and units in the line could send 25 per cent or more – up to 50 per cent if circumstances permitted – home.

Haig attacks again

The news of the failure of the French attacks prompted renewed British attacks around Arras on 23rd April. These resulted in a gain of one to two kilometres, but with no hope of a breakthrough.

1st DCLI

Haig reported in his Dispatch concerning 24th April:

> In the minor operation south-west of Lens Cornish troops [1st DCLI, 5th Division] established themselves on the railway loop east of Cité des Petits Bois, and succeeded in maintaining their position in spite of numerous hostile counter-attacks.
>
> In the course of these operations of 23rd and 24th April we captured a further 3,000 prisoners and a few guns. On the battlefield, which remained in our possession, great numbers of German dead testified to the costliness of the enemy's obstinate defence.

The British too had sustained heavy losses, and troops were exhausted as they continued the struggle into May to maintain pressure on the Germans.

Casualties

Battle statistics again vary. British losses are generally given as some 150,000, and German losses estimated at about 100,000 – but there are no reliable statistics for the German forces. From unquoted sources, John Laffin in his *Western Front Companion* gives the smallest losses – his are 84,000 for the British and 70,000 for the Germans. French losses are again uncertain, some say because of the trouble in the army it was not considered politic to reveal the true figures, but somewhere in the region of 150,000 plus,* and the Germans opposing them again doubtful, but 163,000 has been mentioned.

*Martin Marix Evans gives the French losses as 187,000 and the Germans 163,000.

Haig, on the whole, seems to regard the battles as having a successful outcome although his mind was still firmly fixed on his proposed Flanders campaign. He does reveal his disappointment in the French attacks and results, as he wrote in his dispatch on the campaigns of 1917:

> The decisive action which it had been hoped might follow from the French offensive had not yet proved capable of realisation; but the magnitude of the results actually achieved strengthened our belief in its ultimate possibility.
>
> On the British front alone, in less than one month's fighting, we had captured over 19,500 prisoners, including 400 officers, and had taken 257 guns, including 98 heavy guns, with 464 machine-guns, 227 trench mortars, and immense quantities of other war material. Our line had been advanced to a greatest depth exceeding five miles on a total front of over twenty miles, representing a gain of some sixty square miles of territory. A great improvement had been effected in the general situation of our troops on the front attacked, and the capture of Vimy Ridge had removed a constant menace to the security of the line.
>
> I was at length able to turn my full attention and to divert the bulk of my resources to the development of my northern plan of operations [Messines].*

*On 4th and 5th May a conference in Paris gave agreement for Haig's plan to go ahead and to abandon Nivelle's plan. Ten days later Nivelle was replaced by Pétain.

An aerial digression

Although my concern is primarily with ground forces, the month of April 1917 was not only a time of heavy casualties once again for French and British troops, but also in the air on the Western Front for the Royal Flying Corps; and this certainly deserves at least a passing mention, not least because Nivelle's battle was a major cause in what for the Royal Flying Corps would become known as 'Bloody April'.

The German withdrawal from the 1916 battle line to the Hindenburg Line, and the Allied preparation for the coming attack, had added extra miles for RFC patrols to fly, and made increased demands for aerial reconnaissance. Unfortunately this coincided with a time when the Germans were superior in both aircraft and experienced men to fly them.

There was, it has been said, discord among the British navy and army chiefs and civilians in the administration of this junior service. And the French, who had manufactured and supplied nearly all the rotary engines to the British* (and it was rumoured darkly, kept the best ones for themselves) were falling behind with their contracts. To aggravate the position, new engines and aircraft from British factories were slow in coming through the production lines to meet the needs at the front.

*The rotary engine had the advantage of compactness and a good power-to-weight ratio. Originally invented in 1907 by Laurent Séguin, it was superseded by an improved rotary engine, the Le Rhône. British versions were made later by W.H. Allen Son and Co. Ltd., and further rotaries came into being such as the 130 hp Clerget, and finally W.O. Bentley's 150 hp BR1 (which found fame in the Bentley version of the Sopwith Camel). Water-cooled engines such as those in the famous scout (fighter) the S.E.5A gradually came on line and these were based on a design of the Hispano-Suiza Company (a V-8 largely aluminium engine which was increased in power from 140 hp to 200 hp with a negligible weight increase). The engine weighed 442 lb compared with the 160 hp Beardmore and the 160 hp Mercedes, which each weighed 600 lb or more. Negotiations for purchase and licence to manufacture these engines in England – although started in 1915 – took time, and it wasn't until the end of 1916 that they were in production aircraft (source: Purnell's *The First War Planes*).

The airmen

The RFC squadrons, with their poorer aircraft at this time, seemed to have no answer to the experienced and better equipped German airforce that was killing our new pilots and observers before they had time to develop the vital skills of observation and combat flying techniques necessary to stay alive. Many trainees with 10 hours solo flying experience were despatched to France and sent up on patrol with little or no time for training and familiarisation flying, and they were expected to fly five or six hours a day over enemy lines as the battle for Arras and Nivelle's offensive opened. The strain was immense on the experienced pilots as they tried to carry out their allotted tasks and at the same time guard these fledgling replacements.

Many of these inexperienced pilots, among them 18-year-olds, died before they reached the level of skill required to 'read' the sky and ground to stay alive. The big German 'flying circus' formations roamed the skies looking for just such tyros and before the end of May 1917, 316 British airmen would be reported missing or killed.

V.M. Yeates (see *Winged Victory* above), a very experienced Sopwith Camel pilot with 248 flying hours over the Western Front, and who died in 1934 of what was technically known as 'Flying Sickness D', speaks through the words of one of his characters to illustrate clearly what it was like – for both guardian pilot, and brand new novice – as the experienced pilot briefs the new man:

We're going to look at the lines without crossing into Hunland, so you need not bother about anything but not running into me and map reading. I expect we'll have plenty of trouble tomorrow, so we'll do our best to keep clear of it today. I'd be very careful for the first month you're on jobs. That's the dangerous time. You'll find 80% of casualties are fellows who've done less than, say twenty jobs. War flying is a trade you've got to learn and however much you fancy yourself as a pilot, remember that's only part of the trade. The great thing is to see things and, believe me, until you have had a month's practice over the lines there'll be a deuce of a lot going on that you ought to know about but won't. Many a fresh pilot is shot down before he even knows there is a Hun within miles. Push your goggles up when you are over the lines if your eyes will stand it and practise looking around you so you study every square foot of the earth and sky every two minutes. Watch the region round the sun specially; it's not a

463

bad idea to put your thumb against the disc of the sun. You've got to know exactly what to look for; what an aeroplane looks like against the sky above you and below against the ground, and they look a bit different against every variation of background. Remember that aeroplanes approach each other at four miles a minute, and concentrate at first on seeing in time. Never mind about shooting down Huns; if one gets in your way shoot at it but make quite sure first that there is no other Hun is getting into position to put in a burst at you. You'll get your Huns later, and do a lot better than if you rushed into the war all heroic. Drop your bombs where the leader drops his, and keep close to him all the time; it's his job to look after you. And when you've got to the stage of seeing everything and keeping your head in a scrap and knowing when to fight and when to clear out, if you ever get do get to that stage, then you can begin to take an active part in the war and do some fighting if you feel inclined. But give yourself a chance. Anyone can shoot you down if you don't see him coming, but it takes a wonderfully good Hun to bag a Camel if the pilot is expecting him.

Richard Townshend Bickers says in his *The First Great Air War*:

Both the Allies and the Gemans had been learning since the year began that it was not numerical superiority that decided air battles: it was the performance of the aircraft. This was chasteningly demonstrated now. Between 4th and 8th April [1917], seventy-five British machines fell. Nineteen lives were lost, thirteen aircrews wounded and seventy-three went missing. At the same time hasty training of pilots, who were not fully competent when they arrived at the Front, resulted in the wrecking of fifty-six machines in accidents. These new pilots averaged only $17\frac{1}{2}$ flying hours, a mere ten solo, and had no experience of the types they were to fly in operations.

The aircraft

Many of the British aircraft in use were long outmoded, and no match for the enemy they were sent up against. Bickers describes the position:

When these travesties [he is referring to BE.2cs, RE8s, DH2s etc.] were beating into the strong headwinds of a delayed spring they were like sitting ducks to a poacher with a double-barrelled twelve-bore.

New models and improved versions of existing aeroplanes *were* coming, but in too small numbers and too late and, as with the tanks on the Somme, some because they were unusual machines were not being used to their advantage and potential. A specific and tragic example of this was the Bristol Fighter. This aeroplane was, I believe, the first two-seater designed primarily as a scout or fighter and not as a reconnaissance or bombing machine. Bickers describes it as:

> A big strong machine over twenty six feet long, with a wing-span of nearly forty feet. The crew sat closely back-to-back in a shared cockpit. There was a Vickers [machine gun] synchronised with the propeller for the pilot, and a Lewis mounted on a Scarff ring for the observer to protect flanks and rear.
>
> The first Brisfit [Bristol Fighter] squadron, No. 48 arrived in France in late March [1917], initially equipped with only six [aeroplanes]. Had there been time for the crews thoroughly to familiarise themselves with the aeroplane before taking it into action, its impact on the enemy would have been as startling and gratifying as the RFC expected. Tragically, instead of raising the Corps's morale and lowering the enemy's, the reverse happened. On 5th April – much too soon – a flight commander, Captain Leefe Robinson, who had won a VC for shooting down a Zeppelin near London, had to lead all six on their first patrol. Five albatross DIIIs, led by Richthofen, intercepted them.
>
> The British pilots, following the standard two-seater routine, turned away from the enemy and took no evasive action, trying to give their observers a stable gun platform. Nobody had had time to find out that the excellently manoeuvrable Bristol Fighter could be thrown about like a single-seater: and that it was the pilot's heavy Vickers machine-gun that should be used as the main weapon; with the movable and lighter Lewis as a means of defence, not attack.

As a consequence of this staid old-fashioned manoeuvre, Richthofen was able to shoot two Bristols down while his wing men took out two more. Of the two that got away, one was badly damaged. Leefe Robinson had gone down and was taken prisoner.

Interviewed by the press, Richthofen described the Bristol Fighter with contempt. This was no service to his comrades, who thenceforth attacked it over-confidently. The British pilots and gunners quickly learned how to fight their aircraft effectively. The manufacturers progressively gave it a more powerful engine, until its speed reached 125 mph. In a very short time it became enemy doctrine never to attack three or more Brisfits, even when outnumbering them two or three to one. In order to tempt them to fight, Bristol Fighters used to go out in pairs and singly; but the Germans remained reluctant. This remarkable aeroplane, perhaps the best and most versatile of the war, remained in RAF service until 1932.

Another complimentary view of the Bristol Fighter, containing a longer and differing description of the episode above, and with a less than lauditory portrait of William Leefe Robinson VC, is given by Alan Morris* in his *Bloody April*.

*Morris is one of the 1960s 'butchers and bunglers' school of authors e.g: 'Blunders were plentiful that April. Usually they could be traced to red tabbed staff wallahs with curried livers and monsoon-steeped minds.'

PART FORTY-TWO

When Haig dined with Pétain in Paris in March 1919 his host informed him that 'the state of the French Army was much worse than he had dared to tell me'.

Cyril Falls, *The First World War.*

French pressure on the British in 1917 to take the offensive

The French armies slowly recovered from the mutinies, but for the rest of 1917 they were in no fit state to do much other than hold where they were, and pray no big attack would be launched against them. Pétain appealed to Haig to keep the enemy engaged by every means within his power although he did not reveal to Haig just how bad things were in the French army.

Westerners' dilemma

1917 became an agonising time for the Westerners, as Robertson reveals below. Intelligence reports, especially from information supplied by Charteris, were saying German prisoners were now of a much lower physical standard, and German morale was low, and all that was needed was one more big push to break them.

Neutral sources were indicating that Germany was open to consider peace negotiations, and in fact was suggesting proposals; but now, with Russia finished as a fighting ally of the British and French, Germany, unless pressure was maintained strongly in the west, might well soon be in a position to launch a major attack on the Western Front. And even if unsuccessful such an attack could strengthen their conditions for a peace settlement – especially when the French Army mutinies were known to the outside world.

Also there was a very realistic fear that if nothing in the way of a major assault was planned and put into effect, troops could be drained away to other war zones by the 'Easterners', and all the bloodshed, money, and materials used on the Western Front up to now would be for nothing. So, 'just one more push,' said the Westerners. 'Don't let this opportunity slip by.'

A Royal proclamation

At home in Britain in July 1917 the King, following consultation with his Privy Council and Dominion Ministers signed the following proclamation:

By the King
A Proclamation

Declaring that the name of Windsor is to be borne by his Royal House and Family and relinquishing the use of all German titles and dignities GEORGE R I

Whereas we, having taken into consideration the name and title of our Royal House and Family shall be styled and known as the House and Family of Windsor:

And whereas we have further determined for ourselves and for and on behalf of our descendants and all other the descendants of our Grandmother Queen Victoria of blessed and glorious memory to relinquish and discontinue the use of all German titles and dignities

And whereas we have declared these our determinations in our Privy Council:

Now, therefore, we, out of our Royal Will and Authority, do hereby declare and announce that as from the date of this our Royal Proclamation our House and Family shall be styled and known as the House of Windsor, and that all the descendants in the male line of our said grandmother Queen Victoria who are subjects of these realms, other than female descendants who may marry or may be married, shall bear the said name of Windsor;

And do hereby further declare and announce that we for ourselves and for and on behalf of our descendants and all other the descendants of our said grandmother Queen Victoria who are subjects of these realms, relinquish and enjoin the discontinuance of the use of the degrees, styles, dignities, titles and honours of Dukes and Duchesses of Saxony and Princes and Princesses of Saxe-Coburg and Gotha, and all other German degrees, styles dignities, titles, honours and appellations to us or to them heretofore belonging or appertaining.

Given at Our Court of Buckingham Palace, this seventeenth day of July, in the year of our Lord One thousand nine hundred and seventeen, and in the eighth year of our reign.

God save the King.

On the same date Mr Winston Churchill became Minister of Munitions.

Flanders, 1917, the operations begin

Although Flanders held the strategic objectives that the Somme area did not, the terrain remained unpromising. The flooded drainage ditches, inside the belt of what had been reclaimed marshland before the Belgians reflooded it, criss-crossed the area like a giant spider's web and spilled out over the countryside. Further inland the ground improved, but the subterranean water level was still high.

Messines

Haig, with the departure of Nivelle, and now free to pursue his plans in Belgium, decided that the narrow ridge dominating the plain east of Ypres – Messines Ridge – could be taken first as a separate operation and, according to Gough in his book *Soldiering On*, Haig did not have sufficient heavy artillery to tackle the whole of the Flanders offensive in one go anyway.

Troop formations involved in the offensive in Flanders in 1917

Captain E.A. James says of these battles:

> The Battles Nomenclature Committee has defined a common geographical boundary for the eight individual battles of the Battles of Ypres, 1917 and the compiler has adhered to this boundary in deciding which formations qualify for the various battles... It would have been more satisfactory if a separate geographical boundary had been assigned to each battle as was done for the Battles of the Somme, 1916.

None of my battalions appears to have been actively engaged in the opening phase – the battle of Messines 7th to 14th June 1917, but in the main battles of Ypres from 31st July to 10th November 1917, the 4th, 5th, 7th, 8th and 61st Divisions were all involved.

4th Division which included the 1st Rifle Brigade went into action as part of the Fifth Army, XIV Corps, in the battle of Polygon Wood 26th September – 3rd October.

5th Division, part of X Corps in the Second Army, included 1st DCLI and 1st Devonshires were also engaged in Polygon Wood as above.

7th Division, 8th Devonshires, 20th Brigade, X Corps, were involved in the battle of Polygon Wood, 26th September–3rd October; the battle of Broodseinde, 4th October; the battle of Poelcappelle, 9th October, and the second battle of Passchendaele, 26th October–10th November. (After all that it was no wonder that the remnants of the battalion were sent to Italy a week later.)

8th Division was transferred from the Second Army to the Fifth Army on 11th June, The Division now became part of the Second Corps and under the command of Lieut.-General Sir C.W. Jacob.

The 2nd Devonshires,* as part of 23rd Brigade, and the 2nd Rifle Brigade, as part of 25th Brigade (in the 8th Division, Fifth

470

Army), were in action at the battle of Pilckem, 31st July–2nd August, and the battle of Langemarck 16th–18th August.

*The 2nd Devons had received few reinforcements during the spring. By now, although they had received 200 replacements, most of them had been in the army only a few weeks and needed all the training they could be given.

24th Division, part of the Fifth Army, which included the 3rd Battalion, Rifle Brigade, 17th Brigade, took part in the battle of Pilkem 31st July–2nd August, and the battle of Langemark 16th–18th August.

61st Division, also part of Gough's Fifth army, XIX Corps, with 1/5 DCLI as Pioneers, was involved with the Second Army in the battle of Langemarck between the 16th and 18th August.

Training for the battle for Messines Ridge

The British troops practised their proposed great breaking-free operation during the long months prior to the offensive while still suffering almost helplessly under the guns of their tormentors ringed around them on the slopes. Behind each of the three corps training areas had been constructed a model of the entire ridge, laid out in a field about the size of a tennis court.* Various of the twelve divisions had also made table-top replicas of their individual sectors.

*The reported size of the model varies from a tennis court to two croquet courts to more than an acre of ground depending on the reporting by different war correspondents. Whatever its actual dimensions there is no doubt the model was big and very detailed as all accounts agree.

As the training programme progressed commanders from General Plumer down visited the front daily, and saw to it that the movements of troops, as small as corporals' sections, were understood by the men and coordinated with the larger plan. Patrols increased their activitity, seeking new information, and there was a sense of optimism despite the fact that the German positions looked impregnable. The Germans held the ridges full of guns, and webbed with row after row of sandbagged trenches. The ridges were armed with thousands of machine-gun emplacements, pillboxes, and snipers' positions. The British tunnels and mines would have to do their job almost impossibly well to overcome these seemingly unpassable barriers.

471

There had been a prolonged artillery barrage with guns openly displayed from 18th to 30th May. Leon Wolff writes in *Flanders Fields*:

> The greatest artillery mass of the war had been arrayed against enemy lines between Ploegsteert Wood and Observatory ridge, about a mile north-east of Hill 60. Over 2,400 guns and howitzers were to participate, fully a third of which were heavy pieces: one gun to every seven yards of front... In single file the heavies were hauled directly to the frontal area from the rear towns and assembly points. Behind them jostled the little field guns, galloping up without the slightest caution, a wild collection followed closely by their ammunition wagons. They were emplaced wheel to wheel with no attempt to hide them. From 18 to 30 May the guns rumbled forward, and on the latter day they began shelling in earnest the enemy's wire entanglements, his roads, camp areas, supply dumps and in particular the routes and points where it was known that water and food were being delivered to troops up front.
>
> In the final days gas shells were thrown in vast numbers to force the enemy to don masks and lose sleep.

False indications of the impending attack were given as twice the barrage grew in crescendo and silenced. By the 7th June the British were thoroughly rehearsed, and every gun was on its target. Tanks were ready, and some three hundred RFC aircraft were flying sorties to take photographs and act as spotters for the artillery.

The battle begins

The battle opened well for the British. The heavy artillery bombardments, and the detonating of 19 of the massive 21 mines that had been in preparation by tunnelling companies for so long, could be heard in England.

The mines

British, Canadian, Australian and New Zealand men of the tunnelling companies had been digging for more than a year and shafts from

472

concealed positions, as far as 2,000 yards from the German lines, were sunk to allow mines to be placed up to 100 feet below the German trenches. The combined power of the detonation of these mines was the greatest ever effected until the advent of the nuclear bomb. The explosives had been brought up by night in backpacks weighing 50 lbs and hauled through the tunnels to be packed into place and fused.

One million pounds of ammonal was eventually placed in the workings divided between 21 mines, and 933,200 exploded in the 19 mines that went up. The German troops in the front line were literally shattered. Estimates vary, but the figure of 10,000 German soldiers being killed or buried alive in those few seconds is frequently mentioned. War correspondents who were present found difficulty in describing that terrible awe-inspiring event of the exploding of the mines that heralded the attack – the attack that Plumer and his chief of staff 'Tim' Harington had been preparing for so meticulously and for so long. This could be no surprise attack except for that unbelievably well-kept secret of the mines.

Martin Farrar quotes William Beach Thomas, representative for the *Daily Mirror* and *Daily Mail*, reporting from the battle, dazed by the magnitude of the opening bombardment:

This morning General Plumer's army, which for nearly two years has fought a fine stonewall battle, took in hand its biggest and boldest attack of this war. I come back from the sight of it dazed and battered by the fury of engines of war, new and terrible and grouped in untold mass.

I have seen several of the heaviest bombardments ever conceived by scientific imagination; none of them approached this in volume or variety or terror, and one moment of it will live forever in the mind of all who were in range as a spectacular miracle of the world. An hour before dawn, as we stood over the dim valley, where the black tree-tops looked like rocks in a calm sea, we saw what might have been doors thrown open in front of a number of colossal blast furnaces. They appeared in pairs, in threes, and in successive singles. With each blast the earth shook and shivered beneath our feet. 'It is worse than an earthquake,' said someone who had known one of the worst.

Thunderclouds of smoke rose in solid form to immense

473

heights from Hill 60, from Wyteschaete Wood, and other places, and while our eyes were full of the spectacle a thousand guns opened. Was ever such a signal for such an upheaval? The air shook as the earth shook, and where the earth and air met incredible explosions set the world on fire.

The Daily Chronicle for Friday 8th June relates:

BATTLE DIN HEARD IN LONDON.
MR. LLOYD GEORGE CALLED TO LISTEN.

Mr. Lloyd George, who was staying at Walton Heather on Wednesday night, was called at three o'clock yesterday morning in anticipation of the explosion with which the battle opened and of the exact hour of which he had been notified.

He and others heard clearly the tremendous shock. Sleepers in the district were awakened by it, and even in London some heard shortly after 3 am what they judged to be heavy guns across the channel till the account of the firing of the ponderous mine told them what it really was.

On the evening before the battle Plumer's chief of staff, Major General Harington, brought the accredited war correspondents to the Second Army's headquarters for a lecture on the strategies for Messines Ridge. Martin J. Farrar, in *News From The Front*, says that Lytton, a correspondent censor with GHQ, commented:

General Harington began his lecture with the momentous words, 'Gentlemen I don't know whether we are going to make history tomorrow, but at any rate we shall change geography'.

Leon Wolff says of Harington:

He [Plumer] was fortunate in possessing an extraordinary chief of staff, the cultured and wise Major-General Sir Charles ('Tim') Harington – also a cautious planner, but perhaps with an extra dash of imagination and verve. He was tall and thin, nervous, had a card-index mind and a sense of humour. The combination of the two men had proved outstanding in the war to date.

474

Leon Wolff continues:

During the evening the men marched silently in columns of fours like groping tentacles towards the communication trenches, and thence to the front, where white jumping-off tapes lay on the soft wet ground of No-Man's-Land. They were troubled and wearied by the need for wearing their masks, for gas shells were plopping all about them, laying low the unwary and careless as well as many pack animals gasping and heaving in the poisoned air. It was a warm night. Fog lay on the Salient like a heavy caress, and in it not a breeze stirred. Overhead forked lightning played, accompanied by the mutter of thunder. At midnight a sharp thunder shower broke. It lasted only a few minutes, and when it passed a three-quarter moon floated regally in a nearly clear sky. Now brilliant flashes against the enemy slopes could be seen, and the steady whamming of the big guns sounded perceptibly loud as the blanket of smoke melted away.

Half-an-hour before Zero Hour the British guns stopped firing and the night became so still that one could hear nightingales singing in the nearby woods. The men fixed bayonets and removed their gas masks. Officers changed to other ranks' tunics and kept peering at their wrist watches. Zero Hour would be 3.10 am.

...A few seconds before 3.10 some of the heavy guns rearward began to fire. Then each of the nineteen land mines exploded almost in unison. The earth quaked, tumbling and staggering the British soldiers as they rose in awe to see the rim of the hated ridge burst skyward in a dense black cloud, beneath which gushed nineteen pillars of flame that lit the salient with the red glare of hell.

The Times correspondent, Mr Perry Robinson, tried to find the words to describe this awful and awe-inspiring scene in a long dispatch to his readers:

I watched the attack from a very advantageous position, but the dim light of the early dawn, and, still more, the volumes of smoke which enveloped the whole battlefield, made it impossible to see what was happening. From what one can

475

learn from the various quarters, however, the attack was perfectly successful everywhere, and while there was hard fighting from the start on many parts of the line, our casualties on the whole are extremely light, and everything which we had set ourselves to win was won even more rapidly than we had dared hope.

One of the two mines that did not explode in 1917 went off in 1955. The location of the remaining mine is unknown.* The combination of the exploding mines at 3.10 am on 7th June, and the intensity of the barrage had a demoralising effect on the surviving German troops as the British, Australian, and New Zealand divisions pushed forward. As always resistance stiffened after the first shock, but the British troops gained all their objectives.

*A battlefield guide of my acquaintance claimed, while we were standing in the vicinity, that he had a very good idea where it is, but he did not elaborate beyond this, and we did not linger very long.

Anthony Eden* who took part in the opening of the battle of Messines said in his memoirs (as quoted by Andy Simpson):

> ...our attack succeeded beyond our wildest dreams. The Dammstrasse [trench] on our front had been virtually obliterated, as Harington [Plumer's chief of staff] had promised, and the Fusilier battalion on our left captured their stretch without loss. Even so, the dug-outs built into the bank and invisible from our side were immensely strong. Evidently we owed much to those 9.2" howitzers... The artillery bombardment and the barrage were excellent.

*Anthony Eden, future Foreign Secretary in Winston Churchill's cabinet during and following the Second World War. Later, after Churchill, he himself became Prime Minister. Sadly he ended his political career – and his life – a sick and rather tragic figure. Two of his three brothers were killed in the First World War, Jack in 1914 and Nicholas in 1916.

Eden is extremely complimentary of the staff work and, unlike Sassoon in his poem *The General* quoted above where at Arras *'we're cursing his staff for incompetent swine'*, Eden writes:

> During the five hours which our advance was planned to last, we were scheduled to attack a series of lines, red, blue and black

476

on our maps. The rate of our advance and the length of the pause at each captured objective was perfectly timed to give us just long enough to regroup before the barrage moved on again and the enemy no sufficient opportunity to rally and fight back.

Plumer and his staff were renowned for their meticulous planning and operation. Haig, it has been said, felt Plumer was at times too meticulous and cautious in his approach, and that was why he brought in Gough for the later attacks by the Fifth Army.

Messines, the casualties

The success of the operations at Messines was bought at considerable cost. Martin Marix Evans gives the casualties for the British troops as 24,562 of whom 10,521 were ANZAC. 11 tanks were lost. The German figures, he says, were 23,000 of whom 7,264 were taken prisoner. They also lost 154 guns, 218 machine-guns and 60 mortars.

Haig in his report of the campaigns of 1917 does not refer to British casualties for the assault, but gives the following:

> The rapidity with which the attack had been carried through, and the destruction caused by our heavy artillery, made it impossible at first to form more than a rough estimate of our captures. When the final reckoning had been completed, it was found that they included 7,200 prisoners, 67 guns, 94 trench mortars and 294 machine-guns.

Post Messines

For six weeks after the success at Messines the weather held fair day after day, and men and matériel were moved in large numbers and huge amounts for the second phase of the offensive planned to include both British and French forces.

During this period the labour corps, pioneers, and ordinary infantry were engaged in the constant task of building and repairing roads as the continuous stream of motor lorries bringing up the materials and supplies played havoc with already damaged road surfaces. It was not possible to hide the fact that another massive attack was being prepared and the Germans, from aerial reconnaissance and from their overview from the 'heights' they held, saw it all developing.

The Germans attack. Mustard gas

Despite being savagely attacked at Messines the German troops themselves went on the attack on 10th July at Nieuport, on the extreme of the line on the Belgian coast, taking more than 1,000 prisoners. And on 12th July they shelled the salient, firing 50,000 rounds and introduced a new horror, mustard gas.

Martin Marix Evans says in *Passchendaele* that nearly 2,500 soldiers were gassed, and the mustard gas shells continued falling on British lines for the next three weeks claiming another 14,726 victims. He continues:

> Staff Nurse C. Macfie describes the scene at Godwaersvelt Casualty Clearing Station: 'The mustard gas cases started to come in. It was terrible to see them. I was in the post-operative tent so I didn't come into contact with them, but the nurses in the reception tent had a bad time. The poor boys were helpless and the nurses had to take off their uniforms, all soaked with gas, and do the best they could for the boys. Next day all the nurses had chest trouble and streaming eyes from the gassing. They were all yellow and dazed. Even their hair turned yellow and they were nearly as bad as the men, just from the fumes from their clothing.'

Passchendaele, the prelude. Haig and Lloyd George at odds

Haig was keen to continue with his programme, but the Prime Minister, Lloyd George, still harboured doubts about the operation despite the success at Messines. He distrusted the intelligence information coming from Haig's headquarters, and was extremely reluctant to release more troops to Haig; in fact, as mentioned before, he had instructed Haig to send some of his precious divisions to Italy to bolster the flagging Italians.

Additionally, Lloyd George would not sanction further attacks on the Western Front without a guarantee of the French adding supporting troops, but when it came to it the French were not really able to offer much support; they were, as I have said, more concerned for the British to take the pressure off *them* following the mutiny by their troops after Nivelle's failed offensive in April. They also had their own plans further south at Verdun again.

Should Haig have continued?

Haig was proceeding on the assumptions that: (a) the fine summer weather would hold until the onset of autumn; (b) the Germans would be unable to transfer troops from the Russian Front in time for his next attack – even if they were in a position to do so, and (c) the intelligence reports from Charteris concerning the morale and quality of the Germans in Flanders following the attack at Messines were correct.

So, if all went to plan, the next phase of the attack – on the Passchendaele Ridge – would enable the Allied forces to sweep across the ridge and on towards Bruges and Ghent. The preparations for the attack were to be in place and the attack ready to start on 16th July. But the long delay following the success at Messines was to prove tragic, especially as during that period the weather had held fair.

Lloyd George did not give Haig sanction to proceed until 25th July, and even then it was somewhat half-hearted. It was also clear that the French could offer only limited support and further, they would not be able to attack until the French First Army on Gough's left was ready, and this would not be before 31st July.

Haig, despite the delays, still appears to be optimistic. Maxse, at this time the Commander of XVIII Corps, describes Haig visiting the Division's HQ on 21st July:

> D.H. was in great form, better than I have ever seen him – full of confidence and – for him – communicative and genial. Though it must have bored him, he consented to go round all my Staff Officers and crack suitable jokes with the humbler members of staff including all the NCOs and clerks ... some were in shirtsleeves and no one was standing too rigidly to attention – and DH did his part excellently well and produced a very good impression on all.

479

The weather

The critics of Haig's plan and timing maintain he should have been aware of the coming bad weather, and strangely it would seem many base support for their criticisms on remarks published by Haig's chief of intelligence, John Charteris, the man blamed so much for over-optimism when forecasting proposed attacks.*

*Philip Warner, in *Passchendaele* quotes General Sir James Marshall-Cornwall, who worked on Haig's staff in intelligence in 1917:

> Haig must be blamed for giving too much credence to the exaggerated estimates of German deterioration which were daily instilled into his ear by Charteris, whose counsels certainly warped Haig's judgement and induced the illusion that only one more push was needed to achieve final victory.

Charteris wrote in his biography of Haig:

> The date of the attack was to be July 25th – the earliest date by which preparations could be completed. Haig was already anxious about the weather conditions that were to be anticipated. Careful investigation of the records of more than eighty years showed that in Flanders the weather broke early each August with the regularity of the Indian monsoon; once the autumn rains set in difficulties would be greatly enhanced.

A different view regarding the weather, according to Richard Holmes in his *The Western Front* comes from John Hussey in *Passchendaele in Perspective*. Hussey, says Holmes, states that from a meteorologist's standpoint 'August might be expected to be reasonably dry, not abnormally wet'. And Haig's chief meteorologist Lieutenant Colonel Ernest Gold later observed, Holmes continues, 'that the rainfall during the five months of the offensive [in Flanders] was over five times heavier than for the same period in 1915 and 1916.'

Haig was now really caught in a dilemma because, to quote Charteris again:

> If the weather broke, progress would naturally be slow, and at the same time conditions of tide and sea limited the opportunity for the amphibious attack to the circumscribed period of the high tides of the month of August or, at the latest September.*

If the attack took place on the 25th July there was some justification for anticipating at least a week of good weather, which would carry the greater portion of the British line out of the low-lying ground on to the ridge, where the rain would not materially impede further operations. Each day's delay in opening the attack would inevitably give further opportunity for German troops to reach the threatened area and for the organisation of defence ... the commanders from the front line urged delay. A few more days were required to move forward more artillery with complete aerial observation of the enemy's battery positions.

Haig's decision

Between these conflicting requirements Haig had to make a decision, and at the end of a conference of army commanders a few days before 25th July, Haig decided to postpone the attack until 28th July. He was not happy however, and expressed doubt about this decision. To bedevil him again, the clear weather now gave way to a dense mist which meant that the aeroplanes could not complete their reconnaissance, and both the British and French armies were unable to complete their artillery registration. On the day of the attack, 31st July, over three-quarters of an inch of rain fell, soaking the battlefield, and the rain then continued to fall for four days without a break. And so, as on many occasions earlier, the weather cruelly, and on time, gave the Germans support in their belief '*Gott mit uns*'.

PART FORTY-THREE

I have just returned, last night, from a visit to Brigade Headquarters up the line, and I shall not forget it as long as I live. I have seen the most frightful nightmare of a country more conceived by Dante or Poe than by nature, unspeakable, utterly undescribable.

Extract from a letter written on 18th November 1917, after the battle, by Paul Nash, official war artist.

An opinion of the Fifth Army and its commander in 1917

Leon Wolff says Gough was saddled with a fairly incompetent staff, and that tiresome meticulous paperwork to ensure coordination between battalions and divisions was hardly a speciality of Fifth Army headquarters. Nor, Wolff goes on to say, was Gough's Fifth Army the keenest blade in Haig's arsenal. Formerly the Reserve Army (see the Somme above), it had a bad reputation for always being pushed and pulled here, there, and everywhere, and thrown into the most dangerous fighting. It suffered far and away the heaviest casualties of any British army in the war. It was in fact, Wolff says, a vast sprawling collection of shock troops. Men hated it and feared to be assigned to it.

By the summer of 1917, Wolff continues, it was an amazing hodgepodge of regulars, reservists, conscripts, territorials, volunteers and assorted units dropped into the cauldron for lack of any better idea what to do with them at the moment. Whether this harsh description is fair or valid – and certainly Maxse, a renowned trainer and commander of meticulous thoroughness, does not seem to share this view – one has to decide for oneself on the evidence available, and I have included elsewhere in my narrative expressed opinions of Gough and his command from serving soldiers. Of Gough at this time, Leon Wolff says: 'Gough himself was a balding but boyish chap of high military quality, always half smiling, invariably courteous, witty and personable.'

31st July, the battle begins

When the battle began at 5.30 am on July 31st there were as usual mixed fortunes. The Tank Corps as such was only four days old, and until then it had been known, for reasons of secrecy, as 'The Heavy Branch, Machine Gun Corps'. Most of the 136 tanks taking part immediately got bogged down in the glutinous mud resulting from the saturating rain and the churned up ground. Lord Carver records that one member of a tank crew heading for Zonnebeke described the mud as coming in through every hole in the tank's armour: 'It was like sausage meat of fantastic shapes and sizes – round and rectangular dollops to get about our feet and legs. We slipped and slid about, and more and more came in the further we went.' It took them nearly nine hours to reach their objective.

The supporting French troops and the Guards Division got off to a good start, but on their right, the 38th Division and the 51st Highland Division met solid resistance from the fortified farms and pillboxes. The 39th Division, alongside them and to the south-east, with the support of four tanks which were still operating, were advancing towards Kitchener's Wood. At the end of the day only one tank of the four was able to record any real success. It reached its objective, the strong-point known as Alberta, and assisted the infantry in taking it, and then took part in a gunnery duel with an armoured light train on the opposite side of the Steenbeek, and put it to flight.

E.W. Grew, writing in volume 6 of *European History*, mentions in passing, of the opening of the battle, something that I have not been aware of before, that the British employed a new weapon – a combination of oil and thermit – 'which was a vast improvement on the crude flame throwers of the Germans'.

484

8th Division

2nd Devonshires and 2nd Rifles. Everything went well at the start for the 2nd Devons in the 23rd Brigade. The Second Corps had four separate objectives ending in the Broodseinde cross-roads. The Devons were mainly concerned with the first two – the Blue Line (Bellewerde Ridge) and then the second, the Black Line (Westhoek Ridge). Behind an excellent barrage they made splendid progress over the front line without a check and swept on over the second and third lines, and by 4.50 am the Blue Line had been taken.

Unfortunately things were not going so well on their right; the division on that flank were not able to keep pace with the 8th Divison, the Black Line was not reached as the Germans enfiladed with heavy machine-gun fire, and the 24th Brigade could not advance further. The Devons did eventually make the Black Line, passing through the Middlesex and coming under heavy machine-gun fire.

Losses

The Devons' losses had been heavy, mainly owing to shell-fire on 1st August, and to the miscarriage of the order suspending its advance beyond the Black Line. The colonel was killed along with 3 other officers, and 59 men were killed or missing, 8 officers and 170 men were wounded, and of the 20 officers who had gone into the attack only 8 remained unhurt, and with 'B' Company having all its officers hit. The Devonshire's Regimental History states:

> Since July 31st, heavy rains had been almost incessant. The downpour had made it quite impossible to exploit the advantages then gained. It had hampered consolidation, almost prohibited moving guns and ammunition forward, and allowed the Germans to relieve shattered formations, improve their defences and re-adjust their artillery. Not until August 16th could the attack be resumed, and the ten days' delay had gravely impaired the chances of success.

2nd Rifles, in 25th Brigade, were not able to continue their advance further without the support of the Devons. About 4.45 pm the 25th Brigade was ordered to retire, and the Devons had to consolidate the Black Line in the expectation of a German counter-attack which duly took place in force on 1st August. The Devons held on and even managed to counter-attack the Germans and recovered some lost ground. They were relieved that night when the 26th Division relieved the 8th Division, and the 2nd Devons trudged back in pouring rain to Dominion Camp on the far side of Ypres.

The 8th Division suffered 3,000 casualties on 31st July, and fourteen days later the battalions were back in the line, returning to relieve the 25th Division on 13th August, and the attack, despite the appalling weather conditions, was to be resumed.

The offensive continues

Although fighting had gone on continuously, on 16th August the attack resumed on a nine-mile front north of the Ypres – Menin Road crossing Steenbeek river. Again the 23rd and 25th Brigades got off to a good start, but the 16th Division was held up, and the 8th Division could barely hold on to their gains. By nightfall they had to withdraw to their original start lines.

Robertson writes to Kiggell

Haig was still confident of success, but appears to have been playing his cards close to his chest and was uncommunicative. Robertson, concerned about the lack of information reaching him, wrote to Haig's Chief of Staff, Kiggell,* on 17th August, asking for more information, and included a touch of the whip:

> ...but I would like to have a few lines occasionally giving your opinion as to how matters are progressing – of course with the knowledge of the Commander-in-Chief. Not unnaturally the Cabinet ask me my opinion every morning as to how matters are going and it is rather difficult for me to say much as I have nothing to rely upon but the Communiqué and the slight additions you occasionally send me. It would well be worth while for you to drop me a line once or twice a week during the operations and give such information as will enable me to show that things are going satisfactorily.

486

On the 18th August the 8th Division was relieved and placed in reserve. On 21st August the 2nd Devons were inspected by the Commander-in-Chief, and on 29th moved to Neuve Eglise, prior to going into trenches astride the Douve, which the 8th Division had taken over from the New Zealand Division. Aubrey Smith in his *Four Years on the Western Front* wrote of those August days:

> We ourselves laid the blame at nobody's door in particular. God knows it was not the fault of the regimental command, nor, I suppose – since other divisions suffered similarly – was our brigade or division to be censured. We were really not in the least interested as to who our army or corps commander might be, since we were continually being transferred from one to another, and it is far from me to criticise anyone in particular ... after the Third Battle of Ypres, in August, it was certainly the feeling of the rank and file that the Passchendaele Ridge was not worth the sacrifice involved.

The French

The French, apart from their assistance in Flanders, were fighting elsewhere, and on 20th August carried enemy defences north of Verdun – their third offensive – on an 11-mile front capturing 5,000 prisoners. By 28th August they had almost restored the front to its original position before the great German Verdun offensive of 1916.

Second thoughts on the Flanders offensive

Both sides in Flanders continued fighting despairingly but grimly day after day in the terrible conditions, and with ground changing hands and back again. Philip Warner, quoting the Australian historian C.E.W. Bean, says that because of the losses incurred, and the little gains actually achieved after the initial opening attacks, Lloyd George, by 23rd August, had resolved to stop the offensive in ten days' time and divert the Allies' efforts to the Italian theatre. Bean gives casualties for the British forces in the period 5th August to 9th September as 109,000, with 11 Corps figures alone as 27,300.

By the later part of September 1917, Robertson was also having second thoughts about the offensive in Flanders. He was concerned not only because of the conditions and difficulties in the battle area, but because of what was happening in Russia, and the strong probability of Germany reinforcing the Western Front with troops no longer needed on the Eastern Front. He said that opinions were being expressed that it would be exceeding difficult to bring about a decision in the west in view of this.

War correspondents now free to name British regiments in dispatches

There was a policy change in September, one that was certainly welcomed by war correspondents; at long last they could name British regiments in their dispatches. The complaint, up to now, had been that because of the existing restrictions the Imperial troops got all the mentions, and this made it seem as if they were doing all the work.*

During the resumption of the Flanders offensive on 20th September, for the first time the military authorities allowed the county names of the English Regiments to be published in the correspondents' dispatches, and they were printed from 22nd September.

*One correspondent, William Beach Thomas, said that the standard answer from the military authorities up to now had always been that no name must be mentioned that would hint to the enemy the constitution of our battle line unless there was evidence or a reasonable presumption that the enemy already knew what division faced them. In practice this meant that the only divisions that remained continuously in one corps were the Canadian and Australian.

The enemy was always supposed to know which corps was in front of them, so it came about that after most engagements the war correspondents were informed that they could mention the Canadians and Australians. This had the effect of piling up the impression that the whole burden of fighting was on the shoulders of the overseas troops.

Haig buoyant

Despite the stalling progress of the offensive, Haig's mood, at least ostensibly and publicly, continued to be one of optimism, and Phillip Warner records that on 4th October Haig wrote in his diary:

Glass fell $\frac{1}{2}$ inch from mid-day yesterday to mid-day to-day. High wind all night with slight rain, increased to gale during the day. Storm in channel so boats did not cross. Wet afternoon, fine night.

Attack was launched at 6 am this morning by eight divisions of Second Army [Plumer] and four divisions of Fifth Army [Gough]. On the right of the attack was 37th Division (9th Corps) south of the Menin Road. Next on the north was 10th Corps with the 5th, 21st and 7th Divisions. Some hard fighting took place here. To-day was a very important success and we had great good fortune in that the enemy had concentrated such a large number of Divisions just at the moment of our attack with the very intensive artillery barrages.

Over 3,000 prisoners and six guns already reported captured. In order not to miss any chance of following up our success if the enemy were really demoralised, I met with Generals Plumer and Gough with their staff officers at my house in Cassel at 3 pm Plumer stated that in his opinion we had only up-to-date fought the leading troops of the enemy's Divisions on his front. *Charteris, who was present, thought that from the number of German regiment represented amongst the prisoners, all divisions had been seriously engaged and that there were few more available reserves* [my italics].

After full discussions I decided that the next attack should be made two days earlier than already arranged provided Anthoine* could also accelerate his preparations. At 4 pm I saw the latter. He was most anxious to do everything possible to hasten matters. Finally it was found only possible to advance the attack by *one* day.

*The commander of the French First Army.

4th October, the 5th and 7th Divisions arrive

After the earlier strenuous fighting of the Arras offensive the 5th Division enjoyed a spell of comparative quiet until moved to the battle area of 'Third Ypres' at the end of September. The Division (with 2nd DCLI and 1st Devonshires) came into the line on the night of 1st–2nd October, but the 1st Devons remained in reserve until 3rd October.

The 5th division was the second division from the right resting that flank on the Menin Road and having as its objectives a spur SW of Reutel and the Polderhoek ridge between the valleys of the Reutelbeck and Sherriabeck. The Devons' History says:

> The country which confronted the Fifth Division was anything but good going. The shelling had shattered the trees, had blocked ditches and streams with debris, had torn the surface of the ground to an extent which disorganised completely the ordinary drainage, and would anyhow have reduced the ground near the brooks to swamps but when the disorganized drainage had to cope with the abnormal rainfall of 1917, conditions became infinitely worse, and the attack had almost more to fear from the ground than from the Germans, skilful and stubborn as their opposition was.

The 1st Devons advanced to the assembly position just east of Veldhock on 3rd October and as they slipped and slid in the mud and under heavy shell-fire both the colonel and adjutant were hit and killed. Next morning, at 6 am on 4th October, the Devons assaulting troops went over with the DCLI on their left. The fighting was very hard as the Germans opposite – as they learned later from prisoners – were in fact lining up for an attack themselves and this involved three divisions (the Bavarian 10th, 19th Reserve, and 25th). The history of the Devons says:

> The 1st Devons, attacking astride the Reutelbeck with three companies south of it and one on the left bank, were to realize fully the obstacle of the water logged ground. To keep up with the barrage was most difficult, to keep direction quite impossible, for in places men would have been swallowed up in the swamps had they gone straight ahead. Several morasses had to be turned, and in the smoke and confusion of an attack troops found their proper line hard to recover.

The 7th Division

Meanwhile, the 7th Division had the hamlet of Noordemdhoek as its objective. The right wing though was not to strike the main blow, but to cover the flank of the main advance which was to be made to the centre and the left.

The 8th Devonshires, as part of the 7th Division, like their 1st Battalion in the 5th Division, were also having a most unpleasant time. They were back on what had been the 7th Division's old 1914 stamping ground of Polygon Wood. The 8th Devons, in the 20th Brigade, had moved up from their bivouacs at Château Sigard an hour before sunset on 2nd October, threading their way to Hooge Crater (created by one of Plumer's massive mine explosions of Messines in June) first by paved roads and then by conduroy* tracks.

*Sometimes printed as 'conduroy' and sometimes 'corduroy'.

Ground conditions

After passing Hooge it was a question of sticking to the conduroy or duck-board tracks or sticking in the pools of mud and water which otherwise monopolised the scene. The whole place was an ocean of mud, in which every other feature seemed to have been obliterated except the pill-boxes and the butte* in Polygon Wood.

*Butte (North American) an abrupt, isolated hill or peak.

Special mention at this time was given to the 8th Devonshires' transport officer in his determination and resourcefulness to get through: 'He rose superior to even the most formidable obstacles and difficulties and never failed to get the rations up or keep his horses fit.' One can barely imagine the difficulty all transport sections had of getting supplies up the front troops in the appalling conditions. Sometimes it would take eight or ten hours to cover a distance measurable in yards, and then to load up and start again.

Edwin Campion Vaughan, an officer in the Royal Warwickshire Regiment, described the conditions in his account of the conflict *Some Desperate Glory* (quoted by both Richard Holmes and Martin Evans) thus:

From the darkness on all sides came groans and wails of wounded men; faint long sobbing moans of agony, and despairing

491

shrieks. It was too horribly obvious that dozens of men with serious wounds must have crawled for safety into new shell holes, and now the water was rising about them, and powerless to move, they were slowly drowning.

A New Zealand artillery man (like Horace Cobb mentioned earlier, who was killed here, and whose niece I met on a visit to Flanders) said, as quoted by Martin Evans:

C and D guns went forward first, and didn't they have a time getting them through the sea of mud and slush! They had to have eight horse teams to do the job ... we only managed to get four guns out of our six gun battery forward.

Another New Zealander (again quoted by Martin Evans) describes conditions at the time:

It was a terrible night. We dug in as best we could at the bottom of the Bellevue Ridge – but the idea of digging in was ridiculous. You can't dig water! My section managed to throw up a ridge of slush, but the water from the shell-holes around just poured into it. You couldn't squat down, we just stood there in the rain and wind waiting for our guns to open up with the barrage.

The British attacks on 4th October hit the Germans hard, and Ludendorff is reputed to have said: 'We only came through it with enormous losses. It was evident that the idea of holding the front line more densely was not the remedy.'

PART FORTY-FOUR

We could not believe that we were expected to attack in such appalling conditions. I never prayed so hard in my life. I got down on my knees in the mud and I prayed to God to bring me through. My whole life went before me and I couldn't see any future. I really prayed, believe me.

Private Pat Burns, 46th Canadian (South Saskatchewan) Infantry Battalion, of the attack on Passchendaele October – November 1917. (Recorded from The Flanders Fields Museum *No Man's Land Audio Visual Display* in the Cloth Hall, Ypres.)

6th November: capture of Passchendaele and the ridge

Thus the preliminary to Passchendaele Ridge, the battle from Broodseinde southwards to Hollebecke, including Polderhoek and Tower Hamlets Ridge – and these objectives included the notorious Polygon Wood – began. Haig, buoyed with enthusiasm fuelled by the reports from Charteris, but Plumer and Gough more doubtful.

Conditions

Field Marshal Lord Carver, quotes Albert Conn, a private soldier in the 8th Devons, who had been wounded in 1916 on the Somme, and who would be wounded again here at Passchendaele in November 1917. Conn describes the conditions in November, as the battalion moved up to relieve another regiment, thus:

The weather and conditions were now at their worst, we had

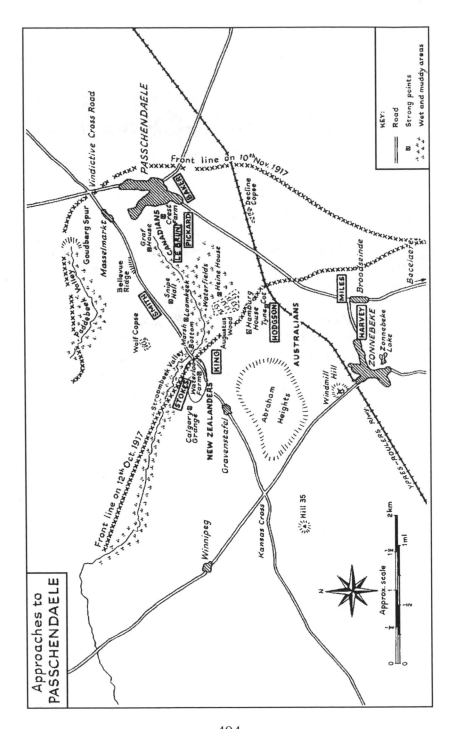

Approaches to PASSCHENDAELE

PASSCHENDAELE

Front line on 10th Nov. 1917

Front line on 12th Oct. 1917

Vindictive Cross Road

Goudberg Spur

Masselmarkt

Bellevue Ridge

Paddebeek Valley

Wolf Copse

Graf House

Crest Farm

CANADIANS

LE BLUN

PICKARD

BAKER

Snipe Hall

SMITH

Marsh Bottom

Laamkeek

Waterfields

Waterloo Farm

Heine House

Augustus Wood

Hamburg House

Tyne Cot

HODGSON

AUSTRALIANS

Decline Copse

Broodseinde

MILES

Bacelaere

HARVEY

ZONNEBEKE

Zonnebeke Lake

Windmill Hill

KING

STOKES

Calgary Grange

NEW ZEALANDERS

Gravenstafel

Abraham Heights

Stroombeek Valley

Winnipeg

Kansas Cross

Hill 35

YPRES—ROULERS Rlwy.

KEY:
Road
Strong points
Wet and muddy areas

N

Approx. scale

0 ½ 1 1½ 2 km
0 ½ 1 ml

494

advanced towards Passchendaele Ridge, there was a series of wooden tracks leading up to the front, used only at night. Guns had sunk down to their axles in the mud and the badly wounded who could not help themselves died in the mud. We used to start off from Abraham Heights in the evening laden with our ammunition and picks and spades on to the old track and trudge several miles to be met finally by guides from the regiment we were due to relieve. We would then flounder through the mud to the shell holes half filled with water occupied by two or three men facing the Germans. The conditions were so bad that men were only kept there for forty eight hours then relieved. The wide tracks were a nightmare, they were continually under fire and we stumbled over objects underfoot awash with mud. Sometimes the track got a direct hit and we would run past screaming men and plunging mules. The artillery used pack mules to carry the ammunition up to the gun positions, dead mules were dragged off the track into the mud surrounding it. Isolated pill boxes stood out like islands in a sea of mud.

Edwin Sharpe Grew, in his history published in 1920, writes of the battle:

Again the London and Naval Divisions ploughed their way through the mud; again the Canadians fought tooth and nail to win the goal of Passchendaele. They reached the outskirts, and on the spur west of it beat off five German efforts to dislodge them. The reward of their tenacity came to the Canadians a week later, on 6th November, when in one final, almost anguished, effort they won the right to put the name of Passchendaele on the flags of their regiments by capturing the village and the high ground immediately north and north-west of it.

The hold on the ridge where this stronghold stood was consolidated on subsequent days, but Passchendaele, with its toll of men's lives sacrificed to obtain it, and its dubious value, must stand as an emblem of the latter part of the Flanders campaign of 1917. Sir Douglas Haig most truly describes it as an offensive maintained for three and a half months under the most adverse conditions of weather, entailing almost

495

superhuman exertions on the part of the troops and all arms and services. The greatest tribute to it was not the number of its prisoners, though these reached 25,000 together with 75 guns, nor the ground captured, though much of it was of the highest tactical value, but the fact that 78 German divisions had been employed from first to last in holding back assaulting columns of British divisions which at times had to struggle through mud, waist high to reach the defence.

Haig's Dispatch

Sir Douglas Haig, whatever the views of the troops on the ground, seemed to be satisfied at the conclusion of the year. He began his report dated 25th December, 1917:

> General Headquarters,
> British Armies in the Field,
> 25th December, 1917.

My Lord,

I have the honour to submit the following Report on the operations of the Forces under my Command from the opening of the British offensive on the 9th April, 1917, to the conclusion of the Flanders offensive in November. The subsequent events of this year will form the subject of a separate Dispatch, to be rendered a little later...

1. The general plan of campaign to be pursued by the Allied Armies during 1917 was unanimously agreed on by a conference of military representatives of all the Allied Powers held at French General Headquarters in November, 1916...

Working his way steadily through the Flanders campaign, he says of Passchendaele:

60. At this date the need for the policy of activity outlined above [in the preceeding fifty-nine paragraphs not included by me here] had been still further emphasised by recent

496

developments in Italy. Additional importance was given to it by the increasing probability that a time was approaching when the enemy's power of drawing reinforcements from Russia would increase considerably. In pursuance of this policy, therefore, two short advances were made on 30th October and 6th November, by which we gained possession of Passchendaele.

That last matter of fact sentence does not reveal the misery and the horror of the battle. Haig however, in his report of the Passchendaele battle which follows his comments above, is well aware of the conditions prevailing. He writes:

Farther north, [than the successful attack by the 4th and 3rd Canadian Divisions on Crest Farm which included the beating off of five German counter-attacks] battalions of the same London and Naval divisions (58th and 63rd Divisions) that had taken part in the attack on 26th October again made progress wherever it was possible to find a way across the swamps. The almost impassable nature of the ground in this area, however, made movement practically impossible, and it was only on the main ridge that much could be affected.

During the succeeding days small advances were made by night south-west of Passchendaele, and hostile attack on both sides of the Ypres-Roulers Railway was successfully repulsed.

At. 6.0 am on the 6th November Canadian troops (2nd and 1st Canadian Divisions) renewed their attack and captured the village of Passchendaele, together with the high ground immediately to the north and north-west. Sharp fighting took place for the possession of 'pill-boxes' in the northern end of the village, around Mosselmarkt, and on the Goudberg Spur. All objectives were gained at an early hour, and at 8.50 am a hostile counter-attack north of Passchendaele was beaten off.

Over 400 prisoners were captured in this most successful attack, by which for the second time within the year Canadian troops achieved a record of uninterrupted success. Four days later, in extremely unfavourable weather, British and Canadian troops (2nd and 1st Canadian Divisions and 1st Division) attacked northwards from Passchendaele and Goudberg, and captured further ground on the main ridge, after heavy fighting.

Haig continues in paragraph 61 of his report:

> This offensive, maintained for three and a half months under most adverse conditions of weather, had entailed almost super-human exertions on the part of the troops of all arms and services. The enemy had done his utmost to hold his ground, and his endeavours to do so had used up no less than seventy-eight divisions, of which eighteen had been engaged a second or third time in the field, after being withdrawn to rest and refit. Despite the magnitude of his efforts, it was the immense natural difficulties, accentuated manifold by the abnormally wet weather, rather than the enemy's resistance, which limited our progress and prevented complete capture of the ridge.
>
> What was actually accomplished under such adverse conditions is the most conclusive proof that, given a normally fine August, the capture of the whole ridge, within the space of a few weeks, was well within the power of the men who achieved so much.

Summary

This campaign following after Messines had been a brutal slogging battle of attrition, fought doggedly and with incredible bravery by both sides in conditions that words cannot really describe. It is the photographs of the ground of the offensive of Third Ypres that convey a glimpse of the nightmare it was for men and beasts.

A private soldier, R.A. Colwell, gives a vivid description of the area as he saw it in January 1918, two months after the end of the battle:

> There was not a sign of life of any sort. Not a tree, save a few dead stumps which looked strange in the moonlight. Not a bird, not even a rat or blade of grass. Nature was as dead as those Canadians whose bodies remained where they had fallen the previous autumn. Death was written large everywhere. Where there had been farms there was not a stick or stone to show. You only knew them because they were marked on the map. The earth had been churned and re-churned. It was simply a soft, sloppy mess, into which you sank up to your neck if

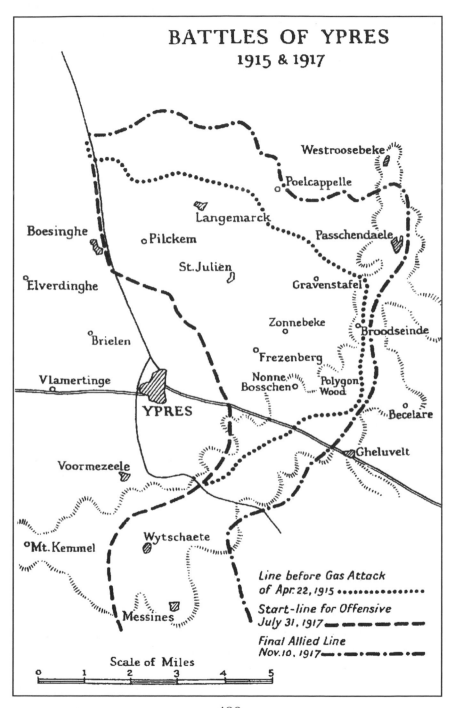

BATTLES OF YPRES
1915 & 1917

Westroosebeke

Poelcappelle

Langemarck

Boesinghe

Pilckem

Passchendaele

St. Julien

Elverdinghe

Gravenstafel

Zonnebeke

Brielen

Broodseinde

Frezenberg

Nonne
Bosschen

Polygon
Wood

Vlamertinge

Becelare

YPRES

Voormezeele

Gheluvelt

Mt. Kemmel

Wytschaete

Line before Gas Attack
of Apr. 22, 1915 ••••••••••••

Start-line for Offensive
July 31, 1917 — — — —

Final Allied Line
Nov. 10, 1917 —•—•—•—•—

Messines

Scale of Miles

0   1   2   3   4   5

you slipped off the duckboard tracks – and the enemy had the range of those slippery ways. Shell hole cut across shell hole. Pits of earth, like simmering fat, brimful of water and slimy mud, mile after mile as far as the eye could see. It is not possible to set down the things that could be written of the Salient. They would haunt your dreams.

PART FORTY-FIVE

Cambrai is an important battle, still awaiting a full academic survey. The British failure in late November is important, though valuable lessons were learnt from the experience.

Nigel Cave, from his Introduction to *Cambrai The Right Hook* by Jack Horsfall & Nigel Cave.

Cambrai, 20th November–7th December 1917

Edwin Sharpe Grewe, whom I have quoted from above, in Volume VI of *European History*, describes the reasoning behind the decision to deliver a blow in this area while the battle in Flanders, like the troops engaged in it, died in a welter of mud:

Several reasons contributed to Sir Douglas Haig's consent to deliver a blow here [Cambrai]: the chief of which was that the redistribution of German forces, as the result of divisions brought from, or exchanged with, the quiescent Russian front, as well as those which would be available when the autumn campaign of the British and French ceased, was not yet being made. Another reason was that owing to the Caporetto disaster* Italy was clamouring for French and British assistance, to be rendered directly or indirectly. It was judged, and rightly judged, to be probable that a surprise attack on a defined and limited scale might be undertaken at some weakened section of the German line and might secure good results in the forty-eight hours before the German organisation could reinforce the sector attacked.

501

The general idea of the attack was to burst through by the aid of Tanks without employing any artillery preparation to give warning; and if a break should be thereby made, to pass through it cavalry whose mission should be to do the largest amount of damage to the enemy's communications in the shortest possible time. Otherwise the tactical object of the break-through was to secure, if possible, a position from Bourlon and eastwards which would be a perpetual threat to Cambrai – the essential supply-junction of the German army of General von Below. Cambrai itself was not, and was not believed to be, within reach of any attack such as was proposed.'

*Sir William Robertson writing to Haig on 4th November, 1917 prior to making his way back from the conference in Italy at Rapallo where the decision was to establish a 'Supreme War Council', gave his usual trenchant view of the Italian war effort (and opinion of the proposed Council):

Of course the Italians have lost their heads and so have our own people, evidently. Foch is playing the game correctly and takes the line that Italy must defend itself, though we will help. Twice I have been asked by War Cabinet to send more Divisions and twice I have declined... A more disgraceful sight than the returning Italians, without arms and equipment, was never seen. They are not for it.

Haig's assessment (dispatch February 1918)

The assessment by Edwin Sharpe Grew is very much on the lines of Haig's Dispatch dated 20th February 1918:

As I pointed out in my last Dispatch, the object of these operations was to gain a local success by a sudden attack at a point where the enemy did not expect it. Our repeated attacks in Flanders and those of our Allies elsewhere had brought about large concentrations of the enemy's forces on the threatened fronts, with a consequent reduction in the garrisons of certain other sectors of his line.

Of these weakened sectors the Cambrai front had been selected as the most suitable for the surprise operation in contemplation. The ground there was, on the whole, favourable for the employment of tanks which were to play an important part in the enterprise, and facilities existed for the concealment of the necessary preparations for the attack... The capture of

502

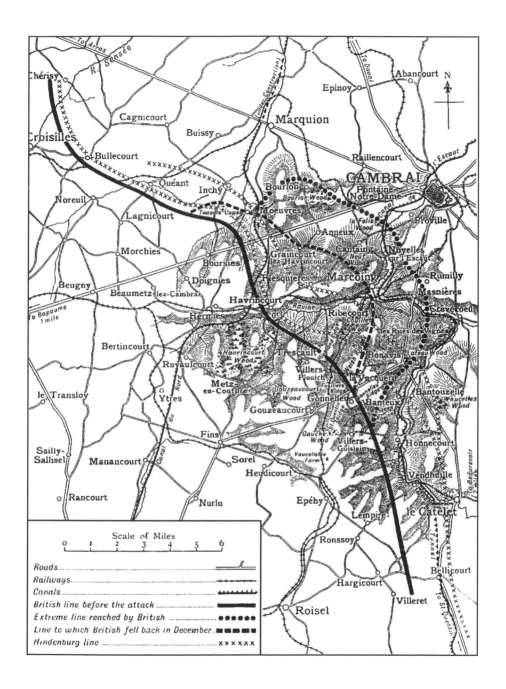

To Arras
R. Sensée
To Douai

N

Chérisy
Cagnicourt
Buissy
Marquion
Raillencourt
Abancourt
Epinoy

Croisilles
Bullecourt
Quéant
Inchy
Bourlon
Bourlon Wood
CAMBRAI
Fontaine
Notre-Dame
l'Escaut

Noreuil
Lagnicourt
Toapole Copse
Moeuvres
la Folie Wood
Canal de
Proville

Morchies
Boursies
Anneux
Graincourt
lez-Havrincourt
Cantaing
Neu Wood
Noyelles
sur l'Escaut
Rumilly

Beugny
Beaumetz-lez-Cambrai
Doignies
Flesquières
Marcoing
Masnières

To Bapaume
1 mile
Hermies
Havrincourt
Ravine
Ribecourt
Wood
les Rues des Vignes
Steveroed

Bertincourt
Ruyaulcourt
Havrincourt
Wood
Trescault
Bonavis
Lateau Wood

le Transloy
Ytres
Metz
en-Couture
Douzeaucourt
Wood
Villers
Plouich
Fusiliers
Ridge
la Vacquerie
Bantouzelle
Vaucelles
Wood

Sailly-
Sallisel
Manancourt
Fins
Sorel
Gonnelieu
Gouzeaucourt
Banteux

Rancourt
Nurlu
Heudicourt
Gauche
Wood
Vaucellette
Farm
Villers-
Guislain
Honnecourt
Vendhuille

Epéhy
Lempire
le Catelet

Ronssoy
Villeret

Hargicourt
Bellicourt
Roisel

Scale of Miles
0   1   2   3   4   5   6

Roads
Railways
Canals
British line before the attack
Extreme line reached by British
Line to which British fell back in December
Hindenburg line

Cambrai itself was subsidiary to this operation, the object of our advance towards that town being primarily to cover our flank and puzzle the enemy regarding our intentions.

...Against these arguments in favour of immediate action I had to weigh the fact that my own troops had been engaged for many months in heavy fighting, and that, though their efforts had been successful, the conditions of the struggle had greatly taxed their strength. Only part of the losses had been replaced, and many recent drafts, still far from being fully trained, were included in the ranks of the Armies. Under these conditions it was a serious matter to make a further heavy call on my troops at the end of such a strenuous year.

On the other hand, from the nature of the operation, the size of the force which could be employed was bound, in any case, to be comparatively small, since success depended so much on secrecy, and it is impossible to keep secret the concentration of very large forces. The demand made upon my resources, therefore, should not be a great one.

...The success of the enemy's offensive in Italy subsequently added great force to the arguments in favour of undertaking the operation, although the means at my disposal for the purpose were further reduced as a consequence of the Italian situation.*

*Haig had been forced by Lloyd George – despite the efforts of Robertson – to send five divisions to Italy and so further reduce his supply of troops drastically. This would cost him dearly in the spring of 1918.

Eventually I decided that, despite the various limiting factors, I could muster enough force to make a first success sufficiently sure to justify undertaking the attack, but the degree to which this success could be followed up must depend on circumstances.

Success hailed for tanks

Undoubtedly Cambrai was seen initially as a resounding success – particularly by the tanks used here in far larger numbers than in 1916, and here over ground that was particularly suited to them. Also this, the first really planned cooperation between tanks and infantry on a large scale, was generally successful – apart from the episode involving the 87th Brigade of the 29th Division mentioned below.

The *Daily Mail* correspondent in a dispatch that appeared in the paper on 22nd November* commented, with a gardener's eye, on this suitability of the battle location ground for the tanks:

The tanks were in no danger of being bogged, as they must have been in the frightful quagmires of Flanders. They could move across nice, firm, thirsty soil in which plants such as the yarrow, cow parsnip, and ragwort, and great masses of docks and darnels flourish. On some of this ground one noticed that the tank in passing scarcely left its stamp. Such soil is the very thing for tanks so long as the weather holds up – it has several times threatened us rather ominously this afternoon, by the way – and it is excellent too for the movements of troops.

*Source, Martin J Farrar, *News from the Front*.

Jack Horsfall and Nigel Cave in *Cambrai The Right Hook* have this to say about the tanks:

Elles* amassed the largest concentration of tanks ever seen on a battlefield, denuding the rest of the front of every tank which he could make serviceable. He was determined that the tank should be seen for what he fervently believed it was – the decisive weapon of the war. He managed to pull together 476 tanks. They would fight in nine battalions, each of those consisting of 36 tanks with six in reserve. These 378 fighting tanks would be supplemented by 54 supply tanks (petrol, oil, water and ammunition); 32 tasked with dragging barbed wire obstacles away, making paths for the cavalry; nine for communications, fitted with wireless; two with bridging equipment and one to bring telephone cable forward as the advance progressed.

*Brigadier-General J.H. Elles, described by Horsfall and Cave, as 'the young (forty years old) and dynamic Royal Engineer officer commanding the Tank Corps in France.' (J.F.C. Fuller, who I have mentioned and quoted several times, was his Chief of Staff.)

It has been said that Elles wanted the tanks to be used as spearheads leading the infantry, but the infantry commanders wanted them to attack on a broad front. Elles led the battle in person in his tank

'Hilda' having issued his special order number six the previous evening:

> Tomorrow the Tank Corps will have the chance for which it has been waiting for many months, to operate on good going in the van of the battle. All that hard work and the ingenuity can achieve has been done in the way of preparation. It remains for unit commanders and for tank crews to complete the work by judgement and pluck in the battle itself. In the light of past experience I leave the good name of the Corps with great confidence in these hands. I propose leading the attack of the centre division.

Aircraft

Another innovation was the number of aircraft, a mixture of scouts (fighters) and bombers available for the attack, and to be used for a variety of tasks, not least the reporting of German troop movements coming to reinforce the battle area, as well as attacking enemy aircraft, artillery spotting, and attacking ground targets including concentrations of enemy troops and railway junctions.

Like the British, the Germans also brought forward large numbers of aircraft in support of their infantry when they began to counterattack: Co-operative tactics between arms were certainly evolving, with tanks, infantry, and aircraft working together.

Cavalry

After a breakthrough had been achieved the cavalry was poised to use its speed and flexibility to isolate the town of Camrai from the east. However, as had happened so often before, despite initial British success, once the Germans had overcome their initial surprise – and shock of facing large numbers of tanks appearing almost without warning with infantry attacking alongside them – they were able to rally and pour in reinforcements in large numbers. Gradually the attacking British forces, suffering heavy losses, became exhausted and lacking reinforcements to keep up the pressure, they were forced to halt their attack and go to the defensive. Once more the cavalry were not able to be deployed.

506

Perhaps Haig was over-optimistic in pushing on and changing what had been envisaged initially as virtually a large-scale raid on the Hindenburg Line to show the Germans it could be penetrated and overcome, and so force a concentration of German troops to stay there. No doubt the great success of the early break-through by the tanks, which enabled the infantry to advance ten thousand yards on a front of eleven thousand yards in ten hours, was so overwhelming that the feeling must have been 'at last! we can really break through' and then to go for it.

However, the fatigue of the British troops, and the durability and stubbornness of the Germans, combined with their ability to bring up fresh troops, rapidly drew the battle to the usual stalemate. And so, on 27th November, Haig called a halt to the offensive and consolidated the salient – nine miles wide by four miles deep – resulting from the battle.

Initially church bells had been rung in England for the first time since war had been declared three years earlier, and the country rejoiced in this first real break-through of the war, until word of the German counter-attack on 30th November, and the ensuing stalemate, was brought home.

Philip Gibbs, as quoted by Martin J. Farrar, described the initial successes in a dispatch that appeared in the *Daily Chronicle* on 22nd November, and one that reflected the pervading spirit of optimism:

> One of our battalions, the Royal Fusiliers,* gained their objectives without a single casualty. Other battalions of English county regiments had very light losses, and they were mostly from machine-gun bullets. At the field dressing-station on the southern part of the attack they had only received 200 walking wounded by eleven o'clock in the morning – five hours or so after the battle began...
> In strategy, it seems to me the battle may prove the best adventure we have had, and the enemy was utterly deceived.

*Presumably the Royal Fusilier battalion mentioned by Gibbs was either the 8th or 9th Royal Fusiliers, 36 Brigade, 12th Division, both of whom were attacking between La Vacquerie and Banteux.

By early December the war correspondents were beginning to alter the tone of their original very optimistic and hopeful accounts of the attack. For example, the *Daily Mail* on 3rd December 1917:*

I do not modify a word I have written of the splendid skill and striking power of our offensive of November 20, which yielded us 10,000 prisoners and Bourlon Wood. That success stands, to apply a famous phrase, but neither must we question or belittle the strength and daring of this huge army on the West. People at home must draw their own moral out of this new German thrust. My present duty is to give as good account of it as I can. It will be some days before we can clear up the confusion of various accounts.

*Quoted again by Martin J. Farrar in *News from the Front*.

Investigation

An official Court of Inquiry convened to investigate 'The Action fought south of Cambrai on November 30th'. The President of the Court of Inquiry was Lieutenant-General Sir Alexander Hamilton-Gordon of IX Corps, with Major-General Pinney, and Ivor Maxse, Commander of XVIII Corps. Maxse signed the report but was not satisfied with it. John Baynes in his biography of Maxse says Maxse felt the overall picture of the Cambrai outcome was becoming unbalanced, and while the court was sitting wrote home to his wife:

The nonsense talked about Cambrai, both here and at home, makes me despair of British intelligence. The whole battle was a ten days British success which was only marred by one incursion, on one date, at one place. Everywhere else on the same date on a front of ten miles in violent fighting the Hun was badly done down – but to hear people talk one would suppose the Hun had really won a great victory! What he did on the 30th was to gain a local success.

Captain J.C. Dunn,* reporting on comments at the time going around in his battalion of the Royal Welch Fusiliers, has the following to say about the 30th November and the Court of Inquiry:

The GOC [General Officer Commanding] is bubbling over with news and gossip about the 'regrettable incident' at Cambrai as it would have been called in S. African days. Some generals find an unholy joy in the disasters of others. Praise be we were not there. Two of our regimental Brigadiers were in the collapse; they appear to have come out with credit; it's all one of them came out with, for he had to set fire to his HQ, kit and all. The Government Enquiry would be more promising of good if an outspoken coroner and a candid finding were feasibilities. It is plain that the southern re-entrant was so thinly held that it invited attack. German preparations were reported on each of the three previous days; the GOC who reported them had his Division stand-to each morning. Will the Enquiry show why nothing of the sort was done, no move was made by others? Why gunners were killed in pyjamas? – the Germans did not attack until daylight: why a GOC had to escape in pyjamas, leaving his Yellow Book and other confidential papers to be captured? Do the high Commands know of the unfitness of not a few of their immediate subordinates? Is it owing to the continual circulation of divisions through Corps that duffers escape detection, or deletion if detected? – yet a good average GOC may be dismissed rather arbitrarily.

It should be said that his battalion was still up in the Ypres sector at the time, not at Cambrai, so it was indeed 'grapevine' gossip.

*The War The Infantry Knew.

The results of the enquiry were announced on 15th January 1918, as follows:

War Cabinet is of opinion that High Command was not surprised by attack of November 30th; that all proper dispositions were made to meet it, and that public discussion of the affair is detrimental to national interests.

12th Division at Cambrai

I mentioned earlier the comments a colleague of mine made concerning the renowned RSM Brittain of the Coldstream Guards. The first written reference to him I have found, before he reached this exalted rank, was when he was a drill-sergeant. The occasion relates to the German counter-attack at Cambrai on 30th November, when his unit came across men of the 12th Division who had broken and given way before the German onslaught. This reference occurs in the diaries of a young Coldstream Guards officer, Lt. William St Leger, writing in 1917 and as reported by Michael Moyniham:

> Look at them, sir! said Drill Sergeant Brittain. Soldiers, sir! SOLDIERS! 'Ardly CREDITABLE, sir! To think that British soldiers could do a thing like that, sir!

The 12th (Eastern) Division, an all 'New Army' division under the command of Major-General A.B. Scott, consisted of the 35th Brigade, 36th Brigade and the 37th Brigade. They were part of the attack from the beginning of the battle, and their objectives on the first day involved taking possession of ground (including the formidable 'Hindenburg Line') of a defensive depth of some five thousand yards.

Despite the Germans' ability to look down on the British positions from their strong points, the heavily fortified village of La Vacquerie, and a series of heavily fortified farm buildings, the 12th Division with its tanks – 25 of which were knocked out or ditched – went forward and achieved all objectives in an advance of 5,000 yards. The division's initial task was completed by midday although with many casualties, particularly in the 6th West Kents.

The men to whom the then Drill Sergeant Brittain refers could have been from the 35th Brigade, whose commander, Brigadier-General B. Vincent, discovered when the German counter-attack barrage started on 30th November that all signal wires connecting him with forward elements of his brigade some two thousand yards to the north west were broken, and the Germans were in the village at 7.30 am. He proceeded to pull together a composite force of his staff, some Royal Enginers, and a Vickers machine-gun crew from the 235th Machine Gun Company, before beating a hasty retreat. They managed to fight a withdrawal to the west, gathering about 100 or so men – lost survivors and stragglers – to the relatively security of a railway cutting and embankment where the little force managed to put up a sustained rate of rifle-fire and to hold the enemy off.

Alternatively, the men referred to could have been from the 36th

Brigade who had been forced out of the village of Gonnelieu by the German 7.30 am attack, and where again all communications were broken. To avoid being overrun the HQ of 36th Brigade moved back down the valley soon after fighting began. One of the battalions, the 7th Suffolks, was vitually wiped out. The Guards Division, of which Drill Sergeant Brittain was part, recaptured Gouzeaucourt towards the end of the day.

The 29th Division. Newfoundlanders honoured

The 29th Division was the only division not to be broken on that fateful day of 30th November. The Newfoundland Regiment, a unit of the 29th Division, for its actions on the Somme in 1916, 3rd Ypres in the summer of 1917, and in November and early December 1917 at Cambrai, was granted the award of the title 'Royal', and became officially from then onwards 'The Royal Newfoundland Regiment'. This regiment was the only regiment to be granted the title 'Royal' during the war, and only the third ever – the other two occasions being in 1695 and 1885 respectively.

Cambrai casualties

After the first huge success with gains of up to four miles on the first day, the impetus of the attack was lost, and the Germans counter-attacked. As a result, much of the ground captured by the British troops was retaken by the Germans – and in the south, they penetrated the original British start line. The battle had resulted in some 48,000 British and 53,000 German casualties.

George Coppard mentions the number of letters he received after the publication of his book in 1968 *With a Machine Gun to Cambrai*, and I have included several of these later, but there is a particularly dignified and poignant one from a Mrs Beatrice Buckley, written in October 1971, that seems appropriate to include here:

...I am an old woman now (81). My husband joined the forces early in 1916. He was passed only for home service. But after training in England and Ireland he was sent to France in august 1917. He was forty years old then. After some time in and

out of the trenches, the 1st King's Own Scottish Borderers*
were sent to the Cambrai area. They met a strong attack, near
Masnières, and my husband was killed on 30th November
1917. He has no known grave. He was a private.

...We had a daughter – now nearly 57, and a son now nearly
55. Their father would have liked to see them grow up. Please
excuse me if I have trespassed on your time.

*1st KOSB at Cambrai

The 1st King's Own Scottish Borderers was a regular battalion in the acclaimed 29th
Division, and forming part of the 87th Brigade under the command of Brigadier-General
C.H.T. Lucas. The task of the brigade on 21st November was to cross the canal, take
Flot Farm and break through the Masnières – Beaurevoir line south east of Noyelles.
The start was not a happy one for the brigade as Jack Horsfall and Nigel Cave relate:

> For some reason the tanks did not go forward to crush the enemy wire for the lead
> battalions, but rather cruised up and down the German lines blazing away at the
> German defenders with very limited success... There were, not surprisingly, a large
> number of Tank Corps casualties.

Frustrated by uncut wire by dusk the infantry troops were back at their start line.

Poor Mrs Buckley's husband was probably one of the unfortunates
who, because of the desparate shortage of men to fill the drafts for
France and Flanders to replace those lost in the earlier 1917
campaigns, and because of the enforced departure of the five
experienced divisions to Italy, and despite being categorised 'fit for
home service only,' found himself in a draft bound for France, to
the front, and to his death at Cambrai.

Armoured vehicles

For those unfamiliar with the tanks of those days, the name
'tank' was a coded designation for reasons of secrecy – although
Sir Frank Fox (otherwise 'G.S.O.' above) seems unaware of this
for he says:

> 'The Tank' was the great mechanical find of the war, and it
> was an all British find. High authority had many fine name
> proposals for the useful monsters, but Tommy took the matter
> into his own hands and coined the word 'Tank' and 'Tank' it
> remained.

The original specification called for a minimum speed of 4 mph, rapid all-round manoeuvrability, and a range of 20 miles or better. The Mark IV 'female' tanks – of which 'Deborah' below was one – were armed with 6 machine-guns while the Mark IV 'males' carried 2 six pounder guns and 4 machine-guns. The Royal Navy had been using armoured cars in France from early days and were considering the development of 'landships'. The ideas were passed in a memorandum to Winston Churchill at the Admiralty via Colonel Hankey (mentioned above, the brother of Donald and Secretary to the British Committee for Imperial Defence) on 26th December 1914. Churchill seized upon the idea, and the project was launched. However Lord Kitchener, I have read, thought little of the idea and was said to have regarded them as 'pretty mechanical toys'.

I assume the lighter armament of machine-guns only was considered more feminine, and those tanks so fitted became designated 'female' tanks. They were given girls' names by their commanders. The 'males' were given all types of names and possibly one of the best known of them was the male tank 'Fray Bentos' (after the tins of corned beef of that name).

The resurrection of Deborah. A tank interlude concerning Cambrai

In October 2000 I was staying in the Hotel Beatus in Cambrai, and the owner, M. Phillipe Gorczynski, very kindly escorted me, and two other visitors, around the battle area of 1917. He included a special treat for us, and that was to see the Mark IV female tank 'Deborah' he had excavated from a field two years earlier. The excavation had followed his long search and enquiries among local farmers for the location of a relic of the battle, a buried tank.

We were ushered into a barn where Deborah now stood under spotlights on her own plinth. She was as she came from the battlefield when she had been knocked out at Flesquires in 1917; mud stained, holed and battle scarred. To me she looked splendid and noble, but at the same time a sad and lonely sight, for she had returned to the world in 1998 (eighty-one years after her last appearance on the surface), and to a world so very much changed from the one in which she had been built, and in which she had fought and been buried.

Deborah had been commanded by Second Lieutenant R.A. Jones who was killed in the action that knocked Deborah out, and lies in Flesquires Hill Cemetery. Monsieur Gorczynski told me he had invited the grandson of 2nd Lieut. Jones to come to see the tank after she had been brought to the surface and identified. In the course of conversation M. Gorczynski asked Mr Jones if his grandmother's name had been Deborah. The grandson replied that it was not, and M. Gorczynski, with Gallic tact, said to me: 'I thought it best not pursue the matter.'

Autumn and winter 1917. Departure of the 7th Division

As 1917 drew to a close, the 8th Devonshires, licking their wounds after Third Ypres and with the gaps in their ranks filled by some of their returning sick and wounded, but mainly by newcomers – those combed out from other units such as ASC and AOC, together with many untrained recruits – found themselves entrained for Italy with the rest of the 7th Division.

After the nightmare of mud and death of France and Flanders, what a contrast and relief it must have been for the division when they billeted in villages north of Castelfranco, 17 miles from the Italian front line. How Horace Westlake and his fellow dead comrades of Loos in 1915, the Somme in 1916, and Third Ypres in 1917 would have been delighted to have shared this unexpected experience. It must have seemed like paradise to be in another country, free from the Western Front, and in a location unscarred by signs of war, and under clear skies. So here I leave them as they leave my story.

The Supreme War Council

Lloyd George, in an effort to gain more support and views from people other than those whose focus was centred entirely on the Western Front, created 'The Supreme War Council'. This council comprised representatives from all the Allied nations, and its stated purpose was to 'Watch over the general conduct of the war'. The inaugural meeting of the council was held on 1st December 1917 at Versailles, and Sir Henry Wilson, detested by Robertson and no friend either of Haig, had been selected by Lloyd George as the British military representative. Foch represented the French, General Cadorna the Italians and General Bliss the USA.

The battles rumble to a close in Flanders

The 2nd Battalion of the Rifle Brigade and the 2nd Battalion of the Devonshire Regiment, in Flanders as part of the 8th Division, were still in action on 2nd December, fighting and dying in tidying up operations in the aftermath of Third Ypres. They were attacking at Passchendaele Ridge where the objective of the 25th Brigade was to open out a salient round the Ridge, and at the same time carry the British line sufficiently far northwards along the ridge to give observation into the valleys running up to the Passchendaele plateau from the north and east.

On the night chosen for the attack there was bright moonlight, and the divisional commander was of the opinion that hostile machine-gun fire was more to be feared than any artillery barrage. The enemy, because of the moonlight, would see the advancing troops who were to move forward *before* the 'zero' hour of 1.55 am and the opening of the barrage. He requested a change in the timing. Unfortunately he was overruled.

The 2nd Rifles *were* spotted before the barrage opened, and they ran into the anticipated heavy machine-gun and rifle fire. To make matters worse, a strong point was discovered still in enemy hands, and the Rifles made only about 100 yards in advance of their original line. Over 50 per cent of their effectives became casualties, including 10 out of 12 officers. The operation was not a success.

The 2nd Devonshires were also involved in this failed operation, and their commanding officer was mortally wounded. Divisional losses amounted to 40 officers and 584 other ranks.

America declares war

On 7th December the USA declared war on Austria–Hungary.

Cecil Westlake, December 1917

That winter there was published news of Cecil Westlake. The *Supplement to the London Gazette, 18 December, 1917. 13237* under the heading *Mentioned in Dispatches* printed the following:

Duke of Cornwall's Light Infantry. Westlake No. 240201 Sergt. C.H. (Launceston).

A faded and yellowing cutting from the *Western Morning News* shows it had picked up the story and under the heading 'Mainly Personal' reported:

Sergt. C.H. Westlake, DCLI (Launceston) is among those recently mentioned in dispatches by Sir Douglas Haig.

Other December news

By the end of December the month had seen the dismissal of Charteris (Haig's Chief of Intelligence), and the resignation of Kiggell (Haig's Chief of the General Staff). Lloyd George was plotting to begin the removal of Robertson as CIGS, and he also hoped to get rid of Haig at the same time as Robertson, but in this he would not be successful.

Unlike other authors, Phillip Warner's view is that Lloyd George and Robertson got on well, and shared similar views, for he writes: 'Doubtless he [Robertson] and Lloyd George saw eye to eye on most things, even though one was an orthodox soldier and the other a subtle politician.' I cannot think how he arrived at this conclusion.

Christmas

The 8th Division was relieved and moved south of St Omer for training in the rest area, and then on Christmas Day the 2nd Devonshires returned wearily to Passchendaele. Meanwhile the War Diary of the 1/5th Duke of Cornwall's Light Infantry records their Festive Season:

24th December 1917. The battalion marched from the Beetroot

Factory Camp arriving at Marly Camp at 12.45 am. [They had left Bray-sur-Somme at 5.30 pm the previous day and de-trained at Plateau Station at 9 pm and marching until their arrival at Marly Camp at 12.45 am.]

25th December 1917, The battalion was employed during the day in the improvement of the billets.

26th December 1917, Kit Inspection and Rifle Inspection.

These men were the lucky but very weary survivors of the battalion's pioneering and fighting activities in Flanders and France during the year. Unfortunately for these Cornishmen there would be no respite in the spring of the coming year.

The Divisional History of the 8th Division gives an insight into the work that both the pioneers, and the infantry generally, were engaged upon in Flanders that autumn and winter when they were not fighting:

The shelling of the forward areas at this time was indeed more severe than any which the division had yet experienced, while the mud and water and discomfort of life East of Ypres were indescribable. To get from Ypres to the front line entailed a walk of several miles along duck-boards. One step off the duck-boards meant sinking to the knees in mud from which it was impossible to extricate oneself unaided. Men got into this mud in the dark, and after many hours exposure, died of cold and exhaustion despite every effort made by rescue parties to save them. The old battlefield was one vast tormented bog, seamed by narrow lines of conduroy or duck-board tracks* which, marked down by the enemy's artillery, were swept with high explosive and shrapnel by day and night. The mere work of repair kept large numbers of men continuously employed, both in the huge workshops where 6-foot lengths of duck-boarding were made and in the more arduous and dangerous task of restoring the gaps blown by the enemy's shells.

*Duck-boards were slatted wooden planking used for flooring trenches or muddy ground, and a conduroy (sometimes written 'corduroy') road was a temporary road surface made by laying chords of wood at right-angles to the direction of the path or track.

The History of the Division records dejectedly:

So in bleak and bitter weather the year ebbed away with the battle lines still locked, mile after dreary mile from Switzerland to the sea, in their deadly and seeming purposeless embrace. The experience of the 8th division in each of the three engagements in which they had taken part in the Flanders offensive [1917] had been harsh and disappointing. Endeavour had been dogged by misfortune, and effort brought to naught by circumstance. As had been the case with the great offensive itself, the immediate objectives for which the troops had striven had constantly eluded them.

The end of 1917

In France and Flanders the year ended once again as it had begun; heavy frost and snow carpeting the battle lines shrouding the tortured landscape of craters, barbed wire, debris and detritus with a gentle melancholy, mantling the unburied dead of men and beasts, and deadening the sound of movement. And so, in the wording of official communiqués:

All quiet on the Western Front.

PART FORTY-SIX

We have accepted the Government in order to conduct the war with redoubled energy... We shall carry out this programme... There will be no consideration of persons or partisan passions – no more pacifist campaigns, no treachery, no semi-treachery – only war. Nothing but war!

Georges ('The Tiger') Clemenceau in his speech to the French Chamber of Deputies on his election to Premier in November 1917.

1918. 'Nothing but war'

John Toland began the prologue of his book *No Man's Land The Story of 1918* by saying: 'On New Year's Day, 1918, Europe was close to bankruptcy after almost three and a half years of a war which had killed and maimed millions of soldiers, ravaged the land and brought hunger and misery to countless civilians.'

It was not an auspicious start for a year that would actually end with an armistice and bring silence to the guns along the whole of the Western Front for the first time since 1914.

Conditions and weather

Malcolm Brown, in *1918 Year of Victory*, describing conditions as portrayed in the contemporary media at the start of the new year at home, writes of violent gales lashing the coast of southern England on New Year's Day 1918, while damage to shipping was matched by sporadic damage on land, with many trees denuded of their branches. 'Much snow had fallen,' he said, 'and though in

519

some places skaters emerged to celebrate their seasonal skills, in London a bitter wind under leaden skies drove most people to seek sanctuary indoors ... warnings of meatless days to come and an announcement that the Food Controller had now forbidden the making of ice cream.'

Brown added that the harsh winter affected everywhere. In Germany the Rhine-Weser-Leine Canal froze trapping forty-five fully laden coal ships in the ice. And as far afield as Miami snow had fallen, while New York was reported as being wrapped in driving mist. In Paris the Seine froze and fuel was in short supply. Cinemas and theatres were shut four days a week to conserve fuel, and cafes and restaurants closed early.

Food rationing in Britain

Britain, faced by worrying food shortages caused by the heavy shipping losses, had a rationing scheme put into effect before the end of January 1918, and January saw the first commodity to be rationed, sugar. Meat and bacon followed in April, together with butter, lard and margarine.

Although some of the commodities were rationed, prices were not controlled and the financially better off fared better than the poor. In an attempt to make matters fairer 'National Kitchens' were opened in the poorest part of London, and by August there were 623 across the country. The meals purchased were exchanged for ration coupons* and a typical range of food offered by a National Kitchen – as quoted by David Bilton in his book *The Home Front* – included oxtail soup, Irish stew, potatoes, beans, bread, jam roll and rice pudding. Some of the National Kitchens did have eating areas, but, according to David Bilton, the intention was for the meals to be eaten at home.

*The smooth introduction to rationing and ration books in the Second World War was no doubt due, at least in part, to the experience gained from 1918. Although initially, in January 1918, ration cards were issued they were then replaced in July by ration books.

National Kitchens did not appear in WWII. The nearest to them were the 'British Restaurants', but unlike the National Kitchens these were actually places that served subsidised meals to be eaten there and then (at one school I attended during the Second World War the kitchen and dining hall also served as a British Restaurant).

Interestingly and perhaps surprisingly, Winston Churchill, despite his experience at the Admiralty in the First World War and faced by the very real threat posed to merchant shipping from both surface and U-boat raiders in the Second, was, when he was once again at the Admiralty, opposed to the introduction of rationing in the opening months of the Second World War. His stand, according to E.R. Chamberlin in *Life in Wartime Britain*, was backed strongly by the *Daily Express*:

> The public should revolt against the food rationing system, that dreadful and terrible iniquity which some of the ministers wish to adopt. There is no necessity for the trouble and expense of rationing because there may be a shortage of this or that inessential commodity. Why should old women be forced to wait here and there before the shops for their supplies? This form of folly is difficult to understand.

Germany

Conditions were far worse in Germany in 1918, and what food supplies there were from vessels that escaped the British naval blockade were directed towards the armed forces. The bulk of the civilian population, other than the wealthy landowners, endured a diet that included acorns, chestnut flour, and stews made up of almost anything including pine kernels. Potatoes rotted in the icy ground, the little meat there was for the civilians was mainly bone and gristle, and there were reports of dogs and cats being eaten. Germany's vaunted railway system was beginning to fail because of lack of maintenance as railway staff had been called away to serve in the army. Parts of the Fleet had mutinied at Wilhelmshaven, and there were doubters in the German political world about the war.*

*Prince Lichnowsky, the late German ambassador to London, had published a pamphlet that absolved the British Foreign Minister for responsibility for the war, and his former colleague, von Kuhlmann, the Foreign Minister, made a declaration that no decision of the war by military action alone was likely.

Germany prepares to attack

Despite talk of mutual assistance nothing much seemed to be happening between the French and British, and the discussions and manoeuvring between Pétain and Haig had brought no tangible results.

The war dragged on. The Allies were hoping for a vast injection of new, enthusiastic and non battle-weary troops from the USA, but they were very slow in arriving, and as a result the Germans felt they could launch and succeed with their big offensive before the Americans arrived. 'They have no wings and cannot fly,' said an Admiral in the Prussian Diet. 'They cannot swim: they will not come.'

The German military heirarchy had good grounds for confidence. They now had nothing to fear from Russia; in addition they had once again rescued their incompetent partner, Austria-Hungary, and had immobilised the Italian armies by the remarkable and unexpected victory at Caporetto. At last they were free to mass their strength on the Western Front, and to give their men training in new tactics for a forthcoming all-out offensive; and this they did with thoroughness.

Supreme War Council meeting

On 2nd February, Robertson wrote from Versailles to Lord Derby, Secretary of State for War, providing a fascinating insight of the conference he and Lloyd George, the Prime Minister, were both attending:

> We had our final meeting this morning. The most important questions discussed at the Conference were Palestine, taking over the line, and the formation of Inter-Allied General reserves... The question of Palestine was bound up with the question of our ability to hold the Western front. In this discussion the question of Man-Power was much to the fore and Foch made a very long statement showing the great things the French had done and the small effort that had been by England, and pointed out the great reserves of men still in the country, in Ireland, and in the colonies, and alluded to the fact that we had as yet called up none of the older classes. The Prime Minister replied at some length explaining the other demands that are made upon us. Foch returned to the charge rather vehemently and in the end the Prime Minister appealed to the President to stop the discussion as he declined to be further criticised on matters of government and policy by a foreign General...*

*Foch, it would appear, had by now changed his tune more than somewhat from his conversation with Wilson in 1910, described earlier above.

We passed on from the figures [showing that there would be a considerable shortage of men in 1918] to the question of Palestine, the Prime Minister suggesting that the recommendation of the Versailles people to take the offensive there with a view to annihilating the Turk should be adopted in principle. This was supported by Orlando [the Italian Premier]. Clemenceau proposed however that it should be rejected because it was quite obvious from the figures regarding man-power that we should with difficulty hold our own on the West Front. Upon this the Prime Minister made a long speech much on the lines of his Paris speech, alleging great want of courage, imagination and so forth, and pointing out the admirable position we should now have been in if we had but knocked out Turkey, as we could have done a year or more ago. Clemenceau made an equally vehement reply which was to the effect that that he could not for a moment think of supporting any such enterprise in Palestine when the enemy was practically knocking on the doors of Paris In fact he might have been Maxse by the way he spoke with respect to side-shows, and he added that there had been too much imagination and that if there had not been so much we might have saved many hundred of thousands of men in Palestine, Mesopotamia, and Salonika, and by now won the war.

Robertson, I feel sure, must have enjoyed that outburst from Clemenceau which was so much in tune with his own views, and he added, with satisfaction, that the Prime Minister was very badly mauled: 'I never saw him so knocked out.' To rub salt into Lloyd George's wound Robertson said he also felt it incumbent on him to make some observations, and expressed his well-known opinions on 'side shows'. The Prime Minister, he said, did not agree with him and was much annoyed. Robertson added prophetically that he thought Lloyd George would contemplate taking action against him before long.

Lloyd George refuses to send more men to the Western Front

Despite massive building up of German forces on the Western Front now many of their troops were released from the Russian Front, and despite the warnings of an anticipated all-out German offensive – the warnings coming from many sources* – Lloyd George refused Haig's urgent pleas for more men. He and his colleagues in the War Cabinet had made it clear they would pour no more troops into a front that in their view had already squandered the cream of Britain's manhood.

*On the subject of the warnings, Robertson wrote in 1926 (quoted by John Baynes in *Far from a Donkey*):

> The warnings with respect to the continuous arrival of German reinforcements on the Western Front, and the prediction that a desparate attempt to snatch victory would probably be made by the enemy on that front not later than February, were, for all practical purposes, disregarded [by the War Cabinet].

The lack of replacements and additional troops led to an enforced reorganisation of Haig's armies. A War Office order on 10th January compelled reorganisation whereby some battalions were broken up to reinforce others and, as I have mentioned earlier, infantry brigades were reduced from 4 battalions to 3, and so divisions were reduced from 13 battalions to 10.

These measures were deplored by the military generally, and chaos occurred at a time when cohesion was paramount. The German armies increased in might immensely, while the British armies shrank, and if that were not enough, they had to take over even more of the front line from the French. John Terraine in *To Win a War* describes the operation thus:

> It need hardly be said that such reorganization meant disorganization to a fearful degree. This entire astonishing and demoralizing exercise took time – time during which the roads of France were filled with British units seeking a new home in strange divisions, and during which an *esprit de corps* built up over years of common experience was thrown away, while all existing tactical principles and schemes had to be scrapped. Of the four British Armies comprising the BEF in 1918, the First Army completed its reorganization by 19 February, the Fifth Army by 25 February, the Third Army by 27 February, and the Fourth Army (in Flanders) not until 4 March.

As a final complication, it must be added that the governments of Australia, Canada and New Zealand declined to adopt similar measures, with the result that the ten Dominion divisions on the western Front retained their twelve battalions each; this turned out to be most fortunate.

So we find the extraordinary spectacle of the British army facing the most formidable offensive of the war, actually disbanding units and thrown into confusion by the ensuing arrangements.

See Haig's dispatch below for a more measured, but equally angry, response to the order.

There was anger too among the military leaders in France who believed far too many British troops were being retained on the Home Front. One of the reasons given for this retention was that they would be needed in Ireland if the situation there deteriorated further; and, as has been described, Lloyd George and some of his cabinet collegues were still favouring sending any 'spare' troops to other theatres of war to take the pressure off the Western Front.

Robertson sacked

On 17th February 1918, Lloyd George struck at Robertson – and Robertson writing again to Lord Derby,* this time in wounded indignation, had this to say:

> You will remember that on Thursday evening you informed me that the appointment of CIGS had been offered to General Plumer, and that pending a reply you wished me to continue to carry on the duties. Last evening you informed me that he had not accepted the offer, and I then reminded you that I awaited your further instructions. These you promised to give me in due course, and in the meantime you requested me to continue to carry on the duties of CIGS. About 8 pm last evening a Press representative brought to my house a Press Bureau notice to the effect that the Government had accepted my resignation. I informed him that I had not resigned, and this is so.
>
> Now however that it has been publicly announced that General Sir H. Wilson is to become CIGS will you please say when you wish me to hand over the duties to him.

Not only had Robertson been sacked, but to rub salt into the wound, he was replaced by the man he could not tolerate, Sir Henry Wilson. Lloyd George remarked to Lord George Riddell, on 24th March, that one of the disasters of the war was not appointing Henry Wilson earlier to high command. 'They have wrongly regarded him as a farceur, just because he will joke on all occasions. But what does that matter?' Later though he was to complain that he found Wilson whimsical almost to the point of buffoonery, and also although he regarded Wilson as very able, and especially good at explaining military problems with lucidity to non-military people, he could not be pinned down when decisive decisions and actions were needed; not a charge that could be laid at the door of Robertson.

An undated typescript headed 'War Office', minuted by Robertson, puts his position clearly:

For some months before I ceased to be CIGS the advice I gave to the War Cabinet on certain vital questions of strategy and general military policy was either unheeded or rejected, and it daily became more evident that, for practical purposes, I did not possess their confidence. On the 11th February last [1918], when the Secretary of State for War informed me that two days earlier he and the Prime Minister had decided to replace me as CIGS he told me that the P.M. could not 'get on' with me, and the Prime Minister himself, in my final interview with him on 16th of February, told me that, not withstanding our friendly personal relations, we had for some time past differed on important military questions... The military situation is, in my opinion, now so grave and difficult as to demand that the War Cabinet shall, subject to the general policy of the Allies, leave the responsible Generals they employ absolutely free and unfettered in the conduct of military operations, and for this it is obvious that they must have complete confidence in those Generals. It would be idle, in view of what has been said above, to pretend that they have any confidence in me, or that I have faith in the methods which they have hitherto pursued in the military conduct of the war.

Cecil Westlake, Croix de Guerre

Lower down the military hierarchy there were better tidings for some in those early winter days of 1918. An extract from the War Diary of 1/5th DCLI dated 6th February, 1918, recounted the following:

Holnon Wood, from 61st Division Routine Orders, dated 4th February 1918 (DRO No. 1571).

The Divisional Commander has much pleasure in notifying that His Majesty the King has approved the awards of Belgian Decorations as under, placed at his disposal by His Majesty, the King of the Belgians.

Croix de Guerre No. 240201 Sergt. C.H. Westlake 1/5 Bn. DCLI (P).*

*Three other names are also listed. The History of the Regiment records that there were only eleven recipients of this award in the regiment during the war.

The information was also recorded in the *Supplement to London Gazette* 12th July 1918, under the listing of 'Awards of the Belgian Croix de Guerre'. And a clipping from a local West Country newspaper of that time gave the information as follows:

'*Croix de Guerre.*' Most hearty congratulations to Corpl. [*sic*] C.H. Westlake, who has been recommended for the above decoration. We are awaiting particulars of this rare honour, coming as it does so soon after Corpl. [*sic*] Westlake was 'mentioned' in a recent Dispatch from our own Commander-in-Chief.

PART FORTY-SEVEN

The German accession of morale is not of a permanent character and is not likely to stand the strain of an unsuccessful attack with consequent heavy losses... If Germany attacks and fails she will be ruined.

British GHQ intelligence analysis 7 January 1918. Quoted by John Terraine, *To Win A War 1918 The Year of Victory.*

The Emperor's battle (*Kaiserschlacht*)

With the collapse of Russia there had been long discussions in the German High Command about where a 'last chance' great offensive in the west should be aimed. One possibility that was rejected was another attack on the French at Verdun. A second proposal was to attack the British in Flanders and this seemed a promising possibility, but March was too early for the weather and ground conditions in this low-lying region, and time was of the essence. Finally the choice was made to strike in an area between Arras and Péronne, towards the coast.

German strength had begun to build up in the west in November 1917. At the beginning of that month there were an estimated 150 German divisions on the Western Front. By 22nd March 1918, British Intelligence at GHQ identified 190, and the tally rose to 208.

The calm before the storm

As did the Germans on the Somme in 1916, so the British troops in early 1918 knew a major attack was coming, but were not sure just where.* Unlike the German army in 1916, who were in secure well prepared defensive positions, the British in 1918 were exposed and under-defended. The French promised reinforcements to the British troops once they were sure that the British front was where the real thrust would be, but British and French opinions on this were divided.

*There are stories told of German troops on the Somme in 1916 prior to the start of the battle holding up placards in the front-line trenches opposite the British bearing the words 'When are you coming over?'

Haig was very conscious of the problems facing his armies, and he wrote in his Dispatch dated 20th July 1918:

> Already at the beginning of November, 1917, the transfer of German divisions from the Russian to the Western Front had begun. It became certain that the movement would be continued steadily until numerical superiority lay with the enemy.
>
> It was to be expected, moreover, that large numbers of guns and munitions formerly in the possession of the Russian Armies would fall into the hands of our enemies, and at some future date would be turned against the Allies.

In the area around the village of Ham the German High Command had planned a series of three attacks code named 'St Michael' from 1 to 3. 'St Michael 3' was to be launched from their line just in front of the St Quentin Canal, with its left flank on the banks of the river Oise where it flowed through La Fere, and this was to be the flank of the whole offensive. (The Crozat Canal would act as a very convenient line upon which one southern attack group could rest and guard its flank while the remainder of the army broke the British front on each side of St Quentin, and flooded forward between Ham and Peronne.) General Ludendorff had said that if this blow succeeded the strategic result might indeed be enormous as his armies could then separate the bulk of the English army from the French, and crowd it up with its back to the sea (as would happen in 1940 at Dunkirk).

With seventy-one divisions readied by Germany the scene was set for the battle to be fought for the ultimate stakes. Three German armies, the Eighteenth, Second and Seventeenth would deliver the attack, and facing them were two undermanned and over-stretched British armies, the Third Army commanded by General Sir Julian Byng, and the Fifth Army commanded by General Sir Hubert Gough.

The March offensive: The British

On 19th March Haig gave lunch to a party of visitors from England that included Winston Churchill, Minister of Munitions. Churchill announced that the War Cabinet had given approval for more tanks and he was proceeding with the manufacture of four thousand of them.

Malcolm Brown mentions that a Lieut. Frank Warren of the 17th King's Royal Rifles also noted the occasion, and wrote in a letter of this visit by Churchill and others – among them the Duke of Westminster and General Tudor, GOC 9th (Scottish) Division – saying: 'Winston, who can never be like other mortals, wears a French helmet with a khaki cover; the Duke of Westminster is content with a cloth cap, although well within the area where a "tin hat" is compulsory.'

After dinner that evening, General Lawrence, Haig's chief of staff who had replaced Kiggell, reported that based on the interrogation of prisoners, it looked as though the attack would be launched on the 21st. Toland writes: 'Haig felt prepared. Batteries had received their allotment of ammunition for the battle, 1,200 shells including 300 gas shells, and a large number of aircraft were being held in concentrated numbers along the front.'

Haig's wife had given birth to a son on 15th March, and Haig had written to her to say that in the present circumstances he had better delay his proposed visit to see them; adding that everyone was in good spirits, and only anxious that the enemy should attack. Gough too was appearing reassuring. Toland says Gough wrote to his wife: 'I expect a bombardment will begin tomorrow night, last six or eight hours, and then will come the German infantry on Thursday 21st... Everyone is calm and very confident. All is ready.'

There appears to have been an almost relaxed 'let them come' attitude expressed in public by members of the British High Command just prior to the German onslaught, although this was at variance

531

with the worries felt and expressed in meetings. For the British commanders there were very real concerns over the lack of sufficient troops to hold their positions, and equally worrying was the generally very poor defensive state of the front facing the expected attack. In addition there was the uncertainty of exactly where the real thrust of the attack would be aimed.

Outnumbered and ill-prepared defences

Heavily outnumbered, the British were attempting to hold ill or barely prepared lines stretching 125 miles, and this included a 28 mile extension hastily taken over from the Third French Army in late January. Gough's Fifth Army was attempting to hold 42 miles of front and as he had the least number of men of any British commander his resources were vastly overstretched.

South of the river Oise, part of Gough's inheritance from the French included marshlands that should have been a strong deterrent to an attack of any strength. Unfortunately a long spell of dry weather had made the marshes easily passable and this help no longer existed; the Oise had almost dried out and the French had built only the sketchiest of defences. The cleverly devised German retirement to the 'Hindenburg Line' in 1917 had left utter devastation in its wake, and the British had not been able to make good the damage done.

Like Gough, Byng's army also faced a dismal and devastated horizon to the front, and behind lay the devastation of the Somme battlefields of 1916.

Gough and Maxse meet

Brigadier-General Freyberg recorded details of a meeting at which he was present between Gough and Maxse at Ham (headquarters of XVIII Corps):*

The conversation between General Gough and General Maxse made a great impression on me. I had never before heard a plan of campaign discussed by two such senior commanders and I gathered from their conversation that:

532

(a) The Fifth Army had been given an impossible task to do. That they had too few men either to hold the line in its present condition, or to put it in a satisfactory state of defence before the Germans launched their attack in the spring, and

(b) That even if we had sufficient men to dig the necessary defences, we hadn't sufficient engineers' material (i.e. wire and pickets etc.).

I learned also that the British General Headquarters Reserves available in event of a crisis, after the Fifth Army moves were completed, would not be more than seven weak divisions.

*Biography *Bernard Freyburg V.C.* quoted by John Baynes in his study of Sir Ivor Maxse *Far from a Donkey.*

The plan for defence

So despite Gough's assertion to his wife that everyone was calm and very confident and all was ready, all was certainly not ready. In December 1917, GHQ had issued instructions on the way in which defence should be arranged. There were to be three zones: 'Forward', 'Battle' and 'Rear'. They were to be prepared and each organised in depth. In reality the 'Rear Zone' was little more than a piece of ground reconnoitred and marked out, and usually called 'The Green Line'. The 'Forward Zone' was actually a strengthened existing front line trench, albeit with a good supply of machine-guns, while the 'Battle Zone', which in theory was to be the main defensive area and with a depth of between two and three thousand yards of mutually supporting positions on the best ground available from which to destroy the enemy attack, was little prepared. Richard Holmes said that when the Germans began their attack there were no dugouts in the Battle Zone, and it was incomplete south of St Quentin.

Almost every infantry battalion in the British Fifth and Third Armies was undermanned and the surviving experienced soldiers were worn out from the battles of 1916 and 1917. Battalions although officially resting and training when pulled out of the line, in practice were put to work on road building and maintenance – including trench building, road rebuilding, and general labouring renovation and construction tasks. The newcomers to the battalions, often a combination of a low medical category and very young conscripts, were untrained for the

533

tasks that would await them, there was no time for familiarisation in quiet sectors placed alongside experienced troops.

British troops and defensive action

Unlike the Germans, the British troops were not used to, or properly trained for, defensive action. The emphasis in training, throughout the war, had been on attack, and trenches however well maintained were regarded as places from which to launch an attack. Now depth of defence was an absolute necessity.

There were just not enough men, materials, or time to make the properly constructed defences in depth as envisaged by the instructions from GHQ. In addition there was still a strong feeling among many British troops that it was better to fight from a continuous front line of well constructed linking trenches, than the proposed series of individual strong points that could be outflanked and attacked from the rear and sides.

Maxse had tried to instil his belief in the 'in depth defence' into his lectures, and said:

> The main lesson learnt [at Cambrai] was the futility of putting all your eggs into the front line basket and of neglecting distribution in depth. For two years GHQ and others preached depth. The French learnt it. We British agreed to it in principle, but not one division in ten carried out depth on the actual ground. But you shall. Many commanders cling to the silly idea that successful defence implies firing every weapon into no man's land.

Haig, in his dispatch, makes his views clear:

> 4. The strenuous efforts made by the British forces during 1917 had left the Army at a low ebb in regard both to training and numbers. It was therefore of the first importance, in view of the expected German offensive, to fill up the ranks as rapidly as possible and provide ample facilities for training.*

*Para 4 actually began as follows: 'The lack of adequate reinforcements and my consequent inability to keep the ranks of the fighting units within a measure of their establishment gave me cause for anxiety.' This sentence was deleted by the Government, and it was not allowed to be reinstated after the war when the dispatches were published.

Haig continued in Paragraph 4:

> So far as the second of these requirements was concerned, two factors materially affected the situation. Firstly, training had hitherto been primarily devoted to preparation for offensive operations. Secondly, the necessity for maintaining the front line systems of defence and the construction of new lines on ground recently captured from the enemy had precluded the development of rear line systems to any great degree.
>
> Under the new conditions the early construction of these latter systems, involving the employment of every available man on the work, became a matter of vital importance. In consequence it was difficult to carry out any elaborate course of training in defensive tactics.

In the same dispatch, Haig has a swipe at the enforced, detested, reorganisation of his troops:

As regards our requirements of men, deficiencies were not being made good, and this necessitated a change in the organisation of the forces. Under instruction from the Army Council, the reorganisation of divisions from 13 battalions to a 10 battalion basis was accordingly undertaken and completed during the month of February. Apart from the reduction in fighting strength involved by this reorganisation, the fighting efficency of units was *lowered at a crucial moment.**

*The wording in italics was also, as in the other part above, cut from the Government version of his dispatch.

The German CIC's prediction

Now that the British had been forced to take over more of the line, the strike, when it came, would be right at the juncture of the French and British Armies. The Germans intended the attack principally to strike the British troops, and the German Commander in Chief predicted accurately:

It need not be anticipated that the French will run themselves off their legs and hurry at once to the help of their Entente comrades. They will first wait to see if their own front is not attacked also and decide to support their ally only when the situation has quite cleared up.

The German assault

The assault was to be very heavy in terms of numbers – somewhere between 190 and 200 infantry divisions, with reinforcements available from the east and south as movement developed. A possible total of effectives in the region of 1,500,000 rifles with another 1,000,000 in the artillery, cavalry and auxiliary services. The number of machine-guns had been dramatically increased so that the first line of attack was almost a machine-gun line. A system of intensive training had accustomed part of the light artillery to go forward with the infantry.

The German preparations for the attack on 21st March were imaginative in conception, and successful in operation. They moved their artillery batteries constantly, laid dummy batteries to confuse the British reconnaissance aircraft, caused the British artillery to fire at the dummies, and then moved them again. This went on for weeks the whole length of the front. In addition the Germans had devised the use of 'shock' or 'storm troopers' for the attack when it was launched. Malcolm Brown quotes from Stephen Westman's *Surgeon in the Kaiser's Army*, on the subject of these troops:

> The men of the storm battalions were treated like football stars. They lived in comfortable quarters, they travelled to the 'playing grounds' in buses, they did their jobs and disappeared again, and left it to the poor footsloggers to dig in, to deal with counter-attacks and to endure the avenging artillery fire of the enemy. They were so well trained and had developed such a high standard of team work that their casualties were almost nil. They moved like snakes over the ground, camouflaged, and making use of every bit of cover, so that they did not offer any targets for artillery fire. And when they reached the

barbed-wire entanglements of the positions opposite they had special torpedoes with which they blew up the defences – dangerous people to come up against.

Dr Stephen Bull (see also above) in his second publication covering trench warfare in the First World War, *World War 1 Trench Warfare (2) 1916–18* quotes a German staff directive outlining the method of attack to be adopted for the battle:

> Troops were to be massed for the attack in secret to penetrate the enemy position rapidly, to the furthest possible objective on the *Schwerpunkt* (centre of gravity) of the attack, usually on a frontage of two to three thousand metres per division... Reserves were to be committed on successful sectors, not where resistance was most stubborn.
>
> Artillery preparation would no longer consist of an all-out bombardment lasting days, but was more concentrated in relation to time and space in order to increase surprise and moral effect. Trench mortars, infantry guns, and batteries firing over open sites would not be used prior to the day of the attack, so as to maintain surprise.* The preface to the assault would last from minutes to hours depending on the circumstances. Pauses, sudden bursts of shells, and the 'fire waltz' back and forth across the target were all useful ruses.

*Despite the difference in scale, the opening strategy proposed for the German offensive in March 1918, particularly with regard to artillery preparation, where targets had been registered well beforehand and there was to be no prior prolonged barrage to herald the attack, was similar in some respects to those planned by the British at Neuve Chapelle in 1915 (see above), and where initially they were very nearly successful.

The failure in 1915 can be blamed, at least in good part, on the severe shortage of both artillery and ammunition, together with the lack of up to date and reliable information as the battle progressed. There were no reserves to push through the enemy lines when and where the break occurred. These factors had given the Germans the chance to rally from their shocked surprise and hurriedly bring in reinforcements to shore up the line when the British did not follow through. And unfortunately in 1915, the flexibility that would have permitted the British troops, at least those who were in a position to do so, to continue the advance once and where the way was open, was not allowed by the commander – to the frustration and anguish of those troops. The contingency for independent initiatives to break through and push on was not only envisaged but also encouraged in the German approach of 1918. And of course in 1918 the Germans had vast numbers of artillery and shells unlike the British in 1915. Also unlike 1915, the poor weather conditions in 1918 would favour the attackers – although Ludendorff expressed concern about the possible lack of visibility when the attack started.

The German infantry were to advance immediately behind a creeping barrage despite the risks of 'shorts'. The objective was to shoot the enemy into a condition where they were ripe for attack. It was not to be an artillery barrage aimed at pure destruction.

For the infantry, the scope for independent action and initiative was expressed right down to private soldier level, and it was the job of senior officers to state objectives and provide the resources without the constraints of too many orders. (There were echoes back to the Roman army, as the instructions spoke of assault detachments often organised into eight-man squads led by an NCO – a Roman army tactic.)

With the enemy positions thoroughly penetrated the main body of the infantry could follow, feeding the advanced detachments, widening the breakthroughs, and destroying the isolated and demoralised pockets of opposition.

PART FORTY-EIGHT

Rendered blind by fog, overwhelmed by one of the most violent bombardments of the war, General Gough's eleven divisions, weak from lack of reinforcements, were driven out of indifferent entrenchments, recently taken over from the French, by the attack of two German Armies, with 22 divisions in the front line and 22 in support.

The Official History for the 21st March 1918.

'Operation Michael', Thursday 21st March to Thursday 28th March 1918

Although the weather had been fair, fog and mist began to shroud the strangely quiet front. On the Wednesday night, a British raiding party from the 61st Division brought thirteen prisoners in from No Man's Land. Several spoke freely and revealed that a preliminary barrage would start at 4.30 am in the morning [Thursday]. Gough wrote:*

The night of March 20th every man in the Fifth Army whose duty allowed him to do so, lay down calmly enough for a night's sleep, but all of us felt perfectly certain that we would be awakened before morning by the roar of battle. And so we were!

*Extracted from *Fifth Army*.

A German officer, Lieutenant Rudolf Binding (see also below), writing home, described the battle preparations as:

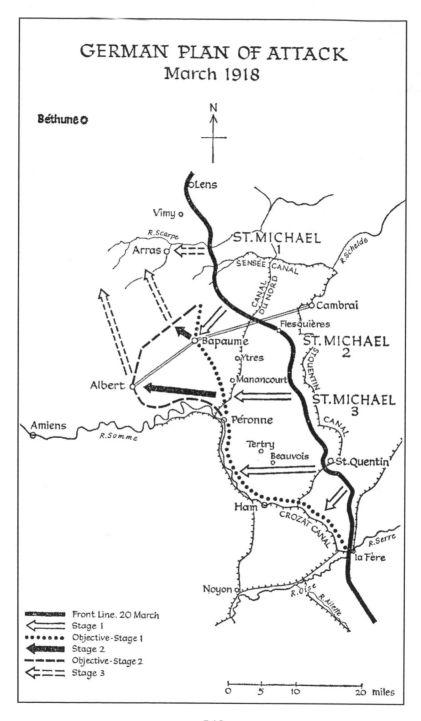

GERMAN PLAN OF ATTACK
March 1918

Béthune o

N

oLens

Vimy o

R.Scarpe

ST.MICHAEL
1

Arras o

SENSÉE CANAL

R.Schelde

CANAL DU NORD

o Cambrai

Flesquières

o Bapaume

ST.MICHAEL
2

S.QUENTIN

o Ytres

o Manancourt

Albert o

ST.MICHAEL
3

CANAL

Amiens

Péronne

o

R.Somme

Tertry
o

Beauvois

o St.Quentin

Ham o

CROZAT CANAL

R.Serre

la Fère

Noyon o

R.Oise

R.Aliette

Front Line. 20 March
Stage 1
Objective-Stage 1
Stage 2
Objective-Stage 2
Stage 3

0   5   10   20 miles

540

Quite inconceivable in detail, and can only be described as the last word. The troops are packed in position so tight that those in front have been there for the last ten days. For weeks past ammunition has been hauled and hauled, night after night, to be piled in mountains round the guns. All that is to be poured out on the enemy in four hours from now.

The opening bombardment

The bombardment when it came was the most massive there had ever been in the history of the war. Along a front of more than fifty miles, in the thick fog, some 6,000 guns, more than 2,500 of which were heavy or superheavy, simultaneously began pounding the British Third and Fifth Armies.

The deafening noise sundered the air, and the force and pressure of the explosions sucked air from lungs, distorted vision and disorientated minds. Unheard in the screams of approaching shells and the roar of explosions were the plop of gas shells, and soon the sickly odour of mustard gas began to entwine with the smoke from the high explosives and the increasing fog.

The ferocity and sound of the bombardment beggared description. Particularly for those inexperienced British replacement troops who had no prior experience of being under heavy shell-fire, let alone such a barrage as this, it must have been the most unbelievably frightening nightmare experience. An experience that not only induced mind-numbing shock, but horror and terror from which there was no escape – nowhere to run to, nowhere to hide, nowhere to be safe. All around them defences crumbled, the ground shook and split as though by earthquakes. Soldiers were torn to pieces by shell fragments and others buried alive among the debris and cratered earth.

Ernst Jünger wrote of this opening of the bombardment, as seen from the German front line among his storm troopers, that they knew they would be entering a witches' kettle and that its pre-dawn was like a *Walpurgisnacht*: 'The wavering movement of the dark masses in the depths of the smoking, glowing cauldron exposed for a second the utmost abyss of pain, like the vision of a hellish dream.'

Richard Holmes says the German guns fired over three million

541

shells that day, and hc and others quote a German artillery officer, Lieut. Herbert Sulzbach, who said: 'It sounded as if the world was coming to an end... During the firing I often have to interrupt my fire direction duties because I can't take all the gas and the smoke.'

Malcolm Brown describes the bombardment as:

> Meticulously planned, and so precisely registered that it could go ahead in any kind of visibility, was aimed at a whole range of targets; artillery positions, unit headquarters, telephone exchanges, telegraph cables, wireless stations, railway stations, every kind of strong points, dumps, key roads.

The German troops advance

Of the scene following the initial barrage John Terraine writes:

> Five hours after the opening of this pulverizing bombardment the German infantry came over in thick fog which extended all along the fronts of the Fifth and Third armies. In the Fifth Army sector particularly, where the defenders were very thin on the ground, continuous trenches were virtually non-existent, and rear positions pious hopes rather than military realities, great store had been set by mutually supporting machine-gun posts. To be effective, however, these needed to communicate, and preferably to see each other; the bombardment cut out communications, the fog blotted out vision. The German tactic of infiltration succeeded in these circumstances beyond all the dreams of its devisers.

The British front line infiltrated

The history of the 8th Division confirms this analysis of the opening of the attack saying that the dense white fog, which lasted until 1 pm, favoured the attackers; the defenders of the British lightly held forward zone depended largely on the cross-fire of carefully sighted machine-guns and forward field guns, but the lack of visibility rendered these guns more or less useless and so, to a great extent, destroyed the defensive scheme. Not only this, but detachments holding the forward positions were in many cases overwhelmed or surrounded before they had even realised that the hostile assault had been delivered, and before they could pass back the information.

Private Arthur Wrench, 51st Highland Division, writing up his diary for the 21st March 1918, seems close to despair:

> We are getting it now all right. It is absolute Hell here. Cold-blooded murder and mass slaughter. The Germans in their mass formation get it from our Lewis and machine-guns while they give it to us unmercifully with their artillery. The fatigue is awful and the strain from holding on tremendous and God knows how long it will go on. Our line is getting thin while the Germans seem to be coming on in inexhaustible numbers and must surely get through.

The British troops overrun

As the Germans infiltrated through the fog and smoke, British units lost touch with their flanks, or found there was nobody on their flanks. Battalion headquarters were overrun, Brigade and Divisional HQs could not get through to the front line – where it still existed, to establish what was happening and where. In the next few days the British front crumpled and gave way under the onslaught.

The regimental history of the Rifle Brigade laconically states of the 21st March (as quoted by Toland): 'About 4.40 am the enemy bombardment opened ... from that moment nothing was heard of, or from, the Seventh Battalion.' The war diary entry of the 9th King's Royal Rifle Corps recorded: 'By the evening of the 21st the battalion ceased to exist.' The 12th Royal Irish Rifles entry reads: 'The battalion itself was gone, killed, wounded and prisoner.' The 15th Battalion of the same regiment said simply: 'Battalion surrounded. 22 officers and 566 men missing'.*

*The last three entries quoted by Malcolm Brown.

The attacks were renewed in great strength all along the line on the 22nd. Again there was a thick morning mist and the Germans succeeded in exploiting the advantage they had gained in the sectors south of St Quentin and in the Cologne Valley, and by late afternoon and evening the centre of the Fifth Army, deeply outflanked to both south and north, was compelled to give further ground.

3rd and 2nd Rifles

For the Rifle Brigade, the 3rd Battalion fought for 36 hours without food, and in gas masks for four consecutive hours. 'C' Company saved the battalion from destruction by stopping the enemy, and at one point they were almost entirely surrounded and with no other British troops within a quarter of a mile of them. Lt.-Col. H.S.C. Peyton, Commander of the 2nd Battalion, was killed and the medical officer wounded and taken prisoner died of his wounds.

The Fifth Army retreats

By now the situation was really serious. The Fifth Army had no reserves left at all and the Third Army, also fighting for its life, could spare not a man to help. The third and final defensive zone of the Fifth Army had been breached, and an immediate retreat to the bridgehead positions east of the Somme covering Ham and Péronne, and linking with the Third Army on the Nurlu Plateau, was ordered late that night.

The 8th Division holds the line

Gough, however, decided to retreat at once to the western bank of the Somme believing that the line had already been forced at Jussy. With his troops exhausted and no reserves he wished to avoid a complete rupture of the line. Unfortunately this decision by Gough meant that the troops of the 8th Division were called upon to undertake an active defence of the river line directly they arrived upon it. They went straight into battle 'fortified', as the Divisional History describes it, 'only by the knowledge that upon them depended the fate of the Fifth Army'.

On the 23rd March, the enemy reached the river at Ham, found the railway bridge east of the town intact and crossed. Like all the 8th Division both the 2nd Rifles and the 2nd Devons were fully engaged, and by the end of the 24th March they were still holding firm in the centre while the retreat continued on both flanks.

Pétain

Pétain meanwhile was still obsessed with the defence of Paris, and still convinced the main German attack would fall on his own armies. On the night of 24th March, Pétain came to Haig's advanced HQ 'looking very much upset, almost unbalanced and most anxious' and told Haig that he, Pétain, acting under instructions from the commander of the groupe d'armées de reserve (GAR), intended to fall back south-westwards to Beauvais in order to cover Paris. Haig, appalled, asked Pétain if he meant to abandon Haig's right flank. Pétain nodded assent, and added that it was the only thing possible if the enemy compelled the Allies to fall back further.

Haig wrote in his private papers that following this exchange, keeping in touch with the British army was no longer a basic principle of French strategy, but in *his* opinion the British army's existence depended on keeping the French and British armies united. He returned to his HQ to report the information to Henry Wilson (the new CIGS) and to the Secretary of State for War Lord Derby.

A digression. The appointment of a generalissimo

When Ludendorff began his March assault, as winter gave ground to spring, Lloyd George was dining with the American ambassador, Walter Hines Page.* No doubt pleased that having got rid of Robertson he could now put into effect his plan to oust Haig, he announced at the dinner: 'This battle [the German offensive 'Michael'] means one thing, that is a "Generalissimo".' And the man he had in mind for the position was Foch.

*The same Mr Page to whom King George had made his despairing comment on 4th August 1914.

Foch, who was engaged in as bitter a feud with Clemenceau as Haig was with Lloyd George, had meanwhile seen in his mind a danger of two distinct battles being fought when the anticipated big German offensive began; one by Haig to protect the Channel ports, and one by Pétain for Paris – which to the consternation of the French in general, and the Parisians in particular, had just been shelled by German artillery. This state of affairs, Foch foresaw, would surely result in a separation of the two armies and bring about certain defeat. He composed a note to Clemenceau calling his attention to the danger of the present coalition warfare in the present crisis with no generalissimo to direct a unified battle.

On 26th March, at the Hôtel de Ville in Doullens, the British and French commanders met. According to Toland, Haig was the first to arrive, looking exhausted and anxious having had little sleep in forty-eight hours. The French arrived a little later while the British commanders were discussing events. While waiting, Clemenceau, speaking with Poincaré, the French President, expressed his annoyance with Pétain's pessimism. 'Do you know what he told me? And I would not repeat it to anyone but you. He [Pétain] said: "The Germans will beat the British in open country; after that they will beat us too". Do you think a general should talk, or even think like that?'

Haig's response to appointment of a generalissimo

When the meeting of the allied military and government leaders began soon after noon, Haig explained that he was fully determined to stand his ground as long as he could, and with some assistance from the French on his right flank, he believed he ought to be able to do so. His entire object, he explained, was to have a fighting French general in supreme command who would hold Amiens. (A dig at Pétain it would seem.) He also added, 'I can deal with a man, but not with a Committee.'

Haig, despite Cabinet fears, appeared quite happy for Foch to take over the whole operation in France during this time. He knew a British overall commander would be unacceptable to the French and he said that arrangements should be made for Foch – or some other determined general who would fight – to be given supreme control. Foch, he added, was a man of great courage and decision, as he had shown during the fighting at Ypres in 1914, and he, Haig, was agreeable to go along with Wilson that Foch should be the man in control.* Haig wrote in his diary: 'Foch seemed sound and sensible, but Pétain had a terrible look. He had the appearance of a commander who was in a funk.'

And so, by agreement with both French and British governments, Foch became Generalissimo. The press reported on 30th March that the Prime Minister, in his statement at the Conference of Doullens [17 miles north of Amiens] on March 26th, had said:

Since the present battle began, the decision has been taken to appoint General Foch to coordinate the action of the Allies on the Western Front. This appointment has cordial cooperation of the French and British Commanders in Chief.

Back to the battle

All my battalions were heavily involved during the period 21st March to 5th April. The 2nd Rifles and 2nd Devons fighting a desperate rear guard in the 8th Division. The 3rd Rifles, as part of the 24th Division, were at the Somme Crossings 24th – 25th March, as were 1/5th DCLI. The 3rd Rifles and 1/5th DCLI were again at the Battle of Rosières, 26th–27th March.

'Operation Michael', 1/5th DCLI cut off

On 21st March, the battalion had been in the thick of the battle and now, just west of Ham, the battalion while digging in were suddenly ordered to attack the village of Verlaines. Picking up their weapons, they moved forward in artillery formation and heard the band of the 7th Cornwalls playing them on as they advanced. Two miles further on the 1/5th reached the village and despite being hot, hungry, and exhausted from all their previous efforts, they extended into open order, fixed bayonets, and continued their advance.

Captain Tyacke urged on the weary men and as they reached the crest of a rise they came under heavy rifle and machine-gun fire. Tyacke was hit and died, and many of his men as they attempted to find cover were also killed or wounded. Stretcher bearers trying to reach the wounded were also killed.

The following record appeared in both *The Western Morning News* and *The Western Mail*:

In his dispatch this week, Sir Douglas Haig, describing the fighting near Ham at the end of March refers to the work of the Cornish Territorial Battalion, the 1/5th Pioneers of the DCLI, stating that they materially delayed the enemy's advance.

The following is an account of the incident received immediately from a correspondent in France immediately after the battle:

'The – Battalion [cut for censorship reasons] DCLI (Pioneers) went into action on March 21st under the command of Major Courteney Edyvesyn, a regimental band playing them into action [7th Cornwalls].

'The CO Colonel Carus Wilson, was at this time on leave, and hurriedly rejoined a few days later, when he took other companies into action and was mortally wounded.

'The two companies were separate. The first companies were heavily engaged in the thickest of the fighting from 21st to 27th, during which they counter-attacked an important village, and took another village, after what is described as a splendid fight, our men fighting like devils.

'Eventually they were cut off for four days with very little food and the loss of all kit.

'On 27th the enemy swarmed around them in overwhelming numbers, and after repelling many attacks were forced to retire.

'After marching and fighting for 25 miles, they succeeded in reaching their division [61st Division], which had given them up. The men have fought magnificently, and the spirit of the Army is wonderful.'

Sir Douglas Haig said the men fought like devils and materially delayed the enemy's advance.

A new British line was established by early morning on the 26th, but under heavy pressure from determined German attacks, the line was forced back still further as a breach was threatened between French and British forces. Foch, who had now taken over as Generalissimo, ordered the Fifth Army to hold the line at all costs until French troops would arrive to relieve them.

61st Division

Martin Middlebrook says in his book *The Kaiser's Battle* that the 61st Division was one of the 'Second Liners' territorial divisions.* This meant that they arrived on the scene late and a high proportion of their earlier volunteer recruits had been sent to the first line battalions in France and replaced by conscripts. Their divisions had then come out to France themselves, and were the least experienced part of the British Expeditionary Force. Their reputation was not high although their efficiency varied from unit to unit. In early 1918 he says the 61st Division reckoned it had been unlucky at everything it had attempted so far, and called itself the 'Sixty worst'. Whatever the truth about alleged feelings of low esteem held up to then by the 61st Division, they came out of the fighting in 1918 with an enhanced reputation.

*Middlebrook is referring to the 59th, 58th, 61st, and 66th Divisions, all part of Gough's Fifth Army. He continues: 'They were somewhat derisively known as "Conscript Divisions", and it is reputed that a British corps or army commander once said, "God save me from the New Army and Second Line Territorials".'

Malcolm Brown in his *1918 Year of Victory* mentions one officer of the 61st Division (Captain Geoffrey Christie-Miller of 2/5th Gloucesters) who, while returning to France from a Senior Officers' course on 31st March, was worried where the reserves of men could be found for the present emergency. He said, 'One saw thousands of boys being poured across the channel. Were they fit to be plunged straight into one of the severest battles of History?'

According to Christie-Miller countless tragedies arose over the improvisation of units being flung together to be sent straight up the line as men disembarked from the leave boats. 'They were pushed straight into the battle,' he said. 'Their nominal roles were incomplete and sometimes non-existent. Thousands went missing and it is not known to this day to what units they were sent, or in what part of the line they were fighting.'

German troops break through

As the German troops broke through on both sides of the junction between the Third and Fifth Armies the British troops withdrew in disorder. The German advance was now threatening Bapaume and Péronne, and in some respects the withdrawal was like the 1914 retreat from Mons all over again. John Toland quotes a British soldier, Private R.D. Fisher of the London Regiment:

> It was terrible not because of the danger, for the enemy was following us with a half mile's distance, but because of the utterly exhausted condition of the men, after half a week without sleep, moving, moving, digging, digging, and having little to eat or drink. As we went along other men appeared from all sides to join us, so that in half an hour we had grown from a small party into an immense line numbering thousands of retreating men, tramping dejectedly along, across open country. We could see neither the front nor the rear of the column, nor did we have any idea where it was going.

Toland again quotes a British soldier, but this time not one in retreat. Lieutenant Richard Gale was one of the reinforcements heading east towards the crumbling front. Gale, a machine-gunner with the 42nd Division, wrote:

> Dumps of kits and valises lay by the side of the road, disorganized transport and guns were moving to the rear, all intermingled with pathetic groups of refugees... This was a retreat with all the horrors of panic. There was, as far as we knew, nothing behind us and the Channel ports, save this wretched rabble that seemed to have lost all cohesion and will to fight.

As in 1914 there was the same distressing sight of civilians mixed among the retreating troops; old men and old women, young girls and small children, carrying, wheeling or dragging whatever of their cherished possessions and farm animals they could take, all heading away from the battle as the troops fell back.

In their hurried retreat the British troops left large dumps of supplies behind them, and the German officer mentioned above, Rudolph Binding, recorded in his book *A Fatalist at War* that on 23rd March: 'Our cars now run on the best English rubber tyres, we smoke none but English cigarettes, and plaster our boots with lovely English boot polish – all unheard of things which belong to a fairyland of long ago.'

28th March. The next step, 'Operation Mars'

Following the successful launch of 'Michael', on 28th March Ludendorff put into effect his next phase of the offensive, 'Mars'. Here he was aiming towards Vimy Ridge, and with the final intention of reaching Boulogne. And here he came unstuck. Cyril Falls in *The First World War* explains why:

> If this had gone as well as the attack on 21st March, the war might have been nearly as good as won. Unfortunately for the gambler Ludendorff his nine divisions assaulting astride the Scarpe on 28th March struck four British as good as Britain could show and of all types of her Army: regular, New Army, and Territorial. These were the 3rd and 4th Divisions, the regulars, the 56th (London) Territorials, and the 15th (Scottish) New Army.
>
> The defences north of the Scarpe were intact. All were well dug and wired. The Germans attacked with sparkling vigour and skill. They were fought to a finish and beaten by a defence at once elastic and resolute. Ludendorff stopped the fight that very night.

Falls expressed the opinion that the above British achievement should be inscribed in gold letters on Britain's roll of honour, adding: 'The defence of 28th March not only killed Ludendorff's plan to expand the battle but virtually ended the battle itself.' On Friday, 5th April, Ludendorff halted all the attacks of the battle that had continued to rage along the front . His men were now like the British, exhausted,* and in addition they had outrun their artillery and most of their transport and supplies. Both sides had suffered extremely heavy losses, and the Germans were finally stopped just nine miles from Amiens.

*Field-Marshal von Hindenburg wrote in his memoirs that the German advance became slower and slower, and if only they could have reached Amiens a decisive victory would have been possible, 'our strength,' he said, 'was exhausted'.

Despite this setback, a vast bulge had been driven into the allied line; and on the same ground, as John Terraine says, that had been bought by the Allies at a fearful cost in 1916, and was now lost again. In his view summing up the whole battle of 21st March to 5th April:

> For Germany it had been a magnificent tactical victory, but not a strategic success to anything like the same extent... Still, he had done what nearly everyone had come to believe was impossible and had taken 90,000 prisoners. He had inflicted a loss of 240,000 (British 163,000 French 77,000) on his foes. But his own casualties were at least as great as, if not greater than, the sum of these totals.

Winston Churchill wrote: 'It has been touch and go on the front. We stood within an ace of destruction.'

Rifle Brigade, early April

By 4th April the casualties suffered by the 7th, 8th and 9th Battalions of the Rifle Brigade caused them to cease to exist, and the remnants were formed into one composite battalion as a training cadre. Later in the spring the 16th Battalion ceased its fighting career and became a training battalion for the American Expeditionary Force.

Gough departs

For Haig, the month facing him looked bleak; he had hardly any reserves after the March attack by Ludendorff – one division out of the sixty. Two of his sixty were the Portuguese. Sixteen of his divisions were being cobbled together and mainly composed of

552

inexperienced lads between 18 and 19 years of age; and to make matters worse, one of the commanders he had staunchly defended, Gough, was sent home and replaced by Rawlinson.* Rightly or wrongly Wilson, now CIGS, was blamed for this decision. Rawlinson promptly re-named the Fifth Army as the Fourth Army, after his previous field command, leading many to think that the Fifth Army had vanished.

*Rawlinson, prior to this appointment, had been at Versailles to replace Sir Henry Wilson as a member of the Supreme War Council when Wilson was made CIGS.

Another German April offensive, 'Georgette'

The losses and fatigue of his troops sustained in the 'Michael' and 'Mars' operations caused Ludendorff to modify his next planned offensive. This, originally code-named 'George', was now because of its reduction in scale called 'Georgette'. This reduced attack was to be aimed at the northern half of Haig's lines in the Flanders plains, a stretch of some twenty-five miles between La Bassée Canal and Ypres. Armentières was planned to absorb the main thrust, and once the city was taken, the German spearhead would drive on to take the vital rail centre of Hazebrouck. From this Haig would have his back to the English Channel and face the threat of evacuation to England.

So now, in early April, the British troops could not afford to lose ground as they had in March where there had been nothing of strategic value around, just the debris from 1916. Now they *had* to make a stand, come what may.

Haig expresses his concern to Foch

Haig wrote to Foch, 'All information points to the enemy's intention to continue his efforts to destroy the British army. With this object in view he appears to be preparing a force of 25 to 35 divisions to deliver a blow on the Bethune-Arras front.'

Haig wanted Foch either to start an offensive in the next few days, or to replace British troops on the Somme front with four French divisions, and so release the British troops to Haig. Haig

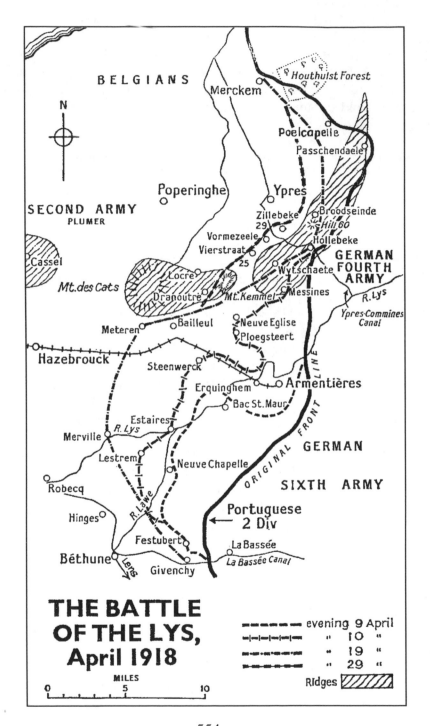

BELGIANS

Merckem

Houthulst Forest

N

Poelcapelle

Passchendaele

Poperinghe

Ypres

SECOND ARMY
PLUMER

Zillebeke
29
Broodseinde
Hill 60

Vormezeele
Vierstraat
Hollebeke

Cassel

25

Wytschaete

GERMAN
FOURTH
ARMY

Mt. des Cats

Locre

Messines

R. Lys

Dranoutre

Mt. Kemmel

Ypres-Commines Canal

Meteren

Bailleul

Neuve Eglise

Ploegsteert

Hazebrouck

Steenwerck

Erquinghem

Armentières

Bac St. Maur

Estaires
R. Lys

O
R
I
G
I
N
A
L

F
R
O
N
T

L
I
N
E

GERMAN

Merville

Lestrem

Neuve Chapelle

Robecq

SIXTH   ARMY

Hinges

R. Lawe

Portuguese
2 Div

Festubert

La Bassée

La Bassée Canal

Béthune

Lens

Givenchy

THE BATTLE
OF THE LYS,
April 1918

MILES

0   5   10

evening 9 April
"   10 "
"   19 "
"   29 "

Ridges

554

met with Foch, but came away with the feeling that neither Foch or Pétain had any intention of putting French divisions into the attack.

The Portuguese

One of Haig's many worries was that the sector just above the canal was held by the two Portuguese divisions, and Portugal was no longer a reliable ally. A revolution was going on in Portugal, and its anti-war expression had many sympathisers among the Portuguese troops in the sector. In addition the men, unlike their officers, were allowed no home leave, and they had just experienced a miserably cold and wet winter. All in all, any enthusiasm they might once have had for the war had now gone.

In these circumstances, doubting their reliability, Haig planned to move the two Portuguese divisions from the centre of the zone where he expected the attack would be likely to fall. One of the Portuguese divisions was due for relief on the night of 9th April, and General Sir Henry Horne, the commander of the First Army, because he was restricted for available troops, let the Portuguese out unrelieved that morning. This left the remaining Portuguese division forced temporarily to hold a very wide front.

9th April, the Germans attack

The formidable German artillery, including 137 heavy batteries, moved north to Flanders to open the new attack. The frontage covered by 'Georgette' was now only twelve miles – from Armentières to the La Bassée Canal, but with the option of, if all went well, extending the attack to just south of Ypres.

The pattern of this attack followed that of the 21st March offensive, but this time, on the right of the attack, the German waves were shot to pieces by a well trained and rested British division. Unfortunately however, under the tremendous bombardment, the Portuguese evacuated their trenches and took flight, and the Germans broke through, rolling back the now unprotected flanking British troops – who were mainly from divisions exhausted by their fighting experiences of 'Michael'. Battalions of the Scottish Highland

555

(51st) Division were hurried forward to take the place of the Portuguese.

Two companies of 1/5th DCLI transferred to help the 51st Division

The Scots had been refitting and absorbing drafts, a process only half complete. One of the battalions in the division, the 7th Gordon Highlanders, had been to all intents and purposes destroyed in March, having sustained casualties of 714, and its ranks were now full of 'boys' and with hardly a trained non-commissioned officer left. Yet this division began by sharply checking the enemy's advance, and it was at this point the 1/5th DCLI were ordered to transfer two companies, 'A' and 'B', to this Scottish Division (the 51st Highland).*

*Cecil Westlake was a member of 'A' Company (see below for what befell them).

By nightfall on 9th April the enemy had made a big dent in the British line and reached the eastern bank of the Lys river, though in many places the bridgeheads were still held. The 61st Division was hastily transferred from the Somme front to the northern front. The 1/5th DCLI were among the first troops to arrive in the Steenbecque area.

The condition of the 1/5th DCLI

Like other pioneer battalions, the Cornishmen were suffering from a supply of replacements containing men who were considered unequal for the physical demands expected of them, and who – in the words of an *Extract of Reports of C.E. & CRE on Recent Operations, August 1917* – 'lacked the engineering knowledge and the capacity for manual labour, and who consequently break down easily.' K.W. Mitchinson, *Pioneer Battalions in the Great War*, relates that in March:

> One draft of over 400 men [for] the 1/5 Duke Cornwall's Light Infantry, mostly aged 19 or under and entirely untrained for

556

active service conditions, arrived at their new battalion. The draft had left Etaples under the command of a major, a CSM, and a CQMS to march to their new battalion. When they stopped for the night it was discovered that the men had no idea how to cook in their mess tins. Having already concluded that the draft were totally devoid of discipline and training, the major and his two NCOs viewed the prospect of the next day's 12 mile march with kit with some misgivings. It was obvious that the troops were far from fit, and current regulations applying in Britain stated that B1 [a medical category] men should not march more than five miles… The fears of the major were soon realised. Within 30 minutes, 20 had fallen out and when the column reached the first hill, hordes of boys collapsed on either side of the road.*

Despite this less than auspicious start to their overseas service, within a week of their arrival the [1/5th] battalion was to hold ferocious German attacks upon Merville for over 48 hours and suffer over 450 casualties in the process.

*The history of the Duke of Cornwall's Light Infantry, says that with this new and inexperienced draft from the 4th battalion in England, 1/5th strength was brought up to 24 officers and 944 other ranks. It continues: 'But on the whole the draft were youths without any experience of real warfare and the change practically from the barrack-square to the firing line against a well-trained, war bitten enemy was a terrible experience.'

It was not only the pioneers that suffered from poor replacements. Rudolf Binding, commenting on the quality of the opposing British troops, said: 'In 1915 their high quality compensated for their small numbers, but later in the war prisoners were rickety, alcoholic, degenerate, ill-bred and poor to the last degree.' Richard Holmes says that by 1918 many observers, British and German, testified to the number of schoolboys in the ranks.

The 1/5th DCLI War Diary

TRIENNES. April 10th. Occupied billets at TRIENNES. At midnight orders received to embuss at 2 am

TRIENNES. April 11th. 'A' and 'B' Coys embussed and went forward joining the 153rd Brigade, 51st Division. Under orders of the GOC 153 Brigade, a line was taken up from Q23 Central to Q17 Central (Ref sheet 36A). This was subsequently altered, and the line was extending commencing from Q.11.d.4.8. along line of road to X roads at Q.11.b.8.5 thence junction of road and railway at L.31.c.3.5. This line was worked on and held all day. HQ were established at Q.11.b.7.3. Owing to the advance of the enemy, digging in was rendered very difficult and heavy casualties were caused by shelling and machine-gun fire from PARADIS the wood W of L'EPINETTE, wood west of LESTREM and approaches to these villages. About this time 'C' Coy arrived and took up a position with its left flank on the little river ANCNE LYS (K.3.5.d.3.0). As soon as it was dark HQ were shifted to Q.11.b.3.7. and the support half Coy were moved into line to strengthen the right. This line was held throughout the night, although troops on either flank withdrew. Just before dawn on 12th HQ were again moved to LE CORNETAULOUPS.

The regiment's history says:

...the enemy had got through Calonne in considerable strength and, working forward, had penetrated the junction of the forward companies of the 5th Gordons and 9th Royal Scots (both of the 51st Division) with the result that the Gordons and the 1/5th DCLI had to fall back across the canal. The crossing was effected under heavy rifle and machine-gun fire and casualties were heavy. A line was then taken up west of Le Sart and held up to midnight when, under orders, the Pioneers withdrew to rejoin the 61st Division. The pioneers had put up a splendid fight, but their losses were again heavy. No less than sixteen officers and 467 other ranks had been killed, wounded or were missing.

The 1/5th War Dairy describes the actions:

April 12th 1918. At 7.30 am the whole line was attacked and the enemy worked around both flanks. A line was taken up in front of CALONNE approximately across the bend in the river from Q.4.b.4.0. to Q.10.a.0.5. This line was held for $1\frac{1}{2}$ hours, although no troops were in touch on the right flank, but although no formed unit, many men of Scotch battalions were on the left flank.

A withdrawal was necessary from this position, and a line was taken along the railway bank Q.3.d.0.7 to Q.4.a.3.2.

The battalion fought on this line for ½ an hour, when the right flank was again turned, and a withdrawal was made to the canal, here again the battalion held the enemy for about 1½ hours, although the right flank was open all this time.

Meanwhile the enemy having worked round the outskirts of MERVILLE, a position was taken up along the side of the village of LESART, astride the road in K.33.a. and continuing westward.

During the course of arranging this line, the troops on the left withdrew leaving the left flank again open. Very severe machine-gun fire was now opened from MERVILLE and casualties had now become very heavy. At about noon orders were received to hold a sector from X roads at K.26.c.7.1 along the road to the forest K.19.d.8.1. This line was held till midnight when instructions were received to rejoin the 61st Division.

In accordance with instructions received the Battalion withdrew Head Quarters to P.3.c.8.0 and three company billets along the road running W of Bn. HQ The day was spent cleaning up billets etc.

The British retreat continued

The Germans had broken through on both sides of the junction between the two British armies and threatened Bapaume and Péronne. Foch visited Haig on the evening of 10th April, and attempted to assuage Haig's worries of having no reserves to stem the German advance by saying he was assembling a French relief force behind Amiens. The German advance continued and despite being described as 'not satisfactory' by Ludendorff, Hazebrouck was seriously threatened. Hoping, but not sure of when the French could help, Haig composed his famous order of the day.

Field Marshal Haig's Order of the Day, 11th April 1918

To All Ranks of the British Forces in France.

Three weeks ago to-day the enemy began his terrific attacks

against us upon a fifty-mile front. His objects are to separate us from the French, to take the Channel Ports and destroy the British army.

In spite of throwing already 106 divisions into the battle and enduring the most reckless sacrifice of human life, he has yet made little progress towards his goals.

We owe this to the determined fighting and self-sacrifice of our troops. Words fail me to express the admiration which I feel for the splendid resistance offered by all ranks of our army under most trying circumstances.

Many amongst us are now tired. To those I would say that Victory will belong to the side which holds out the longest. The French Army is moving rapidly and in great force to our support.

There is no other course open to us but to fight it out! Every position must be held to the last man: there must be no retirement. With our backs to the wall, and believing in the justice of our cause, each one of us must fight on to the end. The safety of our Homes and the Freedom of mankind alike depend on the conduct of each one of us at this critical moment. *

D. Haig. F.M.
Commander in Chief,
British Armies in France.

General Headquarters,
Thursday, April 11th 1918.

*The last paragraph of Haig's message above (in which the italics are mine) is doubtless the best known of any British commander's exhortation to his troops next to Nelson's 'England expects' signal, and Shakespeare's Henry V's: 'Once more unto the breach, dear friends, once more; or close the wall with our English dead!'

It is uncertain how many of those engaged actually received the message that day, but John Toland quotes an Australian subaltern of the 1st Australian Division brought up to plug the gap below Bailleul, who *was* inspired by the simple emotional words coming from a stolid cool figure, and who told his men 'If the section cannot remain here alive, it will remain here dead'.

Charteris doubts strongly the French will turn up

Haig's former Chief of Intelligence, Brigadier-General Charteris in his book *At GHQ* expressed the opinion that he thought this order of Haig's unwise because if, as in 1914, the French never came it would arouse false hopes. It would hearten the enemy; and in any event he believed the British army needed no such exhortation. Charteris wrote:

> The news from the battle is not good. The Germans are making a big effort, and the French are doing nothing. Foch said two days ago that he had at last made up his mind that the big German attack was against the British army, and that he would send a large French force to take part in the battle, but so far nothing has happened. It looks as if we should have to fight this battle alone, and we have no reserves... D.H. [Haig] has issued a finely worded appeal to the army to fight to the last, saying the French troops are hurrying to our assistance. I wish they were. It is all so like 1914 when we told the 1st Corps the French were coming and they did not come. Yet then we won alone, and I believe we shall now. All the same I wish D.H. had *not* issued his order. It will immensely hearten the Germans when they hear of it, as they must. I do not think our own men needed it to make them fight it out. If the French are really hurrying to our assistance, they should be here in a few days, almost as soon as the order will reach the front-line troops. If they are not, it may have a really bad effect to raise false hopes in the troops' minds.

Jubilation in Germany

The German gains were, naturally enough, greeted with delight and acclaim at home. German newspapers were celebrating the victory in the west, and Toland quotes the *Deutsche Zeitung*:

561

Away with all petty whining over an agreement and a reconciliation with the fetish of peace. Away with the miserable whimpering of those people who even now would prevent the righteous German hatred of England and sound German vengeance The cry of victory and retaliation rages throughout Germany with renewed passion.

12th April, 1/5th DCLI overrun

Sergeant Westlake and the rest of the survivors of 'A' Company were not among the men of the battalion who rejoined the 61st Division following 12th April. At some time on the 12th, during the desperate and exhausting conditions so matter of factly described in the War Diary, where amid the confusion of units losing touch with each other in the smoke and fury of exploding artillery shells, the hissing and crackle of machine-gun and rifle fire, and bursting grenades, and with stragglers – mainly Portuguese passing through them to the rear – the 1/5th DCLI with their ranks full of young untrained and untried replacements were valiantly trying to hold a line with both flanks exposed and with no supporting troops on either side. They fought grimly until the hordes of advancing grey-clad figures encircled and overran them, and the surviving members of 'A' Company were trapped and taken prisoner.

The remnants of the battalion who got clear received orders at midnight to return to 61st Division, and on rejoining wearily once again laid aside their rifles. As the War Diary relates below* during the following days they resumed their interrupted tasks, engaging once more in their pioneer duties – digging, unloading and carrying wiring materials, preparing posts and fire bays and traverses under instructions from Royal Engineer officers.

*Example of entry from War Diary:

> 16th April. 250 yards of trench dug, ORs [other ranks] wiring and digging and throwing up earth for parapet (mainly near LA HAYE). Later LES AMUSOIRES. Digging, revetting, wiring posts.

It doesn't sound as though they (or any other troops who had been engaged in the exhausting desperate struggle to stem the overwhelming advancing horde of German storm troops and infantry) were taken away for rest or therapeutic counselling sessions following their traumatic March and April defensive battles in the face of great odds.

The 1/5th Battalion lost sixteen officers and 467 other ranks either killed wounded or missing, over half of their effective strength.

By the end of April the German offensive on the _ys had definitely failed.

PART FORTY-NINE

*I thought I might be killed or wounded. But I never thought
of being taken prisoner. And it broke my heart. I thought
I was a better man than Gerry, man for man. But there
it is. It broke my heart.*

A sergeant in 1st Battalion, King's Royal Rifle Corps,
on being taken prisoner in a minor action in the early days
of trench warfare after the battle of First Ypres.
Quoted by Malcolm Brown.

Prisoner of war

The following is undated article cut out from either the *Western
News* or *Western Morning Mail*:

Sergt. C. Westlake, of Western Road, Launceston, is a prisoner
of war in Germany. He was captured on 12th April and the
news reached his mother yesterday (Thursday), to her relief,
as he had been reported missing for some time.

Richard Van Emden in his book *Prisoners of the Kaiser* says:

Statistically, the vast majority of soldiers were, as one
might expect, never taken prisoner. While 50 per cent of all
those who served could expect to be killed or wounded, only
around 2.8 per cent, or approximately 170,000 British
servicemen, were captured on the Western Front, over half of
these being taken prisoner only during the last eight months
of the war.

He propounds the view that being taken a prisoner was not something a soldier really thought about. If one were not unscathed then death and being wounded rather than capture were the expectations that came to mind. The notion of surrender he says was quite foreign to their minds, and those who were taken prisoner had no idea of what to expect or what to do in the event of being captured. He goes on to say:

> The transition from soldier to prisoner has always been a precarious one. History is littered with evidence of POWs being maltreated and even killed, and no amount of legislation, national or international, has guaranteed survival, or ever will . . . It took a great deal of trust for an unwounded man to hand over his weapons. Placing such trust in the good nature of a captor, to whom no good had ever been ascribed, was difficult under any circumstances; in a pitched battle such a gesture was an act of faith tantamount to leaving survival in the lap of the gods.*

*Personally, I would have thought there was little option for prisoners other than to hand over their weapons, and in most cases where troops were overrun and unable to avoid capture I would not imagine that 'trust' was operative here. Fear and apprehension more likely perhaps, especially when captured troops (on both sides) were sent back unescorted overland with shells and bullets falling around them from their own side, as well as the uncertainty concerning the intentions of their immediate captors. The history of the Devonshires mentions an occasion in October 1917, at Passchendaele: 'Nearly 250 [German] prisoners were taken by the 95th Brigade, though the majority were caught and wiped out by the German barrage on their way to the divisional cage.'

Richard Van Emden continues:

> Enemy soldiers, pent up and aggressive, often gave prisoners short shrift during intense action. It was easier to kill than remove potentially dangerous prisoners from the battlefield no matter how compliant they might seem when their hands were in the air.

General Jack during the battle of the Marne in September 1914 speaks of:

> Stupid incidents due to our troops leaving their trenches to 'accept the surrender' of Germans approaching under a white

flag. Others of the enemy having no intention of giving in, thereupon opened fire on friend and foe with dire results to both.

He is not condemnatory of the Germans who were not surrendering, but of the actions of the British troops leaving the safety of their trenches in the circumstances. He and others also instance cases where German troops had surrendered, but when the advancing troops were unable to provide escorts rearwards, or were reluctant to take them back through the still falling barrage, some of the Germans picked up their rifles again and fired into the rear of the troops that had overtaken them.

Malcolm Brown says of those taken prisoner in the Great War:

It [becoming a prisoner of war] was one of the many possible consequences of enlistment. It was part of the job description. Yet however honourably acquired, the POW label was inevitably a pejorative one.*

Returning POWs received documents from the War Office and the King and Queen relieving them of blame, but few were happy with such formal consolation. They had not taken up arms to end up behind bars. As POWs they had to suffer the humiliation of being entirely at the enemy's mercy and they could have no idea when their freedom would be restored . . . Some POWs were treated well, others badly.

*To illustrate the difference in attitudes towards prisoners of war today; in the 2003 Iraq War, seven soldiers of an American maintenance unit lost their way, came under fire, and were captured by the Iraqi forces. They were later released and on returning to the USA they were hailed by the media as 'The Magnificent Seven'.

POW diary

My cousin Pamela Westlake discovered a tiny pencil-written notebook of her father's in which he had recorded some details of his experiences during his captivity. She very kindly loaned this invaluable record to me and I have written below the items I could decipher in the order and page number in which they were written in his notebook.

There are gaps in the narrative in places because I cannot always decipher the handwriting, but there is enough material to get a feeling of the conditions he and his fellow prisoners endured. Some of the place names I cannot decipher either, partly because the notes are in pencil and written 84 years previously in this tiny notebook, and sometimes, in addition, because the formation of some alphabetical letters is rather different from the style of today, and the place names are unfamiliar to me anyway. The explanatory notes in italics are mine, and are not part of his text.

Sgt. C.H. Westlake
A Coy. 1/5th DCLI
Gardelegen
Stammologen [*Not sure of this word*]
Germany.

Page 5 [*although actually headed 'page 1'*] of the notebook reads:

Notes on the Way: Captured 12th April at Merville. Assisted a wounded man to dressing station a distance of 2 miles. Treated fairly well. Carried wounded German another two miles.

Marched to [*not clear. Looks a bit like Marquille?*]
12th April. Barley water and slice of black bread for breakfast the morning 13th 8 am. 13th marched to [*Wari—-? Cannot decipher*]. Carrying shells all day from the station to village.*
Our airmen had bombed the station the previous night and blew up ammunition, trucks and rails.

*Prisoners of war were not supposed to be ordered to engage in tasks that could be considered as aiding their captors against their own troops – such as the carrying of shells. It was never clear just where the dividing line came, and both sides had prisoners unloading and loading vehicles and trains and clearing roads as well as the 'allowed tasks' such as the carrying of wounded soldiers – both friend and foe.

Michael Young in his book on the ASC (see above), says that until the battle of the Somme German prisoners of war were sent back to England, but subsequently under the Labour Directorate, POW companies were organised, each consisting of four platoons of about 100 men. In the early part of the war, there were several companies at the ASC Heavy Repair shops, but then the number of captured rose so that the prisoners were sent to a main POW pen in Abbeyville. From these numbers skilled units were formed for work in quarries and roads. Bavarians and foresters were drafted into POW Forestry Companies, while skilled units were formed for workshops of the ASC, Royal Engineers, Army Ordnance Departments and locomotive shops.

Left work 7 pm. Marched to [*La Heine?*] Men slept like pigs in a sty. Nothing to eat all day.. Breakfast next morning 14th a slice of black bread and water. Had a wash in a ditch. No soap, no towel. Dinner a drink of barley water. Rusty tin picked up [*see below, this was to be his only eating and drinking utensil for the rest of the time while in captivity*].

I [*cannot decipher*]. Tea time burnt barley water and a slice of bread. Slept that night as previous one. In morning 15th breakfast barley water, slice of bread. Carried shells all day.

(Page 4) Still at same place. Sanitary conditions awful. Remained at the farm. Men in awful condition. No clean clothes or boots. Several men died in the camp. Men were absolutely weak, dropping down faint. Impossible to say how many men died in hospital. We started with 500 men in the camp [*see below for further description of conditions*]. (Page 5) and finished up with 1/3rd. German guards changed every 14 days. Plenty of [*indecipherable*] in the camp. We paid for all writing paper $\frac{1}{2}$ a mark for a packet of five. We sent 4 cards and two letters a month. Several of our men escaped which caused a lot of excitement to us. The meat we (Page 6) had was either horse flesh, wild boar flesh, whale or porpoise. One of our [*cannot decipher*] dinners consisted of black [*bread?*] peas, maize meal, horse beans.

Adjoining field on 27.6.18 German plane brought down by one of our airman. We had been writing home for three months, on the 3.7.18 we were told none of it had gone.

(Page 7) On 5.7.18 the men refused to go to work owing to the awful rotten dinners we had. Officer drew his revolver, all the guards loaded their rifles, but things quietened down.

12.7.18. We were gassed by [*cannot decipher*] gas from shells. Used blankets for gas masks. Wooden clogs issued in place of boots.

(Page 8) We had some shirts, toe rags, pants and towels, Austrian trousers, caps [*I can't decipher*] and some worn out boots given to us. The bandages they used for our men now made of paper. Men were starving broke into [?] cook house and stole 15 loaves. The camp were punished by having their bread stopped the next day.

[The following undated and without page numbers is headed 'Our Camp' and it seems appropriate to insert it here where it fits with the above.]

It was a French farm, all buildings were partly knocked down, we slept on about 3 feet of manure. The smell was simply awful which caused a lot of sickness. We had nothing to have our meals in. I myself used an old rusty tin [*see his reference above on page 3 of his notebook*] which had been lying in the manure heap probably for months. We had some Portuguese troops with us.* We had no blankets to sleep with. And in the morning places where it rained were worse inside than out.

*These troops were most likely from the Portuguese Division who broke under the German onslaught on 12th April and left a gap in the line through which the Germans poured to outflank the British troops and caused the Cornishmen to be overrun.

The food we received was not so good as what we should give to a pig at home. It was awful, words cannot explain the condition of the men.* They were catching moles and eating them. Picking up potato peelings from the manure heap and cooking them. If one of the Germans had two or three spoonfuls of his dinner left our boys were that hungry that they would all scramble and fight for it, and the Germans standing by laughing at them. Washing in an old ditch the water was absolutely black. The sickness was terrific, but still they were made to work.

*As I mentioned earlier Cecil Westlake was diagnosed as suffering from beriberi when he reached home. Malcolm Brown quotes an officer POW, a Lieutenant of the Royal Navy Division who was in a camp in Germany at a time when the British blockade was most effective who said:

The quality of the food was extremely poor and very meagre inasmuch as the Germans, at that period of the war, had very little of their own. The good food of course went up the line to the soldiers and what we had, particularly in the towns where I was a prisoner, was minimal... Malnutrition and so on meant a considerable loss of body weight in all of the prisoners. To give an indication of how weak one became; there was a flight of stairs – not very steep stairs – up to my particular bedroom and after a while I could negotiate the first two steps standing upright, the remainder of the steps I had to do on my hands and knees.

Officers, as a rule, suffered less hardship in captivity and unlike the other ranks prisoners did not have to engage in manual labour.

(Page 9) Another German plane brought down in flames. One man came down in a parachute. [*As I mentioned earlier, British airmen were not allowed parachutes, they were issued only to observers in static observation balloons.*] Weather is very wet. Now dinners were made of boiled beetroot.

About a 100 of our planes bombed the village of [*can't decipher. Looks like Santel*] put the wind up Jerry. On 28.8.18 we left the farm and made our camp at [*again can't make out. Think it might be Lesquint?*]

(Page 10) Men worked 8 hours every day on ammunition and ration dumps. Eighteen sergeants left for Germany arrived at [*Dort?*]. Lille [*Fort McDonald?*]. 5.10.18 [*Bais??e*] we left there on the march for Brussels [*?*] a distance of 80 kilometers. We marched 20 kilometers every day.

9.10.18. Entrained at [*can't decipher starts like Hal?*] for Gardelegen 19.10.18 we left a village called [*Bysingham?*] for [*can't decipher*] Germany and we reach [*again cannot make it out*].

Page 11 [*Name of a place I can't decipher*] where we get into a passenger train. We reach Gardelegen* about 9 pm the same day.

*Gardelegen is described – according to a reprint I have by the Imperial War Museum of a publication by, I think, The Journal of the Central Prisoners of War Committee – *Map of the Main Prison Camps in Germany and Austria* by Mrs Pope-Hennessy, as: 'An old town with dilapidated walls (pop. 8,500) near Stendal on the line Hanover-Berlin. A large camp, to which many prisoners have been sent since September 1914. The centre of many working commandos [work Kommandos]). 4th army corps.'

Next day we received an emergency parcel each which was a Godsend as our rations for the journey had been a slice of bread a day and water. On 24.10.18 we move to [*Weshan? or*

571

Werhen? or Werbian?] An NCO camp where (Page 12) we get another parcel. Then every ten days we get one until the Armistice is signed and then we get six [*groceries?*] each 3 bread and a biscuit parcel. On 17th December three others and myself left the camp and proceeded to Havelberg,* a nice little town where we stopped at an hotel called The Kronprinz. Of course we took our own food with us. 9.30 same evening I had a [*can't decipher*] time, everything was extra special. Came back to camp next day.

*Havelberg is described in the map and guide of prison camps I mentioned above as: 'Small town population 6,200 with Romanesque cathedral. Near it is placed a camp for civilian prisoners, which consists of hutments surrounded by high wire netting. There are 4,500 of all nationalities there. Prisoners from Ruhleben are occasionally sent to this camp. Nearly 400 British Indians are on the register. 3rd Army Corps.'

On 22nd December two of our officers visited the camp, a Major and a Lieutenant. Told us we were leaving for England on Boxing Day. Went to village theatre. Very Good. Paid one mark. Christmas Day (Page 14) the Germans had a parade to see whether everyone had the correct clothing. Some of our boys were still away. In the afternoon went to our hotel, went back to tea [*presumably to the camp*] came out again at six went to same hotel. Played billiards, piano playing and singing. Left [*Werben? Werlham? etc. see above*] camp on 27th and arrived [*looks like Stettin*]. Embarked on the (Page 15) 'Dronning Maud' [*or 'Dronning Maid' not clear*] a Danish steamer at 9 o'clock. We had two meals on the boat. Disembarked at Copenhagen at 8 o'clock on 29th December. We went to [*can't decipher*] by train. We were welcomed by the civilians more than I expected. On 30th we were issued out with khaki and each man received a bath. 6 am On 31st we had a glorious time plenty to eat and (Page 16) [*not actually numbered but follows previous page*] plenty of singing and more than we could drink of whisky and soda. On 1st January 1919 I went to Copenhagen had a lovely time. Every night after I went to a village called [*Birkerod? It is not clear and I can't decipher next bit*] some pleasant evenings. Left [*cannot read name*] for Copenhagen and went aboard ship 'Frederick VIII' on 7th January. The first two evenings we've a good concert each night. Landed Hull 10 am. On 11th. Went to [*Ripon?*] 2 days.

572

And so here, with this last diary entry, the third of my four 1914 enlisted soldiers departs from the story. He was unwell as I have said, but it is encouraging to read that his final days on the Continent were of happiness and good cheer following the awful times he and his fellow prisoners suffered during the months of their captivity.

Other POWs' recorded experiences

Another soldier, a professional musician who had been conscripted into the 2nd Battalion the Rifle Brigade, and fought in the battle for Passchendaele in 1917, was taken prisoner on 24th April 1918 at Villers-Brettoneux. Like Cecil Westlake he managed to keep a diary in a tiny notebook, and he wrote on Thursday 2nd June when he and fellow POWs were being transferred back to Germany:

> Oh! For a cigarette, or something solid to eat, something to read or write a letter to you, but no, nothing now but distracted thoughts, prowling around the cage, just waiting for meal times. Filthy from lying on the dirty yard, overrun with lice, grimy through want of soap, unshaven and I feel now one of God's lowest of creatures. May God bring Peace to the world soon.

Lance-Corporal E.J. Dungey, 7th Battalion, Somerset Light Infantry, who was taken prisoner at the St Quentin Canal, not far from Cecil Westlake and some two and a half weeks earlier than Cecil, seems to have experienced a different captivity according to his diary which his son, Mr William F. Dungey, reproduced in the September 2003 issue of *The Great War Magazine.* He records for example that on 14th July 1918:

> Today is the anniversary, I believe, of the French Republic and there is great jollification by the French officers, with plenty of grub knocking about, and spouts of music. We had a most enjoyable time. The French are a very light-hearted lot, different to the British, and do not feel captivity so much evidently.
> Nearly all the boys here are down with Flemish Fever. I

hope I shall not get it, as there is an epidemic among the civil population at Rastatt

20th July, 'Received four letters from England, two from mother and two from Topsy. Also received a pack of twenty-four biscuits from the British Help Society.

22nd July, Great excitement because a not bad looking girl came into the block with the farming people with the cart for our waste soup etc. we never see any females here, except the old woman that comes from the farms to empty the latrines. Women do everything in Germany; stokers, coal heavers, the jobs I shouldn't like my women-folk to do anyhow.

4th August, I got news that there were dozens of parcels for me at Mannheim by mistake. Worse luck! I shall get most of them in time I expect.

12th August, We've had some jolly fine feeds in the evening from our parcels... Last night we had baked beans and fried bacon with biscuits fried in fat, then pea soup and then English tea with biscuits and jam, it was jolly good. We all feel ten times better for it.

From the remarks in the diary generally it seems the Germans in this camp were meticulous in passing on the food and other parcels to their prisoners. Conditions too for the prisoners sounded better than in most camps, certainly far better than the others described above, including those of Cecil Westlake and his comrades.

As an inconsequential footnote to the German spring offensives in March and April 1918, and to being taken prisoner, Rudolf Binding writes in his *A Fatalist at War*, according to *Anthology of Armageddon* edited by Newman and Evans, of a rather strange encounter during this March/April German offensive:

There was a corner of a little wood where the English put up a desperate resistance, apparently with a few machine-guns, and finally with only one. When the defence was broken down, out from the lines of our advancing infantry, which I was following, appeared an English general, accompanied by a

574

single officer. He was an extraordinary sight. About 35 years old, excellently one can almost say wonderfully – dressed and equipped, and he looked as if he had just stepped out of a Turkish bath in Jermyn Street. Brushed and shaved, with his short khaki overcoat on his arm, in breeches of the best cut and magnificent high lace-boots, such as only English bootmakers make to order, he came to meet me easily and without the slightest embarrassment... I said 'Good morning, you have given us a lot of trouble; you stuck it for a long time.' To which he replied: 'Trouble! Why we have been running for five days and five nights!' It appeared that when he could no longer get his brigade to stand he had taken charge of a machine-gun himself, to set an example to his retreating men. All his officers except the one with him had been killed or wounded and his brigade hopelessly cut up. I asked him his name, to remind me of our meeting, and he gave it. He was General Dawson, an Equerry of the King.*

*I can find no record of a General Dawson at this time, or any other mention of the incident. Perhaps Binding means a Brigadier General as he talks of a brigade, but unfortunately I have no listings of these officers. It makes a splendid story, but it seems somewhat unlikely to me that when the army was being overrun, with his brigade routed and on the retreat non-stop for five days and five nights, and with all his staff casualties, the intrepid [Brigadier?] General mans a machine-gun to the bitter end, and as the German troops advance on his position he has the time to emerge bathed, shaved, unscathed and immaculately turned out, complete with polished boots. Superman could hardly have done a better change of clothing in the time!

PART FIFTY

Civilian morale is a question of potatoes. We no longer have any meat. We cannot deliver potatoes because we are short 4000 cars every day. We have absolutely no fats left. The misery is so great that it is like asking a complete riddle when one asks one's self: What does North Berlin live on and on what does East Berlin exist? As long as the riddle cannot be solved, it is impossible to elevate the popular morale. It would be the height of dishonesty if we left anyone in doubt on the question.

Secretary of State Scheidemann at a meeting between
Ludendorff and German civilian ministers on
18th October 1918.

Leaving the campaigns of 1918

The Royal Air Force, as it had now become, hampered the German troops on the 12th April, and although they secured Messines Ridge the German advance began to lag. General Plumer had been put in command of the whole defence in front of Ypres and withdrew from dearly bought ground to the Steenbeck. On the 17th his forces held and repulsed the Germans who suffered bloody losses, and on the same day the German troops north of Ypres, opposite the Belgians – who had not been engaged in a major battle since 1914 – were utterly defeated.

On 24th April the German High Command switched down to the Somme again and here occurred the only real 'tank versus tank' engagement – thirteen German and thirteen British, although seven of the British were only light tanks.

577

Haig and Foch

A coolness developed between Haig and Foch. Haig felt the French were still dragging their feet although Foch had been moving four fresh divisions north to defend Mount Kemmel. Here they were engaged, suffered severe losses, and lost Kemmel on 25th April. It had been successfully defended by worn-out British divisions and was lost by relatively fresh French divisions assaulted as they were by seven German divisions. Falls was scathing about the loss of Kemmel. He wrote:

> There was no getting away from it the [French] defence was feeble. Next day, when a counter-attack was launched by the Allies, the British advanced alone and the French did not move.

Later that day though the French did begin to resist in earnest and the Germans made little more progress.

Haig suffered an anxious time, and he must have been mentally drained by now. His divisions were often ghosts, and his young soldiers caused him concern as the attacks on them mounted and he had no room to manoeuvre.

On 27th and 28th April there was a pause in the German offensive. Foch did not believe that they had made their final effort and moved his reserves further north. He was right, and the German Fourth Army attacked at 5.40 am on the 29th. This time the French responded well and their artillery and machine-guns were well organised and staggered the attackers by the weight of their fire, and the Germans gained only two slight successes. Elsewhere the assault was smashed with heavy loss. It was the end, and the channel ports were saved.

Summing up

Falls* wrote, in summing up the British troops in the period of the March–April offensive, that the Germans regarded the battle of the Lys as a failure (*Misserfolg*). Strategically, he said, it was a worse failure than the March offensive although the Germans fought brilliantly, if not quite as well as in March. The majority of the divisions released from Russia had never faced the British and found them unexpectedly tough – even though the majority of the British troops were now only shadows of the old army; half trained, immature, weakly led at the lowest level, and often hardly knowing their lieutenant-colonels by sight. Falls said of them:

> But for that factor and the failure to relieve the Portuguese in time there would not have been cause for grave anxiety. Even as things were, it must be said that these lads, many of them none too well fed before enlistment, gave a good account of themselves. As in most of the great battles in the west, the losses of the opposing forces ... appear to have been extraordinarily similar, in the two offensives combined about three hundred and fifty thousand on both sides.

*Falls served throughout the war on the Western Front, first with the Royal Inskilling Fusiliers, and later on the General Staff and as Liaison Officer with the French forces. He was twice mentioned in despatches and awarded the French Croix de Guerre with two citations. After the war he worked on the official war histories and at the onset of the Second World War he became military correspondent of *The Times*. From 1946 to 1953 he was Chichele Professor of the History of the War at Oxford University and a Fellow of All Souls College.

Holding on

After March and April, with both sides reeling from the effects of those desperate, and for the Allies, nail-biting days of British and French retreats, the line held. As the weeks passed the British and French rallied their so weary forces, and later in the year, joined by the long awaited fresh and eager American troops, the Allies began their advance towards victory.

There was much fighting still to come. The German troops in places still fought hard grimly contesting every mile. In others they had had enough. Conditions were very bad at home, and the tired troops were now getting less supplies of food and equipment and in such circumstances morale deteriorated. General Ludendorff, when meeting with German ministers in October, underlines this point:

> I come to another point ... the morale of the army. It is very important ... The [41st] Division absolutely refused to fight on the 8th August ... The morale was bad at that time. The

579

division had *grippe*, it had no potatoes. The spirit introduced by the men from home was also bad. The drafts arrived in a state that in no way correspond to order or discipline. There were gross cases of insubordination.

Moving forward

For the Allies, more and new types of equipment arrived. Tactics and attacking skills involving greater coordination between different arms and services became more sophisticated. The RAF had at last been equipped with new machines and even with an armour-plated fighter for attacking ground troops (the Sopwith TF2 Salamander, a development of the Sopwith Snipe). Unfortunately though there were actually only a few of the final version of the Salamander in operation in France in October 1918.*

*Previous losses among ordinary squadron machines had run up to 30% when used for ground attacks, and the pilots hated 'ground strafing' patrols knowing how vulnerable they were from machine-gun and rifle fire when attacking ground forces in aeroplanes that had no protection at all underneath. Sopwith Dolphins also came into service, and were involved in the fighting from March onwards in bomber escort and ground attacking duties.

There were now different types of tanks at the front, and many more armoured cars were in use and making attacking and reconnaissance patrols. Break-throughs were made as the tired German troops fell back. And gradually the British troops became accustomed to advancing in open territory after four years of thinking of advances in terms of yards rather than miles, and now the infantry worked closely with the armoured vehicles and cavalry as they advanced.

Interestingly Ludendorff, at the same meeting mentioned above and from the same source,* says of the British troops who were, as has been universally agreed, nothing like the quality of 1914–1916:

The Americans must not be rated too highly. They are pretty dangerous, but up to the present [18th October 1918] we have beaten them back. They make a difference to the relative number, it is true, but our own men do not worry about the Americans; it is about the English. Our Army must be relieved of the feeling of isolation.

580

* Jay Winter and Blaine Baggett, *The Great War and the Shaping of the 20th Century.*

Here, in the spring 1918, although there are still hard campaigns on the Western Front ahead, with two of my four soldiers long dead, one a POW, and one who, apart from bouts of malaria, was still full of beans in India and moving towards the North West Frontier for the Third Afghan War and his first and last spell of action; this seems an appropriate time to leave the campaigns on the Western Front.

PART FIFTY-ONE

The fires of hell have been put out, and I have written my last message as war correspondent. Thank God!

Sir Philip Gibbs writing from Mons
on 11th November 1918.

The war ends

At 6.50 am on the morning of 11th November 1918, the following message was sent to the British Armies:

> Hostilities will cease at 11 hours today, November 11th. Troops will stand fast on the line reached at that hour, which will be reported by wire to Advanced GHQ. Defensive precautions will be maintained. There will be no intercourse of any description with the enemy until receipt of instructions from GHQ.

It seems rather fitting, or at least 'tidy' that British troops were engaged at Mons when the hostilities ceased. Barrie Pitt (*1918 The Last Act*) says:

> The British managed to finish the war as many of them would have liked to conduct it, with a cavalry charge. At 10.50 am and with only minutes to go, a squadron of the 7th Dragoons was sent forward to capture a bridge over the river Dendre at Lessines, the official reason given that a bridgehead was required over the river in case the Germans chose to violate the terms of the armistice. Along a straight road lined with trees, and in

perfect formation, the squadron galloped forward – and even had the war been over, they would have presented to the German machine-gunners a most tempting target. But the war was not over and the machine-guns were manned by the toughest and now bitterest of the German troops. These opened fire – together with some like-minded riflemen – and although the impetus of the charge carried some of the horsemen on to the bridge, the position was not taken until 11 am, when the machine-gunners ceased fire in accordance with their instructions.

I take issue with Pitt's assertion: 'as many of them [the British] would like to conduct it'. Also it would appear the 7th Dragoons were actually being asked to secure a bridge within the last few minutes of the war, not to conduct a cavalry charge. However if the operation was carried out as he describes it, it certainly seems both tragic and unnecessary. The cavalry were operating in the advance in 1918, but in their traditional role scouting ahead of the infantry – sometimes in cooperation with armoured cars and tanks as I have said.

William Pressey, a gunner in the Royal Artillery, as quoted by Michael Moynihan (see also above), *did* witness a cavalry charge in 1918. This was near St Quentin during the Allied retreat in the spring, and the reaction to it was far from the assertion expressed by Pitt. This charge was conducted by the French (Pressey's division was operating on the extreme right of the British line where it linked up with the French) and Pressey writes:

On the morning of the fifth day we had seen Uhlans [German lancers] on either side of us and we got out in a flaming hurry. Shells followed us as we had a hectic gallop through the village and dropped to a walk on going over the hill. Out of sight of the Germans over this hill we were walking along when we saw an unforgettable sight.

Coming towards us were a troop of French cavalry. I should say a hundred and fifty or two hundred strong. Gosh, but they looked splendid. I think word must have got to them about the German cavalry harassing us and they had come to put a stop to that. They could never have been told about the machine-guns. They laughed and waved their lances at us, shouting 'Le Bosch fini'. What a picture they made with the sunlight gleaming on their lances. We slowed down as they trotted briskly past, and everyone looked back at them.

Before reaching the top of the hill they opened out to about six feet between each horse and in a straight line. We hardly breathed. Over the top of the hill they charged, lances at the ready. There was not a sound from us. Then, only a few seconds after they disappeared, the hellish noise of machine-guns broke out. We just looked at each other. The only words I heard spoken were 'Bloody hell' ... That's what it must have been over that hill, for not one man came back. Several of their horses did, and trotted beside us, and were collected at our next stopping place.

If only the cavalry officer had stopped for one minute and talked to our officers they would have told them of the mounted machine-guns, and that it was certain death over the hill from where we had come... If they [the conditions] were known, did anyone think the Germans would leave their machine-guns and fight evenly, lance to lance? What an awful waste of husbands, brothers, sons.

Why, I wonder, did not the British officers call out a warning to the French officers? Perhaps the French were moving by them too quickly intent on their task.

Sir Esmé Howard, the British ambassador in Sweden on his way back to Britain, recounts in his book *The Theatre of Life** of arriving in Paris on 11th November 1918:

I reached Paris very early in the morning. The Gare de Lyon seemed almost deserted. An old porter took one of my handbags, I took the other. We made our way slowly to the exit of the station. As we reached it he suddenly dropped my bag and held up his hand: '*Écoutez*', he cried. '*Les canons du Mont Valérian. Ils sont signer.*' The guns of Mont Valérian were telling the people of Paris that the Armistice would be signed that day. November 11th.

Many have recounted their experiences of Armistice Day but few, I think, can have been as touched as I was by that old porter with tears of emotion in his eyes. If I had not been a unhappy Anglo-Saxon suffering like all my people from inhibitions regarding the expression of emotion of any kind, I should have flung my arms around the old man's neck. As it was I dropped my bag and clasped hands for some moments in a silence that meant much more than words. Then he told me he had lost two sons in the War but had two more whom he hoped to see again.

*Quoted by Hugh Cecil and Peter H. Liddell, editors of *At the Eleventh Hour*.

General Jack, on that fateful day, paraded his battalions and after a short address of congratulations shook hands with all the recipients of decorations during his period of command, and expressed the hope that the behaviour of the brigade under peace conditions would remain unsullied as it had been in the field. In the evening he and his officers were entertained to dinner by the Burgomaster of Cuerne and his Council. On retiring to bed, tired and very happy but unable to sleep he says:

How far away is that 22nd August 1914, when I heard with a shudder, as a platoon commander at Valenciennes, that real live German troops, armed to the teeth, were close at hand – one has been hardened since then. Incidents flash through the memory: the battles of the first four months: the awful winters in waterlogged trenches, cold and miserable: the terrible trench-war assaults and shell fire of the next three years: loss of friends, exhaustion and wounds: the stupendous victories of the last few months: our enemies beaten to their knees.

Thank God! The end of a frightful four years, thirty-four months of them at the front with the infantry, whose company officers, rank and file, together with other front-line units have suffered bravely, patiently and unselfishly, hardships and perils beyond even imagination of those, including soldiers, who have not shared them.

In 1918, William Linton Andrews had been sent home for officer training although up to then he had resisted efforts to send him for a commission. He completed the course and passed out soon after the Armistice was declared. He said: 'So I became an officer after all. Demobilised at Crystal Palace on 8th January 1919, with the rank of second lieutenant, unpaid.'

And my regiments, where were they? And what happened to them as the war closed?

The Regulars

The Rifle Brigade

The 1st Battalion, still part of the 11th Brigade, 4th Division, as they were when they landed in France in August 1914, came to a stop at Haspres, north-west of Solesmes.

The 2nd Battalion still with their 'unlucky' 8th Division, and still part of the 25th Brigade, finished the war in Belgium, at Pommeroeul, near Mons.

Alfred Watts' 3rd Battalion grounded their arms at Bavai in France, still members of the 17th Brigade. And as a matter of interest, according to Basil Harvey, when the 3rd Battalion of the Rifle Brigade, sailed for home from France in 1919 (it had incidentally been fighting up to 7th November 1918) only two officers of those who went to France with the battalion in 1914 were still serving with it; Lt. Col. Kewly DSO, MC, and Capt. L. Eastmead MC, both had been subalterns in 1914. I wonder why Eastmead had not gained more promotion over the years? I wonder too if they had to revert to their substantive ranks after the war – assuming they stayed in the army.

The 4th Battalion, 80th Brigade, 27th Division, who had been transferred to Salonika in November 1915, were in Macedonia, at Rabrovo, NW of Lake Doiran when the armistice was declared.

The Devonshire Regiment

The 1st Battalion, 95th Brigade 5th Division had returned to France from Italy in April 1918. The war ended for them at Le Quesnoy.

The 2nd Battalion, still like the 2nd Rifles, part of the 8th Division, and still with their 23rd Brigade, were also near Mons, west of Mons at Terte.

The Duke of Cornwall's Light Infantry

The 1st Battalion were in France and the same as the 1st Devons. The 2nd Battalion were the same as the Rifles 4th Battalion, in Macedonia.

The Territorials

1/5th Duke of Cornwall's Light Infantry – Cecil Westlake's battalion. Still the Pioneers of 61st Division, they finished very close to their 1st Battalion at Parquiaux, NW of Le Quesnoy.

The 1/1st Kent Cyclist Battalion – Joseph Edward Holley's battalion – lucky to the end, were in India, not yet engaged in the Third Afghan War, and lucky too in that unlike their fellow brigade members, the 1/9th Hampshires, they were not sent to Siberia.

'Kitchener's Army'

8th 'Service' Battalion, The Devonshire Regiment – Horace Westlake's battalion – ended the war in Italy at Cisterna, east of Gradisca still with the 7th Division, and without returning to France.

PART FIFTY-TWO

The Central Powers had lost the war. The Allies had won. The victors, especially 'the Big Three' – Great Britain, France and the United States of America, would decide the peace. This would be shaped by idealism, pragmatism and fear. The idealism would be largely (though not entirely) American, the pragmatism largely (though not entirely) British, and the fear largely (though not entirely) French.

John Bourne (see above) describing – as 'simple' – the
principal consequence of the Armistice.

The Armistice and the aftermath

Criticism from Clemenceau

True to the end, the French continued to denigrate the British. In his *Personalities of the Peace Conference* Clemenceau says

> To be quite candid, there was no serious opposition to the harshest clauses of the Armistice except among our British Allies, who were applying themselves heartily to the task of sparing Germany – fearing nothing so much as that the balance of power might too markedly swing over to the advantage of her 'ally' France. In his book, *The World Crisis*, Mr Churchill, who is very far from being our enemy, relates how he dined with Mr Lloyd George on the evening of the Armistice, and how the conversation turned on the sole topic of the best way of helping Germany.* At such a moment perhaps it might have been more natural to think first and foremost of

589

succouring France, so cruelly ravaged by the German soldiers.

...The new men on the other side of the Channel have not yet perceived that since those days [August 1914] there have been many changes. They were fully aware, however, that the invasion of Belgium meant that they were directly menaced in their most vital parts by a Germany that was declaring that *her future was on the water*. They decided to save England with our assistance, at the risk of freeing France at the same time. They gallantly fulfilled their part, and we treasure up for them a gratitude they mistrust, through fear that we may make it an excuse for securing those future advantages which still haunt the dreams of some of our warlike civilians. Our fate seems to be settled for an invading America has taken it into her head to pay us visits the aims of which are commercial, and Great Britain may yet suffer more from this than the insight of her latter-day politicians yet allow them to suppose.

*I can find no mention of this in my copy of *The World Crisis 1911–1918*. In my copy Churchill writes only this of the occasion:

> My wife arrived, and we decided to go and offer our congratulations to the Prime Minister, on whom the central impact of the home struggle had fallen, in his hour of recompense. But no sooner had we entered our car than twenty people mounted upon it, and in the midst of a wildly cheering multitude we were impelled slowly forward through Whitehall... It was with feelings which do not lend themselves that I heard the cheers of the brave people who had borne so much and given all, who had never wavered, who had never lost faith in their country or its destiny and who could be indulgent to the faults of their servants when the hour of deliverance had come.

There is no mention at all of his actually arriving at number 10, or of any conversation with Lloyd George if and when he got there.

Churchill says in *Great Contemporaries*, at what appears to have been his last visit to Clemenceau, that Clemenceau remarked:

> Mr Lloyd George, he is now an enemy of France. He told me himself the English will never be friends with France, except when she is weak and in danger. I am angry with him, but all the same I am glad he was there while these things were going on.

At the signing of the Peace Treaty of Versailles one of the German delegates turned to Clemenceau and said, 'I wonder what History will have to say about all this?' There was a pause while Clemenceau eyed the speaker with cool deliberation. 'History,' he replied, 'will not say that Belgium invaded Germany.'

Dr John Bourne, writing in *At the Eleventh Hour*, says:

The First World War has had a bad press, especially in the English-speaking world. During the 1920s and 30s a considerable literature of disillusionment derided wartime idealism as naïve, even reprehensible. Patriotism was not enough. These views lodged themselves firmly in popular memory where the war is commonly recalled as avoidable, mismanaged and futile. They were reinforced by the perceived experience of the Second World War as an inevitable and necessary struggle against evil and tyranny, a 'people's war' which achieved a 'people's peace'. Distance may lend perspective but it can also distort. For those who fought it, the First World War was clearly about doing something. It mattered who won and who lost. This was not simply a matter of patriotism and national survival, so clear-cut in countries like Belgium, France and Serbia, which had been invaded and occupied by enemy forces. It was also a question of ideology. The ideology of war is constantly underestimated. It was the last crusade of nineteenth century liberalism. This was nowhere more true than in Great Britain and, eventually the United States.

'Shell shock'

I have mentioned earlier that the poets Graves, Sassoon and Owen in common with many other men – many of whom had shown courage and leadership – as a result of their experiences on the Western and/or other fronts, became emotionally and mentally drained, and suffering from what was then called 'shell shock.' This was actually a war neurosis, often the result of intense and/or prolonged exposure to the battlefields and combat. It was a little known or understood medical condition at the time and some who suffered the condition were just accused of cowardice, or 'wind up' in the early days at least. Several were shot having been accused of cowardice.

The 'lucky' ones were sent to special mental hospitals and convalescent nursing homes for a while by the army medical service, but it took years for them to recover from their experiences, if they ever did. After the war, to the outside world on a casual daily basis they may have seemed 'normal', but mentally they were often scarred for life by their experiences.

The musician, composer and poet Ivor Gurney* (see also above, Ovillers 1916) enlisted as a private soldier in 2/5th Gloucesters in February 1915 on his second attempt. He had been rejected earlier because his eyesight was below the standard then acceptable. Serving on the Western Front he suffered from a combination of a wound, the effects of a gas attack, and mental illness in September 1917, and as a result of these experiences he was invalided home. In fairness he had shown signs before the war of depression, but there is no doubt that his war experiences exacerbated his condition, and he was discharged with 'delayed shell-shock' in October 1918 following an attempted suicide. He was committed to a mental asylum in Gloucester in 1922. He died in 1937.

*In 1990 Gamut Classics produced a CD of some of his hitherto unrecorded piano pieces, and tragically the pianist who recorded the works, Alan Gravill, was killed in an accident very soon after the release.

Often soldiers, particularly other ranks, were just patched up and returned to the front with only the hope of either being wounded again or killed to put them out of their misery. *The Times* in an article dated 28th June 2001, records the death of David Ireland in his home town of Cupar, Fife:

> He was 103 years of age. He joined the Cyclist Battalion of the 3rd Royal Highlanders, The Black Watch, just after his 18th birthday. He was wounded in the shoulder by fire from a German aircraft in 1916. He returned to the front in time for the Battle of Arras in April 1917 where he was shot again, in the knee. After discharge from the army in 1919 he worked as a gardener, but entered Stratheden Hospital in 1925 suffering from 'shattered nerves', and never left it until he died.

W.L. Andrews recalls a sad little event involving a shell shocked 15 or 16 year-old lad following the battle of Neuve Chapelle in 1915. He says:

I was given charge of a boy of fifteen or sixteen who had been with us in action but now sobbed uncontrollably, and could not be quiet. Later we would have called it shell shock. I had not seen the boy whilst we were in action, but I believe he carried on well, and had spent most of his time at the side of our old battalion tailor, a big elderly ex-regular. The youngster, Private X, was a pathetic sight, his face swollen with crying. He had black hair, black eyebrows, and a round face which normally would be cheerful and perhaps comic. It was now childish and frightened.

'Don't take me back to they shells, corporal,' he said again and again. 'For God's sake get me out of this. I can't face they shells. I don't mind they bullets, but I can't face they shells.' NCOs had told him he must cheer up or he would be shot for cowardice, but this did not steel his shattered nerves, nor did my reasoning with him, and my attempt to cheer him with chocolate.

Andrews took the lad to the medical officer saying 'what am I going to do with him, sir?' The doctor, although a kindly soul, could do nothing. Andrews said the poor lad had no spirit left and that he must have been knocked down or shaken by a big shell exploding near him. Andrews had to leave the lad at the first aid post and did not see him again.

One can only hope that Private 'X' received the same treatment as George Maher (mentioned earlier) who says, having been discovered in tears after his unit had been bombed by aircraft when they were encamped near Amiens:

I was lying on my ground sheet crying in the tent when this man said 'what are you crying for?'. Then it all came out, that I was thirteen. He went and reported what I had said and I was taken to see the major. I can see him now, wringing wet, with rain dripping from his helmet. He swore at me. 'You bloody fool, it costs money to get you out here and you bloody well cry.' He had no option but to have me arrested by the Military Police and to send me home, but I wasn't the only one going back. When I was being taken under escort to the railway station I found I was one of five under-age boys from different regiments being sent back to England, and one of thcm I discovered was even younger than myself. A little nuggety bloke he was too! We joked that he could never have seen over the trenches, that they would have had to have lifted him up.

Maher was not punished and the authorities took no action against him. He was given a new suit and a little amount of money that was owing to him and the chance to rejoin the regiment as a bandsman. He said he jumped at the chance, he was given a month's paid leave and told to rejoin in November on 'boy service' and, he said, thankfully took no further part in the war.

Andrews also mentions shell shock again when talking about the battle of the Somme. He says:

> When the battalion returned to the line it had a long and trying spell. There were few dug-outs, just shell holes linked up, opened to a fire that never died down. I saw many cases of shell-shock, poor fellows who trembled all the time, and could not stop it, and were very terrified.

In the Second World War, some aircrew in particular, especially those in bomber command after repeated operations, suffered from a similar strain of combat fatigue and could not continue with their duties. Many personnel who suffered managed to stick it out to the end, but for those who did not and were taken off operations it was referred to kindly as 'LMF' (Lack of Moral Fibre).

Gordon Corrigan (see above) spends some time on the subject of 'shell shock' and says the term was coined by a Dr Charles Myers in 1914. Corrigan quotes from the *Report of the War Office Committee into the Causation and Prevention of Shell Shock* held at the PRO at Kew (Document WO32/47/48) and published in 1922 by HMSO. Also at Kew – where the PRO is now known as The UK National Archives – for those interested there are the papers in sections CSC/ 5/93 and FD 2/1–5.

'The Haunting Years'

William Linton Andrews, having served the whole war on the

Western Front, writing in the Foreword to his book *The Haunting Years*, recalls the immediate post-war years in terms so similar to those feelings expressed by Robert Graves. And he too must have been suffering from the same war neurosis that afflicted Graves and so many others:

I call them haunting years, for nothing in our time will haunt us like the war. Our dead comrades live in our thoughts, appealingly, as if afraid to be forgotten. Peace came, but not at once for those who survived. The War pressed down on some of us like a doom for years after the last shot was fired... For some years after the War, like many others who had been there a long time, I woke almost every night in terror from a nightmare of suffocation by gas, or being trapped by a bombardment from which I ran this way and that, or of fighting a bayonet duel with a gigantic Prussian Guardsman.

The specialists told me the best thing I could do was to forget the War and build up with hearty feeding – porridge, apples with their skins, potatoes with their jackets, oatmeal cakes, wholemeal bread... The advice on diet jumped with my humour, and one of the happiest moments of the peace for me was when we were at last allowed to go to a dairy and drink a glass of milk straight off. The specialists approved heartily. But the other part of the specialists' advice, to forget the War. How was I to do that? How could any of us? By what effort of will could I blot out the memory of those years of flame and death, and of life in trenches that were like clay graves, and often were graves, and of wounded men trampled to death in Somme mud by a panic rush, and of seeing men killed horribly by shells or going mad under the murderous strain?

How *could* the men forget? Perhaps Matthew Arnold in his poem *Absence* found the words:

> And we forget because we must,
> And not because we will.

Memories – good and bad

But memories have a strong part to play, and time for most of the surviving soldiers of those war-riven years did have a healing quality by bringing about a simple and sometimes guilty wonderment many years later that they had survived when so many of their friends did not. A casual move to the left by one man while talking to another, and one of them is hit by a bullet or a chunk of shrapnel and dies. A soldier leaves his dug-out for a moment, it is hit by a random shell and the other occupants die, while he is shaken but alive. A particularly ghastly example is described by Edmund Blunden:

> A young cheerful lance-corporal of ours was making some tea as I passed one warm afternoon. Wishing him a good tea, I went along three fire-bays; one shell dropped without warning behind me; I saw its smoke faint out, and I thought all was lucky as it should be. Soon a cry from that place recalled me; the shell had burst all wrong. Its butting impression was black and stinking in the parados where three minutes ago the lance-corporal's mess tin was bubbling over a little flame. For him how could the gobbets of blackening flesh, the earth-wall sotted with blood, with flesh, the eye under the duckboard, the pulpy bone be the only answer? At this moment while we looked in horror, the lance corporal's brother came round the traverse.

I find it very moving when reading letters from one old ex-soldier to another recalling those days when they were young. And poignant comments in letters from the families. There is a simple dignity about the people from that generation, and so often one is struck by how little they asked or expected from life, despite many of them suffering from hard times in the subsequent 'Depression' of the inter-war years.

As I mentioned, George Coppard printed some of the letters he received in the period 1969 to 1973 after the publication of his book *With a Machine Gun to Cambrai*. I have taken the liberty of extracting comments from some of them in addition to the one already quoted under the 'Cambrai Battle' heading in Part Forty-five:

You are to be envied with two lovely daughters. I had no family and my wife died ten years ago. At 79 I am keeping fit and a five-mile walk is nothing. My greatest joy is growing dahlias. [An ex-soldier who enlisted in September 1914 into the 6th Buffs.]

I too was born in 1898, and joined the army, like you, very much under age in 1914... So I have been very lucky in life, which I often find surprising when I think back to the sort of life we led as youths in the war. I have really enjoyed reviving memories in writing to you of those days of so long ago. It is, of course, mainly the good things one remembers most and this is just as well. Time is marching on for us both, but I do wish you well and hope you have many pleasant years ahead.

My wife and I are quite fit and still enjoy life [he was gassed in 1917], gardening etc – just pensioners but we get about quite a lot... We aren't well off but we get along. I've never been without a bob or two in my pocket all our married lives and usually a cigarette in my mouth and a dog at my side.

PART FIFTY-THREE

Today is the sixty-ninth anniversary of the assassination of the Archduke Franz Ferdinand at Sarajevo, the date from which the world changed. At the time no one realised what it meant, though I often think of that prize-winning spoof headline in the New York Daily News in 1920· 'Archduke found alive, World War a mistake'.

Alan Clark; entry in his diary on 28th June 1983.

So, what *did* you do in the war, Daddy?

Wherever they served, and in whatever capacity, they are virtually all gone now, the survivors of those once carefree young men who set off in 1914 for the 'great adventure'. So too their mothers and fathers, their sweethearts,* their wives and widows, their commanders, the kings and queens and all the political figures of those years; the leaders and the led, the powerful and the ordinary people of those times.

*It is so sad to think of those young women who never had the chance to marry and raise a family because the war ripped from them their potential husbands, and they were left with only memories of what might have been.

Cabinet documents, departmental minutes, and once secret government instructions lie dormant and mainly neglected within the 100 miles or more of shelving in the Public Records Office, and in other institutions. Tragically many of the documents of 'The Great War', particularly the records of soldiers, were destroyed by incendiary bombs in the Blitz in London in the Second World War, and these are referred to at Kew as 'the burnt documents'.

599

An article in *The Times*, 9th April 2003, reported a meeting at the PRO on the previous day attended by nine of the forty believed remaining survivors of the war. Their ages ranged from 102 years to 108 years. Two of them were ex-DCLI – Jack Davis and Harry Patch – and one an ex-2nd Lieutenant in the Artists' Rifles aged 105.

The cost

How can one evaluate the cost of such a war? Even in terms of 'facts and figures' not only do these vary according to the sources, but according to when the figures were collected. And how can they be interpreted and costed in terms of human suffering, and the ruinous destruction of towns, villages and countryside?

How does one evaluate the appalling waste of food, materials and equipment that ended on the sea bed? As far as Great Britain alone goes, she lost nearly eight million tons of merchant shipping. The majority of the vessels destroyed were laden with desperately needed cargoes as they sank to the ocean floor spilling their precious cargoes to rot and rust, and with them went 15,313 seamen and fishermen in over 3,000 vessels.

Peace treaty signed

A letter addressed to King George V by the Prime Minister dated 28th June 1919, written at La Galerie des Glaces, du Chateau de Versailles, reads:

> Mr Lloyd George, with his humble duty to Your Majesty, has the honour to announce that the long and terrible war, in which the British Empire has been engaged with the German Empire for more than four years, and which has caused so much suffering to mankind, has been brought to an end this afternoon by the Treaty of Peace just signed in this hall.
>
> He desires on behalf of all the Plenipotentiaries of Your Majesty's Empire to tender their heartfelt congratulations to Your Majesty on the signature of a Treaty which marks the victorious end of a terrible struggle which has lasted so long,

and in which Your Majesty's subjects from all parts of the Empire have played so glorious a part.

The League of Nations

E.S. Grew, the author of *Volume VI The Great War European History* published in 1920, wrote prophetically:

> The Peace Treaty is, in itself, an instrument of such ramified structure, and so dependent for its fulfilment on factors that are yet hidden from many who took a part in framing it, that its consequences can neither be forseen nor indicated. It rests for its accomplishment on the design of a League of Nations which was the ideal of the President who brought America into the war, thereby seeking not merely to end it, but to end all wars.

The unknown warrior comes home

The following passage is taken from *The Long Trail* by Brody and Partridge:

> From places near Ypres, Arras, Cambrai, on the Marne and 'in two other salients', six shell-torn and unrecognisable British corpses were disinterred by an impartial commission; placed in six coffins, all exactly alike. The unknown remains were placed in a hut, each draped with the Union Jack. All concerned then retired to a distance. Lastly a 'British officer of very high rank' was blindfolded, led into the hut, which he had not previously entered. Groping about, he finally touched one of the coffins and so selected the Unknown Warrior who was buried in Westminster Abbey on Armistice Day 1920 with simple and solemn funeral rites.*

*The inscription on the tomb reads: 'Beneath this stone rests the body of a British warrior unknown by name or rank, brought from France to lie among the most illustrious of the land and buried here on Armistice Day, November 1920, in the presence of His Majesty King George V, his Ministers of State, and the Chiefs of his Forces, and a vast concourse of the nation. Thus are commemorated the many multitudes who during the Great War of 1914–1918 gave the most that man can give, life itself, for God, for King and country, for loved ones, home and Empire, for the sacred cause of justice and the freedom of the world. They buried him among the Kings because he had done good towards God and towards His House.'

Disarmament

Naval

The reduction in naval and military forces was soon well under way. By November 1921 the limitations of naval armaments were being proposed at the Washington Conference. The USA was to scrap all new capital ships now under construction and on their way to completion. This included six battle-cruisers, seven battleships plus two battleships launched. The total of capital ships to be scrapped was 30.

Great Britain to stop further construction on four new battleships of the Hood class and scrap her pre-Dreadnought second line battleships, first-line battleships up to, but not including, the King George V class.

Japan was to abandon her programme for the building of ships not yet laid down.

M. Briand explained that the French could not adopt a policy of disarmament; Germany had 6,000,000 to 7,000,000 ready to wage war anew at a few weeks' notice.

The Royal Air Force

The editor of *The Aeroplane* writing with a degree of pride and satisfaction in 1921 claimed that in operations on the North-West Frontier of India half a dozen aeroplanes of the RAF had accomplished in three weeks what a very considerable punitive expedition on the ground failed to accomplish in three months. In Mesopotamia, he continued, the RAF had demonstrated that it could do with a very few aeroplanes more to produce quietude among insurgent Arabs than can be done by a very large army. As a result the policing of Iraq had now been handed over completely to the RAF. In Equatorial Africa, where one tribe or another was constantly causing trouble, several small disturbances had been promptly crushed by the appearance of only two or three aeroplanes over the villages of the disaffected tribes. Throughout the war with the Irish

Republican army the RAF assured the carriage of official documents and service mails which could not be conveyed by road or rail owing to Sinn Fein action. And, warming to his theme, the writer continued:

It is gradually becoming evident to those in authority that there are certain types of war in which the RAF can deal with the whole business just as in other types of war the Army or Navy is the predominant power, and thus the importance of the RAF in the scheme of our widely dispersed Empire is becoming properly defined.

It is obvious that the British Isles cannot be attacked except by water or by the air. A thousand aeroplanes of the largest bomb dropping or torpedo-carrying type can be bought for the price of one battleship. Moreover such aeroplanes located in the centre of England can reach any part of the coast within a few hours, while any hostile fleet must take many more hours at sea before it can reach our coast. And no conceivable fleet could withstand the attack of a thousand bombing or torpedo aeroplanes.

Finally, if one looks to 1940 and the Battle of Britain, perhaps he was not so far out when he said:

It is reasonable to argue that the defence of Great Britain by sea and air may justifiably be committed to the RAF.

It is also fascinating that although times and methods of warfare have changed in the 80 odd years since he wrote the above summary of 1921, the main trouble spots of the world as I write are still the same now as they were then: the Balkans, Iraq, Africa, and Northern Ireland. *Plus ça change, plus c'est la même chose.*

Following the war a number of aircraft manufacturers went out of business, among them the Sopwith Company, the builder of famous scout aircraft such as the Sopwith Triplane, Sopwith Pup and of course the Sopwith Camel. The Avro Company was taken over by the Crossley Motor Company, and the Martinsyde Company went into the hands of a liquidator. Others flourished, at least for a while, among them the Bristol Company, the Westland Company, the Gloucestershire Company and the Fairey Company, all of whom continued to design and build aircraft for the RAF up to and including the Second World War.

C.G. Grey makes an intriguing statement, one I have never heard before in relation to the RAF (and presumably the RFC too as the RAF only came into existence on 1st April 1918). He writes:

The RAF at home is steadily demonstrating its fitness for the high responsibilities which are to be put upon it. *The officers and men have already lived down all the reproaches that were made against them during the War and after the Armistice* [my italics].

I cannot recall having read of any such reproaches and I wonder what they were about? In the Second World War the Royal Air Force suffered jibes from soldiers in 1940 – until the Battle of Britain quelled them – 'Where was the RAF at Dunkirk?' But I know of no adverse remarks or accusations passed about them during or following WWI.

A number of private airlines grew rapidly into existence soon after the end of the war, mainly using cheaply obtained ex-military aeroplanes in the first instance. By the end of 1920 a number had gone broke. Among the casualties were: Air Transport & Travel Ltd, Instone Airline which although it continued for a while closed its cross-Channel service in December, and in the early spring of the following year Handley-Page Transport Ltd, also ceased to exist.

The post-war army

Excluding India, the number of men on the army establishment for the year 1921–1922 was 341,000 and planned to fall to 235,000, including colonial and native Indian troops serving outside India. This compared to 525,000 in 1920–1921.

Not forgotten, the departure of the last of my four soldiers

My father once said to my wife Ann in his later years: 'Life began for me in 1914 when I was 16 and joined the army.' On 29th October 1919, together with the other 1914 men of the 1/1st Kents, he left Daghasi for the long journey home, and sailed from Bombay on 12th November 1919. In January/February 1920, in England, the 1/1st Kents received their 'Certificates of Disembodiment on Demobilisation'. If a new emergency broke out they were instructed to rejoin at Shorncliffe.

Home was a totally different world in which they now found themselves in 1920. Gone were those five years of comradeship. People at home were doing their best to put the war behind them. Jobs were few and far between and nobody was interested in the arrival of these sunburnt soldiers. The battalion demobbed, split up and went their ways, and although grateful to have escaped the 'sausage machine' of France and Belgium – which they could barely comprehend – with their comrades of six years gone they were all bereft and felt strangers in their own land for a while to come.

Joseph Edward Holley rejoins in 1939

Possibly in the hope that he would recapture the feelings of those days when he and his young companions marched all over India, where their world was full of the heat and colour, the smells and wonders of that subcontinent, so different from the muted tones and colours of the suburbs and city of London, my father joined the army again in 1939.

On his demobilisation in 1945 he told me he had hated every minute of it. Alas, a married family man twenty-five years later cannot recapture the youth and the innocent wonder of a sixteen-year-old who enlisted in 1914. But those First World War years still played a great part of his memories in the last years of his life, and he often spoke of them, and his comrades, with affection. He and they were the lucky ones, as I said earlier; the blind chance of the draw led them to India and the Northwest Frontier while nearly all his school chums died or were maimed in one or other of the London Territorial or 'Kitchener' battalions on the Western Front, particularly on the Somme in 1916.

Nearly 30 years after my father's return from India, while I was serving aboard the troopship *Empire Windrush*, we brought home the last of the British troops from India (following Lord Mountbatten's overseeing of the partition of India and Pakistan). We sailed from Bombay and Karachi for Southampton where we disembarked the troops and passengers, and then sailed up the Channel and round to our berth at Tilbury. The trooping days to India were over, and the Raj had departed the Indian continent forever.

My father died on 23rd November 1991.

Demobilised, and looking back

Rowland Fielding, *War Letters to a Wife*, had this to say while waiting to be 'demobbed':

> The raging desire still continues to be demobilised quickly. Nevertheless, I feel pretty sure that, for many, there will be pathetic disillusionment...
>
> After all, there was a good deal to be said in favour of the old trench life. There was none of the mean haunting fears of poverty there, and the next meal – if you were alive to take it – was as certain as the rising sun. The rations were the same for the 'haves' and the 'have nots,' and the shells fell without favour, upon both.
>
> In a life where no money passes the ownership of money counts for nothing. Rich and poor alike stand solely upon their individual merits, without discrimination. You can have no idea, till you have tried it, how much pleasanter life is under such circumstances.
>
> In spite – or partly perhaps because of the gloominess of the surroundings, there was an atmosphere of selflessness and a spirit of camaraderie the like of which has probably not been seen in the world before – at least not on so grand a scale. Such is the influence of shells!
>
> The life was a curious blend of discipline and good-fellowship; wherein men were easily pleased; where even a shell when it had just missed you produced a sort of exultation; – a life in the course of which you actually got used to the taste of chloride of lime in tea.
>
> In short, there was no humbug in the trenches, and that is why – with all the disadvantages – the better kind of men who have lived in them will look back upon them hereafter with something like affection.

Arthur Behrend too, looking back from 1963, remembers those

comrades and years, with some affection and nostalgia:

> I am not ashamed to confess that I look back upon my time with the 90th [Artillery] Brigade in Flanders and France as by far the most fulfilling eighteen months of my life. My home ties were slight, and I was neither married nor engaged. I had an absorbing job, [adjutant] responsibility well beyond my years, the companionship and friendship of men better and older than myself, and days if not weeks of excitement which often, yet not too often, were spiced with danger. No man in his early twenties can ask for more.

Churchill completes the story

Early in my story I quoted a passage from Winston Churchill, and it seems neatly fitting to end it with another passage from the same author writing some years after the 1914–1918 war. He says:

> The curtain falls upon the long front in France and Flanders. The soothing hands of time and Nature, the swift repair of peaceful industry, have already almost effaced the crater-field and the battle lines which in a broad belt from the Vosges to the sea lately blackened the smiling fields of France. The ruins are rebuilt, the riven trees are replaced by new plantations. Only the cemeteries, the monuments and stunted steeples, with here and there a mouldering trench or huge mine crater-lake, assail the traveller with the fact that twenty-five millions of soldiers fought here and twelve million shed their blood or perished in the greatest of all human contentions less than twenty years ago.
>
> Merciful oblivion draws its veils; the crippled limp away; the mourners fall back into the sad twilight of memory. New youth is here to claim its rights, and the perennial stream flows forward even in the battle zone, as if the tale were all a dream.

Postscript

When, on 3rd September 1939, German troops and tanks rolled

into Poland, and Britain and France were again at war with Germany, a British Expeditionary Force prepared to embark for France for the second time within living memory. This time there was no euphoria, no excitement, just a sense of impending tragedy and a feeling of *déjà vu* across the land, and perhaps too the ghostly echo of dead soldiers' voices:

> What's the use of worrying,
> It never was worthwhile.
> So pack up your troubles
> In your old kit bag
> And smile, smile, smile.

APPENDIX:
Bibliography* and specialist publishers

*Books from my own collection I have used as reference material.

General reference material

Anthology of Armageddon, edited and compiled by B. Newman and I.O. Evans. 1935.
Army Service Records of the First World War, Public Record Office Guide No. 19.
Army Records for Family Historians, Public Record Office Guide No. 2.
At The Eleventh Hour, Hugh Cecil & Peter H. Liddle, 1998.
A Western Front Companion 1914–1918, John Laffin, 1994.
Brasseys Companion to the British Army, Antony Makepeace-Warne, 1995.
Britain's Army in the 20th Century, Field Marshal Lord Carver, 1998.
British Battalions in France and Belgium 1914, Ray Westlake, 1997.
British Battalions on the Western Front 1915, Ray Westlake, 2001.
Business in Great Waters, John Terraine, 1989.
British Battalions on the Somme, Ray Westlake, 1994.
Chronicles of the Great War. The Western Front 1914–1918, Peter Simkins, 1999.
Chronology of the Great War 1914–1918, ed. by Lord Edward Gleichen, 1998. (Originally published in 3 volumes between 1918 and 1920.)
Dictionary of Military Biography, Wordsworth Reference.
GHQ (Montreul-Sur-Mer), 'G.S.O.', 1920.
History of the First World War, Liddell Hart, 1930.
Identifying Your World War I Soldier from Badges and Photographs, Ian Swinnerton, 2001.
Look to your Front. Studies in the First World War, British Commission for Military History, 1999.
Military Badges, John Gaylor, 1971.
Mud, Blood and Poppycock, Gordon Corrigan, 2003.
News From The Front, Martin J. Farrar, 1998.
Stalemate!, J.H. Johnson, 1995.

Testimony of War 1914–1918, Peter Liddle, 1979.
The British Army, Iain Swinnerton, 1996.
The British Army 1914–1918, Fosten, Marrion and Embleton, 1978.
The British Dominions Year Book 1922, editors E. Salmon and J. Worsfold, 1922.
The First World War, Cyril Falls, 1960.
The First World War, The Essential Guide to Sources in the UK National Archives, Ian F.W. Beckett. PRO 2002.
The German Army 1914–1918, Fosten, Marrion and Embleton, 1978.
The Great War and the Shaping of the 20th Century, Jay Winter & Blaine Baggett, 1996.
The Home Front in the Great War, David Bilton, 2003.
The Imperial War Museum Book of The First World War, Malcolm Brown, 1991.
The Long Trail – what the British soldier sang and said in 1914–1918, J. Brophy & E. Partridge, 1931.
The MacMillan Dictionary of the First Word War, Stephen Pope & Anne Wheal, 1995.
The Price of Pity: Poetry, History and Myth in The Great War, Martin Stephen, 1996.
The Register of the Victoria Cross, This England, 1981.
The Smoke and the Fire, John Terraine, 1980.
The Soldier's War 1914–1918,* Peter Liddle, 1988.
The World Crisis 1911–1918, Winston S. Churchill, 1923.
The World War One Source Book, P.J. Hathornthwaite, 1992.
Tracing Your First World War Ancestors, Simon Fowler, 2003.
Trench Warfare 1914–1918, Tony Ashworth, 1980.
War Facts and Figures, The British Dominions General Insurance Co. Ltd, 1915?
War Underground, 1914–1918, Alexander Barrie, 1962.
World War One A Chronological Narrative, Philip Warner, 1995.
World War I Trench Warfare 1914–1916, Dr Stephen Bull, 2002.
World War I Trench Warfare 1916–1918, Dr Stephen Bull, 2002.

Regimental Histories and Studies

Army Service Corps 1902–1918, Michael Young, 2000.
British Regiments 1914–1918, Brig. E.A. James, 1978.
British Territorial Units 1914–18, Ray Westlake & Mike Chappell, 1991.
The Devonshire Regiment 1914–1918 Vol. 1, C.T. Atkinson, 1926.
The Devonshire Regiment 1914–1918 Vol. 2, C.T. Atkinson, 1926.
The Duke of Cornwall's Light Infantry (History of) 1914–1919, Everard Wyrall, 1932.
The 8th Division 1914–1918, Lt. Colonel J.H. Boraston and Captain C.E.O. Bax, 1926.

English and Welsh Infantry Regiments, Ray Westlake, 1995.
Histories of 251 Divisions of the German Army 1914–1918, London Stamp
　Exchange Ltd, 1989.
The Kent Cyclist Battalion 1908–1920, Cyril Bristow, 1986.
The London Scottish in The Great War, Mark Lloyd, 2001.
For Love of Regiment Vol. 1, Charles Messenger, 1994.
For Love of Regiment Vol. 2, Charles Messenger, 1996.
Military and Naval Silver, Roger Perkins, 1999.
Pilgrimage. A guide to the Royal Newfoundland Regiment in World War One,
　W. David Parsons, 1994.
Pioneer Battalions in the Great War, K.W. Mitchinson, 1997.
Princess Patricia's Canadian Light Infantry, Jeffrey Williams, 1972.
The Queen's Own Hussars (3rd and 7th), Brassey's Defence Publishers, 1985.
*The Rifle Brigade Chronicles for 1914, Col. Willoughby Verner, 1915.
The Rifle Brigade, Basil Harvey, 1975.
Sepoys in the Trenches The Indian Corps on the Western Front 1914–1915,
　Gordon Corrigan, 1999.

*Borrowed, not in my collection.

The Generals

1914, Field Marshal Viscount French of Ypres, 1919.
Bloody Red Tabs, Frank Davies and Graham Maddocks, 1995.
Field Marshal Earl Haig, Brig.-Gen. John Charteris, 1929.
General Sir Ivor Maxse. Far From a Donkey, John Baynes, 1995.
Haig's Command A Reassessment, Denis Winter, 1991.
Sir Douglas Haig's Dispatches, 1915–1919, J.H. Boraston. Editor, 1919.
The British Field Marshals 1736–1997, T.A. Heathcote, 1999.
The Great War Generals on the Western Front, Robin Neillands, 1999.
The Military Correspondence of Field Marshal Sir William Robertson, David
　R. Woodward, Ed., 1989.
The Swordbearers, Correlli Barnett, 1963.

The Years

The Guns of August. August 1914, Barbara W. Tuckman, 1962.
1914, James Cameron, 1959.
Liaison 1914, Edward Spears, 1930.
The Donkeys (1915), Alan Clark, 1961.
1915 The Death of Innocence, Lyn MacDonald, 1993.
1916 Year of Decision, James Cameron, 1962.
In Flanders Fields (1917), Leon Wolff, 1959.
1918. The Last Act, Barrie Pitt, 1962.

To Win a War 1918 The Year of Victory, John Terraine, 1978.
The Imperial War Museum Book of 1918, Malcolm Brown, 1998.
No Man's Land The Story of 1918, John Toland, 1980.

The Battles. Western Front

Mons. The Retreat to Victory, John Terraine, 1960.
Le Cateau, 1914, Michael Gavaghan, 2000.
Ypres 1914. The Death of an Army, A.H. Farrar-Hockley, 1967.
1915 Campaign in France – Aubers Ridge, Festubert and Loos, Lieut. Col.
   A. Kearsey, 1929.
*A Record of the Battles and Engagements of the British Armies in France
   and Flanders 1914–1918*, Captain E.A. James, 1924.
The Battle of Neuve Chapelle, Geoff. Bridger, 2000.
The Battle of Loos, Philip Warner 1976.
Loos 1915, Micheal Gavaghan, 1998.
The Price of Glory. Verdun 1916, Alistair Horne, 1962.
When the Barrage Lifts, Gerald Gliddon, 1987.
The Big Push. The Somme 1916, R.B. Gardner, 1961.
The Somme, A.H. Farrar-Hockley, 1964.
The First Day of the Somme, Martin Middlebrook, 1971.
Guillemont, The Somme, Michael Stedman, 1998.
The Battles of the Somme (1916 & 1918), Martin Marix Evans, 1996.
The Imperial War Museum Book of the Somme, Malcolm Brown, 1996.
Cambrai (1917), Jack Horsfall & Nigel Cave, 1999.
Passchendaele, Philip Warner, 1987.
To the Last Man (Spring 1918), Lyn MacDonald, 1998.
The Kaiser's Battle (Spring 1918), Martin Middlebrook, 1978.
Advance to Victory 1918 Somme, Micheal Steadman, 2001.
The Western Front (Book and 2 Videos], Richard Holmes, 1999.
The Evolution of Victory, Andy Simpson, 1995.

Autobiographical and Biographical (reminiscences and diaries etc.)

Alchemist of War the life of Basil Liddell Hart, Alex Danchev, 1998.
As From Kemmel Hill An Adjutant in France and Flanders 1917 and 1918,
   Arthur Behrend, 1963.
A Student in Arms, Donald Hankey, 1916.
*Cameos of the Western Front South Ypres Sector 1914–1918. A Walk Round
   Plug Street*, Tony Spagnoly & Ted Smith, 1997.
Cameos of the Western Front. Salient Points One. Ypres Sector 1914–1918,
   Tony Spagnoly & Ted Smith, 1995.
Cameos of the Western Front. Salient Points Two. Ypres Sector 1914–1918,
   Tony Spagnoly & Ted Smith, 1998.

MacMillan of MacMillan, Colonel of the Regiment Argyll and Sutherland Highlanders, 60–61

McMillan, Private Archibald, 15th Battalion, Royal Scots (Lothian Regiment), 29 Highlanders, 60–61

Maher, George, Private, 2nd King's Own Royal Lancashire Regiment, 593–594

Malcolm, Major-General, Neil, Gough's Chief of Staff, 235

Mallins, Geoffrey, Official War Photographer, 420–421

Mallory George, mountaineer, 203

Marconi, Guglielmo, pioneer in the invention and development of wireless telegraphy, 100

Marne, the battle of, 306

Marshall-Cornwall, General Sir James, member of Haig's intelligence staff, 480

Marten, Howard, member of the Non-Combatants Corps, 26–27

Martin, Captain, D.L., 9th Battalion the Devonshire Regiment, 423

Masefield, John, Poet Laureate, 38

Mason, A.E.W., author, 39

Mason, Major K.S., Divisional Machine Gun Officer, 16th (Irish) Division, 170–171

Maude, Brigadier-General Sir F. Stanley, Commander 14th Brigade (later General in Mesopotamia), 310

Maxse, General Sir Ivor, 171, 209, 405–406, 479–480, 483, 532–533, 534

Maxwell, Brigadier-General, F.A.M., VC, CSI, DSO & Bar, 248–249

Merville, 559

Mesopotamia (Iraq), 391, 567, 602–603

Messines, 75, 164, 469–477

Micheler, General Alfred (Commander, French 5th and 10th Armies), 459

Military Service Acts 1916 and 1918, 74

Militia Act, 68

Milner, Lord Alfred (replaced Lord Derby as War Minister), 526, 547

Ministry of Defence (MoD), 29

Moltke, Field Marshal, Helmouth Johann Ludwig von, 67, 183, 295, 306, 308

Mons, 295, 296, 298, 299, 301, 303

Montgomery, Field Marshal Bernard, 63, 181

Moore, Major-General, Director of Veterinary Services, 285

Morland, Lieutenant-General Sir T.L.N, Commander 5th Division and later X Corps, 142, 422

Mountbatten, see Battenberg, 66, and Lord Louis, 605

Murray, Sir Archibald, 82, 172, 197, 305

Myers, Dr Charles, 594

Nash, Paul, official war artist, 483

National Kitchens, 520–521

National Service League, 73

Neuve Chapelle, battle of, 10th–13th March 1915, 329–336

Newbolt, Sir Henry, 216

Newfoundland, 11, 41–43

Newton, Lord, Foreign Office, 38

New Zealand, 45–46, 267

Nietzsche, Friedrich Wilhelm, German philosopher, 223

Nivelle, General Robert Georges, 178–179, 448–450, 453–455, 459, 461

Noble, Reginald, acting Corporal VC, 2nd Battalion Rifle Brigade, 335

Officer Training Corps (OTC), 53

Oh What a Lovely War, 225–226

Old Comrades Associations, 51

Old Contemptibles, 325

Orlando, Vittorio, Italian Prime Minister, 523

Owen, Wilfred, 55, 204, 212, 214–216, 591

Page, Lieutenant, Royal Artillery, 418

Page, Walter Hines, American Ambassador to Gt Britain, 110, 545

Painlevé, Paul, French War Minister and Premier, 455

parachutes, 72, 571

Passchendaele, see Third Ypres

Patch, Harry, DCLI veteran, 600

Peace Treaty, 600

Pennefather, Lieutenant, 2nd Battalion Rifle Brigade, 333

623

BRITISH MILITARY INDEX

628

Ernst Jünger and Germany Into the Abyss 1914–1945, Thomas Nevin, 1997.
Forgotten Men [Video], Sir John Hammerton, 1999.
Four Years on the Western Front, Aubrey Smith ('Rifleman'), 1922.
General Jack's Diary – War on the Western Front 1914–1918. The Trench Diary of Brig. General J.L. Jack, Ed. John Terraine, 1964.
Goodbye to All That, Robert Graves, 1929.
Great Contemporaries, Winston S Churchill, 1937.
Great Push An Episode of the Gt. War [Loos], Patrick MacGill 1917.
Haunting Years, William Linton Andrews, 1930.
Old Soldiers Never Die, Frank Richards, 1933.
Old Soldier Sahib, Frank Richards, 1936.
People at War 1914–1918, Michael Moynihan (Ed.), 1973.
Prisoners of the Kaiser, Richard van Emden, 2000.
Remembrances of Hell, Norman Ellison, 1997.
Robert Graves – Life on the edge, Miranda Seymour, 1995.
Scots Guard on the Western Front, 1915–1918, Wilfrid Ewart, 1934.
The Burgoyne Diaries (1914–1915), G.A. Burgoyne, 1985.
The Mint, T.E. Lawrence, 1936.
The Veterans. The Last Survivors of the Great War, Richard Van Emden/Steve Humphries, 1998.
The War The Infantry Knew 1914–1919, Captain J.C. Dunn, 1938.
Undertones of War, Edmund Blunden, 1928.
Voices from the Western Front [Video], Imperial War Museum.
Wearing Spurs, Lord Reith, 1966.
Wilfred Owen, Dominic Hibberd, 2002.
With a Machine Gun to Cambrai, George Coppard, 1968.
Without Parade. The Life and Work of Donald Hankey, A Student in Arms, James Kissane, 2003.

Fiction (including autobiographical 'faction')

Birdsong, Sebastian Faulks, 1993.
The General, C.S. Forester, 1936.
Covenant With Death, John Harris, 1961.
The First Hundred Thousand. 'K1', Ian Hay, 1916.
Her Privates We, Frederic Manning, 1929.
All Quiet on the Western Front, Erich Maria Remarque, 1929.
War, Ludwig Renn, 1929.
Verdun, Jules Romain, 1938.
Memoirs of a Foxhunting Man, Siegfried Sassoon, 1928.
Memoirs of an Infantry Officer, Siegfried Sassoon, 1930.
Siegfried's Journey, Siegfried Sassoon, 1946.
Sherston's Progress, Siegfried Sassoon, 1944.
The Patriot's Progress, Henry Williamson, 1930.
How Dear is Life (1914), Henry Williamson, 1954.
A Fox under my Cloak (1915), Henry Williamson, 1955.

The Golden Virgin (1916), Henry Williamson, 1957.
Love and the Loveless (1917), Henry Williamson, 1958.
A Test to Destruction (1918), Henry Williamson, 1960.

Poets and Poetry of the First World War

First World War Poetry, Wordsworth Library, 1995.
Violets from Overseas, Tonie & Valerie Holt, 1996.
Collected Poems, Siegfried Sassoon, 1959.
The Collected Poems of Wilfred Owen, C. Day Lewis, 1963.
Wilfred Owen, Dominic Hibberd, 2002.

Battlefields – Guides, Walks, Maps and Museums

A Guide to Military Museums and other Places of Military Interest, Terence & Shirley Wise.
A Military Atlas of the First World War, Arthur Banks, 1975.
Bray-Sur-Somme (Serie Bleue), IGN.
Location of Hospitals and Casualty Clearing Stations BEF 1914–1919, Imperial War Museum.
Longueval Trench Map, reproduced from an original by W.H. Smith & Son, 1916.
Map of the Main Prison Camps in Germany & Austria, Imperial War Museum.
Military Operations France and Belgium 1915, Imperial War Museum.
Routledge Atlas of the First World War, Martin Gilbert, 1970.
Somme, Major and Mrs Holt's Guide, 1996.
Battle Map of the Somme, Major and Mrs Holt, 1995.
The Somme Battlefields, Martin & Mary Middlebrook, 1991.
Topography of Armageddon. Trench map atlas of the Western Front, Peter Chasseaud, 1991.
Trench Map Archive on CD ROM, Imperial War Museum & The Naval & Military Press, 1997.
Ieper 1914–1918, Flanders Field Museum Shop.
The Battlefield Guide to the Ypres Salient, Major and Mrs Holt's Guide, 1996.
Battle Map of the Ypres Salient, Major and Mrs Holt, 1997.
The Ypres Salient, Michael Scott.
Walking the Salient, Paul Reed, 1999.
War Walks, Richard Holmes, 1996.
The Western Front From The Air, Nicholas C. Watkins, 1999.

War in the Air

A Few of the First, Bruce Lewis, 1997.
Bloody April (1917), Alan Morris, 1967.

Bombers 1914–1939, Purnell's History, 1971.

Death in the Air. War Diary and photographs of a Flying Corps Pilot, unknown, 1933.

Fighter Aircraft of the 1914–1918 War, W.M. Lamberton, 1960.

Fokker V5/Dr1, Wolfgang Schuster & Achim Sven Engels (English Ed., 1998).

Full Circle, J.E. 'Johnnie' Johnson, 1964.

In the teeth of the wind, C.P.O. Bartlett, 1974.

Jane's Fighting Aircraft of World War One, Jane's Publishing Company, 1919.

Royal Flying Corps Communiques 1915–1916, Christopher Cole, Ed., 1969.

Royal Flying Corps Communiques 1917–1918, C. Bower, Ed., 1998.

The Achievement of the Airship, Guy Hartcup, 1974.

The British Bomber since 1914, Peter Lewis, 1967.

The First Great Air War, Richard Townshend Bickers, 1988.

The First War Planes, Purnell's History, 1971.

The Royal Flying Corps in France – from Mons to the Somme, Ralph Barker, 1994.

The Royal Flying Corps in France – from Bloody April 1917 to Final Victory, Ralph Barker, 1995.

Wind in the Wires, Duncan Grinnell-Milne, 1966.

Winged Victor: A Biograpy of Victor M. Yeats, F.A. Atkins, 2004.

Winged Victory, V.M. Yeats, 1934.

Wings over the Somme 1916–1918, Gwilym H. Lewis, 1976.

Winged Warfare, Lt. Col. William Bishop RFC, reprinted 1975.

WWI German Aircraft [Video], Eagle Rock Entertainment PLC 1918, Edited by S.M. Ulanoff (75).

Publishers

Many general publishers have published, and continue to produce books on the period, but for those interested there are publishers/book sellers who specialise in books on military history. Among them, and whom I have found very useful, are:

Pen and Sword (Leo Cooper). The Naval and Military Press. Ray Westlake Military Books. Osprey Publishing. The National Archives (Public Records Office). The Imperial War Museum. Battlefront Books (specialising in secondhand books).

There is also an interesting little magazine, published quarterly since September 2001 by the Great Northern Publishing Company, called *The Great War*.

In addition there are people who will attempt to find copies of out-of-print books. I have found one company very successful in this: 'Booksearch UK'. (NB Out-of-print books can be expensive.)

GENERAL INDEX

Acland, Captain A.N. Adjutant, 1st DCLI, 301–303

Afghan War, 6, 581, 588

Aisne, end of mobile war, 12th–15th September, 1914, 306–308

Albert 1, King of Belgium, Commander-in-Chief, Belgium Army, 181–182

Alexander, Lt.-Col. R., 3rd Battalion, Rifle Brigade, 327

Alexiev (Alexeiff), General Mikhail Vasilevich, Chief of staff to Emperor Nicholas II, 432

Allen, Chesney, stage partner of Bud Flanagan, 225

Allenby, General Sir Edmund, Commander, 3rd Army, 165–166, 171, 296, 298

American Expeditionary Force (AEF), 98, 552, 580

Anthoine, General François, Commander French First Army, 489

ANZAC (Australian New Zealand Army Corps) Day 24, Anzac Cove, 33, 477

Armentières, The Battle, 13th October–2nd November, 1914, 311–313

Armitage, Lieutenant, AEF, 261–262

Army Council, 81

Arras, 28, 86, 457–461, 476

Artillery – definition of, 273–274

Asquith, Herbert Henry, Prime Minister, 81,117, 153, 305

Atkins, Ernest A, Private, 16th King's Royal Rifle Corps, 247, 263, 266

Attenborough, Richard, actor and film director, 225

Aubers Ridge, *see* Neuve Chapelle, 329–336

Australia and Australian troops, 45, 100, 266–267, 457, 524

Bairnsfather, Bruce, 325

Baker-Carr, Brigadier-General, 299

Balfour, Arthur, Prime Minister, 66

Barnett, Reuben, Rifleman, 1st Battalion Rifle Brigade, 314

Battenberg, Admiral, Prince Louis, 66

Beatty, Admiral Sir David, 396

Beaverbrook, Lord (Sir W. Maxwell Aitken), journalist, Minister of Information, 152–153

Beitzen Kurt, commander of submarine *U75*, 151

Belgian Army, 95–96

Belgian Refugees, 114–115

Below, General Otto von, served as an army commander on three fronts, 502

Benella, P&O Branch Line vessel, trooped 1/1st Kents to Bombay 1916, 392

Bennett, Captain E.P. VC, MC, 2nd Battalion, Worcestershire Regiment, 379

Bertie, Sir Francis, British Ambassador to France, 254

Bethmann-Hollweg, Theobold von, German Imperial Chancellor, 108–109

Birdwood, Lieutenant-General, Sir William (replaced Gough as 5th Army Commander), 171

Bishop, William, Lieutenant-Colonel, RFC ('Billy Bishop') VC, 45

617

Falkenhayn, General, Erich, von, replaced Moltke, 183–184, 198, 308, 339, 387, 389, 391

Felstead, Bertie, Private, 15th Battalion, Royal Welch Fusiliers, 382–383

Fergusson, Sir C. Bart, Major-General, Commander 5th Division, replaced by Major-General Morland, 142, 303, 307

Festubert, 336,

Fisher, Admiral, John Arbuthnot, 1st Baron Kilverstone, 65–67, 120, 150

Fisher, R.D., Private, The London Regiment, 550

Flanagan, Bud, stage partner of Chesney Allen, 225

Fletcher, Raymond, journalist and MP for Ilkestone, 226

Foch, Marshal, Ferdinand, 102, 121, 180–181, 402, 502, 522, 526, 545–547, 549, 553–554, 578

Fokker, Anthony, aircraft designer and manufacturer, 71

Forde, Florrie, entertainer, 126

Fox, Sir Frank, General Staff Officer, *GHQ*, 55–56, 234, 285, 286–287, 512

Frederick II, King of Prussia (Frederick the Great), 1

French Army, structure, 96
Plan XVII, 121, 178
Mutiny, 1917, 460, 487, 532

French, Field Marshal, Viscount of Ypres (Sir John French), *1914*, 76, 82, 97–98, 117–119, 154–157, 159, 165, 172, 174–175, 230, 238, 240, 304–306, 309, 330, 336, 365, 379

French view of the British, 253–255

Freyberg, Bernard, Brigadier-General VC, 406, 532–533

Frommelles, 337–338

Fuller, J.F.C., Major-General, GSO1, 208, 227, 228, 232, 233, 260, 447–448

Gale, Richard, Lieutenant, Machine Gun officer, 42 Division, 550

Gallipoli, 33–34

Garratt, Brig-Gen. Sir F.S., Director of Remounts, 285–287

Garretson, Major, AEF, 262

gas, 339, 367, 478

Gault, Hamilton, 43

Geddes, Sir Eric, Major-General (also held honorary title of vice-admiral), 276

George V, King, 102, 110, 123, 399, 449, 468–469, 600

German Army, structure, 96–98

Gibbs, Sir Philip, 230, 231, 295, 317, 401, 507, 583

Gladstone, William Ewart, Prime Minister, 50

Glen, William, Corporal, 15th Battalion, Royal Scots, 29

Gobar Sing Negri, VC, Rifleman, 2/39th Garwhal Rifles, 333

Godley, General, commander of the New Zealand troops on the Western Front, 45

Gold, Ernest, Lieutenant-Colonel, Haig's chief meteorologist, 480

Gommecourt, 414

Goodyear family of Newfoundland, 41

Gorczynski, Phillipe, 513

Goshen, Sir Edward, British Ambassador to Germany, 109

Gough, General Sir Hubert, 81, 168–171, 470, 483, 489, 493, 531, 532, 539, 552–553

Graves, Robert, Captain Royal Welch Fusiliers and author (*Goodbye to All That*), 63–64, 75, 76, 92, 203–207, 249, 591

Gravill, Alan, 592

Great War, magazine published by Great Northern Publishing, 573

Green, Acting Corporal, 2nd Battalion, Rifle Brigade, 312

Grenfell, The Hon. Julian DSO, Captain 1st Royal Dragoons, 228, 293

Grey, C.G., editor, *The Aeroplane*, 69–71, 604

Grey, Sir Edward, Foreign Secretary, 105–109

Grierson, Sir James, BEF Corps Commander, II Corps, 82, 161

Grogan, Brigadier-General, G.W. St G., Commander 23rd Infantry Brigade, 453

Gurney, Ivor, poet and composer, 2/5 Gloucester Regiment, 425, 592

620